For Tom Graham,

THIS TERRIBLE SOUND

OWNER OF ONE OF THE
MOST DELIGHTFUL BUILDINGS

IN CHICAGO
WITH THANKS FOR KEEPING
THE PAST ALIVE

Pete Cozzens

THE BATTLE OF CHICKAMAUGA

THIS TERRIBLE SOUND

Peter Cozzens

Illustrations by Keith Rocco

UNIVERSITY OF ILLINOIS PRESS
Urbana and Chicago

© 1992 by the Board of Trustees of the University of Illinois
Manufactured in the United States of America
C 5 4 3

This book is printed on acid-free paper.

Library of Congress Cataloging-in-Publication Data

Cozzens, Peter, 1957–
   This terrible sound : the battle of Chickamauga / Peter
Cozzens ; illustrations by Keith Rocco.
   p.   cm.
   Includes bibliographical references and index.
   ISBN 0-252-01703-X (cl)
   1. Chickamauga (Ga.), Battle of, 1863. I. Title.
E475.81.C78 1992
973.7'35 — dc20   92-725
                                                              CIP

For my mother

CONTENTS

MAPS

ILLUSTRATIONS

ACKNOWLEDGMENTS

WHERE so many have been helpful, it is hard to adequately express my gratitude. One of the most pleasant aspects of writing a book of this sort is the contact it brings with professional librarians and archivists. I would like to thank several who went out of their way to help me locate manuscript items. They are Anne B. Shepherd of the Cincinnati Historical Society; Catherine Kidd of the Greene County District Library, Xenia, Ohio; Linda McCurdy of the William R. Perkins Library, Duke University, Durham, North Carolina; Ruby Shields of the Minnesota Historical Society, St. Paul; Martha Clevenger of the Missouri Historical Society, St. Louis; Wendy Greenwood of the Ohio Historical Society, Columbus; Herbert Hartsook of the South Caroliniana Library, University of South Carolina, Columbia; Ann Alley of the Tennessee State Library and Archives, Nashville; and Julia Hodges of the Howard-Tilton Memorial Library, Tulane University, New Orleans. James Ogden III, Historian at the Chickamauga and Chattanooga National Military Park, not only directed me to manuscript sources at the park library but shared his extensive knowledge of the campaign with me.

I am also very grateful to Carley Robison, the archivist of Knox College, Galesburg, Illinois, for her kind assistance in providing me with photocopies of materials from the fine Ray D. Smith Civil War Collection.

My special thanks go to Paul Yon, Ann Bowers, Steve Charter, and Marilyn Levinson of the Center for Archival Collections of Bowling Green State University, Bowling Green, Ohio. They are true professionals who are refreshingly enthusiastic about their collections, and with good reason. The center's William P. Sullivan Collection of Twenty-first Ohio Papers represents the finest grouping of letters anywhere pertaining to the Battle of Chickamauga. The acting regimental commander during the battle, Major Arnold McMahan, devoted much time in his later years to gathering evidence pertaining to the regiment's role on the second day of the battle. In so doing, he corresponded with numerous officers and enlisted men, North and South. I recommend this collection to anyone interested in the fighting on Horseshoe Ridge.

I would also like to thank several other individuals for their assistance. Charles Van Adder of Forked River, New Jersey, graciously provided me with information pertaining to Captain John Sloan of Wood's Confederate Brigade, as well as other materials from his private library. Laurence Strayer of Dayton, Ohio, made available to me the correspondence of Dr. J. T. Woods, historian of the Ninety-sixth Ohio, from his extensive personal collection of materials pertaining to Ohio's participation in the war. Richard Sauers of Harrisburg, Pennsylvania, made available that portion of his exhaustive hand-written index of the *National Tribune* pertaining to the Chickamauga Campaign. Dr. Sauers's index is an invaluable tool that merits publication. Sharon Miller of Ravenna, Michigan, provided information she had gathered on soldiers from the area of Muskegon, Michigan, who served at Chickamauga. Adrienne Hanrahan of Oak Park, Illinois, brought to my attention the letters of Colonel Silas Miller. Robert Younger, the owner of Morningside Press in Dayton, Ohio, made available to me materials from his library pertaining to Ohio units at the battle. My gratitude also goes to Dan Weinberg, proprietor of the Abraham Lincoln Book Shop, Chicago, who helped me first get into print.

I am especially indebted to Kenneth Bandy of Beloit, Ohio, a true gentleman and a friend. Few can claim a greater understanding of Chickamauga, and certainly no one has a deeper appreciation of the suffering and sacrifice that occurred there. Ken shared his knowledge openhandedly throughout my writing of *This Terrible Sound*. He read the manuscript as well, and I deeply appreciate his suggestions and comments.

I would also like to express my gratitude to James Bier of Champaign, Illinois, for the fine battle maps, which add immeasurably to the book, and to my editor, Carol Bolton Betts, with whom it is a great pleasure to work.

To my friend Keith Rocco of Downers Grove, Illinois, sincere thanks for providing the evocative sketches that appear in this book and for a great painting for its jacket.

To my wife, Dee Ann, my warmest thanks for her gentle support and patience while I wrote the manuscript.

A final note: In referring to places on the battlefield, I've tried whenever possible in the text to retain a contemporary flavor. Thus, Snodgrass Hill is treated as the Snodgrass hill, Dyer Field as the Dyer field, and so on. Before 19 September 1863, no one had any cause to honor them with proper names.

CHAPTER ONE

MY DEAR GENERAL, YOU ARE THOROUGHLY OUTDONE

DEFEAT was in the wind. It rose from the steaming bayous of Mississippi, crept through the deep gorges of the Tennessee River, drifted over the rolling fields of southern Pennsylvania.

It touched Major General Daniel Harvey Hill as he sat under the hot July sun in the yard of a mansion on the outskirts of Richmond, carrying his thoughts to dark corners. In two short weeks, Lee and the Army of Northern Virginia had marched into and been thrown out of Pennsylvania. In the South, the reaction was swift and severe. Disaster. Massacre. Terrible. Useless. These were some of the words Lee's subordinates used to describe the climactic Battle of Gettysburg. The Charleston *Mercury* carped that the invasion of the North could not have been "more foolish or disastrous." The common soldier registered his views with his feet. On 4 July 1863, while the victorious Army of the Potomac hung dangerously close, some five thousand able-bodied Confederates simply turned their backs on their regiments and melted into the long train of wounded that rumbled south toward Virginia.

Hill may have been grimly satisfied with all this. He had predicted such a defeat in June, when he learned of Lee's plans, and he later wrote: "The drums that beat for the advance into Pennsylvania seemed to many of us to be beating the funeral march of the dead Confederacy."[1]

From Mississippi came a blow equally crushing. The river citadel of Vicksburg had fallen on the Fourth of July. This Hill had foreseen as well. When Lee started northward, Hill had confided his fears to his wife: "General Lee is venturing upon a very hazardous movement; and one that must be fruitless, if not disastrous. It would have been infinitely wiser to have brought his army back to Richmond and held it with a small force while his main strength went to the relief of Vicksburg. As it is, there seems to be no ground to hope for Vicksburg."[2]

Nine days later the garrison surrendered, and "Federal gunboats were now plying up and down the Mississippi, cutting our communications between East and West. . . . The end of our glorious dream could not be far off," Hill mused. Yet he was strangely serene. "The bitterness of death had passed with me before our great reverses on the Fourth of July."

Although Hill probably gave them little thought, affairs were no better in the Confederate heartland. After lying inert for six months along the Duck River in southern Tennessee, the Confederate Army of Tennessee in late June suddenly found itself fleeing south over the Cumberland Mountains and across the Tennessee River to Chattanooga. After just eleven days, and at a cost of only 560 men, the Army of the Cumberland had swept its old foes nearly out of the state in one of the most brilliant campaigns of the war. Braxton Bragg and his generals were left dazed and befuddled, only temporarily safe in Chattanooga, with the river and mountains between them and the Federals.

Hill's attention was drawn to a gaunt man in a plain brown suit galloping up to the yard. The general listened as President Davis explained the reason for his unexpected call.

"Rosecrans is about to advance upon Bragg; I have found it necessary to detail Hardee to defend Mississippi and Alabama. His corps is without a commander. I wish you to command it," Davis said.

"I cannot do that," Hill pointed out, "as General Stewart ranks me."[3]

"I can cure that by making you a lieutenant general. Your papers will be ready tomorrow. When can you start?"

"In twenty-four hours."

If Hill paused before answering, it must have been for only a moment. Never one to accept authority easily, the petulant North Carolinian had been constantly at odds with Lee during his service with the Army of Northern Virginia. Not surprisingly, he was soon relegated to the Department of North Carolina, a backwater command. Charged with protecting the vulnerable Confederate interior, Hill had too few experienced troops and too much ground to defend. It was an assignment leading nowhere.[4]

So Hill told the story of the circumstances that sent him west out of exile. If Jefferson Davis was as agitated during their conversation as the general would have us believe, then Hill had seen the president in a rare moment of true distress over affairs in Tennessee. Normally, Davis was profoundly preoccupied with events in Virginia. He and Secretary of War James Seddon tried to play a kind of balancing game in the West, shifting forces from place to place to meet the greatest Federal threat of the moment, rather than concentrating their own armies against the weakest Federal army in order to seize the offensive at a time and place of their own choosing, a policy long advocated by General Pierre G. T. Beauregard, Senator

Louis Wigfall, and other members of what has been called the "western concentration bloc."[5] When Davis did turn his attention westward, it was all too often only after a crisis had turned acute. This was particularly true where the Army of Tennessee was concerned.

Sadly, Davis's actions to date had only made matters worse. After the failure of the invasion of Kentucky in the fall of 1862, a wave of unrest swept over the Army of Tennessee. Corps commanders Leonidas Polk and William Hardee, with at least the tacit support of most of their lieutenants, demanded the ouster of Bragg. Davis permitted Bragg's detractors an audience but decided to retain the general in command. This decision was not unwise under the circumstances, but the president's failure to discipline or transfer at least Polk, the leader of the dump-Bragg movement, was deplorable. The next time Davis acted in Tennessee, it was to strip the army of nearly one-sixth of its infantry to reinforce the defenses of Vicksburg. The timing of this move could not have been more unfortunate, for it came on the eve of a major Federal thrust against Middle Tennessee. Defeat followed. After three days of bloody and inconclusive fighting at Murfreesboro, Bragg abandoned most of the state and fell back to a line of defense behind the Duck River in early January. Major General William Starke Rosecrans and his Army of the Cumberland remained in Murfreesboro.

But if the Union army was content to remain inactive, Bragg's opponents in the Army of Tennessee were not. Led by Polk, they redoubled their efforts to secure his removal. Again they failed. Davis sustained Bragg, in part because he lacked a suitable successor. The overall commander in the West, Joseph E. Johnston, did not want the job. Davis apparently saw no one to his liking within the Army of Tennessee, and the only other available general officer of appropriate rank and prestige, Pierre G. T. Beauregard, was an implacable foe of the administration and its policies. Once again, Davis stopped short of transferring Polk, an error that was to have grave consequences.

By the spring of 1863 it was obvious that there could be no reconciliation between Bragg and Polk. Both were proud, unyielding men, and both were friends of the president. Polk and Davis had been classmates at West Point. Although Davis apparently did not make friends readily while a cadet, he and Polk developed a friendship that would prove lifelong. And the president's loyalty to friends, especially those made during his formative years at West Point, was unwavering.[6]

Polk answered a higher calling after his graduation from the Military Academy. At the first opportunity, he resigned his commission to enter the Episcopal ministry, in which he rose to become Missionary Bishop of the Southwest. While quite successful as a cleric, Polk had little Christian charity where Braxton Bragg was concerned. In his eyes, Bragg was "a poor, feeble-minded, irresolute man of violent passions ... uncertain of the soundness of his conclusions and therefore timid in their executions."[7] Polk sought Bragg's removal not because he coveted his command — he actually advocated replacing Bragg with Joseph E. Johnston — but simply because he judged him incompetent, a "weakling, without the qualities requisite for his station."[8]

While Polk certainly was the most vocal of Bragg's critics inside the army, he was hardly the only one. Opposition to Bragg ran deep and sprang from varied and complex sources, some of which had little to do with Bragg himself or his fitness for command. Fellow corps commander William Hardee, never as outspoken as the bishop, urged Bragg's removal because he believed the army had lost faith in his generalship. Generals Patrick Cleburne and St. John Liddell quietly supported the anti-Bragg movement for the same reasons. Others, of whom Tennessean Benjamin Franklin Cheatham was the most notable, held personal grudges against Bragg that stemmed from the commanding general's unfortunate penchant for seeking scapegoats in the wake of defeat. In Cheatham's case, Bragg had good cause. Bragg censured him for being drunk at Stones River, which he evidently was, and blamed the faulty execution of the Confederate attack on the first day of the battle in part on Cheatham's intoxication. All too often, however, Bragg's accusations were baseless. Certainly this was the case when he held John C. Breckinridge accountable for the failure of the climactic attack on the second day at Stones River, which, though made by Breckinridge's division, had been faulty in its conception by Bragg.

Breckinridge and fellow Kentuckian William Preston were estranged from Bragg for other, equally personal reasons as well. Both resented Bragg's undisguised contempt for the Kentucky soldiers in his army, whom Bragg's troubled mind somehow held to blame for the collapse of his invasion of their home state. Also, both were related to Joseph E. Johnston. They resented the favoritism Davis showed in retaining his friend Bragg in command while shelving Johnston, with whom the president did not get along, and they directed their anger at Bragg.

Had Bragg exercised even the most rudimentary tact in dealing with his subordinates, he might have been able to defuse some of the opposition. But while he could speak and write warmly, even tenderly, of his lieutenants to others, he would not permit himself to bestow praise directly. Neither would he tolerate anything less than total devotion to duty, perhaps because he gave so much of himself to the cause. Even William Polk, the son of Bragg's greatest defamer, admitted that "in all matters touching his private duty to the cause of the South he was unselfishness itself. No man loved it better, no man gave it more devoted service, none laid his all upon the alter more ungrudgingly, and no one would have laid down his life for it more cheerfully."[9]

Bragg never wavered in his attention to duty, even though chronic ill health was gradually but unmistakably breaking him. Years earlier, as a lieutenant chasing Seminoles in the miasmal swamps of Florida, Bragg had had to come to terms with his unusual susceptibility to disease. While nearly everyone in that campaign suffered from the sun, insects, and fevers, Bragg was unusually hard hit, especially for a young man of twenty-one. After eight months in Florida his health gave out completely, and he was sent home to recover. From then on he suffered from one ailment or another. Dyspepsia, dysentery, and chronic headaches all plagued him — often striking in concert, and always most pronounced when he was under stress or despondent, as he had been most of the time since taking command of the Army of Tennessee. His biographer has speculated that Bragg's ailments were partly psychosomatic.[10] Whatever the cause, they had taken a dramatic toll. Although just forty-six, Bragg looked years older. He appears to us in contemporary photographs haggard and cadaverous, a prematurely gray beard and bushy black eyebrows the only distinguishing features of a severe, almost puritanical countenance.

More disturbing than his physical decline were the early signs of mental and emotional collapse. Major General Richard Taylor, son of former president Zachary Taylor and a keen observer, suggested that Bragg "furnished a striking illustration of the necessity of a healthy body for a sound intellect."[11] Bragg had been in command just two months when Taylor saw him in the late summer of 1862. Six months later the strain of two humiliating defeats and an army of contentious subordinates had nearly wrecked him. He was having trouble concentrating, and his notorious temper was growing even shorter. Always suspicious, Bragg seemed now to relish clashes with his opponents.

What did all this mean in battle? Without a doubt, the certainty that Bragg would be hunting for scapegoats should the day be lost made his subordinates reluctant to take the initiative. And where oral orders from Lee often sufficed in the Army of Northern Virginia, Bragg's generals insisted on getting everything in writing, no matter how much time might be lost in the process.

To his credit, it must be said that Bragg had an excellent strategic mind. His campaigns were well conceived. It was in the execution that he faltered. Lieutenant Colonel Archer Anderson, who came west with Hill as his adjutant general and wrote in a spirit of fairness, summed up the problem best: "General Bragg seemed to know always what ought to be done, to possess the decision and the will to order it to be done, but, by some strange lack of gift, where so many gifts abounded, he could not do it himself and he could not make others do it."[12]

So Bragg could plan well enough but could not inspire others to carry out his orders. And though his plans were sound, Bragg could not anticipate probable enemy courses of action or responses to his designs. As Major General Simon Buckner complained: "General Bragg as a military man . . . is wanting in imagination. He cannot foresee what probably may occur. When he has formed his own opinions of what he proposes to do, no advice of all his officers put together can shake him; but when he meets the un-expected, it overwhelms him because he has not been able to foresee, and then he will lean upon the advice of a drummer boy."[13]

On the field of battle, Bragg's greatest failing was his detachment from the fighting. With battlefield communications slow and uncertain during the Civil War, an army commander had to keep in touch with his lieutenants without exposing himself to undue personal risk. As D. H. Hill observed: "Whenever a great battle is to be fought, the commander must be on the field to see that his orders are executed and to take advantage of the ever-changing phases of the conflict."[14] In this Bragg failed. He habitually re-mained too far to the rear, drifting into a strange mental withdrawal when-ever the vagaries of combat compelled a change in plans.

William Gale, a nephew of Polk and a member of his staff, summed up Bragg as his opponents saw him: "Bragg was obstinate yet without firmness, ruthless without enterprise, crafty yet without stratagem, suspicious, en-vious, jealous, vain, a bantam in success and a dunghill in disaster."[15]

In marked contrast to the caldron of ill will and suspicion that was the high command of the Army of Tennessee, the leadership of the Army of the Cumberland worked together with a harmony unusual in a day when armies were led by a mixture of professionals, volunteers, and political hacks. "If there was a characteristic of our army in which we felt a pride, it was in the fact that we never had any dissensions or crass purposes to distract the harmonious execution of the orders of our commanding officers," the army provost marshal, Colonel John Parkhurst, wrote proudly. Dr. Fer-dinand Gross, medical director of the Fourteenth Corps, agreed: "It was the general sentiment and constant boast of the officers and men . . . that the Army of the Cumberland was singularly united and free from dissensions."[16]

Of course, the army's success certainly helped to blunt any potential discord, but credit must go primarily to its commander, Major General William Starke Rosecrans. Rosecrans was no less eccentric than Bragg; indeed, he was probably the most eccentric army commander the war produced. However, unlike Bragg, he was a very likeable man who inspired — and returned — the loyalty of his generals and troops. In fact, Rosecrans was loyal to a fault. His sense of obligation to his subordinates prevented him from removing corps commanders Alexander McCook and Thomas Crittenden, both hopelessly inept, because he "hated to injure two such good fellows."

Rosecrans had a countenance as pleasant as his disposition, with a kindly if rather plain face. The journalist and financier Henry Villard left an engaging description of the man: "General Rosecrans was of middle stature, with a broad upper body and rather short, bow legs (owing to which peculiarities he presented a far better appearance when mounted than on foot); a head not large, with short, thin light-brown hair; a narrow, long face with kindly blue eyes, strong nose and mouth, and scanty full grayish beard. His general expression was very genial."[17]

But there was a dark side to Rosecrans's personality. Normally genial and voluble—even gregarious—Rosecrans had a hair-trigger temper that exploded at the most inopportune moments. He was apt to fly into a rage in situations that scarcely merited vehemence and then forget the incident just as readily. Rosecrans's emotional intemperance, his tendency to lash out or speak his mind before contemplating the consequences, would keep him constantly in ill favor with the War Department.

Despite his personal shortcomings, in the aftermath of the victory at Stones River few doubted Rosecrans's military ability. Indeed, D. H. Hill respected him as one of the finest generals in the North. None questioned his talents as a strategist, nor his tremendous capacity for work. The same nervous energy that produced outbursts of rage made him a voracious worker under routine conditions. "Labor was a constitutional necessity with him," wrote W. D. Bickham of the Cincinnati *Commercial*. In the field, to the dismay of his staff, the commanding general was apt to be the first out of his blankets in the morning and the last to dismount at night. "He scarcely ever gets to bed before two or three in the morning, nor do those of his immediate personal staff, who are always by him and never separate from him," a tired aide-de-camp, Colonel John Sanderson, wrote in his diary. He "gets up about ten and takes breakfast between eleven and twelve, then goes to work until three or four, takes lunch, rides out on a tour of inspection, on his return he takes supper and then again goes to work."[18] Nor did the completion of a day's work, in garrison or in the field, necessarily promise a respite for Rosecrans's weary staff. As Bickham observed while a guest at army headquarters: "When lectures were concluded, orders executed, correspondence all disposed of, somewhere about midnight—an hour earlier or later was altogether immaterial—dull care was dismissed and pleasure assumed supremacy."

For Rosecrans, pleasure lay in conversation, and his unfortunate staff was a captive audience. The general was a tireless talker with an inquisitive intellect. He thought nothing of chatting the night away with his drowsy aides on whatever subject came to mind. Most often the topic was religion, one of the driving passions in Rosecrans's life. Having embraced Catholicism over the objections of his staunchly Methodist parents while a cadet at West Point, Rosecrans displayed the sort of dogmatism common in adult converts to any faith, and he dismissed all other theological systems as mere corruptions of the church. So as not to be separated from its sacraments, he took his friend and confidant, the Reverend Father Patrick Treacy, with him to the field.

Rosecrans had met Treacy while serving under Grant in Mississippi the year before. Before the war, Treacy had wandered through the West, setting up congregations wherever he found enough members of the faith. In 1860, illness led him to seek a parish in the South, and he eventually settled in Huntsville, Alabama. While his ministrations to wounded Rebel soldiers were appreciated, his Unionist sentiments were not, and Treacy finally was forced to flee into Federal lines, where he met Rosecrans. The two felt an instant rapport, probably because the thirty-six-year-old Irish immigrant was as odd as Rosecrans. Treacy became the general's constant companion, keeping him apprised of the latest camp rumors when not tending to his spiritual needs. While he made himself useful, helping the surgeons with the wounded and sick, Treacy's obvious influence over the commanding general was deeply if quietly resented by many of his Protestant subordinates.[19]

The tremendous energy that allowed Rosecrans to work all day and ruminate well into the night was also his curse. He became excited easily. Under pressure, particularly the strain of combat, he was susceptible to near-manic mood swings. Wrote Major General Jacob Cox, whose opinion of Rosecrans was formed long before Chickamauga: "Rosecrans's perceptions were acute and often intuitively clear. His fertility was great. He lacked poise . . . and there was the fatal defect of the liability to be swept away by excitement and to lose all efficient control of himself and of others in the very crisis when complete self-possession is the essential quality of a great general." Apparently, he also stammered when under stress. Said the New York *Herald* correspondent William Shanks: "I have known him, when merely directing an orderly to carry a dispatch from one point to another, [to] grow so excited, vehement, and incoherent as to utterly confound the messenger. In great danger as in small things, this nervousness incapacitated him from the intelligible direction of his officers or effective execution of his plans."[20] Shanks wrote with an acid pen that spared few. However, even Rosecrans's admirers acknowledged the general's impulsiveness, which, in direct contrast to Bragg, led him to issue far too many orders during combat. His impatience also caused Rosecrans to undermine his own chain of command. Even in relatively routine situations, he often gave orders directly to division or even brigade commanders without informing their superiors of what he had done.

Unlike Bragg, Rosecrans was fortunate to have a loyal second in command who more than compensated for his shortcomings. Where Rosecrans was impulsive and excitable, George H. Thomas was methodical and phlegmatic; where Rosecrans was voluble and moody, Thomas chose his words carefully and seemed always in good spirits. After seeing him almost daily for several months, Colonel Sanderson concluded that Thomas was "a model man, and a true soldier. He is a man of few words, and plain and simple as a child in his manners. I have yet to see him for the first time in bad humor. His amiability is a matter of general notoriety." Even the crotchety Shanks had nothing but praise for Thomas: "The self-control and coolness of Thomas under fire, and amid the excitement and angers of battle, is absolutely superior. . . . I did not believe that human nature was capable of it."[21]

Rosecrans appreciated Thomas's talents. He had the highest regard for his counsel and as often as not would defer to it. Rosecrans probably knew he had no reason to fear that Thomas coveted his job. In a service where so many put personal advancement above the good of the cause, Thomas was a breath of fresh air. He "never made the least effort for personal preferment, and rather shunned than sought higher commands," said Henry Villard, who speculated that Thomas's humility stemmed from "modest doubts of his competency."

That Thomas held his commander in equally high regard was perhaps the finest tribute to Rosecrans's ability. Their mutual esteem was lifelong. After the war, in a letter to the *National Tribune,* Rosecrans mourned the untimely death of "Corinthian Thomas." His passing, said Rosecrans, was a "national calamity. . . . Few knew him better than I did, none valued him more." Reminiscing about him in a letter to Alexander McCook nine years later, Rosecrans wrote: "Having first been attracted to him when in the Military Academy, two years my senior, by what I thought his remarkable resemblance to Stuart's portrait of Washington, I always retained for him both friendship and respect."[22]

Rosecrans by nature trusted his subordinates implicitly. This was fine where Thomas was concerned, but it was unwise in the extreme when it came to his other infantry corps commanders, Alexander McCook and Thomas Crittenden. At Stones River, Rosecrans had allowed McCook great discretion in placing his forces on the field, a mistake that almost cost him the battle. But Rosecrans was learning. While he could not bring himself to replace McCook or Crittenden, Rosecrans knew he had to keep a tighter rein on them.

McCook was a disappointment in part because so much had been expected of him. A former instructor of tactics at West Point, he had won promotion for gallantry at Bull Run and Shiloh. Too, he came from a distinguished family, the "Fighting McCooks" of Ohio. His father, Major Daniel McCook, and his uncle John had nine sons, all of whom served in the war.[23] Although he was a hard fighter who could handle a brigade or division competently, McCook clearly was in over his head as a corps commander. Few were taken in by his bluster. A former staff officer thought him "much set up with his elevation." A veteran of the Fifty-ninth Illinois came away with the same impression after a chance meeting with the general: "While the column was passing, General McCook and staff came dashing by in magnificent style. They came, they were seen, and they were gone. Like most his rank, he prides himself on being General McCook."[24] Good-natured and jovial, with "twinkling bright china-blue eyes," McCook was a wonderful storyteller and fine singer. To many, however, he came across as undignified, even coarse. John Beatty, a talented brigade commander in Thomas's corps, thought McCook "a chucklehead" with a grin that excited "the suspicion that he is either still very green or deficient in the upper story." Nadine Turchin, the wife of a Russian emigré brigadier general and a constant presence in camp and field, dismissed McCook as "an imposter of a general."[25] In marked contrast to Thomas, who despite his sterling record seemed constantly to have been troubled by self-doubt, there is no evidence that McCook for one moment thought himself anything less than deserving of his high rank and responsibilities.

Major General Thomas Crittenden was the third of Rosecrans's infantry corps commanders. Like McCook, he was notorious for his profanity; in the same manner, noted Beatty, he was capable of blowing his own horn exceedingly well. Crittenden was a lawyer by profession, whose sole military experience prior to the war had been as a volunteer aide on the staff of Zachary Taylor during the War with Mexico. But he had other credentials. As a member of the powerful Crittenden family of Kentucky he exercised great influence in the state. His commissioning as a brigadier general in 1861 was politically motivated, an acknowledgment of the state's critical role during the early days of the war.

Crittenden did not perform badly at Stones River, he just was largely invisible. Decisions involving his corps mostly were made for him by others, which tended to validate Shanks's assertion that Crittenden "never on the battlefield had an opinion of his own, or ever assumed any responsibility that he could possibly avoid."[26]

Into this harmonious if not altogether competent circle in January 1863 came James A. Garfield, the first potentially discordant personality. The young Ohioan was a consummate politician of burning ambition. In his first thirty-one years, Garfield had overcome every obstacle thrown before him. He was left fatherless as an infant, and his formative years were marked by deprivation and drudgery. While he worked at menial jobs to help provide for his family, he somehow succeeded in getting an education, and he graduated from Williams College at the age of twenty-five. Garfield's charming manner and natural gifts as a speaker and debater carried him to the Ohio senate just three years later.

When war broke out he helped recruit the Forty-second Ohio Infantry. For his efforts, Garfield was appointed colonel of the regiment in December 1861. Garfield threw himself into the military arts with his customary zeal, impressing his Regular Army associates with his quick mastery of the manuals and his ability to turn raw recruits into soldiers. Promotion came quickly. In January 1862 he was handed command of a brigade and promoted to brigadier general. He served capably at Shiloh and seemed to have a bright future in the army until that summer, when ill health forced him to quit the field. In typical fashion, Garfield turned this setback into opportunity. While recuperating in Ohio he devoted his time to politics and offered himself as a Republican candidate for Congress. When the party's prospects for the fall elections darkened, Garfield traveled to Washington in the hope of securing a field command.[27]

It proved the best decision of his young life. While waiting for a command, he made the acquaintance of Kate Chase, who introduced him to her father, Secretary of the Treasury Salmon B. Chase. The secretary was deeply impressed with Garfield and his rise from "a laborer on a canal" to a "conspicuous part as a Republican leader" in Chase's home state of Ohio, and Chase at once set about to try to help "this fine young officer" however he could. Garfield genuinely liked his newfound benefactor as well. "Chase is, I believe, by far the strongest man in the administration and he seems to be thoroughly imbued with a moral and religious sense of the duties of government in relation to the war," he wrote in late September.[28]

He and Chase saw each other almost daily. They shared an interest in chess, and for two or three weeks averaged five or six games a day. At one point, Garfield moved into the Chase residence for several weeks. Although Garfield was anxious to return to field duty, things were going his way. Despite his earlier pessimism, he won a seat in Congress handily, and by November his health had returned. Finally, on 14 January 1863, he got his orders: "Brigadier General J. A. Garfield is assigned to duty in the Army of the Cumberland under Major General Rosecrans to whose headquarters he will repair and report in person." Garfield wrote Chase that same day: "I am exceedingly sorry not to see you again before leaving Washington, but I must start to-day for Tennessee to report to General Rosecrans. I choose that field because I believe there is more life and work in the west and that the chief hope of the country rests in that army. I wish you to add another to the many kindnesses you have shown me. I will be particularly obliged if you will write a letter to General Rosecrans. . . . Of course I take my chances of having only a brigade, though I would like a division." And he added, prophetically, "If there should ever be anything in which I can serve you I hope you will command me."[29]

Garfield arrived at Rosecrans's headquarters on 25 January. His first interview with his new commander was a tremendous success, and he won over the general as readily as he had Chase. "He was very friendly and received me with the familiarity of an old friend," Garfield wrote his wife of their first encounter. "I am greatly pleased with some features of General Rosecrans's character. He has that fine quality of having his mind made up on all the questions which concern his work. The officers whom I have met since I came here seem to have the most unbounded confidence in Rosey and are enthusiastic in his praise."

But even Garfield, who was accustomed to making friends of influential people quickly, was dizzied by the pace at which their relationship was developing. Garfield had been with the army only a few days when, one night around midnight, he awoke to find Rosecrans standing over him. Although he had been bedridden with a severe cold, Rosecrans insisted on making conversation. He kept Garfield engaged for over an hour, before his servant came and gently led him off to bed.

From that evening on, Garfield was fated not to get a good night's rest. "Last night," he wrote his wife, "I went into the General's room to see him and he insisted I should sleep in the room. We sat up til two o'clock notwithstanding his illness and my frequent remonstrances that he should go to bed." That night, the topic of conversation was religion. "I do still curse and damn when I am indignant but I never blaspheme the name of God," Rosecrans told the sleepy brigadier. He wanted an authorized supernatural teacher and the best claimant was the Roman Catholic church. As Rosecrans rambled, Garfield had a chance to study him more closely. "He is the most Spanish-looking man I know of—a kind of Don Menendez face. He carries a cross attached to his watch seal and as he drew his watch out of his side pants pocket his rosary, a dirty-looking string of friar's beads, came out with it. Before retiring he took out his rosary and knelt for five or ten minutes before his bed. It was three o'clock before our conversation ceased," Garfield wrote his wife, adding hopefully, "I expect a command will be assigned me today or tomorrow."

Garfield was disappointed. The days passed with no assignment in sight. Weary of what appeared to be his sole function as the commanding general's chief interlocutor, Garfield tried to sneak quietly out of headquarters and take up residence in Murfreesboro. Just after bedding down for his first uninterrupted night's sleep, Garfield was awakened by an orderly who handed him an order peremptorily directing the Ohioan to return to head-quarters; he was to be Rosecrans's roommate.

Finally, in mid-February, Rosecrans made clear his intentions. "Garfield, I have now got a division ready for you, but I want to ask what you think of staying here with me and taking the place as my chief of staff," he asked, almost pleading. "I am almost alone in regard to counsel and assistance in my plans, and I want a power concentrated here that can reach out through the entire army and give it unity and strength." So Garfield remembered the conversation, perhaps embellishing it a bit egotistically. Nevertheless, the request was worded in such a way that he knew he could not refuse.[30]

Among his brother officers, Garfield was not a popular choice for chief of staff to fill the vacancy left by the death of the well-liked and intensely devoted Julius Garesche, whose brains had been splattered on Rosecrans's coat by a cannonball at Stones River. Garfield's colleagues saw him for what he was—an ambitious man who would measure his loyalty to his commander by its utility in furthering his political or military career. Few were as taken with Garfield's military abilities as he himself seemed to be. Wrote Colonel Sanderson: "Garfield, though a smart, is by no means a strong man, and with less confidence and assurance of his own superiority, would be a much safer and more valuable chief advisor than I think he is. He . . . does not possess in any great degree, genuine business capacity, being without order or apparent system." Major General David Sloane Stanley, Rosecrans's blunt-speaking chief of cavalry, thought Garfield "had no military ability, nor could he learn anything."[31] If he did nothing else well as chief of staff, however, Garfield quickly developed a knack for explaining the intentions of the commanding general more clearly than could Rosecrans himself. Orders written by Garfield were models of clarity.

Before one feels too much sympathy for Rosecrans as a trusting innocent, it must be said that he knew of Garfield's political connections and should easily have been able to read his ambition. Indeed, he may have calculated that they could serve him as well. Rosecrans was doubtless impressed by the Ohioan's letter of introduction from Chase, and, as Garfield's biographer has speculated, Rosecrans probably reckoned the political advantages that might accrue to him from having patronized an officer bound for Congress.[32]

Regardless of what else might be said of Garfield, he knew exactly what Washington expected from the Army of the Cumberland: Action. Although President Lincoln and General-in-Chief Henry Halleck directed the main Federal effort in the West in the spring of 1863 toward the capture of Vicksburg and the opening of the Mississippi, they expected Rosecrans to move forward from Murfreesboro in order at least to prevent Bragg from reinforcing Johnston in Mississippi.

Rosecrans, however, refused to budge until he was sure the army was ready, and the general had a very exacting idea of what constituted readiness. As he had done before advancing from Nashville the preceding December, Rosecrans began after Stones River to importune Washington for every conceivable type of supply to rebuild his army. He was especially concerned with the state of his cavalry, which, despite some improvements made under the competent if erratic tutelage of David Stanley, was still markedly inferior to that of the Army of Tennessee. A truly innovative thinker, Rosecrans hit upon the idea of arming his mounted troops with repeating rifles to compensate for their inferior abilities. His requests for repeating rifles, as well as for horses and mules by the thousands, went unfilled, and Washington answered instead with reminders that Bragg too faced shortages and that Rosecrans was delaying his advance against Bragg's Duck River defenses needlessly. Rosecrans's response was to renew his requisitions and complain to his generals that the War Department treated field commanders unjustly.[33]

The majority of Rosecrans's generals agreed that an advance was imprudent. Thomas tried to calm Rosecrans and make him understand the administration's perspective; most of the others did nothing more constructive than agree with their commanding general that Washington was run by scoundrels bent on destroying him. However, there was one young colonel who, when he heard that Rosecrans was anxious to increase his mounted force but could not get horses, looked for a creative solution. This officer had been impressed by the speed and impunity with which the Confederate raider John Hunt Morgan moved his cavalry around Kentucky. Anxious to give his unit the same kind of mobility, he went to the general to request permission to raid the countryside for mounts for his brigade of infantry. Always fond of audacity in younger officers, Rosecrans gave his consent at once, and thus was born the Lightning Brigade of Colonel John T. Wilder.[34]

Wilder was the quintessential volunteer officer, innovative and brave with no interest in army red tape or procedures. He had raised eyebrows by his unorthodox actions in defense of Munfordville, Kentucky, during the Confederate invasion of that state. Wilder had been ordered to hold the town and protect the railroad bridge over the Green River against Bragg's advance. When J. R. Chalmers showed up before the fortifications with a brigade of Mississippians and demanded surrender, Wilder replied calmly: "We'll try fighting for awhile." Chalmers attacked and was torn apart, losing 283 men to Wilder's 37. Confederate reinforcements converged on the town, and two days later Wilder and his 4,000-man garrison found themselves surrounded by the bulk of Bragg's army.

Simon Bolivar Buckner, a native of Munfordville, commanded the Confederate forces investing the town from the south. He was deeply troubled by the prospect of having to destroy his hometown and was contemplating ways it might be spared when a blindfolded Federal officer was ushered into his presence. It was none other than Wilder himself. A startled Buckner inquired as to the nature of his call. Wilder told Buckner, a West Pointer, that he had heard the Kentuckian was an honest gentleman. Not being a military man himself, Wilder had come to ask Buckner's advice. Should he surrender the town? "It appealed to me at once," Buckner recalled. "I wouldn't have deceived that man under those circumstances for anything." Buckner honestly explained to Wilder what he was up against, which was a force of twenty-two thousand infantry and one hundred guns, and explained the Yankee's options as he saw them. Wilder was silent for a few minutes, then said, "Well, it seems to me that I ought to surrender." The next day, Wilder and his garrison marched out with full military honors. Wilder spent two months as a prisoner of war before being exchanged.[35]

Wilder's men took every horse and mule they could find around Murfreesboro, and by mid-April the brigade was mounted. Wilder, however, was not yet satisfied. Like Rosecrans, he was enamored of repeating rifles and wanted desperately to arm his men with the best weapons available. When Christopher Spencer paid a visit to the army in March to hawk his new lever-action, seven-shot repeating rifle, Wilder knew he had found what he wanted. Calling his men together, Wilder put the matter to a vote: Did they want to carry this remarkable new rifle? He got a unanimous yes. Once again Wilder showed his contempt for red tape. On his own authority he wired his hometown bankers for a loan to enable him to buy enough Spencer rifles to arm the brigade. His men offered to reimburse him, and each signed a note for thirty-five dollars. Wilder cosigned the notes and sent them to the bank. The guns were ordered, and Wilder's men, armed with what one officer called "the most effective and complete weapon for actual service ever placed in the hands of soldiers," were soon out foraging and scouting with an esprit unmatched in the army.[36]

Meanwhile, Rosecrans was still entreating Washington for supplies. In March, Henry Halleck tried a new approach to prod Rosecrans. He sent his field commanders a letter offering a major general's commission in the Regular Army to the first of them to win a decisive victory. It was a stupid ploy, and one that Grant quietly ignored. Rosecrans, on the other hand, exploded with rage at the implicit suggestion that he could be bribed into moving before he was ready. "I never saw him so angry as when he received that letter," a staff member told a reporter from the New York *Tribune*. With his anger still white hot, Rosecrans penned an intemperate reply expressing his disgust at "such an auctioneering of honors." Though certainly justifiable, Rosecrans's response merely widened the breach between him and the authorities in Washington.[37]

By the end of May, it looked as if Grant would win the promotion. That month, he succeeded in turning Vicksburg and reaching the east bank of the Mississippi below the city. Richmond responded by diverting to Mississippi five thousand troops intended for Bragg, and ordered Johnston, as commander of the Department of the West, to leave Bragg's headquarters to take personal charge of operations around Vicksburg. Confederate Secretary of War Seddon, after failing to shake loose troops from Lee, appealed to Bragg for help. He obliged cheerfully, sending Breckinridge and his division to Johnston. It was one of Bragg's shrewder moves. He gained favor in Richmond and at the same time rid himself of the powerful and troublesome Kentuckian.

Now more than ever, Union hopes for victory in Mississippi depended on Rosecrans doing something to prevent any further contribution by Bragg to the defense of Vicksburg. Lincoln tried to nudge him forward. On 28 May, he wrote Rosecrans, gently but firmly: "I would not push you to any rashness, but I am very anxious that you do your utmost, short of rashness, to keep Bragg from getting off to help Johnston against Grant." Rosecrans's laconic reply bordered on the disrespectful: "Dispatch received. I will attend to it." When he did not, Halleck dropped all pretense and on 2 June issued the Ohioan an ultimatum: Move against Bragg or have part of your army detached to Grant. A week earlier, Halleck had stripped Ambrose Burnside's Department of Ohio of half its forces to reinforce Grant, so Rosecrans knew this was no idle threat.[38] Nonetheless, Rosecrans would no more yield to bullying than he would be tempted by the prospect of promotion. Before telling Halleck as much, though, he decided to canvass his generals to be sure of their support in case of a showdown. Rosecrans instructed Garfield to gather in writing the answers of his corps and division commanders to the following questions:

1. Has the enemy in our front been materially weakened by detachments to Johnston, or elsewhere?
2. Can this army advance on him at this time with strong, reasonable chance of fighting a great and successful battle?
3. Do you think an advance likely to prevent additional reinforcements being sent against General Grant by the enemy in our front?
4. Do you think an immediate advance advisable?
5. Do you think an early advance advisable?[39]

The answers were mixed to the first three questions, but to the fourth, the only one in which Rosecrans probably had a real interest, his fifteen commanders were unanimous in believing an immediate advance unwise.

That just two chose to address the final question, and they both in the negative, was immaterial. Rosecrans had made up his mind to move at the end of the month, though he apparently told no one but Garfield.

The replies certainly met Rosecrans's needs, but they were not what Garfield had hoped for. Impatient for an immediate advance, he received permission from Rosecrans to write his own response. Rosecrans got more than he bargained for. Pointing out (correctly) that Bragg's army was the weakest it had been since Stones River, Garfield bluntly counseled an immediate offensive, suggesting that there were no longer legitimate reasons for deferring it.

Rosecrans was mortified. He regretted "the indelicate tone" of Garfield's letter and, since Garfield already knew Rosecrans's plans, surmised it was "intended for outsiders." He was probably right. Garfield had kept up a detailed correspondence with Chase, who clearly saw Garfield as "his man" in Rosecrans's camp. Two weeks earlier, Chase had written the brigadier: "My trust in you is as complete as that of the good deacon in his minister. I can sleep if it is you who preach."[40] And right now Garfield was preaching the sermon Washington wanted to hear.

Rosecrans once wrote that "the most fatal errors of this war have begun in an impatient desire" for action. "The next fatal mistake," he admitted, was "to be afraid to move when all the means were provided."[41] By 23 June, Rosecrans was finally satisfied that the means were at hand.

The Army of Tennessee had accommodated Rosecrans nicely by remaining dormant on the north side of Duck River. The two armies were separated by a range of foothills that rose sharply from the Middle Tennessee countryside. Through these hills the major roads connecting Murfreesboro and Tullahoma passed at three defiles: Hoover's, Guy's, and Liberty gaps. Polk's corps was at Shelbyville, some twenty-five miles south of Murfreesboro, resting behind strong entrenchments completed during the six-month hiatus. Twenty miles southeast of Polk lay Tullahoma, site of Bragg's headquarters and his forward supply depot. The Confederate right under Hardee was deployed at Wartrace astride a branch line of the Nashville and Chattanooga Railroad and held the passes at Liberty, Hoover's, and Bellbuckle gaps.

Preoccupied by his quarrels with his generals and weakened by the detachments to Johnston, Bragg was thinking only of defense. If an attack came, he believed it would be directed against his entrenchments at Shelbyville. Rosecrans, however, had no intention of accommodating his opponent and instead devised a grand turning movement. He would hold Polk in place with a feint against Shelbyville by Stanley's cavalry, supported by a newly created Reserve Corps under Major General Gordon Granger. Meanwhile, the corps of McCook, Crittenden, and Thomas would concentrate against the Confederate right. By turning Hardee's right and seizing the railroad bridge across the Elk River, astride Bragg's line of retreat, Rosecrans hoped to prevent the Confederates from merely falling back to equally strong entrenchments at Tullahoma.[42]

Bragg and his generals were completely deceived. On 23 June, Stanley and his troopers rode forward in an ostentatious demonstration against Shelbyville, conveying the impression that a major infantry advance was to follow. It was enough to hold Polk in check for two days. Concurrently, Thomas moved against Bragg's right. His first objective was Hoover's Gap, through which columns of infantry could be funneled into Bragg's rear. Wilder's mounted brigade was put to the test, with orders to ride through the gap. The impetuous Hoosier, anxious to prove the utility of his mounted brigade, obeyed his instructions literally. In the predawn twilight of 24 June, Wilder swept down on the handful of Confederate cavalry pickets who guarded the mouth of the gap, scattering them easily. Although the head of Thomas's infantry column was six miles behind him, Wilder kept on. His men galloped to the summit of the gap, where William Bate's brigade of infantry was reported to be lying in wait. Instead, they found it empty. Gazing down into the valley below the gap, Wilder saw the tents of Bate's encampment, the troops at rest and most of the officers at a nearby spring holding a Masonic picnic. By the time Bate organized his brigade, Wilder's men had dismounted and were firmly in command of the gap, which Wilder was determined to hold despite orders from the commander of Thomas's lead division, Joseph Reynolds, to fall back. The Spencer rifles tore apart every Confederate effort to reclaim the gap, and Wilder held out handily until the infantry came up.

When Wilder spied Rosecrans and Thomas galloping up to his position, he decided to try to preempt the inevitable rebuke. He rode out to meet Rosecrans halfway and told him what his men had done and how he had taken the liberty of disobeying Reynolds's order; he had felt certain he could hold the gap and was sure the general would have agreed had he been there. Rosecrans was delighted. He grasped Wilder's hand and, as he pumped it, laughed: "You took the responsibility to disobey the order, did you. Thank God for your decision. It would have cost us two thousand lives to have taken this position if you had given it up." Just then Reynolds rode up. Rosecrans checked him before he could utter a word. "Wilder has done right. Promote him. Promote him." From that day on, Rosecrans's confidence in Wilder and his men — officially christened "Wilder's Lightning Brigade" after the battle — was unbounded.[43]

Rosecrans could afford to be generous. He had completely out-generaled his opponent. Bragg was not even aware of the overwhelming force moving on his right until 27 June, and by then Thomas was at Manchester, twelve miles in the rear of Hardee, with a Federal detachment moving against the railroad, Hardee's only viable line of retreat to Tullahoma.

Bragg was in a precarious position, but at this moment of extreme peril, nature smiled on the Confederates. A driving rain began early on 25 June, pounding the roads into a pasty ooze and slowing the Federal advance to a crawl. It rained for three days, allowing Bragg to withdraw Hardee and Polk by rail to Tullahoma.[44]

There he intended to make a stand, or so he told Polk when the bishop went to army headquarters on the morning of the twenty-eighth for orders. Bragg also told St. John Liddell as much when the ubiquitous brigadier paid him a call a few hours later. Riding back to his bivouac, Liddell told Colonel Daniel Govan, one of his brigade commanders, of Bragg's resolve to hold fast at Tullahoma.

"No, General, he will not fight here," Govan said quietly.

"But, Colonel, I have General Bragg's word for it."

"No matter."

"But Bragg would not so positively assert to me such a thing," Liddell insisted.

"No matter, General, I don't believe it, and I will go an oyster supper on it," countered Govan.

Govan guessed correctly. The shock of Rosecrans's unexpected advance had completely enfeebled Bragg physically, and to his normal litany of ailments was added a painful attack of boils. At 3:00 P.M. on 28 June, he called his corps commanders to a conference. By then his resolve had weakened, and he looked to Polk and Hardee for answers. Polk counseled retreat, fearing that Rosecrans would cut the railroad in their rear, hemming them in and leaving the Federals free to march on Chattanooga. Hardee was noncommittal, and the conference adjourned without a decision.[45]

Bragg did nothing until the thirtieth when, finally learning that the whole of the Army of the Cumberland was converging on Manchester, he ordered a withdrawal across the Elk River. On the evening of 1 July he again turned to Polk and Hardee for advice. He wrote: "The question to be decided instantly: shall we fight on the Elk or take post at foot of mountain at Cowan," just twenty miles from the Tennessee River. Polk and Hardee both advised the latter course. Hardee was deeply troubled by Bragg's vacillation and obvious weakness, and wrote Polk of his fears: "I deeply regret to see General Bragg in his present enfeebled state of health. If we have a fight, he is evidently unable either to examine and determine his line of battle or to take command on the field. What shall we do?"[46]

Rosecrans saved Hardee the worry. He was content to halt just below the Elk, and the Army of Tennessee fell back unmolested.

Bishop Charles Quintard, chaplain of the Army of Tennessee and confidant to its high command, saw Bragg as the general and his staff rode into Cowan. Quintard joined the party. He addressed Bragg bluntly. "My Dear General, I am afraid you are thoroughly outdone."

Bragg took no offense. "Yes," he said wearily. "I am utterly broken down." Leaning over in the saddle, he whispered to Quintard of the loss of Middle Tennessee: "This is a great disaster."

"General, don't be disheartened, our turn will come next," Quintard replied with an assurance probably he alone felt.

Seeing another who needed his ministrations, Quintard dismounted and walked over to Colonel Walters, Bragg's adjutant general, who lay in the corner of a rail fence "looking the very picture of despair."

"My dear colonel, what is the matter with you?" Quintard asked.

"How can you ask such a question, when you know as well as I do what has happened?" Walters moaned.

"My dear colonel, I am afraid you've not read the Psalms for the day."

"No," Walters said. "What do they say?"

Quintard answered in the words of the first verse of the Eleventh Psalm: "In the Lord put I my trust; how say ye then to my soul, that she should flee as a bird unto the hill?"[47]

Bragg indeed fled unto the hill — and beyond, not stopping until the Army of Tennessee was tucked safely in Chattanooga. From there he continued his personal flight, riding on to Ringgold, Georgia. There he checked himself into a hospital and temporarily turned his back on the burden that was breaking him.[48]

CHAPTER TWO

GOLDEN MOMENTS ARE PASSING

ROSECRANS was disgusted. In eleven days and at a cost of fewer than six hundred men, he had advanced eighty miles and swept Middle Tennessee clean of Confederates. But instead of praising him, Washington only badgered Rosecrans to keep moving—that he might "give the finishing blow to the rebellion," as Secretary of War Stanton put it. Indeed, the War Department seemed not even to take notice of his brilliant success. Genuinely wounded, Rosecrans wrote Stanton of his hope that the department "may not overlook so great an event because it is not written in letters of blood." Lieutenant Henry Cist of the general's staff understood the truth, even if his commander in his pique did not. "Brilliant campaigns without battles, do not accomplish the destruction of an army," he observed. "A campaign like that of Tullahoma always means a battle at some other point."[1]

That point could be none other than Chattanooga. The river city had a strategic value of its own, independent of its role as host to a demoralized Army of Tennessee. It was the door to the Deep South, a gateway that could lead in several directions. Seize Chattanooga, and the Federals could block any future invasion of Middle Tennessee or Kentucky. Hold it, and they could walk through the southern, and easiest, entrance into East Tennessee, the chief source of coal for Southern manufacturing and a region that, because of its decidedly Unionist sentiments, Lincoln was anxious to liberate. Most important, however, was the fact that no Federal army could even contemplate an advance into Georgia or Alabama with the city in enemy hands. Of lesser significance but not inconsequential was the status of Chattanooga as a center of industry. Ironmaking thrived and the surrounding mountains, which had been opened by the building of the Nashville and Chattanooga Railroad, were being exploited for their rich veins of coal. Finally, Chattanooga was a key railroad hub. Three critical railways came together there: the Nashville and Chattanooga Railroad, northern lifeline of the Army of the Cumberland; the East Tennessee and Georgia Railroad, which ran through Knoxville and into Virginia, affording Bragg direct communication with Lee's army; and the Western and Atlantic Railroad, which touched every other rail artery then under Confederate control on its way to the Gulf of Mexico.[2]

The preparations Rosecrans demanded prior to the advance on Tullahoma paled beside what would be required to operate successfully against Chattanooga. Just reaching the Tennessee River would be a tremendous undertaking. Between Tullahoma and the river, a distance of thirty miles as the crow flies, loomed the rugged Cumberland Mountains—barren, sparsely settled, devoid of forage, and offering but scant water. Scattered through the wild vista of desolate oak ridges, cedar thickets, and dark gorges were a handful of crude log farms, inhabited by simple folk trying to scratch out a living from small parcels of land on which they raised corn or wheat.

Rosecrans would find similar conditions once he crossed the river. Little of the land around Chattanooga was cultivated, and the long, high ridges that paralleled the river on the east side were as barren as the Cumberlands to the west. What few roads crossed them were little more than narrow wagon trails, described by a contemporary observer as "rough, stony and [ascended] in steep zig zags."[3]

Obviously, the army would have to carry enough food to sustain it through a potentially protracted campaign, supplementing its rations with what it could glean from the meager corn crops. A secure line of supply to the rear was imperative, as were forward depots to stockpile supplies for an army of sixty-six thousand. Rosecrans was keenly aware of this, even if Washington was not, and he set about with unusual alacrity to lay out a logistical grid over the rough countryside.

The lifeline of the army would be the Nashville and Chattanooga Railroad, and logic dictated that supply depots be located on or near the railway. From Tullahoma, the railroad carved its way southeast through mountains and past towns not much bigger than their names: Decherd, Cowan, Tantallon. At Stevenson, Alabama, just three miles from the Tennessee River, the tracks veered sharply to the northeast, crossing the river at Bridgeport and passing Shellmound—a speck on the map that consisted of one brick depot house—before winding their way into Chattanooga.[4]

The first step was to repair the railroad as far as the Elk River, the second, to extend repairs to Stevenson and Bridgeport so that supply depots could be positioned there to meet the needs of the army after it crossed the mountains. Colonel William Innes and his First Michigan Engineers—just 677 men to attend to eighty miles of track—worked with commendable speed to complete both tasks. They were helped immeasurably because

Bragg, in his dazed state, had neglected during his retreat to do the one thing that might have forestalled a Union advance for months. Just below Cowan, the railroad ran through a long tunnel in the mountain. It would have been simple to cave in or at least damage the tunnel, but Bragg did not think of this, and no one apparently suggested it. By 13 July the line was open to the Elk River bridge, and twelve days later trains were hauling supplies all the way to Bridgeport.[5]

Now came the task of stockpiling. The army's daily needs were moved forward in sixty carloads of freight; another six hundred had to be on hand to support the advance. While plans for this were being made, Rosecrans showed his clear intention to advance by sending Phil Sheridan's division of McCook's corps to Stevenson and Bridgeport at the end of July. Sheridan secured the towns, and commissary and quartermaster stores began to roll in.[6]

Rosecrans, however, was not moving fast enough to suit the administration. Lincoln and Halleck saw Gettysburg, Vicksburg, and Tullahoma as not the end but merely the beginning of a sustained Union offensive designed to break the back of the Confederacy. Unfortunately, the momentum quickly died. Meade moved with tortoiselike caution after Gettysburg, and a long-planned offensive against the defenses of Charleston ran aground in the middle of July. Meanwhile, Grant, after months of puzzling over Vicksburg, ran out of fresh ideas when it finally fell. He merely waited in the hope of getting instructions from Washington, content to launch minor strikes against the Confederate logistic network in the area.[7]

Rosecrans suddenly found himself the focus of far more attention from Washington than he cared for, most of it negative. Tullahoma had done nothing to raise Rosecrans in Stanton's estimation. Major General Lovell Rousseau and Colonel John Sanderson felt the secretary's continuing hostility first hand. In July, Rosecrans sent them to Washington with an appeal for reinforcements to protect his vulnerable line of communications and a plan to reenlist ten thousand two-year veterans as mounted infantry, a scheme heartily endorsed by several governors. At their first interview, Rousseau handed Stanton the general's written proposals. "I would rather you would come to ask the command of the Army of the Cumberland. He shall not have another damned man," snapped the secretary. Halleck, too, was "violent against granting our wishes," wrote Sanderson. Rousseau concluded that Rosecrans's professional demise was but a matter of time.

Lincoln was more agreeable and seemed disposed to grant Rosecrans's requests, but his good offices were not enough to turn Stanton around, and so Rousseau and Sanderson left with nothing more than the secretary's grudging consent to mount Rousseau's division — on mules, not horses.[8]

On 4 August, Rosecrans received a personal reminder of the War Department's impatience. Just ten days after he had repaired the railroad to the river, Halleck told him: "Your forces must move forward without delay. You will daily report the movement of each corps till you cross the Tennessee River." Colonel Henry Boynton of the Thirty-fifth Ohio neatly summed up the general's reaction: "To a commander who was building boats, opening mountain roads, rushing the accumulation of stores, getting out material for four thousand feet of bridges, preparing to leave his base carrying provisions for twenty-five days, and ammunition for two battles, and crossing three mountain ranges and a deep and broad river, in an enemy's country, and in the face of an army, this dispatch was not only astounding but discouraging and exasperating to the last degree."[9]

Although Halleck was far more conciliatory in private channels, Rosecrans's mercurial temper got the better of him, and he telegraphed Halleck angrily: "Your dispatch ordering me to move forward without delay, reporting the movements of each corps till I cross the Tennessee, is received. As I have determined to cross the river as soon as practicable, and have been making all preparations and getting such information as may enable me to do so without being driven back, like Hooker, I wish to know if your order is intended to take away my discretion as to the time and manner of moving my troops." Yes, Halleck responded: "The orders for the advance of your army, and that it be reported daily, are peremptory."[10]

Rosecrans decided to call Halleck's bluff and offer his resignation: But as he had before Tullahoma, Rosecrans now wanted to be sure his lieutenants were firmly behind him before he forced a confrontation with Washington. He called Thomas, McCook, Crittenden, Granger, and Stanley to his headquarters at Winchester Springs. In the presence of Garfield, Rosecrans read them Halleck's showdown dispatch, which, he added, was obviously instigated by "that unprincipled Secretary of War." He then reiterated the three things that had to be done before the army could move against Chattanooga, bringing down his right forefinger rapierlike to drive home each point. First, the army had to carry across the Tennessee River twenty days' rations and ammunition sufficient to fight one great battle, with enough to spare for contingencies. Second, the growing corn, sparse in the best of times and predicted to be unusually poor this season, had to be ripe enough to subsist the cavalry once it rode beyond its forage. Third, the enemy had to be deceived as to the point at which the bulk of the Army of the Cumberland would cross the river.[11]

His lieutenants were at one with him. "They all saw the danger," Rosecrans recalled acidly. "The same recklessness, conceit and malice which dictated the order might easily lead the Secretary blindly to push the army into danger to cover this mistake." Rosecrans obviously relished the moment.

As his generals nodded their agreement, he read them the telegram he intended to send Washington:

General Halleck: My arrangements for beginning a continuous movement will be completed and the execution begun Monday next [17 August]. We have information to show that crossing the Tennessee between Bridgeport and Chattanooga is impracticable, but not enough to show whether we had better cross above Chattanooga and strike Cleveland, or below Bridgeport and strike in their rear. The preliminary movement of troops for the two cases are very different. It is necessary to have our means of crossing the river completed, and our supplies provided to cross sixty miles of mountains and sustain ourselves during the operations of crossing and fighting, before we move. To obey your order literally would be to push our troops into the mountains on narrow and difficult roads, destitute of pasture and forage, where they would not be able to maneuver as exigencies may demand, and would certainly cause ultimate delay and probable disaster. If, therefore, the movement which I propose can not be regarded as obedience to your orders, I respectfully request a modification of it or to be relieved from the command.[12]

Rosecrans finished. Thomas was the first to react: "That's right," he agreed with uncharacteristic animation. "Stand by that and we will stand by you to the last."[13]

Not quite. Garfield was as impatient for an advance as he had been in June. And he made no secret of his feelings. Recalled William Shanks of the New York *Herald*: "He often deprecated to me personally — with no prohibition of publication, although he knew me as a newspaper correspondent — the inactivity of the army."[14] Such grumbling about headquarters, though indiscreet, was excusable; a certain familiarity inevitably grew between officers and those correspondents fortunate enough to be welcomed at headquarters. Generally, they were careful not to print anything that might cost them their privileged access.

But no excuse could be made for what Garfield did on 27 July, when he took his anxiety to Washington. "I cannot conceal from you the fact that I have been greatly tried and dissatisfied with the slow progress we have made in the department since the battle of Stone's River," he wrote Chase. First he set himself up as the only clear thinker at headquarters, telling Chase precisely what the administration wanted to hear: "For many weeks prior to our late movement I could not but feel that there was not that live and earnest determination to fling the great weight of this army into the scale and make its power felt in crushing the shell of the rebellion. . . . The army had grown anxious, with the exception of its leading generals, who seemed blind to the advantages of the hour. . . . I was the only one who urged upon the general the imperative necessity of striking a blow at once. . . . I have since then urged, with all the earnestness I possess, a rapid advance while Bragg's army was shattered and under cover." He closed with almost heroic pathos: "My personal relations with General Rosecrans are all that I could desire. . . but I beg you to know that this delay is against my judgment and my every wish. Pleasant as are my relations here I would rather command a battalion that would follow and follow and strike and strike than to hang back while such golden moments are passing. . . . If this inaction continues long I shall ask to be relieved and sent somewhere where I can be part of a working army."[15] Assuming the best—that he wrote out of genuine patriotic conviction that more could be done in Tennessee and with no thought to wounding his chief—Garfield was nevertheless politically sophisticated enough to know that Chase, himself an admirer of Rosecrans, had an obligation to act on such information in counseling the president, even if he did not reveal the source.

Rosecrans sent his telegram, and the effect in Washington was electric. Lincoln's private secretary, John Hay, called it "one of the worst specimens of epistolary literature I have ever come across." But the president was willing to stick with Rosecrans for the time being and so tried to calm him. Lincoln assured Rosecrans that he had read more into Halleck's letters than was intended. For his part, Lincoln went on, he thought of Rosecrans "in all kindness and confidence" and was not watching his general "with an evil eye." But, Lincoln said, he could not mask his anxiety for East Tennessee. Rosecrans had only to think of military considerations, while he was beholden to a thousand demands that the general could not possibly appreciate. The same day he wrote to Rosecrans, Lincoln penned a letter to a group of East Tennesseans who earlier had tried to hand him a petition, circulated in stealth among the loyal mountain folk and purportedly signed by thousands, pleading for Union forces to deliver them from the depredations of marauding Confederates. What could Lincoln tell them? He had sidestepped a meeting with them because he had known it would do no good. "I do as much for East Tennessee as I would, or could, if my own home and family were in Knoxville. You know I am not indifferent to your troubles. . . . The Secretary of War, General Halleck, General Burnside, and General Rosecrans are all engaged now in an effort to relieve your section."[16]

By the time Lincoln's fatherly letter reached Rosecrans, only the lack of a single locomotive stood in the way of an advance of the army. Rosecrans recognized that he could not supply his entire army from Bridgeport and Stevenson and still disperse it across a front wide enough to deceive Bragg as to the Federal river-crossing sites. So he chose the little hamlet of Tracy City, high atop the Cumberland Plateau, as the supply depot for Crittenden's corps, on the left of the army. A branch railroad jutted east from Cowan to connect the town to the main line, but the branch line had been uniquely designed to bring coal down from the mountains, not haul supplies up, and

the steep grades and sharp curves could only be tackled by a special type
of engine. The only one available had broken down on the way from
Nashville. Three more days passed before it was repaired and supplies began
to flow to the plateau depot.[17]

At Chattanooga, the Army of Tennessee idled away the long, hot weeks
of July and early August in a torpor "more demoralizing than the retreat
had been." Rations were scarce and the foraging poor. "We could not even
get a piece of bacon for a sick captain," a Texan wryly recalled. Food was
available in town for those with money, but already prices were climbing.
Georgia peaches went for two dollars a pound; a dull meal of soup, bread,
meat, and unsweetened coffee cost a dollar. To break the tedium and perhaps
scare up a meal, some soldiers hired out to local farmers; most, however,
seemed resigned to lie about camp, take an occasional swim in the Tennessee
River, and wait for their commanders to act.[18]

Bragg, however, did nothing to interfere with Rosecrans's preparations.
Sick, perplexed, and depressed, he seemed at a loss to act at all. The army
had "backed to the last jumping-off place and could go back no further with
any hope of success," Bragg admitted to St. John Liddell.[19] But while he
could not retreat, neither would he advance against Rosecrans. In a fleeting
moment of aggressiveness, Bragg actually contemplated a merger of forces
of the sort long advocated by the western concentration bloc. Convinced
that Rosecrans would not move for some time, he wrote Johnston on 17
July with an offer to bring his army west so that the two might deliver a
quick punch at Grant. Johnston was cool to the idea; the time for such
action had passed. "Such a combination might have been advantageous
before or during the siege of Vicksburg, but not after its disastrous termi-
nation," he wrote Bragg bitterly. After learning from Hardee that Johnston
had only eighteen thousand infantry, Bragg realized his suggestion had been
impractical and so let the matter rest.[20]

The pall over the army deepened. "It was clearly apparent now that we
had receded until all chances of success had passed by. The turning points
of the war had been fatally overlooked or were given up without sufficient
effort and strategic concurrence," observed Liddell, who tried but failed to
convince Bragg to grant him a transfer west so that he could await the end
near his Louisiana plantation.[21]

The atmosphere of gloom enveloped Daniel Harvey Hill like the summer
heat when he arrived at headquarters on 19 July to take command of
Hardee's corps, the more so because he had come west with high hopes,
happy to be in the field once again. His first interview with Bragg disturbed
him deeply. He had last seen his new commander in 1845, when Hill and
George Thomas had been lieutenants in Bragg's battery of artillery. Before

him now was a mere ghost of the man Hill had known: "He was silent and reserved and seemed gloomy and despondent. He had grown prematurely old since I saw him last, and showed much nervousness. His many retreats . . . had taken away that enthusiasm which soldiers feel for the successful general, and which makes them obey his orders without question, and thus wins for him other successes." And gone at once was Hill's enthusiasm. With Bragg at his worst and Hill quick-tempered and sensitive by nature, it was only a matter of time before they would come into conflict.[22]

Ironically, Richmond was looking hopefully to the Army of Tennessee at the same time Hill was souring on it. With the fall of Vicksburg and the defeat of Lee at Gettysburg, the Davis administration was open to suggestions, even from its foes in the western concentration bloc. Beauregard was ready with a plan. The previous spring, the Creole had written: "We must take the offensive . . . not by abandoning all other points, but by a proper selection of the point of attack — the Yankees themselves tell us where." He had selected Middle Tennessee as "the most favorable strategic point for the offensive" and had advocated concentrating forces there from South Carolina, Mississippi, and Virginia.[23]

That was still his plan, and in the troubled summer of 1863 he found takers aplenty. Lieutenant General James Longstreet, Lee's talented but controversial second in command, was outspoken in support of a western concentration, largely because it complemented his own desire for an independent command. In mid-August he wrote Secretary of War Seddon privately that he thought the Army of Northern Virginia should remain on the defensive while he led heavy detachments to Tennessee to combine with Bragg. There, together with reinforcements from other quarters, they would strike "a crushing blow" against Rosecrans. Longstreet sought and received political support for his crusade. Tennessee Senator G. A. Henry obliged him nicely, writing Seddon: "I say to you we want some fighting generals in the Army of Tennessee. As sure as you are born that army is better than its commanders, and you will see my statement verified if men of more nerve are put in its command. Can't Longstreet be sent there?" On 18 August, Longstreet wrote to Senator Wigfall, the civilian leader of the western concentration bloc and a personal friend of Seddon, asking him to use his influence with the administration as well. "I am not essential here," he complained. "I hope that I may get west in time to save what there is left of us. I have no personal motives in this," he was quick to add, "for with either Bragg or Pemberton's army I should be second to Johnston and therefore in the same relative position I am at present."[24] Longstreet could play coy because he knew Johnston wanted nothing to do with the Army of Tennessee and that Wigfall already regarded him as a likely successor to Bragg.[25]

From the Army of Tennessee itself, Polk had begun lobbying for a move into Middle Tennessee after Johnston rejected Bragg's offer of reinforcements. Hoping Hardee would raise the subject with his new commander, Polk wrote his former colleague on 30 July: "In reflecting on the situation, it seems to me that things are not wearing a promising aspect, and that some change in our program might not be amiss." Polk suggested that Johnston's army be brought to Chattanooga and consolidated with the Army of Tennessee and with Simon Buckner's Department of East Tennessee. With Johnston in command, the combined Confederate forces would take the offensive, crush Rosecrans, and retake Middle Tennessee. Polk also wrote President Davis of his plan, adding that it reflected the views of "the most intelligent circles" in the army.[26]

Those circles apparently did not include Bragg. Perhaps in response to Polk's letter to the president, Adjutant General Samuel Cooper wrote Bragg on 1 August: "If we can spare most of Johnston's army temporarily and reinforce you, can you attack the enemy?" Maybe, Bragg replied, "if a fight can be had on equal terms," although he feared the same geographic obstacles that gave Rosecrans pause. His fears got the better of him, and four days later he wrote Cooper that "it would be unsafe to seek the enemy," even if reinforced by both Johnston and Buckner. To Johnston he privately confided his doubts: "The defensive seems to be our only alternative, and that is a sad one."[27]

Indeed, the time for a strategic counterstroke had all but passed. Rosecrans was on the move. On 15 August, orders were issued from army headquarters at Winchester explaining with textbook clarity the precise missions of each corps in the general movement toward the Tennessee River, which would begin on the morning of the sixteenth. Ironically, Garfield lay on his cot violently ill, unable to draft the instructions for the advance he had so anxiously awaited.[28]

Rosecrans and the Army of the Cumberland were about to embark on one of the most ambitious and perilous operations of the war. It was hard to say which would prove the greater obstacle to taking Chattanooga—the Army of Tennessee or the terrain. Just getting to the river looked daunting enough to the Federals as they gazed on the lofty Cumberland Mountains rising sharply before them. The Cumberland range formed a continuous plateau that ran to the very bank of the Tennessee River southwest of Chattanooga and dropped abruptly into the narrow Tennessee River valley northwest of the city. About fifteen miles due west of Chattanooga, the Sequatchie Valley extended a narrow, jagged finger fifty miles long to the northeast. It split the plateau of the Cumberland Mountains in two, creating an elevation between the Sequatchie and Tennessee River valleys known locally as Walden's Ridge. Opposite Chattanooga, Walden's Ridge abutted the river in dizzying bluffs.[29]

The terrain was no more promising on the Chattanooga side of the river. North of the city, the countryside, though comparatively level, was ribbed with a seemingly endless string of hills and ridges running north to south. South of the city, the mountains continued their rugged course from northeast to southwest in four distinct ridges, each separated from the other by a valley through which ran one or more creeks that emptied into the Tennessee. Nearest the river was Sand Mountain, called Raccoon Mountain at its northern extremity just west of Chattanooga. Sand Mountain hugged the bank of the Tennessee and was about fifteen miles wide, its plateau a barren oak ridge brushed with coarse, weedy grass and nearly devoid of water. East of Sand Mountain stood Lookout Mountain, wildly beautiful as it loomed one thousand feet above the valley floor. Between Sand and Lookout mountains was Lookout Valley. At the center of the valley rose a small elevation called Valley Head. There two streams took their source: Lookout Creek, which flowed north to the Tennessee, and Wills Creek, which ran south through the valley.

Stretching for one hundred miles below Chattanooga, Lookout Mountain took the shape of a hand—forefinger on the west and thumb to the east— as it neared the city. At the base of the finger it narrowed from a width of twelve or fifteen miles to less than three, becoming higher and rockier on its northward course. Some thirty miles south of Chattanooga, the thumb threw off a narrow spur called Pigeon Mountain that ran north about eighteen miles. Tucked between Pigeon Mountain and the forefinger of Lookout was a relatively fertile valley known as McLemore's Cove. The cove was just six miles wide at its head, where it spawned Chickamauga Creek, a sometimes sluggish, sometimes rushing stream that emptied into the Tennessee River northeast of Chattanooga. Northwest of Pigeon Mountain was the fourth ridge, known as Missionary Ridge. Rising from the Tennessee River about five miles northeast of Chattanooga, it followed a course due south for fifteen miles before leveling off in McLemore's Cove. On the west side of Missionary Ridge, separating it from the forefinger of Lookout Mountain, was Dry Valley and Chattanooga Creek. No more than a rugged, heavily forested hill five or six hundred feet high, Missionary Ridge could be crossed anywhere along its length with relative ease. Not so Lookout Mountain, where the roads were few and rocky and the gaps through which they ran were gaps in name only—not dips in the mountain but only small breaks in the rugged escarpment along Lookout's rim.[30]

Such was the country before the Army of the Cumberland. Its ruggedness meant the army would have to traverse a wide front to the Tennessee; once at the river, there were three options open to Rosecrans, each of which presented its own advantages and risks. First, he could operate against Chattanooga from the north. This course had several things to recommend it. The Army of the Cumberland would be closely supported by Ambrose Burnside's Army of the Ohio, which was to advance into East Tennessee at the same time. Also, it would find itself among friends, the loyal mountaineers whom Lincoln was so eager to liberate. Finally, on this flank Chattanooga could be approached over comparatively level ground. Rosecrans, however, rejected this approach for three reasons: it would mean moving the bulk of the army over a long, exposed, and difficult path, first over the wide plateau of the Cumberland Mountains, then across both the Tennessee and the swift-running Hiwassee rivers; it would expose the army's rail supply line; and, as Rosecrans correctly surmised, Bragg would expect him to advance from that direction.[31]

Rosecrans's second alternative was to concentrate his army directly across the river from Chattanooga, lay bridges under enemy fire, and fight the battle in the heart of town. This had too much the ring of Fredericksburg about it for Rosecrans's taste.

The third option was to cross the river south of town and try to flank Bragg out of Chattanooga much as Rosecrans had done at Tullahoma. The potential rewards were as great as the hazards. If successful, Rosecrans might turn Chattanooga and, concealed initially by the mountains, drive east and cut Bragg's railroad communications with Atlanta and points south before Bragg knew what had happened. But the mountains were a fickle temptress, promising conquest and threatening destruction in about equal measure. For the army would have to cross in several columns, widely separated and without secure communications, exposed to defeat in detail should the Confederates learn of Rosecrans's designs too soon.[32]

In the heady aftermath of Tullahoma, Rosecrans felt fortune was with him. He had duped Bragg once and saw no reason why he could not do so again. His confidence was based in part on intelligence reports that estimated Bragg's available infantry at between 28,000 and 30,000 (he actually had on hand some 37,000). Rosecrans, on the other hand, mustered about 60,500 infantry exclusive of the Reserve Corps, which could rapidly introduce another 20,500 men to the field. The cavalry forces of the two armies were at least numerically equal at some 12,000 troopers apiece, although Stanley's Federals still had a long way to go to match Forrest's and Wheeler's men in efficiency and esprit. Rosecrans was also encouraged by exaggerated reports of the poor state of morale in the Army of Tennessee. One supposedly loyal Unionist, just returned from Chattanooga, told the Ohioan that Bragg's army was "little, if any, better than a mob," adding that the common soldier felt overawed by the Federals and that "the prevailing opinion with officers and men is that Bragg will retreat as soon as an advance is made."[33]

So self-assured was Rosecrans that he thought he could trick his foe with a clumsy ruse. A reckless and homesick Rebel lieutenant had been captured while visiting his family near Federal headquarters at Winchester. Rosecrans sent for him. "You have been taken under circumstances which, were you to be tried by court-martial, would convict you of being a spy," Rosecrans told him; but, because he was young and had a family, Rosecrans said it would be a shame to have to hang him. Having thoroughly frightened the young officer, Rosecrans made his pitch: "I think I can propose something for you to do which would be fair and right, and will enable you to escape trial. I am willing that you should return to the Confederate lines and tell what you have seen and heard. And more, I will guarantee that everything you hear will come true, so that your service to General Bragg will be a real and substantial one, and he will unquestionably be disposed to allow you to return and try your luck a second time. But I require this: that if you are permitted to come back to me you shall answer such questions as I put to you truly." With his only alternative the rope, the lieutenant agreed. The next morning, after placing the young Rebel in the hall next to his office so he might overhear any conversation, Rosecrans called in his quartermaster for transportation and loudly commanded him to repair the McMinnville branch railroad with haste so that supplies might be concentrated there for an advance into East Tennessee north of Chattanooga. The credulous Confederate was then released.[34]

While the lieutenant made his way to Chattanooga, Rosecrans set about completing his plans. To lend credence to the deception, Crittenden was given the task of crossing the plateau of the Cumberland Mountains and demonstrating on the west bank north of Chattanooga. His Twenty-first Corps was to advance in three columns extending over a twenty-mile front and descend into the Sequatchie Valley, where it was then "to encamp and make as much smoke and general appearance of a numerous army as he possibly could." Once in the valley and no later than 19 August, the attached cavalry brigade of Robert Minty was to ride rapidly to the Tennessee River and begin reconnaissance operations between Washington and Blythe's Ferry, some thirty-five miles north of Chattanooga. At the same time, Colonel Wilder's Lightning Brigade, on detached service reporting directly to army headquarters, was to demonstrate against Chattanooga and Harrison's Landing, driving "everything across the river clear into Chattanooga, to fire on that place if he thought proper, and make all the row he could." To support Wilder and enhance the illusion of an approaching army, one brigade apiece from the divisions of Thomas Wood and John Palmer would move out of the Sequatchie Valley and over Walden's Ridge to the river, there to reconnoiter "with a show of modest concealment, indicating strength."[35]

To Thomas fell a much simpler mission. He was instructed to move his Fourteenth Corps as rapidly as possible from its encampments at Decherd and Cowan directly toward the river. The divisions of James Negley and Absalom Baird were to halt along the railroad behind Stevenson, those of Joseph Reynolds and John Brannan were to march down the narrow Battle Creek Valley and take up concealed positions near the mouth of the creek; once there, they were to begin building boats for a crossing. Unlike Crittenden, Thomas was to maintain the utmost secrecy in his movements.

McCook and his Twentieth Corps, on the army right, had the easiest task. With Sheridan already near the river at Stevenson, it remained only for Richard Johnson to advance his division to nearby Bellefonte and Jefferson C. Davis to come up behind Sheridan before the corps would be ready to cross.[36]

Sunday, 16 August, dawned ominously. A warm rain was falling. Lightning danced over the Cumberland Mountains, which rose darkly to the east of the Federal camps. Across a sixty-mile front, long columns of blue began snaking their way up wet mountain roads. At eleven o'clock, Wilder's mounted infantry saddled up and began the ascent. They turned their faces from the driving rain, cursed the mud thrown up by their horses, and slowly climbed the rocky road amid a cascade of rushing water.

At army headquarters, a spirit of quiet confidence prevailed despite the weather. The crossing of the mountains had begun, Rosecrans wired the War Department. "I think we shall deceive the enemy as to our point of crossing. It is a stupendous undertaking. The Alps, with a broad river at the foot, and not fertile plains, but seventy miles of difficult and mostly sterile mountains beyond," before reaching Chattanooga, "a point of secondary importance to the enemy, in reference to his vital one, Atlanta."[37]

Well could Rosecrans be hopeful. Bragg and his generals were wholly unaware of the blue whirlwind rising out of the Cumberland Mountains. Not a single Confederate cavalryman picketed Walden's Ridge or the northwest bank of the Tennessee. Forrest was in East Tennessee watching the ferries and fords toward Kingston. South of Chattanooga, Wheeler's cavalry lay scattered between Gadsden, Alabama, (eighty miles southwest of Stevenson) and Chattanooga. Only a single infantry brigade under Patton Anderson was deployed west of the city. Without firing a shot, Bragg had not only conceded every crucial point from Bellefonte to the Sequatchie Valley but had left his army blind to happenings across the river. None of this seemed to trouble Bragg or most of his senior lieutenants. Hill was horrified by this lethargy that permitted Rosecrans to go about his business unmolested. He could not help but contrast the western army to the Army of Northern Virginia: "The want of information at General Bragg's headquarters was in striking contrast with the minute knowledge General Lee always had of every opponent in his front, and I was most painfully impressed with the feeling that it was to be a hap-hazard campaign on our part." More typical was Polk's smug assurance. To his sister he wrote on 14 August: "Rosecrans we hear is preparing to move forward, but he is certain to risk nothing if he can help it."[38]

CHAPTER THREE

I HAVE NEVER FELT SO GLAD
TO BE A SOLDIER

PRESIDENT Lincoln was taken with the Spencer rifle and its "quiet little Yankee" inventor, who had come to Washington to peddle his new weapon. The president admired the rifle's simplicity and the ease with which seven shots could be squeezed off in less than thirty seconds. Lincoln; his private secretary, John Hay; and Spencer passed an enjoyable evening on Friday, 21 August, shooting the new rifle. "The president made some pretty good shots," recalled Hay.[1]

On the hills across the river from Chattanooga, John Wilder and his men were getting in some shooting of their own with their Spencers. That morning, the brigade had crested Walden's Ridge to a spectacular, blue-skied panorama of the Tennessee Valley. Twelve miles to the south and clearly visible was Chattanooga.

Wilder prepared his demonstration. He sent the Ninety-eighth and Ninety-second Illinois with a section of Eli Lilly's Eighteenth Indiana Battery off toward the landing opposite Harrison. Right on schedule, the brigade of William Hazen, on detached service from Palmer's division, marched on the same spot. With the remainder of his brigade, Wilder descended the ridge and cantered down the valley toward Stringer's Ridge, opposite Chattanooga. As planned, George Wagner's brigade of Wood's division was coming up in support.[2]

Captain Mercer Otey took his work as chief signal officer of the Army of Tennessee seriously. After the army fell back into Chattanooga, Otey carefully placed signal stations on high ground around the city: one each on Sand, Lookout, and Raccoon mountains, and a fourth across the river from Bridgeport. He equipped each four-man post with a powerful telescope, flags to communicate with one another by day, and torches to do so by night. Otey tied off the line with his own station in the city and waited for a chance to prove the worth of his little command.

He got it sooner than expected. Glancing toward Raccoon Mountain that Friday morning, he was startled to see his signalmen frantically waving word of the approach of Wilder and Wagner. Otey immediately rushed off a message to army headquarters. The report could not be true, came the reply, scouts had sighted no Federals for miles around. Before a flustered Otey could scratch off another message, a shell whizzed overhead and fell into the heart of town, then another and another, and headquarters had its answer. "Ah, then and there was hurrying to and fro, and gathering tears and tremblings of distress," recalled Otey.[3]

Otey might have gotten a more satisfactory reply had someone in authority been at headquarters. But Bragg was back at the army hospital at Cherokee Springs, near Ringgold, trying to restore his jangled nerves and something of his battered health; his wife was with him, also ill, perhaps from having suffered through the physical decline of her husband.[4] The rest of the high command was in church, for President Davis had declared this to be a day of prayer and fasting for the crumbling Confederacy. Officers and civilians had thronged into the local Presbyterian church to hear the eminent Reverend B. M. Palmer of New Orleans entreat the Almighty for Southern salvation. An early shot from Lilly's battery sailed overhead during the opening prayer, exploding in the street and breaking the leg of a little girl. Parishioners began heading for the door. "Do not be alarmed. It's our gunners practicing," General Cheatham assured the congregation. "There's not a Yankee within fifty miles of here." The next shot skimmed the rooftop, and the stampede was on. An intrepid few remained to hear the minister out — "the longest prayer I ever heard," remembered Henry Watterson, editor of the Chattanooga Rebel.[5]

Across the Tennessee, Wilder's men were having a high time. They had achieved complete surprise. They captured one hundred dumbfounded teamsters and their wagons foraging on the west bank, overwhelmed an infantry picket station and wounded most of its relief who were caught midway across the river in their rowboat, sank the steamer Paint Rock, disabled a second ferry boat, and tore up a pontoon bridge. Lilly's gunners fired into the city with impunity until one three-gun Confederate section finally mustered a volley. The Hoosier gunners quickly silenced it, but not before a well-placed solid shot sliced off the leg of Corporal Abram McCorkle, who, remarkably, was lying asleep next to his cannon — making him the first Union fatality of the campaign. Filled with the import of the moment, Wilder picked up the spent shot and later mailed it to the governor of Indiana.[6]

To the north, demonstrations proceeded according to schedule. Minty had his brigade galloping about near Blythe's Ferry. The other half of Wilder's brigade was making its presence known to the Confederate picket posts opposite Harrison, while Hazen marched ostentatiously across the Tennessee Valley to join them. That night and for several to come, Wilder had details out working to create the illusion of a gathering army. They banged boards together, hammered on barrels, and sawed countless planks, which they tossed into streams to simulate castoff lumber from an imaginary flotilla under construction. Bugles blew for fictitious commands, and bands serenaded phantom bivouacs. Hazen played out the same charade farther upriver.[7]

Rosecrans's deception was a huge success. Bragg returned from Cherokee Springs on the night of 21 August convinced that Hazen's feint heralded the start of a major thrust by the Army of the Cumberland against the rear of Simon Buckner's command in East Tennessee. Burnside had advanced his twenty-thousand-man army into the Cumberland Mountains, one hundred miles west of Knoxville, on 20 August, and Bragg assumed he would maneuver to hold Buckner in place. Buckner was also deceived. To Bragg, he wrote: "Burnside's main column is expected to co-operate with Rosecrans's left. Rosecrans designs to cross the Tennessee above the Hiwassee."[8]

Bragg's initial moves flowed from this assumption, and so every order he gave was the wrong one. He called in Patton Anderson's brigade from the Hog Jaw Valley opposite Bridgeport, effectively blinding the army to any crossing by Thomas. Only the Third Confederate Cavalry Regiment remained to picket the river from Bridgeport to Gunthersville, Alabama, a distance of nearly fifty miles. Next, he ordered Hill, who was also duped by Hazen's feint, to deploy Cleburne's division so as to cover every ford and ferry from the mouth of Chickamauga Creek to the mouth of the Hiwassee. Two days later, Bragg sent Stewart's division to reinforce Buckner.[9]

Bragg may not have known where the Army of the Cumberland was but he did know he needed reinforcements. Richmond was still mulling over the propriety of a western concentration, so Bragg decided to nudge the process along by appealing directly to Johnston for help. He had every reason to expect it; earlier in the summer Johnston had promised to send eleven infantry brigades to Chattanooga if Bragg were threatened. But now, when it came time to make good his offer, Johnston balked. First, he went through the formality of wiring Richmond for permission, even though, if Bragg was correct about Rosecrans's intentions, every hour counted. Perhaps because the administration was not yet sold on the idea of a concentration around Chattanooga, it left the decision with Johnston. Without actually ordering him to do anything, the War Department advised Johnston: "By all means help General Bragg as far as you are able to do so."

Johnston was slow to act. Reneging on his earlier promise of eleven brigades, he agreed to send only two divisions, for a total of six brigades. The first, under Major General W. H. T. Walker, left Mississippi by train on 23 August. Though Johnston assured Bragg that both divisions had left by the twenty-fourth, John C. Breckinridge and his division did not begin the return trip to their old army until 25 August. Johnston's niggardliness was reflected in his telegram to Bragg: "I sent 9,000 infantry and artillery. . . . This is a loan to be promptly returned." The long-awaited and much-heralded western concentration was off to a rocky start.[10]

After moving Anderson and Cleburne in the wrong direction and sending for reinforcements, Bragg was at a loss what to do next. He turned to Hill for ideas. The day after Wilder's bombardment, Brigadier General William Mackall, who only four days earlier had taken up his duties as army chief of staff, penned the first of what were to be many expressions of his commander's anxiety during the upcoming campaign. Unlike Garfield, Mackall was a consummate professional. He had had a good record in the Regular Army and had served as chief of staff to Confederate General Albert Sidney Johnston early in the war. At some point Mackall ran afoul of the administration, and he was relegated to backwater district commands. His old friend and West Point classmate Bragg came to his aid, requesting his services as chief of staff in early August. Mackall made a good impression at headquarters; Colonel George Brent judged him "a plain, straightforward, earnest officer."[11]

Mackall now wrote Hill: "General Bragg . . . wishes you to know that his general plan is to await developments of the enemy and when his point of attack is ascertained, to . . . fall on him with our whole force. He further instructs me to say that he hopes you will at all times, in person or by letter, give him any suggestion that may occur to you in furtherance of this great and common cause. You cannot, general, offend even by importunity."[12]

Bragg's openhanded note, certainly meant in the best spirit, probably was a mistake. Hill was too new to the theater of operations to have anything to contribute. More important, Bragg's letter unduly raised Hill's expectations about his influence at headquarters, a dangerous thing given Hill's temperament. As Arthur Manigault aptly observed, the general "had always borne the unenviable reputation . . . of having his own way and doing things only as pleased him, and, were it otherwise, throwing obstacles in the way."[13] When Hill finally did offer a suggestion a few days later, Bragg spurned it, and the rift between them opened.

Bragg and Hill were on good terms for the moment, but the North Carolinian had already worn out his welcome with his brother officers. Hill had a dry sense of humor, bordering on the perverse, that few appreciated. Two examples will suffice to show why he fast developed "a most unenviable reputation" in the western army. Soon after his arrival, Hill was handed a leave request from one particularly talented quartermaster. There was just enough room on the endorsement for Hill to write approved or disapproved and sign his name. But he could not leave well enough alone: "Approved," he scrawled, "as I think he can well be spared from the numbers of quartermasters that infest the army." A few days later, Hill outdid himself. On a furlough application from a Georgia soldier, he wrote: "Approved because if the soldiers are not allowed to go home occasionally, the next generation will be the offspring of skulkers and cowards." Major General W. H. T. "Hell Training Billy" Walker, a man of more emotion than intellect, took the joke as a slur upon the virtue of the women of his state.[14]

Chattanooga was fast emptying of its civilian inhabitants. At midnight on 21 August, Bragg ordered noncombatants to leave town. Few needed to be told twice. For the next several days, train after train chugged south loaded with civilians, hurried on their way by Lilly's continuous bombardment. By 25 August, only the office staff of the Chattanooga *Rebel,* a handful of defiant citizens, and the army remained.[15]

At his new headquarters at Stevenson, Rosecrans was in fine spirits. He even joked with his staff about Washington politicians, whom he dubbed "the peace party," "white-rag faction," and the "not-another-man-or-dollar conspiracy." Deserters, particularly disaffected Tennesseans unwilling to fight outside their state, were coming into his lines in large numbers, which added to the prevailing optimism and led young Captain Horace Porter of the general staff to speculate that, when the river no longer separated the two forces, "half of Bragg's army will desert."[16]

That remained to be seen. For the moment, all serious thought at headquarters was given over to the challenge of crossing one of the major rivers on the continent. The task was stupendous. To men accustomed to the open farmlands of Ohio, Indiana, and Illinois, it seemed nearly impossible. The sheer palisades and narrow river valley, so deep that the sun licked its waters only in the late morning and left abruptly in the early afternoon, overawed them. In the back of their minds was the gnawing realization that, once they crossed, the Tennessee River would bar their retreat and attenuate their supply line.[17]

Even Rosecrans seems to have been momentarily taken aback. Finding bridges burned and boats sunk or impounded under Rebel batteries in Chattanooga, he hesitated, uncertain where to cross. "I wish to cross below, if not hindered; may try above, if enemy moves to suit," he told Burnside on 22 August. He was unable to believe that no Confederates lurked behind the mountains below Chattanooga. A reconnaissance of the river restored his confidence, however, and preparations for a crossing of the army southwest of the city soon began in earnest.[18]

For ten days the work went on. By day, roads were improved, fieldworks built to cover the crossing sites, fords pinpointed, supplies unloaded, and pontoons laid out. By night, patrols rowed quietly across the river to sweep back the handful of Rebel cavalry pickets on the far bank. Mostly, however, they found no one. Opposite Bridgeport, the great Federal supply depot, Yankee cavalry scouts reported not a single Confederate.[19]

With pontoons in short supply, expedients were used, and each division commander was pretty much left to his own devices. Joseph Reynolds fared the best. He sent a raiding party across the river to seize Shellmound, and in so doing his men were lucky enough to find eight or nine flatboats. With these the general put together a scratch flotilla capable of crossing four hundred men an hour. Less fortunate were the men of Brannan's division, crowded around the mouth of Battle Creek. They were reduced to cutting down trees and scrounging scrap lumber to build rafts.[20]

To Phil Sheridan went the critical task of bridging the Tennessee at Bridgeport. The railroad bridge to Long Island, midway across the river, lay in ruins; only the brick supports and a bit of trestle remained.[21] There was no time to repair it, so work began on a substitute. In the temporary absence of Sheridan, the job devolved on Brigadier General William H. Lytle, the senior brigade commander present. A better choice could not be had. He was one of the finest and best-loved generals in the army, a born leader with military instincts as sharp as those of John Wilder. Soldiering was in the blood of the Lytles. His great-grandfather had fought first the French in 1750, then the British during the Revolutionary War. Still looking for a fight, he took his family to Kentucky in 1790 and chased Indians. The old man passed on his Indian-fighting skills to Lytle's grandfather, who commanded a company in Daniel Boone's division at the age of fifteen. Lytle's father later followed more urbane pursuits and represented the district of Cincinnati in Congress. Young William took after his father, making a name for himself in Ohio as an orator and lawyer. It was as a poet, however, that he captured the heart of the nation, and his "Antony and Cleopatra" with its poignant opening line, "I am dying, Egypt, dying," was recited in parlors North and South. Lytle certainly looked more the poet than the soldier. Said a contemporary admirer: "His head . . . was covered with masses of long silken brown hair. His complexion was so fair as to be almost effeminate." But the martial spirit of his forebears was in him. At the age of twenty, Lytle left his law practice to lead a company of the Second Ohio Volunteers in the War with Mexico, and at the outbreak of the rebellion he was tendered command of the Tenth Ohio Infantry. He performed splendidly in the West Virginia campaign of 1861 under the admiring eye of Rosecrans, who rewarded him with a promotion to brigade command. For one who had accomplished so much in just thirty-seven years, Lytle was refreshingly modest. "I never saw a general with so few fancies and who seemed to think so little of [him]self," wrote his aide, Lieutenant Alfred Pirtle.[22]

Colonel Innes reported his Michigan engineers to Lytle, and together they tackled the imposing task of bridging the Tennessee. Pontoons had not yet arrived. They would be too few to span the entire river in any case, so Innes set about constructing a trestle to bridge the difference. Lytle sent hundreds of his men with axes into the woods around Bridgeport, and in two days they delivered fifteen hundred logs to the engineers. Other details took up floorboards and planks from surrounding houses and barns. Rosecrans rode up each day from Stevenson to watch the progress. Pontoons arrived on the thirtieth and were quickly laid across the river and connected with the trestle. On 1 September the job was finished. Sheridan rode into Bridgeport the same day to assume division command. A tired Lytle breakfasted early, yielded to his staff's request for a group photo, then retired to get some rest before the next morning's crossing.[23]

Colonel Hans Christian Heg was another of the gifted young volunteer officers in the Army of the Cumberland. His was the not uncommon story in mid-nineteenth-century America of an immigrant boy made good. With his parents, Heg had left his native Norway for a Norwegian colony near Muskego, Wisconsin. Heg moved on to California to pan gold with the forty-niners just nine years later. He stayed in the goldfields for two years, when his father's death drew him home. His mother had died eight years earlier, so it fell to Hans to raise his younger siblings. The time spent in California apparently had satisfied his wanderlust, as the young Norwegian soon married and settled down to farm. He made a name for himself in state politics and was elected state prison commissioner on the Republican ticket. Heg was an enlightened reformer. "Experience has confirmed my conviction that a mild and merciful application of the rules of discipline is sufficient in all cases to reduce the most hardened offenders to obedience," he wrote. Heg applied a similar brand of discipline with his first military command, the Fifteenth Wisconsin Infantry, a Norwegian regiment that boasted 115 members named Ole, including three Ole Andersons in Company B, three Ole Ericksons in Company E, and four Ole Olsons in Company F. His men did not love him, but, as fellow Scandinavians, they respected and appreciated his strict leadership.[24]

Now a brigade commander in the division of Jefferson C. Davis, Heg was to lead the first crossing of the Tennessee River, set for dawn, 29 August. At midnight on the twenty-eighth, his men silently assembled on the riverbank under a bright, cool, moonlit sky. The campfires of Rebel pickets flickered on the opposite bank, five hundred yards distant; none knew how many Confederates lay in wait behind them. All through the waning hours

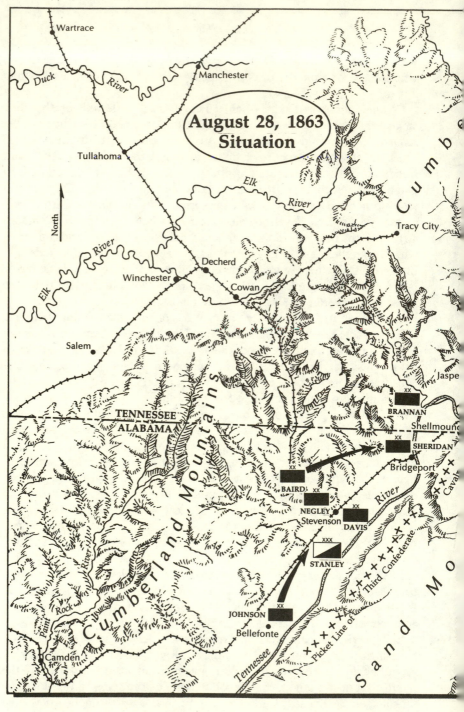

Map Symbols

	Corps	Division	Cavalry brigade	Infantry brigade	Cavalry regiment	Infantry regiment	Infantry battalion	Artillery battery
UNION	McCOOK	VAN CLEVE	MINTY	DODGE	Pa	Ill	US	A-1 Ohio

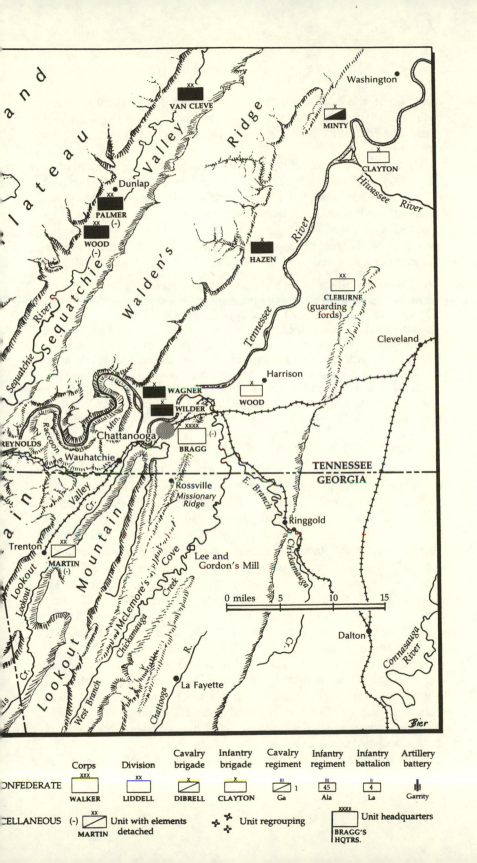

VAN CLEVE

Washington

MINTY

CLAYTON

Hiwassee River

Dunlap

PALMER (-)

WOOD (-)

Walden's Ridge

HAZEN

Tennessee River

CLEBURNE (guarding fords)

Cleveland

Harrison

WOOD

WAGNER

WILDER

Chattanooga

BRAGG (-)

REYNOLDS

Wauhatchie

Raccoon Mtn.

TENNESSEE
GEORGIA

Rossville

Missionary Ridge

E. Branch

Ringgold

Trenton

MARTIN (-)

Lookout Valley

Cr.

Lookout Mountain

Lookout

McLemore's Cove

Chickamauga Creek

Lee and Gordon's Mill

Chickamauga Cr.

0 miles   5   10   15

Dalton

Conasauga River

West Branch

Chattooga R.

La Fayette

Bier

	Corps	Division	Cavalry brigade	Infantry brigade	Cavalry regiment	Infantry regiment	Infantry battalion	Artillery battery
CONFEDERATE	XXX **WALKER**	XX **LIDDELL**	X **DIBRELL**	X **CLAYTON**	III 1 **Ga**	III 45 **Ala**	II 4 **La**	**Garrity**

MISCELLANEOUS   (-) XX **MARTIN** Unit with elements detached   ✦✦ Unit regrouping   XXXX **BRAGG'S HQTRS.** Unit headquarters of the night, the Pioneer brigade quietly unloaded and assembled pontoon boats, while the two regiments chosen to lead the crossing—the Eighth Kansas and Fifteenth Wisconsin—assembled beside them in groups of twenty-five per boat.

Day dawned bright and chill over the palisades. Scattered on the riverbank was a "disjointed mass of boats [and] timbers." Heg's infantrymen crouched in bushes farther back. Army headquarters had assured them they would meet little resistance, but headquarters had been wrong before, and most expected to be blasted out of the water. Heg gave the signal, regimental and company officers took it up, and the troops scampered to their boats. Heg recorded what followed:

> The boats gradually slid down the steep embankment, and before a person had time to realize the beauty of the sight, the word "Forward" was given. My pen will fail to describe the reality of the scene before me. The beautiful scenery of the country, the mountain tops glittering in the sunshine, the thick misty cloud just rising from the still blue waters of the river, forced to leave its light couch by the rays of the rising sun, the sharp command "Forward" as it resounded along the river bank, and was taken up by the mountain echo. All this requires a better pen than mine to portray. There was something grand and beautiful in this sight, something emblematic of the great cause in which we are engaged. All this, I say, was so inspiring that I almost forgot how terribly those men were exposed, should the enemy be in condition to take advantage of the opportunity.[25]

But the Confederates were not. Only the gentle swishing of oars and barking of commands broke the morning stillness. The startled pickets of the Third Confederate Cavalry managed a ragged volley when the boats landed, then darted up the bluffs, leaving behind burning campfires and half-eaten ears of corn. Heg deployed his skirmishers and started up Sand Mountain after the Rebels. By nightfall, division trains were across and encamped high atop the mountain, five miles from the river.[26]

Everywhere the army crossed, the story was the same. Concealed in underbrush near the bank, the men fought a fear that grew as the moment of crossing neared, recalled a participant. Then came the rush to the boats and a "rowing for dear life." On the far bank, the Yankees tumbled out of the boats to find nothing but a few frightened Rebel pickets.[27]

On the right, there was little excitement after Heg braved the waters. McCook had the divisions of Johnson and Davis across by nightfall on 31 August; they encamped on the east bank near Caperton's Ferry to await the crossing of Sheridan, who was delayed until 2 September by work on the bridge at Bridgeport. Stanley crossed part of his cavalry at Caperton's Ferry, the rest splashed across at a ford a few miles downriver.

In the center, where the current was rapid and the banks soft and treacherous, Brannan's division provided all the thrills. His jerry-built flotilla pushed off from the mouth of Battle Creek simultaneously with Heg, and a stranger collection of boats could not be imagined. On the rafts, priority went to the artillery and ammunition train. The luckier infantrymen found places on the rafts or in canoes, so crowded with screaming soldiers that waves broke over the gunwales, making it an open question whether the paddlers could keep the boats from drifting downstream with the current. Those unable to find places in the boats stripped, bundled their clothing, lashed their rifles to fence rails, and swam the four hundred yards across the river. Strong swimmers pushed the rails ahead of them while the weaker hung on and drifted with the current.[28] Had the Confederates been on the opposite bank in force, few Yankees would have gotten across alive; certainly those who did would have been in no condition to fight.

Reynolds's division crossed handily in their flatboats at Shellmound about the same time as Brannan. Negley got over at Caperton's Ferry after McCook, but a collapse of a portion of Lytle's trestle bridge delayed the crossing of Baird until 4 September.

Crittenden's corps was the last across. His orders were to move down the Sequatchie and follow Thomas over, but neither of his division commands nearest the river could get across. When Wood reached Shellmound on 3 September, he found the way blocked by Reynolds's trains. Palmer had been promised use of the ferry when he reached Battle Creek, but he could not wrest the boat from Brannan who, happy to finally have real transportation, was using it to cross his trains.[29]

These delays irritated Rosecrans. Early intelligence speculated that Bragg would abandon Chattanooga without a fight, and the Ohioan was anxious to press his presumed advantage. Wilder reported that "the universal cry . . . on the other side of the river is that they are not going to fight us this side of Atlanta." Deserters told the same story. A bit of this may have been part of Bragg's own deception plan. Already, in the early hours of the campaign, he was putting into action the standard operating procedure in the Army of Tennessee of planting "deserters" in the enemy's camp with false information. Among Rosecrans's staff, opinion was divided as to whether Bragg would fall back to Atlanta, move northward into East Tennessee, or attempt to turn the Federal left flank and advance into Middle Tennessee. Rosecrans, giddy with his early success, accepted the stories of impending flight at face value and wired Burnside on 30 August that all indications pointed to an early retreat by Bragg to Atlanta. Now more than ever, Rosecrans wanted to begin his push through the mountains into Bragg's rear, not only to compel the evacuation of Chattanooga but perhaps even to beat Bragg to Atlanta.[30]

While Rosecrans fretted over delays, those troops already across the river enjoyed themselves as only soldiers can. Since they were rarely clean while in the field, the first order of business was a bath in the Tennessee. "The whole river as far as one could see seemed to be alive with men in bathing," remembered an Illinois private. Some invariably overdid it and got sunstroke, so swimming became forbidden after ten in the morning.[31] After a day or two the soldiers began drifting off, in organized details or individually, in search of food to supplement their dull rations of bacon and biscuits. Those over the river first found foraging good, and sweet potatoes, pumpkins, apples, peaches, chickens, and hogs all made their way into camp.

It was in their search for food that the Yankees first met the loyal population of eastern Tennessee and came face-to-face with a side of war they would rather have missed. All the mountaineers were friendly, and most had suffered brutally for their loyalty. With the coming of the Army of the Cumberland, men who had hidden for months in caves and in deep mountain crags to dodge Rebel conscription agents emerged with their families to get their first look at Federal soldiers. Although dirt poor, "they vied with each other in bestowing upon the boys their kindness—sweet potatoes, all kinds of vegetables, ducks, chickens, pies, cakes, honey, and applejack brandy were among the gifts," recalled Colonel Smith Atkins of the Ninety-second Illinois fondly. "All the men want to act as guides for us, and three hundred have just enlisted in our ranks," Horace Porter wrote his sister. Hans Heg was sickened by the suffering of these good but ignorant people at the hands of the enemy. "I have never felt so glad to be a soldier as I have since I came into these mountains where we could do so much good to the poor down trodden people," he wrote his wife, Gunhild. One woman who came into camp to sell some chickens said her husband, a Union man, had been made to dig his own grave before conscript agents shot him. Another woman with six young children to feed wandered into Heg's headquarters almost dead with hunger and consumption. Two weeks earlier, her husband had been tied with a rope and gunned down before her eyes. Heg gave her some flour and a chunk of maple sugar Gunhild had sent him. Captain Porter and a few fellow staff officers stopped at a cabin near headquarters one afternoon simply to beg a little cool water to drink with their rations. Instead, the lady who greeted them ushered the officers in, sat them down, and brought out butter and milk "which made our eyes dance. Her little children ran to us each with a U.S. flag, waving it in great glee. I asked the woman where these flags came from. She said they have been hidden away for more than two years."

So the liberator had come. Lincoln's promise to the East Tennesseans was being played out. But in the mountains, malice toward none had no meaning. "Some of the houses of those men that have helped to torment these poor fellows have already gone up in smoke—and more will be apt to follow," wrote Heg.[32]

Rosecrans's patience ran out quickly. With or without Crittenden, he was determined to push on. In the wee hours of the morning on 3 September, Garfield drafted the orders that would take the army deep into the mountains and beyond. On the right, General Stanley was directed to take up post with the cavalry at Rawlingsville, Alabama, in the southern reaches of Lookout Valley (or Wills Valley, as that portion of the valley was sometimes called). From there, he was to "push forward with audacity" across the state line toward Rome and Alpine, Georgia, to "ascertain the position and intentions of the enemy," making "a strong diversion" in the process.

McCook received orders to concentrate just north of Rawlingsville at Valley Head. Davis and Johnson were to take the direct road over Sand Mountain from Caperton's Ferry; Sheridan would take the valley road from Trenton, unless he could find a suitable path over the mountain. Once his corps was reunited, McCook was to open communications with Thomas and seize Winston's Gap on Lookout Mountain.

By that time, Thomas presumably would be twenty miles up the valley at Trenton, with orders to seize Cooper's (also called Frick's) and Stevens's gaps. (Lookout Mountain was the final and greatest barrier to an advance on Chattanooga from the south. The mountain was impassable except at scattered gaps, of which Cooper's and Stevens's were the best.) Thomas, in turn, was to open communications with Crittenden who, if all went well, would be at Whiteside astride the railroad. From there the Kentuckian was to threaten Chattanooga. The forces opposite and north of the city—consisting of the brigades of Hazen, Wagner, Minty, and Wilder—were placed under the supervision of Hazen with orders to keep up the ruse of a major crossing and to cooperate with Crittenden. Rosecrans set a stiff deadline of midnight on 4 September for everyone to be in place. As an afterthought, he ordered Granger to concentrate at Bridgeport such of his Reserve Corps as could be spared from guard duty in southern Tennessee.[33]

At his headquarters in Chattanooga, Bragg was as despondent as Rosecrans was elated. It was the same old story with the Confederate high command: sketchy and unreliable intelligence reports, a dazed uncertainty among the generals, and an embarrassing lack of will. Precious days slipped by and still Bragg knew nothing of Rosecrans's intentions or whereabouts. Everyone failed him. Mercer Otey's signal station opposite Bridgeport was oddly quiet during the crossing. Bragg's highly touted secret service—really just an odd mixture of poorly disciplined scouts and spies—could offer nothing; they had no idea where the Federals were or what they were up to. The cavalry should have compensated for this, but Wheeler's cavalry was in no position to help. While Bragg must be held to blame for conceding the northwest bank of the Tennessee and relegating Wheeler to a defensive posture on the near side, he had instructed his chief of cavalry to watch closely the potential crossing sites and report any telltale activity immediately. As noted earlier, Wheeler had not taken his orders seriously. He deployed only one regiment to watch over fifty miles of river, choosing this of all times to withdraw his two divisions for rest and refitting.[34]

The only good news was the arrival of the first reinforcements from Johnston's army on 27 August. Part of Walker's division came in that evening and was ordered into camp at Chickamauga Station, ten miles east of the city. Breckinridge's division arrived next, on 2 September. Bragg certainly was not happy to see the contentious Kentuckian, but he still had faith in his ability even if he did not relish his politicking. Despite their quarrels, after the war Bragg would still call Breckinridge "as gallant and true a man as ever lived." He assigned Breckinridge's division to Hill, who placed it at Tyner's Station. Fortunately Hill and Breckinridge, who had never met, hit it off nicely.

Despite their keen dislike for Bragg, Breckinridge's men were glad to be out of Mississippi, where they had wasted away on rancid meat and putrid water. Georgia was heaven by contrast. Recalled John Jackman of the Orphan Brigade when their train chugged into a depot near Atlanta: "I looked out at the platform in front of the depot where there was such a jam of white crinoline and such a chattering of women, I thought at first I was in another world. We had a fine time as the ladies stayed at the depot until midnight." Although rations were short and the country had been picked clean by Bragg's army, "it was a treat for us to rest awhile on the grand mountains of Georgia and let Mississippi, with its heat and sand, fade into a bad memory."[35]

These reinforcements helped, and Bragg now mustered a little over 35,000 infantry, exclusive of Buckner's divisions in East Tennessee. Bragg understood Rosecrans to have some 70,000 troops of all arms and Burnside another 25,000 men. What he desperately needed were the troops from Virginia.[36]

There was no sign he would get them. Lee continued to oppose the idea and as late as 31 August spoke of taking the offensive against Meade. Longstreet was still trying to bring him around to a western concentration. On 2 September he wrote Lee, who was in Richmond conferring with the president on this very question: "I know but little of the condition of our affairs in the West, but am inclined to the opinion that our best opportunity for great results is in Tennessee. If we could hold the defensive here with two corps and send the others to operate in Tennessee with that army, I think that we could accomplish more than by an advance from here."[37]

Meanwhile, Buckner had abandoned Knoxville to Burnside's advancing army and had fallen back on Loudon. Bragg, whose authority had been enlarged to encompass the Department of East Tennessee earlier in the summer, initially tried to help the Kentuckian despite his own need for troops, sending Stewart's division to rendezvous with him at Loudon. When it became clear that Buckner would be unable to stop a juncture of Burnside and Rosecrans, Bragg ordered him to withdraw to the Hiwassee River.[38]

Bragg was beginning to get better intelligence from his scouts and secret service, although Wheeler remained out of touch. For instance, Bragg knew on 27 August that Rosecrans's headquarters was at Stevenson. Two days later, he was told that an enemy corps was at Bridgeport. Nevertheless, he and his lieutenants clung to the notion that Rosecrans would cross north of the city; they could not imagine he would sever himself from Burnside and plunge into the wilds south of Chattanooga. Hill was sure the major crossing would be at Harrison. The very day Heg was braving the Tennessee River, Bragg and his staff assumed the corps at Bridgeport had withdrawn northward into the Sequatchie Valley preparatory to crossing the river at Washington.[39]

Finally, on 30 August, Bragg learned—"almost accidentally" as Hill put it—that the Yankees had crossed in strength at Caperton's Ferry. The news came not from Wheeler's troopers but from a resident of Stevenson who had made his way to headquarters. The next day, Lieutenant Colonel T. H. Mauldin of the Third Confederate Cavalry confirmed the story with a report that the enemy was in "very heavy force" on Sand Mountain. Although he and his generals were loath to abandon their belief that the major Federal push would come north of Chattanooga, Bragg could not ignore the evidence, skimpy though it was, of a crossing southwest of the city. Consequently, on 1 September he ordered Buckner and Forrest to fall back on Chattanooga, leaving Knoxville and East Tennessee to Burnside.[40]

More than this Bragg dare not do until he had a better idea of what was happening in the mountains beyond his left flank. To get it he gave Wheeler a hard nudge. As early as 30 August, army headquarters had ordered Wharton's division to fan out from La Fayette to watch the passes of Lookout Mountain; two days later, Martin's division was instructed to closely reconnoiter the enemy across from Bridgeport. Nothing came of it, however, as Wheeler seems to have disregarded his orders. Not until 2 September did he have even a picket line on Lookout Mountain, and he made no effort to guard the passes of Sand Mountain. By then, Bragg had run out of patience. Mackall administered the rebuke: "I am uneasy about the state of affairs," he told the twenty-seven-year-old chief of cavalry. "It is so vitally important that the general should have full and correct information. One misstep in the movement of this army would possibly be fatal. Your line of pickets now occupy on Lookout Mountain about the same advantages they possessed on the river or Sand Mountain. The passage at Caperton's Ferry broke the line, and a week has passed and we don't know whether or not an army has passed. If this happens on Lookout and the enemy obtain that as a screen to their movements, I must confess I do not see myself what move we can make to answer it."[41]

The soldiers of the Army of the Cumberland were working hard to administer just such a blow. Their first move, the scaling of Sand Mountain, was a nightmare of unremitting toil in blazing heat and ankle-deep dust, set incongruously against a backdrop of profound natural beauty. Wagons slipped and tumbled down the rocky slopes, killing mules and scattering supplies into the valley below. Teams were doubled on artillery limbers; it took twelve horses to pull a single gun up the slope. Men fainted in the ninety degree heat. Virtually all the trails up the mountain had to be widened and smoothed over, and many more had to be cut from scratch. One regiment per brigade was given picks and shovels, and the luckless infantrymen found themselves felling trees, moving boulders, and leveling grades for the artillery and wagons. Some tried to make sport of it, recalled Captain F. W. Perry of the Tenth Wisconsin. His men "slung their guns over their shoulders and marched up the mountain side, taking their places at intervals, stacked their arms, and, with cheers and jovial good spirits, made an attack charging with picks in advance upon trees, rocks, and dirt." Even the generals got caught up in the spirit and dismounted to join in. The portly James Negley and his staff pushed cannons and caissons over rocks alongside their men.

The majesty of the mountains awed the midwesterners. "Suffice it is the prettiest view I ever saw," recalled James Suiter of the Eighty-fourth Illinois.[42]

Aching muscles and a bed of stony soil, called "Alabama feathers" by the tired Federals, were the rewards for a day's work. Brigadier General John Beatty, an Ohio banker turned brigade commander, long recalled his first night on the mountain:

> I have no blankets, and nothing to eat except one ear of corn which one of the colored boys roasted for me. Wrapped in my overcoat, about nine o'clock, I lay down on the ground to sleep; but a terrible toothache took hold of me, and I was compelled to get up and find such relief as I could in walking up and down the road. The moon shown brightly, and many camp-fires glimmered in the valley and along the side of the mountain. It was three o'clock in the morning before gentle sleep made me oblivious to aching teeth and head, and all the other aches which had possession of me.[43]

Once up the western slope, the men found that the going was easier across the broad and generally level Sand Mountain. But true to its name, the mountain plateau was sandy and the roads deep with dust. The few streams had dried in the summer heat, "and immense boulders of limestone weighing thousands of tons, worn into fantastic shapes, were lying about in groups."

When they came to the eastern slope of Sand Mountain, recalled a Union cavalryman, the weary soldiers saw before them the next hurdle: "The lofty and rocky sides of Lookout Mountain extending north and south as far as the eye could see."[44]

Needless to say, the army had fallen behind Rosecrans's rigid schedule. Not only had Crittenden failed to get into position, but the last of his divisions did not cross the Tennessee until the night of 4 September. It was mid-afternoon on the fifth before his corps moved out toward Whiteside. Two days later, Crittenden directed the captious Thomas Wood to make what should have been a routine reconnaissance in force along the railroad to the base of Lookout Mountain to threaten Chattanooga and develop the enemy's intentions. Wood balked. No other Federal units had approached that near Chattanooga, and Wilder was now reporting some fifty thousand Confederates concentrated in and around the city. Under the circumstances, Wood saw no reason why he should expose his command, and so he simply ignored the order. He apparently failed to appreciate the importance of keeping Confederate attention focused on their immediate front and away from the mountain passes toward which McCook and Thomas were struggling. When Crittenden prodded him with a reminder that the order emanated from army headquarters, Wood complained of the hazards in a testy and pedantic reply: "All the dangers and difficulties of my position increase as I advance toward the enemy; the valleys widen, making it utterly impossible to protect my flank and rear. With them secured I could push boldly up to the enemy's front. I cannot believe General Rosecrans desires such a blind adherence to the mere letter of his order for the general disposition of his forces as naturally jeopardizes the safety of the most salient portions of it, and certainly cripples the force and vigor and accuracy of its reconnaissances." He bent a bit, however, and sent Harker's brigade forward two miles to a point across Lookout Creek. At dusk he withdrew Harker, then pulled his entire division back four miles to what he considered a more tenable position.

None of this probably would have amounted to much, had Wood let the matter rest. When Rosecrans asked why the reconnaissance had not taken place, Crittenden replied with Wood's own words. Wood, he said, had neglected his duty by delaying the reconnaissance because he felt a "blind obedience to orders" would have imperiled his command. There the affair should have ended, but Wood insisted on submitting a long epistle to Garfield complaining that Crittenden had slandered him unjustly and implying that "fatal disasters are likely to befall us" if army and corps headquarters did not better inform themselves of local circumstances before issuing instructions.

Rosecrans was not amused. Garfield wrote Wood: "The general commanding ... directs me to say that he sees nothing in the endorsement of General Crittenden ... which warrants your complaint. The general commanding was disappointed that your reconnaissance was not made earlier, and he is still uninformed of the place where you found the enemy, the strength of the force which you encountered, and the distance to which you pushed the reconnaissance."[45]

The upshot of all this was to prove far more serious than a mere falling out between a corps commander and his lieutenant. Wood had a sensitive ego and was not one to forget a slight, perceived or real. If "blind obedience to orders" was what the commanding general wanted, that was what he would get, reasoned Wood. It was a sentiment that was to bear bitter fruit on the battlefield of Chickamauga.

Far off on the army's right, nearly forty miles to the south, the jovial McCook was sending better tidings, even if they were not entirely true. "All goes on swimmingly, and our part will be well done," he assured Garfield on 3 September; and again the next day: "All goes on well. The Rebel cavalry has all moved toward Chattanooga." Jefferson C. Davis hurried his division across Lookout Valley and took Winston's Gap without resistance and according to schedule on 4 September; Richard Johnson was right behind him with his division. Sheridan, however, was still twelve miles away, having lost a bid for the only useable road to the trains of Negley's division.[46]

In the center, the going was slow. Nightfall of 4 September found Baird at the western foot of Sand Mountain and Brannan and Reynolds just across. Only Negley had reached Trenton. With the towering heights of Raccoon Mountain lying between his corps and that of Crittenden, Thomas hesitated to advance farther.[47] His caution was compounded by the lack of a cavalry screen, which meant that his infantry would have to grope blindly once they closed on the gaps of Lookout. For this, Rosecrans was to blame. The Ohioan had mismanaged his cavalry during the advance on Murfreesboro and apparently had learned little in the intervening nine months. For reasons never made clear, Rosecrans had concentrated all but the brigades of Minty and Wilder on the right flank of the army.

Had Stanley pushed his troopers aggressively to create "a strong diversion" deep in the Confederate rear as Rosecrans had intended, the faulty disposition of the cavalry might have been less censurable. But Stanley, who after the war said Rosecrans had had "no idea of the use of cavalry," was doing little better himself. Colonel Edward McCook sent a scouting party from his division into Rawlingsville on 4 September that returned to report the town empty. The next morning Brigadier General George Crook, whose division had reached Winston's Gap with Davis, reconnoitered over Lookout Mountain and into Broomtown Valley. His scouts reported fewer than two hundred Rebels in the entire valley.

With the picturesque and fertile Broomtown Valley apparently clear of Confederates, the way was open for Stanley to push north toward La Fayette, east toward Resaca, or southeast toward Rome. Any one of those courses would have given Rosecrans the strong diversion he demanded. It also might have drawn Wheeler away from the gaps of Lookout Mountain and certainly would have complicated matters for Bragg. Yet for three days, from the sixth to the ninth, Stanley's troopers did nothing more aggressive than wait for their trains and shoe their horses. Rosecrans was livid. "The cavalry for some reason was not pushed with the vigor nor to the extent which orders and the necessities of the campaign required," he wrote in his after-action report.

The torpor of the cavalry stemmed from a lack of strong leadership. Stanley was desperately ill with dysentery and confined to an ambulance. His senior division commander, Robert Mitchell, was himself absent on sick leave and not expected back for at least another week. Ill as he was, Stanley dreaded the prospect of turning command over to Mitchell when he returned. Stanley had no use for Mitchell, a prominent Free State politician in Kansas before the war who had been forced on him by Garfield. Mitchell "was always thinking of the votes he could make in Kansas," complained Stanley.[48]

Not until 6 September did Thomas feel comfortable turning Negley loose. Even then, the movement toward the gaps was tentative. Negley detached the brigade of John Beatty to seize Cooper's and Stevens's gaps, while he followed up the mountain with the remainder of the division. The going was hard, and it took Beatty the better part of two days to reach the summit of Lookout. What little Rebel cavalry there was on the mountain put up meager resistance — being "very timid," as Negley told Thomas — and nightfall of 8 September found the Federals in control of both gaps. As the sun set behind Lookout Mountain, Beatty peered down into McLemore's Cove and beyond. What he saw both pleased and troubled him: "While standing on a peak . . . we saw far off to the east long lines of dust tending slowly to the south, and inferred from this that Bragg had abandoned Chattanooga, and was either retiring before us or making preparations to check the center and right of our line."[49]

Beatty surmised correctly. After four days of doubt and anxiety, Bragg had abandoned Chattanooga. On 2 September, he had summoned his corps and division commanders to a council of war. While all present seemed to agree that two Union corps had crossed the Tennessee in the vicinity of

Stevenson and Bridgeport, no one came forward with a plan to challenge the Federals. Uncertain of the enemy's strength north of Chattanooga, all were disinclined to attack the two corps. Hazen's "dumb but noisy show," as he called it, was thus paying handsome dividends. For the past ten days, he had been moving his field musicians around the Tennessee Valley with orders to sound tattoo, reveille, and calls to parade as if for a corps. So convincing was his demonstration that even now Bragg believed the enemy to be in corps strength north of the city, and Hill maintained the main crossing would be made there. The council adjourned, having decided nothing.[50]

For the next two days, a fog hung over headquarters. "It is said to be easy to defend a mountainous country, but mountains hide your foe from you, while they are full of gaps through which he can pounce on you at any time," a befuddled Bragg complained to Hill. "A mountain is like the wall of a house full of rat-holes. The rat lies hidden at his hole, ready to pop out when no one is watching. Who can tell what lies hidden behind that wall?" he said, pointing to the Cumberland range across the river.[51]

Certainly not the Confederate cavalry. Wheeler continued to display a singular lack of enterprise. True, he finally had drawn a picket line across Lookout Mountain. But he failed to guard the passes of Sand Mountain, thereby surrendering both Lookout Valley and the chance to develop the enemy's intentions early on. Despite the sparse intelligence, by 4 September Bragg seemed reasonably certain that McCook and Thomas had crossed south of the city and that Crittenden lay opposite Chattanooga. He also surmised Rosecrans's objective to be Atlanta or Rome, Georgia, which lay astride the railroad deep in the Confederate rear. However, in the absence of effective scouting by the cavalry, doubts lingered. A nervous Buckner was passing along reports that a large force from Rosecrans's army had effected a junction with Burnside as far north as Kingston. Were the movements north of Chattanooga really just a feint? No one knew. "It seems truly wonderful that no reliable information can be had," George Brent complained to his diary that night.[52]

The strain was beginning to tell on Bragg. One moment he was full of fight, ready to take the initiative, as when he wrote Hill on the morning of the fourth of his desire to attack Crittenden's corps:

> There is no doubt of the enemy's position now; one corps opposite you, and two this side of the river from Shellmound by Bridgeport to Caperton's, the point of first crossing. A part of the latter are reported moving down Will's Valley toward Gadsden or perhaps Rome; Wheeler is gone to develop them and Walker goes by railroad to Rome to head them off from our communications.
>
> If you can cross the river, now is our time to crush the corps opposite.

What say you? Or if we could draw the enemy over. We must do something and that soon. . . . The crushing of this corps would give us a great victory and redeem Tennessee. Can you be the instrument to do it? Consult Cleburne. He is cool, full of resources, and ever alive to a success. Then give me your views, or call with Cleburne and see what our resources are.[53]

Later that very morning, he despaired of taking the offensive in a letter to President Davis: "With our present dispositions we are prepared to meet the enemy at any point he may assail, either with a portion or with the whole of his forces, and should he present us an opportunity we shall not fail to strike him. My position is to some extent embarrassing in regard to offensive movements."[54]

The tone of both letters is as alarming as the contents are contradictory, suggesting nothing less than the frenzied excitement of a man nearing his breaking point.

Despite Bragg's self-assured air in his letter to Hill, army headquarters really was still only guessing as to the whereabouts of Rosecrans's army. Not until 5 September did Bragg get his first solid intelligence. A recent issue of the Chicago *Times* had found its way to him; in it was a detailed exposition of Rosecrans's entire plan of operations as reported by the paper's special correspondent at Federal headquarters. It said in part: "If Crittenden succeeds well in his efforts upon Chattanooga and will not need re-enforcements, Thomas and McCook will move rapidly upon Rome, Georgia. . . . Rosecrans will, if possible, whip Bragg in detail, disperse his forces. . . . Twenty days from this time, if I mistake not the signs, will see Georgia redeemed and thoroughly regenerated."[55]

There it was. Bragg had no doubt of the authenticity of the newspaper report; too much of what it foretold — the crossing of McCook and Thomas south of Chattanooga, Crittenden's movements opposite the city — had come to pass. It remained now to find out from which hole the rat would emerge. Positive orders were dispatched to Wheeler to attack and drive in Federal pickets, wherever located, and then to develop the enemy's strength "at all hazards."

Bragg knew he could no longer wait passively in Chattanooga for the Federals to appear behind him. As he had told Davis in his letter of 4 September: "In a country so utterly destitute we cannot for a moment abandon our line of communications, and unable to detach a sufficient force to guard it, we must necessarily maneuver between the enemy and our supplies." On the morning of 6 September, Brent drafted orders for a movement of the army toward Rome in four columns "in order to meet the enemy and strike him." Bragg had no fixed notion of where or when this might be, he simply had determined "to meet him in front whenever he should emerge from the mountain gorges."

The movement was to begin at nightfall. Polk would march out of the city on the La Fayette road via Rossville and La Fayette to Summerville. Hill was to follow on the same route. With his recently created Reserve Corps — consisting of his own division and a new two-brigade division under Liddell — General Walker would move on a parallel road to the east via Greysville and Ringgold. Buckner was ordered to follow Walker. Forrest was told to gather at least one brigade and ride rapidly to overtake the infantry to screen its movements. With luck, the Federals would present Bragg with an opportunity to give battle before his army had fallen back all the way to Rome, but he was taking no chances. To Johnston he wired: "Hasten a division of infantry to Atlanta if you can spare it only for a few days. It will save that depot and give me time to defeat the enemy's plans."[56]

True to character, Bragg vacillated when it came time to act. Wheeler did not receive the order to attack into Lookout Valley until mid-afternoon on 6 September. Instead of complying, Wheeler sent a long-winded, feeble rejoinder pointing out the dangers of such a move: he risked uncovering Rome should he descend into the valley, his scouts could see as much from atop Lookout as they could learn by engaging the Federals, and the march down the rocky slope would wear out his horses. At the same time, Buckner's scouts reported incorrectly that Burnside had turned south to join Rosecrans. Finally, Crittenden had begun his demonstration against Confederate outposts on the northern tip of Lookout Mountain. All this was too much for Bragg, and at dusk he ordered the movement suspended.[57]

The next morning brought no change. Once again, doubts arose as to the nature of the Federal threat west of Lookout Mountain. Wheeler estimated the enemy to be there in force. Major Pollock Lee of the general staff, whom Bragg had sent to Alpine to gather intelligence, disputed Wheeler's conclusions. In desperation, Bragg summoned his lieutenants to a second council of war. They had little to offer. Lieutenant W. B. Richmond of Polk's staff probably echoed the bishop's frustration when he scribbled in his notebook: "The feeling is one of great doubt as to the movements of the enemy, all want to fight him but the question is can we make him fight us." Polk and Hill counseled against abandoning Chattanooga, and for the moment Bragg yielded to their views. Scarcely had the generals returned to their commands, however, when orders came to begin the withdrawal at dark, this time with Hill in the lead.[58]

Although his subordinates probably spent the waning hours of 7 September waiting for orders that would again cancel the movement, this time there was to be no turning back. Bragg's deep apprehension over the strategic implications of a Federal thrust beyond his left and rear had finally overcome his hesitancy. As the sun sank behind the rugged Cumberland Mountains, the first Confederate soldiers filed onto the dusty road out of the city.

Emotions ran high as the army abandoned Chattanooga and headed south to few knew where. "A restive feeling exists," George Brent recorded in his diary. Some were confident of success. "The army marching in the very best of spirits under the conviction that we are to have a fight," observed Lieutenant Richmond. "Today is my birthday and I am twenty-five years old and am celebrating by marching in the dust . . . to meet the enemy — the ruthless invaders of our soil — better than to be celebrating it over the wine cup and luxurious dinner though," Captain Daniel Coleman of the Fifteenth Mississippi Battalion Sharpshooters wrote in his diary with youthful exuberance. Hard-bitten Texan William Heartsill of Deshler's brigade was skeptical. "This may not be a retreat, but it looks very much like one, but if General Johnston (as reported) is in command; then we have no fears, if however Bragg is maneuvering, then we will not be surprised to wake up one of these September mornings and find the entire army at or near Atlanta." A fellow Texan, Lieutenant R. M. Collins, agreed: "The idea of our army giving up the city of Chattanooga, the gate to the center of the Confederacy, was trying on our confidence in General Bragg and all others in authority over us, and the saying of all the boys was: 'If we can't check them and whip them with advantages of the river and the mountain-locked passes on the right and left of Chattanooga, where is the place we can?' And this added to the recent fall of Vicksburg made the outlook gloomy indeed."[59]

With the Tennessee troops there was an ominous near-unanimity of opinion. "You may be well assured that it was almost like drawing eye teeth for those brave and daring Tennessee soldiers to give up our most beloved native state. . . . after crossing the state line many Tennesseans refused to serve our country longer thinking that we were on the retreat and shamefully deserted our army," recalled George Dillon of the Eighteenth Tennessee. Probably to stave off mass desertions, General Stewart issued an address to his Tennessee division the day after the withdrawal began, assuring his men that they would soon "meet the enemy in deadly conflict." Even Forrest was losing men from the Tennessee regiments of his celebrated cavalry corps.[60]

Among the generals, opinion was divided. Hill, who grew more disputatious with each passing day, thought Bragg should have left a division in Chattanooga to strike at or at least neutralize Crittenden's corps and forestall any combination of forces by Rosecrans and Burnside. Stewart, although certainly loath to turn his back on his home state, doubted that Bragg had sufficient forces to both garrison Chattanooga and fight Rosecrans. Polk,

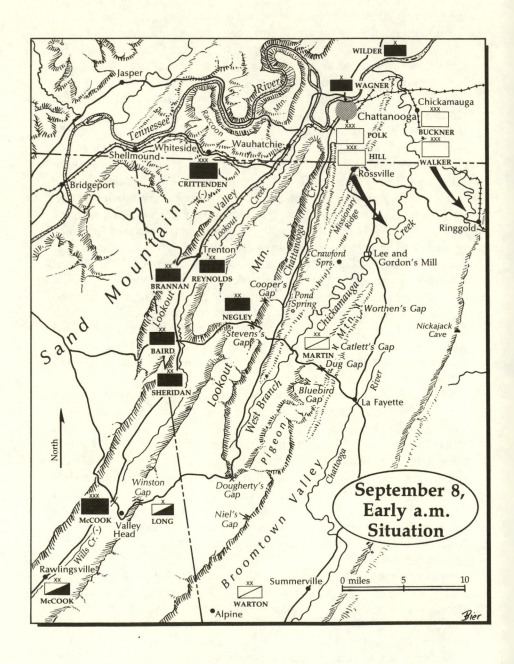

September 8,
Early a.m.
Situation

who was suffering from a severe attack of rheumatism, probably gave the matter little thought.[61]

Under the circumstances, the decision to abandon Chattanooga and give battle to Rosecrans as he emerged from behind Lookout Mountain was a sound one. Whether or not Bragg and his lieutenants fully realized it, Rosecrans already had effectively turned their left flank. To have tried to hold the city—with one division or with the entire army—would have accomplished nothing. Crittenden probably could have recrossed the Tennessee before Bragg organized an attack, and Bragg lacked the pontoons and boats needed to cross the Tennessee River himself. Moreover, with no effective opposition then remaining in East Tennessee, Burnside could have easily swung southward and kept the Army of Tennessee occupied while Rosecrans drove on toward Rome and Atlanta. Finally, Bragg was still badly outnumbered in infantry. In response to Bragg's latest appeal for aid, Johnston had agreed only to send two more small brigades under Evander McNair and John Gregg, and these only for a few days. Bragg did not yet know that Richmond had at last decided to reinforce him from Virginia.[62]

President Davis and General Lee had deliberated for five days. Each passing hour threatened to wreck the entire scheme, but Davis, convinced that Rosecrans would not move without first uniting with Burnside, felt no need for haste. Not until 5 September, after much foot-dragging by Lee, did they agree to send two divisions under Longstreet to Tennessee. By then, Knoxville had fallen, severing the direct rail line through East Tennessee. A rail movement now would have to be made indirectly over several lines in varying degrees of disrepair, south through the Carolinas, west to Georgia, and then north to Bragg's army, a total of 775 miles as opposed to 540 miles via the direct route. When the Army of Tennessee marched out of Chattanooga on 7 September, any chance for a western concentration leading to the kind of strategic counteroffensive envisioned by Beauregard and his supporters passed. The most that reasonably could be hoped for was to halt Rosecrans and throw him back across the Tennessee.[63]

On 5 September, unaware that Davis and Lee had that very day concluded to send the bulk of his corps west, Longstreet laid his cards on the table. To Lee, he wrote: "I think that it is time that we had begun to do something in the west, and I fear if it is put off any longer we shall be too late. If my corps cannot go west, I think that we might accomplish something by...putting me in General Bragg's place and giving him my corps. We would surely make no great risk in such a change and we might gain a great deal. I doubt if General Bragg has confidence in his troops or in himself either. He is not likely to do a great deal for us."[64] When he learned of the president's decision to retain Bragg, Longstreet was deeply pained.

The plan finally approved by the War Department, termed "Westward

Ho," called for the divisions of John Bell Hood and Lafayette McLaws, accompanied by Colonel E. Porter Alexander's twenty-six-gun artillery battalion, to move secretly and swiftly to northern Georgia under the command of Longstreet. The execution, however, was neither swift nor secret. Not only were the Southern railroads in poor repair, but they were of varying gauges, which promised long delays while the troops changed trains. Rolling stock was at a premium. Troops were squeezed into and on top of boxcars. Flatcars were added to accommodate the overflow. The men nibbled on biscuits and uncooked bacon, slept as best they could, but mostly just hung on as the cars jolted over the deteriorating roadbeds of the Deep South.

The element of surprise was lost on 9 September, the same day the first train steamed out of Richmond, when the New York *Herald* ran a surprisingly accurate story detailing the movement, right down to the units involved and the routes to be taken. That the War Department in Washington put little stock in the story, Richmond could not know.[65]

Longstreet had little time to sulk while preparing to depart. He was at Lee's headquarters every moment, or Lee was at his. Once Lee had resigned himself to the plan, he could talk of nothing else. "General, we must have a great victory out there. The success of our cause depends on it. We need only inflict one great disaster upon the Federal army to recover everything that has been lost," he told his lieutenant repeatedly.

On the day he was to leave, Longstreet rode over to army headquarters to bid his commander farewell. Lee followed him to his horse. As Longstreet put his foot in the stirrup to mount, Lee rested a hand on his shoulder and told him earnestly: "General, you must beat those people out there." Longstreet forgot his personal disappointment long enough to reassure Lee that Rosecrans "shall be beaten if I live."[66]

Not until he was aboard the train and alone with his thoughts did Longstreet give vent to his frustration. To his friend and political patron Senator Wigfall he wrote: "I don't think that I should be under Bragg. And I would fight against it if I had any hope of setting anyone in the responsible position except myself."[67]

So the days passed and the troop trains jolted and chugged through the Carolinas. With luck, they would arrive before the Army of the Cumberland poured out of the mountains and battle was joined. Regardless of when they came, the veterans of the Army of Northern Virginia would have at their head another powerful recruit for the anti-Bragg forces.

CHAPTER FOUR

A GLIMMER IN THE TWILIGHT

COLONEL Smith D. Atkins of the Ninety-second Illinois was troubled by self-doubt. He had enlisted as a private two years earlier "without a particle of military schooling." Promotions came quickly to the young lawyer—too quickly, Atkins himself thought. "I always had a larger command than I believed myself capable of handling," he later wrote. But of one thing Atkins was certain in the summer of 1863. He wanted out from under the command of Major General Gordon Granger at any cost. In June, Granger had ordered Atkins's division commander, Absalom Baird, to turn him over to civil authorities to be tried in a Kentucky court on trumped-up charges of "stealing niggers," as Atkins, who claimed that his black servant was freeborn, put it. When the officers of the court came for him, Atkins chased them off at gunpoint. Baird sympathized with his angry young colonel, and Granger, having a change of heart, seemed willing to let the matter rest. He recognized talent when he saw it and actually offered Atkins a brigadier general's commission and command of a division in his Reserve Corps. Still deeply offended, Atkins replied that he would rather resign from the army. He was prepared to make good on his threat when John Wilder happened on the Ninety-second in camp one day. Wilder took a fancy to the regiment and told Atkins he would try to have it transferred to the Lightning Brigade. Atkins was delighted. Without waiting for Wilder to act, Atkins took the matter all the way to Rosecrans, who reluctantly consented to the transfer. Wilder gave Atkins the surplus Spencers of the brigade, 140 in all, and helped him round up horses from the countryside. On the day the Ninety-second rode out of camp to join the brigade, Atkins was handed a message from Granger ordering him to assume command of the division he had earlier been offered. Atkins decided the order was illegal and went on his way.[1]

Atkins was enjoying himself immensely in the campaign around Chattanooga. His regiment was on detached service with Thomas, who, having no cavalry of his own, needed mounted scouts desperately. The Ninety-second was attached to the division of Joseph Reynolds and kept constantly in the saddle. On the afternoon of 8 September, a detail of fifty men on handpicked horses and armed with Spencers rode off on a scout to the northern tip of Lookout Mountain to confirm rumors that the Confederates had evacuated the city. Climbing up a rocky, neglected bridle path in dust that swirled to their stirrups, the Illinoisans surprised and drove a handful of Rebel pickets all the way to the summit. The view from the top was everything they had hoped for: Only a small Rebel rear guard was visible in Chattanooga. Turning their horses, Atkins's men hurried back down the mountain to report the evacuation of the city.[2]

At army headquarters near Trenton, Rosecrans already had received similar reports. General Wagner had telegraphed at noon from the heights opposite the city that deserters were telling of the evacuation of Chattanooga and flight of the Rebel army to Rome. A highly trusted scout returned with the same story. By 8:30 P.M. Wagner considered the matter settled: "The enemy has evacuated Chattanooga. They left to-day. Will occupy the place to-morrow," he wired headquarters.[3]

Rosecrans acted at once. He telegraphed McCook that the enemy was moving south and ordered him to send out a brigade of infantry in support of a cavalry reconnaissance into the Broomtown Valley and, if safe, beyond to Summerville; "We must know as speedily as possible which route he is taking." At the same time, he told McCook to prepare to advance the entire corps. To Crittenden he sent orders for a strong reconnaissance of the northern spur of Lookout at daylight, telling the Kentuckian to hold his corps ready to enter the city at a moment's notice. He told Thomas to have the Ninety-second link up with Crittenden.[4]

Reynolds sent the Ninety-second on its way after midnight on Wednesday, 9 September. Colonel Atkins imperiously dropped by army headquarters en route to Crittenden, presumably for last-minute orders. He found Rosecrans brimming with enthusiasm. Anxious to share his good fortune, the commanding general amended Atkins's orders on the spot. He gave the young colonel written instructions to lead the way into the city, supplementing them with a caution to all infantry commanders to yield the road to the Ninety-second. "The flag of the Ninety-second will wave first in Chattanooga," he called out to Atkins as they parted.[5]

Although it was 3:00 A.M. before Atkins left, Rosecrans gave no thought to sleep. Instead, he told Garfield to send for Thomas. Awakened by the arrival of the courier, Thomas wiped the sleep from his eyes and read the summons: "The general commanding desires you to call on him at once to consult in regard to arrangements for the pursuit." Thomas dressed and rode into the darkness for headquarters deeply troubled. He would of course hear his commander out, but already he felt strongly against any hasty advance beyond Chattanooga.[6]

Rosecrans laid out his plan. He believed Bragg was retreating toward Rome and incorrectly assumed he had taken the direct road through Ringgold and Dalton. Early information suggested the Rebel army was badly demoralized, and one supposedly loyal citizen had assured Rosecrans that, if pursued vigorously, Bragg would not stop short of Atlanta. This was music to the general's ears. His easy success to date was getting the better of him. Rosecrans acted as if Bragg were incapable of action; or, as General Richard Johnson wryly observed, he "seemed to imagine that the enemy had disappeared from the face of the earth" and that he could move with impunity. The enemy was in rapid retreat, Rosecrans told Thomas. They must strike the Confederate army in the flank before it reached the entrenchments at Rome.'

Thomas interrupted. He strongly urged a concentration of the army at Chattanooga to gather supplies and improve communications before beginning a pursuit. To push three widely separated corps over the mountains was to invite disaster, he argued. Already it took nearly nine hours for orders to reach McCook from army headquarters. Lateral communications between the center and right of the army were tentative at best; between the left and right they were nonexistent. Thomas also was concerned by the reinforcements Bragg already had received from Mississippi and was troubled by the persistent rumors that more help was on the way from Virginia.[8]

None of these arguments had any effect on Rosecrans. Thomas agreed to let the matter rest, asking only that Wilder be returned to him. Shortly before 10:00 A.M., messages went out from headquarters modifying the orders of the night before to reflect "a general pursuit of the enemy by the whole army." Crittenden was now ordered to detach a brigade to garrison Chattanooga, then press immediately on toward Ringgold and Dalton to harass the retreating Confederate army; he should attack the enemy's rear whenever he thought he could do so "with a fair opportunity to inflict injury upon him." Forty miles to the south, McCook was to move his entire corps "as rapidly as possible" to Alpine and Summerville to intercept the Confederate retreat. With luck, McCook would strike the enemy in the flank; in any event, he should hold him in check to allow Thomas time to cross McLemore's Cove and deliver the knockout punch somewhere near La Fayette or Dalton, depending on which route Bragg had chosen.[9]

Rosecrans had grown so disgusted with his chief of cavalry that the instructions he sent Stanley were a mere afterthought. For four days Rosecrans had exhorted the cavalry to vigorous action, but every mission was either bungled or fatally delayed. Now he simply told Stanley to operate according to his own discretion, asking that, if he do nothing else, he at least protect the extreme right flank of the army.[10]

The day before, Rosecrans had personally rebuked Stanley in writing. "It is a matter of regret to me that your command has done so little in this great movement," he scolded. "If you could do nothing toward Rome, nor toward the railroad, you might at least have cleared the top of Lookout Mountain to Chattanooga and established a patrol and vedette line along it, which I should have ordered had I not trusted your discretion."[11]

Rosecrans might as well have been lecturing his horse. Stanley's health had taken a turn for the worse, and he was so sick with fever and dysentery that he could barely stand up. Mitchell had not yet reported in, however, and Stanley was apparently unwilling to relinquish command to either of his division commanders. Rosecrans must not have known of Stanley's incapacity; if he had, he presumably would have peremptorily ordered the Ohioan to the rear rather than issue him a reprimand that he was probably too sick to read.

For nearly two weeks there had been no rain. The marching columns of infantry stirred dust that rose to their knees. In the ninety degree heat it stung the eyes and clung to sweat-soaked uniforms, coating the soldiers of both armies with a tan film and slowing the rate of march to a drowsy shuffle. Those on horseback suffered less, being generally able to keep above the clouds of dust.[12]

Atkins was playing the weather to his advantage. Determined to be the first into the city, he drove his men hard on the morning of 9 September. The long columns of infantry dutifully yielded the road to the Illinoisans; all, that is, except the division of Tom Wood. Equally anxious to get into Chattanooga first, Wood had no intention of ceding the way. Atkins triumphantly waved his orders from headquarters in Wood's face. Wood read them, swore at them, but in the end let Atkins pass.

Atkins dismounted his skirmishers at the foot of Lookout Mountain. They scampered up the slope and easily drove back the remaining Rebel pickets of the First Tennessee Legion. More troublesome was Wilder's artillery on the opposite bank of the Tennessee. Mistaking the Illinoisans for Confederates, Eli Lilly had opened fire with his guns the moment Atkins's men showed themselves near the summit. Atkins halted and called for two strong swimmers to cross the river and call off Lilly's gunners.

While Atkins fretted over the lost time, a young boy of Company F who had served in the signal corps quietly offered to send a message to Wilder. Atkins bade him proceed. The soldier tore his handkerchief in two, tied each piece to a hazel stick, climbed up on a rock jutting over the valley, and, amid the bursting shells, asked Atkins what message to send. "Ninety-second Illinois," replied the colonel. The boy waved the words, the guns fell silent, and in a moment a loud cheer was heard from across the river.

Just as Atkins was about to descend into the city, a staff officer galloped up and breathlessly ordered him to report to Wood. A suspicious Atkins ordered his men forward before riding to see the general. "Did you send for me?" Atkins asked. "Yes, Colonel: I wanted to say to you, that if you have any difficulty I will reinforce you," Wood stammered lamely. "Oh, is that all?" Atkins snapped before hurrying back to his command.

Wood refused to give up. Just after Atkins sent a detail into town with his regimental flag, Wood rode up with General Wagner and his brigade colors. He ordered Atkins to march straight for Rossville and stay clear of Chattanooga. Too late, Atkins replied, pointing to the colors of the Ninety-second Illinois floating above the Crutchfield house, where only the day before the banner of Bragg's headquarters had flown.[13]

Bragg was miserable. His health worsened with each step his army took southward. "In the first week I suffered much and in all my service never have undergone such hardship and privation," he later wrote his wife of his condition after he abandoned Chattanooga.[14] With the commanding general enfeebled and introspective, opportunity would have to knock loudly to be heard at headquarters.

It rapped first in the early morning hours of 8 September, when Brigadier General William Martin, whose cavalry division guarded Stevens's and Cooper's gaps, reported that Negley's advance had pushed his troopers into McLemore's Cove. Martin had withdrawn to Pigeon Mountain, the only barrier remaining between Thomas and Bragg's retreating army, and was busy fortifying and blockading Bluebird, Catlett's, and Dug gaps. In the turmoil of retreat, Martin's warning went unheeded. He followed it with similar messages throughout the day and into the night. Bragg finally ordered a halt of the army midway between Chattanooga and La Fayette, but took no further action for the moment.

Martin, in the meantime, had sent the Third Alabama Cavalry back into the cove to develop the enemy. On the afternoon of 9 September, he sent Bragg a final, desperate message: an isolated fragment of Thomas's corps (Negley's division), believed to number between four and eight thousand, then lay at Davis's Cross Roads, just ten miles from Lee and Gordon's Mill, and appeared vulnerable to defeat in detail.[15]

That got Bragg's attention. With commendable swiftness, during the afternoon of the ninth he formulated plans to crush Negley in a double envelopment. Aware that the opportunity might be lost at any moment, Bragg understandably chose the nearest available units for the job. Before sundown he told Major General Thomas Hindman, whose division was resting near army headquarters at Lee and Gordon's Mill on Chickamauga Creek, to prepare to advance that night in conjunction with a division from Hill. Written orders followed at midnight. Hindman was enjoined to move immediately on Davis's Cross Roads from the northeast; Hill was ordered to send Cleburne, then near La Fayette, through Dug Gap. Once united, Hindman was to assume overall command and strike both of Negley's flanks simultaneously. Hindman was then thirteen miles from the cross-roads, Cleburne perhaps six; an easy night march for both.[16]

While Bragg's vigor was praiseworthy, his choice of Hindman to lead the attack was deplorable. "Poor Hindman, he was a pleasant gentleman and kind, a nice ladies' man, but utterly unfit to command a division of fighting men," lamented Lieutenant Colonel B. F. Sawyer of the Twenty-fourth Alabama. In Hindman, wrote A. P. Stewart after the war, "the right man was not there in command."[17]

Hindman was a man of violent passions, thoroughly committed to the cause of Southern independence. He had distinguished himself as a lieutenant in the Mexican War and later as a member of Congress from Arkansas, but he was a complete failure to date as a general officer. Hindman had kicked about in the Trans-Mississippi Department for nearly two years before joining the Army of Tennessee that summer to replace the ailing Jones Withers. About all there was to recommend Hindman for the assignment was his close friendship with Cleburne, whom he ranked.

Theirs was a friendship cemented in adversity. Cleburne had come to America from County Cork, Ireland, in 1849 after serving three years as an enlisted man in Her Majesty's Forty-first Regiment of Foot. He made his way to Helena, Arkansas, to take a clerkship in a local drugstore, a bashful young man whose brogue must have sounded odd to his Arkansan neighbors. In 1855 an epidemic of yellow fever devastated Helena. All who could fled for the country. Only two doctors remained to care for the scores of sick. Their plea for nurses was answered by only three men: a young Methodist preacher, Hindman, and Cleburne. Day and night the three made the rounds of the stricken, baking bread, boiling tea, and performing a hundred menial tasks. That experience was the basis of their friendship. A year later, it endured an even greater test. Hindman had become a successful Democratic congressman. During a stump speech, he indiscreetly accused a hotheaded member of the local party of selling out to the Know-Nothings. The accused went home, vowing to return with his brother and kill Hindman. Hindman armed himself and ran to Cleburne's drugstore. "I want you to accompany me, and see that I have fair play," he implored his friend. Cleburne picked up his derringers, and the two walked out of the store and into an ambush. Hindman went down with a bullet in the left breast. Turning to look for the source of the shot, Cleburne was struck in the lower back by a blast from a doorway behind him. Cleburne fell firing and killed his assailant. Both Cleburne and Hindman suffered immensely, and after recovering followed one another's fortunes with brotherly concern.[18]

At first, Hindman undertook his mission aggressively. An hour after receiving his written orders he had his men on the road, and by dawn his division was within four miles of Davis's Cross Roads. Then the problems started. Hill did not get his orders until 4:30 A.M. on 10 September, five hours after they were written. He immediately replied with a list of reasons why he could not obey them: Cleburne had been sick in bed all day and a third of his division was still on picket duty along Pigeon Mountain; moreover, it would take hours to clear the obstructions in Dug Gap placed there earlier by Martin's cavalry. Bragg accepted Hill's arguments. Not wanting to "lose this favorable opportunity," he told Buckner at 8:00 A.M. to hurry forward two divisions to reinforce Hindman and compensate for Cleburne's absence. Bragg informed Hill and Hindman of his decision, then sat back to await the arrival of Buckner, whose lead division was still a half-day's march to the north.[19]

Meanwhile Hindman had grown cautious. It was daylight and he had heard nothing from Hill. Civilians encountered along the march had warned of two Federal divisions awaiting him between Stevens's and Dug gaps, adding that the latter gap, through which Cleburne must pass, was heavily blockaded. (Apparently no one had bothered to tell Hindman that Martin had thrown obstructions across the gap.) Hindman halted to await word from Hill. He had lost any interest in taking the initiative and had convinced himself that he need not act until Hill launched his attack. Bragg did nothing to nudge him forward so as to at least hold Negley in place, even after Hill changed his mind about cooperating and reported Cleburne on the move at 1:30 P.M.[20]

Major General James Scott Negley was another of the many talented, high-ranking volunteer officers in the Army of the Cumberland. Heavyset, with twinkling eyes and a cherubic face, Negley cared deeply for the welfare of his soldiers, who, recognizing their good fortune, nicknamed him "Commissary General Negley." If Negley had shown any flaw to date, it was his reluctance to commit troops aggressively in risky situations.

Negley had dropped out of college at the age of nineteen to enlist in the First Pennsylvania for service in the Mexican War. His well-connected parents tried to stop him. When that failed, they procured an honorable discharge for him from the War Department. Negley refused it and served on until his regiment came home. He maintained an active interest in military affairs, rising to the rank of brigadier general in the state militia before the Civil War. His first love, however, was gardening, and by 1861 he had made a name for himself as one of the most accomplished horticulturists in the nation. Recalled a bemused William Shanks: "When in the field of war his leisure hours were devoted to the study of various fruits, flowers and shrubs in which the Southern fields and woods abounded. Many a march, long, tedious, exhausting, has been rendered delightful to his staff by his interesting descriptive illustrations of the hidden beauties and virtues of fragrant flowers and repulsive weeds. I have known him, when on the march, frequently to spring from his saddle to pluck a sensitive plant."[21]

McLemore's Cove was a horticulturist's delight. From Stevens's Gap to Davis's Cross Roads the only traces of man were a narrow dirt road and a hamlet of log cabins known locally as Bailey's Cross Roads. Otherwise the forest reigned supreme, spilling down the sharp crest of Lookout Mountain at Stevens's Gap and rolling over rocky knolls on through the cove.

Tempted though he might be, Negley dared not dismount to pick flowers. Throughout the day and into the evening on 9 September, reports had come in from scouts and residents telling of an entire Rebel corps gathered on the far side of Pigeon Mountain. Although Negley initially discounted the information, he recognized that his division was dangerously isolated in McLemore's Cove. The nearest support was Baird's division, a day's march away on the west side of Lookout Mountain. It had taken Negley the better part of a day to get his trains down through Stevens's Gap, which his men found to be "about as high as any place in the mountain." Going back up would be no easier. "All the information I have from other sources confirms the report that there is not more than a brigade of cavalry at La Fayette," Negley wrote Baird early in the morning. "But I would suggest, general, that you push forward your division within supporting distance."[22]

Thomas too was worried. Rosecrans's plan of pursuit compelled him to instruct Negley to take up the march through Dug Gap and on to La Fayette at daybreak on 10 September, but his heart was not in the order. He sensed trouble and was in the saddle and on his way to McLemore's Cove before sunrise.[23]

Rebel bullets modified Thomas's orders for him. At 10:00 A.M., under a bright blue sky that promised another day of searing heat and suffocating dust, Negley led his division forward from Bailey's Cross Roads. Confident there were no Rebels nearer than Dug Gap, he rode at the head of the column with his staff. He told Lieutenant Colonel Archibald Blakely, whose Seventy-eighth Pennsylvania led the march, not to bother deploying skirmishers.

Off they went down the narrow, cedar-lined country road. Within minutes, Blakely recalled, "the enemy's pickets opened fire on us; the division and brigade commanders, with their staffs, wheeled, rushed back on us pell mell, yelling, 'Into line, Colonel; into line!' Bullets were flying through the cedars thick as flies and dropping all around us."[24]

From then on it was skirmishing every step of the way. By mid-afternoon the Federals had broken clear of the dense cedar thickets into the open meadows that surrounded the Widow Davis plantation. From a high knob east of the house they had a clear view of the gorge leading up to Dug Gap, less than one thousand yards to their front. Negley knew he was in grave danger. A few minutes earlier, a loyal citizen had told him that Hindman was advancing from Catlett's Gap, just three miles away, to envelop his left. Negley could clearly see men from S. A. M. Wood's brigade, the vanguard of Cleburne's division, at work clearing the fallen trees and rocks from Dug Gap. An officer of the Thirty-second Mississippi, who had stumbled into the Federal lines while searching for his picket post, was generous enough to advise Negley to advance no further or "he would get severely whipped." Negley took the hint. He threw out a strong skirmish line, made a brief demonstration toward the gap in a feeble effort to convince the Confederates that he outnumbered them, then earnestly prepared a defensive line around Davis's Cross Roads.[25]

Thomas arrived as Negley was deploying his troops. A quick reconnaissance was enough to convince him that Negley had been right to halt. Having smelled danger all along, Thomas now decided not to go on until his corps was united. He dispatched a courier to hurry along Baird, sent instructions to Reynolds and Brannan to move over the mountain via Cooper's Gap at daylight and come in on the left of Negley and Baird, then returned to his headquarters to send Rosecrans the bad news. At 9:00 P.M., he wrote the commanding general of his decision to stop until he had gathered his forces. Anticipating Rosecrans's anger, he added: "By this arrangement I hope to drive the enemy beyond Pigeon Ridge tomorrow night." Thomas closed the letter with a jab: "I very much regret not having Wilder's brigade, as I believe if I had had it I could have seized Dug and Catlett's Gaps before the enemy could have reached those places."[26]

Rosecrans was not pleased. Assuming that the Virginian was stalling, he dictated a reply the moment he received Thomas's note. An aide-de-camp transcribed Rosecrans's testy admonition: "The commanding general . . . is disappointed to learn . . . that his forces move tomorrow morning instead of having moved this morning, as they should have done, this delay imperiling both extremes of the army. Your movement on La Fayette should be made with the utmost promptness." And in case Thomas missed the point, he added: "Your advance ought to have threatened La Fayette yesterday evening."[27]

Never before had Rosecrans expressed such displeasure with the general for whom he professed lifelong admiration. He refused to entertain for a moment the possibility that Thomas might be right; that his grand pursuit might be about to take a dark turn. In his mind, the Confederates were in panic-stricken retreat, their army disintegrating.

Thus Rosecrans was duped in part because he wanted to be. It did not help that Halleck was asking him to confirm absurd rumors that Bragg had further weakened himself by detaching troops to reinforce Lee. Most of the credit, however, must go to Bragg. On abandoning Chattanooga he had put into play a simple but successful deception plan. Volunteers were solicited from the ranks of the army to "desert" into Federal lines. There they were to fill the ears of their interrogators with wild tales of the imminent collapse of the Confederate army, then make their way back to Confederate lines with whatever intelligence they could gather. Some saw through the charade. Recalled Smith Atkins:

> Along the road were found, every now and then, a Rebel soldier claiming to be a deserter; and, by orders from General Rosecrans, they were not arrested, but told to go on their way home. It was apparent to every soldier in the Ninety-Second that these straggling Rebels were spies, and not deserters; they were clean, well clad, in good health, and . . . the brightest soldiers of the rank and file of the Rebel army. Such men are not often deserters; it is the ill-clad, unwell, downhearted, home-sick men who desert their colors. But orders were orders, and these straggling Rebels were left unmolested to watch the movements of the Union troops on every road.[28]

Most, however, accepted the stories the Rebels told, and "the impression prevailed that all we had to do was to advance against the enemy and he would flee as he had done at Shelbyville and Tullahoma," admitted Sergeant Alexis Cope of the Fifteenth Ohio.[29]

Bragg too was vexed by recalcitrant subordinates and disturbing intelligence. Forrest's rear guard reported that Crittenden was marching rapidly on Ringgold. Early on the morning of 10 September, troopers from the First Tennessee Cavalry had stampeded Polk's bivouac, claiming that the pursuing Federals were only a mile and a half away. The story proved false, but the nearness of Crittenden reminded Bragg that he would have to act fast if he were to trap Negley. Equally worrisome were dispatches from Wheeler, who was finally reconnoitering aggressively near Summerville. He reported the advance of McCook to Alpine and correctly speculated that his objective was Summerville.[30]

With pressure growing against both his rear and his line of retreat, Bragg could ill afford any further delays. At dusk, he moved his headquarters to La Fayette, to better direct affairs in the cove. Before departing from Lee and Gordon's Mill, he left instructions for Polk to march as far south as Dr. Anderson's house on the La Fayette road, to cover Hindman and Buckner and buy time in case Crittenden turned south. He and his staff entered town a few minutes before midnight. His first action was to send orders to Hindman to attack "and force your way through the enemy . . . at the earliest hour that you can see him in the morning. Cleburne will attack in front the moment your guns are heard."[31]

Though tired and ill, Bragg sought out Hill at his quarters to explain what was expected of him in the morning. The gathering quickly grew to include Generals Walker, Liddell, and Martin. Before he could begin, Bragg was interrupted by the arrival of an emissary from Hindman, Major James Nocquet, formerly of the French army. Earlier in the evening, Bragg had twice forwarded to Hindman the reports of Crittenden's advance, so as to impress upon him the need for rapid action in the morning. There had been nothing alarming in Bragg's messages. First at 6:00 P.M.: "The general commanding instructs me to say that Crittenden's corps marched from Chattanooga this morning in this direction, and that it is highly important that you should finish the movement now going on as rapidly as possible"; and then at 7:30 P.M.: "The enemy is now divided. Our force at or near La Fayette is superior to the enemy. It is important now to move vigorously and crush him." But Hindman had lost interest in his mission. He had convinced himself that some unknown enemy force was about to fall on his rear, and he also believed that the Federal operations in the cove were merely a feint to mask a major thrust from Alpine. Consequently, Hindman saw in Bragg's mention of Crittenden a further rationale for recommending cancellation of the attack. Buckner, whose division had come up shortly before sunset, was too new to the situation to offer him any advice.[32]

Hindman could not have chosen a worse messenger. Bragg had relieved Nocquet one month after appointing him chief engineer of the army in November 1862. Since then, the incompetent Frenchman, who was now serving on Buckner's staff, had been loudly critical of both Bragg and the entire Southern war effort. In addition to being obnoxious to the commanding general, Nocquet could barely speak English.

Bragg and his lieutenants listened now as Nocquet somewhat incoherently relayed Hindman's concerns. The general, Nocquet said, had "heard that the enemy were moving in a particular direction and [thus] thought it advisable to modify the orders he had received." Bragg turned to Martin. There was absolutely nothing to Hindman's story, Martin assured him, no enemy forces threatened his rear and Thomas was definitely moving toward the cove and was not at Alpine. Bragg addressed Nocquet emphatically: He was to return to Hindman and tell him to attack even if he lost his entire command in doing so.[33] Pushing himself relentlessly, Bragg rode out a couple of hours later to watch Cleburne's progress at Dug Gap.[34]

He should have ridden fifteen miles farther to supervise Hindman. Although Bragg's attack order reached him at 4:00 A.M., Hindman chose to await Nocquet's return before acting. Even after Nocquet returned two and a half hours later, Hindman refused to budge. In his after-action report, written in early October, he claimed Nocquet told him that Bragg's orders had been discretionary. Nocquet was a convenient scapegoat, since he was not present to defend his actions. Grown tired of the Confederate cause, he had disappeared through Federal lines shortly after Chickamauga with $150,000 earmarked for construction projects.[35]

As the first rays of sunlight filtered into McLemore's Cove, the men of Wood's brigade filed through Dug Gap, "crawling under, around or over trees, logs and brush that had been cut on the road through the gap." James Deshler's Texas brigade followed. By 8:00 A.M., Cleburne had the two brigades drawn up within a half mile of the crossroads. A single ridge separated the opposing forces. Hill and Bragg joined Cleburne, and together the three listened for the opening guns of Hindman's attack.[36]

The hours passed in silence. A few hundred yards to the west, Thomas came on the field with his staff. Up went their tents in the Widow Davis's meadow, and Thomas "sat down to business as undisturbed and impassive as the craggy mountains around." He watched the brigades of John Stark-weather and Benjamin Scribner arrive and march into place behind Negley's infantry. When scouts reported the advance of Wood and Deshler, Negley prepared to withdraw his trains from the cove and to retire his infantry to Bailey's Cross Roads.[37]

What of Hindman? At daylight, for reasons apparent only to him, Hind-man decided to flip-flop his forces and advance with Stewart's division of Buckner's corps in the lead. As his own division blocked the road, an hour or more was lost while Stewart's Tennesseans struggled to get to the front, and it was 7:00 A.M. before he had his long column in motion along the narrow dirt road that led the last three miles from Gowan's (Gower's) Ford to the crossroads. Halts were frequent. "This don't look like marching to 'attack the enemy when we shall find him,' but rather as though we were afraid he would find us," said a staff officer ruefully.[38]

At 10:00 A.M., a lieutenant of engineers reported to Hindman that he had seen Negley's trains on the near side of Stevens's Gap and doubted that they could turn around easily. This enlivened Hindman temporarily, and by 11:00 the head of his column was within cannon shot of the crossroads and Negley's left flank. As his division commanders began their final deployment, a courier from Bragg handed Hindman the following note: "If you find the enemy in such force as to make an attack imprudent, fall back at once on La Fayette by Catlett's Gap, from which obstructions have now been removed. Send your determination at once and act as promptly." Moments later, a second dispatch arrived from headquarters estimating the enemy force in front of Dug Gap to exceed twelve thousand.[39]

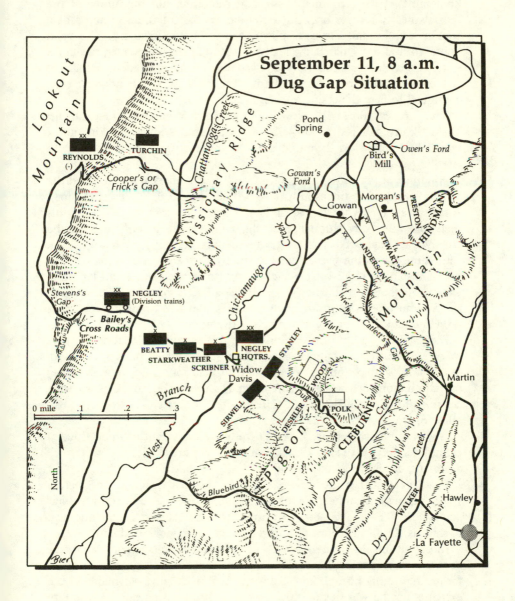

September 11, 8 a.m.
Dug Gap Situation

Lookout Mountain

REYNOLDS (-)

TURCHIN

Cooper's or Frick's Gap

Chattanooga Creek

Missionary Ridge

Pond Spring

Bird's Mill

Owen's Ford

Gowan's Ford

Morgan's

HINDMAN

PRESTON

STEWART

ANDERSON

Gowan

Creek

Stevens's Gap

NEGLEY (Division trains)

Bailey's Cross Roads

Chickamauga

Catlett's Gap

BEATTY

STARKWEATHER

SCRIBNER

NEGLEY HQTRS.

STANLEY

Widow Davis

WOOD

Mountain

Martin

POLK

0 mile   .1   .2   .3

SIRWELL

DESHLER

Dug Gap

CLEBURNE

Creek

Branch

North

West

Pigeon

Duck

Creek

Bluebird Gap

Gap

Dry Creek

WALKER

Hawley

La Fayette

Bier

An aggressive commander would have pressed on to develop the enemy, knowing that the combined Confederate columns still outnumbered the Federals nearly four to one. But Hindman halted his infantry and sent a courier back around the east end of Pigeon Mountain (a ride of several hours) to find out what Bragg really wanted. Three hours later, he sent a second dispatch asking that he be allowed to withdraw. That done, Hindman sat down on a log to await a reply. Buckner, who was at Hindman's side, continued to play the silent partner.[40]

The sun was already dipping below Lookout Mountain when Captain Taylor Beatty galloped up at 4:00 P.M. with Bragg's answer: "The attack which was ordered at daybreak must be made at once or it will be too late."[41]

Hindman at last turned his men loose. Patton Anderson's brigade led the attack. "Never were troops in better spirit and more eager to meet the foe," Anderson recalled with mixed pride and regret. For six hundred yards his men tore their way through briar-choked underbrush, only to find the enemy had disappeared. Their anger led them on across Chickamauga Creek "at a time when the men were extremely thirsty, but not a man halted for an instant to slake his parched tongue from the limpid and tempting waters." As they neared Bailey's Cross Roads a Federal battery barked a volley that wounded two men in the Forty-first Mississippi. With darkness coming on, Hindman told Anderson to stop for the night.[42]

Back at Dug Gap, the frustration was palpable. Hill galloped to S. A. M. Wood's skirmish line the moment he heard the scattered firing from Hindman's front and personally led the skirmishers forward, "thus attracting our admiration for the lieutenant general who was not afraid to go with his front line," recalled Captain Coleman of the Fifteenth Mississippi Battalion Sharpshooters.

It was an empty gesture. A volley from the Nineteenth Illinois, hidden behind a stone wall along Chickamauga Creek, knocked down thirty Alabamians, checking Wood's advance.[43]

Bragg met Buckner and Hindman at the crossroads at sunset. His greeting was anything but cordial. "General Buckner, where are the enemy?" Bragg demanded. "They have escaped through Stevens's Gap," muttered Buckner. Bragg was furious. In front of all present, he upbraided Hindman.[44]

Most felt he deserved the rebuke. Said Arthur Manigault, a brigade commander under Hindman: "The opportunity offered General Hindman for distinguishing himself and striking a terrible blow was favorable in the extreme, but he was not up to the work, it being far beyond his capacity as a general. Had there been a proper man to manage for us, I have little doubt but that a most brilliant success would have been achieved." Part of the blame, however, rests with Bragg. Bragg's resolution weakened during the day as he imagined Crittenden and McCook were closing in on his flanks. His mistake was not in harboring such fears but rather that he shared them with Hindman.

The men in the ranks recognized that a golden moment had passed. "Hill's corps, every man of which had realized the enemy's situation the day through, was in ecstasies of grief. Men and officers swore, some were almost in tears, many were in despair," recalled Captain Buck of Cleburne's staff. "We can never get a better chance and perhaps never again one as good," lamented Taylor Beatty.[45]

About the only damage done the Federals that afternoon was to the ego of Colonel Benjamin Scribner. He was a good-natured man, with a round, jolly face and muttonchops. Just as Wood's skirmishers opened fire on his brigade line, the Indianian was stricken with an attack of hay fever. "I wore dark goggles to protect my eyes, as the glare of the light without them was unendurable," he wrote. "My horse disturbed a hornet's nest in front of my line and became unmanageable, and so slashed me about in the underbrush that my glasses were lost. Overwhelmed with a disaster which would have completely disabled me, I called to my men with much earnestness to find them for me, which they soon did, to my great relief. The men tell this incident with decided relish, that I 'stopped the fight to find my spectacles.' "[46]

Sitting beside their campfires at Bailey's Cross Roads, beneath the glowering summit of Lookout Mountain, Negley's men realized how close they had come to annihilation and that they were not yet out of danger. Everyone expected a hard fight in the morning, and few slept. John Beatty passed the entire night nervously checking and rechecking his lines. Just before dawn, his commissary sergeant handed him a bottle of wine to calm his nerves. Beatty welcomed the bottle. "Well, let's drink," he sighed. "We may not be able to a few hours later."[47]

CHAPTER FIVE

WE ARE IN A TICKLISH PLACE HERE

THE NEAR destruction of Negley and Baird failed to dent Rosecrans's consciousness. While the fate of the two divisions hung in the balance on the morning of 11 September, Rosecrans was telling Crittenden that all evidence "confirmed . . . the belief that the mass of the enemy's force has retreated on Rome." Not until that night, by "sheer repetition of the warnings," was Thomas able to convince Rosecrans that a considerable portion of Bragg's army was drawn up around La Fayette ready to give battle.[1] Nevertheless, as late as the morning of 12 September Rosecrans remained convinced that Negley had withdrawn from Davis's Cross Roads "more through prudence than compulsion."[2]

Though he did not yet understand how exposed his three corps were to defeat in detail, Rosecrans had begun to effect a concentration of his scattered forces in spite of himself. Sharp skirmishing with Forrest's cavalry before Ringgold and along Pea Vine Creek on 10 September, combined with early reports from his scouts, had been enough to convince Crittenden that the bulk of the Confederate army had retreated along the La Fayette road rather than toward Dalton. Rosecrans consequently ordered him to pursue no farther than Ringgold and to reconnoiter toward Lee and Gordon's Mill on 11 September, a first step toward uniting two of his three corps.[3] Although relations between the two had grown frosty, Crittenden was too long in the habit of relying on Tom Wood to do differently now. He gave the reconnaissance mission to his willful subordinate, who in turn passed it on to his most trusted brigade commander, Charles G. Harker.

A better choice could not be had. At twenty-seven, the New Jersey native was both the youngest and the most promising brigade commander in the Army of the Cumberland. Orphaned as a child, Harker went to work as a clerk in the store of Nathan Stratton, a two-term member of Congress who rewarded his hardworking young employee with an appointment to the Military Academy. Harker graduated from West Point in 1858. After serving three years on the northwestern frontier, he was sent to Ohio to drill volunteers at the outbreak of the war. He quickly parlayed that tedious assignment into the colonelcy of the Sixty-fifth Ohio, which he personally trained. Harker had served brilliantly to date, though he stumbled a bit on the first day at Stones River. Graced with boyish good looks, Harker's military prowess was exceeded only by his social charms. A connoisseur of fine wines, the young colonel was among the army's more eligible bachelor officers.[4]

Harker took his mission seriously. Scarcely had he begun when his men captured a mortally wounded private from Forrest's command. With his dying words, the Rebel confessed to Harker that a large force of Confederate infantry lay near Lee and Gordon's Mill. Harker passed the warning on to Wood, who told him to continue on the La Fayette road from Rossville to the mill, where Wood would join him with the remainder of the division. Harker moved cautiously. He reached the mill at 4:30 P.M. without incident and brushed away the enemy cavalry guarding the fords across Chickamauga Creek. Wood rode up after nightfall. "When I arrived at Gordon's Mill . . . the enemy camp fires could be distinctly seen on the other side of the creek," he recalled. "Their light, reflected over a wide section of the horizon, and extending upward on the heavens, told that the foe was present in considerable force."[5]

By 10:00 P.M., Rosecrans was sufficiently concerned to order Crittenden to move his remaining two divisions and Wilder's brigade from the vicinity of Ringgold to Lee and Gordon's Mill at once and there open communications with Thomas. Still loath to abandon his pursuit, Rosecrans did not bring up McCook but instead bucked the matter to him and Thomas to work out between themselves. Most of Bragg's army was assumed to lie opposite Pigeon Mountain, Garfield wrote McCook. "In view of this fact," he continued, "the general commanding suggests that you close up toward General Thomas to within supporting distance. . . . He does not, however, give a peremptory order; but leaves your course to your own discretion, if you find the facts different from what is now supposed." And to Thomas, Garfield wrote: "In case you find the enemy concentrated in heavy force, it will be best to draw General McCook to within supporting distance."[6]

Thomas must have found this all a bit ridiculous. Had he not been telling headquarters for nearly twenty-four hours that the Rebels were massing east of McLemore's Cove? And summoning McCook would be problematical. Without cavalry, Thomas had been unable to open communications with the Twentieth Corps. By the morning of 11 September, he had been compelled to entrust the delivery of his messages to purportedly loyal civilians.

McCook never got them. Nightfall of 11 September found him totally out of touch with developments to the north. In fact, for the past three days he had been operating pretty much on his own. What few dispatches he received from army headquarters were delayed between eight and eighteen hours en route. On arriving at Alpine on 10 September, McCook had tried to communicate with Thomas by way of Broomtown Valley. It was not until his couriers ran into Rebels that McCook realized that Thomas had failed to reach La Fayette. Although he had heard nothing of consequence from Rosecrans, McCook wisely stopped his advance short of Summerville. Concerned but not alarmed, McCook held his divisions in camp around Alpine for the next forty-eight hours.

McCook was happy to await developments; Phil Sheridan, his fiery division commander, was not. Twice in as many days he had shared his anxiety with Colonel Luther Bradley. "This is all wrong," he fretted. "We have no business here, we ought to be in Chattanooga. If we whip Bragg down here we've got to fall back to the Tennessee for supplies. We can't advance till we rebuild the railroad."[7]

Sheridan took it upon himself to find out what was going on behind enemy lines. He sent his trusty scout "Card" to comb the area for a loyal mountaineer willing to spy for the Federals. "Card" returned with a volunteer, who asked only that Sheridan agree to buy up all his livestock and help him migrate west if he survived the mission. Sheridan assented. The mountaineer entered Bragg's lines at La Fayette and was promptly captured, but somehow he escaped. He eluded a search party by crawling on his belly through the Rebel picket lines and grunting like a wild boar. Making his way back to Federal lines on 11 September, he told Sheridan the disturbing truth: Bragg was preparing to turn on the Federals at La Fayette. Much to the chagrin of McCook and his staff, a lieutenant of the First Alabama Cavalry captured near Summerville later that night confirmed the story and volunteered the news that Longstreet's quartermaster had arrived in Atlanta and was gathering railroad cars to bring up Longstreet's corps. "Up to that moment we believed the enemy to be east of us retreating toward Resaca," admitted Lieutenant Colonel Horace Fisher of the corps staff."[8]

Anticipating an order to withdraw, McCook halted his trains on top of Lookout Mountain on the morning of 12 September and sent those few wagons that had made the descent back up the mountain. At 4:15 P.M., McCook finally received Garfield's ambiguous instructions of the night before; they had been eighteen hours in transit. While he puzzled over their meaning, McCook received new, definitive orders through Thomas shortly after midnight, via a newly opened courier line, to move north to McLemore's Cove and unite with the Fourteenth Corps as rapidly as possible.[9]

Rosecrans at last recognized that his grand pursuit had gone tragically awry—that if he failed to gather his forces rapidly he might well find himself the pursued. Every voluble prisoner, every intelligent contraband, every loyal civilian told the same story: Dug Gap had been no rear guard action. The Army of Tennessee had stopped, turned about, and was full of fight. And now it appeared it would have help from Virginia. Rosecrans later claimed that the cooperative cavalry lieutenant captured by McCook had provided the "first certain intimation" he had that Longstreet was coming. Since the War Department not only had dismissed early rumors of Longstreet's detachment but failed even to inform Rosecrans of them, this is probably true. In any case, Rosecrans soon obtained corroborating intelligence from General J. J. Peck, the Federal commander in North Carolina, who said he was sure "large bodies of troops have gone south by us over the road."[10]

Shortly before noon on 12 September, Rosecrans called Granger up from Bridgeport with an admonition to make haste: "The enemy has concentrated in vicinity of La Fayette. . . . We are concentrating the army to support General Thomas and fight a general battle. Come to this place immediately with Steedman's division. . . . If all reports are true, we have not a moment to lose."[11] Later in the day he asked Thomas to summon McCook's Corps. That McCook did not get this order until early on 13 September was a consequence of Rosecrans's vacillation; Thomas did not know from one moment to the next what the commanding general wanted. "I have just sent orders to Generals McCook and Stanley to close in to my support," Thomas told Rosecrans that morning. "I should have done that before had I known that you desired me to do so, but from the tenor of the communications received from you yesterday noon, I was led to believe that you would give orders for McCook to close in to my support."[12]

With the tables turned, Rosecrans suddenly remembered Burnside. While he thought Bragg was in panicked retreat, Rosecrans scarcely had deigned to keep the commander of the Army of the Ohio informed of his own movements or whereabouts. Now he pleaded with Halleck to order Burnside down toward Chattanooga to protect his left flank. While he tried not to sound overly alarmed—"I trust I am sufficient for the enemy now in my front"—he also asked Halleck to order elements from Grant's army to move to Tuscumbia, Alabama, in order to protect his right flank should Bragg try a grand envelopment toward the Tennessee from that direction. Halleck prodded Burnside, who since capturing Knoxville wanted only to resign from the army, and instructed Grant to send whatever troops he could spare to cooperate with Rosecrans. Unfortunately, the telegram went astray and did not reach Grant until five days after Chickamauga.[13]

Well might Rosecrans fear the consequences of even the slightest misstep. For into his camp on 11 September had come a man able to ruin him with the stroke of a pen, Assistant Secretary of War Charles A. Dana. Stanton had chosen Dana to be his assistant after the journalist lost his job as managing editor of the New York *Tribune* for having too vigorously defended the secretary in print against criticism from the newspaper's owner, Horace Greeley.

Earlier that summer, Stanton had sent Dana to Mississippi to observe Grant, "about whom at that time there were many doubts, and against whom there was some complaint," as Dana explained his mission. The fall of Vicksburg ended Dana's duties. He returned to New York in hopes of resuming private business, but Stanton persuaded him to go to the headquarters of the Army of the Cumberland. Dana may not have known a cap from a cartridge, but he knew what Stanton wanted. He was to apprise the secretary confidentially on a regular basis of all he saw and heard, to pass judgments freely on the commanding general and his subordinates and their management of the campaign. Clearly, Stanton hoped to use Dana as the instrument of Rosecrans's destruction. "His part was something like that of the committees which the Convention in the first French Revolution kept at the headquarters of the armies in the field," mused Henry Villard.[14]

When they met, Dana handed Rosecrans the following letter of introduction from Stanton:

> General: This will introduce to you Charles A. Dana, Esq., one of my assistants, who visits your command for the purpose of conferring with you upon any subject which you may desire to have brought to the notice of the department. Mr. Dana is a gentleman of distinguished character, patriotism, and ability, and possesses the entire confidence of the department. You will please afford to him the courtesy and consideration which he merits, and explain to him fully any matters which you may desire through him to bring to the notice of the department.[15]

Stanton's disingenuous letter fooled no one. Gordon Granger dismissed Dana as a "loathsome pimp." Smith Atkins labeled him an "interloper, a marplot, a spy upon rival generals." "He was received by the army as if he was a bird of evil omen," snorted rival journalist William Shanks. "It was whispered at headquarters that he had come as the spy of the War Department, and to find justification for Rosecrans's intended removal. The rumor spread through the army; officers looked upon him with scowls, and the men ridiculed him by pretending to mistake him for a sutler, calling after him as he rode by with Rosecrans, 'Hey, old sutler! When are you going to open out?'"[16]

Despite the presence of Dana and the warnings from Thomas, the prevailing mood at headquarters was remarkably optimistic, even manic. One school of thought still held Bragg's abortive attack at Dug Gap to have been no more than a rear guard action. Thomas's own assistant adjutant general regarded the Rebel concentration as "no doubt a feint by the Rebel rear guard to cover their retreat." Colonel Sanderson found the enthusiasm contagious when he returned to camp from his failed mission at the capital. "It may be that Bragg will give us battle at Dalton, but I do not believe it. . . . My own belief is that there will be no engagement this side of Rome," was his first impression of the state of things. Horace Porter wrote his mother with reckless confidence on 13 September that "the Rebel army is retreating through Georgia, and we are following as fast as we can drag our artillery and supplies over a country with little more than mountain paths to advance upon. Bragg's army has been reinforced by Johnston and Lee, but Rosy is more than a match for him still."[17]

Dana later said that Rosecrans assumed that Bragg simply was making a pretense of taking the offensive in order to check the Federal pursuit; that he would flee to Rome as soon as he found Rosecrans had collected his army in McLemore's Cove. Perhaps Rosecrans still shared some of his staff's confidence. As late as 13 September, he told Thomas and Crittenden that he intended to attack Bragg at La Fayette if McCook were able to come up quickly enough. But if headquarters was reluctant to face the changed reality, one irreverent military telegrapher had no trouble neatly summarizing the hard truth in a wire to Washington: "The enemy are between Thomas and McCook on the south and Crittenden and Granger on the north and the day before yesterday gave Negley a thrashing. . . . We are in a ticklish place here."[18]

The fiasco at Dug Gap initially paralyzed Bragg. All he could think of well into the night of 11 September was McCook at Alpine and the danger of an attack from that quarter, not knowing that McCook himself was so confused and ignorant of the whereabouts of both the Confederates and the rest of his own army that he was afraid to move in any direction. So Bragg's first impulse was to order his army to fall back from Pigeon Mountain and converge on La Fayette.[19]

By 3:00 A.M. on the twelfth, Bragg's anger at Hindman and fear of McCook had subsided enough for him to see that he had been granted a second chance to strike Rosecrans while the Federal army was still divided. When Brigadier General Frank Armstrong's cavalry pickets reported the appearance of Harker at Lee and Gordon's Mill, Bragg sensed the time was ripe for a blow against Crittenden.

Polk's corps was nearest the enemy. At 3:00 A.M., Bragg instructed the bishop to accompany Cheatham's division to Rock Spring Church, which lay six miles southeast of Lee and Gordon's Mill at the junction of the State and Pea Vine Church roads. Early in the afternoon, Bragg directed Hindman's division and Walker's Reserve Corps to reinforce Cheatham.[20]

Meanwhile, Crittenden was moving quickly to reunite his corps. The division of Brigadier General Horatio Van Cleve marched from Ringgold to Lee and Gordon's Mill without incident. Major General John Palmer moved via the Pea Vine Church road. He found "a few enemy troops" watching his movements but nothing to prevent his effecting an easy junction with Wood. Before doing so, Palmer sent the brigade of Brigadier General Charles Cruft up the valley toward Pea Vine Church to clear his flank.[21]

Cruft knew Palmer was giving his brigade a chance to redeem itself. Two days earlier, it had led the march on Ringgold. Palmer had ridden with Cruft's advance regiment, the First Kentucky. As they crested Pea Vine Ridge, Palmer had noticed a large column of Confederate cavalry kicking up dust across his line of march, with a small detachment blocking the road just a few hundred yards ahead. He told his senior aide, Captain D. W. Norton, to take forty troopers from his escort, the Fourth Michigan Cavalry, and brush away the Rebels, who belonged to Pegram's brigade. Off they rode. In the meantime, the First Kentucky filed past and into a skirt of timber near the creek to support Norton if needed.

A few minutes later Norton returned and told Cruft the cavalry, which he estimated at two hundred men, was too strong for him to drive off alone, but that a section of artillery could probably do the job. Just then a whoop and a yell pierced the air. Glancing to the front, Cruft and Norton saw a swirling cloud of dust settle over the First Kentucky. When it cleared just five minutes later, there was no sign of the galloping Confederates it had masked or the fifty-eight men of the First Kentucky who had laid down their arms without firing a shot and surrendered.

Palmer had watched it all. Years later the memory still pained him. "I have never suffered from disease or other cause the agony produced by this event," he wrote. "Not a gun was fired, but the Rebels, at full speed, rode up and captured all these men with loaded muskets in their hands."[22]

Cruft was taking no chances now. At Pea Vine Church he ran into Pegram's pickets. Satisfied that they screened a body of infantry too strong for him to fight alone, Cruft withdraw quickly to the mill.[23]

Cruft's reconnaissance more than made up for the fifty-eight captured Kentuckians. Pegram mistook it for an advance of Palmer's entire division and so informed headquarters. The prospect of netting a lone division with three of his own excited Bragg. At 6:00 P.M., he sent Pegram's note to Polk. You have "a fine opportunity of striking Crittenden in detail, and I hope you will avail yourself of it at daylight tomorrow," he told the bishop. "This division crushed, and the others are ours. We can then turn again on the force in the cove." Perhaps recalling how Hindman had used discretionary orders as an excuse for delay, at 8:00 P.M. Bragg dictated a second order specifically directing Polk to attack at dawn.[24]

Bragg was wasting his breath. Polk was no more inclined to attack than Hindman had been. He did not even leave camp until 4:00 P.M., and by the time he joined Cheatham at Rock Spring Church, night had fallen. There was still no sign of Hindman, whose instructions had said he need move only after his men were "refreshed"; it would be another ten hours before his division sauntered into camp. Walker's corps arrived at 8:00 P.M.

Polk rode into the darkness to reconnoiter his lines as best he could. Thanks to poor intelligence from Pegram's cavalry, which somehow had lost track of Van Cleve and Palmer during the last few miles of their march to Lee and Gordon's Mill, the bishop completely misread the situation. At 8:00 P.M. he set down his conclusions in a message to Bragg. He faced not a single division but Crittenden's entire corps reinforced by Wilder's brigade. Polk erroneously placed one division on the road to Lee and Gordon's Mill, a second on the Pea Vine Church road, and the third on the road to Ringgold, with Wilder covering the entire movement. Polk had no idea that Crittenden's corps was actually concentrated in defensive positions near the mill or that Wilder, who had nearly ridden into an ambush set by Pegram at sunset while screening the infantry, had slipped away silently after dark to join Crittenden. He also believed that another corps lay behind Crittenden's.[25]

Polk was convinced the Federals would advance at dawn. Tossing aside Bragg's order, the bishop told him that he could not attack without heavy reinforcements — say Buckner's corps — and that in any case he could not possibly be ready to move at dawn. Only if he were reinforced and the Federals did not attack first would he move.[26]

Ironically, Polk was about to get his own lesson in what fractious subordinates could do to a commander's nerves. Before dispatching his message to Bragg, the bishop called Generals Walker and Liddell to a council of war to explain his intentions and the part he expected the Reserve Corps to play. Instead, he ended up defending his proposals to Walker, who found nothing but fault with "Old Polk's" dispositions. Polk tried to change them to appease Walker, but the Georgian only raised new objections.

Polk was thoroughly perplexed. One of the bishop's staff officers pulled Liddell aside and begged him to call Walker off. Liddell got his corps commander as far as the front door when Walker suddenly broke loose and resumed the dispute. Seeing no way of ending Walker's "pertinacious quibbles," Liddell asked Frank Cheatham to try his hand with him. Cheatham walked over to where Polk and Walker were talking and listened for a moment to the Georgian. Suddenly, he turned and stormed back to Liddell, "saying with an oath he would not serve two hours under Walker to save his life."

"Walker stayed until he had pretty much exhausted rhetoric and expletives. He came grumbling away, greatly to the relief of General Polk, who was completely badgered. This was the man Bragg had placed over me, with whom he was himself at a loss, as he said to me, 'worn out and disappointed,' " sighed Liddell.[27]

By now it was nearly 10:30 P.M. Remembering the unsent dispatch, Polk summoned Lieutenant Richmond and ordered him to take it to headquarters "with great haste." Richmond covered the eight and a half miles in thirty-five minutes, and Bragg had the message in hand by 11:00.[28]

Polk's gloomy note caught Bragg off guard. His reply, sent at midnight, was oddly worded and vague. "Your position seems to be a strong one for defense, but I hope will not be held unless the enemy attacks early. We must force him to fight at the earliest moment and before his combinations can be carried out." Bragg did, however, promise to order up Buckner.

Once again, the Confederate high command was bedeviled by chimeras. A vigorous demonstration by Crook's Federal cavalry that afternoon had thoroughly unnerved Hill, who feared an attack by McCook's infantry would follow. Bragg shared his concern. At 12:30 A.M., he repeated his admonition to Polk: "The enemy is approaching from the south, and it is highly important your attack in the morning should be quick and decided. Let no time be lost."[29]

Bragg's words were lost in the night. Not until 3:00 A.M. did Bishop Polk order Walker into line on the right of Cheatham. Hindman finally strolled into corps headquarters at 4:30 A.M. Not only did Polk fail to reprimand his tardiness, he did not even bother to order Hindman into position until 6:00 A.M., thirty minutes after the first glimmer of morning twilight. Then, true to his word, he waited for Crittenden to attack.[30]

A sharp exchange of rifle fire broke the stillness at sunrise. Polk sent his inspector general, Captain Frank Wheless, to look into the source of the shooting. A banker in Nashville before the war, Wheless was an honest and reliable volunteer officer. He reconnoitered all the way to Cheatham's picket line. Returning to headquarters, Wheless told Polk that the firing had been nothing more than "a picket skirmish and that an advance of the enemy in force was not possible." Polk was neither convinced nor particularly anxious to press the issue. Two hours passed before he again made an effort to learn what was happening to his front. This time he sent Wheless up the road to Pea Vine Church, where there presumably was a Federal division.

All Wheless found was a tired civilian who complained that he had been forced to guide Crittenden and Wilder's men across Chickamauga Creek during the night. Wheless galloped back to Rock Spring Church to tell Polk conclusively that Crittenden had disappeared from the Pea Vine Church road. A little while later, Pegram sent word that the Ringgold road was clear as well. That left only the road to the mill. A little after 9:00 A.M., Polk sent Strahl's brigade down it to develop the situation.[31]

Bragg stormed into Polk's headquarters a few minutes later. Whatever he might have said to Polk, it produced no attack. Strahl ran into Crittenden's skirmish line a little after noon, then fell back to try to draw the Federals out. Nothing else of consequence occurred. Walker's orders to wheel to the left and attack were canceled after Wheless reported Pea Vine Church clear of Federals. Bragg ordered Buckner to retrace his steps to La Fayette, then himself started back shortly before sunset.[32]

Twice in as many days the Army of Tennessee had allowed nearly certain victory to slip through its grasp. Yet even as Bragg and his staff rode back to La Fayette on the evening of 13 September, Rosecrans's army remained dangerously fragmented. Ten miles separated Crittenden at Lee and Gordon's Mill from Thomas's left flank at Cooper's Gap. Although Thomas had his entire corps up, he in turn was separated from McCook by nearly thirty miles of uncertain mountain trails. Gordon Granger, meanwhile, had just crossed the Tennessee at Shellmound with Steedman's division; only by pushing his men relentlessly over rocky mountain roads and through suffocating clouds of dust did he succeed in reaching Rossville on 14 September.[33]

There was to be no third try at the Federals. Bragg had grown weary of playing the shuttlecock between Rosecrans's scattered forces. Throughout the day on 13 September, he had been troubled by recurring reports from Hill warning of an imminent attack on his corps. When it became evident that Crittenden had escaped the trap at Pea Vine Church, Bragg's only thought was of Hill's two small divisions and vulnerable park of reserve artillery and wagon trains at La Fayette.

For Hill, it had been a day of "great anxiety." At dawn, Brigadier General John Wharton, whose cavalry division watched McCook, sent Hill a note warning him that the Federals were preparing to advance on La Fayette. When a brisk fire opened just two miles from Hill's headquarters moments after the courier handed him Wharton's dispatch, the North Carolinian assumed the worst. "It is to be South Mountain over again," Hill yelled to his staff as they galloped to the sound of the fighting. (A year earlier, Hill had defended the gaps through the Maryland mountain with one sadly depleted division against two Federal corps while Lee hurried to gather together the Army of Northern Virginia at Sharpsburg.)

At the front, Hill met Brigadier General Dan Adams, whose skirmishers had just repulsed a wild charge by two regiments of Union cavalry. "The boldness of the cavalry advance" convinced Adams that "an infantry column was not far off." Hill hurried reinforcements to Adams, and "every disposition was made to celebrate appropriately the next day—the anniversary of South Mountain."[34]

The Federal cavalry thus was beginning to redeem itself. By 13 September, Stanley was completely bedridden with dysentery.[35] When orders came for a reconnaissance in force to fix the enemy forces at La Fayette and mask McCook's withdrawal, Stanley weakly passed the mission on to Brigadier General George Crook, who would one day earn fame fighting Geronimo's Apaches in Arizona.

An unassuming man who "rather underrates than overrates his successes," Crook shined in his fleeting role as chief of cavalry.[36] Crook gave Colonel Edward McCook (another of the "Fighting McCooks") two brigades of cavalry and ordered him to ride toward La Fayette via Summerville, while he with the remaining two brigades would parallel the Ohioan along the direct road. Ten miles outside La Fayette, McCook's lead regiment, the Ninth Pennsylvania, struck Wharton's picket line. Colonel Archibald Campbell yelled "charge," and in a matter of minutes the Pennsylvanians had swept up seventeen startled pickets. After that there was no stopping them. For the next six miles the Ninth drove Wharton's confused troopers relentlessly while the remainder of Campbell's brigade struggled to catch up. "It was exceedingly hot . . . and the great clouds of dust raised by our industrious cavalry were at times almost unbearable . . . cavalrymen's faces were caked with dust, streaked with perspiration," recalled Lieutenant William Carter of the First Tennessee Cavalry, whose misfortune it was to trail the Pennsylvanians.[37] But that same cloud of dust also saved Yankee lives. So effectively did it conceal the cavalry that a Rebel battery, which ordinarily could have decimated it, sent its shells sailing harmlessly overhead. Nine men from Adams's skirmish line surrendered in the confusion, and more were sure to follow, when Campbell was handed orders to break off the attack and return to Alpine.[38]

Bragg and his generals passed a fitful night. "Reports of the enemy's advance from all quarters, and in all directions. They come on as thick as autumnal leaves," a harried George Brent scribbled in his diary. Although dawn of 14 September did not bring the attack from the south Hill so feared, Bragg used his own continued uncertainty regarding McCook's intentions as an excuse to order a general withdrawal of the army to La Fayette. There he took up defensive positions. The initiative passed to Rosecrans. For the next two and a half days, he would be free to gather his scattered corps unmolested.

Bragg was exhausted. He had slept but little since abandoning Chattanooga, and the strain was beginning to tell. Polk thought he looked weaker than he had at any time since the retreat from Tullahoma. "Bragg seems sick and feeble. The responsibilities of his trust weigh heavily upon him," Colonel

Brent noted with concern in his diary.[39] Fundamentally, however, Bragg gave up because he could no longer trust his generals to obey his orders. The command structure of the Army of Tennessee was near collapse. The sudden accretion of new commanders and units had strained the fragile patchwork. Weighed down by distrust and contempt, it now ripped apart completely. Hill summarized the problem from the point of view of Bragg's subordinates:

> The nightmare upon Bragg . . . was due, doubtless, to his uncertainty about the movements of his enemy, and to the certainty that there was not that mutual confidence between him and some of his subordinates that there ought to be between a chief and his officers to insure victory. Bragg's want of definite and precise information had led him more than once to issue "impossible" orders, and therefore those intrusted with their execution got in the way of disregarding them. Another more serious trouble with him was the disposition to find a scapegoat for every failure and disaster. This made his officers cautious about striking a blow when an opportunity presented itself, unless they were protected by a positive order.[40]

Rosecrans would need every minute Bragg was willing to give him to draw his army together, since McCook was fast turning what should have been a one-day forced march into a three-and-a-half-day odyssey. Rosecrans, Thomas, and McCook all must share the blame for this delay, which might have meant the end of the Army of the Cumberland had Bragg not slumbered.

From Alpine, the most direct route into McLemore's Cove was a trail that ran along the summit of Lookout Mountain to Dougherty's Gap. At the gap, the trail joined a good country road that ran due north to Bailey's Cross Roads. A twelve- or fifteen-mile march over this route would have put McCook on Thomas's right flank in the cove.

McCook began moving his trains at dawn on 13 September with every intention of marching along the direct route to Dougherty's Gap. He sent Colonel Thomas Harrison's Thirty-ninth Indiana Mounted Infantry to reconnoiter the trail and open communications with Thomas by way of the gap. Then problems arose. Sometime during the afternoon he received orders from Garfield directing him to join Thomas at Stevens's Gap. The intent was the same; Garfield simply had picked the wrong landmark on which to orient the march. But McCook, who seldom knew from one moment to the next where army headquarters was, much less the maneuver elements, took the message to mean that Thomas no longer controlled McLemore's Cove. Harrison had not returned and McCook, now thoroughly befuddled, sent Thomas a dispatch at 5:00 P.M. saying that he would have to recross Lookout Mountain and march north through Lookout Valley to enter the cove at Stevens's Gap, a distance of nearly fifty miles. McCook, who had failed to reconnoiter Lookout Mountain during his stay of nearly a week at Alpine, was unaware that a good road ran along the mountain from Dougherty's to Stevens's Gap, which would have cut at least twenty-five miles off the trek.[41]

It was 6:00 A.M. on 14 September before Thomas received McCook's dispatch. He too was unaware of the road between Dougherty's and Stevens's gaps. Intimating that the Confederates, who held Dug and Catlett's gaps, could strike the flank of McCook's column should he march north through the cove, Thomas agreed that "the route by Winston's Gap . . . is the only practicable one."[42]

McCook had his troops on the road before sunrise, so that they were already atop Lookout Mountain when orders came to continue west toward Winston's Gap. They pushed on relentlessly through yet another day of choking dust and heat. Sergeant William Newlin of the Seventy-third Illinois recalled that nearly every man in his regiment fell out before the column halted at sunset.

This rest, welcomed by the sun-dazed soldiers, was unplanned. It came because McCook was at wit's end. Minutes earlier, he had been handed a dispatch from Garfield expressing Rosecrans's "regret" that he had chosen to march by way of Lookout Valley instead of taking the mountain road from Dougherty's to Stevens's Gap. Garfield disputed Thomas's contention that the Rebels controlled the gaps along Pigeon Mountain and ordered McCook to turn around and take the direct route into the cove.[43]

McCook replied angrily: "I was placed under the command of General Thomas . . . who requested me to join him at Stevens's Gap. . . . I at least supposed that General Thomas would know the condition of the country and roads for a few miles on his right. . . . By his approval I am on this route. I will be pained to take my troops over the route again; they certainly would feel as if I were trifling with them. I will suspend the movement until I hear from you."[44]

When he got McCook's testy note the next morning, Rosecrans backed down. He bade McCook come along through the valley and asked only that he detach two brigades to guard Dougherty's Gap. McCook sent William Lytle with two brigades to watch the gap and see the corps baggage trains over the mountain, and for the next thirty-six hours pushed his corps forward harder than most had ever marched before. Private Levi Wagner of the First Ohio estimated his regiment covered twenty-six miles "over very rough ground" on 16 September alone. Nonetheless, it was well after dark before the first soldiers of the Twentieth Corps filed wearily down the mountain from Stevens's Gap into the cove.[45]

Meanwhile, Bragg had begun slowly to shed his lethargy. Perhaps the prospect of imminent reinforcements was overcoming his disappointment and fatigue. Evander McNair's brigade already had arrived at Ringgold, where it was placed in a provisional division under Bushrod Johnson. John Gregg's brigade was expected from Mississippi momentarily, and the first troops from Virginia were just two days out. All told, Bragg could count on 7,600 more infantry for an eventual total of approximately 68,000; hardly the impressive concentration of forces tradition has held it to be, but enough to tip the numerical balance slightly in Bragg's favor. Like most field commanders, Bragg overestimated the strength of his enemy. He was convinced that Rosecrans had some 70,000 infantry, when in fact he had present for duty only 63,816 soldiers of all arms. And on 14 September Bragg was given "very reliable" intelligence that 20,000 men from Grant's army had already passed Stevenson, Alabama, en route to the Army of the Cumberland. Add to this Burnside's 25,000 troops idling in East Tennessee, and what is amazing is not that Bragg let three days pass without acting but that he chose to act at all.[46]

On the morning of 15 September, Bragg called his corps commanders together and announced his intention to resume the offensive. He contemplated a rapid march north and then west to interpose the Army of Tennessee between Chattanooga and the Federals. Thus outflanked, Rosecrans would be forced either to fight to regain the city or to fall back across the Tennessee to preserve his line of supply. All present apparently agreed with the general outline, and Polk contributed the specifics. Polk suggested a strong demonstration be made against Crittenden at Lee and Gordon's Mill. While Rosecrans's attention was fixed there, the rest of the army should move quickly by the right flank as far as Reed's Bridge and the nearby fords over Chickamauga Creek. Once across, they should seize Rossville (Polk may not have known of Granger's presence there), then swing south and close the valley from the creek to Missionary Ridge. Polk suggested that the provisional division of Bushrod Johnson, along with whatever troops from Virginia might have arrived at the Ringgold station, move west to support the crossing. Bragg agreed with everything except the point of crossing; he preferred to cross closer to the mill. The council adjourned, and the generals returned to their commands to await marching orders.[47]

None came. Bragg hesitated, perhaps to allow time for the troops from Virginia to arrive but more probably because he was emotionally unprepared to enter battle at the head of an army of recalcitrant subordinates. The orders that finally emerged on the evening of 16 September were oddly tentative and contained no instructions for a crossing of Chickamauga Creek. They read in part:

VII. Buckner's corps and Walker's reserves will move at daylight tomorrow and take position from Pea Vine Church, north along Pea Vine Creek.

VIII. Polk's corps will move at 8 A.M. tomorrow and take post on Buckner's left, and occupy the ground to near Glass's Mill, so as to command that crossing.

IX. Forrest's cavalry will cover the front and flank of both these movements.

X. Wheeler's cavalry, leaving a small force to observe the road south, will pass through Dug to Catlett's Gap, press the enemy, secure some prisoners if possible, and join our flank near Glass's Mill.

XI. Reed's Bridge, Byram's Ford, Alexander's Bridge, and the fords next above, will be seized and held by our cavalry.[48]

Bragg's scheme of maneuver would put Buckner and Walker well north of the Union left and anywhere from one to three miles east of Chickamauga Creek.

To cut Rosecrans off from Chattanooga, Bragg would have to cross Chickamauga Creek rapidly enough to close at least one of the two roads between the creek and Missionary Ridge that led from McLemore's Cove to the city. The road nearest the creek was known locally as the La Fayette road. It crossed the creek at Lee and Gordon's Mill and ran north to the Rossville Gap, a distance of nearly eight miles. From there, it ran west through the gap, passing Rossville and continuing on for another four miles before entering Chattanooga. Relatively well maintained, the La Fayette road was the natural route of withdrawal for Crittenden's corps. Crossing the creek about three miles upstream at Owens's Ford was the Dry Valley road, more an expanded trail than a true wagon road. Five miles from the ford, the Dry Valley road bumped up against Missionary Ridge, then followed the trace of the ridge for two miles before passing through it at McFarland's Gap. From there, the Dry Valley road ran north to Rossville, where it joined the La Fayette road. Either road would serve the needs of Thomas's corps in a withdrawal. McCook's corps at Bailey's Cross Roads could escape along a third road that followed the trace of Chattanooga Creek, west of Missionary Ridge.

The country itself was only four decades removed from a state of nature. It had been home and hunting ground to a fierce band of Cherokee Indians, runaway slaves, fugitive Tories, and dispossessed Creeks, whose primary pastimes were ambushing river traffic along the Tennessee and murdering pioneers foolish enough to erect cabins in the isolated forests. To distinguish them from more pacifistic elements of the Cherokees, frightened settlers labeled these troublemakers "Chickamaugas," a name taken from the creek alongside which they built their villages. It was a fitting name for a band of river pirates and bandits: "Chickamauga" loosely translated from the Cherokee meant "River of Death."

In 1838, the Chickamaugas and their Cherokee brothers were driven westward to Oklahoma by President Andrew Jackson over the infamous "trail of tears," and settlers at last entered the region confident of keeping both their land and their lives. The succeeding thirty years had witnessed few improvements to the countryside, however. Like most early pioneers, those who scratched out a homestead in the cedar glades and pine forests of northern Georgia did only what was needed to keep alive. Most farmhouses were one- or two-room cabins indifferently built of logs or clapboard; more prosperous farmers tried to add a small barn and stable. Fields were laid out haphazardly and were poorly cleared. Tree stumps checkered most farmland. Corn was planted carelessly, and cattle and hogs were generally turned loose to fend for themselves in the nearby forest. Split-rail fences sometimes marked the boundaries of a farm, other parcels of land merely melted into the surrounding timber.

The terrain was hardly conducive to agriculture. Missionary Ridge threw off a series of spurs in the direction of Chickamauga Creek, the highest of which ended at the Snodgrass farm, one-half mile west of the La Fayette road. In fact, the road itself neatly separated the rolling country that extended west to the base of Missionary Ridge from the low-lying, more thickly forested land nearer the creek.

Where cattle grazed and hogs rooted, visibility in the forest east of the La Fayette road might exceed one hundred yards; in many places, however, briar-laced underbrush cut it to almost nothing. As George Thomas said in his report, the "surface . . . is covered with original forest timber, interspersed with undergrowth, in many places so dense it is difficult to see fifty paces ahead." Here and there, the forest gave way to cedar glades, the dry and alkaline soil of which killed all but the most hearty plants. Visibility and footing were better in the glades.

Only two structures of consequence graced the area. One was the John Ross house, around which a tiny village had grown up. Though only one-eighth Cherokee, Ross had been raised as an Indian by his father, the trader Daniel Ross around whose river trading post the city of Chattanooga grew, and his mother, Mollie McDonald Ross. The Cherokees not only accepted him but for forty years recognized John Ross as the head of their nation. A man torn between two cultures, young John Ross kept the white man's post office in his house and a cave to accommodate secret meetings of Cherokee chiefs beneath it. Ross stayed clear of the hated Chickamaugas, so that he was able to sell his property in 1826 and peaceably move to Rome, Georgia. He remained a Cherokee at heart, and when his people were driven west twelve years later, Ross went with them.[49]

The other building of note was the beautiful but oddly out of place Gordon-Lee mansion, a bit of Southern grace amidst backwoods crudity. When the Cherokees ceded their land to the government in 1836, James Gordon and his two brothers hurried west from coastal Georgia to buy up all they could. Gordon purchased 2,500 acres of cheap "lottery tracts" and set up a milling operation and sawmill on Chickamauga Creek with one James Lee. Lee and Gordon's Mill prospered, and in 1840 Gordon began work on what was to be a twelve-room, two-story red-brick mansion. The completed home boasted four Doric columns of wood and was flanked by a brick smokehouse and six slave cabins in a region where few owned a single black man. Gordon chose the site well. Directly opposite the house bubbled up Crawfish Springs, the best source of fresh water for miles around. Soldiers who passed it came away impressed. "Crawfish Springs is one of the best I ever saw," marveled Sergeant John Kane of the Seventy-fifth Indiana. "It is a river, clear as crystal and cold as ice. An army might get water at this spring." Colonel Sanderson agreed: "The spring here is a magnificent one, affording an abundant supply, for man and beast of the entire army, of cool, soft, delicious water. It runs out of a hill and forms a very large creek."[50]

Although its waters were neither clear nor swift nor especially deep — certainly no more than ten feet deep during rainstorms — Chickamauga Creek was an effective barrier to east-west movement. Its banks were steep and rocky or low and swampy. Even in the drought-ridden summer of 1863, all wagons, cavalry, and large bodies of infantry would have to cross over one of the five bridges or nine fords that offered access to the prospective field of battle.

No Confederates would be crossing for the time being, nor even preparing to cross. In the early morning hours of 17 September, Bragg backed away from even the limited movement dictated in his orders of the evening before. At 3:00 A.M. he issued instructions countermanding them. "The first 'As you were' went forth," lamented Brent. "What uncertainty and vacillation."

By mid-afternoon on the seventeenth, Bragg had again changed his mind. He retreated even further from his stated intention of sweeping across Chickamauga Creek and blocking the way to Chattanooga. Buckner was now ordered to move north no farther than Pea Vine Church, while Bushrod Johnson and Forrest at Ringgold were to march by way of Leet's Tan Yard toward La Fayette, rather than to the creek, as had been the understanding at the council of war on 15 September. Polk would continue to hold the center between Rock Spring Church and Glass's Mill, while Hill on the left kept an eye on the gaps, with orders to withdraw from Pigeon Mountain at dawn on 18 September and move northward behind Polk toward Lee and Gordon's Mill. New marching orders went out, confused corps commanders put their men on the road, and at 2:00 P.M. Bragg and his staff started for Leet's Tan Yard to set up headquarters.[51]

No one had ever accused Major General Gordon Granger of vacillating over anything. To the contrary, the forty-year-old Regular Army officer had an opinion about everything and never hesitated to express it. On the field of battle, Granger was a keen, alert observer who made quick and generally correct decisions. He had more than average ability and should have risen higher, but he was his own worst enemy. Simply put, Granger did not know when to keep his mouth shut. He "would as quickly criticize General Grant as a private soldier," recalled a former staff officer. William Shanks, the scurrilous journalist, penned one of his few truly insightful character sketches when he wrote: "Granger was a man equally courageous morally as physically, and pursued an object, or criticized a subject or person without the slightest regard to others' opinions. He never shirked a responsibility — in fact, would rather act without authority than not, as giving zest to the undertaking. Granger was almost always gruff, not only in his criticisms, but in his language, and never disliked a man without showing it."[52]

To date, Granger had succeeded in alienating Grant, Sherman, and apparently even Thomas. When Thomas heard that Rosecrans intended to retain Granger as commander of the Reserve Corps for the Chickamauga campaign, he went at once to army headquarters to learn if the rumor was true. "Yes," Rosecrans smiled. "I know what you think — you think he is a blatherskite and in one sense he is so, but you will find him a great man in battle because the preponderance of his observing faculties which ordinarily make him full of suggestions . . . serve him in battle while the danger leads him to settle down to what is necessary."[53]

Granger had two other handicaps. He had a great love of artillery and could not resist the temptation to dismount in the heat of battle to sight a cannon, and his men despised him.

On 14 September their antipathy for Granger's cruel and unyielding brand of discipline erupted with near-tragic consequences. In its rapid march from the Tennessee River, the infantry of Steedman's division had far outpaced its wagon train, so that the men went into camp at Rossville with no rations and no immediate prospect of drawing any. Granger had issued strict orders against foraging. Under the circumstances, even his officers thought the orders unreasonable, and they quietly ignored them. "Get to the woods boys and keep out of sight," Colonel Dan McCook told his men as watched them go off in search of food. Every troop commander in the division apparently turned a blind eye to the foraging, leading the men to assume it was open season on the Georgia countryside.

Drowsing in front of his tent in the afternoon heat, Granger happened to notice two privates from the One Hundred Twenty-fifth Illinois stroll by with an armload of fresh meat. Granger cornered them. He reminded the soldiers of his orders against foraging and ordered them to drop the meat. As punishment, he told them to pick up rails and march around a nearby tree. Granger had just sat down again when an entire squad walked by loaded down with everything from hams to yams. Granger gave them the same lecture, this time more heated, then stormed into the tent of his adjutant and ordered him to send out a mounted patrol to arrest every forager it could find. Offenders were brought in by the score. Granger exploded. He threatened to make an example of every man who had disobeyed his orders, and soon soldiers from every regiment in the division were hanging by their thumbs from trees around his tent.

The word spread like wildfire. Mutiny was in the air. The officers of the Ninety-sixth Illinois and Fifty-second Ohio regiments marched to Granger's headquarters and demanded the release of their men. Behind them the crowd of angry soldiers grew. Granger called on a nearby section of artillery to open fire with blank cartridges and, if that failed to disperse them, to mow the group down with canister. The artillerymen refused and walked off. The crowd grew louder and nearer and Granger matched them oath for oath. Fortunately General Steedman and Colonel McCook stepped forward with a promise to mediate. The prisoners were untied and released. The crowd slowly dispersed, and Granger "slunk away into his tent, damning everybody." Granger's soldiers never forgave him. "From that day our dislike for Granger was intense; he had proved himself a tyrant, and a man of ungovernable passion, and we fairly hated him," recalled a young lieutenant.[54]

While tempers simmered in the Reserve Corps, Rosecrans was putting the final touches on his line of battle in McLemore's Cove. On the morning of 16 September, he set up headquarters at the Gordon-Lee mansion. From its stately parlor that evening came the first order intimating that battle was imminent. To all corps commanders, Garfield wrote: "The general commanding directs you to see that your men have three days' rations in their haversacks, and as near twenty rounds of ammunition in the pocket of each man, in addition to having his cartridge box full. There are some indications that the enemy is massing for an attack on our left."[55]

Thursday, 17 September, dawned clear and warm. A strong breeze offered the only hope of relief from yet another day of blistering heat. With each passing hour the signs of impending battle grew clearer, although some still chose to ignore them. Robert Minty, as fine a cavalry officer as the Army of the Cumberland produced, had his brigade posted on the western slope of Pea Vine Ridge covering the approach to Reed's Bridge, with pickets covering every road in the Pea Vine Valley. The day before, strong Rebel scouting parties had driven in his patrols near Leet's Tan Yard and on the Ringgold road. Minty was certain that a concentration of Confederate infantry against the Federal left flank was imminent. He galloped to the headquarters of the Twenty-first Corps to pass on his concerns, only to have Crittenden dismiss them out of hand.

One by one on the morning of the seventeenth, Minty's patrols returned with the same report: the Rebel army was preparing to mass northeast of the Union left flank. Minty went again to Crittenden's headquarters and was told the Kentuckian had gone on to the Gordon-Lee house. Minty followed and gave his report in the presence of the commanding general, including information from Rebel stragglers that Longstreet had arrived.

At the mention of Longstreet, Crittenden laughed. "Longstreet is in Virginia."

"Pardon me, General Crittenden, Longstreet, with a considerable force from the Army of Northern Virginia, is now at and near Ringgold," Minty remonstrated.

Noticing that Rosecrans seemed inclined to credit the report, Crittenden sprang up and exclaimed: "General Rosecrans, I will guarantee, with my corps, to whip every rebel within twenty miles of us."

Repelled by Crittenden's histrionics, Minty left headquarters "with a heavy heart."[56]

Minty was half right. Hood's famous Texas Brigade, now under the command of Brigadier General Jerome Robertson, did chug into Catoosa Station near Ringgold early in the afternoon. Brigadier General Henry Benning was a few hours behind with his brigade of Georgians, and John Gregg's brigade showed up from Mississippi about the same time. Division commander John Bell Hood was still a day away, however, and Longstreet, traveling with his second division under the temporary command of Brigadier General Joseph Kershaw, was at least forty-eight hours out.

The Texans were in fine spirits and full of fight. Their trip had been "one grand ovation." The enthusiasm of the populace more than made up for the rickety railroads. At every station, "old men slapped their hands in praise, boys threw up their hats in joy, while the ladies fanned the breeze with their flags and handkerchiefs. At the towns which we were forced to stop for a short time great tables were stretched, filled with the bounties of the land, while the fairest and the best women on earth stood by and ministered to every wish and want," one veteran recalled wistfully. The soldiers had never had it so good. "Rags and dirt seemed to be a recommendation where gilt and brass failed to excite attention," wrote John West of the Fourth Texas. As civilian passenger trains passed slowly in the opposite direction, the frolicking Texans made a game of snatching hats off unwary well-wishers, so now Robertson's men marched into Ringgold sporting everything from top hats to ladies' bonnets.[57]

Every report that reached Federal headquarters during the afternoon of 17 September suggested that the Rebels were up to something. Beyond that,

Rosecrans and his staff could make little sense of them. Signal stations on Lookout Mountain spotted vast columns of dust swirling north along the State road but could offer no suggestion as to the destination of the marching columns. They mistook the dust stirred by Wheeler's cavalry as it probed through Dug and Catlett's gaps for that raised by a major force of infantry, leading Rosecrans momentarily to fear a thrust against McCook in the cove. Tom Wood, whose division lay directly behind Lee and Gordon's Mill, passed the afternoon watching dust clouds draw near from the south.[58]

By late afternoon, Rosecrans had concluded correctly that a large Confederate force was gathering in the neighborhood of Rock Spring and Pea Vine churches. In response, he shifted his entire line of battle to the northeast in order to better cover the La Fayette road. Crittenden, who had the divisions of Van Cleve and Wood deployed at Lee and Gordon's Mill, moved Palmer north from Gowan's (Gower's) Ford to Glass's Mill to make room for the Fourteenth Corps. Thomas in turn edged his entire command by the left flank along Chickamauga Creek. Negley came into line with his right at Bird's Mill and his left touching Palmer. Baird extended the line to Gowan's Ford, and Brannan rounded it out as far south as Pond Spring. Reynolds lay in reserve with Turchin's brigade thrown forward to cover Catlett's Gap. McCook originally had been ordered to concentrate between Gowan's Ford and Pond Spring, but when it became evident that Thomas could hold the line himself, the Ohioan was halted at the base of Missionary Ridge. His corps covered the roads to Dug and Catlett's gaps. Colonel Edward McCook's cavalry division, which had relieved Lytle's brigade at Dougherty's Gap on 16 September, trotted down into the cove and made camp southwest of his cousin's corps. General Stanley at last relented and turned over the cavalry to Robert Mitchell. He started home for Ohio on 17 September, hobbled by fever and dysentery. It would take a month of nursing by his wife and a strict milk diet before he would be able to rejoin the army.[59]

Evidence of a threat north of the army's left was minimal beyond that brought in by Minty's patrols, and so Rosecrans was reluctant to move farther in that direction. However, Minty's frequent warnings convinced him at least to order Granger to reconnoiter the Ringgold road. The results were inconclusive but disturbing.

In the early morning twilight of 17 September, Steedman broke camp with six regiments and a battery of artillery and started along the road. Two miles west of Ringgold, his skirmishers ran into pickets from the Fifth Tennessee Cavalry of Scott's brigade. The Tennesseans quickly gave way. The Federals splashed across East Chickamauga Creek and chased them to within one mile of Ringgold. There Steedman halted his column and opened fire with Battery M, First Illinois Artillery, from a high hill overlooking the town. The streets emptied of Rebels, and Steedman was about to order an advance, when a Confederate battery unlimbered to his front and returned the fire. It belonged to Bushrod Johnson's Tennessee brigade, now commanded by Colonel John Fulton. The Tennesseans deployed across the road to challenge Steedman, while Johnson hurried up Gregg's brigade, just arrived from Mississippi, to support them. At the same time, Robertson's Texas brigade hastened forward from Catoosa Station toward Steedman's right flank. Steedman descried the billowing clouds of dust that betrayed their movement. Concluding "that large bodies of troops were moving," Steedman fell back six miles and bivouacked for the night just west of Pea Vine Creek. Scott's cavalry pursued the Federals and, for good measure, threw six rounds of shell into their camp at midnight.[60]

Rosecrans reacted ably to this evidence of a Confederate buildup at Ringgold. At dusk, he borrowed Wilder's brigade from Thomas, who had just gotten it back after days of pleading, and placed it at Alexander's Bridge. To Wilder, Rosecrans gave firm orders to use his Spencers to prevent any attempted crossing of the bridge or the four fords between it and Lee and Gordon's Mill. Minty, who had begun to feel alone and forgotten out on Pea Vine Ridge, was delighted to receive "the cheering information that Colonel Wilder, with his splendid brigade of mounted infantry, was at Alexander's Bridge."[61]

Six miles away at Leet's Tan Yard, Bragg worked deep into the night perfecting new plans for 18 September. His own intelligence reports correctly placed the left of the Union army at Lee and Gordon's Mill, its front along the creek into McLemore's Cove. With the bulk of his army now opposite Rosecrans's left, Bragg at last was ready to commit himself to a crossing of Chickamauga Creek north of the Federals. But he still came up one step short. The directive that emerged shortly after midnight simply ordered Walker to cross at either Alexander's Bridge or Lambert's Ford at 6:30 A.M., while Buckner waded the creek at Thedford's Ford on his left and Polk distracted Crittenden at the mill. It said nothing about what Walker and Buckner were to do once across. And there were other problems. The crossing sites were far too close to Crittenden, the two corps selected for the task were the weakest in the army, and no role was assigned Bushrod Johnson's division or the troops from Virginia then at Ringgold.[62]

During the night the temperature plummeted to near freezing. Clouds formed. A hard wind blew through the deep forest. Soldiers who had perspired through two weeks of blazing heat now fumbled in the dark for wool blankets to cover themselves.[63]

Few slept. Too much had happened during the past twenty-four hours. "All day a feverish, mysterious, nervous foreboding had seemed to pervade the camp; everyone was conscious of it and apprehensive that everything was not in order as it should be," remembered Lieutenant Colonel Judson

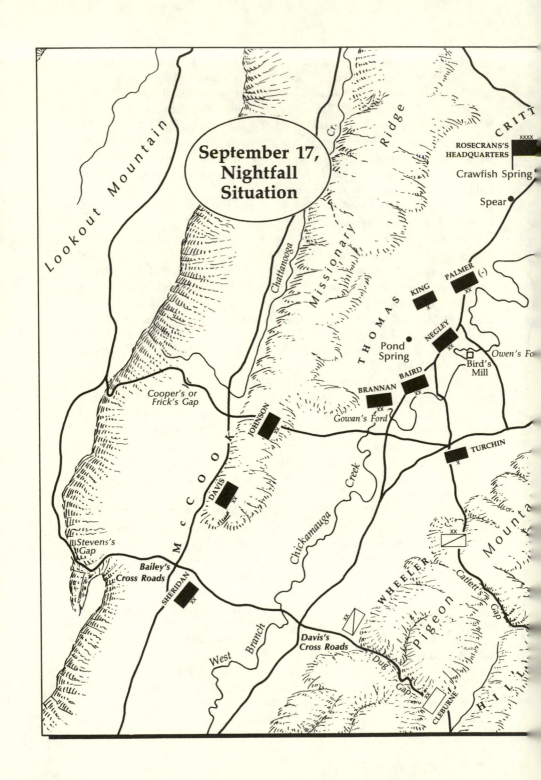

September 17,
Nightfall
Situation

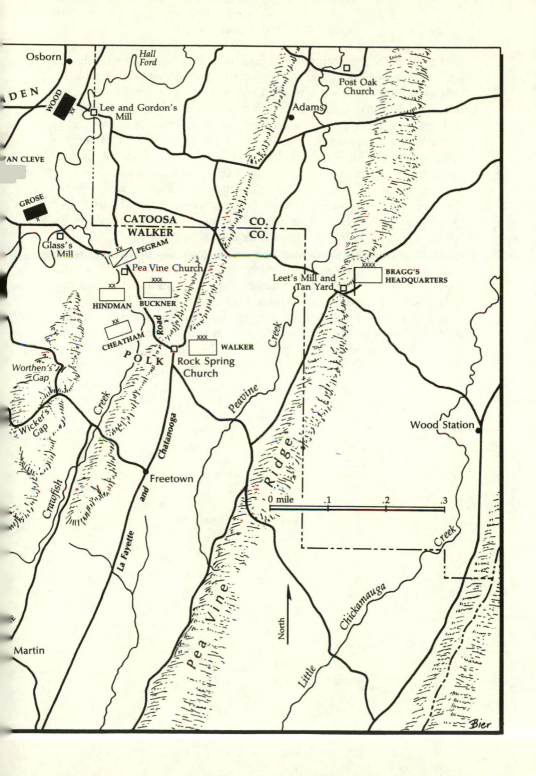

Osborn

Hall
Ford

DEN

WOOD
xx

Lee and Gordon's
Mill

Post Oak
Church

Adams

AN CLEVE

GROSE
x

Glass's
Mill

PEGRAM
xx

CATOOSA
WALKER

CO.
CO.

Pea Vine Church

Leet's Mill and
Tan Yard

BRAGG'S
HEADQUARTERS
xxxx

HINDMAN
xx

BUCKNER
xxx

Creek

CHEATHAM
xx

Road

WALKER
xxx

P O L K

Rock Spring
Church

Worthen's
Gap

Creek

Peavine

Wood Station

Wicker's
Gap

Crawfish

Chatanooga

Freetown

0 mile   .1   .2   .3

La Fayette

and

Peavine

Ridge

Martin

North

Little

Chickamauga

Creek

Bier

Bishop of the Second Minnesota. Sergeant Louis Simmons of the Eighty-fourth Illinois agreed: "Upon high points or mountain tops the signal lamps were swinging, and it was speedily known by every subaltern and private in the whole army that a momentous conflict was about to take place." In their growing dread, the men accepted every rumor, no matter how absurd. In the Federal camps it was whispered that the enemy had been reinforced by Longstreet and Early, and that Rosecrans was "hourly expecting aid from Burnside, and even that Sherman and McPherson with divisions or corps were coming with all possible speed."[64] In the Confederate camps, where the disappointment had been greater, the rumors were more fantastic. England had recognized the Confederacy, it was said, and a French division had marched into Texas to drive out the Yankees.[65]

By the flickering light of the campfire Sergeant Simmons watched the faces of the men around him. "Many while resting would pencil a few hasty lines to the loved ones at home, and many would take from their knapsacks and cartridge boxes their last letters received from dear and cherished sweethearts, wives and mothers, read them slowly over, and then tear them into a hundred pieces, or use them to light the inevitable pipe — a soldier's indispensable solace."[66]

CHAPTER SIX

SOUNDS OF ILL OMEN

SOME MEN are born losers; others become losers through the choices they make. Brigadier General Bushrod Rust Johnson was both. Born in 1817 on a small farm near Morristown, Ohio, to Quaker parents of deep and abiding faith, Johnson was nurtured in the quiet, peace-loving traditions of the Society of Friends. He was taught that war and slavery were abhorrent. His elder brother grew to become a vocal abolitionist; young Bushrod chose to attend West Point. He stuck it out over the strong and continued objections of his family and graduated with William T. Sherman and George Thomas in the class of 1840. Duty took him far from his Quaker roots to a variety of posts in Florida, and the South "cast a magic spell" over the young lieutenant that was to prove lifelong.

His troubles began during the war with Mexico. As an infantry company commander, Johnson fought in four battles without earning a single brevet. Johnson was made acting commissary officer of Winfield Scott's invading army just before the fleet landed at Vera Cruz, effectively removing him from the front line. The war went on without him, and peace found Johnson still a lieutenant and nearly dead of yellow fever. He recovered, but illness and resentment had chinked his moral armor. When local Mexican merchants offered him sums far in excess of his meager salary to procure and transport merchandise for them from New Orleans disguised as government shipments, Johnson succumbed. He then made the fatal mistake of offering his superior officer a cut in the profits from a shipment, which, he wrote, "you will understand would have to be shipped Commissary property." That clinched it. He was court-martialed and found guilty of profiteering. Only Johnson's poignant and personal appeal to President Polk saved him from being cashiered, and he was allowed to resign.

Instead of returning home to seek solace in the Society of Friends, Johnson accepted an instructorship at the Western Military Institute in Georgetown,

Kentucky. He stayed in the South, rising to chairmanship of the Literary Department of the University of Nashville in the fall of 1855. So completely had Johnson come to identify with the South that he offered his services to the Confederacy in the spring of 1861. Ill fortune would plague Johnson in the final months of the war, until he suffered the ultimate indignity of being relieved from command by Robert E. Lee just days before Appomattox. But he had done well to date, and now was about to go into battle at the head of a division for the first time. True to his luck, however, Johnson was given an improvised command made up of four brigades that had never even marched together before: his own Tennessee brigade, commanded by Fulton, the two brigades from Mississippi under Gregg and McNair, and, for the moment, Robertson's Texas brigade.[1]

Johnson had his men on the road from Catoosa Station at 5:00 A.M., just as morning twilight opened the curtain on a cool and cloudy Friday. Lacking more recent instructions, he moved toward Leet's Tan Yard in accordance with the marching orders of 16 September. The head of his column was three miles out of the station when Colonel Brent galloped up and handed Johnson new orders. He was to retrace his steps to Ringgold and there pick up the road to Reed's Bridge, where his division was to force a lodgment on the west bank of Chickamauga Creek. General Forrest would cover his front and right flank on the march. Forrest, who had no idea these orders were coming, was back at Ringgold.

Despite Forrest's absence, Johnson complied, and he soon had his infantry marching toward Reed's Bridge, which lay eight miles to the west. Minutes later, Johnson received supplementary orders that must have both startled and flattered him. He was now to turn south after crossing Reed's Bridge and sweep along the creek toward Lee and Gordon's Mill, picking up Walker and Buckner as he went along. To the luckless Ohioan had been given the task of initiating the attack on the Federal left.[2]

This was to be the final revision of Bragg's plan of battle. In the early morning hours of 18 September, it had dawned on him that his midnight orders to Walker and Buckner had the two corps crossing the creek too close to Crittenden's left. Consequently, Bragg added a crossing point at Reed's Bridge, as Polk had suggested three days earlier, and he finally instructed his generals what to do once they were across. The amended orders read in part:

1. Johnson's column (Hood's), on crossing at or near Reed's Bridge, will turn to the left by the most practicable route and sweep up the Chickamauga, toward Lee and Gordon's Mills.
2. Walker, crossing at Alexander's Bridge, will unite in this move and push vigorously on the enemy's flank and rear in the same direction.
3. Buckner, crossing at Thedford's Ford, will join in the movement to the

left, and press the enemy up the stream from Polk's front at Lee and Gordon's Mills.

4. Polk will press his forces to the front of Lee and Gordon's Mills, and if met by too much resistance to cross will bear to the right and cross at Dalton's Ford, or at Thedford's, as may be necessary, and join in the attack wherever the enemy may be.

5. Hill will cover our left flank from an advance of the enemy from the cove, and by pressing the cavalry in his front ascertain if the enemy is re-enforcing at Lee and Gordon's Mills, in which event he will attack them in flank.

6. Wheeler's cavalry will hold the gaps in Pigeon Mountain and cover our rear and left and bring up stragglers.[3]

Although certainly the best plan Bragg had yet devised, its hasty conception was evident. Presumably, Bragg hoped for an early crossing, yet he set no hour for the movement to begin. More problematical, Walker and Buckner were expected to use the same road to reach their respective crossing sites. The inevitable entanglement occurred, and it was early afternoon before the two corps neared the creek.[4]

Robert Minty felt trouble coming. All through the night of the seventeenth he had sent Crittenden dispatch after dispatch warning him that train whistles were blowing from the direction of Ringgold. From his outpost atop Pigeon Ridge, he could plainly hear the rumble of trains into Catoosa Station. All night long it went on. Minty tried to warn Crittenden, but the Kentuckian had grown tired of the annoying cavalryman. "The Rebel army is retreating, and are trying to get away some of their abandoned stores; they have nothing but dismounted cavalry in your front," snapped Crittenden. It was his way of telling Minty to let him get some rest.[5]

Minty believed in his scouts and in his intuition. He had his men out of their bedrolls and in the saddle long before daybreak. At 6:00 A.M. Minty sent Captain Heber Thompson with a detail of one hundred troopers from the Seventh Pennsylvania Cavalry down the road toward Ringgold to look for the enemy he sensed was close by.

The Pennsylvanians found the Rebels nearer than expected. Pulling rein at Peeler's Mill just east of Pea Vine Creek, Thompson and his men watched a long column of Butternut emerge silently out of the morning fog. The Yankees galloped back over the bridge and took cover a hundred yards west of the creek, apparently unnoticed.[6]

Johnson was moving at a crawl. Residents had warned him that Yankees were just over Pea Vine Ridge, and without a cavalry screen he hesitated to press on. Halting at the mill, Johnson waited while Lieutenant Colonel Watt Floyd of the Seventeenth Tennessee and his adjutant rode forward with their skirmishers to reconnoiter over the bridge. Tucked safely behind a cabin near the creek, Private Samuel Walters of Company F, Seventh Pennsylvania Cavalry, had a clear view of the Rebel officers. He raised his Smith carbine, took aim, and fired the first shot of the Battle of Chickamauga.

Walters missed. Floyd and his adjutant had no desire to give the trooper a second chance. They galloped back to report the far bank bristling with Federal pickets. Johnson overreacted, ordering his entire column off the road and into line of battle to await Forrest's arrival. An hour passed, perhaps more. When Forrest finally rode up, he had at his side only one hundred men from his personal escort, far too few to provide an effective screen. Pegram and Davidson were still miles in the rear. Johnson sent Floyd forward again, this time reinforced with skirmishers from the other regiments of Fulton's brigade, Forrest's little band, and Everett's Georgia battery of artillery.[7]

Thompson sent a courier back to Minty for help and tried valiantly to hold on. His men peppered the Tennesseans as they neared the creek, without hitting anyone. The Rebels returned the fire and drew first blood at Chickamauga, killing Private John Ward. Everett's guns boomed, and four more Yankees fell dead. That was enough for the Pennsylvanians. Thompson and his men slipped out of the bushes and galloped back toward Pea Vine Ridge, taking cover behind the Fourth Michigan Cavalry, a battalion of the Fourth United States Cavalry, and a section of the Chicago Board of Trade Battery, all sent forward down the east slope of the ridge by Minty to buy time.[8]

Floyd's reinforced skirmish line, with Forrest's dismounted escort on its right, inched its way tentatively across Pea Vine Creek, while behind it Johnson's half-mile-long line of battle waited. Two guns of the Chicago Board of Trade Battery barked their greeting and again the Confederates stumbled. Johnson ordered up his artillery reserve, and another hour slipped by.

From atop Pea Vine Ridge, Minty and his staff peered through field glasses at the long line of Confederates. If Minty felt vindicated, he had no time to gloat. Counting fifteen stands of regimental colors flapping in the breeze, he feared the Confederates might grow tired of his cavalry and divert toward Dyer's bridge and ford, both of which lay unprotected one mile to the north. Shortly before 11:00 A.M., Minty sent a courier to Wilder to request reinforcements to cover the unguarded crossing points. Then he wrote Crittenden and Granger to report the appearance of the enemy.[9]

While his second line slowly fell back up over the ridge, Minty worked feverishly to improvise a third line. He formed the Fourth Michigan Cavalry, two battalions of the Fourth United States Cavalry, and the remaining companies of the Seventh Pennsylvania Cavalry in a cornfield astride the road, just four hundred yards east of Reed's Bridge. With the third battalion of regulars and two sections of the Board of Trade Battery he galloped back another two hundred and fifty yards to the Reed house, hiding the cannon and troopers in an orchard behind the cabin. Then he ordered his inspector general, Captain Joseph Vale, to take his trains to safety and tell Crittenden or Wood what was happening. At that moment, Wilder answered his appeal. Colonel Abram Miller arrived with the One Hundred Twenty-third Illinois, seven companies of his own Seventy-second Indiana, and a section of Lilly's battery, a most welcome distraction. Minty paused to order them northward to Dyer's bridge and ford. Less welcome was the presence of Mrs. Reed and her three small children. Minty begged and pleaded, but she flatly refused to leave her house. Giving up, Minty told her to stay indoors and rode back to his brigade.[10]

As reports came in from his skirmishers, now atop Pea Vine Ridge, Johnson finally realized that for nearly four hours he had allowed 973 cavalrymen to dictate the progress of his four brigades. But knowing this did not end his troubles. The gap in the ridge cut by the Reed's Bridge road could accommodate only a movement in column, which would canalize Johnson's forces and prevent them from reacting to a counterattack. Minty knew this too, and just as the first of Fulton's Tennesseans ran through he sent the Seventh Pennsylvania and Fourth Michigan galloping toward them with sabers drawn. The Tennesseans retreated, and Johnson's entire skirmish line spilled back off the slope.

Growing frustrated, Johnson ordered a general advance in line of battle. More time was lost while the men clawed their way up the ridge. Once again Minty's troopers halted those unfortunate few who poked through the gap, but Gregg's brigade came over the ridge and eventually outflanked his right.

Now it was Minty who was in trouble, and he had to act fast. "My only means of crossing the creek was Reed's Bridge, a narrow, frail structure, which was planked with loose boards and fence rails, and a bad ford about three hundred yards farther up," he recalled. By the time Minty's first squadron trotted across, the head of the rebel column was only five hundred yards away, "carrying their arms at right shoulder shift, and moving at the double quick as steadily as if at drill." Mrs. Reed stood on her porch and jeered the troopers as they rode past her house. "You Yanks are running! Our army is coming! Our friends will not hurt me!" Just then Bledsoe's Missouri battery swept the house with canister, throwing her mangled body against the door.

As the Rebels swept past the cabin, Minty sprang his ambush. The four guns of the Board of Trade Battery hidden in the orchard raked the Rebel flank with canister. The Confederates halted to redeploy, and in the ensuing confusion Minty's troopers galloped across the bridge. Minty unlimbered the Chicago Board of Trade Battery on the west bank to cover the crossing

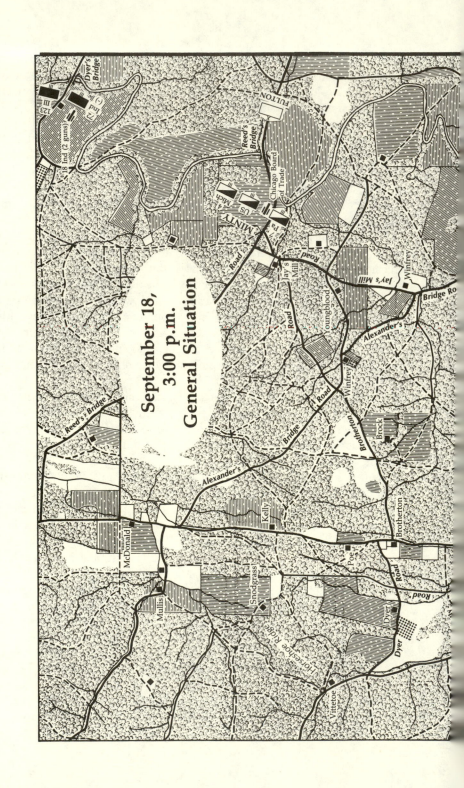

September 18,
3:00 p.m.
General Situation

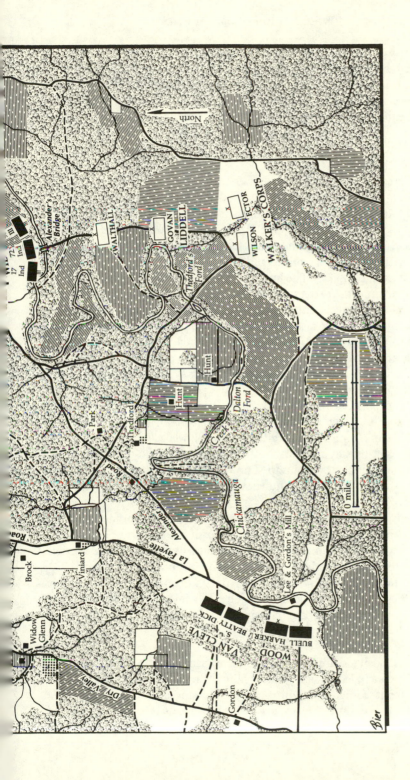

North

17 72 WE
Ind Ind

Alexander's
Bridge

WALTHALL

GOVAN
LIDDELL

Thedford's
Ford

ECTOR

WILSON

WALKER'S CORPS

Hunt

Hunt

Dalton's
Ford

Chickamauga Creek

Thedford

Park

La Fayette & Alexander Road

Lee & Gordon's Mill

Road

Viniard

Brock

Widow
Glenn

Dry Valley

VAN CLEVE

BEATTY DICK

S.

HARKER

BUELL

WOOD

Gordon

0 mile   .5   1

Bier

of the last squadron of the Fourth United States Cavalry. The Regulars dismounted long enough to tear up a few planks and fling them into Chickamauga Creek, then hurried over. Behind them, the Twenty-third Tennessee raised the Rebel yell and made a dash for the bridge. Shots rang out. Five Tennesseans crumpled around the bridge, including the color bearer, but the rest pushed across it. It was 3:00 P.M. when the first Rebel from Johnson's division set foot on the west bank of Chickamauga Creek.[11]

Up the creek at Alexander's Bridge, the morning had begun quietly for Wilder. Perhaps because they held a naturally strong position, his men felt none of the tension that gripped Minty's troopers. The north bank, where the Seventy-second Indiana and One Hundred Twenty-third Illinois rested, was low and marshy. The ground rose just enough to give both regiments a clear field of fire across the bridge and into the fields beyond. The opposite bank was steep and slippery. The bridge itself was a rickety, wooden structure that tottered some thirty feet above the creek on two wooden supports. Wilder's second-line regiments, the Ninety-eighth Illinois and Seventeenth Indiana, were posted back near the Alexander house. Lilly's battery sat atop a high knoll next to the house, about five hundred yards from the creek.[12]

Those not on picket or other duty drifted into the surrounding countryside to forage for breakfast. The more intrepid among Wilder's men crossed the bridge and foraged on the south side of the creek, and a breakfast of eggs, chickens, and potatoes was the reward for their daring. A few wandered back over the bridge at 10:00 A.M. to gather food for dinner. Lieutenant Joseph Barnes of Company A recalled what followed: "In a few moments they came back like flying birds, with Rebel pursuers close at their heels, yelling and shouting at every jump. The Rebels got the advantage of them, cut them off from the bridge, and they had to plunge into the creek and swim across."

The hapless foragers had stumbled across the path of Brigadier General H. B. Davidson's cavalry brigade on its way north to join Forrest near Reed's Bridge. A few volleys from the Seventy-second easily repelled those troopers who came too near the bridge, and Davidson continued on his way.[13]

A few minutes later, Wilder received Minty's urgent appeal for help. He gave it selflessly, and in so doing was left with fewer than one thousand men. He well knew that any crossing of Alexander's Bridge would be attempted by many times that number.

St. John Liddell's opinion of his corps commander had not improved. Walker, he concluded, was a "crackbrained fire-eater, always captious or cavilling about something whimsical and changeable and hardly reliable.... It was my duty to obey his orders, regardless of consequences and they were often destitute of common sense. The only satisfaction that I had was that our official relations would end with the next battle."[14]

Liddell also could take satisfaction in the knowledge that his own column was led by a solid brigade commander, Brigadier General Edward Cary Walthall. Raised in comfort on a plantation in Holly Springs, Mississippi, Walthall had studied law and was admitted to the state bar in 1852. Four years later, at the age of twenty-five, the talented young lawyer was elected district attorney for the Tenth Judicial District of Mississippi, an office he held until resigning to join the Confederate army as a lieutenant in the Fifteenth Mississippi. Walthall proved just as capable as an army officer and in the spring of 1862 was elected colonel of the Twenty-ninth Mississippi. As a brigade commander Walthall quickly became known for his steadiness under fire, and even Bragg had nothing but praise for him.[15]

Word of Davidson's brush with Wilder reached Walker and Liddell a little before 1:00 P.M. With Walthall less than one-half mile from Alexander's Bridge, Liddell ordered the Mississippian to deploy in line of battle with his left on the Alexander's Bridge road and advance, guiding steadily to the left. Walthall formed his five Mississippi regiments with the Thirty-fourth on the left, the Twenty-fourth on the right, and the Thirtieth, Twenty-ninth, and Twenty-seventh in between. Skirmishers dashed ahead two hundred yards, and the brigade stepped forward into a dense thicket.

The line swung to the left, forcing the right regiments to sprint to maintain their alignment with the rest of the brigade. The men of the Twenty-fourth ran nearly a mile in a desperate effort to keep up. The dense forest and tangled undergrowth played havoc with the regimental line, and the men scattered. The Twenty-seventh Mississippi at least kept together, but it too fell far behind the rest of the brigade.

Walthall thus lost two regiments before the first shot was fired. With the remaining three, he entered a cornfield three hundred yards southeast of the creek. His skirmishers were sprinting so hard to keep ahead of the main line that they ran headlong into Wilder's skirmishers. The Federals were equally startled. "We had to return on a trot to keep them from cutting us off, they followed us [so] closely," recalled Private Alan Griest of the Seventy-second Indiana.[16]

On the north bank, Wilder's men swung into action. With Company F of the Seventy-second on the skirmish line and the rest of the regiment gone to reinforce Minty, the thirty-seven men of Company A were left to their own devices. Running out onto the bridge, they tore up the flooring, carried back the heavy planks, and quickly fashioned a small lunette astride the road,[17] behind which they crowded for cover. Wilder ordered the Seventeenth Indiana to move down to the creek on the right side of the road and the Ninety-eighth Illinois to move in closer on the left. On the knoll beside the Alexander house, Lilly's four rifled guns opened fire with long-range canister and shell.

Captain William Fowler's Alabama Battery returned the fire from a hill a half mile away. The first Rebel shell arched toward Lilly's gunners with an "awful, unearthly screeching. It seemed as if it never would strike it was so long coming. . . . We all knew, from the sound of it, that it would strike some place close by," recalled cannoneer Henry Campbell. The shell crashed through the trees. It bounced in front of gun number two, ricocheted off the corner of the Alexander cabin, then fell back among the horrified artillerymen with the fuse sizzling. Private Sidney Speed coolly picked up the shell and heaved it over the cabin, where it burst harmlessly on the other side. An amazed Captain Lilly cited Speed for gallantry in his after-action report.[18]

Meanwhile, down at the creek, the fighting had begun in earnest. The Thirty-fourth and Thirtieth Mississippi lay down in the cornfield and traded volleys with the Seventeenth Indiana, which was almost invisible in the dark wood and thick underbrush of the far bank. It fell to the Twenty-ninth Mississippi to try to force a lodgment on the north bank. The Mississippians repeatedly edged toward the bridge only to be driven back by tiny Company A of the Seventy-second Indiana and its rapid-fire Spencers, 37 men tearing apart a regiment of 368. By the afternoon's end, the Twenty-ninth would count 56 men dead or wounded.[19]

For three hours the struggle went on. Due to a sharp turn in the creek, there was no room to maneuver Govan's brigade effectively on Walthall's left, where help was needed. Rather than search for a ford farther north, Walker and Liddell let Walthall pound away at the bridge.

John Bell Hood could have stayed in Virginia. By any reckoning one of the finest division commanders then in the Confederate service, the thirty-three-year-old Kentuckian had taken a bullet at Gettysburg that rendered his left arm useless. For a month he lay in hospitals in the Shenandoah Valley, thinking less of his command than of Sally Preston, a pretty but fickle young Richmond socialite with whom he was in love. Although only partially recovered, he traveled to Richmond in early August to court her.

The night before his men boarded the trains at Richmond, bound for northern Georgia, they met Hood in tearful reunion. Hood's lieutenants begged him to come along and command the division. The sad-eyed major general consented. The next morning Hood put his horse on the train and saw his men off; he had one matter to settle before he joined them at their first stop in Petersburg.

Hood rode by carriage with Sally Preston and Mary Chesnut, who recorded what followed as assiduously as she did every other happening in wartime Richmond. As he stepped from the carriage to board the train, Hood turned to Sally and proposed. She would say neither yes nor no. Hood persisted. "I am engaged to you," he told her as though issuing a field command. "I am not engaged to you," she countered. There, for the time being, the matter rested.

Certainly Hood's thoughts were with young Sally as he rode the trains south, and his disappointment must have been great. Perhaps, though, Hood should have considered himself lucky that she had not accepted his proposal. Men who loved Sally Preston often ended up dead. Her first fiancé had fallen in a duel, a second died at Gaines's Mill, and yet a third was killed at Fredericksburg. Mary Chesnut's brother admonished men that it was safer to face a Union battery than to fall in love with Sally Preston. If a man was in love with her, then "Look out! You will see his name next, in the list of killed and wounded."[20]

Hood arrived in Ringgold shortly after noon on 18 September in dramatic fashion. As the train entered the station, a courier from headquarters handed him a note from his new commanding general. Angry at Johnson's failure to cross Chickamauga Creek and obviously forgetting that his own frequent changes in plan were partly responsible for the delay, Bragg directed Hood to proceed at once to the front and take command of the right column from the hapless Ohioan. Hood hurried to the freight car that held his horse. With his left arm in a sling, he mounted and held onto the reins with his right hand. Hood applied the spurs, and his horse leapt from the train and galloped out the Reed's Bridge road.[21]

A thousand cheering Texans greeted Hood when he reached the front. He rode past his old brigade and came alongside Johnson a little after 3:00 P.M., just as the Twenty-third Tennessee raised the Rebel yell and charged across Reed's Bridge. Davidson's cavalry brigade had reported in a few minutes earlier and now splashed across Fowler's Ford a half mile south of Minty's right flank. Captain Vale spotted them on his return from Lee and Gordon's Mill. He galloped on to tell Minty that he was flanked; in his excitement, Vale embellished the story and said that Wilder already had withdrawn. Minty concluded that he had done all he could with only 953 cavalrymen. He called in Colonel Miller's detachment, and together the two commands fell back along the Brotherton road, not stopping until they reached Lee and Gordon's Mill.

Vale was still excited when they got there. While Minty redeployed his command near the Thedford house, the young captain reported to General Wood that Minty "had been attacked at 7:00 A.M. and had been fighting for three or four hours." Wood asked him what time he thought it was. "About eleven o'clock," replied Vale. "Look at your watch," said Wood with a smile. It was five in the afternoon. "Time flies when we are so engaged," recalled Lieutenant Colonel Robbins of the Fourth Michigan Cavalry.[22]

Minty rode up a few minutes later.

"Well, Minty, what have you been doing all day?" asked Wood.

"Fighting pretty sharply, General." Vale had told him this much; Wood wanted to know more.

"What have you been fighting?"

"Infantry and artillery," replied Minty.

"Where are they?" Wood asked offhandedly.

"Close to your position."

"What! On this side of the creek?"

"Yes, sir, on this side of the creek."

"Well, come along, and we'll drive them across to their own side," answered Wood, smug in his conviction that Minty had exaggerated the situation. Off he rode with Minty, two staff officers, and a handful of orderlies to throw five Confederate brigades back across Chickamauga Creek.[23]

Minty's withdrawal had left Wilder in a tight spot. A little after 4:00 P.M., a courier brought him word of Minty's withdrawal. Moments later, riders from the Ninety-eighth Illinois reported the approach of Bushrod Johnson's division down the Jay's Mill road in his rear. Before Wilder could react, the left flank companies of the Ninety-eighth came under fire from Forrest's cavalry.

Clearly it was time to leave. Lilly's cannoneers fired their final volley at 4:30 P.M., then limbered up and headed down the road toward Lee and Gordon's Mill. The Seventeenth Indiana covered their withdrawal. The Ninety-eighth fell back fighting, the last Federal unit to clear the field.[24]

Almost. The gallant thirty-seven of Company A, Seventy-second Indiana, were still pouring it on from behind their little lunette. By the time it dawned on the Hoosiers that they were alone, Walthall's men had crept to the edge of the opposite bank. Forrest's troopers closed in on the Indianians from the rear. Their own horses were tied to trees thirty yards away.

Some panicked and shot their horses to prevent their capture, then ran into the woods, where they wandered lost for two days before stumbling into friendly lines. A few made a dash for their mounts. Sergeant Joseph Higginbotham tried it and was shot five times in twenty-five yards. One by one, the Indianians abandoned the lunette until only two were left—a sergeant named Stewart and a private named Bailey. Stewart recalled their predicament: "[Bailey] was a boy seventeen years old, had fought bravely, and being the last to get the word to fall back, would not go but turned and shot a Rebel who fell; another Rebel ran up to aid the fallen man and Bailey shot him also. I, having got a shell fast in my gun, kept urging Baily to fall back. I got the shell out and we both gave the enemy a farewell shot and ran. My horse was killed where he was tied, but Baily's was not, and cutting him loose he mounted and rode away in a shower of bullets." Both made good their escape.[25]

Walthall's Mississippians had nothing to show for four hours of fighting. Alexander's Bridge was in ruins. "It was on fire, but what was more serious, the flooring had been torn up and was floating down stream between high banks on both sides," lamented Captain Joseph Cumming, Walker's chief of staff. Many years later, Cumming delighted in goading Wilder into reliving the defense of Alexander's Bridge: "He was disposed to take all things seriously, and when I would 'start something' by remarking casually: 'General, when you and I opened the battle of Chickamauga, and we whipped you down there at Alexander Bridge. . . .' He replied with heat: 'I whipped you!' 'Why then,' I asked, 'Did you run away and leave the bridge?' 'I didn't run away. I destroyed the bridge and then moved off to whip some more of you at another place.' There was much truth in the old fighter's statement," Cumming admitted.[26]

Walthall's men turned their backs on the burning bridge and their 105 fallen comrades and rejoined their corps in a march north to Lambert's Ford. There the men stripped off their sweat-soaked uniforms and plunged into the icy waters at dusk. It would be morning before the last of Walker's Reserve Corps was across the creek. Buckner, who had seized Thedford's Ford at 2:00 P.M., idled away the eighteenth of September waiting for Walker to appear on the far bank.[27]

Meanwhile, out on the Alexander's Bridge road, Hood and Forrest were pushing their five brigades — all there was of Bragg's grand enveloping force on the west bank — hard in the direction of Lee and Gordon's Mill. The temperature had not risen above sixty-two degrees all day, and as the sun set a chill bit the air. Brigadier General John Gregg's brigade led the march. As the last hint of twilight melted into darkness his skirmishers ran into a fire so sharp and steady it caused Johnson to halt and begin the tedious process of deploying his two-and-a-half-mile-long divisional march column into line of battle.

Hood and Johnson had just had their first taste of Spencer rifles. Wilder had halted his brigade only a few minutes earlier and formed a hasty line of battle from the Viniard field to the Thedford house, square across the path of Johnson's advance. His men dismounted, sent their horses to the rear, threw together breastworks with whatever rocks and logs lay nearby, then waited.

Wood and Minty rode up beside Wilder a few seconds later.

"Well, Wilder, where are they?" demanded Wood.

"Ride forward a dozen paces, General, and you will see them!" replied Wilder hopefully.

As Wood trotted forward a crackling of rifle fire pierced the night air. It was Gregg's skirmishers. "By God, they *are* here!" Wood cried, then rushed back toward the mill with a promise of reinforcements.[28]

Wood kept his word. While the Confederates continued to deploy, Colonel George Dick came up with two regiments from his brigade. Wilder shifted his line to the northwest, and Dick placed the Forty-fourth Indiana and Fifty-ninth Ohio on either side of the Alexander's Bridge road. An hour later, the Rebels were ready. They stepped noisily through the underbrush in three lines. Gregg led the way, with McNair and Fulton trailing in line of battle and Robertson's Texans bringing up the rear. It was nearly 9:00 P.M. The men of the Fifty-ninth Ohio lay quietly until the enemy was just fifty yards away, then lit up the forest with a volley that sent the Confederates scattering for cover. Gregg's left regiments kept on past the right flank of the Fifty-ninth, which fell back one hundred yards into a ravine to await the next attack.

It never came. Badly shaken by the unexpected opposition, Johnson halted his entire division: "The whole Yankee army was in our front, on our right flank and rear, while our army was still on the east side of the Chickamauga." Hood had no desire to press on over strange ground in the dark, and so he allowed Johnson to bivouac his command where it had stopped, some eight hundred yards east of the Viniard farm. Forrest returned with Davidson's brigade to Alexander's Bridge to bed down, and all was silent.[29]

For Wilder's troopers it was a miserable night. When their horses were sent rearward their tents and blankets had gone with them. Sergeant McGee of the Seventy-second Indiana recalled the long hours of darkness and uncertainty:

> We lay all night behind our works without blankets, tents, or a bite to eat; the night was so cold that frost fell on the leaves and grass and we suffered severely. Sleep was out of the question. The night was clear, and thousands of sounds for many miles around were audible; while those coming from the south were omens of good to us, those coming from the north and east were presages of disaster and defeat. Between these conflicting sounds and the feelings engendered by each in turn we wore the hours of night away.
>
> As soon as the firing ceased . . . we could hear at the creek . . . the sounds of thousands of axes engaged in constructing bridges across the creek, making roads through the forests and building defensive works. All night long we could hear thousands of troops moving into the woods and taking up positions north of us; while the rumbling of the enemy's artillery and ammunition trains never ceased. . . . These were sounds of ill-omen.[30]

All Rosecrans had heard all day long were ill omens. The first had come from Wood. At 10:30 A.M. he reported a strong force of skirmishers advancing on him from across the creek. It was Hindman's division moving forward, late as usual, to begin the demonstration against the Federal left at the mill. The signal stations at Stevens's Gap confirmed the advance against Wood and warned that large clouds of dust were moving north toward the bridges. Later in the morning came the first report from Minty, followed shortly after 4:00 P.M. by a note from Wilder alerting headquarters to Minty's withdrawal and adding that he too would have to fall back soon.[31]

Rosecrans's first response came shortly before noon, when he ordered Steedman to send a brigade to support Minty. Steedman had only just returned to Rossville from his reconnaissance of the day before, and so it was 3:30 P.M. before he had the brigade of Dan McCook, yet another of the "Fighting McCooks," on the road to Reed's Bridge. (For some reason Granger was loitering about the Gordon-Lee house, leaving Steedman in command of the Reserve Corps well into the next morning.)

As the evidence of a Confederate movement to turn his left grew, Rosecrans prepared to shift his entire army northward along the line of the La Fayette road to cover his routes of withdrawal to Chattanooga and forestall any Rebel thrust west from Chickamauga Creek. He intended to accomplish this by leapfrogging Thomas over Crittenden. First, Crittenden was to move the divisions of Van Cleve and Palmer to the left of Wood. Thomas, in turn, would post one division near Crawfish Springs to relieve Van Cleve and Palmer. With his remaining three divisions, he was to move north on the Glenn-Kelly road past Crittenden's new position as far as the home of the Widow Glenn. There he was to face east and move his corps to the La Fayette road, where it would form line of battle with its left extending obliquely across the road near the Kelly farm. Alexander McCook, meanwhile, was to close on Thomas and take position at Crawfish Springs to protect Crittenden's right and act as a general reserve. Mitchell's cavalry was to fall in on McCook's right, with instructions to watch the crossing sites to the south and act on McCook's orders. Rosecrans admonished his generals to move quickly and "very secretly."[32]

The most obvious flaw in Rosecrans's plan was that it did not extend the Federal line far enough north to cover effectively the roads leading to Rossville from the Ringgold, Dyer's, and Reed's bridges. Rosecrans apparently intended the Reserve Corps to cover these three approaches once the cavalry fell back, but at best this would place a brigade astride each avenue of approach. A gap of nearly a mile would exist between any force covering the Reed's Bridge road and Thomas's left, and McCook's reserve at Crawfish Springs would be at least five miles away.

The execution was halting and uncertain. Crittenden had Van Cleve on the road by 11:45 A.M., but for some reason he directed Palmer to march to Wood's right rather than to his left. McCook received his movement orders shortly before 2:00 P.M., only to be handed a telegram a moment later advising him simply to hold his corps "in *readiness* to move" [italics mine]. "Which order will I obey?" a befuddled McCook wired back. Forty minutes passed with no answer. He repeated the message. At 4:15 P.M. came a two-word response signed by Rosecrans: "Move up." Another forty-five minutes were lost before corps headquarters dispatched marching orders to the divisions. Thomas apparently did not get his instructions until mid-afternoon, and those told him only to move his corps to Crawfish Springs and relieve Crittenden; there was no mention of a continued march to the north. It was 3:30 P.M. before marching orders were in the hands of his division commanders and 4:00 P.M. before the lead division under Negley started for the springs.[33]

The problems grew as the afternoon wore on. When it became apparent that Minty was about to lose Reed's Bridge, Rosecrans ordered Steedman to send a second brigade in that direction. Steedman complied and by 5:00 P.M. had the brigades of Dan McCook and Mitchell on the road. Whitaker's brigade, meanwhile, had already moved off toward the Ringgold Bridge and was at that very moment locked in a skirmish with Scott's cavalry brigade a mile and a half west of Chickamauga Creek. Steedman was thus compelled to stretch three brigades over a three-mile front, and he had no troops to spare to cover the wagon road from Dyer's Bridge.[34]

Far more serious were the troubles closer at hand. Negley found the first of Palmer's brigades, commanded by Hazen, near Glass's Mill at sundown. Negley sent an aide, Captain Alfred Hough, to the Gordon-Lee house to report his location, then rode off with John Beatty to find General Hazen, whom Beatty was to relieve. They came across the Ohioan lounging in the grass behind his lines. Hazen was very sorry, but he had no orders to move from his position. Negley pleaded with Hazen, who just as emphatically refused to budge. Thoroughly disgusted, Negley turned and rode off to army headquarters for answers.

Negley was in no mood for games. The strain of the Dug Gap affair had wrecked him. As soon as his division had marched clear of danger on 12 September, he had reported himself sick, and for the next four days lay in bed with acute diarrhea. He was on horseback now, but an ambulance stood by just in case.

Rosecrans reiterated to Hough his orders for Negley immediately to relieve Palmer's division. Palmer was present, and he sent a staff officer with Hough to help him locate the positions of his three brigades.

The comedy continued. Major James Lowrie, Negley's chief of staff, ran into John Beatty on the Crawfish Springs road. Beatty complained that, as Negley had not returned from the Gordon-Lee house, he had no idea what to do with his troops. Lowrie rode away in the dark to find Negley but instead ran into a bewildered Colonel Timothy Stanley. Colonel William Grose likewise had refused to yield his position, leaving Stanley's troops to stand in the road with nowhere to go.

For four and a half hours Negley, Hough, Lowrie, Beatty, and Stanley rode around looking for one another while Palmer's brigade commanders refused to move. What Palmer did during all this time is unknown, although he later claimed to have sent his brigade commanders written orders at 6:30 P.M. to move at once. In the meantime, Thomas's trailing divisions stacked up along the road behind Negley. And behind Thomas, McCook waited to bring his corps off Missionary Ridge.[35]

The hours slipped away and the soldiers waited. Hans Heg used the delay to pen a letter to his wife. "Once more I have an opportunity to write a few words. . . . The Rebels are in our front and we may have to fight him a battle — if we do it will be apt to be a big one," he wrote, quickly adding a few words of reassurance: "Do not feel uneasy for me. I am well and in good spirits and trusting to my usual good luck. I shall use all the caution and courage I am capable of and leave the rest to take care of itself."[36]

The poet general, William Lytle, sat down beside a campfire among his soldiers and began conversing with his aide, Lieutenant Pirtle, while they waited for Colonel Laiboldt to move his brigade out ahead of them. Lytle had caught a terrible cold the night before. He had napped when he could during the day, and now sat wrapped in a buffalo robe, huddled close to the flame. The moment was magic. The soldiers, recalled Pirtle,

> kept a cheerful blaze, listening with great respect and rapt attention to the general's conversation which was addressed to me entirely, and in the beginning was lively, genial, and full of fun, and they enjoyed it very much, but when it gradually took a more serious turn, the poor fellows finding it was not intended for them, went off, leaving us alone. As invariably followed when the general and I had a talk by ourselves, his mind turned to home and friends. He spoke of his sisters, wondering where they were that night, as he knew they were absent in Cincinnati. He recalled many incidents of society in Louisville, in those balmy days when he used to visit our city. The whole scene and circumstances of this long and delightful conversation are indelibly impressed on my mind and heart.
>
> I can see the general sitting on a rail before the fire, his reins slipped over his arm, the firelight glancing from his sabre. . . . The hours passed on almost unheeded. The fire burned low and at length we determined to hunt up Laiboldt and learn when he would move.[37]

Among the soldiers, death insinuated itself into every effort at conversation. Scores recorded an eerie phenomenon, as comrades and officers who had survived a dozen battles and skirmishes without a care suddenly paled with premonitions of their own impending deaths. Some could pinpoint where the death bullet would strike. There was nothing anyone could say to these men. Sergeant Chauncey Castle of the Seventy-third Illinois made the mistake of trying to strike up a conversation with the regimental adjutant, Captain Winget. There was no braver officer in the regiment, boasted Castle. The two had grown up together, and Winget now unburdened himself to the sergeant. A great and bloody battle was about to be fought, he said, one that he would not come out of alive. For the next hour he meticulously reviewed with Castle every detail of his personal affairs "that he hoped I might be able to attend to, while he believed that he should not." Two days later, Winget was dead.[38]

While Negley was stalled along the road, Thomas belatedly learned that the remainder of his corps was expected to march to the left of the army. At 10:30 P.M., the Virginian took matters into his own hands. He ordered Negley off the road and into bivouac near Crawfish Springs. That opened the way for the rest of the corps to march to the Widow Glenn house. Getting there, however, would require a night march that might last until sunrise. At this point, Rosecrans hesitated. How effective would an army of somnambulates be in blocking the Confederates? Rosecrans pondered awhile but ultimately decided that he had no alternative. He ordered Thomas to continue the march at all hazards and McCook to come on to Crawfish Springs. Then he and Thomas walked out of the Gordon-Lee house to watch the troops start on their way.[39]

Few would forget this march; it had a weird, almost surreal quality. The forest deep and dark closed in on the moving columns. The temperature fell to near freezing. Scouts rode ahead and set fences ablaze to light the way. Smoke mixed with rising dust to burn the eyes and sting the nostrils of the sleepy soldiers. All night long it went on: stopping, starting, stopping, starting—all night to march five miles. At each halt the men sank into the dust or rested in place, asleep on their feet.[40]

Soldiers hated night marches in principal. Sergeant Simmons of the Eighty-fourth Illinois best explained their effect on the troops: "It is not a little remarkable, how strongly the situation and surrounding circumstances impress the mind of the soldier. A march upon a bright, clear morning is full of hilarious mirth; the lively story is told, jest succeeds jest in rapid succession. . . . A march on a rainy, dismal day elicits no small amount of repining. . . . A march at night is invariably silent; scarcely a word will be spoken for hours, and when one does address a comrade it is in a quiet, suppressed voice, such as is heard in the sick room."[41]

Silence and doubt. A fear unspeakable. It took a poet to ease the tension. Along the way, General Lytle remarked to Lieutenant Pirtle that he was hungry. Pirtle obediently reached into his pocket to offer him some food, and as he pulled it out a valuable ring spilled onto the ground. Pirtle dismounted. Halting the long column of infantry behind them, the lieutenant lit a candle and began groping in the dust while Lytle rode on. Pirtle galloped up a few minutes later waving the ring. Lytle laughed: "A man who can lose a ring at midnight and find it in six inches of dust, on as dark a road as this, is not going to be hit in the coming battle."[42]

The hours passed and still the columns crept on. Everyone seemed to understand that failure to reach the La Fayette road before daylight might well mean the end of the army.

At the Gordon-Lee house there was nothing to do now but wait. "The camp is perfectly quiet and orderly, just as much as if no great events were in anticipation for tomorrow," wrote Colonel Sanderson before retiring. He closed his journal with an invocation that spoke the heart of every Union soldier: "Be the events, or the results of tomorrow, as yet beyond all human ken, what they may, it is my hope and prayer that the same kind Providence, which has successfully shielded and preserved this army thus far . . . sustain and uphold it and give it another victory, fruitful to the overthrow of this unholy rebellion. . . . And finally, be the part devolving upon me, ever so great or so small, may that same kind Providence aid and sustain me in its faithful performance and protect me against all dangers."[43]

At his headquarters at Leet's Tan Yard, Bragg was strangely serene, while on the west bank of Chickamauga Creek all was confusion. Hood and Johnson had followed as best they could Bragg's vague instructions to sweep south but in doing so had created serious problems of command and control. Walker, who spent the entire night shepherding his Reserve Corps across the creek, was now on the extreme right of the army instead of in the center. More important, Hood's decision to halt for the night east of the Viniard farm forced Buckner's corps into a tiny pocket on the west bank, with the creek on three sides and Johnson's division on the fourth. Buckner's front was completely blocked by a sharp bend in the creek.

The Confederates would become even more cramped. During the night, Bragg ordered Polk to send Cheatham's division north, with discretionary authority to cross the creek "as circumstances may demand." Hindman would remain opposite Lee and Gordon's Mill. Bragg then ordered Hill to shift his corps closer to the mill to compensate for the detachment of Cheatham. The choice of a crossing site apparently was left to Cheatham, and he understandably picked the first one he came upon, which was Dalton (Hunt's) Ford. Unfortunately, it was also the one Buckner had chosen, so that when Cheatham crossed his large four-brigade division at daylight, he had barely enough space to squeeze into line behind Buckner.

The second and third brigades of Hood's division, commanded respectively by Colonel James Sheffield and Brigadier General Henry "Old Rock" Benning, came on the field during the early hours of the morning and with Robertson's Texans were placed on the right of Johnson's division. Brigadier General Evander Law, as ranking officer, was placed in command of the division. In Longstreet's absence, Hood assumed command of the corps.

Apart from moving Cheatham and Hill, Bragg did nothing during the night. His intelligence reports still placed Rosecrans where he wanted him, with his left at Lee and Gordon's Mill and the rest of the Union army strung out southward into the cove. Having no inkling of Thomas's night march, Bragg concentrated his effort on opening the battle against what he assumed to be the Union left flank with all the troops he could muster. He gave no serious thought to what if any Union forces might lie beyond his own right flank until dawn, when he ordered Forrest to take a ride up the Jay's Mill road and reconnoiter west of the mill. Issued as an afterthought, this order was to shape the course of the battle.[44]

CHAPTER SEVEN

WITHDRAW IF NOT ALREADY
TOO LATE

COLONEL Daniel McCook was slowly being consumed by the fire of his own ambition. For fourteen months a brigadier general's silver star had glittered just out of reach. His military career was in the doldrums and it galled him. Brother Alexander, only three years his elder, had been handed his second star only two days after Daniel made colonel. William T. Sherman, his law partner in Leavenworth, Kansas, before the war, already commanded his own army. Add to insatiable ambition a high-strung, nervous intensity, and in Dan McCook one had an officer dangerous both to himself and his troops.[1]

McCook sensed his opportunity was at hand. His brigade had arrived at the intersection of the Reed's Bridge and Jay's Mill roads on the evening of 18 September just in time to gobble up the tail of Bushrod Johnson's column hurrying toward Lee and Gordon's Mill. Two or three teamsters, a handful of straggling privates from McNair's brigade, and a startled regimental band quietly surrendered to the equally surprised Federals. To their credit, the captured Rebels were close-mouthed, and McCook learned only (and incorrectly) that they represented regiments from Arkansas, Texas, and Louisiana. Somehow, from this paltry information, he concluded that a Confederate brigade lay in the forest to his front, lost and alone and willing to stay put until dawn to be captured.[2]

By the time Colonel John Mitchell came up with his brigade at 3:00 A.M., McCook could talk of nothing else. He implored Mitchell to give his men only the briefest rest and to breakfast them quickly, so that they would be ready to support his attack at sunrise. McCook was leaving nothing to chance. An hour earlier he had hunted up Lieutenant Colonel Joseph Brigham and told him to take his Sixty-ninth Ohio and burn Reed's Bridge at once, so to deny the Confederates a route of escape.

Brigham could not have been pleased. His regiment had just come on the field from guard duty in the rear. The Sixty-ninth belonged to Negley's division and was only temporarily under McCook's command, yet McCook expected it to march down a strange road in the dark of night and place itself behind an enemy brigade. Brigham reluctantly started down the Reed's Bridge road. To present a less conspicuous target, he turned the regiment off the road a few hundred yards shy of the bridge and plunged into the forest.

Brigham's skirmishers stepped warily from the forest and slipped down to the bridge as the first rays of sunlight glinted on Chickamauga Creek. There was not a Rebel in sight. The Ohioans piled fence rails on the flooring and set the bridge aflame.[3]

McCook was in the saddle early. He met Mitchell, and the two rode forward toward McCook's line in the rapidly melting morning twilight.

McCook's regimental commanders seemed not to share his enthusiasm for a dawn attack, as none yet had their troops in line of battle. Most of the soldiers were still quietly sipping their morning coffee. The thought foremost in their minds was water, and how they would fill their canteens before the impending battle. When word spread that the pickets of the Eighty-sixth Illinois had come upon a spring near Jay's Mill, a rambling sawmill that cut lumber for local farmers, the clamor was more than their officers could ignore. Lieutenant Colonel Magee of the Eighty-sixth Illinois tried to instill some order in the process. He told his company commanders each to select three men to gather the canteens of the company and form a detail to go to the spring. Lieutenant William Faulkner of Company D was placed in charge. At his own picket line, Faulkner was confronted by a mob of thirsty soldiers from every regiment in the brigade, begging to go along. Faulkner told those with guns to fall in, and with canteens clanging his ragtag detail started across the Jay cornfield toward the spring.[4]

It was 6:00 A.M. McCook was about to give the order to fall in, when he was distracted by a galloping horseman. It was a messenger from corps. He drew rein on his foaming horse and handed McCook a dispatch from Rosecrans to Granger. It read: "Withdraw McCook and Mitchell if not already too late." McCook was stunned. Too late for what?

Unbeknownst to McCook, his encounter with the tail of Johnson's column had alarmed rather than reassured headquarters. Rosecrans was concerned over the exposed position of McCook and Mitchell and so ordered Granger to withdraw them at sunrise. Steedman had had the same thought during the night and had drafted his own orders to pull the two brigades back to the McAfee church. He simply appended Rosecrans's message when received and sent the messenger on to McCook.

McCook was crestfallen. He told Mitchell to take his brigade back to the

La Fayette road; he would be along shortly. As they talked, the two noticed a column of dust rise from beyond the forest, in the direction of the La Fayette road a mile behind them. Hoping for a reprieve, McCook galloped off to meet the troops behind the dust.[5]

McCook and Mitchell had glimpsed the dust raised by the head of Brigadier General Absalom Baird's division closing on the ratty little homestead of Elijah Kelly—a two-room log cabin, barn, outhouse, and played-out cornfield that was the object of their nightmare march. There Baird faced his column to the right and deployed it in line of battle east of the road, with King's Regular Brigade on the left, Scribner in the center, and Starkweather withdrawn a bit on the right. Five thousand jaded Yankees stumbled into line, then collapsed in place, some to sleep, others to throw together a hasty breakfast of bacon and coffee.

Brannan's division trudged up the road behind Baird, continuing past him to extend the Federal line north from the Kelly field toward the Reed's Bridge road. Thomas and his staff rode at the head of the column. Reynolds's division, which had spent the night in a traffic snarl with Palmer's troops, was still four hours away.[6]

Thomas met McCook just as Brannan's men began filing off the road. Pointing toward the bridge, the Ohioan breathlessly told him that a lone Confederate brigade lay ripe for the picking. McCook begged Thomas to overturn Rosecrans's orders and allow him to attack. Thomas declined but, intrigued by the possibility of bagging a thousand Confederates easily, decided to send a brigade from Brannan's division forward to develop the enemy. The wisdom of sending a single brigade into dense woods on the strength of an excited colonel's report is clearly open to debate; certainly Thomas was exceeding his orders in moving beyond the La Fayette road. Be that as it may, he had taken the first tentative step toward seizing the initiative from Bragg.

On the way back to his brigade, McCook passed Colonel John Croxton, to whom Thomas had given the mission of finding the Confederates. The Ohioan paused long enough to vent his spleen on the unsuspecting colonel. McCook told Croxton that "he had supposed, when he received his temporary assignment to the command of General Steedman, that he had been placed under a fighting officer who would afford him a chance to win distinction; but he had, instead, proved to be his evil genius, and had just plucked from his shoulder a star, for had it not been for the inopportune receipt of this detested order he would have moved on and whipped the indiscreet rebel command, and thus deserved promotion." Riding on, he met Captain Seth Moe of the division staff. To Moe, McCook mewled that Croxton would "do the work and get the coveted prize (a star)."[7]

McCook was in for a surprise. While he was away, Brigadier General

H. B. Davidson appeared with his Confederate cavalry brigade near Jay's Mill, ordered there by Forrest in response to Bragg's order that he reconnoiter beyond the army's right. Davidson had joined the brigade only six hours earlier, so division commander John Pegram rode along to keep an eye on things. Davidson dismounted his troopers in a hollow behind the mill, where they set about preparing their breakfasts, then sent a detachment from the Sixth Georgia Cavalry into the timber to form a skirmish line at the edge of the cornfield. Less than two hundred yards away, members of Lieutenant Faulkner's little detail were quietly dipping their canteens in the mill spring.

The Georgians ran into Faulkner's skirmishers, and a few rifle cracks split the morning air. The rest of Faulkner's men kept filling canteens—a little faster now—until the thunder of hooves announced the arrival of an entire regiment of cavalry in line of battle.

Pegram had ordered the First Georgia to ride to the front with a gun from Gustave Huwald's battery the moment Davidson's skirmishers became engaged. Badly outnumbered now, Faulkner and his men scattered. A few were captured, but enough made it back to sound the alarm.

Down at Reed's Bridge, Private William Rea of the Sixty-ninth Ohio looked past his steaming cup of coffee at what he thought were friendly cavalry trotting up the Jay's Mill road to reconnoiter across the creek. "How will them fellows get back, as there is no bridge," Rea asked his company commander. His answer came from the rifle barrels of Davidson's troopers, and the Ohioans forgot their breakfasts and scurried through the woods toward the La Fayette road.[8]

McCook rejoined his brigade to find everything in confusion. He rode first to the Eighty-sixth Illinois, which was taking fire from Huwald's cannon, and ordered Lieutenant Colonel Magee to fall back by the right flank at once. Magee reminded McCook that his pickets were still out. No time to recall them, McCook replied, they would have to fend for themselves. Colonel Caleb Dilworth, commander of the Eighty-fifth Illinois, glanced to his right to see the Eighty-sixth filing off to the right, so he ordered his men to fall in. McCook's adjutant rode up and told him to follow the Eighty-sixth, and Dilworth hastily withdrew. By then, the lead horsemen of the Sixth Georgia had edged around his left.

In McCook's second line, Colonel Oscar Harmon was thoroughly confused. He saw the Eighty-sixth fall back past his right but having no orders himself decided to hold his One Hundred Twenty-fifth Illinois in place until someone told him what was happening. Finally a courier from McCook arrived with word that the brigade was withdrawing, and Harmon faced his men about and marched off. The Fifty-second Ohio did the same, and what was to have been an easy advance degenerated into an embarrassingly hasty retreat.[9]

The First Georgia Cavalry began a leisurely pursuit up the Reed's Bridge road until Pegram, who was running the brigade for Davidson, called it back. He sent the Tenth Confederate Cavalry, on detached service from Scott's brigade, out to reconnoiter the ground between the Reed's Bridge and Brotherton roads, then rode back up the Reed's Bridge road himself accompanied by General Forrest. The remainder of the brigade rested along a slight, wooded ridge about two hundred yards west of the mill.[10]

The men of Croxton's brigade were not at all happy about missing breakfast. The call to arms came while they were boiling their coffee. "The grand rush now made by those who had abandoned their coffee boilers to regain possession of them, and secure the benefit of the much needed stimulant was enlivening," recalled Captain I. B. Walker of the Tenth Kentucky. "To see the attempts made to swallow the hot beverage while marching over the rough road was ludicrous in the extreme. Many among our regiment went into battle with both hands full of something to eat or drink."[11]

Though the men grumbled about missing their meal, they had no cause for complaint where their brigade commander was concerned. Just twenty-six years old, Colonel Croxton already had won the esteem of both his troops and his superiors. The son of a wealthy Kentucky planter, Croxton had graduated from Yale with honors in 1857. He set up a law practice in Paris, Kentucky, and was one of only two men in the town to vote for Abraham Lincoln in the election of 1860. Croxton had distinguished himself while serving under Thomas in the Battle of Mill Springs early in the war; perhaps this explains why Thomas felt comfortable sending Croxton in alone. Certainly the Virginian trusted him implicitly. "Croxton is the best soldier Kentucky has furnished to the war," he once remarked to a group of officers.[12]

Croxton was about to have that estimate tested. He moved his brigade column a mile down a farmer's lane that he mistook for the Reed's Bridge road but which was actually a parallel trail between it and the Brotherton road. Then he formed line of battle in a pine forest thick with tangled underbrush. The Fourth Kentucky deployed to the left, the Tenth Indiana held the center on the trail, and the Seventy-fourth Indiana came into line on the right. The Fourteenth Ohio and Tenth Kentucky formed the brigade reserve. Skirmishers from the Tenth Indiana darted forward to cover the brigade front.

The officers of the brigade were confident. No one doubted McCook's story. Before their regiment advanced, Captain Walker heard his major joke: "We have a soft snap here. A rebel brigade has crossed the creek to this side, and our forces have destroyed the bridge behind them, and we are now going to gobble them up."

For a few moments nothing could be heard but the swishing of vines and crunching of dead leaves underfoot. Then came a pop-pop from the skirmish line, growing gradually to a steady drumming. Bullets began striking the front line. Walker heard a dull thud and winced. A minie ball had struck a private standing beside him. It was "followed almost immediately by the most inhuman sound that ever escaped the vocal organs of a man. . . . His arms went up, his gun flew far from him, and he fell in his place with the dead wound in his groin." By then, the skirmishers had run in. It was too hot out there, their commander yelled as he pressed past Walker.

Up over a rise and right behind them thundered the Tenth Confederate Cavalry. "Steady boys, wait for the word," cautioned Colonel William Carroll of the Tenth Indiana. On came the Rebels, oblivious to Croxton's line of battle. At a range of 150 yards all three frontline regiments opened fire: a thousand rifles trained on perhaps 250 horsemen. The results were predictable. "At first all was smoke, then dust from struggling steeds, a few riderless horses were running here and there save which nothing was seen of that cavalry troop," remembered Sergeant Peter Kellenberger of the Tenth Indiana. The front line fixed bayonets, skirmishers redeployed, and the advance resumed.[13]

Back on the ridge near the mill, Davidson's more fortunate troopers were cooking breakfast or relaxing. No one expected trouble. Private Jay Minnich of the Sixth Georgia Cavalry recalled how his regiment was "resting, rearranging saddles and girths, and incidentally munching hardtack, some smoking, some chatting . . . all resting easy that there was not a Yankee within cannon range — when we were suddenly brought up standing by two volleys delivered in rapid succession and with such precision as is attained only by practiced and seasoned troops. One of our boys yelled, 'By thunder! That's infantry!' " Back over the ridge galloped the fugitives of the Tenth Confederate Cavalry, throwing the Sixth Georgia and First Tennessee Legion into confusion. "Stop them, stop them!" Colonel C. T. Goode of the Tenth yelled to the Georgians. When that had no effect he told them to knock his men off their horses. Minnich raised his rifle to strike a terrified trooper bearing down on him, but when he saw the man close up — riding hatless clutching his horse's mane with both hands, eyes bulging "as big as goose eggs" — the Georgian stepped aside and fell to the ground laughing. Goode was beside himself. "Sixth Georgia, I'm going to stay with you. You are men, by God. My men are a set of damned cowards. Damn them!"[14]

Forrest and Pegram had returned from the Reed's Bridge road. With Colonels Hart of the Sixth Georgia and Goode, they were frantically trying to restore order to the brigade left when Croxton struck that portion of the line. They managed to form a scratch line along the ridge, to which men were added as they rallied, and Croxton's Yankees gradually were brought to a halt in a thick fringe of black oak saplings at the base of a second ridge opposite the Confederates.[15]

Croxton sent back word of his encounter. Brannan responded by ordering Van Derveer's brigade to move down the Reed's Bridge road to turn the Rebel right flank. Gradually but inexorably, Thomas was being drawn into a battle.

Like their comrades in Croxton's brigade, the soldiers of Van Derveer's command were cooking breakfast when the order came to move out. Captain Jeremiah Donahower, the twenty-six-year-old commander of Company E, Second Minnesota, had already downed his coffee and was enjoying a can of pineapple when he saw the messenger from division tip his hat to Van Derveer and draw from his belt the long envelope Donahower surmised contained the order to advance. For a moment, recalled Donahower, those who had not yet eaten forgot their fear of death. Swearing profusely, they grabbed their cups "and drank their coffee seasoned with the dust of the road as they marched." All this cursing over coffee was too much for the chaplain of the Second Minnesota. "Dreadful, dreadful," he moaned as the air grew blue. "But think," laughed a nearby soldier, "how dreadfuller it would be to go into battle and get killed with all those curses in 'em."

Van Derveer's men marched up the La Fayette road to the McDonald farm. There they turned onto a wagon trail that led to the Reed's Bridge road. Brannan was on hand to see the Second Minnesota off with a smile and a gentle admonition: "Now Minnesotans, step out." It was his way of saying that there were Rebels ahead to be hit, and hit hard.

Maybe so, but Van Derveer had no idea where he was going. "Being without a guide and entirely unacquainted with the country," he elected to play it safe. Soon after his column passed Brannan, the forty-year-old Ohioan deployed the brigade into two lines of battle, which would slow his march to a crawl but lessen the risk of being taken by surprise. Caution was fundamental to Van Derveer's nature. The balding and bespectacled Mexican War veteran, who looked more the schoolmaster than the soldier, followed the principals of reconnaissance and picketing with excruciating exactness.[16]

While Van Derveer crept along and gradually let slip the chance to envelop Davidson's right, Croxton continued to engage the troopers in front. In the deep forests and tangled thickets, it was fighting more by feel than by sight. "We never saw a single foe, so completely were they concealed by the underbrush in our front," remembered Private Minnich. But their invisible foes were taking a heavy toll on the Rebel troopers, who hugged the ground and returned the fire as best they could. Forrest was among them, in his element. A major who had never before seen Forrest in battle marveled at the change that came over him when the shooting started: "His face flushed until he bore a striking resemblance to a painted Indian warrior, and his eyes, usually so mild in their expression, flashed with the intense glare of the panther about to spring on its prey. In fact, he looked as little like the Forrest of our mess-table as the storm of December resembles the quiet of June."

Although his troopers were holding their own, Forrest recognized that they could not long withstand one of the largest infantry brigades in the Union army. He dispatched a courier to Polk's headquarters to request that the bishop release Brigadier General Frank Armstrong's cavalry division to him, then rode down the Jay's Mill road in search of infantry. Near the Alexander house he ran into Colonel Claudius Wilson, who had just gotten the last of his brigade across the creek and was allowing his men to cook breakfast before moving into position behind Hood's corps. It was 8:00 A.M. Forrest begged Wilson to join him, but Wilson declined pending authorization from Walker.

Walker had been sitting on a log conferring with Hood when the roll of musketry from the right drew him back to his command. But instead of turning Wilson over to Forrest, the punctilious Georgian insisted on obtaining Bragg's approval.[17]

Bragg had risen early. At sunrise he and his staff had ridden to Thedford's Ford, where they set up headquarters behind Buckner's corps and watched Cheatham's division wade across Dalton Ford at 7:00 A.M. Bragg was in good spirits. "If he had been in a dazed condition for the few days previous there were no lingering traces of bewilderment visible then. For he was self-possessed, bright and confident," recalled Captain Wheless of Polk's staff. Bragg's only thought was of crushing the Federal left, which he still believed to be at Lee and Gordon's Mill. His first written order from Thedford's Ford was to Polk, asking for a status report from the bishop's front and alerting him to the planned advance by Buckner and Hood. Bragg sketched out the locations of the Confederate lines of battle on the west bank for Wheless, and admonished the captain to "report this to General Polk and say to him I will move forward in a few minutes and attack the enemy wherever I can find him, and as soon as he hears any guns, he must come at once with the rest of his command."[18]

Forrest's appeal for help effectively ended Bragg's planned attack. Bragg immediately authorized Walker to dispatch Wilson to aid the cavalry, but the unexpected fighting from an area he thought empty of Federals unnerved him. The old doubts and vacillation returned. Bragg surrendered the initiative, and from that moment his overriding concern was to match the Federals blow for blow wherever they might appear.

To speculate on what might have been, had Bragg gone ahead and attacked, Hood and Buckner would have walked into a two-mile gap between Crittenden at the mill and Thomas near the Kelly farm. Only Wilder's brigade, which had thrown up breastworks west of the Viniard farm, would have stood in the way of two and a half Rebel corps. Once past Wilder, Buckner and Hood could have struck the flank of Reynolds's and Johnson's moving divisions.

Forrest rode part of the way back to Jay's Mill with Wilson and his Georgians before his anxiety got the better of him. Enjoining Wilson to choose a suitable position near Davidson, he galloped ahead to encourage his men to hold on.

Forrest returned to a slightly improved but still desperate situation. Polk had agreed to release only the Tennessee brigade of Colonel George Dibrell from Armstrong's division. Dibrell lost no time, and he had his troopers dismounted and in line on Davidson's right before 9:00 A.M. Dibrell's brigade extended north far beyond Croxton's left flank, and the added firepower of his Tennesseans strained Croxton's line. Croxton called on the Tenth Kentucky to move up from the second line to the left of the Fourth Kentucky to meet the threat and gave up any thought he may have had of continuing his advance.[19]

Dibrell quickly tired of the Kentuckians. He pushed his dismounted cavalry up the Reed's Bridge road to search out Croxton's rear. Instead, they ran headlong into Van Derveer. Captain Donahower, in command of the Second Minnesota's skirmishers, was among the first to see the Tennesseans coming: "During a few minutes the quiet of the forest was undisturbed save by the cracking noise of dead limbs as they broke under the tramp of the men, until the voice of a corporal on the left of the skirmish line sang out, 'There they are' and others saw the enemy and repeated the warning." The opposing skirmish lines met four hundred yards to the left and rear of Croxton. Van Derveer edged his brigade down the slope of a gentle hill. At its base, he ordered his regiments to lie down to escape the fire of their still unseen foe. The Second Minnesota took cover on the left front and the Thirty-fifth Ohio hit the ground on its right. The Eighty-seventh Indiana, in reserve, had nowhere to lie except on the crest of the ridge, and there they took a severe peppering from bullets passing over the front line. Van Derveer called up a section of Battery I, Fourth United States Artillery, and wedged it between his frontline regiments. Then the wait began.

For fifteen minutes the skirmishing continued, drawing steadily nearer. At last the skirmishers rushed in, then "over the little rise in the woods in front appeared the heads of a solid line of men in gray" and the

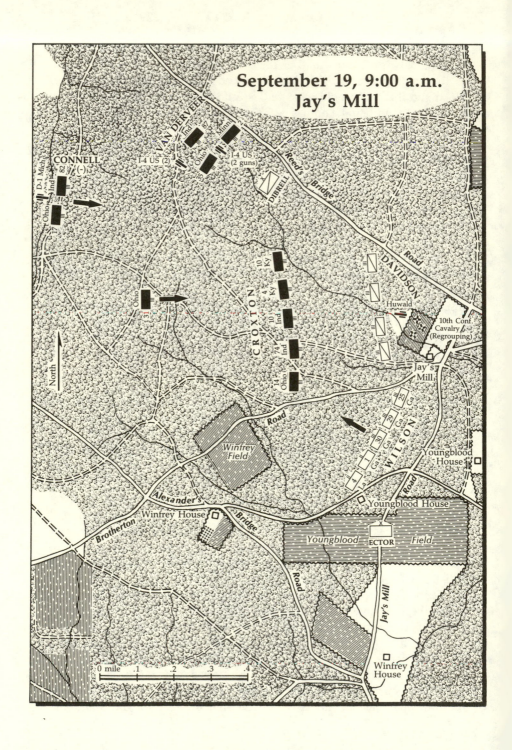

"Ki.. yi.. Ki.. yi" of the Rebel yell split the air. At 125 yards the Minnesotans and Ohioans let go their first volley, and Dibrell's front line melted away. His second line came up to return the fire, and the two sides were soon blanketed in smoke. For thirty minutes it went on. The Thirty-fifth Ohio was losing men at the rate of two a minute when the fire finally slackened and Dibrell's Tennesseans backed away some time after 9:30 A.M. As the woods fell silent, Van Derveer's men hastily reloaded and peered through the smoke for signs of another Confederate assault.[20]

The first sounds of skirmishing from Van Derveer's front caused Brannan to order his remaining brigade to its feet. This brigade had fallen on hard times. Its commander, Colonel Moses Walker, was under arrest; the acting commander, Colonel John Connell, was in terrible health; and the officers and men were restive. The Thirty-eighth Ohio had been detached to guard the division supply train, leaving Connell with just three regiments and a battery of artillery. Aware of the brigade's problems, Brannan was taking no chances. He met Connell at the Kelly house, ordered the Thirty-first Ohio left behind in case Croxton needed help later, then rode with his ailing colonel as what remained of the brigade stepped into the woods east of the farm.[21]

On the ridge near Jay's Mill, Davidson's troopers were still suffering. Dibrell's inadvertent clash with Van Derveer had allowed Croxton again to turn his full attention toward Davidson. Three times the Rebels fell off the ridge, only to be shooed back into line by Pegram and his colonels. Nearly a third of the brigade was dead or wounded. Huwald's battery had lost most of its horses, and the cannoneers could see the bottoms of their ammunition chests.

Forrest was everywhere, reassuring the men that help was on the way. Up and down the exposed ridge he rode. "Hold on, boys, the infantry is coming; they'll soon be here to relieve you," Forrest repeated to each unit he passed; as he neared Huwald's guns, the key to his line, both the plea and assurance became more emphatic: "Stay by the battery, men; support the battery. General Walker will be here in five minutes to help us."

Forrest was masterful. Few generals could both inspire frontline troops and retain a perspective on the larger tactical situation as ably as he. No act was too small if it would boost morale. "Just as Forrest came to where I was standing, a stripling of my company had just finished loading and was in the act of setting the cap intent only at what was ahead of him in the bushes beyond," said Private Minnich. "Forrest leaned over and patting him on the shoulder said 'Go to it my little man.' I'll never forget the look in Bob [Brison's] eyes as he turned and saw who it was addressing him. He rushed forward to a big pine, laid his gun against the side of it and let drive. . . . But the fun was in the fact that the night before Bob's horse had

"Hold on boys, the infantry is coming." General Forrest reassures
his tired troopers.

stepped on his gun and bent the barrel about five degrees, so that if he fired at Croxton . . . [Van Derveer] on his right was in danger."[22]

Croxton was about to find himself in graver danger than Minnich or his grimy and thirsty comrades could have imagined. A little after 9:00 A.M., Wilson's Georgia Brigade swept north across the Brotherton road toward Croxton's right. On the brigade right with his Seventy-fourth Indiana, Colonel Charles Chapman was the first to spot the Georgians. As his skirmish line melted away, Chapman struggled to retire his right flank companies to meet the enemy. In the din his order was misunderstood, and the entire regiment began to withdraw. Chapman was saved by the quick thinking of Croxton, who sent the Tenth Kentucky at the double-quick time from the brigade left to shore up the fast-disintegrating right. The Kentuckians pushed past Chapman's confused Hoosiers and lined up in time to deliver a volley that momentarily halted Wilson. Chapman gathered up his men and reformed on the right of the Tenth. Meanwhile, Croxton disengaged his remaining regiments from their pointless shooting match with Davidson's cavalrymen and filed them by the right to meet Wilson. Croxton now had a single line in the thickets north of the old weed-infested Winfrey cornfield, facing south to confront Wilson head on. It was a fine bit of maneuvering under fire, but Croxton's men were too exhausted from two hours of continuous fighting to offer much resistance. Slowly but steadily, they began to fall back.[23]

Now it was Croxton who sought succor. Tradition has it that the Kentuckian, convinced by the audacity of Forrest's stand and Wilson's unexpected attack that he faced an overwhelming force of infantry, sent Thomas a sardonic dispatch asking which of the four or five enemy brigades in his front was the one he was supposed to capture.[24]

Thomas was not so easily ruffled. Croxton's message found the Virginian seated at a table in the woods on the west side of the La Fayette road opposite the Kelly farm, "taking his breakfast as calmly and coolly as anyone could be who was seated in a much less dangerous locality."[25]

Thomas interrupted his repast to ride forward and look the situation over for himself. The sound of heavy and gradually nearing rifle fire from the right convinced him that Croxton was indeed in trouble. With two brigades engaged and a third (Connell's) nearing the fight, Thomas realized that he was committed to the contest. He therefore sent orders to Absalom Baird, whose division still rested in line of battle south of the Kelly house, to move rapidly to the relief of Croxton, who he said was "hard pressed and almost out of ammunition."

It was a sound decision under the circumstances. Not only would Baird's advance relieve the pressure on Croxton, but the right of his line would likely take the attacking Confederates in the left flank. Guessing correctly that the real threat would come from the southeast and not from Davidson's weary troopers to his front, Thomas hoped to wheel Baird's division to the right and sweep south once Wilson was defeated. Before Baird could do so, someone would have to apply pressure on the enemy to prevent him from sending any more reinforcements to Jay's Mill. Reynolds was still a good two hours away, so Thomas scribbled an appeal directly to Palmer, commander of Crittenden's nearest division, to advance and hold the Confederates in place while he moved against their flank. "The Rebels are reported in quite heavy force between you and Alexander's. . . . If you will advance on them in front while I attack them in flank, I think we can use them up." Thomas sent word of his intentions to army headquarters but apparently not to Crittenden, then waited for Baird to make contact.[26]

The first trace of a fog that was periodically to envelop Federal decision making during the day now rolled in. Crittenden had anticipated a request for help, but not in the way Thomas intended. With the best of intentions and uncharacteristic initiative, he ordered Palmer to send a brigade north at the first sound of firing to reconnoiter the La Fayette road and open communications with him. Palmer passed the mission on to fifty-year-old Colonel William Grose, a reliable brigade commander whom age had not slowed down. Grose had his men on the road a little after 8:00 A.M. A courier from Bragg's headquarters inadvertently stumbled upon his column and was taken prisoner; from him Grose learned only that the Rebels were in force on the west bank. Pushing on, the Ohioan found the way clear. He came into line on Baird's right just minutes before that division went in.

The fog thickened. Thomas was unaware that Grose had already arrived on his right when he penned his note to Palmer. Palmer, in turn, felt he lacked the authority to recommend an advance to Crittenden until Grose returned. Grose was caught in the middle. He applied to division headquarters for permission to attack with Baird, but Palmer ordered him to return. Two precious hours were lost while Grose marched back and forth along the La Fayette road.[27]

Rosecrans's response was no more helpful. Although Colonel Sanderson had been with Thomas two hours earlier and heard the opening guns of Croxton, Rosecrans seemed unprepared to credit fully either Thomas's analysis of the situation on his front or the colonel's ears. He declined to commit the rest of Palmer's division as Thomas wished but had too much respect for the Virginian to forbid him to use his discretion in deploying his own troops. In the end, he simply urged caution: "The general commanding does not think you should commit yourself to any considerable movement before we hear from our extreme left. The rumor that the enemy is between

Alexander's and Reed's bridges can hardly be true.... The general commanding directs you to reconnoiter thoroughly before moving out in force."[28]

Forrest was taking a more direct approach to getting reinforcements. Ector's brigade of the Reserve Corps was only a half mile away in the Youngblood field. If Walker was an impediment to swift action, Forrest would simply ignore him. When Dibrell made contact with Van Derveer, Forrest called up Ector himself. Like Thomas, Forrest was searching out his opponent's flanks. Ector reported in at 9:30 A.M. Wilson was driving Croxton smoothly on the left, so Forrest sent Ector's Texans in to shore up Dibrell's flagging attack on the right.

Brigadier General Matthew Ector was a man whom Forrest could understand. Like Forrest, Ector had risen from the ranks. A prominent attorney and member of the Texas state legislature before the war, the forty-one-year-old native Georgian eschewed an officer's commission and enlisted as a private in Hogg's Texas brigade in 1861. His talents were too obvious to go unnoticed, and he was soon plucked from the ranks and made brigade adjutant. Promotions came swiftly. He was handed the colonelcy of the Fourteenth Texas Cavalry in August 1862 and two weeks later won a brigadier general's commission for gallantry in action during the invasion of Kentucky. At Stones River, Ector's brigade had helped crush the drowsy and unsuspecting troops of the Union Right Wing in the early morning hours of New Year's Eve, 1862.[29]

Here at Chickamauga, the going would be tougher. Van Derveer was ready for Ector. "We on the left of our line heard the steady and heavy tramp of many feet a full minute before they came into sight, and the warning was sent along the line," recalled Captain Donahower. The Rebels emerged from the smoke, and Van Derveer's frontline regiments opened fire. This was the critical moment for Ector: whether to rush the enemy and try to sweep him away by shock and audacity or halt and hope to wear him down in a slugging match, trading volley for volley. Ector chose the latter course. He halted his line and returned the Federal fire.

Ector's men never had a chance. Lieutenant Frank Smith's Regular battery tore gaping holes in their lines, and the Georgian had no battery of his own with which to reply. Captain John Morton, Forrest's youthful chief of artillery who was celebrating his twenty-first birthday under fire, tried to support Ector, but his gunners overshot their mark and landed only a few rounds amidst the luckless Eighty-seventh Indiana on the crest of the ridge. The unequal contest lasted perhaps thirty minutes before Ector withdrew, shortly after 10:30 A.M. So handily was he repelled that many Federal officers did not recognize his as an attack distinct from that of Dibrell; Captain Donahower said his company fired only five volleys in the skirmish.

Connell made a belated appearance with his demi-brigade just as the smoke cleared. Ironically, Brannan's presence had hindered his arrival. Brannan could not make up his mind who to reinforce—Van Derveer or Croxton—and so for nearly ninety minutes had compelled Connell to march and countermarch through the dense thickets. Brannan finally settled on dispatching only the Thirty-first Ohio to Croxton, and Connell was at last able to march uninterrupted to Van Derveer. Once there, Connell tried to be helpful. He placed Church's Battery D, First Michigan Artillery, and the Seventeenth Ohio on Van Derveer's right and held the Eighty-second Indiana in reserve. Even with these additional forces, Van Derveer gave no thought to seeking out the enemy. He merely replaced the Thirty-fifth Ohio with the Eighty-seventh Indiana and waited.[30]

The arrival of the Thirty-first Ohio to support Croxton was a bit more timely. The Ohioans dropped their knapsacks at the Kelly farm, and "the boys looked anxiously at the pile . . . as we moved away, leaving our wardrobe forever." For the Thirty-first it was a steady march "through the woods right toward the wicked noise, which had increased to a steady roll. . . . The regiment went on and on into the depths of the wilderness of pines, remembered Sergeant S. A. McNeil of Company F. "We could smell burnt powder. The little birds seemed frightened as they flew among the branches above us. A deafening crash, followed by the familiar rebel screams, was the prelude to a double-quick step that sent us forward." The regiment halted behind Croxton's line while their colonel reported them present. In those brief moments, recalled a member of Company I, "thoughts of home came rushing through our brains. A few days before we had been jubilant at the thought of meeting the enemy soon, but now the zip and whiz of the bullets coming so near dampened our ardor very decidedly. Visions of contraband chickens we had appropriated for the good of the service floated before our eyes and we wondered who would eat them if we didn't."[31]

Croxton was able to insert the Thirty-first Ohio into the left of his line moments before Wilson attacked, but the extra regiment made little difference. His own men were nearly out of ammunition and had already retired four hundred yards, having left behind a mortally wounded Colonel William Carroll of the Tenth Indiana, the first field officer of either army to fall. It was an open question how much longer they would hold on before giving way altogether.

Help came not a moment too soon. First to arrive was the Regular Brigade of Brigadier General John King. The Regulars were something of pariahs in the army. At the outbreak of the war, Congress had passed legislation calling for the creation of ten new regiments for the Regular Army. Each regiment was to consist of three battalions of eight companies, making the battalions large enough to fight as independent commands when necessary. While the field officers were drawn from the old army, line officers and enlisted men were volunteers. Nonetheless, Regular service was stigmatized, and the volunteers often poked fun at the Regulars for their incessant drilling and fastidiousness in camp.[32]

All that was forgotten in the heat of battle. Croxton's men were only too happy to see the Regulars come up behind them. The two brigades began what was one of the most difficult of battlefield maneuvers—a passage of lines while under fire. It began smoothly but rapidly degenerated. Captain George Smith moved his First Battalion, Eighteenth United States Infantry, by the right flank and filed rapidly through the left of Croxton's line. His men deployed into line and opened fire on Wilson's Georgians. Unfortunately, the retreat of Ector's Ninth Texas across their front had distracted the remaining battalions of the Regular brigade, causing them to incline too far to the east. As a result, Smith was left to face Wilson's entire brigade alone.[33]

Smith, though, had nothing to fear. Concerned that Wilson might overextend himself, Forrest ordered the Georgian to break off the pursuit. Before Wilson could comply, Scribner came into action against his left flank, which folded at the first fire of Scribner's skirmishers. Unaware that Ector had gone into battle an hour earlier, Wilson sent a staff officer to the Youngblood farm to urge him to reinforce his left. When the officer returned to report nothing but dead cornstalks in the Youngblood field, Wilson tried to retire his left regiments, only to find they had disintegrated. The Thirtieth Georgia in the center gave way moments later, leaving Wilson with only the Twenty-fifth and Twenty-ninth Georgia on the right, and they too were beginning to waver. Wilson steadied them and then galloped down his line to rally the Thirtieth Georgia, while Scribner continued to march around his left. When the Yankee skirmishers entered the Winfrey field through which Wilson had charged less than half an hour before, Wilson gave up and withdrew. Nearly half his men lay dead or dying in the woods north of the Brotherton road. That night, fewer than 450 men would answer the brigade muster.[34]

Only the prevailing confusion among Baird and his subordinates spared Wilson from annihilation. Baird had advanced with King on the left, Scribner on the right, and Starkweather's brigade in reserve. After Baird moved a few hundred yards Thomas had ordered him to incline to the left in order to come in behind Croxton's line as it fell back. Baird got King and Scribner headed in the right direction, and they attacked Wilson, but somehow he lost track of Starkweather, who had received an order to relieve Croxton directly from Thomas. Starkweather got lost in the woods and marched aimlessly for nearly an hour. He eventually settled on a gradual wheel to the right, passing Croxton as the Kentuckian fell back for ammunition. It was after 11:00 A.M. by the time Starkweather's brigade came to rest along a bare ridge three hundred yards northwest of Winfrey field.[35]

Meanwhile, Scribner was having problems of his own. Grose's well-intentioned appearance on Baird's right before he moved out had given rise to a rumor that Palmer's entire division was advancing across Baird's front, leading Baird to forbid Scribner from firing on Wilson's left flank. By the time the rumor was dispelled, any chance to catch Wilson had passed. Still, Scribner tried to inflict what damage he could. He waved Lieutenant George Van Pelt's Battery A, First Michigan Light Artillery, forward in the hope of throwing a few shells at the departing Confederates. Scribner's infantry hurried after the bouncing limbers, but both were too late. The Georgians escaped across the Winfrey field, hurried along by a few scattered volleys from the Second Ohio.

After Wilson left, Scribner deployed his brigade in a single line on the forward slope of a wooded ridge, behind a worm rail fence at the edge of Winfrey field. His men were unimpressed with their colonel's choice of a position. "We had our knapsacks on and were lying down at full length on our faces with heads down hill. Everybody felt that this was wrong as we could not roll over to reload in that condition," recalled August Bratnober of the Tenth Wisconsin, whose added misfortune it was to be lying directly in front of one of Van Pelt's guns. Neither Scribner nor his regimental commanders apparently took much notice of their soldiers' predicament, nor did the colonel realize that he was missing an entire regiment. Just as Brannan had meddled in the affairs of Connell's brigade, so too did Baird interfere with Scribner's direction of his command. He had told Major Rue Hutchins, commander of the Ninety-fourth Ohio, in the second line on the left, that the brigade was inclining too much to the right. Hutchins consequently wheeled his regiment to the left under the watchful eye of his division commander at the same moment the rest of the brigade was sprinting toward the right after Wilson's retreating Rebels. Then Baird rode off, leaving Hutchins and his Ohioans alone in the deep woods with no sign of their own or any other friendly brigade.[36]

It was 11:00 A.M. For the first time in four hours a hush fell over the forest, broken only by the cries of the wounded and the rustling of moving Federal infantry. On the Confederate side, Wilson and Ector had slipped into the woods south of the Brotherton road to count their losses and regroup. Davidson's exhausted troopers snatched a few minutes' rest on the ridge near Jay's Mill, and Dibrell's Tennesseans reformed across the Reed's Bridge road. On the Union side, Van Derveer and Connell were content to hold their ground, and Croxton had retired to draw ammunition. Baird was busy tinkering with his line and looking for Starkweather. No one on the field cared to renew the contest. If there was to be more fighting, it would have to be started by the thousands of troops, Blue and Gray, then hurrying north toward the smoke-shrouded forest and tiny sawmill.

CHAPTER EIGHT

THEY ARE COMING LIKE A PACK OF WOLVES

As the low thunder from the attack of Wilson and Ector rolled over the Gordon-Lee mansion, Rosecrans became convinced that Thomas had been right. At about the same time, the "strapping tall Butternut" courier from Bragg's headquarters whom Grose had captured an hour earlier was ushered into Rosecrans's presence. He confirmed Thomas's supposition that the Rebel army lay between the La Fayette road and the creek, and offered Rosecrans an additional bit of information, liberally embellished: Bragg, he said, had a huge army that had been reinforced by thirty thousand from Virginia under Longstreet. Rosecrans was in a receptive frame of mind and he completely reversed his thinking. Thirty minutes earlier, he had dismissed Thomas's petition for help as unwarranted. Now he feared that Bragg may have interposed a large force on the Ringgold road with a view to turning the Virginian's left and sealing off the La Fayette road. Rosecrans acted on this assumption, that the battle would be fought on Thomas's front. When Brigadier General Richard Johnson showed up at Crawfish Springs with his division a little after 10:00 A.M., Rosecrans sent him on to Thomas, then set about looking for a new headquarters site nearer the action. Before Johnson's infantry had a chance to clog the road, Rosecrans started north with his staff and cavalry escort "at a most fearful speed, raising a dust that was frightfully suffocating," recalled Sanderson.[1]

Their destination was the little log cabin of Eliza Glenn and her two-year-old son and infant daughter. Her husband, John, had enlisted in the Confederate army just seven months earlier, leaving her pregnant with their second child. He never returned. John fell ill and died in a hospital in far-away Mobile two months after enlisting. From that day, young Eliza was known simply as the "Widow Glenn."

Her home was ideally situated for a headquarters. Perched on a high hill behind what was to become the Union center, it fronted a large cornfield that offered an unobstructed view as far north as the Dyer house and east almost to the La Fayette road. No better vantage point could be had on that part of the field. The journalist William Shanks later ridiculed Rosecrans unfairly for locating his headquarters too far to the rear. In the tangled thickets and deep forest that prevailed on the field of battle, his presence any nearer the front would have accomplished nothing. Indeed, Colonel Sanderson would write that, by late afternoon, the line of battle "was entirely too near for anyone to be there as a looker-on indisposed to hearken to the singing sound of shots and shells or the whistling of bullets." Less than an hour after Rosecrans's arrival, the army's field telegraphers had opened communications with Thomas's headquarters, and by mid-afternoon Dana was able to wire progress reports to Stanton in Washington.

Rosecrans's first act on reaching the Glenn house was one of kindness. He pulled Eliza aside and admonished her to move herself and her children to a place of safety. The frightened widow piled her family and meager furniture into an oxcart, then drove away to pass the battle at the home of the Vittetoe family.[2]

The firing from Thomas's front had shaken Crittenden into action just as it had Rosecrans. Laying aside his orders to hold Lee and Gordon's Mill at all cost, he told Palmer to march rapidly to the aid of Thomas and vigorously attack the enemy in the flank; he could pick up Grose on the way. Crittenden sent word of his action to Rosecrans, who heartily concurred. Crittenden was learning his job, at last.

Palmer's column passed along the La Fayette road in front of the Widow Glenn house at 11:45 A.M. Rosecrans sent a courier to Palmer to suggest he attack "en echelon, keeping your right refused and closing your left well up on Reynolds." Unfortunately, Reynolds's division was not in the front line as Rosecrans assumed but rather three-quarters of a mile to the west of Palmer on the Vittetoe road, just north of the Glenn house. Rosecrans had seen Reynolds pass but in the excitement apparently had wished him into position a good hour before Reynolds could possibly get there. In any case, three Union divisions—those of Reynolds, Palmer, and Johnson— were now rushing to the aid of Thomas. Still, Rosecrans feared for his left. Again he turned to McCook for help. McCook was at Crawfish Springs with Davis's division, awaiting the arrival of Sheridan, who was still two hours to the south. A little before 10:30 A.M., Rosecrans ordered McCook to send Davis on to the Glenn house and to assume command of the right wing of the army, which by then had dwindled to his cousin Edward McCook's cavalry division, Negley's infantry division at Glass's Mill, and Sheridan.[3]

Bragg too had heard the thunder from Jay's Mill. Before Walker could complain that Forrest had filched Ector, Bragg told the Georgian to send him Liddell's division as well. Then, true to character, Bragg hesitated. He had two alternatives, either of which offered a strong promise of success. He could hold to his original plan and attack that part of the Army of the Cumberland still at Lee and Gordon's Mill, or he could strongly reinforce his right and turn Thomas's flank, as Rosecrans feared he would. For nearly an hour Bragg brooded. In the end, he settled on a middle course of committing his troops piecemeal. At 11:00 A.M., he sent word to Frank Cheatham, ordering him to move to the right to support Walker. This was forty-five minutes after Rosecrans had urged Johnson on in the same direction, and, as Colonel Archer Anderson of Hill's staff lamented, "minutes in war decide battles."[4]

For once, Walker and Liddell were thinking alike. They mistook Baird's division for a corps and, giving him credit for an aggressiveness he did not feel, concluded that Baird was about to attack the Confederate right. To forestall it, they agreed to strike first.

Walker and Liddell took every precaution to guard against surprise. Liddell's division was resting along the Alexander's Bridge road a half mile west of the creek when Walker received Bragg's order to move. Although he was nearly three-quarters of a mile south of the Brotherton road and the nearest Federals, Liddell formed his two brigades in line of battle on the spot, with Govan on the left and Walthall on the right, and advanced north through the forest.

Liddell's line had been moving only a few minutes when Walker galloped up to Walthall to report Wilson and Ector badly outnumbered and cut up, and to urge him to move faster. Liddell similarly admonished Govan, cautioning him to look to his left at all times for any sign of Federal reinforcements.

A little after 11:00 A.M., the division passed the Winfrey house, five hundred yards south of Scribner's unsuspecting Federals. There the men halted to dress their lines and cap their rifles. Walthall's brigade was restive. Through an administrative error, the brigade had drawn ammunition too large for the bores of the .57 caliber Enfields most of the men carried; during the fight with Wilder the day before, many of the rifles had choked after firing only a few rounds. While the men loaded and cursed their weapons, Walthall called together his regimental commanders. Wilson and Ector had lost their advantage by stopping to return fire, he told his colonels. He would not repeat their mistake. The brigade was to hold its fire and advance at the double-quick until within one hundred yards of the enemy, at which point the men were to drop to the ground and rest. At Walthall's command, the entire line would rise up and rush the enemy without firing.

At 11:30 A.M., Govan crossed the Brotherton road under the cover of the

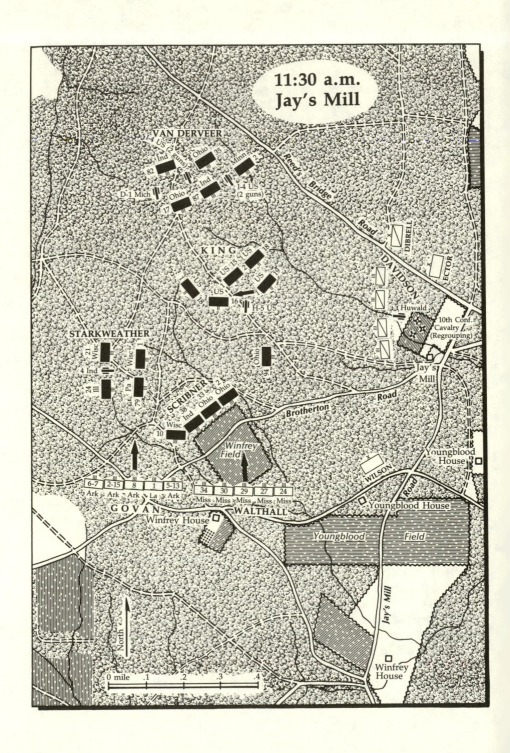

11:30 a.m.
Jay's Mill

VAN DERVEER

82 Ind / Ohio / Minn
D-1 Mich / Ohio / 87 Ind / I-4 US (2 guns)
17

KING
US / US / US
US / US
US
16 / H-5 US

STARKWEATHER

21 Wisc / Wisc
4 Ind / Pa
24 Ill / 79
Ohio / 94

SCRIBNER
38 Ind / 33 Ohio / 2 Ohio
Wisc
10

DIBRELL
DAVIDSON
ECTOR
Huwald
10th Conf.
Cavalry
(Regrouping)
Jay's Mill

Reed's Bridge Road

Brotherton   Road

Winfrey
Field

WILSON

Youngblood
House

6-7 / 2-15 / 8 / 1 / 5-13
Ark / Ark / Ark / La / Ark
GOVAN
Winfrey House
WALTHALL

34 / 30 / 29 / 27 / 24
Miss / Miss / Miss / Miss / Miss

Youngblood House

Youngblood   Field

Jay's Mill

Winfrey
House

North

0 mile .1 .2 .3 .4

forest in a single line of battle. The Sixth and Seventh Arkansas held the left, the Second and Fifteenth Arkansas the left center, the Eighth Arkansas anchored the center, the First Louisiana marched on its right, and the Fifth and Thirteenth Arkansas occupied the right flank.

Walthall's Mississippi brigade stepped into the southern edge of the Winfrey field a few moments later. It too swept forward in a single line, with the Thirty-fourth on the left, the Twenty-fourth on the right, and the Thirtieth, Twenty-ninth, and Twenty-seventh Mississippi in between.[5]

On the far side of the field, Scribner and his colonels were in high spirits. The rout of Wilson had been too easy. "We were all now very happy," recalled the Hoosier. Colonel Oscar Moore of the Thirty-third Ohio laughed and yelled: "They can't fight us; the Bloody First [Brigade] is too much for them." While all were in this "congratulatory state of mind," Scribner noticed his brigade surgeon approach, looking downcast.

"What is the matter, Dr. Miller," he asked.

"I have just been in the hands of the enemy," Miller answered.

"What do you mean?"

"I mean to say that the enemy is in your rear and on your right. They have taken my field hospital with all the wounded. They have captured the provost guard and all the prisoners and are coming down upon you like a pack of wolves," warned Miller.

"The shock of these words and their dreadful import can be better imagined than described. Bracing myself up to meet the impending crisis, every staff officer was dispatched in a different direction," remembered Scribner. "First order of battle, face to the right," the Indianian screamed in an effort to withdraw his right regiments before they were rolled up by Govan. The Thirty-eighth Indiana pulled back to form a right angle with the Thirty-third Ohio on its left. The Tenth Wisconsin followed and formed on the right of the Thirty-eighth, and Van Pelt turned his guns to meet the threat from the south. Private Bratnober found himself once again lying downhill with a cannon looming over his shoulder.[6]

It was a short, bitter fight at close range; the "country being covered with a thick undergrowth of wood was such that it was impossible to see the enemy until we were very close upon him," wrote Lieutenant Colonel John Murray of the Fifth and Thirteenth Arkansas, upon whose regiment the brunt of the fighting fell.

Van Pelt's cannon roared. Bratnober and his comrades grimaced: "The concussion of the guns was terrific and we were fairly bumped against the guns at every discharge." But the gunners were firing too high and the Rebels closed rapidly. Bratnober saw the Eighth Arkansas and Fifth and Thirteenth Arkansas regiments emerge from a timbered ravine less than fifty yards away. The Rebels looked unstoppable. "After the front line fired the next line passed through them, the first line reloading as they came on," said Bratnober, who watched them while awaiting the command to return fire. When it came, the Arkansans recoiled. They rallied and returned the fire, compelling Bratnober and his comrades to stand up under fire to reload. It was more than the Yankees could bear, and they began to run, individually at first, then by squad, until finally the entire regiment broke. The Thirty-eighth Indiana was right behind them. Left without infantry support, Lieutenant Van Pelt and his artillerists stood by their guns firing canister until overwhelmed at the point of the bayonet. Van Pelt and five of his gunners were killed, nineteen were wounded or captured, and nearly all his artillery horses were dead. To the Eighth Arkansas and First Louisiana went the credit for overrunning the Yankee battery.[7]

While Govan battled Scribner's right, Walthall's aggressive charge "worked like a charm" against the Hoosier's left, recalled Captain J. D. Smith of the Twenty-fourth Mississippi. As planned, Walthall's entire line of Mississippians, seventeen hundred strong, lay down in the Winfrey field a hundred yards from the Yankee line to catch their breath, then rose and charged with a yell.

The Second Ohio and Thirty-third Ohio had no chance. Walthall's three right regiments swept past their left, and Govan poured a murderous enfilading fire into their right after capturing the battery. Scribner was too stunned to be of much help. Twenty-four years later, writing of the moment reduced him to incoherent babble: "It seemed as though a terrible cyclone was sweeping over the earth, driving everything before it. All things appeared to be rushing by me in horizontal lines, all parallel to each other. The missiles of the enemy whistling and whirring by, seemed to draw the elements in the same lines of motion, sound, light and air uniting in the rush."

Scribner lost nearly half his men, four hundred of whom surrendered. The rest ran all the way back to the McDonald farm on the La Fayette road. As if the anguish of watching his brigade evaporate was not enough, Scribner faced a personal tragedy when he reached the rear. Lieutenant Colonel Obadiah Maxwell of the Second Ohio, his dearest friend in the brigade, lay on a stretcher beside the McDonald house, blood bubbling and hissing from a bullet hole in his lung. Scribner helped lift Maxwell into an ambulance. Tears clouded his eyes as he laid his friend down. "He wore a light buff vest which was soaked with his blood, which made him a ghastly spectacle to look upon," wrote Scribner. "He was not dead, and ignoring my cause of grief, tried to console me for the reverses of the day, and encourage me with hope of ultimate victory."

No officer in the Army of the Cumberland yet living could possibly have had worse luck than the gallant Maxwell. At Perryville a bullet had broken his leg. He recovered, and was shot in the throat at Stones River. Again he recovered, only to be shot through the chest here at Chickamauga. A third time he recovered and was appointed colonel of a new Ohio regiment. He took a bullet in the groin in its first skirmish. After the war, Maxwell was appointed to a quiet job as an assessor of internal revenue. But fate found a way to wound him even then. While showing some friends a device that a peddler had sold him to prevent burglars from tampering with locks through the explosion of a percussion cap, the contrivance went off unexpectedly. A piece put out one of his eyes. Scribner last saw his old friend at a meeting of the Society of the Army of the Cumberland in Dayton. Maxwell was master of ceremonies and seemed very happy to see his old comrades again. A few weeks later, Scribner opened the newspaper to Maxwell's obituary. He had been found dead in a hotel room with an empty revolver in his hand. "The poor fellow had great trouble, and had lost all his money, and when his comrades departed his mind plunged again into his misfortunes and his balance was lost," Scribner wrote sadly.[8]

Brigadier General John Starkweather was about to experience Scribner's nightmare. The thirty-three-year-old Wisconsin attorney with muttonchops and a warm, bright countenance could not have been in a worse position to receive the Confederate attack had Govan placed his command for him. Govan was coming from the south, but Starkweather's brigade lay atop a hill in two lines, facing due east. The First Wisconsin held the left and the Seventy-ninth Pennsylvania anchored the right of the first line. The Twenty-first Wisconsin, Fourth Indiana Battery, and the Twenty-fourth Illinois formed the second line. Whatever advantage he gained from the high ground, Starkweather lost to the forest and undergrowth, which cut visibility to fifty yards.

Starkweather tried to correct his line when he heard the firing from Scribner's front. He ordered the battery forward and the infantry to face to the south and form a semicircle, then told his adjutant, Lieutenant Charles Searles, to ride to Baird with news of his predicament. The words were scarcely out of Starkweather's mouth when Govan's Arkansans struck and Searles threw up his hands, muttered "Good-bye, General," and rolled off his horse, dead.

The little hill was a whirl of chaos and fear. Lieutenant John Johnston of the Seventy-ninth Pennsylvania had his senses overwhelmed. Somewhere behind him he could hear Starkweather barking commands, but in the din the words were a meaningless garble. Closer at hand, his company commander was weeping. "Steady boys, steady, for God's sake, don't run away," he sobbed, until a bullet cut him down. Another captain fell, then two lieutenants, until the regiment "melted into a panic-stricken mob."

The Pennsylvanians kicked and pushed their way back through the

Twenty-fourth Illinois, which tried desperately to get off a few scattered shots before it too gave way. On the brigade left, the Rebel whirlwind swept everything in its wake, and just minutes after beginning their attack, Govan's Arkansans were regrouping atop the hill among dead and dying Federals and the abandoned guns of the Fourth Indiana Battery.

Lieutenant Johnston choked back the tears as he ran toward the rear: "We are whipped ... disorganized and demoralized. I keep near the colors, and try to gather stragglers around them, but my heart's in my mouth. I feel more like crying than anything else. The 'Old Brigade' that we have all been boasting about is disgraced, and we, who never ran before, are completely broken up—not a regiment or company left."

While the men caught their breath along the La Fayette road, Starkweather rode up and down swearing through his grief: "The old Second Brigade has run away from the enemy today. It never ran before, and by God it shall never run away again, or if it does I will leave my body on the field! I tell you here that you hold my life in your keeping, for if there is any more running I'll be damned if I run with you!"[9]

Scribner had lost half his brigade. Starkweather had watched his unravel in the wink of an eye. Now it was Brigadier General John King's turn to feel ashamed. Baird was with him, helping King swing his line around to meet Walthall's onslaught. They got only Battery H, Fifth United States Artillery, and the First Battalion, Sixteenth United States Infantry, into position before the Mississippians struck. Walthall's attack was over almost before it began. Before being engulfed, Battery H fired just four rounds, one of which sent the top of a black oak tree spinning down on Walthall and his horse, causing him more entanglement than injury. The Thirty-fourth, Thirtieth, and Twenty-ninth Mississippi all converged on the battery. "Every regiment capturing artillery in battle was entitled to the crossed cannon and name of the battle on their regimental flag, and that was a grand inducement to get men to charge batteries where it looked like instant death," explained R. A. Jarman of the Twenty-seventh Mississippi.

Death came instead to the battery commander, Lieutenant Howard Burnham, and twelve of his gunners, who stood by their pieces to the last. The Federal infantry gave a slightly better account of itself here than it had in support of Van Pelt, but to no avail. Lying in front of the guns, the Sixteenth United States was quickly surrounded, and of the 258 Regulars who marched into battle that morning, only 62 escaped.[10] Captain Henry Freeman of the First Battalion, Eighteenth United States Infantry, was chatting with a friend in the Sixteenth when the attack came. He ran to his horse and slipped a foot in the stirrup just as a bullet whizzed by the animal's head. It jumped suddenly, Freeman fell on his back, and the horse galloped toward the enemy lines dragging the captain by the foot. As he bounced over the ground and through the bushes, Freeman glimpsed the Rebels drawing near. He kicked and pulled until his foot came free and he rolled to a stop. Freeman lay perfectly still while the Rebel line marched past him, then began edging his way through the woods toward the La Fayette road. When he rejoined the battalion later in the day, he found his horse standing in its usual spot next to the battalion commander.[11]

Freeman was lucky to have missed the fighting. His battalion lost over one hundred men while firing scarcely a shot in return. It was the same throughout the brigade. Outflanked and confused, Regulars surrendered by the score.[12]

Those who could, ran. Their flight led them toward the brigades of Van Derveer and Connell. Lieutenant Colonel Bishop of the Second Minnesota watched as the terrified Regulars stampeded his line: "The firing broke out again; first the scattering fire of skirmishers—then the terrific file firing of regiments, then the artillery, then the Rebel yell, and the firing gradually approaching us. We stood attentive and expectant for a few minutes, then a straggling line of men in blue appeared coming toward us in wild retreat, their speed accelerated by the firing and yelling of the exultant Confederates who were close behind them. I do not remember any more appalling spectacle than this was for a few minutes." Regulars screamed, "The whole Rebel army is before us; we will all be killed," as they entered Van Derveer's lines. Even the officers panicked. They shouted to the volunteers to save themselves and retreat, and Van Derveer smiled approvingly when Private Robert Savage of Smith's battery flattened one of them with his sponge for having run into his cannon.

The survivors of the Eighteenth United States stumbled toward Captain Donahower's company. "We yelled, come in men, and they did come but seemed confused, not knowing what to do next, but we said go back and reform," wrote the Minnesotan. He watched in disgust as the color-bearer tossed aside the regimental colors fifty yards in front of his line. Donahower and his first sergeant shamed a sergeant and two soldiers from the Eighteenth into running the gauntlet of Rebel fire to retrieve their standard.[13]

The panic did not affect Van Derveer's or Connell's men. They had replenished their cartridge boxes after Ector's attack and now lay quietly while the Regulars ran through their ranks and the cheering Rebels drew near. When the Mississippians had closed to within forty yards, the Federals rose up and delivered a volley that brought the stunned Mississippians to an abrupt halt. The ten guns of Church's and Smith's batteries swept the field with canister, and Walthall's line began to back out of range.[14]

At that moment Colonel Gustave Kammerling rode up behind the Second Minnesota at the head of his Ninth Ohio Infantry. It was an all-German regiment, using German tactics and speaking only German. The Ninth began the day in the rear, guarding the corps ammunition train, a duty that Kammerling and his men resented as an ethnic slur. At the first sound of firing, Kammerling "raved and tore around about . . . attacking every general officer he met and asking to be ordered to his command, until finally he succeeded in getting an order to rejoin his brigade."[15]

Now Kammerling feared he had missed the action. "Where dem got tam rebels gone," he yelled angrily at no one in particular. Someone pointed to the front. Without hesitating a moment, Kammerling formed line of battle and led his men past the bemused Minnesotans on the run. Van Derveer yelled at him to come back, but his voice was drowned out by the German cheers. Van Derveer sent his adjutant, Captain John R. Beatty, after Kammerling and then saw to it that no one else tried to join in the fun, halting the Eighty-seventh Indiana the moment it started forward. The hapless Connell, on the other hand, merely watched as his Seventeenth Ohio disappeared into the woods after the Ninth.[16]

Kammerling and his 502 Germans must have looked like a brigade to Walthall's tired Mississippians. They struck the Twenty-seventh and Twenty-fourth Mississippi head on and completely lapped Walthall's right flank. The Mississippians fell back rapidly past Burnham's ruined battery, and the Germans swarmed around the abandoned cannons.

There, a little before noon, Captain Beatty caught up with Kammerling. "I found the 'Bloody Ninth' in possession of a six-gun battery and all talking at once. I will never forget how the bully Dutchmen looked, all in one big mass around the captured guns and all talking," smiled Beatty. "I had lost my hat in the rough ride, and shouted orders to Kammerling to bring his regiment back quick. He yelled: 'I have gaptured a battery, vot shall I do mit dis battery?' " The orders to withdraw were peremptory, explained Beatty, and the Germans started back, leaving the cannons to stand sentinel over the dead and dying.[17]

Kammerling had not yet returned when Van Derveer's brigade faced its fourth attack of the morning, this time from a new and wholly unexpected direction. Forrest had ordered Dibrell to march his dismounted troopers by the right flank north across the Reed's Bridge road and assault Van Derveer's left and rear the moment Ector showed signs of wavering.

Out on the brigade skirmish line, Captain Donahower was the first officer to spot the movement. Concerned for the safety of his left, Donahower had sent a corporal with a small detail into the woods beyond the flank to reconnoiter. A private returned breathlessly a few moments later. The corporal, he said, had spotted a long column of Rebels crossing the road. Donahower followed the private to where the detail was peering through the trees. He stooped down and pushed aside the brush. Confederate battle flags flapped in the breeze just beyond. Donahower ran to Major Davis, who had ridden out to the skirmish line, and passed the warning. Davis galloped back to the regiment with the news, and Lieutenant Colonel Bishop instantly ordered it to change front to the east, then file to the left across the road. The regimental commander, Colonel James George, was hobbled by an attack of rheumatism and could do little more than look on approvingly while Bishop did the hard work. Van Derveer repeated the command down the brigade line.[18]

It was a foot race into position between Van Derveer's Federals and Dibrell's Tennesseans that the Yankees won. In a matter of minutes, Van Derveer had a new line of battle across the road facing north, at right angles to his previous line. He had an imposing force. The Thirty-fifth Ohio held the left. On its right was a two-gun section from Smith's battery. Next came Church's entire battery, then the Eighty-seventh Indiana, the remaining two guns of Smith's battery, and the Second Minnesota. Connell's Eighty-second Indiana formed in reserve. Van Derveer had lost only about 250 men repelling three charges of the enemy; with the addition of the Eighty-second Indiana he now mustered nearly eighteen hundred men to oppose Dibrell's small command of dismounted cavalry. The Tennesseans put on a brave front, winning the admiration of the Federals for their ability to march in "orderly array" through the tangled thicket. But drill and courage were not enough. Church's battery and Smith's left section belched double-shotted canister, and Dibrell's entire front line disintegrated in gore. The Yankee infantry opened fire, and his second line melted into the ground. The Thirty-fifth Ohio wavered, but Dibrell could not exploit even this small success. Van Derveer's right extended beyond Dibrell's left flank, and when the right section of Smith's battery opened into his dazed Tennesseans, they dove into the brush to escape the fire. Dibrell's cavalrymen came no closer than forty yards, and in a few minutes disappeared into the smoke and the forest.

The day was over for Van Derveer's men, who marched back up the Reed's Bridge road to refill their cartridge boxes. They had withstood four separate attacks in as many hours, all over a forested tract of only fifty square acres.[19]

Daniel Govan and his Arkansans ran into trouble about the same time as Walthall. Heeding Liddell's warning to "look well to his left flank," Govan moved more cautiously than had Walthall. He ordered Colonel D. A. Gillespie, commander of his left regiment, the Sixth and Seventh Arkansas, to deploy skirmishers beyond his flank and to swing his entire command in that direction at the first hint of blue.

The Arkansans barely had begun their descent of the ridge from which they had swept Starkweather when they encountered a long line of blue arrayed along the crest of the next ridge to the northwest. A handful of

Arkansans fell back to turn the captured cannon of Van Pelt and Flansburg's batteries on the Federals.

Their new foe was Croxton's brigade, which had been ordered back into action when Scribner was attacked. "The men, although wearied from the loss of sleep and hours [of] hard fighting, responded to the summons with the greatest alacrity," Colonel William Hays of the Tenth Kentucky observed with pride. Croxton deployed his six regiments four hundred yards northwest of King, facing south toward the sound of the fighting. Unable to see the length of a single regiment, Croxton wisely divided command responsibility, assigning the right half of the brigade to Colonel Chapman of the Seventy-fourth Indiana.

For perhaps thirty minutes the two lines traded volleys at will before Liddell's fears for his left were realized, as Govan ironically became the victim of his own precautions. Apparently construing the efforts of the skirmishers of the Sixth and Seventh Arkansas to protect their left flank as the prelude to an attack on his own right flank, Colonel Chapman decided to preempt the move with a charge of his own. Down the slope rushed Chapman and his three regiments. A bullet hit Chapman's mount, and horse and rider collapsed in a heap. Chapman crawled out from under his dead horse with a broken arm. He straightened up and staggered in pain after his men.

The Arkansans knew they were beaten. They broke in confusion, setting off a panic that gradually ran the length of Govan's line. Lieutenant Colonel John Murray, whose Fifth and Thirteenth Arkansas (Consolidated) had been holding their own against the foe to their front, was at a loss to understand the sudden confusion on his left that now threatened his own line. He gave his all to steadying the men until his major, P. V. Green, galloped up to suggest they retreat: the Yankees were not only on their left flank but had suddenly appeared behind them. Murray accepted his major's advice and marched the regiment rapidly off the field by the right flank a few minutes before noon. Govan saw the new enemy line as well and led the rest of the brigade out of danger ahead of Murray.[20]

Croxton's men paused in their pursuit just long enough to savor the capture of what they thought were two abandoned Rebel batteries. A little disappointed to learn that his spoils were actually the remains of Van Pelt's and Flansburg's batteries, Croxton ordered details to drag the cannons to the rear to their rightful owners, and then pressed his brigade forward.[21]

Liddell had also caught a glimpse of the mysterious Union line that was slowly working its way in behind Govan's brigade. The Mississippian need not have felt any shame in ordering his brigades off the field. For the enemy unseen was far greater than he, Govan, or Major Green could have imagined. Stretching nearly a mile, from the Kelly field to the Brotherton farm, and on the move eastward, were the six brigades of Johnson and Palmer. For the moment, Rosecrans was winning the race for control of the La Fayette road.

CHAPTER NINE

WE SHALL SOON BE IN IT

THOMAS was immensely relieved to see the divisions of Johnson and Palmer. Interrogation of prisoners confirmed Thomas's belief that Bragg had been reinforced from Virginia and Mississippi. Now two fears plagued him. As the morning wore on, the Virginian had come to share Rosecrans's suspicion that Bragg might try to envelop his left flank and cut him off from Rossville. To guard against it, he placed Baird's division and the brigades of Connell and Van Derveer between the McDonald house and the Reed's Bridge road once they recovered from the shock of their first combat. At the same time, the attacks of Wilson, Ector, and Liddell had deepened his concern for the two-mile gap between his right flank and Crittenden at the mill. As early as 10:45 A.M., with Reynolds still at least an hour away, Thomas had applied to Crittenden for a second division before Palmer was even on the road.[1]

For the moment, Thomas had given up any notion of turning the Confederate flank and was anxious merely to plug the gap in the Federal lines and attack straight ahead, if at all. This was the mission he assigned to Johnson when he came on the field. Thomas was on hand when the head of Johnson's column shuffled up the Glenn-Kelly road on the last leg of its march. He rode with Johnson to the southern edge of the Kelly field shortly after noon, waved his arm across its expanse and toward the woods to the south, and told him to form line of battle and attack the enemy wherever he found them.

They were simple orders, too vague for many, but for Johnson they were enough. The thirty-six-year-old West Point graduate had served under Thomas on the western frontier before the war, and Thomas had come to trust his judgment implicitly. Johnson hailed from Kentucky. Like Thomas, he had turned down a commission in the Confederate army to stand by the Union. For his loyalty, he was rewarded with a brigadier general's star. Although most shared Captain E. T. Wells's opinion of him as "a man of noble presence, of the greatest personal worth and amiability, and filled with the lofty traditions of the old army," the Kentuckian had fallen on hard times of late. A year earlier, he had vowed to capture the elusive Rebel raider John Hunt Morgan and "bring [him] back in a band box." Instead, Johnson himself was defeated and captured by his numerically inferior foe near Gallatin, Tennessee. He was exchanged just in time to join the army for the march on Murfreesboro, where his division was shattered in the opening minutes of the battle of Stones River. Certainly Johnson was anxious now to prove himself worthy of Thomas's continued confidence.[2]

He arranged his division with great care. The brigade of Colonel Philemon Baldwin filed off the La Fayette road and into a double line of battle on the division left, Brigadier General August Willich led his brigade into a double line on the right, and Colonel Joseph Dodge fell in behind the center as the divisional reserve. Battery commanders were cautioned to keep their guns well behind the infantry, so as not to share the fate of Baird's artillery. The men stacked their knapsacks, pulling out the handful of keepsakes and other precious articles they could not live without in the very likely event they never saw their packs again, then lay down in line to wait. Every impression, every thought was burned into their memories; moments of life were dear where death waited so near. Twenty-three years later, as he recalled those minutes, Sergeant I. K. Young of Dodge's brigade could still see the sunlight sparkling through the trees and smell the Southern pine: "The birds were singing, the butterflies fluttering about, and a cow stood under a tree to our right and lazily chewed her cud and switched away the flies. . . . It was autumn, and the scene was so quiet and peaceful that our eyes would have grown sleepy had we not known that ten minutes more were to change it into a raging hell. In the woods behind us we could hear the tramp of regiments and brigades. In the forest across the peaceful meadow large masses of the enemy were coming into position."[3]

The scenes that Colonel Allen Buckner of the Seventy-ninth Illinois saw while he waited were not of this world. Spare of frame and stern of countenance, Buckner looked every bit the hellfire-and-brimstone preacher he had been before the war. Buckner heard the call at the age of ten and never looked back. A fire swept through him before every battle, just as it first had one March night eighteen months earlier near Elkhorn Tavern, Arkansas:

The evening before we all knew that we must go into battle the next day. I was conscious that I was a coward. We slept in the woods on our arms. That is, others slept. I went to a convenient place from time to time and prayed, asking God to help me. I kept this up all night and was on my knees when the first streak of day appeared, when suddenly my whole being was thrilled by a flood of light and I was assured that I would be able to do my duty and that I never would be killed in battle. With this feeling the dread of personal danger was removed.

The light bathed Buckner here in the Georgia forest, leaving him at peace with his God. Then he looked to his men, "standing in line of battle pale and trembling, fighting the battle with themselves." Buckner rode down the line. At each company he paused and addressed his troops in the somber thunder of the pulpit. "We shall soon be in it and many of us will fall but I hope all will stay in their place and do their duty," he began. Then to his real point. "Boys, if there is anything to settle with your God you better attend to that at once."[4]

Three hundred yards to their right, the same dramas, great and small, were being played out in Palmer's division, which had come up after Johnson. Like Johnson, Palmer was deploying his brigades carefully. He decided to take Rosecrans's suggestion that he advance en echelon, and was forever grateful he had. He ordered Hazen to move his brigade forward in line of battle five hundred yards into the woods and there halt and pull back his right. Then he sent Cruft four hundred yards forward on Hazen's right with the same instructions. Finally he moved Grose up three hundred yards on Cruft's right. Palmer now had his division "en echelon by brigades with the right refused," one hundred yards separating each from the other.

On Hazen's staff, helping to shepherd the regiments into line, was a twenty-one-year-old lieutenant with an outlook perhaps unique among the 135,000 men at Chickamauga; certainly none could better express their vision of humanity. "From childhood to youth is eternity; from youth to manhood, a season. Age comes in a night, and is incredible," Ambrose Bierce would one day write. And of the patriotism that led him into battle, he would later say:

> My country, 'tis of thee
> Sweet land of felony,
>   Of thee I sing —
> Land where my fathers fried
> Young witches and applied
> Whips to the Quaker's hide
>   And made him spring.

Bierce's brutal realism and wicked wit would liberate and transform American fiction; Crane, Lewis, and Mencken would all dip their pens in his bile. But for now, Bierce was just another promising if odd young lieutenant, and with the rest of his command — the famous, the footnoted, and the forever obscure — he stepped off into the forest. If anyone had chanced to glance at his watch, he would have noticed it was 12:35 P.M.[5]

Captain Cumming lost count of the number of times he had mounted and dismounted during the ninety minutes Liddell's division was in action to write Bragg for reinforcements at the behest of General Walker. Shortly after noon, they came. Cumming was as happy as anyone to see the long Butternut column running toward him through the woods, but his stomach turned when he realized that it was Brigadier General John Jackson's brigade of Cheatham's division.

Less than a month before, Cumming had been Jackson's adjutant; now they were bitter enemies. Their falling-out stemmed from the most trivial of causes. One day in August, lost in the numbing routine of his clerical duties, Cumming had approved a voucher for stationery from the brigade quartermaster for twenty dollars. He thought nothing more of it until Jackson stormed into his office waving the voucher. In a tone that implied Cumming had been dipping into brigade funds, the general upbraided him for signing it. The suggestion of malfeasance enraged the captain. He snatched the voucher out of Jackson's hand, tore it up, and said he would pay for the stationery himself. Jackson grew hot. He ordered Cumming to reproduce the voucher. Cumming refused, walked out of the room, and lay down in his tent, expecting to be arrested and brought up on charges.

Nothing happened. Cumming returned to his duties the next morning. Carefully tucked in the stack of papers that he brought to Jackson for the general's signature during the day was his resignation. Jackson endorsed it: "Respectfully forwarded approved. On a recent occasion Captain Cumming failed to obey a positive order I gave him, and I recommend that his resignation be accepted." Cumming read the endorsement and threw it into the fire, shouting "This paper shall not go forward!" Jackson snatched it from the flames.

"General," Cumming said after he regained his composure. "You propose to do me a great wrong. We have just gone through a bloody battle. Anyone reading that endorsement would be free to believe that the order you gave me was on the battlefield, and that I failed to obey from sheer cowardice."

Jackson relented. "I hadn't thought of that view," he admitted, then threw the paper back into the fire. Cumming wrote out another resignation, which Jackson simply forwarded: "Approved."

Now the two were at it again. Jackson ordered his column into line by a movement that Cumming claimed would have taken far more time than was prudent. "I told him that in my opinion the movement was too slow, and that he would be caught in the midst of it as the enemy was near at hand, and that he should pivot on his right and wheel to the right into line. He acted on the suggestion and had hardly gotten into line when he was attacked," Cumming recalled with smug satisfaction.[6]

Walker had ridden off to consult with Cheatham and so was not there to settle the squabble. Like Richard Johnson, Cheatham needed a victory to restore the luster to his tarnished reputation. A hard fighter and a hard drinker, the forty-two-year-old Nashville native was intensely loved by the troops of his division, the majority of whom were Tennesseans like him. Sadly, the bottle sometimes got the better of him, and at Stones River he had appeared before his command blind drunk at the height of the struggle. Bragg despised him, and Cheatham heartily returned his commander's contempt.

Certainly Cheatham looked the part of the warrior. He was squarely built, standing five feet eight inches and weighing a hefty two hundred pounds, and was known in the army for his extraordinary strength. Regardless of what some might whisper of his drinking, none questioned his integrity and courage.[7]

Cheatham was on his own here at Chickamauga — Polk was busy shuttling between army headquarters at Thedford's Ford and Hindman's division opposite Lee and Gordon's Mills — and this time he rose to the occasion. While Cumming helped maneuver Jackson into line behind a hill at the southern fringe of the Winfrey farm, Cheatham arranged his remaining four brigades. The Tennessee brigade of Brigadier General Preston Smith lined up in the forest west of the Alexander's Bridge road on Jackson's left. Brigadier General Marcus Wright formed his five regiments to the left of Smith. Cheatham held the brigades of Maney and Strahl in reserve, and at 12:30 P.M. sent his frontline brigades forward with a reminder that the division could expect no support on either flank.

Cheatham had deployed his division well. His front extended nearly a mile, longer than the tactics manuals suggested but precisely what was needed to confront the advance of Johnson and Palmer.[8]

As Captain Cumming had feared, Jackson's brigade was engaged almost instantly. During their argument, Cumming apparently had neglected to impress upon Jackson the disordered state of Liddell's troops, most of whom had drawn off to the east beyond Jackson's right by then, and the Georgian neglected to deploy skirmishers on the assumption his command constituted a reserve line behind Liddell. The dropping fire of Federal skirmishers quickly convinced him of his error. The Fifth Georgia on the brigade left reeled momentarily before the fire but its commander steadied his line, and in a few minutes the brigade was exchanging volleys with the main line of the enemy.

Jackson had run into Croxton's brigade, which had swept southeast over the scene of Scribner's defeat in pursuit of Govan and was marching toward the Winfrey farm at the same time Jackson moved through it. It was a stand-up fight that Croxton's men lacked the strength to sustain. They had marched all night, missed breakfast, and been in battle for over five hours, with only a short pause to draw ammunition. After thirty minutes of bitter fighting the weary Federals began to give way.[9]

Jackson's men pushed the Yankees steadily for a half mile, across the Brotherton road into the forest beyond. They watched Croxton's brigade vanish behind a long ridge, then scampered over it themselves, intent on continuing the pursuit. What they saw on the other side brought the Rebels to an abrupt halt. Three hundred yards away, Brigadier General August Willich's brigade marched toward them with the quiet assurance of soldiers taught to believe in themselves by a commander they venerated.

There was perhaps no officer in either army more thoroughly trained than the fifty-two-year-old Prussian immigrant, and few who better understood the sacrifices that democracy demanded. Born into German aristocracy as August von Willich, he had entered the military academy at Potsdam at the age of twelve; six years later he was commissioned a second lieutenant in the royal artillery. Willich's unabashedly republican sentiments assured the failure of his military career. Thirteen years passed before his promotion to captain, and his attempted resignation five years later met with a transfer to a lonely outpost in Pomerania. The Prussian persevered. He finally submitted a personal letter of resignation to the king so irreverent that he was court-martialed. Surprisingly, he was acquitted and allowed to resign in 1846. For the next two years he supported himself as a carpenter, a scandalous vocation for one of his class and station. When the tide of revolution swept over Germany in 1848, Willich offered his services to the revolutionists, rising to corps command before defeat at the battle of Candarn forced him to flee to Switzerland.

Willich arrived in the United States in 1853, middle-aged and penniless and fired by a quixotic ambition to raise an army of immigrants to invade Germany and establish the republic of which he dreamed. In the struggle to earn a living he forgot his plans, and by 1858 Willich was a respected member of the German community in Cincinnati, where he at last could freely express his ideals of democratic socialism as editor of the *Deutscher Republikaner*.

At the outbreak of the war, Willich, then fifty years old, humbly enlisted as a private in the Ninth Ohio, a reaffirmation of his commitment to democracy. The commander of the regiment, Colonel Robert McCook, recognized a good thing when he saw it, and immediately pulled Willich from the ranks and promoted him to major. Willich took over the training of the regiment with the blessing of the genial McCook, who was happy to tend to matters of supply and personnel. So completely did the regiment come to rely on Willich that McCook, when addressed as "Colonel" by friends, replied laughingly that he was no colonel, but merely "clerk to a thousand Dutchmen."[10]

As a brigade commander, averred Captain Wells of the division staff, Willich lavished the same "intelligent, fatherly care" on his command that had won him the love of the men of the Ninth. Sergeant Alexis Cope of the Fifteenth Ohio recalled the training that made Willich's one of the most reliable and proficient brigades in the army: "Usually in military operations the regiment was the unit. But with General Willich in command . . . the brigade was the unit. The regiments . . . were skillfully commanded . . . but in time of action all looked to General Willich as the directing mind, trusted him with the utmost confidence and followed him implicitly. We had our company and regimental drills, but the brigade drill was that to which most attention was given, and it was always given with battle movements and battle emergencies in view."[11]

Here at Chickamauga, Willich had the situation well in hand. Seeing that Baldwin had lagged behind on his left and that Hazen had diverted from his right toward the Brock field, the Prussian halted his brigade two hundred yards west of Jackson. He ordered his men to the ground to escape the fire of Scogin's Georgia battery, which was posted on the ridge opposite the Forty-ninth Ohio, then called up a section of his own Battery A, First Ohio Light Artillery, commanded by Captain Wilbur Goodspeed, to silence the Georgians. The two lines settled into desultory firing shortly after 1:00 P.M., each awaiting an opportunity to attack the other.[12]

By then, the entire divisions of Cheatham, Johnson, and Palmer were locked in vicious combat. Hazen had wheeled to the right away from Willich to meet the advance of Preston Smith, whose brigade had driven past Croxton's right and was making for the cornfield of sixty-five-year-old John Brock, whose two sons, John and Roland, wore Confederate gray at Chickamauga. John, the elder of the two, was a good-natured boy who never missed a chance at a joke. Sometime during the course of the battle a bullet plowed a furrow across the top of his head, scalping him but leaving John otherwise unhurt. "If it had been an inch lower it surely would have got you," commented a concerned comrade. "Yes," smiled John, "and if it had gone an inch higher it surely would have missed me." Thankfully, John's father and younger siblings were not at home now.[13]

Hazen won the race for the cornfield. Halting in the woods that fringed its northwest corner, he moved quickly to adjust his lines before plunging across. Already a steady rattle from his skirmish line warned that the Rebels were nearing the field. Shells began shrieking over the farm and bursting among the men, as the cannoneers of Scott's Tennessee Battery felt for the Yankee position. With only the Ninth Indiana and Forty-first Ohio in his first line, Hazen recognized that his narrow brigade front was susceptible to being flanked once he moved into the open. Consequently, he called up the One Hundred Twenty-fourth Ohio from the second line and wedged it into the center of his front line, leaving the Sixth Kentucky as his only reserve. Lieutenant Giles Cockerill kept his Battery F, First Ohio, at a safe distance in the rear.

Hazen certainly would have preferred to leave the One Hundred Twenty-fourth Ohio in reserve as well. It was one of the greenest regiments in the army, having been recruited only nine and a half months earlier. Its commander, Colonel Oliver Payne, tried his best to bring the men forward like veterans, but amid the bursting shells Payne's commands were misunderstood by his frightened and uncertain company commanders. After some coaxing, Payne got seven companies into line on the left of the Forty-first Ohio, but the captains of the remaining three—companies A, H, and D—were either hopelessly confused or terrified. They marched their men in the opposite direction, beyond the right of the Sixth Kentucky, and that was the last anyone saw of them that afternoon.

Captain G. W. Lewis of Company B understood his orders perfectly. Payne told him to take his men out into the field and skirmish with an enemy that lurked somewhere in the forest beyond. His heart pounding, Lewis sprinted forward with his men, all the time thinking that he was more scared than any of them. They took cover in a small skirt of timber that ran through the center of the field just as the skirmishers of Dawson's battalion of sharpshooters drew a bead on them from the forest's edge. Then the horror began. Corporal William Atkins, an ardent abolitionist and former schoolteacher who liked to preach the evils of slavery around the campfire, squeezed off a shot from behind a pine tree next to Lewis. A moment later a bullet tore open his left shoulder. Lewis was aghast. "William, you are badly wounded, go to the rear," he said with as much authority as he could muster. Atkins was not listening; the fever of battle had taken hold of him. Extending his bloody left arm toward Lewis, he replied: "See captain, I am not much hurt, I want to give them another." Lewis merely watched Atkins draw another cartridge from his box, run it down the barrel of his rifle, then fall backward dead when a second bullet ripped through his chest.

A long line of Butternut stepped into the field. Lewis recovered from the shock of seeing the first member of his company killed and ordered the rest to lie down. Behind them, the regiment opened fire on the Rebels. Bullets whizzed overhead in both directions, making it "difficult to tell from which we suffered most, the fire of the enemy, or the bad marksmanship of the line in the rear," remembered Lewis.[14]

There was nothing wrong with the aim of Preston Smith's Tennesseans. Colonel Payne fell, shot through the thigh in the first volley. Colonel George Shackelford of the Sixth Kentucky was knocked off his horse with a minie ball in his right shoulder, and Lieutenant Colonel Richard Rockingham, just returned from sick leave, took over. A cannonball sliced off the leg of

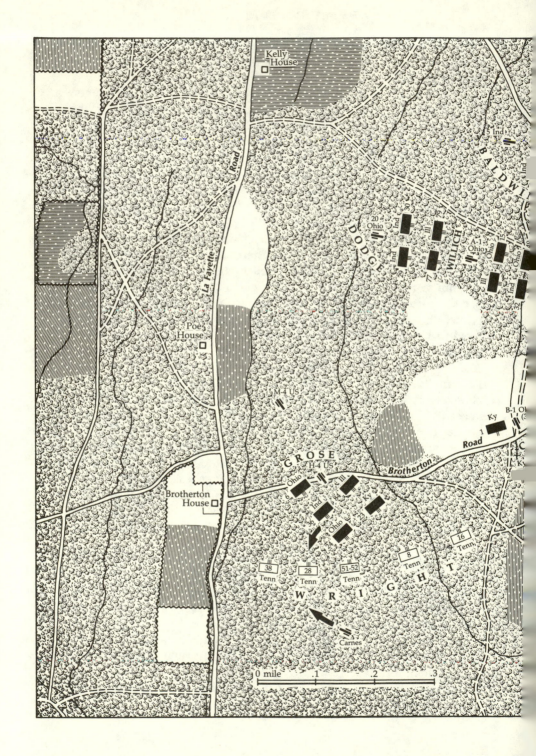

Kelly
House

Road

La Fayette

Poe
House

M-4 US

Brotherton
House

GROSE
H-4 US

Ohio

Ohio

Ky

Ohio

38
Tenn

28
Tenn

51-52
Tenn

8
Tenn

W R I G H T

Carnes

16
Tenn

Brotherton

Road

Ky

1 Ky

B-1 Oh

DODGE

WILLICH

BALDWI

20
Ohio

Ind

30

Ind

Pa

29
Ind

Ohio

A-1
Ohio

Ohio

Ind

89

5 Ind

0 mile   .1   .2   .3

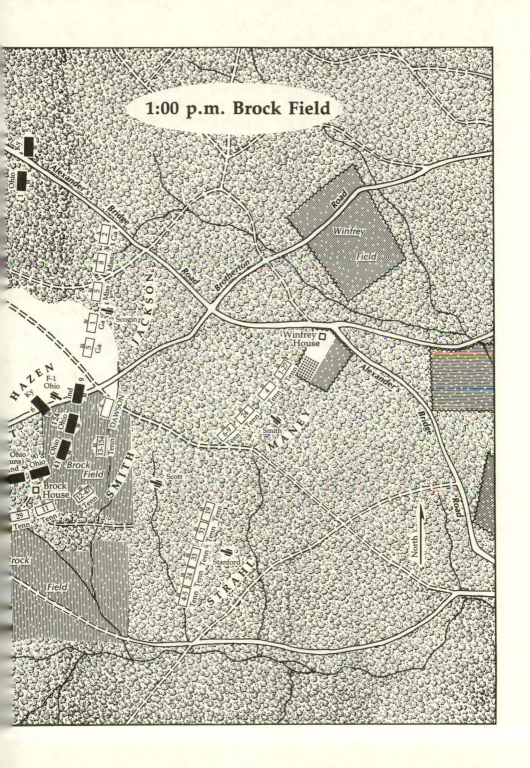

1:00 p.m. Brock Field

Captain Peter Marker of Company G as he walked the line of prone soldiers. Two regimental commanders and countless line officers were down and the brigade main line scarcely had fired a shot, a situation Hazen remedied at once. He ordered the brigade forward, and with a yell it charged into the field. On the other side, Smith's four regiments, arrayed in a single line with Dawson's sharpshooters congregated on the right, threw down the fence at the forest's edge and broke into the open a few minutes later.

Private Jacob Miller of the Ninth Indiana would never forget what happened next. Just as he squeezed the trigger of his rifle, a lead ball bore into his forehead and three buckshot shattered his left orbital bone, leaving the eye dangling from the socket. Miller lay face down a few moments, then slowly stood up. Blood streamed down his shirt. He declined his captain's offer to detail a man to lead him to the rear, stumbled back a few yards dragging his rifle, then blacked out. Hours passed. "At last I became conscious and raised up in a sitting position. Then I began to feel for my wound," remembered Miller. "I found my left eye out of its place and tried to place it back but I had to move the crushed bone back as near together as I could at first. Then I got the eye in its proper place. I then bandaged the eye the best I could with my bandanna. I could hear the firing not far away, some of the bullets even striking near where I was sitting."

Struggling to his feet, Miller searched the field with his good eye for some sign of his comrades. All he saw were the dead and dying. "I did not know which way to go or what to do so I poured some water out of my canteen on the bandage. Then I sat down against a tree with the idea that someone would come past me and would know how to act or what to do." Miller did not have long to wait. Behind him the brush stirred. Out walked a Rebel. "Yank, you got hit pretty bad," the Confederate said with compassion. They talked a few moments, then the Rebel started toward the front to find his unit. Miller watched him go. The kindly Confederate had gone no more than a few yards before a stray bullet struck him dead.

Miller decided to try to find his unit before more Confederates found him. As he rose to his feet, he was diverted from his purpose by a low moaning plea for water. Miller walked to the wounded man, another Rebel. He raised him up and gave him a drink from his canteen. The Confederate looked perplexed. "Well Yank, you come and give me a drink." "Why not?" Miller asked. The embarrassed soldier said he had heard the Yankees were not given to such kindness. Anxious to repay the kindness, the Rebel pointed the direction Miller should walk to avoid the Confederate lines. Miller gave him one last sip and then started on his way, his sight fast growing dim as his good eye began swelling shut.[15]

Hazen and Smith lost control of their brigades in the cornfield as opposing regiments vied for position. Dawson's Sharpshooters and the Thirteenth and

One Hundred Fifty-fourth Tennessee wheeled to the right to challenge the Ninth Indiana and the One Hundred Twenty-fourth Ohio for possession of the northern part of the field; Captain Lewis and his skirmishers got back to the main line just a few steps ahead of the Rebels. Smith's center regiment, the Twelfth and Forty-seventh Tennessee, made for the skirt of timber along a ravine in the middle of the field. The Forty-first Ohio beat the Tennesseans to it and sent a volley into their ranks at short range. Colonel William Watkins ordered his Tennesseans to take cover behind a fence at the southeastern edge of the field and return the fire, and the two lines disappeared in smoke. The cacophony grew. The four guns of Scott's Tennessee battery boomed from the wood-line. Lieutenant Cockerill's Battery F, First Ohio, answered from the woods north of the road.[16]

The Eleventh Tennessee pressed through the western limit of the Brock field, halting in a drainage ditch to Hazen's right, while Smith's left regiment, the Twenty-ninth Tennessee, stumbled through the rocky woods south of the field, skirting past Hazen's flank without even knowing it. It was between 12:30 and 1:00 P.M. The underbrush played havoc with the alignment of the Twenty-ninth, and Colonel Horace Rice paused to reform his line. Suddenly the roar of rifle fire threw his command deeper into confusion. Rice galloped about rather aimlessly as volley after volley ripped through his regiment. Fortunately the Federals had no interest in advancing, and Rice eventually was able to rally himself and his men and return the fire.[17]

Rice had run into the Second Kentucky Infantry of Brigadier General Charles Cruft's brigade. Cruft had kept his place en echelon, and when Hazen came under fire from the right, Cruft wheeled in the same direction. He had with him only three complete regiments, as five companies of the First Kentucky were absent guarding wagons. Cruft formed a single line of battle on the southern extreme of a long ridge west of the Brock field, with the Ninetieth Ohio on the left, Thirty-first Indiana in the center, and the Second Kentucky on the right. Cruft split his artillery, carrying forward one section of Battery B, First Ohio Light Artillery, while leaving the other on the ridge with the remainder of the First Kentucky. Cruft discovered Rice's Tennesseans a couple of hundred yards in front of him. Seeing that his own men were dangerously silhouetted on the ridge, he methodically pushed his line forward to meet the Rebels on level ground.

In battle, Cruft did everything with the same dogged, unyielding persistence that had enabled him to graduate from Wabash College at the age of sixteen and rise to the presidency of the St. Louis, Alton, and Terre Haute Railroad before his thirtieth birthday. In combat, wrote a brother officer, Cruft's manner "was that of a stern business man, who had a colossal enterprise in hand, from which he expected proportionate gains, and the staff officer who did not enter into the spirit of the enterprise was relieved of his position; and he regarded the soldier, who did not do his duty with a will, as the merchant does the man who robs him of his merchandise." Cruft got his men into the Brock field on Hazen's right, but there was no profit to be had here, just long hours of brutal fighting with an equally determined foe.[18]

Colonel William Grose followed the right wheel to a little wooded knoll four hundred yards east of the Brotherton house. His was a powerful command of five regiments and two batteries of artillery, which he now placed with great care. The Twenty-third Kentucky lined up on top of the hill and faced southeast. The Twenty-fourth Ohio formed on slightly lower ground to its right. With the Eighty-fourth Illinois and Thirty-sixth Indiana Grose fashioned a second line, and yet a third line with the Sixth Ohio. He placed Battery H, Fourth United States Artillery, beside the Sixth Ohio and left Battery M, Fourth United States Artillery, on high ground north of the road in general support of the brigade.

The Twenty-third Kentucky came up in support just in time to take the pressure off Cruft's Second Kentucky, which was now being mauled by Wright's Tennessee brigade. Grose's other regiments found only empty woods. With no enemy to their front, the men lay down in the weeds to rest.[19]

Brigadier General Marcus Wright had a lot to prove to his men, especially those of the Sixteenth Tennessee. When sixty-one-year-old Brigadier General Daniel Donelson went home sick after Stones River, most in the brigade assumed that the popular Colonel John Savage of the Sixteenth would take over by virtue of seniority and uniformly meritorious service. But Cheatham had other ideas. He gave the brigade to the thirty-two-year-old Wright, who, although junior in rank to Savage, had won over Cheatham while serving on his staff during the invasion of Kentucky, which happened to be the last time Wright had seen active service with the division. Savage resigned in indignation, making Wright unpopular before he ever set foot in camp. Captain H. H. Dillard of the Sixteenth complained that the officers and men of the brigade "did not and could not comprehend why it was that the reigning powers should ignore the claims of the brigade, go outside of it, and take a stranger to it, a junior in rank, and place him in command as a brigadier. . . . These men could not see any plausible reason for such a strange, unusual course, against their wishes and hopes, and they never did like it."[20]

Wright was off to a very bad start at Chickamauga. To begin with, he was working under two misconceptions. Somehow he had been led to believe that Maney's brigade would advance on his left, rather than remain in reserve as Cheatham intended. More seriously, he thought that Liddell was still engaged somewhere to his front. Wright shared his misapprehensions with his regimental commanders and told them to caution their skirmishers to take care not to fire into the backs of friendly troops. So, shortly before 1.00 P.M., Wright led his brigade into action for the first time, wrongly convinced that his left was protected and his front was clear.[21]

With grim irony, it was the Sixteenth Tennessee that suffered first for Wright's puzzlement. As the regiment stepped through the forest, Private Jim Martin, in the front rank, caught sight of blue uniforms in the trees to his right front. "Yonder they are," he cried. "Don't shoot, they are our men," cautioned the regimental commander, Colonel D. M. Donnell. "Our men Hell," snapped Martin, squeezing off a shot at the same time. A blast from Battery B, First Ohio Artillery, cleared away any doubt about who the Tennesseans faced, as well as most of the left wing of the regiment, which stumbled back fifteen yards before order was restored. Luckily, the Sixteenth had come upon the gap between Cruft's right and Grose's left, and so lost only sixty-seven wounded the rest of the afternoon.[22]

Nearer the brigade left, Colonel Sidney Stanton's Twenty-eighth Tennessee was less fortunate. His regiment, like the rest of the brigade, had been moving at the double-quick for five hundred yards, wheeling steadily to the right after Smith was checked by Hazen, and Stanton's main line now was almost on top of Grose's skirmishers. Any chance of early warning was gone. When just a hundred yards from Grose's line, said Stanton, "somewhat to our astonishment, instead of friends, who were supposed to be in our front, we found ourselves suddenly in contact with the enemy." Stanton ordered his men to lie down. In a few minutes the entire brigade was on the ground, and any chance of driving Grose from the hill was gone.[23]

Meanwhile, Captain William W. Carnes was struggling to get the limbers of his four-gun battery through the underbrush, while ahead of him a crescendo of musketry told him Wright's brigade had met the Yankees. The day before, Carnes had celebrated his twenty-second birthday in bivouac with brother officers. The son of a wealthy West Tennessee planter, he had attended the United States Naval Academy, graduating with the class of 1861. He returned home and served briefly as drill master in Cheatham's original brigade before receiving a commission as a captain of artillery, which made him, at twenty years of age, the youngest battery commander in the Confederate service. A slight young man with raven hair and alert, piercing eyes, the former midshipman showed a rare talent for artillery, becoming known as one of the most reliable battery commanders in the Western army. That reputation would be hard to sustain, however, if Carnes could not get his guns to the front before the fighting was over.[24]

General Johnson also fretted over his reputation, but from where he sat there was little he could do to influence the fighting. "The field of battle was a vast forest, whose dense foliage prevented us from seeing fifty yards distant," he wrote. "No one commander could see the flanks of his regiment even, and so division commanders could only learn how the battle progressed through their orderlies, staff officers, and occasional wounded men brought from various parts of the line. I remember seeing Captain E. C. Ellis, of the Ninety-third Ohio, who was seriously wounded, and I feared mortally; but when I asked him how it was going in his front, with a smile on his face he replied: 'General, our boys are giving them Hail Columbia to our front.' "[25]

Neither Palmer nor Cheatham was much better informed. It did not really matter much, however, as the fighting had settled down into a struggle of wills with little room for flanking movements or other elaborate maneuvers. As his brigades ran into the Federals, Cheatham's front line, stretched out for more than a mile, came to resemble the letter "V." Mutual support or concerted action by the brigades was virtually impossible. The divisions of Johnson and Palmer formed an inverted "V." Cheatham had fought Johnson and Palmer to a standstill. Once again, any decisive work would have to be done by fresh troops.

CHAPTER TEN

GIVE HELP WHERE IT IS NEEDED

THE TINY cabin of the Widow Glenn was a swirl of activity. In one corner, a field telegraph clicked with reports from Thomas, McCook, and Granger. Dana hovered nearby, periodically shoving an update for the War Department under the nose of the telegrapher. In another corner, Brigadier General James St. Clair Morton, chief engineer of the army, hunched over a map. With pencil and compass, he plotted unit locations as best he could from reports and the sound of the firing. Garfield sat at a field desk beside him, scribbling orders amid a retinue of staff officers and orderlies. Back and forth, in and out, paced Rosecrans, field glass in hand, a common blue overcoat draped over his shoulders, and a faded felt hat on his head. Captain William Colton of the Fifteenth Pennsylvania Cavalry, the head-quarters escort, sat on his horse near the cabin and watched it all. "From this position but little could be seen of the fighting lines, but the smoke and dust of the conflict and bursting of shells could plainly be seen above the trees. . . . Orderlies and couriers and staff officers were continually coming and going with orders and reports from the line. Officers were riding up and going off at full speed with verbal orders. . . . It was a scene of great interest and intensity. . . . The General would hurry off a courier here and a courier there, his eyes sparkling, his questions quick and earnest, his orders brief."[1]

Rosecrans's orders could hardly have been otherwise. No one at head-quarters had a firm grasp of the location of the enemy or where he might strike next, which is not surprising on a battlefield where division commanders lost track of their units the instant they entered the forest. All present at least understood that the enemy would have to come from the east, and from this knowledge evolved the single imperative that was to guide Rosecrans's actions the rest of the day: Deny Bragg the La Fayette road. Rosecrans was willing to launch limited counterattacks against Bragg's flanks to throw him off stride, but he would allow nothing to interfere with the defense of the road. In his anxiety to fill the gap between the Kelly field and Lee and Gordon's Mill, Rosecrans tossed aside any consideration of command cohesion: divisions and even brigades were peeled from their parent units and fed into the fight wherever and whenever they were needed. Commanders were thrown into unfamiliar relationships. Left with only Sheridan's division of his own corps, McCook found himself responsible for a division of cavalry and Negley's division of Thomas's corps. Crittenden was about to lose his second division, and Thomas was struggling to exercise some control over the left, where units from all three corps were fast being thrown together.

The commanding general's fixation on the La Fayette road is understandable, to a point. A successful penetration of any part of it would sever the best avenue for lateral communications and movement open to him. Where Rosecrans erred was in assuming it to be his only viable line of retreat to Chattanooga. In the heat of battle, he seemed to have forgotten about the Vittetoe and Dry Valley roads.

Rosecrans was tired and hungry. He had gone to bed after midnight the night before, and was up by 3:00 A.M. His only meal in the last twelve hours had been a biscuit and a few gulps of coffee before daybreak. Already he was operating on adrenalin. For the moment, Rosecrans appeared to have a grip on his emotions, but the strain was beginning to tell.

Smith Atkins caught a glimpse of the other Rosecrans—the explosive, excitable, impulsive Rosecrans—that was lurking dangerously near the surface. During the morning, Atkins's skirmishers brought in a prisoner captured near the Viniard farm. He was a mere boy and badly frightened, but by quiet and gentle persistence, Atkins was able to coax from him the fact that he belonged to Longstreet's corps. Atkins immediately led the boy to the Widow Glenn house so that he might repeat his story to the commanding general. Atkins ushered the young Rebel into the cabin and told Rosecrans he was from Longstreet's corps. What followed shocked the Illinoisan: "Rosecrans flew into a passion, denounced the little boy as a liar, declared that Longstreet's corps was not there. The little boy prisoner was so frightened that he would not speak a word. In sorrow I turned away, and joined my regiment."[2]

Assuming Smith's story to be true, there can be no rational explanation for Rosecrans's behavior. The captured courier from Bragg's headquarters had told the same story an hour earlier, and Minty had made a nuisance of himself for two days with his repeated reports of troop trains arriving at Catoosa Station. The conclusion is sad but unescapable: Rosecrans was coming unhinged.

Nevertheless, things were going Rosecrans's way. His troops were coming onto the field when needed and his corps commanders were taking the initiative. Davis rode up to the Widow Glenn house at the head of his division shortly before noon, as expected. Rosecrans held him at headquarters for perhaps an hour, then sent him into action with the best orders and advice he had to offer: Davis was "to move forward as speedily as possible in the direction of the heaviest firing, and to make an attack with a view, if possible, to turn the enemy's left flank."

Crittenden continued to shine. As soon as Thomas's request for a second division reached him, the Kentuckian sent his versatile chief of artillery, Major John Mendenhall, and Rosecrans's aide-de-camp, Colonel Joseph McKibbin, up the road to see Palmer and find out what was happening. Mendenhall and McKibbin were back minutes later to report that enemy skirmishers had fired on them before they could reach Palmer. Crittenden wrongly concluded that Palmer was surrounded, but his response was sound. He sent a messenger galloping to headquarters to beg Rosecrans's permission to send Van Cleve's division to the aid of Palmer. Once again Rosecrans heartily endorsed Crittenden's initiative. By 1:00 P.M., Van Cleve was on the road with the brigades of Samuel Beatty and George Dick, heading toward the sound of the guns. Colonel Sidney Barnes stayed behind to help Wood guard the ford at Lee and Gordon's Mill.[3]

Rosecrans was concentrating his divisions along the La Fayette road with a decisiveness and speed that Bragg utterly failed to counter. The stress of combat was calling into play his worst traits just as it would those of Rosecrans, only sooner. By early afternoon, Bragg had lapsed into that strange detachment in the face of plans gone awry that so enraged his subordinates. Archer Anderson offered the most charitable explanation for Bragg's tactical apoplexy. "In the depth of that thick woodland . . . he could see nothing with his own eyes, very little through the eyes of others, but every sign must be read through a glass darkly."[4]

Major General Alexander Peter Stewart could read no sign in the orders Major Pollock Lee of the army staff handed him shortly after Cheatham's division ran into trouble. Stewart was to withdraw from the left of the army, march behind Hood, and then "move to the point where the firing had commenced." That was all. There was no mention of what he should do when he reached the fighting, nor any hint of a coordinated effort.

Stewart had no intention of acting on orders so ridiculously vague. "Old Straight," as he was known in the army, was an intelligent man who liked to know the why behind his orders; at the moment, however, he would settle simply for a little clarity as to the what. Leaving his command, Stewart set out for Thedford's Ford, a half mile in his rear.

Stewart was an accomplished gentleman and scholar. He had resigned his commission three years after graduating from West Point to take the chair of mathematics and natural and experimental philosophy at Cumberland University in Lebanon, Tennessee, and at Nashville University. Stewart could not abide secession, and he was a staunch Whig in his politics, but as a Tennessean he could not turn his back on the South and so joined the Confederate army when war came.

Stewart's interview with Bragg was a failure. The Tennessean's pointed request for more explicit instructions embarrassed Bragg, and he fumbled for an answer. Walker was engaged on the right; he was badly cut up and the enemy was trying to turn his flank, Bragg told Stewart. Polk was in command of that wing now, he added, and Stewart should report to him for further orders; in the meantime, he must "be governed by circumstances." Stewart gave up and rode back to his command in disgust.

Bragg had been cruelly disingenuous with the Tennessean. Polk had left Bragg's side only minutes before with Captain Wheless to try to find Cheatham's position himself; certainly Bragg must have known that the odds of Polk and Stewart meeting on ground unfamiliar to both were slim.[5]

There is no rational explanation for Bragg's vague instructions to Stewart. Less than an hour before the Tennessean showed up at Thedford's Ford, Bragg had summoned D. H. Hill to headquarters, proposing to shift one of his divisions from the far left to the extreme right. Bragg clearly intended to continue his efforts to turn the Federal left. Indeed, he was clinging tenaciously to his original plan, despite overwhelming evidence that Rosecrans's left was no longer anywhere near Lee and Gordon's Mill. Throughout the afternoon, opportunities to exploit Federal gaps would slip away because of Bragg's inability to respond to a changing situation.

Hill saw the absurdity of all this. At headquarters, he learned that "while our troops had been moving up the Chickamauga, the Yankees had been moving down, and thus outflanked us and had driven back our right wing." To Hill, the appropriate response was clear. He should be permitted to attack what was now the Union right at Lee and Gordon's Mill with the divisions of Breckinridge and Cleburne. Hill was confident that he understood Rosecrans's dispositions. Early that morning, after a bloody artillery duel, Ben Hardin Helm's brigade had crossed Chickamauga Creek at Glass's Mill and driven in John Beatty's infantry as part of a demonstration to convince the Federals that the real Confederate attack would come from the south. Hill and Breckinridge followed their troops to the west bank. There they saw the clouds of dust raised by Rosecrans's infantry as it hurried north.

Bragg, however, was obdurate. Cleburne was to make the six-mile march from Dr. Anderson's house, near Pea Vine Church, to Thedford's Ford, cross, and move to the far right to continue the attack in that sector. Breckinridge was to withdraw from Glass's Mill and relieve Hindman opposite Lee and Gordon's Mill, who in turn would cross at Dalton (Hunt's) Ford. Hill accepted his instructions with grave misgivings but acted in good faith to carry them out. Orders went at once to Cleburne, and the Irishman had his division on the road to Thedford's Ford shortly after 1:00 P.M.[6]

The battle was going badly for Cheatham. His men were burning up ammunition faster than the Federals, and there was no more on hand. Colonel Rice of the Twenty-ninth Tennessee raised the cry for cartridges first, other regimental commanders repeated it, and soon Smith was inundated with requests he could not fill. To conserve ammunition, at 2:00 P.M. he ordered the brigade to fall back behind the fence that separated the Brock field from the forest. While regimental commanders hastily redistributed what rounds remained in their units, Smith urgently appealed to Cheatham and Strahl for help.[7]

Jackson's problems were even more acute. Like Smith, he faced the prospect of fighting the enemy with empty cartridge boxes. With each round they fired, his men grew more anxious. For some, the strain was too great to endure. The troops of the Second Battalion, First (Confederate) Georgia, took it upon themselves to withdraw when their cartridge boxes grew light. Major James Gordon managed to rally most of them and form a firing line about a hundred yards behind his first position, but he knew it was only a matter of time before he would have to order a retreat. On Gordon's right, Lieutenant Colonel W. L. Sykes had allowed his Fifth Mississippi to withdraw after the Georgians gave way. The Mississippians not only were running out of ammunition, but many had gone into the fight with unserviceable rifles. Sykes halted his regiment alongside Gordon, then was cut down by a bullet. Major John Herring assumed command and had the men pool their remaining cartridges. Eventually the whole brigade joined Gordon and Herring on the ridge.

Jackson knew he could not hold his new position long. Although Willich did not press his advantage, Baldwin had finally shaken off his lethargy and was slowly turning Jackson's right flank, and Richard Johnson had sent Colonel Joseph Dodge's brigade forward on Willich's right. After battering the Fifth Georgia, Dodge made for the left flank of Jackson's reformed line. At 2:00 P.M., Jackson sent a staff officer to beg Maney to relieve him while there was still time.[8]

Cheatham had already decided to commit Maney. He ordered Strahl and Maney into the fight at the same time, but their movements were uncoordinated. Cheatham apparently gave them no instructions except to move forward. Maney assumed Strahl would move with him and protect his left flank. Strahl supposed Maney would do the same for his right flank. Neither took any steps to communicate with the other, and both encountered so

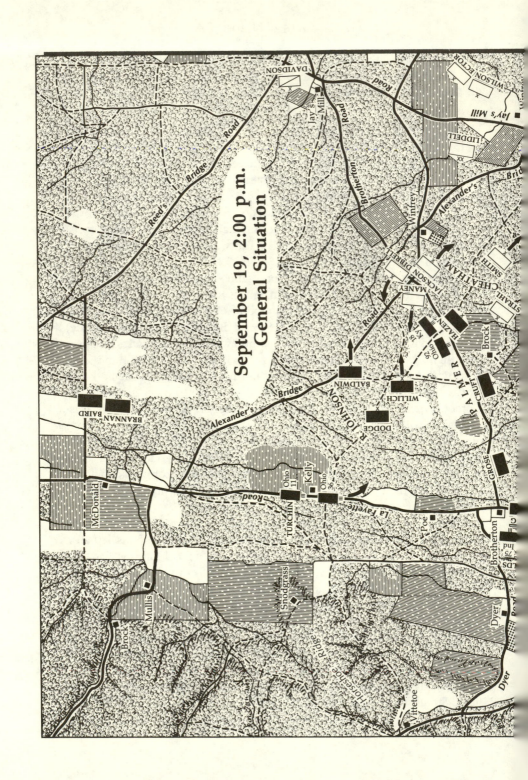

September 19, 2:00 p.m.
General Situation

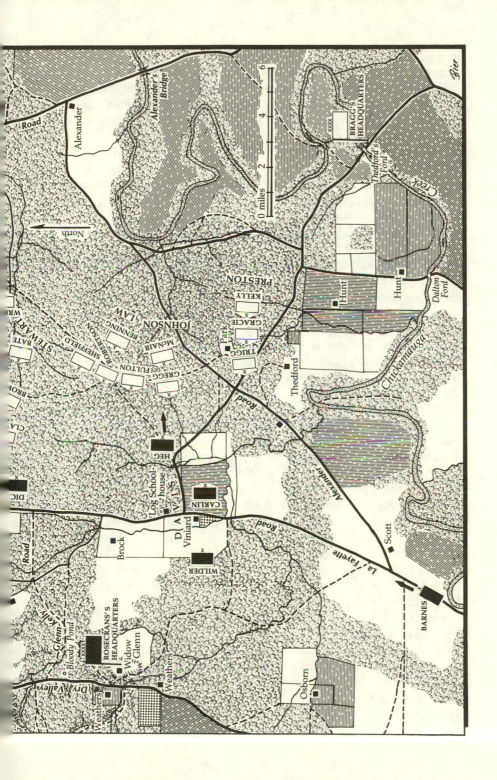

many problems trying to effect a passage of lines with the troops to their front that they had no time to look to their flanks.

Brigadier General George Maney, another of several Tennessee lawyers in the army high command, was a solid brigade commander not easily flustered, but what he found when he moved through the forest to relieve Jackson tested the limit of his patience. Maney had been told he would find Jackson on a "ridge well-wooded," but as he drew within sight of the fighting he saw only a carpet of Butternut where the Georgian's line had stood. Jackson did not stick around long enough to brief Maney, and the Tennessean reluctantly ordered his nine hundred men onto the ridge with no idea of what lay on the other side.

Private Robert Stout of the First and Twenty-seventh Tennessee knew what lurked beyond the ridge. Three nights earlier, he had been visited with a premonition of his own death. Private Sam Watkins noticed the transformation in Stout as the regiment stood in line that evening to draw three days' cooked rations. Stout refused his portion and turned away from his comrades with a "serious, woe-begone expression." Was he sick? "No," Stout answered, then quietly explained: "Boys, my days are numbered, my time has come. In three days from today, I will be lying a corpse. Ah, you may laugh; my time has come. I've got a twenty dollar gold piece in my pocket that I've carried through the war, and a silver watch that my father sent me through the lines. Please take them off when I am dead . . . to give to my father. . . . Here are my clothing and blanket that anyone who wishes them may have. My rations I do not wish at all. My gun and cartridge box I expect to die with."

Some may have laughed at Stout, but not Watkins. "Presentiment is always a mystery," he mused. "The soldier may at one moment be in good spirits, laughing and talking. The wing of the death angel touches him. He knows that his time has come. It is but a question of time with him then. I cannot explain it. God has numbered the hairs of our heads, and not a sparrow falls without his knowledge."

Cresting the ridge, Watkins and his comrades ran into a "perfect hornet's nest. The balls whistled around our ears like the escape valves of ten thousand engines. The woods seemed to be blazing." Watkins shot a glance toward Stout; for the moment at least, he was alive and fighting.[9]

Brigadier General Otho Strahl had even less enthusiasm for the task at hand than did his fellow Tennessee attorney. Like Maney, he had only a vague notion of what to expect. Strahl's brigade lay in the forest east of the Brock field when the order came to advance. Four hundred yards of cornfield and a thin strip of timber obscured the fighting beyond. Shells screeched through the trees, mangling men by the squad. Cheatham rode along the line, speaking words of encouragement between the boom of exploding shells. Slowly, Strahl edged his command into the field. There he found only stragglers and Preston Smith, who breathlessly implored Strahl to hurry toward the right to protect his flank, which was unsupported. Smith assured Strahl that Wright would cover his left, rode down the Tennessean's line to caution Strahl's men not to fire on the soldiers of his own brigade, and then was gone.[10]

A sudden clatter of musketry from the forest to Strahl's left cast doubt on Smith's assurances, and Strahl halted his brigade, hoping Maney might appear on his right and do the job of covering Smith's flank for him. A few minutes later, Smith was back, invoking Cheatham's name. Cheatham, he gloated, now wanted Strahl to relieve his brigade altogether and close the gap with Jackson.

Strahl reluctantly concluded that Maney had been ordered elsewhere. Facing his line of battle to the right, the Tennessean marched across the field toward the ground vacated by Smith's brigade.[11] The tension was agonizing. There was no sign of the Federals, yet with each step the bullets flew thicker. Colonel Francis Walker was at the front of the column with his Nineteenth Tennessee. As his men cleared the strip of timber that separated the two sections of the Brock field, they caught sight of the Yankees. Walker instantly realized the absurdity of the tactics that had brought him by the flank into the field, where he now faced Hazen's entire brigade and was flanked on the right by two fresh regiments of Turchin's brigade. "This movement under a heavy fire was not only a dangerous one but desperate . . . my men . . . being as they were assailed in front and from the right by a murderous fire, which was literally mowing them down," Walker testified in his after-action report. "Being thus exposed without a chance to check the fire of the enemy by our own, and seeing that we were likely to be flanked from the right, I allowed the men to retire slowly, but all the time under a heavy and effective fire from the front and right." In less than fifteen minutes, 75 of the 242 men of the Nineteenth Tennessee who had marched into the Brock field were hit.[12]

Cannoneer John Magee of Smith's Mississippi Battery watched the fight from the tree line. The cannoneers could find no effective firing position and so were spectators to the slaughter of the infantry. "I witnessed it all," remembered Smith. "I never saw so many men fall on so small a space of ground." Nor had Strahl, who concurred wholeheartedly with Colonel Walker's decision to pull out of the field.

On the brigade left, the men of the Fourth and Fifth Tennessee were denied even the satisfaction of seeing their foe. The ever-present Preston Smith had admonished Colonel Jonathan Lamb not to return the fire, unaware that his own Eleventh Tennessee already had cleared out from Lamb's front. Through the smoke, Cruft's Thirty-first Indiana looked very much like the Eleventh Tennessee, so Lamb could only take Smith at his word and watch helplessly as his men dropped around him. After ten minutes, the colonel mercifully received orders from Strahl to fall back into the forest.[13]

Brigadier General John B. Turchin was a nonpareil. No general in either army inspired greater loyalty or more intense hatred than Turchin. "A kinder or a braver commander never led men to battle and to victory," averred Lieutenant Governor Ira J. Chase of Indiana after the war. Recalling his service under the Russian emigré general, Chase continued: "He never hesitated to lead in dangerous places. He was, he is, a hero, and all who knew him wish him peace and happiness." In 1863, most Southerners wished him dead, preferably at the end of a rope. "I cannot close this message without again adverting to the savage ferocity which still marks the conduct of the enemy in the prosecution of the war," Jefferson Davis told the Confederate Congress in his annual message to the legislature. "Their commanders, Butler, McNeil, and Turchin, whose terrible barbarities have made their names widely notorious and everywhere execrable, are still honored and cherished by the authorities at Washington."[14]

Turchin, born Ivan Vasilvetich Turcheninov, and his wife, Nadine, born Nedezhda Lvova to a titled and aristocratic Russian family, had given up much to make the United States their home. A graduate of the imperial military academy at St. Petersburg and a veteran of the Hungarian and Crimean wars, Turchin enjoyed a comfortable and privileged life as a colonel in the Imperial Guards and the husband of an aristocrat. But Turchin's heart was not in Moscow. Both he and Nadine had become imbued with liberal Western philosophy and the ideals of the French Revolution; like August Willich, the Turchins looked to the United States for a chance to live their ideals.

Their early years in America were hard, and as European aristocrats they never quite shed the distaste members of their class felt for the rough-hewn, ill-bred Americans. After living briefly in Philadelphia and on Long Island, the Turchins settled in the prairie town of Mattoon, Illinois, which must have seemed as foreign to them as the moon. There Turchin took a job as topographical engineer for the Illinois Central Railroad. George Brinton McClellan happened to be president of the company, and when war came it was probably he who saw to it that Turchin received a colonel's commission.

Turchin caused quite a stir among his brother officers. He spoke openly of his disdain for army regulations that protected the property of Southern noncombatants, or what Turchin called the "guarding potato patches policy" of "gently fighting the rebels in the field, and at the same time preserving their property from the uses of the army." His convictions got the better of him, and in May 1862 he permitted his brigade to plunder the town of Athens, Alabama, which ironically was known for its large loyal population. Turchin was swiftly brought up on charges of "neglect of duty, to the prejudice of good order and military discipline" and "disobedience of orders" by his commander, Major General Don Carlos Buell, who had grown tired of the querulous Russian. Turchin pled guilty only to the latter charge, which stemmed from his disregard of the regulation prohibiting wives of officers from accompanying their husbands in the field. The court, of which James A. Garfield was president and John Beatty was a member, found him guilty on all counts, and Turchin was dismissed from the service.

There his military career might have ended, had it not been for the intervention of no less a man than Abraham Lincoln. Powerful foreign-born and radical members of the Republican party, who much admired Turchin's fiery abolitionism and no-nonsense treatment of the Rebels, cried for his reinstatement. Lincoln not only obliged them but promoted Turchin to brigadier general. In March 1863, Turchin was ordered to report to the Army of the Cumberland. Although his reputation as the "Mad Cossack" preceded Turchin, Rosecrans took a liking to him, and he assigned Turchin to the command of a cavalry division.

General Stanley, however, had only contempt for the "dumpy, fat, short-legged Russian, who could not ride a horse." When Turchin failed to come to his support during a skirmish near Shelbyville, Tennessee, Stanley went to Rosecrans to demand he be relieved. Rosecrans hesitated. Fine, said Stanley, "If he stays then relieve me." The irascible cavalry chief prevailed, and Turchin was demoted to the command of a brigade of infantry in Reynolds's division.

Turchin had learned nothing from his court-martial. Nadine was still with him in the field, enduring all the discomforts and agonizing over his safety. If Turchin's fellow generals resented her presence, the troops of his brigade certainly did not. This "elegant and rather delicate-looking lady," as Colonel Sanderson saw her, won them over completely. "Dear Madame Turchin! How we all respected, believed in, and came to love her," recalled Captain James Haynie of the Nineteenth Illinois. The esteem was mutual. "Only a free man can endure hunger, cold, and injustice with such boundless patience," she wrote. "A citizen-soldier who feels free by his birthright endures all things because he does not feel obliged to endure them. He has volunteered to serve for the love of liberty." On the other hand, Nadine detested most of the general's colleagues with the intensity of a wife who felt her husband had been wronged: "I would rather see my husband out of this army, which only knows how to die. . . . These fellows may be decorated with titles of marshals, but this does not change the fact that they are supremely ignorant of military matters, and for that reason incapable of appreciating an accomplished officer."[15]

Turchin probably shared his wife's frustration with the general officers of the army as he wandered around the battlefield with his brigade on the morning of the nineteenth. Shortly before 10:30 A.M. Thomas ordered Reynolds's division to deploy near a collection of pits, nitre vats, and shacks used for tanning animal hides that was known as the Tan Yard. A little later, as Thomas's concern for his left flank grew, he changed his mind and ordered Reynolds up the La Fayette road to the McDonald house. Turchin, whose brigade was in the lead, barely had passed the Kelly farm when a courier from division directed him to face his command about and retrace his steps to the Tan Yard. Before he could comply, Reynolds's adjutant informed Turchin that his two rear regiments, the Eighteenth Kentucky and Ninety-second Ohio, had been snatched from his column and sent to the aid of Hazen. Turchin was to follow them with his remaining regiments, the Thirty-sixth Ohio and Eleventh Ohio. Thoroughly disgusted, Turchin turned off the road and plunged into the forest.[16]

Turchin had not been singled out for harassment. Reynolds's entire division was being carved up and fed piecemeal into the battle. After Turchin left, Reynolds paused along the road near the Poe house to wait for someone to tell him what to do with the remainder of his command, which consisted of King's brigade, the Nineteenth Indiana Battery, the Ninety-second Illinois on detached service from Wilder, and four small mountain howitzers from Lilly's battery. Nadine Turchin genuinely liked Reynolds, whom she found to be "an honest man, modest and courteous, without the sign of the impudence and rudeness of the Americans, in his manners or in the discharge of his official duties." Henry Duffield of the Ninth Michigan painted a similar picture of Reynolds, a man "as gentle, both in presence, appearance and manner, almost, as a woman; and it always seemed to me that he, of all our leaders, best illustrated the picture the poet draws in those two beautiful lines: 'The bravest are the tenderest, The loving are the daring.' "[17]

Thomas rode up a few minutes later, at about 1:30 P.M., but he had little to tell Reynolds except that the first two regiments that had gone into action from Turchin's brigade were being badly chewed up. Looking to play a constructive role, Reynolds suggested that he use part of his division to form a reserve upon which Palmer could rally if necessary. Thomas agreed, telling Reynolds to "exercise [his] own judgment and give help where it was needed," then rode off to supervise Johnson and Palmer.

Reynolds knew precisely where to form a reserve line. On the way to the Poe house he had passed a long, north-south ridge that ran the length of a cleared field belonging to George Brotherton, whose one-room cabin sat beside the La Fayette road. Along the ridge, which rose about one hundred yards west of the road, Reynolds placed Captain Samuel Harris's Nineteenth Indiana Battery and Lilly's four howitzers. Heavy timber blocked the view beyond the road, but from their elevated position the cannoneers could throw rounds far into the forest. Reynolds left the Seventy-fifth Indiana, a relatively untested regiment that still numbered over seven hundred men, and the Ninety-second Illinois on the slope to protect the guns, then started down the Brotherton road with the remainder of King's brigade to join Turchin.

Palmer intercepted him. The battle was going well, the Illinoisan said, but Cruft and Grose were almost out of ammunition and he needed help to hold what they had won. In the spirit of Thomas's admonition that he "give help where it was needed," Reynolds turned King's last three regiments—the Sixty-eighth Indiana, One Hundred Fifth Ohio, and One Hundred First Indiana—over to Palmer and then returned to the ridge to busy himself with his reserve force.[18]

Palmer was happy to have the three extra regiments, but as it turned out his appeal for help was premature. The threat to his front had diminished, so Palmer asked Colonel King to take his command down the La Fayette road a couple of hundred yards and then turn east into the forest to extend Grose's right flank, where the Sixth Ohio was fast expending its ammunition in an effort to keep the Thirty-eighth and Twenty-eighth Tennessee regiments from turning the line. King hurried his regiments down the road, but instead of finding empty forest where Grose's right ended, he ran into two fresh Federal brigades. Determined to extend somebody's right flank, King resumed his march toward the end of the new Federal line.[19]

King had met the brigades of Brigadier General Samuel Beatty and Colonel George Dick. Van Cleve had had his division on the road within minutes of receiving the order from Crittenden to move to the aid of Palmer. At 1:00 P.M., Van Cleve directed Beatty to take the lead and double-quick his column the entire mile and a half to Palmer's right. Dick was still on the east side of the La Fayette road with the Forty-fourth Indiana and Fifty-ninth Ohio, near where he had helped halt Bushrod Johnson the night before. His other two regiments were near the mill. Van Cleve started them after Beatty, then sent a courier to tell Dick to fall in as the column passed. Troubled by what Van Cleve might run into, Crittenden accompanied the fifty-three year old on the march north.[20]

Beatty halted a hundred yards south of the Brotherton cabin. Dick had lagged behind while trying to piece together the two halves of his brigade, but Crittenden and Van Cleve both concurred in sending Beatty into the forest anyway. A forty-two-year-old farmer and former sheriff of Stark County, Ohio, Beatty had not had the benefit of much formal schooling, and may never have read a military text before the war, but he was a born fighter.

Beatty quickly but ably faced his brigade to the right into a double-line of battle, with the Seventy-ninth Indiana on the left and the Nineteenth Ohio on the right of the first line, and the Seventeenth and Ninth Kentucky bringing up the second. Captain Alanson Stevens arrayed the limbered cannon of his Battery B, Twenty-sixth Pennsylvania Artillery, behind the Seventeenth Kentucky. The order was passed to fix bayonets, and at 1:30 P.M., Beatty motioned his command off the road.

Beatty's men marched into some of the wildest ground on the battlefield. For fifteen minutes, maybe longer, they stepped over fallen and rotted trees, through knee-high weeds, and around webs of hanging vines without seeing anything but drifting smoke and forest. Gradually the skirmishers of the Seventy-ninth Indiana began picking out Butternut forms through the trees, and as they opened fire, Lieutenant William Mounts caught sight of a Rebel battery standing oddly alone in front of the regiment. Mounts yelled his discovery to Colonel Frederick Knefler, who ordered his men to shoot the battery horses.[21]

Lieutenant Mounts had spotted young Captain Carnes's four-gun battery. For nearly an hour, Carnes had struggled to catch up with Wright's infantry, finally dismounting his cannoneers from their limbers to hack a path through the forest with axes. When he at last came up behind the brigade, there was no sign of Wright nor of any other infantry officer with the time or inclination to tell him where his guns were needed. Carnes sat patiently until three cannoneers were shot off their limbers in rapid succession. That was enough to cause Carnes to act, and he led his limbers forward at the trot toward the left flank of the brigade.

Fate had cast its eye on Carnes. Just as the captain advanced his guns, Wright prepared to withdraw. His men were unhitching their pieces when Carnes glimpsed the Thirty-eighth Tennessee directly in their line of fire, recoiling from another failed charge. Close on their heels were Grose's Federals, who had ventured off their hill to chase the Tennesseans.

While his cannoneers rammed home charges of canister, Carnes galloped toward Colonel Carter of the Thirty-eighth, screaming at him to get the regiment out of the way. Carter understood. "By the right of company to the rear, double quick," he bellowed, and the Tennesseans moved aside. The Yankees now found themselves staring at two six-pound and two twelve-pound howitzers. Their only hope was to charge, which they did, nearly to the gun barrels. Carnes yelled "Fire!" and the blue line melted away in the smoke. Twelve times his cannoneers threw canister at the retreating Federals, until the last of them fled from view.[22]

By this time, Wright's infantry had vanished; all, that is, but Colonel Carter's Thirty-eighth Tennessee. While his men lay in the weeds beside the cannons, Carter walked into the battery "as if for a social visit," to watch Carnes's gunners blast Grose's Yankees. "His lavish display of coolness and his intrepidity were indeed admirable," recalled Lieutenant L. G. Marshall, commander of the left section.

Carter was not risking his life casually. He feared for his left flank and suggested to Marshall that he swing his guns that way. Carnes agreed. Just then, a handful of men from the Seventy-ninth Indiana dove behind a fallen tree a hundred yards to the left of where Carnes and Carter were conferring and began picking off the battery horses. "Captain, if ever there was an occasion for the double-shotted canister we've carried so long, this seems to be the time," said Marshall. Into the guns it went, just as the rest of the Seventy-ninth Indiana showed itself. Carnes turned his guns on them, and with each discharge, every cannon sent 27 iron balls of canister and 170 leaden balls buzzing toward the blue line.

The Seventy-ninth Indiana shivered but stood its ground. The Nineteenth Ohio joined it, and Colonel Carter finally withdrew the Thirty-eighth Tennessee.

Carnes was running out of time. Battery horses shrieked and fell by the team, every officer and sergeant but one was dismounted, and nearly half the cannoneers were down. Lieutenant A. Van Vleck, commander of the right section, took a bullet in the leg. Carnes glanced over to see him standing by his horses cutting open the leg of his trousers. The captain ran to his side and asked if he were badly wounded. "Only a flesh wound through the thigh, and I'd better stay till this is over," answered Van Vleck. As Carnes walked away a shell exploded between them, sending the lieutenant's horse bolting for the rear and Van Vleck to the ground. Carnes waved a team of litter-bearers to his side. "I think I will have to go now," moaned Van Vleck. The litter-bearers picked up Van Vleck, lifting him right into the path of an oncoming bullet that killed the lieutenant instantly.

Carnes realized they all would end up like Van Vleck unless he acted quickly. To Marshall he barked orders to clear the sharpshooters from behind the fallen tree with his left gun. Then he called on his only remaining team to draw off the right gun of the battery. Up came the limber, and in an instant all six horses fell dead in a heap. "We can't save the battery; let the men leave as quick as possible," Carnes told Marshall, then turned to his bugler. The Yankees were sure to recognize the call for "cease firing," so Carnes tried a little deception. He asked the bugler if he could sound the "assembly" over the din. "I'd sound it in hell, Sir, if you'd give the order," he shouted.

While the bugler blew the call, Carnes told the sergeant commanding the left gun to cover the withdrawal. The sergeant did his best, but the moment the first of Carnes's cannoneers started for the rear, every Federal rifle was trained on the sergeant and his crew. "Hurry up, Captain, I can see them in our rear now," begged the sergeant as the last of his crew fell. The sergeant mounted his horse, and Carnes followed. A bullet hit his beloved mount, Prince, in the hip just as Carnes hit the saddle; four more struck the animal as they rode between the Seventy-ninth Indiana and Nineteenth Ohio, which were racing for the honor of capturing the battery.

"Look out, your horse is going to fall with you," a friendly voice cried out as Carnes and his blood-soaked mount stumbled into an advancing Confederate brigade. Prince staggered and collapsed on his side. Carnes removed the saddle, stood by the dead horse a moment, then joined the survivors of his battery who had gathered near him.[23]

Carnes had found refuge behind the brigade of Brigadier General Henry D. Clayton of Stewart's division. Stewart had marched his division by the right flank nearly a mile, past the wreckage of combat. "Wounded men and mangled horses were soon met," Lieutenant Bromfield Ridley, Jr., an aide to Stewart, recalled of the march. "Field surgeons and litter forces were becoming busy; but the spirits of none flagged, but increased with the raging torrents of shot and shell. One man, as he was borne off on a litter, passed us with bowels protruding, yet with animated fervor waved his hat and cried: 'Boys, when I left we were driving 'em!' Limbs were falling . . . the sweep of battle was becoming more terrific and the sound like the roar of the river and the roll of the thunder."[24]

Stewart halted his division about three hundred yards short of the southern edge of the Brock field. It was 2:00 P.M., and Strahl had moved into the field only minutes earlier. Stewart sent messengers in every direction in search of Polk, but none found him. "Fearing to lose too much time, I determined to move upon the enemy across this cornfield," he reported. The Tennessean was about to give the order when Lieutenant Richmond rode up. He too was looking for Polk. Richmond had no instructions for Stewart but before riding off commented that, from what he knew of the nature of the ground and enemy dispositions, "a better point at which to attack them could not be found." Accordingly, Stewart directed Clayton, whose brigade led the march column, to move into the Brock field toward the shooting. Echoing what seemed to be the universal vague command of the day, Stewart told Clayton that "after having more definitely located the enemy, I would have to act for myself and be governed by circumstances."[25]

Clayton stopped before entering the field to correct the brigade alignment. While his men dressed ranks, Clayton's attention was drawn to Colonel Carter of the Thirty-eighth Tennessee, who was running toward him from beyond the brigade left. Breathlessly, Carter warned Clayton that his brigade was heading in the wrong direction and that, unless he changed direction perpendicularly to the left, he would be completely enfiladed by the same Yankee line that had swept over Carnes's battery. Yet another of the Army

of Tennessee's many attorneys-turned-general, Clayton was a talented commander fully capable of acting on his own. He immediately told his regimental commanders to file to the left and form a line facing west.[26]

Lieutenant Colonel A. R. Lankford, commanding Clayton's left regiment,
was already in position. Marcus Wright had caught sight of Clayton's brigade
just as his fell back. The Tennessean had lost his horse, so, like Carter, he
started on foot through the woods to find Clayton. Despairing of reaching
him in time, Wright grabbed the first regimental commander he spotted
and begged him to move to the left to protect his men as they fell back.
Lankford did so at once, and his Thirty-eighth Alabama was engaged with
the lead elements of Dick's brigade by the time Clayton showed up with
the Eighteenth and Thirty-sixth Alabama. Lieutenant Ridley recalled the
moment when the Alabamians ran into Van Cleve's line: "Did you ever
note the thickness of raindrops in a tempest? Did you ever see the destruction
of hail stones to growing cornfields? Did you ever witness driftwood in a
squall? Such was the havoc upon Clayton."[27]

His three Alabama brigades were too few to match Van Cleve's line,
which extended beyond both Clayton's flanks. Dick had come alongside
Beatty in time to deliver a few volleys into the flank of the Thirty-Eighth
Tennessee as it fell back from Carnes's battery. Like the Ohioan, he had
his brigade deployed in two lines, with the Forty-fourth Indiana and Fifty-
ninth Ohio in the first line and the Eighty-sixth Indiana and Thirteenth
Ohio in the second. Captain George Swallow sat on the road with his
Seventh Indiana Battery, afraid to take his command into the forest. Reynolds
solved Swallow's dilemma by putting him on Brotherton Ridge beside Harris's battery, thus increasing his reserve artillery to a respectable fourteen
cannons.

Outnumbered eight regiments to three in front and subject to a galling
fire from Grose in his right rear, Clayton was forced to call a halt just short
of Carnes's abandoned battery at 2:30 P.M. But although he could not advance,
neither would Clayton retreat. His Alabamians took what shelter they could
among the brush and fallen timber, and for the next sixty minutes kept
up a brave if futile fight.[28]

Stewart was well aware of Clayton's predicament. Lieutenant E. T. Harris,
one of Wright's few staff members who still had his horse, had galloped
on to find Stewart while Wright ran about in search of Clayton. Harris told
Stewart of his commander's desperate need for help, and the Tennessean
rode off to confer with Wright in person. Dismounted and disheveled,
Wright indeed looked like a man who had just lost his battery and a fair
share of his brigade. Stewart responded to his plea by diverting the second
brigade in his column, that of Brigadier General John C. Brown, to the

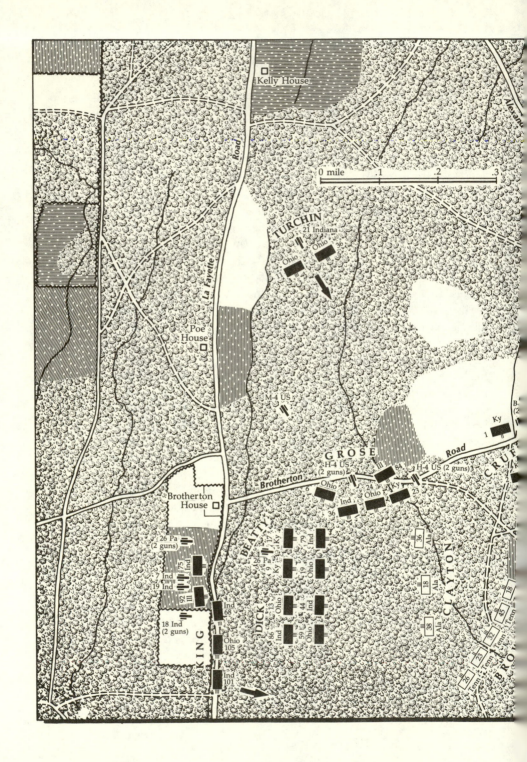

Kelly House

Road

La Fayette

0 mile .1 .2 .3

TURCHIN
21 Indiana
Ohio Ohio
Ohio

Poe
House

M-4 US

Ky
1

GROSE
Road
H-4 US
(2 guns)
Brotherton
6 Ohio
Ind Ohio Ky H-4 US (2 guns)
36
23
CRUF

Brotherton
House
36
Ala

26 Pa
(2 guns)
BEATTY
17
Ohio 79
26 Pa Ky
7 Ind 9 Ky Ind Ohio Ohio
19 Ind
92 Ind
18 Ala

Ind
68
DICK
13 Ind Ind Ohio Ind
86 59 44 Ohio
38 Ala
CLAYTON
18

KING
18 Ind
(2 guns)
Ohio 105

Ind
101

BRO

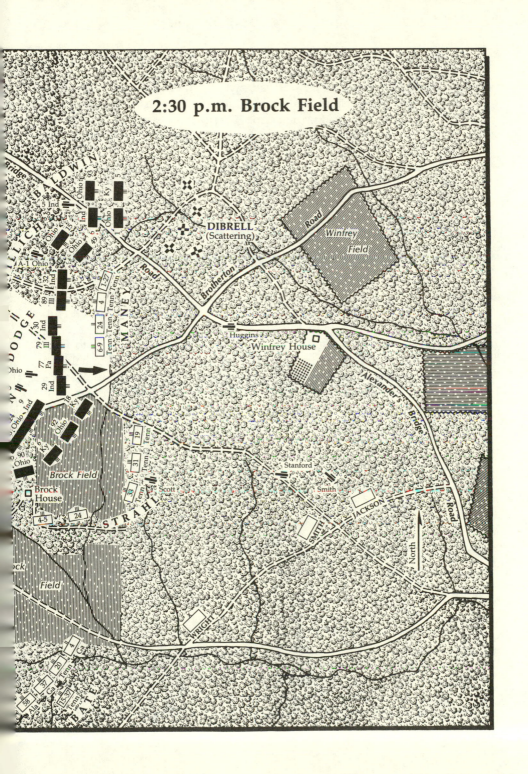

2:30 p.m. Brock Field

support of Clayton. Unwittingly, Stewart had put himself within striking distance of the La Fayette road.[29]

The timely arrival of Stewart had saved Wright, and with him, Cheatham's left. In the center, Strahl had rallied and edged back into the Brock field, where he was holding on against Cruft, Hazen, and Turchin. On the right, however, Maney was bending before heavy pressure in front and on both flanks.

Forrest ordered the survivors of Dibrell's brigade to dismount and move into line on Maney's right to try to stay the advance of Baldwin, but their numbers were too few and resistance too feeble to do more than force the Indianian to reinforce his skirmish line. Only Baldwin's reluctance to outpace Willich and the difficulty his men were having in moving through the heavy timber kept his brigade from gaining Maney's rear.

This was little consolation to the Tennessean. His brigade was too small to cover the entire ridge, and the weight of numbers was beginning to tell. On the brigade right, held by the First and Twenty-seventh Tennessee, Colonel Hume Field had detached his two right companies with orders to report any attempt to turn his flank. Within minutes they were back, pursued by the Forty-ninth Ohio. Field pulled his right wing in to meet the Ohioans from that direction, while his left companies tried to hold the Thirty-second Indiana in front. On the brigade left, Major Frank Maney's Twenty-fourth Tennessee Sharpshooters and Colonel George Porter's Sixth and Ninth Tennessee tried desperately to stave off Dodge's brigade, which had come up in a single line to close the gap between Willich and Hazen and was now pressing inexorably around Porter's flank. Already half of Porter's Tennesseans lay dead or dying.[30]

Maney prepared to withdraw. He rode to Lieutenant William Turner, whose Mississippi Battery was getting the worst of its duel with the rifled cannons of Goodspeed's Ohio Battery. He told the lieutenant to leave one gun with the brigade and take his remaining three back to a wooded knoll three hundred yards south of the Winfrey house. There Maney hoped to make a stand against Willich and Dodge.

The Federals, smelling victory, were not about to oblige Maney. Dodge had grown tired of trading volleys with the Sixth and Ninth Tennessee, and a little after 2:30 P.M. ordered a charge that swept past Porter's left and across the Brotherton road. Porter brought what was left of his regiment down from the ridge. On the reverse slope he ran into Maney, who demanded to know why he had abandoned his position without orders. Porter rattled off the reasons: he was outflanked, out of ammunition, and had lost 60 percent of his regiment. The general let him pass, crestfallen that his controlled withdrawal was turning into a rout.[31]

Things were worse then Maney imagined. Willich had sent his line forward against Maney's right. Sam Watkins and his comrades in the First and Twenty-seventh Tennessee reached for their final rounds as Willich's Yankees closed on them from the front, right, and rear. Colonel Field tried to hold on nonetheless. It took the ever-present Forrest to bring him to his senses. "Colonel Field, look out, you are almost surrounded; you had better fall back," he cried over the din as he braved a storm of bullets to reach Field. The colonel relented and sounded the retreat. There was no time to organize; it was every man for himself. "I ran through a solid line of blue coats," remembered Watkins. "As I fell back, they were upon the right of us, they were upon the left of us, they were in front of us, they were in the rear of us."

Bob Stout ran beside Watkins. "Bob, you weren't killed, as you expected," Watkins chided his friend as they paused to catch their breath. Watkins later recalled, "He did not reply, for at that very moment a solid shot from the Federal guns struck him between the waist and the hip, tearing off one leg and scattering his bowels all over the ground. I heard him shriek out 'Oh, Oh, God!' His spirit had flown before his body struck the ground."[32]

Forrest rode through Field's fleeing Tennesseans to the intersection of the Brotherton and Alexander's Bridge roads, where he had left Captain A. L. Huggins's battery of Dibrell's brigade. Forrest shouted at Huggins to unlimber his guns along the bridge road, one hundred yards west of the Winfrey house.

By the time the last of Field's men cleared the front of the battery, the Federals were only fifty yards away. Huggins let roar a volley of grape and canister that tore apart Willich's Eighty-ninth Illinois and Dodge's Thirtieth Indiana. The three right companies of the Eighty-ninth recoiled in confusion, leaving four officers dead before the guns. Every officer and sergeant in Company D was hit, and only the initiative of a private kept the company intact. The Thirtieth Indiana also wavered, falling back twenty yards into the timber with the Illinoisans to regroup. Meanwhile, Colonel Field had gathered the remnants of his regiment around the colors, held aloft by Joe Campbell, the intrepid color-bearer of the First Tennessee, and pieced together a patchwork line on the left of the battery that momentarily halted Colonel Buckner's Seventy-ninth Illinois. Maney rallied what men he could from the rest of the brigade to the left of Field, placing the cannon he had withheld from Turner on the brigade left near the Brock field, then sent his staff to look for Strahl.

Alone now, Maney grew impatient quickly and soon galloped off to search for Strahl himself. Maney found him at 3:00 P.M., realigning his brigade to extend Maney's patchwork line. That was fine, Maney told Strahl, but not enough: the "emergency [was] critical" and he needed instant succor. Strahl consented. He ordered the Nineteenth Tennessee to change front to the north and charge across the gap between Maney's left and the Brock field, then directed the Thirty-first and Thirty-third Tennessee to redouble its efforts in the field itself. A grateful Maney returned to his brigade.[33]

Strahl had been generous. He was having troubles enough of his own. For the past hour he had been unable to make any headway against Hazen, who seemed to have an endless supply of cartridges. Actually, the Ohioan had had the foresight to bring two ammunition wagons with him. The arrival of Turchin's Ninety-second Ohio and Eighteenth Kentucky shortly after 2:00 P.M. allowed him to rotate regiments out of the firing line without leaving a gap that Strahl might exploit. The Eighteenth Kentucky relieved the Ninth Indiana, and the Ninety-second Ohio spelled the One Hundred Twenty-fourth Ohio. The Sixth Kentucky came up from Hazen's second line to replace the Forty-first Ohio. All this happened moments before Strahl's ill-fated appearance in the Brock field, and it was the firepower of these fresh units that sent Strahl scurrying back to the woods to regroup. Compounding the Tennessean's woes was a lack of artillery support. Captain Stanford's Mississippi Battery never found a suitable firing position and so fired not a single round; by contrast, Cockerill's Battery F, First Ohio, emptied its ammunition chests in support of Hazen.[34]

Strahl's Thirty-third and Thirty-first Tennessee fared no better when they reentered the Brock field at 3:00 P.M. than they had earlier in the afternoon. Turchin had arrived at the head of his remaining two regiments and now sent the Eleventh Ohio into the fight to relieve the Sixth Kentucky, opposite the Tennesseans. Perhaps no men, not even Colonel Buckner's Illinoisans, faced death at Chickamauga better prepared spiritually then these Ohioans. That morning, while the brigade rested near the Tan Yard, Chaplain William Lyle felt compelled to speak "a word of encouragement to the patriot soldiers who were about to enter into the very jaws of death, and many of whom, perhaps, would never hear words of prayer upon earth again." Lyle sought out Colonel Philander Lane to request five minutes to pray with the men before they went into action. "Certainly," Lane replied. "I wish you would have services; I think there will be time." Lyle rode to the front of the line, and Lane ordered the regiment to form in two divisions, with the chaplain in the center. General Reynolds and his staff happened to be passing down the line. They halted when they reached the Eleventh. Reynolds walked his horse next to Lyle's, removed his hat, and waited for the chaplain to begin. Above the screeching shells and too-near rattle of musketry, Lyle spoke in a clear and powerful voice:

> It is but little I can do for you in the hour of battle; but there is one thing I will do — I will pray for you. And there are thousands all over the land praying for you this morning, and God will hear them. You must pray now,

too; for God is a hearer of prayer. And if this is the last time I shall ever speak to you, or if these are the last words of Christian comfort you will ever hear, I want to tell you dear comrades, that GOD LOVES YOU. I pray God to cover your heads today in the battle storm. I pray that he may give you brave hearts and strong hands today. Be brave — be manly! Remember the dear old flag, and what it covers. And if any of you feel uncertain as to your future, O look to the Savior who died for you; and, if any of you fall this day in battle, may you not only die as brave soldiers for your country, but die as soldiers of the Lord Jesus Christ. Let us pray.

A journalist was there to record the scene for his readers. "Instantly every head was uncovered and bowed in reverence, while hands were clasped on the rifles, the bayonets of which were gleaming in the morning sun. The flag, pierced and rent on a dozen battlefields, was drooped, and, strange but glorious sound on a battlefield, a voice of prayer was heard."A low, murmuring "Amen" rose from the ranks as Lyle concluded. Reynolds uttered his "Amen" robustly, which had "a thrilling effect." With tears running down his cheeks, the general shook Lyle's hand warmly. "Sir, I am glad I was here to join you."[35]

Riding behind the regiment as it neared the Brock field, Lyle was deeply troubled for his flock. "I had heard the roar of battle at Bull Run, had felt the earth quiver under the fierce conflicts of South Mountain and Antietam, but the incessant roar of artillery and musketry on this terrible day seemed to exceed all three battlefields combined," he remembered. "The musketry was neither in distinct shots nor in repeated volleys, but ... was one mighty, fearful, continuous roll." Out on the firing line, the men were falling fast. Color Sergeant Rufus Peck was struck by a spent ball in the first fire; his brother, Lieutenant George Peck, scooped up the colors and took them to the front of the line.[36]

Meanwhile, over on the Alexander's Bridge road, Captain Huggins had his Tennessee gunners throwing canister at a frenetic pace. In less than thirty minutes, they fired fifty rounds at the Federals, who clung to the ground to escape the blasts. But there were too many Yankees coming from too many directions for his cannoneers to hold on without support. On Huggins's right, Dibrell's troopers were sneaking off the field before the advance of Willich's remaining regiments. The Prussian had brought up the Fifteenth Ohio and now had his entire brigade in line. Their confidence was unbounded as they pressed ahead, firing and reloading. Willich had taught them this tactic of "advancing firing," as Sergeant Alexis Cope of the Fifteenth Ohio called it, "and it made them feel invincible." They were spurred on by the sight of a battery lying a hundred yards behind Dibrell's troopers. With fixed bayonets, the Forty-ninth Ohio and Thirty-second Indiana charged the guns. The Tennesseans retreated to the battery, where they faced about for a final stand. The Federals kept coming, Dibrell's troopers emptied their weapons, and, for what seemed like twenty minutes to one frightened Ohioan, the two lines merged in hand-to-hand combat. The tired cavalrymen had fought one fight too many that day, and eventually they conceded the battery. The curses must have flowed freely when Willich's men discovered that their prize was not a Rebel battery after all, but only the much-fought-over cannons of Van Pelt's Michigan Battery. Possession on the battlefield as elsewhere being nine-tenths of the law, only one gun ever found its way back to its rightful owners; the rest were quietly appropriated by the battery commanders of Johnson's division.[37]

Captain Huggins faced the prospect of having his battery become a battlefield prize. Already flanked on the right, he had lost his infantry support on the left, where Field's Tennesseans had fled in confusion, this time for good. Matters were no better in front of the battery. "By this time the enemy had got over their surprise and astonishment and began to come on us and then we had to get away as soon as possible," recalled Huggins.[38]

They barely escaped. The men of the Eighty-ninth Illinois stumbled wildly toward the guns, defying all efforts by their officers to keep order. Huggins managed to escape with two cannons, but the Illinoisans captured a third and were going after a fourth that some volunteers from the First Tennessee were struggling to drag down the road. The Illinoisans' ardor had completely broken up the integrity of their regiment, a situation that Willich would not tolerate, even if it meant foregoing the chance to seize a gun. Major William Williams watched Willich do what he and his fellow officers of the Eighty-ninth could not:

> At this point Brigadier General Willich came forward, and, standing in front of the regiment and amid the shower of bullets poured into us, complimented the regiment for its impetuous advance, calmed their excitement, instructed them how to advance firing and maintain their alignment with the advance of the brigade, and by his own inimitable calmness of manner restored order and confidence in the regiment, and after dressing them and drilling them in the manual of arms for a short time, ordered them to advance about thirty paces to the edge of an open space [Winfrey field]. They did so in good order, [then] lay down and kept the enemy in check.[39]

Colonel Dodge's regiments were moving too fast for him to steady them, as the charge he had ordered developed a momentum of its own. With Huggins and Field removed, the rest of Maney's mangled brigade gave way — Maney claims he was ordered to fall back behind the knoll where Turner's battery waited — and Dodge's Federals renewed their running pursuit of the Confederates.

Stahl took his cue from Maney. He pulled the Thirty-third and Thirty-first Tennessee out of the Brock field just as Turchin was sending the Thirty-sixth Ohio in on the left of Lane's Eleventh. The Twenty-fourth Tennessee and Fourth and Fifth Tennessee Consolidated, which was lying behind a swell in the middle of the field, still waiting for the chance to fire its first volley of the day, also withdrew into the woods. Lane led his Eleventh Ohio in pursuit through the field, but Turchin was content to see Strahl go, and in a few minutes the Ohioans rejoined the brigade, bringing with them a group of captured Tennesseans.

As the Brock field fell silent for the first time in nearly three hours, Hazen formally turned its defense over to Turchin, then marched his command out onto the Brotherton road at 3:30 P.M. Palmer was there to meet him. The Illinoisan sent Hazen to the Poe house to rest the brigade and replenish its ammunition. Turchin availed himself of the lull to move his brigade by the right flank through the cornfield in order to close an interval with Cruft's left created by Hazen's withdrawal.[40]

North of the Brock field, the battle raged. Lieutenant Turner and his cannoneers were on the knoll where Maney had posted them, ready to act as the anchor to a new defensive line. Instead of rallying as Maney had planned, however, his Tennesseans poured over and around the knoll, insensible to the artillerymen's calls for them to stop. Suddenly, the gunners were alone. Smith and Jackson had reformed behind the battery earlier, but only trees stood between the cannons and Dodge's cheering Yankees. It was a critical moment for Cheatham's division. Neither Jackson nor Smith was ready to repel an attack, and one more nudge by Dodge might do in Maney's brigade for good. The fate of the division rested on the shoulders of Lieutenant Turner, who had been affectionately labeled the "best artilleryman, but the poorest drilled man in the army" by a captain of Maney's staff. Be that as it may, there was nothing lax in Turner's actions now. He ordered the guns double-shotted with canister, and "when we fired it cut a swath in the advancing lines," wrote a member of the battery.

They raked Dodge's left with fire. The Federals tried to maneuver around the flanks of the battery, but Turner deftly wheeled his end pieces to meet them. Help came. Through the timber, a hundred yards to the southwest, Captain Stanford finally found a chance to do some good with his Mississippi Battery, which had idled the afternoon away watching Strahl's infantry get torn apart in the Brock field. He opened fire on Dodge's right, and the long Yankee line quivered to a halt. Turner and Stanford kept the Yankees at bay until they lost their enthusiasm for a pursuit turned bloody. Dodge had no desire to push the attack, as he already had lost sight of Willich. Having at last regained control of his brigade, Dodge yanked it back to the Winfrey house. There Willich found Dodge, resting his men. The Prussian had reported Dodge's disappearance to Johnson, who told him to break off his own pursuit of Dibrell. Willich had his brigade drawn up along the west edge of the Winfrey field, and he suggested to Dodge that he reform in two lines on his right, south of the Winfrey house. Dodge was happy to oblige. He reassembled his command in its original order—the Seventy-ninth Illinois and Seventy-seventh Pennsylvania in the front line, the Thirtieth and Twenty-ninth Indiana in reserve—refused his right, and then threw a strong skirmish line in the direction of his charge to discourage a Confederate counterattack.[41]

Attack was the furthest thing from Cheatham's mind; he was relieved simply to have escaped destruction. For Turner, Cheatham had nothing but praise. "Lieutenant," he said "you shall be captain of this battery from this time on. I have never seen artillery do such fearful execution in so short a time." Later that day, Cheatham emphatically denied Maney's request that the battery be relieved from the line. "No, let it stay where it is," he told Maney. "For if it had not been for that battery, the Yankees would have been all over this country tonight."[42]

There remained one last drama to be played out on that part of the field before sunset. Bishop Polk, adorned in a "black slouch hat and a faded gray uniform," and Captain Wheless had stumbled upon the right wing of Cheatham's division at 2:00 P.M., just as Stewart was searching in vain for Polk on Cheatham's left wing. "It required but a few minutes to determine we were heavily outnumbered on that part of the field," wrote Wheless, whom Polk sent back to Bragg to report that Cheatham needed reinforcements desperately. The captain returned empty-handed. Wheless told the bishop that Bragg said he had no reinforcements to send, having already dispatched Stewart to that sector; Bragg would, however, order Hood to attack toward the La Fayette road to relieve the pressure on Polk.[43]

So Polk did what he could with the resources at hand. Being on the right of Cheatham's line, he concentrated on the threat to that sector. When Maney relieved Jackson, the bishop asked Walker to send Liddell's division, which had regrouped south of the Youngblood farm, back into action on Maney's right. Had Polk's request come thirty minutes earlier, Liddell could have come up in time to extend Cheatham's line sufficiently to repel the advance of Baldwin and Willich. As it was, he did not get started until 3:00 P.M. By the time Govan's brigade crossed the Brotherton road, Maney had fled and Dibrell's troopers were milling about east of the Winfrey field. Behind a fence on the far side of the field, Willich's infantry rested while Baldwin closed up on its left.[44]

Liddell halted Govan on the north side of the Brotherton road, then faced the division to the left and advanced. For the men of Walthall's brigade it was a nightmare revisited. Before them was the Winfrey field, carpeted with the mangled bodies of comrades lost during their morning retreat.

Willich's skirmishers fell back, and the Mississippians stepped into the field. At the first Yankee fire the entire brigade fell to the ground. On the right, Major W. C. Staples toppled from his horse with a bullet in the back, and command of the Twenty-fourth Mississippi passed to a captain. For fifteen minutes, the brigade endured what one Mississippian called a "murderous fire" from the Federals, before Walthall gave the order to withdraw. The severity of the fire was more imagined than real — the Thirty-fourth Mississippi lost just seven men — but the will to fight had left the Mississippians. There was no attempt at pursuit, which was just as well, wrote Levi Wagner of the First Ohio, for "if they had got the First to advance through that field in line, there might have been none of the First left to blow about their deeds of valor."[45]

Govan's assault showed some initial promise, but it too lacked conviction. Unbeknownst to the North Carolinian, his route of advance led past Baldwin's left and deep into the Federal rear, offering Govan a rare opportunity to completely envelop his enemy. Baldwin saw the danger, but seemed incapable of acting to combat it. Once again, the clear-sighted equanimity of August Willich prevailed. Not only did the Prussian see the danger, but he had anticipated it. A few minutes before Liddell's attack, he rode to Johnson to point out that Baldwin's left was in the air. A division staff officer assured him that Baird's division was on the way to extend the line, and Willich returned to his command.

But Baird never came, so Willich — whom Johnson said was "always in the right place" — suggested to Baldwin that he face his second-line regiments to the left and with them charge to sweep his rear clear of the Arkansans.

Baldwin had the good sense to act on Willich's advice. He sent the Ninety-third Ohio to the left of the Fifth Kentucky, then ordered the Sixth Indiana to the left of the Ohioans. Now it was Govan who was outflanked. The Sixth and Seventh Arkansas held its ground for a few minutes, its volleys sending tremors through the Ninety-third Ohio. But Baldwin had regained his composure. When the regiment's commander fell, Baldwin grabbed the colors and, with a hearty cry of "Rally round the flag, boys," ordered the Ninety-third to charge. The Arkansans gave way in confusion, starting a panic that swept the length of Govan's brigade. The regimental commanders were powerless to stop what they did not understand. Major A. Watkins watched his Eighth Arkansas break and run after facing only a smattering of rifle fire. Lieutenant Colonel John Murray was even more perplexed by the sudden collapse of his regiment, the Fifth and Thirteenth Arkansas. "I am still unable to account for this panic, as during all this time nothing more than a few musket shots, with an occasional shell, were passing over my line, and I could not see the enemy."[46]

Lieutenant John Phelan, commanding a section of Fowler's Alabama

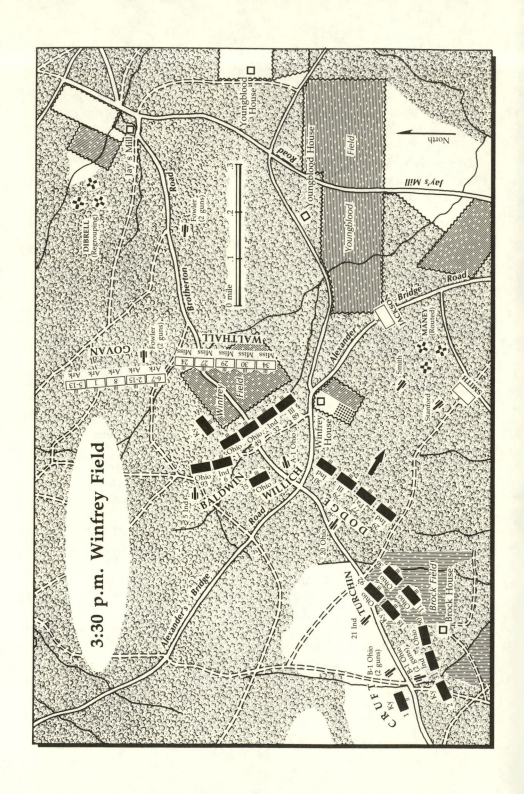

3:30 p.m. Winfrey Field

North

DIBRELL
(Regrouping)

Jay's Mill

Road

Brotherton

Fowler
(2 guns)

0 mile 1 2 3

Youngblood
House

Youngblood
House

Youngblood Road

Youngblood
Field

Jay's Mill

Road

GOVAN

Fowler
(2 guns)

6-7 Ark Ark Ark Ark 8 1 2-15 5-13

WALTHALL

Miss Miss Miss Miss Miss
34 30 29 27 24

Alexander's

Bridge

JACKSON

MANEY
(Routed)

Road

Smith

Stanford

SMITH

Winfrey
Field

Winfrey
House

Ky Ohio Ohio Ind III
32 49 89

III Ind
15

A-1 Ohio

DODGE

Ohio Ind
93 6

5 Ind Ky II

Ohio
32

Road

WILLICH

BALDWIN

Ind
30

20 Ohio

TURCHIN

Ohio
93

Ohio
18

Ohio
90

Brock Field

Brock House

21 Ind

Ky
19

B-1 Ohio
(2 guns)

1 Ohio
(2 guns)

B-1 Ohio
(2 guns)

Ky

CRUFT

Ky
1

Alexander's Bridge

Battery, happened to be behind Govan's brigade when it broke. In a re-markable display of bad judgment, Captain Fowler had ordered Phelan to follow Walthall's infantry into the Winfrey field. Phelan lost his way in the forest and mistook the Sixth and Seventh Arkansas Consolidated for one of Walthall's regiments. He brought his limbers up just as the Arkansans gave way. In a matter of moments, every horse of one team was shot down. Phelan abandoned the gun to the Ninety-third Ohio, and the humiliation of the Confederates was complete.[47]

Willich had hoped for more than a handful of prisoners and a captured cannon. While Baldwin cleared his front of Govan and as Walthall's infantry stumbled back across the Winfrey field, the Prussian looked anxiously for some sign of Baird's division. Not until the last rays of sunlight receded from the smoke-darkened forest did the brigades of Scribner and Starkweather come into line on Baldwin's left. Willich was furious. A rare opportunity had passed. "As we had discovered the flank of the enemy in our first forward move, the great consequence for the success of the day presents itself to every military mind which would have resulted from the spon-taneous advance of the division to our left with our own advance, and by which we could have attacked the enemy's broken flank by changing front to the right. As it was, all I could do was to keep my position and be on the lookout for other attacks."[48]

Few sympathized with Willich just then. After four hours of brutal combat, most of the soldiers of Johnson's division probably hoped only that they had seen the last of the Confederates for the day.

CHAPTER ELEVEN

A BELLYFUL OF FIGHTING

B RIGADIER General Jefferson C. Davis led his division into battle with
no prospect of promotion, regardless of how brilliantly he might command. Like Bushrod Johnson, he had made one tragic mistake that was to
haunt him the rest of his days. Twelve months earlier, while on sick leave
at his home in Indiana, Davis had heard that general officers were needed
in Cincinnati and Louisville to help organize those communities to repel
the invading armies of Bragg and Kirby Smith. Davis volunteered his services
to Major General Horatio Wright at Cincinnati, who sent him on to help
the commander at Louisville, Major General William Nelson.

Anyone who knew the two could have predicted trouble. A man of
"almost gigantic proportions," Nelson was "passionately overbearing and
insulting"; Davis, slight of frame, was "intensely proud and of hot temper."
Perhaps Davis had hoped to see action, although he had no reason to expect
anything but dull duty, which is what he got. Nelson assigned him the
mundane task of arming and training the citizens of Louisville. A couple
of days later, Davis called on Nelson at his headquarters in the Galt House.

"Well, Davis, how are you getting along with your command?" Nelson
inquired.

"I don't know," responded Davis. Nelson continued. How many regiments
had he organized? Davis did not know. How many companies? Davis did
not know. Nelson lost patience with the Indianian's obvious indifference
to his duties.

"But you should know," he remonstrated. "I am disappointed in you,
General Davis; I selected you for this duty because you were an officer of
the regular army, but I find I made a mistake."

Davis replied slowly, choosing his words with care: "General Nelson, I
am a regular soldier, and I demand the treatment due to me as a general
officer." He then called in Nelson's medical director to witness the quarrel.

Nelson repeated the reprimand for the doctor's benefit and ordered Davis to return to Cincinnati.

"You have no authority to order me," Davis rejoined.

Turning to his adjutant general, Nelson said: "Captain, if General Davis does not leave the city by nine o'clock tonight, give instructions to the provost-marshal to see that he is put across the Ohio."

Davis left. When Major General Don Carlos Buell entered Louisville at the head of the Army of the Ohio a few days later, Wright ordered Davis back to the city, this time to report to Buell for duty. Davis returned, glad to have a chance to settle the score with Nelson. In the company of his influential friend, Governor Oliver Morton of Indiana, he burst into the Galt House on the morning of 29 September 1862. Nelson had just finished breakfast and was standing in the hotel office. Davis reminded Nelson of their altercation and demanded satisfaction. Nelson ignored him. Davis persisted.

"Go away, you damned puppy. I don't want anything to do with you," sneered Nelson. Davis snapped. He flipped a paper wad in the face of the burly Kentuckian. Nelson slapped Davis, then glared at Morton. "Did you come here, sir, to see me insulted?" "No," Morton replied weakly, and Nelson walked off. Davis asked for a pistol, and some idiot obliged him. Davis darted after Nelson, who turned and coolly walked toward him. Davis fired. Nelson staggered up the stairs and collapsed.

Tom Crittenden heard the shot. He rushed from the breakfast table to find his friend gasping in a pool of blood. "Nelson, are you seriously hurt?" Crittenden asked as he grasped his hand. "Tom, I am murdered," Nelson answered, and an hour later he was dead.

Both generals had powerful partisans prepared to face off in court. But no charges were preferred, and Davis was released from custody. In October, a civilian grand jury indicted Davis for manslaughter, but released him on five thousand dollars bail. The case dragged on until May 1864, when "it was stricken from the docket, with leave to reinstate." Despite repeated gallantry in action and five brevets, Davis was never promoted. As a fellow general put it: "Perhaps the Administration felt about him as Dr. Johnson did about the American colonists, that he 'ought to be thankful for anything . . . short of hanging.'"[1]

So Davis had the dubious distinction of being the only general officer at Chickamauga free on bail. Sadly, the tragedy had taught him nothing about how to treat subordinates. Brigadier General William Carlin despised him, and Colonel Hans Heg found service under Davis so distasteful that he had threatened to resign from the army at the end of the campaign if not transferred.[2]

Whatever Davis's shortcomings as a human being, none questioned his gallantry. Rosecrans had ordered him to leave the Eighth Wisconsin Light Artillery near the Widow Glenn house and with the rest of his command advance "in the direction of the heaviest firing" to try to find and turn the enemy's left flank. Vague though his instructions were, Davis acted at once to comply. He led his division in column of regiments—Heg's brigade in the lead—down the Glenn hill and into the stubble field of the Benjamin Brock farm at "almost a trot." Davis heard the thunder from Sam Beatty's clash with Wright roll over the forest but misjudged its location. Convinced that his advance would bring him in on Van Cleve's right, when in reality nearly a half mile lay between their flanks, Davis sent Heg across the La Fayette road, telling him to feel for the enemy's left as he entered the forest.[3]

The terrain over which Heg advanced was singularly unsuited for a flanking movement. On the east side of the road, the timber was "heavy . . . thickly grown with jack-oak bushes, making it utterly impossible to see what was going on twenty yards distant," as one regimental commander complained in his after-action report. Where Heg's right entered the forest there stood a single-room, log schoolhouse. Seventy-five yards to the south lay an open field belonging to the Viniard family. It extended five hundred yards along the road to the south and seven hundred yards to the east and was bounded by forest and thickets. On the west side of the road was another field belonging to the Viniards, as well as their house and stable, which were bordered by a weatherbeaten garden fence. North of the Viniard farm was the field and farmhouse of Benjamin Brock. Together, the fields of Brock and Viniard encompassed an open space of nearly half a mile from north to south and two hundred yards east to west, and they were separated by a wooded hollow and a rail fence that ran due west from the log schoolhouse. From the La Fayette road westward, the Viniard field sloped gently downward for one hundred yards until it reached a long, willow-fringed ditch, from one and a half to three and a half feet deep and three to eight feet wide, that ran the length of their property. The ground sloped upward from the ditch to the thick woods that bordered the field on the west.[4]

There, at the edge of the timber, Wilder's Lightning Brigade had passed the morning, watching first Thomas's then Johnson's men hurry along the Dry Valley Road behind them and listening to the sounds of battle away to the north. They had used their time wisely, building a solid barricade of rails, earth, brush, and trees. Now, at 1:30 P.M., they looked on from the safety of their breastworks as Heg's brigade disappeared into the forest and Carlin worked feverishly to deploy his command in the west Viniard field, sixty yards behind and to the right of Heg.[5]

Heg advanced with the Thirty-fifth Illinois, Eighth Kansas, and the Fifteenth Wisconsin in line of battle and the Twenty-fifth Illinois in double column closed on the center in reserve. The Fifteenth was a regiment in name only: disease and battle losses had cut its ranks of Scandinavian immigrants to only 176.

Heg was playing a risky game. For some reason he chose to move without skirmishers, and his twelve hundred men stepped through a tangle of vines, scrub oak, and pines with no one to warn them of what lay ahead. For three, maybe four hundred yards they groped blindly on, down a gentle ridge and into a miserable, humid hollow. There they stumbled on enemy pickets, who turned tail at the sight of the double-line of Yankees bearing down on them. Enough fired their rifles, however, to catch the ear of their brigade commander, Brigadier General John Gregg. It was the misfortune of Lieutenant Colonel J. J. Turner of the Thirtieth Tennessee to be near the general just then. Gregg asked Turner to ride forward and find out why his pickets were rushing pell-mell onto the main line. "I could not get anything out of the pickets or rally them as they rushed past me, so I stopped and took a peep through the thick young pines, and in fifty yards of me two lines of Federals were rapidly approaching," recalled Turner. "Just as I turned to retreat I was shot nearly through my right breast by a minie ball." Turner staggered back to his regiment, and as he collapsed behind it the two lines opened up at close range "with an earnestness and deadly furor that I have never seen equalled."[6]

The slaughter was terrific. In the Fiftieth Tennessee, fifty-seven men were struck down before the regiment moved a step. With mixed horror and pride, Lieutenant Colonel Turner squinted through his pain at the men of his Thirtieth Tennessee, who were falling in windrows: "They were too brave to retreat and would not advance until ordered." After a few minutes, their officers at least had the good sense to allow the men to take cover.

Despite their early losses, the Confederates held the advantage. Heg's Eighth Wisconsin Light Artillery was a mile to the rear at the Glenn house, while Bushrod Johnson had three batteries a stone's throw from the fighting. He put them to good use. Everett's Georgia Battery unlimbered on the extreme left of Fulton's brigade, behind the Seventeenth Tennessee, which was raking the Thirty-fifth Illinois with a terrific enfilading fire. Bledsoe's Missouri Battery opened on the Federals from in front, Culpeper's South Carolina Battery blasted them from the right, and "at once the roar of battle became one steady, deep, jarring thunder," recalled a Kansan.[7]

All this was too much for the Federals. They held on long enough to squeeze off six or seven rounds, then began to back away from the fight. Heg brought up the Twenty-fifth Illinois to extend his right and managed to steady the brigade long enough for it to get off ten or twelve more volleys. With their artillery booming behind them, the Confederates were confident now. Gregg sent his second line forward to relieve the decimated first, then called for an advance of the whole. As the Rebels stepped forward, Heg yelled for a bayonet charge. Nothing happened. The Eighth Kansas had lost five captains, three lieutenants, and nearly 150 men, and the survivors were giving way rapidly. Every regiment was leaking men rearward; a charge was out of the question. Heg reluctantly reversed himself and, at 2:15 P.M., allowed those men still on the field to withdraw slowly, firing as they fell back. The Confederates followed.[8]

Gregg's pursuit was part of a general advance of Bushrod Johnson's entire division. Bragg had made good on his promise to Captain Wheless to send Hood's corps forward to relieve pressure on Cheatham. Hood received the order to move shortly after Heg ran into his front line. He ordered Johnson to extricate himself as best he could from his fight with the Norwegian and to wheel to the northwest. Simply put, Hood was searching for the Federal right flank in order to disrupt the attack against Cheatham in the same way Davis had been feeling for the Confederate left flank to help Van Cleve clear his front. The movement was partially successful. Fulton's brigade, on the division right, glided easily beyond Heg's left toward the unsuspecting Sixty-eighth and One Hundred First Indiana regiments of King, who at last had fallen in on Van Cleve's right. Gregg's brigade, however, split apart. The men of the Third and Forty-first Tennessee regiments managed to keep their "touch of elbows to the right," and so wheeled with Fulton away from their own brigade. McNair, in reserve, kept his place behind Gregg's left.[9]

Left with only four regiments, Gregg found his pursuit of Heg, which he could not break off without endangering his command, slow to a crawl. He pushed the Yankees another fifty yards before Heg, sensing the weakened state of his enemy, reformed his battered line and stopped the Confederates altogether. After having been forced to first give ground, the Norwegian at last had his chance to charge. His battered line moved forward again, and the Confederates began to recede.[10]

Heg had help. Carlin's brigade was in line of battle on the Norwegian's right, and Wilder had left his barricades and crossed the road on Heg's left in response to an order from Crittenden, who had passed by a few minutes earlier en route to the Widow Glenn house.

Crittenden probably rode up and down the La Fayette road more than any other general that afternoon. He was turning in his finest performance as a corps commander, displaying an uncanny knack for knowing exactly where his units were needed and following through to ensure they got there. The Kentuckian was with Van Cleve when his division moved into the forest against Cheatham's left. Sensing that Van Cleve's line was too short, he sent his chief of staff, Colonel Lyne Starling, galloping to headquarters to request permission to bring up Wood. Again Crittenden's instincts were correct; Wood's two brigades would just fill the gap between Van Cleve's right and Davis's left. Starling returned minutes later with Rosecrans's approval. Major Mendenhall left to hurry Wood along. Crittenden rode with him as far as the log schoolhouse, where he stopped to await Wood's arrival. He had done all he could, but still the Kentuckian was troubled. "The enemy appeared to have troops enough to fight us everywhere, and to fill up every interval as soon as my divisions passed," he wrote.

Rosecrans appreciated the enterprise of his normally indolent corps commander, so much so that he formally assigned Crittenden command of the Federal center. Rosecrans relieved him of responsibility for the defense of Lee and Gordon's Mill and gave that mission to McCook, whom he instructed to make Sheridan available, if needed. Grateful at the prospect of having another division to throw against the ubiquitous Confederates, Crittenden rode to the Widow Glenn house to get any final instructions Rosecrans might have for him before Wood came up. Before leaving, he asked Starling to tell Wood when he arrived that "in coming to the field he might have an opportunity, by leaving the road before he reached our position and moving to his right, to strike the enemy on the flank."[11]

Over in the east Viniard field, Carlin had had a hard time getting started. He had his brigade deployed to his satisfaction at 2:00 P.M. The Thirty-eighth Illinois lay in the timber north of the field, the One Hundred First Ohio and Eighty-first Indiana were in the field itself, and the Twenty-first Illinois rested in reserve a hundred yards behind the Indianians. The Second Minnesota Battery remained in the field west of the road. All fronted east. Carlin was ready to start, when Davis rode up and barked out a series of commands that struck the Illinoisan as unwarranted meddling in the affairs of his brigade. The Second Minnesota Artillery should be brought across the road to a low rise that ran the length of the east Viniard field — it was a much better firing position, Davis told Carlin. While he was at it, Davis added, the Illinoisan had better detail a regiment to support the guns. Before he left, Davis took the Twenty-first Illinois with him to support Heg. Thoroughly rankled, Carlin placed the battery in his right rear and pulled the Eighty-first Indiana out of the front line to support it.

That decision, at least, was easy. The Eighty-first had been giving Carlin problems throughout the campaign; its field officers were absent, and the senior captain had shown signs that he was not up to his increased responsibilities. For the moment, the Eighty-first was out of harm's way, tucked fifty yards behind the battery; nevertheless, Carlin was not about to risk it in combat without sound leadership, and so he called on Major James Calloway of the Twenty-first Illinois to assume command of the Indianians. With his two remaining regiments — fewer than seven hundred men in all — Carlin started forward shortly before 2:30 P.M., keeping pace with Heg's right.[12]

The Thirty-eighth Illinois obeyed its orders to guide on Heg too literally, and after moving only a few yards through the timber its left companies became hopelessly entangled with the survivors of the Twenty-fifth Illinois. With the rest of the regiment, Lieutenant Colonel Daniel Gilmer felt his way around the left of Gregg's Fiftieth Tennessee. The two regiments opened on one another at close range. Out in the field, the One Hundred First Ohio was trying to keep abreast of Gilmer's Illinoisans by guiding on the volleys emanating from the woods. "The roar of musketry seemed to be almost constant, sometimes rolling off further to the left, then surging back toward us until it seemed to be at our very elbows, while frequently the crash of cannon by single piece, section, or entire battery, hammered and pounded and shook the very earth, filling the air with shot and shrapnel and bursting shell," remembered Sergeant Day. Gradually its commander made sense of the uproar, and the One Hundred First began a half-wheel to the left. It crossed the fence at the east end of the field and glided into the forest beyond, brushing aside the handful of skirmishers to its front.[13]

Unbeknownst to them, the Ohioans were about to stir up a hornet's nest. A little after 2:30 P.M., Hood had ordered his division, commanded by Brigadier General Evander Law, to wheel to the northwest and follow Fulton toward the La Fayette road, on a collision course with Van Cleve's right flank. Now, a few hundred yards to the northeast of the Ohioans, Brigadier General Jerome Robertson was struggling to bring his brigade on line with that of Colonel James Sheffield, so that the two might move off together after Fulton.

Robertson was a good soldier, but he had a knack of irritating his superiors. A doctor by profession, Robertson had practiced medicine for thirty-four years in Texas, and the Hippocratic oath weighed heavily on him. He could never fully reconcile the needs of the service with those of his men. "On one occasion, General Robertson protested against marching his barefoot men in the snow, when their bleeding feet the day before had left stains along the road, and took upon himself the responsibility of ignoring the order sent down from headquarters," wrote a sympathetic major of the Fourth Texas. "From a humane standpoint, he showed a tender regard for his faithful soldiers, wholly commendable and noble, but from a military standpoint, where unquestioned and blind obedience is the only standard of action, it savored of insubordination and he was relieved of his command and court-martialed."[14]

The affair blew over and Robertson was restored to command; in fact, he led Hood's Texas Brigade for fourteen months, longer than any other officer, and had seen it through the nightmare of Gettysburg. Grateful for his interest in their welfare, Robertson's men gave him the odd nickname of "Aunt Pollie" with the best of intentions. His son Felix, who commanded the artillery reserve of the army, was a miserable sycophant. Unlike his father, Felix would go to any length to ingratiate himself with his superiors. At Stones River, he had led a battery in support of Breckinridge's ill-fated assault on the final day of the battle. The young Robertson falsified his after-action report to slander Breckinridge's conduct of the attack, helping Bragg in his quarrel with the Kentuckian. The commanding general rewarded Felix's shady loyalty with a promotion to major and command of a newly created five-battery artillery reserve. Now father and son were reunited on the field of Chickamauga.[15]

The Texans felt the danger of the forest. For nearly an hour they had lain in line of battle while Yankee shells whistled and burst around them. Rumor had it that the soldiers to their front were "simply standing two or three hundred yards apart, firing at each other as fast as guns could be loaded," and that did not suit the Texans' style of fighting—they preferred to charge and get the business done quickly. One nervous soldier voiced the sentiment of all: "Boys, if we have to stand in a straight line as stationary targets for the Yankees to shoot at, this old Texas Brigade is going to run like hell!"

Few were as callous about their fate as Private William Fletcher, who fell into a deep sleep amid the thunder. "I was shaken and ordered to rise," he recalled, and in a moment the line started forward. Wounded soldiers staggered past. Riderless horses galloped by. Stragglers from Gregg's brigade shoved through their lines. "They came toward us in squads, and, though not running, were not idling by the wayside," observed Sergeant Joseph Polley of the Fourth Texas. "You fellers'll catch hell in thar," shouted one, obviously relishing the chance to taunt the great soldiers of Lee's army. "Them fellers out thar you ar goin' up again, ain't none of the blue-bellied, white-livered Yanks an' sassidge-eatin' forrin hirelin's you have in Virginny that'll run at the snap of a cap—they are Western fellers, an' they'll mighty quick give you a bellyful o' fightin'."[16]

Mighty quick indeed. Robertson had moved less than two hundred yards before Colonel Van Manning reported rifle fire coming from beyond the brigade left. Robertson sent word for him to change front with two companies of his Third Arkansas and clear out whoever was responsible for the firing. The courier had hardly left with the order when the brigade crested a ridge and Robertson discovered Carlin's two regiments bearing down on his left. Robertson halted and sent a staff officer to Law for instructions, while the Federals peppered away at Manning's Arkansans.[17]

Law approved a change of front, and Robertson shifted his line "forward on the left battalion" to confront Carlin. Law held Benning in place, but

Sheffield's brigade became detached and drifted north toward the Brock field. The forest had claimed another division, fragmented in the smoke and bedlam.[18]

Once again, the complaint among the troops was the same: no one could see much beyond his rifle barrel. No fighting that day was more bitter or less organized than that around the Viniard farm. Divisions were irrelevant, brigades unraveled, even regiments splintered in the whirlwind. Sergeant Joseph Polley gave his impression of the universal experience on the first day of Chickamauga: "In timber as thick as that in which the battle raged that afternoon, it was impossible for one in the ranks to see what was happening to right or left. To do his share of the work on hand, he could only look straight before him, and tackle the foe immediately facing him. Doing that with all my might and will, incidents occurred within twenty yards of me, to the right or left, that were wholly unwitnessed by me."[19]

In such circumstances, combat became more personal, and individual actions were magnified. Val Giles of the Fourth Texas noticed a comrade shooting straight up in the air and praying mightily with each shot. His lieutenant suggested he take aim at the Yankees, but the Texan kept on blazing away at the sky. His company commander threatened to cut him down with his sword if he persisted. "You can kill me if you want to, but I am not going to appear before my God with the blood of my fellow man on my soul," the soldier said without flinching. The captain let him alone, and for the rest of the afternoon the pious Texan stood up to every Yankee volley without returning a single shot. Sergeant Polley watched another member of the Fourth step behind a tree and, with his body protected from the flying bullets, extend his arms and wave them frantically. "What in the dickens are you doing, Tom?" someone asked. "Just feeling for a furlough," came the unabashed reply, and the soldier kept up "the feeling process as if his life depended it." S. M. Riggs of Company I did not have to feel for the bullet that struck him. "Oh! Lord! What shall I do?" he gasped as he sank to the ground. "My friend. Place your trust in the Lord Jesus Christ," counseled his captain. He lay a hand on the head of the dying Riggs, then moved on.[20]

Robertson's advance took the pressure off Gregg and brought Heg's counterattack to an abrupt halt. By 3:00 P.M., Gregg's four regiments existed in name only. Together they had mustered only 736 men at the start of the action; now there were perhaps half that number still fighting. Fragments of battalions, companies, and squads were scattered through the forest. The Fiftieth Tennessee, on the brigade left, had entered the battle with only 104 men present. Nearly half fell in the opening volleys, and now the survivors were strung out in a thin skirmish line in a vain effort to reestablish contact with the rest of the brigade, which had sheared off to the north during

Heg's second advance, opening a gap of nearly four hundred yards that gave the tired Federals of Heg's left regiments a brief respite. Slowly, the Texas Brigade drove the Yankees back through the timber and into the east Viniard field. There Robertson lost control of his command. The Fourth and Fifth Texas had been driving what remained of Heg's Fifteenth Wisconsin and Twenty-fifth Illinois and Carlin's Thirty-eighth Illinois. While the Third Arkansas, First Texas, and left companies of the Fourth Texas stepped into the field, the right companies of the Fourth and all of the Fifth Texas continued pushing the Federals through the woods, and Robertson lost sight of them. For the rest of the afternoon, these two regiments fought largely on their own.[21]

Hood had no intention of letting the battle deteriorate into a meaningless slugging match. As soon as Robertson came under fire, he asked Bragg for reinforcements to protect his left. In a rare moment of decisiveness, Bragg sent a courier to Buckner instructing him to help.

The Kentuckian could do little. With Stewart gone, he had on hand only the three brigades of Preston's division. A little after noon, Buckner had ordered Preston to shift his command six hundred yards by the right flank to fill the gap Stewart's withdrawal had created. Preston had had his division in column of brigades west of the Hunt farm, with Gracie in front, then Kelly, and finally Trigg. Rather than move them as Buckner directed, he brought Trigg's brigade from the rear to the right of Gracie. Colonel Robert C. Trigg had been in command only a few weeks, and he arranged his brigade with great care. The Virginian deployed his three Florida regiments and his own Fifty-fourth Virginia along a ridge between the home of the old Widow Thedford and the Park cabin, then sent his right-flank regiment, the First Florida Cavalry (Dismounted), forward three hundred yards as skirmishers. As the right companies edged their way into the southeast corner of the east Viniard field, they ran into the repeating rifles of Wilder's skirmishers. For the next two hours, the badly outgunned Floridians did their best to keep up a strong presence. At 2:00 P.M., the Second Minnesota Light Artillery wheeled into position across the field and for lack of a better target turned their guns on the First Florida. Stung by a hail of grape and canister, the Floridians ran back toward the brigade line.

Since Trigg was on the division right and had already found the enemy, Preston chose his brigade to reinforce Hood. Trigg received his orders at 3:00 P.M. Heavy firing had erupted beyond his right, so the Virginian marched off in that direction, assuming he would run into someone from Hood's division able to show him where he was needed.[22]

Trigg had a better idea of where he was going than did Colonel Sidney Barnes, with whom he was about to clash. Before moving off with Beatty and Dick, General Van Cleve had left Barnes with eight pieces of artillery and "instructions to take care of myself, hold my position, and repel any assault of the enemy." For the next hour Barnes did as he was told, peering across the creek near Lee and Gordon's Mill for any sign of Confederates. A few minutes before 2:00 P.M., Colonel Starling rode up and told the Kentuckian to get into the fight. Barnes asked Starling to be a bit more specific. "I was informed . . . that I was needed immediately to go forward at once and engage the enemy, that they were on the right of the road toward the creek as we went from Lee and Gordon's Mill to the battlefield, that our army was driving them, that I could take them in the flank; to go in and act on my own judgment," recalled Barnes. He formed his brigade in line of battle with the Eighth Kentucky and Fifty-first Ohio in the first line and the Thirty-fifth Indiana and Ninety-ninth Ohio in the second, then instructed his regimental commanders to wheel their companies into route column. With the Third Wisconsin battery and a section of Swallow's battery trailing, Barnes started his brigade north, keeping the La Fayette road centered between the two columns.

Captain James Love of the Eighth Kentucky was lost in dreams of home when the call came to fall in. Since morning, the Kentuckian had been pouring his heart out to his beloved fiancée, Molly, in a letter, while his comrades idled in the grass, brooding or dreaming as their natures dictated. As the regiment came to life, Love scribbled a few last, affectionate words of reassurance:

> Fear not! The Rebels hold not my life in their hands! I long to see you again already and count the days! Why it is four weeks since I bade you a sorrowful goodbye, and now I am at the other end of this great country; but happen what may, I feel that in a few more months I will be with you again a new man! And then? Will we separate much for a long time? Not with my will I assure you. Unless by your advice! But hark the bugle blows the assembly for a march and perhaps a fight, so I bid you a hurried adieu, but hope with God's help to address you again soon with glorious news for the good cause.[23]

A mile up the road, the battle was turning in Hood's favor. Robertson was driving Davis's division relentlessly. In the woods north of the east Viniard field, the Fourth and Fifth Texas had Heg up against the road, while the remainder of the brigade was pushing Carlin toward a slight rise at the western edge of the field.

Colonel Wilder was alert to the danger. He had brought his brigade back to the safety of its breastworks when the firing grew too near. From there, Wilder was able to act as a tactical reserve to Davis, responding to crises and aiming his repeating rifles at any Rebels who might get around the general's flanks. At that moment, it was apparent to the lowliest private in the brigade where Wilder's Spencers were needed. All eyes were on Carlin's front. "The wounded . . . are crawling over the brow of the ridge and sheltering themselves in the ditch by scores. The Rebel bullets have begun to pour across the field . . . in the rear of Davis's now retreating men," observed Sergeant McGee of the Seventy-second Indiana.[24]

In an instant, McGee and his comrades were on their feet and over the barricade, running across the west Viniard field to save the Second Minnesota Light Artillery, its cannons silhouetted along the rise across the road. The One Hundred Twenty-third Illinois went with them. The two regiments swept over the battery and into the southwest corner of the field, where they caught Robertson's Confederates in the left flank just as they were about to make their final rush for the guns. "Aunt Pollie" gathered up his men and fell back into the forest, hurried along by the rapid fire of Wilder's Spencers.[25]

Robertson's anxiety eased when he caught sight of Trigg's column approaching from the south. He sent a staff officer galloping to lay claim to the brigade, which was fine with Trigg, except that the excited messenger did not know where Robertson wanted him. The Second Minnesota Light Artillery shifted its fire to Trigg. As the shells burst ever closer, the flustered staff officer asked Trigg if he would mind waiting while he tried to find out where to deploy his command. With remarkable forbearance, the Virginian assented.[26]

Barnes beat Trigg to the field by fifteen minutes. The racket from the east Viniard field convinced Barnes that he had found the fighting. Guided only by the roll of rifle volleys, he took his brigade off the road into an old field completely overgrown with underbrush, just south of the east Viniard field. He brought his right forward slightly and hoped he was facing the enemy's flank. Reluctant to move, Barnes sent an aide to find Van Cleve for instructions. He returned empty-handed. Barnes told the officer to look for Crittenden. Again nothing. "Not being able to find either, and the fight waxing hotter, I determined to engage the enemy." On the strength of Starling's ninety-minute-old assurance that Wood's division would come up on his right, Barnes started into the brush. Had he waited just a few minutes longer, Barnes would have met Major Mendenhall, who might have been able to convey something of his corps commander's wishes. At the moment, however, Mendenhall was doing what he did best: massing artillery. At Murfreesboro he had arrayed forty cannons along a ridge on the west bank of Stones River just in time to blow Breckinridge's attacking Confederates back to their line of departure. Perhaps the memory of that triumph ran through his mind as he ordered Lieutenant Cortland Livingston, whom Barnes had left on the road, to bring the four ten-pounder Parrotts and two twelve-pounder howitzers of his Third Wisconsin Battery and the two-gun section of Swallow's battery alongside the Second Minnesota Light Artillery.

He was a long way from his Stones River total, but Mendenhall had a respectable force of fourteen cannons trained on the east Viniard field.[27]

Meanwhile, Trigg's wait had been mercifully brief. "While thus halted and under the enemy's fire General Robertson appeared, and hurriedly informing me that his line was very much weakened and would be beaten back unless quickly reinforced, indicated the direction in which I should move," recorded Trigg. "I obliqued to the right until I supposed that my right was opposite to his left. This brought the front of my brigade to the cornfield fence."[28]

Trigg's Floridians hit the fence just as Wilder was reeling in the Seventy-second Indiana and One Hundred Twenty-third Illinois. Believing the Federals to be in precipitate retreat, Trigg waved his men over the fence and into the southeast corner of the field. At the same time, Barnes entered the field from the southwest at a right angle with Carlin's line. The Seventy-second Indiana caused some momentary confusion as it passed through his lines, but Barnes had the situation in hand, and soon the Eighth Kentucky and Fifty-first Ohio were in the field, searching for the Confederate flank.

Carlin had no idea Barnes was coming. Far from appreciating the help, he was angered that this unknown command had masked the right regiments of his brigade. Carlin braved a hail of bullets from Trigg's Confederates, who were just crossing the fence, to learn the identity of the irksome brigade. The knowledge did him no good, however, as Barnes's lead regiments ignored his command to halt and continued across his front. By now they had blocked the field of fire of the right companies of the One Hundred First Ohio as well; to prevent them from masking the rest of the regiment Carlin ordered the Ohioans to conduct their own half-wheel to the left.[29]

Amid this self-inflicted pandemonium, Robertson and Trigg struck. Trigg caught Barnes in the flank, wholly unprepared. On the right, Lieutenant Colonel Charles Wood found his Fifty-first Ohio hopelessly outflanked by "an overwhelming" force, and he immediately ordered his men to withdraw. To his left, the Eighth Kentucky had been trading volleys with Robertson and getting the better of the match, when Wood's Ohioans began to stream across their lines. "We were expecting momentarily to be ordered forward when, to our surprise, we were completely flanked on our right by a heavy force who opened an enfilading fire on us at the same time those on our front opened with a renewed vigor," recalled Lieutenant Thomas Wright of the Eighth. Lieutenant Colonel James Mayhew held the regiment in place until the Fifty-first cleared its ranks, then ordered his Kentuckians to fall back, which they did "in as good order as possible."[30]

Captain Love was not among them. Two bullets had ripped through his thigh, tearing the muscle and jarring the bone. The Kentuckian felt no pain

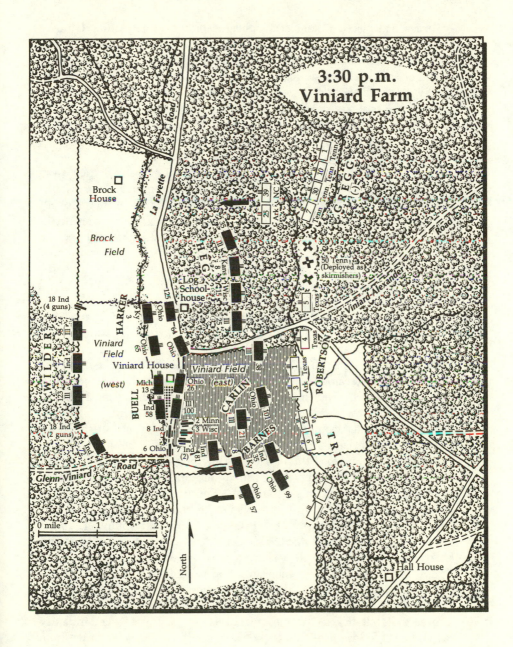

3:30 p.m.
Viniard Farm

as he sank to the ground, only the warm sensation of blood oozing down his leg.[31]

Barnes had placed Colonel Peter Swaine of the Ninety-ninth Ohio in command of the second line of the brigade. The moment he spotted trouble up front, Swaine had the good sense to order his men to lie down until the colors of the frontline regiments passed to the rear. "As soon as our front was cleared of our own men, I ordered an advance, which was gallantly made in the face of a deadly fire of musketry, the Irishmen and Buckeyes keeping up a perfect flame of fire and shower of lead," Swaine reported proudly. Trigg's advance was checked for the moment, and the two lines began blazing away at one another.[32]

Carlin was seething. The retreat of the Eighth Kentucky carried away the right wing of his One Hundred First Ohio, forcing it up the rise. Its colonel managed to steady the remainder of the regiment in the field, but Carlin's problems were far from over. So long as Swaine's two regiments remained in their front, the Twenty-first Illinois and Eighty-first Indiana could contribute nothing to the fight. Carlin thus found himself with only the Thirty-eighth Illinois and the left companies of the One Hundred First Ohio to oppose Robertson's second push for the road. From even these regiments, men had begun to trickle back toward the road.[33]

Davis's entire line was on the brink of collapse. The Fourth and Fifth Texas, still supported on the right by the stubborn survivors of the Fiftieth Tennessee, had fought Heg's Federals to within fifty yards of the La Fayette road. Farther than that the Yankees did not propose to be pushed, and the log schoolhouse became the fulcrum of their resistance. As their regiment gave ground to the Fourth Texas, some twenty Scandinavians from the Fifteenth Wisconsin took shelter inside the dilapidated little cabin and "resolved from that point of vantage to contest the advance of the Texas Brigade as long as possible," recounted Sergeant Polley. "The house stood at the far edge of the wood through which the brigade was making its way, and on account of the intervening timber and undergrowth, could be seen from only a few points along our line. The fire from it was rapid and damaging, but for quite a while our folks failed to discover whence it came."

Julius Glazer of Company D, himself an immigrant volunteer, caught sight of the schoolhouse first. With a yell he sprang from the line and charged toward it. When they realized what he was charging, a squad of Texans ran after him. With their attention turned elsewhere, the Federals had no inkling of Glazer's approach until, just twenty feet from the log schoolhouse, he called on them to surrender. The Yankees replied with half a dozen shots but nicked Glazer just twice. He fired, killing a Federal instantly. Before he could lower his rifle to protect himself, two Yankees darted from behind the house and plunged their bayonets into him. "In all reason,

Glazer should have fallen to the ground, and laid there content. But he did not; he simply sprang back and reached for a cartridge," observed an amazed Polley. "Unwilling to risk a loaded gun in his hands, the two men again rushed at him with levelled bayonets, and in the desperate fight that followed, he placed one of these hors-de-combat. Two more Federals joined the struggle. Bleeding from two bullet wounds and two bayonet jabs, Glazer held all three at bay until his comrades came up, shot two of the assailants, and chased the third into the house."

The Texans repeated Glazer's demand of surrender. "Take us if you can," the Federals yelled from the schoolhouse. They held on until half were dead or wounded before surrendering. As the excitement passed, Glazer felt his pulse slow and the pain surge over him. Only then did he quit the battle. Polley stopped the lieutenant in charge of the Federal squad. Why had they not shot Glazer from inside the house rather than expose themselves trying to bayonet him? "Because he was a mere boy, and after he fired his one shot we thought it would be cowardly to shoot him," the lieutenant answered wearily. "But if the fighting he did against two of our best men at first, and then against three, and that too, after he was four times wounded, is a sample of what you Texans are in the habit of doing, I am going to throw up my commission and return to peaceful pursuits." As a Texan, Polley may be excused for embellishing the story a bit.[34]

Private John C. West of Company E was a few yards to the right of the schoolhouse. He was the only married man in his company and had held a civilian job that exempted him from military duty. He volunteered nonetheless, and here at Chickamauga, like Glazer, his adrenalin got the better of him. With a wave of his hat and a cheer, West sprinted ahead of his company and became "mixed up with the Yanks by being too fast." West paused to pull the bayonet off his rifle; he had bruised his hand trying to reload with it attached. Just as he slid it into the scabbard a bullet struck the handle, knocking it off and driving the splinters into his hip. A wave of nausea rolled over him, the world went black, and the Texan fell, squarely on top of a badly wounded Yankee. When West regained his senses, the Federal he had crushed asked him to unbuckle his belt for him to ease his pain. This "I did with great difficulty, for I was very sick and spitting blood myself. He died before he had time to thank me," recalled West, who turned away and began the long crawl to the rear.[35]

As Trigg slowly rolled back Barnes, and Robertson pressed Carlin nearer the road, Davis faced yet another threat to his attenuated line, this time on the left flank. Bushrod Johnson had been shuttling between Fulton's brigade and that of Gregg, weighing the needs of both before committing McNair's brigade to the support of either. When Heg's counterattack turned the gap between the Fiftieth Tennessee and the rest of Gregg's brigade into a chasm, Johnson acted. At about 3:15 P.M., he ordered McNair to send the Thirty-ninth North Carolina and Twenty-fifth Arkansas into the breech. They came in on the left of the Seventh Texas but were too few to plug the gap, and 250 yards of open space remained between the Thirty-ninth North Carolina and Fiftieth Tennessee.[36]

Robertson was acutely aware of the gap. Although Heg's men were too exhausted to exploit it, Robertson begged Hood to send in troops to close the interval and a battery with which to silence Mendenhall's guns on the rise. Robertson never got his cannons, and the Texans fought the entire afternoon without close artillery support, but infantry reinforcements were on the way. A little after 4:00 P.M., Hood committed his only reserve, the Georgia brigade of Brigadier General Henry Benning, to the battle around the Viniard farm.[37]

Federal reinforcements came apace. Tom Wood showed up with his division at 3:30 P.M., just as Trigg fell upon Barnes and Robertson began his second attack. Wood was puzzled. He had not seen Colonel Starling, so he was unaware of Crittenden's desire that he seek out the Confederate left flank. The last word from Crittenden was that he go to the support of Van Cleve. Wood had known nothing of Davis's engagement and assumed that Van Cleve was a good distance to the north, but from the moment his command stepped onto the road the signs of near and impending disaster were unmistakable. "The hot air, like the breath of a furnace, was heavy with clouds of choking dust," recalled Lieutenant Wilbur Hinman of the Sixty-fifth Ohio. "We passed scores of ambulances filled with wounded, and hundreds of men, bleeding but not disabled, going to the rear in search of hospitals." Lieutenant Howell Trask of the Thirteenth Michigan remembered only the heat as he and his men pushed on at the double-quick time: "It was terribly hot and dusty, the woods along the way were on fire. Some of the men could not stand the rapid marching in the great heat and dust and fell behind, not overtaking the regiment until after they had been fighting some time." For three-quarters of a mile the long division column hurried north, and then "we were near the scene of conflict. Spent bullets began to fall about us. We could hear the cheers and yells of the combatants," recalled Hinman.[38]

Sitting on his horse on the La Fayette road opposite the east Viniard field at 3:30 P.M., Wood could see plenty of Federals evidently in need of help, but no sign of Van Cleve or Crittenden. "The order directed me to take position on the right of Van Cleve, but as I was totally ignorant of his position in the battle, and met no one on my arrival on the field to enlighten me, I found myself much embarrassed for the want of information whereby I could bring my command judiciously and effectively into action," he complained in his after-action report.

Meanwhile, Crittenden had returned from the Widow Glenn house and was looking for Wood. He was in a sour mood. Rosecrans was poorly informed of the happenings around the Viniard farm, and his earlier confidence in Crittenden's judgment had evaporated. Fixated on the fighting on Palmer and Van Cleve's front, he "condemned" Crittenden's design to use Barnes and Wood to strike at the Confederate left flank. Concerned that Starling might have found Wood and sent him forward against Rosecrans's wishes, the Kentuckian rode about trying to find either or both of them.

Davis found Wood first. The Indianian had plans of his own for the division. Heg was sorely pressed and needed support quickly, Davis told Wood. That much was apparent; Wood could see the steady and growing stream of fugitives from the fight around the log schoolhouse skulking across the road into the ravine in the west Viniard field. Davis added that Carlin too was hard pressed to hold his own in the woods bordering the east Viniard field and in the field itself; this was confirmed by the sharp rattle of musketry over the rise where they conferred.

"It was evident a crisis was at hand," Wood reported laconically, and he adapted to the emergency with skill. Major Mendenhall had joined the generals, probably to lay claim to Wood's batteries, but instead Wood sent him off to help Heg rally his troops. Wood agreed with Davis's suggestion that Harker should relieve Heg. Colonel Starling happened by and was sent down the road to bring up the brigade, which was catching its breath at the point where Barnes had gone into action perhaps thirty minutes earlier.

Starling had, in fact, just come from Harker. Knowing nothing of Wood and Davis's conference or of Rosecrans's rebuke of Crittenden, he had invoked his authority as chief of staff and, believing prompt action to be imperative, had taken it upon himself to turn Crittenden's earlier suggestion into an order. He directed Harker to take his brigade into the woods on Barnes's right to help him find and turn the enemy's left. Had Harker been permitted to carry out Starling's instructions, he undoubtedly would have taken Trigg in the flank and put an abrupt halt to the Confederate attack. Certainly Crittenden thought so. "General Wood reached the field but a short time before the enemy attacked our right . . . and had Wood been in the position I suggested, he would have been on the flank of the enemy, and, I think, would have punished him severely." But Davis and Wood felt differently, and just as Harker was about to carry out Starling's orders, the colonel returned to lead him up the road.

Davis was waiting for Harker at the log schoolhouse. Together they posted the brigade. The One Hundred Twenty-fifth Ohio lined up along the road with its left near the schoolhouse. The Sixty-fourth Ohio came into position on its right, and the Third Kentucky and Sixty-fifth Ohio formed a second line on the west side of the road. As Robertson's cheering Texans drew near and Heg's line wavered, Wood told Harker to throw the Sixty-fourth Ohio forward, oblique to the road, to take the Rebels in the flank when they came into range. Just as Harker turned to give the necessary orders, a staff officer galloped up to report that the Rebels had gained the La Fayette road farther to the north and were turning south to roll up Heg's left flank, which in turn would expose Harker's left.[39]

There could be no greater crisis, reasoned Wood. He countermanded Davis's orders and told Harker to charge up the road to check the Confederate advance. Off the Ohioan went, fighting his way north beyond Heg's left flank and into the gap in the Union line. After less than thirty minutes, Harker was thoroughly and understandably perplexed. "There was very great confusion among the troops which had been engaged, and no one seemed to have any definite idea of our own lines or the position of the enemy," he later wrote. "I was compelled, therefore, to resort to my own judgment alone and be guided by the general direction of the firing." So went the battle around the Viniard farm.[40]

Harker of course had no way of knowing, but the emergency on the left had passed even before he put his brigade in motion. It had begun at 3:30 P.M., when McNair's Thirty-ninth North Carolina and Twenty-fifth Arkansas swept across the La Fayette road into the open fields of the Benjamin Brock farm. Right behind them came the Seventh Texas and Thirtieth Tennessee, with a little fight still left in them. At the Brock cabin, McNair's men scattered what was left of the Thirty-fifth Illinois. For an instant, the way was clear to the Federal rear—only eight hundred yards of corn and the Eighth Wisconsin Artillery stood between them and the Widow Glenn house. Then the woods along the edge of the field to their left erupted in a sheet of flame, and the left companies of the Twenty-fifth Arkansas disintegrated. Never before had the Arkansans faced such a fire: volley followed volley with no pause for them to reply. Five bullets hit their commander, Lieutenant Colonel Eli Hufstedler, before he finally rolled off his horse. To complete the Arkansans's discomfiture, Harker's Yankees were hurrying up the road to their left and rear. Retreat was inevitable. As quickly as they had come, McNair's men were gone.

For the second time that afternoon, Wilder's Spencers had saved a Federal flank. It was his sighting of McNair's advance that had led Wilder to withdraw the Seventy-second Indiana and One Hundred Twenty-third Illinois so abruptly from the east Viniard field. The moment they were back, he swung the Seventeenth Indiana and Ninety-eighth Illinois into the timbered hollow south of the Brock cabin. There, with the two cannons of Lilly's left section, they decimated the unsuspecting Arkansans.[41]

Back at the Viniard farm, Colonel George P. Buell was as puzzled as Harker. Before leaving to superintend Harker's charge up the road, Wood told Buell to form on the road behind Carlin. Just twenty-nine years old, Buell had been in command of his brigade only four months. What the young Indianian most needed as he prepared for his first test under fire was guidance. Instead, he found himself oddly alone, gleaning only confused and contradictory rumors from staff officers and orderlies on errands too pressing to permit lengthy briefings. "While my troops were being formed the enemy's balls were whistling about our ears, and the battle, raging most fiercely, seemed approaching nearer, although I had been informed several times by staff officers that we were driving the enemy, and that our force was only needed to finish the rout. I was not informed as to the positions of troops around me, whether we had troops in front and on my left flank," Buell reported with disgust. Left to his own devices, Buell deployed his brigade in two lines parallel to the road. The Twenty-sixth Ohio formed in the southwest corner of the woods behind Carlin's Thirty-eighth Illinois, and the One Hundredth Illinois lined up on the west side of the rise behind and to the left of the Second Minnesota Light Artillery. Buell placed his second line seventy-five yards in the rear, with the Thirteenth Michigan on the left and the Fifty-eighth Indiana on the right, behind the Viniard farmhouse. Assuming the Rebels to be in retreat, Buell ordered Captain George Estep to unlimber the four six-pounders and two twelve-pounder howitzers of his Eighth Indiana Artillery on the rise beside the Twenty-sixth Ohio.[42]

In fairness to Davis and his staff, it must be said that the situation in the Viniard fields was deteriorating too rapidly to make any briefing meaningful. After trading volleys with Trigg for about fifteen minutes, Colonel Swaine found himself flanked on the right by the First and Seventh Florida. "The time had come to retreat," the Ohioan concluded, and he ordered the Ninety-ninth Ohio and Thirty-fifth Indiana to fall back firing toward the road. The Sixth Florida had been waiting for just this moment. Since coming into the field, the Floridians had had their eyes on the cannons of the Second Minnesota Light Artillery and Third Wisconsin Light Artillery silhouetted on the rise to their front, and now they sprinted forward to claim them. Trigg passed the word for a general charge of the entire line, then galloped after the Sixth.

Only three hundred yards separated the Sixth Florida from the guns. For a few minutes the Twenty-first Illinois blocked the Floridians's advance, but when the remaining companies of the One Hundred First Ohio melted away on their left and the very batteries they were trying to defend accidentally threw a few rounds into their backs, the Illinoisans conceded the field. Then, with the batteries his for the taking, Trigg faltered. As the thrill of the chase wore off, the Virginian realized his order to charge had been lost in the din. Instead of closing on the rise with his entire brigade,

Trigg and the Sixth Florida were alone, two hundred yards in advance of any other friendly forces. To make matters worse, Major Calloway had instilled in the Eighty-first Indiana the will to fight, and now his adopted regiment was pouring a withering fire into the left flank of the Floridians. Trigg had no choice but to halt the Sixth and start back for the rest of the brigade.[43]

Matters were brighter to Trigg's right, where Robertson was sweeping everything before him. After two hours of brutal, stand-up fighting, Davis's line finally buckled. Heg's infantry spilled across the La Fayette road, and it was all the Norwegian could do just to herd the survivors into the ditch behind the Viniard farm. East of the road, Carlin's infantry scampered up through Mendenhall's batteries into the field, blocking their line of fire and interfering with their efforts to limber the guns.

Colonel Buell was stunned. "The formation of my command was not yet complete, when everything on my immediate front and left gave way, and hundreds of our own men ran through my ranks crying, 'Fall back! Fall back!' as they themselves were in shameful rout toward the rear." As the first frightened stragglers of Carlin's command stumbled into the road, Buell galloped to his frontline regiments—the Twenty-sixth Ohio and One Hundredth Illinois—and ordered the men to lie down and brace themselves for the stampede. Buell's exhortations lacked conviction. He knew his soldiers would be unable to withstand the shock. Leaving their regimental commanders to cope as best they could, Buell hurried back to the Viniard farm to prepare his second line to launch a bayonet charge to cover the retreat of the first line, when it came.[44]

Buell's fears were realized. Lieutenant Colonel William Young tried desperately to hold his Twenty-sixth Ohio together. As Buell rode away, "dozens, then scores, and finally hundreds, of straggling soldiers came rushing through the woods and over my line in the wildest disorder and most shameful confusion, there seeming to be no effort to either check or control the retreat," said Young. The Ohioans hugged the ground as the panicked survivors of the Thirty-eighth Illinois kicked and trampled a path through their ranks. Bullets stirred the dirt and the Rebel yell grew louder. When the last Yankee cleared his front, Young ordered his men to their feet. He barked out the command to fix bayonets, intending to fire a volley and then charge. "As I was about executing this intention, a mounted officer came galloping to the rear calling out 'For God's sake, don't fire; two lines of our own troops are still in the woods.' " Young hesitated. His men looked to him expectantly. An instant later a volley ripped across his line from the woods beyond his left. Nine bullets struck his horse, and Young fell hard on the ground. His major toppled from the saddle wounded. Screaming Rebels poured out of the timber that was supposed to have held friendly troops. Young kept his composure and his purpose. He again yelled for a bayonet charge. Tragically, just a handful of soldiers near him heard the command. They darted forward with bayonets gleaming, only to be swallowed up in a sea of surging Butternut. Young's regiment was disintegrating around him. His five left companies had lost between half and three-quarters of their numbers. Where the left center company had stood, twenty-four strong, there was now only a pitiful little cluster of five. Four company commanders were down. The Fifth Texas struck his front rank, and the two lines were lost in a tangle of swinging rifle butts and jabbing bayonets.

Only then could Young admit to himself that "defense had become hopeless." Somehow he disentangled his men from the enemy and retreated across the road "under a severe direct and cross fire and the loud cheers of the advancing Rebels." They hopped the fence of the Viniard farm, formed a scratch line, frantically reloaded, then let go a volley that knocked the spirit out of the Texans' pursuit. Young hoped to hold the fence, but when the smoke cleared the Texans were back, in front and on both his flanks. "Already too many noble privates had written themselves heroes with blood stains upon the sod. It was a proud thing to have died there with those that were dead; it was duty to save the remnant of the living for still another struggle," Young conceded. He ordered his men into the ditch behind the farm, already crowded with the wounded and dying of Heg's brigade.[45]

On Young's right, Colonel Frederick Bartleson, the one-armed commander of the One Hundredth Illinois, had held on long enough to allow Captain Estep to bring five of his six guns off the rise, but at a terrible cost. General Wood claimed personally to have ordered the regiment to charge "with a view of checking an exultant enemy." The attempt was feeble, he maintained, through no fault of the Illinoisans: "The bayonets were promptly fixed, and the regiment had just commenced to advance, when it was struck by a crowd of fugitives and swept away in the general melange." Wood did the Illinoisans a gross injustice. They had saved Estep's battery, and nearly one hundred members of the regiment lay in front of the rise to bear silent witness to their stand, however brief it may have been.[46]

Buell witnessed the destruction of the Twenty-sixth Ohio and One Hundredth Illinois from behind the Viniard farmhouse, where he waited with the Thirteenth Michigan and Fifty-eighth Indiana for their chance to live the nightmare. As the men of Young's and Bartleson's shattered regiments streamed into the farmyard, Buell ordered them forward. The Thirteenth Michigan got as far as the fence on the east side of the farm before running into the Fifth Texas. Colonel Joshua Culver fell in the first fire, stunned by an exploding shell. His Michiganders held on for ten minutes, until the Fourth Texas worked its way around their left flank, then they too dropped back into the hopelessly crowded ditch.[47]

Lieutenant Colonel James Embree's Fifty-eighth Indiana made it farther, but at a greater cost. As the Indianians jumped the fence and stepped into the farmyard, they were struck by the bouncing limbers and caissons of Estep's battery. Frothed with terror, the horses resisted the reins of their horrified drivers, who screamed and strained to steer them away from the infantry. Most of the Indianians jumped clear of the limbers, but far too many were crushed under the wheels. Companies B, G, and K veered to the left to avoid the battery and were lost in the smoke and confusion. The remainder of the Fifty-eighth broke up around the farmhouse and stable. "In this condition the regiment undertook to execute the order to charge," lamented Colonel Embree. "No enemy could be seen, they being concealed by the fence, horses, men, and dust in front."

Companies B, G, and K blundered across the road to within a few yards of the men of the Fifth Texas, who were lying in a ditch below the rise. The Texans stood up and opened fire. The Hoosiers replied, and "for a few minutes the air was so filled with smoke that it was impossible to see anyone at a distance of a few feet," a Yankee survivor recalled. The tiny command melted away in the smoke. Company B lost thirty of its sixty-one members in what could hardly have been more than a few minutes' clash.

Colonel Embree claimed he kept the rest of his regiment in the fight for ten minutes, gallantly pouring volleys into the Rebels until hopelessly outflanked. Sergeant D. H. Hamilton of the First Texas, in what certainly was a reference to his regiment's clash with the Fifty-eighth, tells a somewhat different story: "The Yankees in front of us occupied an old farm; they had torn down the rail fences and made breastworks of them . . . and were lying behind this barricade when we charged them. When we got within about one hundred yards of them they arose, fired one volley and ran like turkeys."[48]

Regardless of how long Buell's regiments actually held their ground, their abortive counterattacks succeeded in disrupting the Confederate pursuit and saving Mendenhall's batteries. That Trigg and Robertson were working at cross purposes certainly helped the Federals. Trigg had left the Sixth Florida just short of the rise and ridden halfway back to the Fifty-fourth Virginia and Seventh Florida, which had paused behind a fence midway across the east Viniard field, before he saw them move forward of their own accord. Satisfied that they were coming to help, Trigg wheeled his horse and rejoined the Sixth Florida. In reality, they were moving on an entirely different course under orders from Robertson. The stubborn if brief resistance put up by the Twenty-sixth Ohio and One Hundredth Illinois had induced Robertson to seize Trigg's regiments to support his own wavering line. Lieutenant Colonel John Wade of the Fifty-fourth Virginia apologized to

Trigg in his report: "I . . . was in the act of crossing the second fence when I was met by General Robertson, of General Hood's division, who said he had been sent to conduct the brigade into the fight, we were going wrong, and that our formation should be made on his brigade, in the woods to the right of the field. Knowing that we were to be subject to General Hood's orders, I suffered my regiment to be conducted by him, and moved by the right flank along the cross-fence to the woods." The Seventh Florida and First Florida Cavalry (Dismounted) followed Wade, leaving Trigg with only the Sixth Florida. Reluctantly, he waved the regiment away from the rise, and the Second Minnesota Light Artillery and Livingston's Third Wisconsin Light Artillery made good their escape.

The Sixth Florida had done the only real fighting in Trigg's brigade, which was to contribute little the rest of the afternoon. The Sixth lost 165 men in its unsupported advance. In the First Florida Cavalry (Dismounted), which purportedly skirmished for two hours before the brigade went into battle, the total losses for the day were two killed and fifteen wounded. In the Fifty-fourth Virginia only thirty-eight men fell, and losses were similarly light in the Seventh Florida.[49]

Lieutenant Livingston took his close call as a portent. While the Minnesotans drove their guns into the west Viniard field, Livingston drew off down the road to his original position. There he set up his guns in time to provide a rallying point for Barnes's shattered infantry.[50]

The Viniard farm was awful, a scene of terror tempered by exultation. Hundreds of frightened Federals squeezed together like sheep, wanting nothing more than to find a way out of the farmyard; as many Texans, bent on seeing to it that few left alive, taunted and shot them. Private Fletcher watched the Yankees crowd against the fence that blocked their way to the ravine. "A short distance to the enemy's rear . . . was a high well-built worm rail fence, and as I suppose it was the least of their thoughts of having to return that way, or they would have had it torn down to clear their rear. At this point we were crowding them so close that they had no time to push down the fence or to climb it. . . . A great majority of them were in a pushing motion and jammed and at close range. I got two shots and thought — oh, for a shotgun loaded with buckshot," the Texan recalled with absolute delight.

As Fletcher passed around the corner of the house to get a better shot, a bullet ripped across his left foot, and he tumbled into a hole beside the chimney, out of harm's way. "There had been no pain up to this time, so the idea struck me that I was not wounded and had a coward's position, and I was liable to be seen in it." When he raised himself to get up, Fletcher saw the heel of his left shoe had been shot off. He removed the shoe and found his heel bleeding and badly mangled. The chimney hole offered refuge, but fear of capture sent Fletcher hopping toward the rear. After seventy-five yards he fell against an oak tree to catch his breath. "There was a wounded Yank sitting down, leaning against it. This gave him protection from the bullets . . . and as there was not room enough for two, I gave him a shove, saying: 'The day is ours.' He fell over in a doubled position on his side, made no attempt to move, but was groaning." As soon as he regained his strength, Fletcher continued on his way, hopping until the pain blinded him. Then he would fall, rest a moment, and start the exhausting process all over again.

Wounded though he was, Fletcher had no intention of missing his fair share of battlefield plunder. "This falling continued for some distance," recalled the avaricious Texan, "but all the time I had an eye for a dead Yankee to prowl. I soon was near one and stopped, kneeling, and went through him. . . . He was a poor corpse and it was a poor haul — his knapsack was good but was light." Fletcher settled for it anyway and kept on until he found an ambulance. As he bounced along toward a field hospital, Fletcher opened the knapsack with the delight of a child to whom Christmas had come in September. "I found several well written, sweet letters and from the wording, that fellow sure had some sweet girl stuck on him for she was anticipating a happy meeting and fulfillment of vows when the 'Rebs' were whipped and the cruel war was over." Fletcher felt not a pang of regret or sympathy. "She wanted me whipped — she got that. I wanted dead Yankees — I got that. So both at least got part of their wants satisfied."[51]

While Fletcher, safe in the rear, contentedly rifled the dead Federal's knapsack, his comrades were turning the ditch behind the Viniard farm into a hell for the Yankees who had sought shelter there. Tucked behind the farm fence and a nearby skirt of trees, the Texans poured a cruel volley into the tangled line of blue. Wounded who had crawled into the ditch were struck again and again. Lieutenant Colonel Young of the Twenty-sixth Ohio crouched among them, trying once again to defy the odds and piece together a defense. But nobody was listening, and at last Young gave up the effort and joined the survivors on the run to the woods.[52]

From behind Wilder's barricade, Sergeant McGee of the Seventy-second Indiana watched the panorama of horror laid out before him in the west Viniard field. Crittenden was out there, galloping around within pistol shot of the enemy, trying to rally Buell's mob, insensible to the danger. Wilder sent a company of the Seventy-second to fetch him. From the far side of the field, Robertson's Texans fired on the fleeing Federals. McGee saw many fall only a few yards from the breastworks, shot in the back. The living "reached our works and poured over them like sheep in a panic." McGee now feared for his own brigade. "We know the Rebels will be upon us in a few minutes. It is the supreme moment that tries every man's soul and tests the courage of the stoutest hearts. Panic is infectious, and generally spreads like fire in dry straw," he explained. "Davis's panic stricken troops are clambering over our works of rails and logs and stumbling over us in wild confusion, many of them wounded and bedrabbling us with their hot, dripping blood."[53]

McGee had nothing to worry about. A quick glance at Wilder's breastworks persuaded Robertson it would be foolhardy to lead his Texans across the field. Most of his men agreed and were happy to hide in the ditch or behind the Viniard farmhouse and stable. "Occasionally one would break away and make a run for the woods on the far side," wrote Theodore Petzoldt of the Seventeenth Indiana. "One fellow carrying a flag started on a run for this place. As he came into view from behind the stable I took careful aim and fired at him, sure that I would see him fall. But what was my astonishment to see him keep right on. I had missed him. Before I could fire again he had reached the woods and was lost to sight."

Tipsy with the thrill of pursuit, a handful eluded the efforts of their regimental commanders to hold them back and started up the slope after the Yankees. Wilder's men opened on them the instant the last Federal cleared the breastworks. "In two minutes there is not a man . . . seen upon his feet in our front," wrote Sergeant McGee.

To the nonstop volleys of Wilder's Spencer rifles was added the fire of four batteries. In the northwest edge of the field, Lilly had four guns spitting double-shotted canister into Robertson's right flank as fast as his cannoneers could load. The Indiana captain galloped from limbers to cannons, shuttling canister to his gunners. In the southwest corner, Lilly's remaining section and the Sixth Ohio Battery, left behind by Harker when he hurried north, poured their fire into Robertson's left flank. In between, the Second Minnesota Light Artillery and Estep's Eighth Indiana Battery blasted the Confederates from the front. "The roar is perfectly awful—nothing can be compared with it," wrote Henry Campbell of Lilly's battery. "If ten million pieces of wheat iron were all shaken at once it wouldn't be a drop in the bucket."[54]

Gradually Robertson extricated his regiments from the ditch and farmyard and fell back to the protection of the rise in the east Viniard field. There he renewed his call for infantry reinforcements—Benning had not yet come up—and for close artillery support.

As soon as he reorganized his brigade, Buell started back over the field after the retreating Confederates. Buell's enthusiasm overruled his better judgment, and he ordered Captain Estep to accompany him across the road with his battery. Heg and Carlin pieced together what they could of their commands and fell in on Buell's flanks.

It was between 4:30 and 5:00 P.M. There was no subtlety left to the fighting around the Viniard farm. No searching for flanks. No intricate envelopments. Now it was just charge and countercharge over two worn-out fields. Theodore Petzoldt neatly summarized the redundant slaughter as he witnessed it from behind Wilder's barricade: "At short intervals all day long I would see our troops come up along the road to our right and enter the woods in front of us. After fighting with the Rebels for some time they always fell back across the open field in front of us, followed by the enemy, who . . . were always driven back by our fierce fire."[55]

Brigadier General Henry Benning entered the fray with his brigade just as Buell's Federals crossed the road. A graduate of the University of Georgia (then Franklin College), Benning had had a sterling legal career prior to the war, including six years as an associate justice of the Georgia supreme court. Equally prominent in politics, Benning was elected vice president of the Democratic Convention in 1860. His support for the nomination of Stephen A. Douglas raised eyebrows among his fellow Southern delegates, who knew Benning as a states' rights extremist. Unlike the fire-eaters, however, the Georgian could not countenance secession. Not until the first shots were fired did he throw in his lot with the Confederacy and accept the colonelcy of the Seventeenth Georgia Infantry. Although his Georgians affectionately nicknamed him "Old Rock," Benning tended to excite easily in combat. Nevertheless, he was a first-rate fighter, and at forty-nine, among the most accomplished generals in the Army of Northern Virginia.[56]

Benning's Georgia brigade was a welcome sight to Robertson, whose Texans were about fought out. Benning came up on his right, and Robertson apparently shifted his brigade to the left entirely into the east Viniard field to consolidate his front. Benning's own line of battle extended from opposite Heg's left to the center of Buell's brigade, which was just nearing the road.

Benning evidently did not have his skirmishers out, although they probably would have made little difference. By now the woods were so choked with smoke that no one could see more than a few yards. In any event, recalled a captain of the Second Georgia Infantry, neither side was aware of the other until they suddenly met at pistol range. Captain J. H. Martin of the Seventeenth Georgia literally walked into the ranks of the Eighth Kansas. An equally startled Kansas corporal took a shot at him from ten feet but missed. Martin wisely threw up his hands to surrender.

His captivity was brief. The Georgians rolled over the Federals with ease, and Martin was soon reunited with his regiment.[57]

Sergeant W. R. Houghton of the Second Georgia received a similar shock. Passing around a large oak tree, he bumped into a burly, heavily bearded Yankee who was kneeling at the foot of the tree, in the act of capping his musket. "It was a mutual surprise, for I had no idea any of the foe were so near, and his astonishment caused him to open an otherwise large mouth very wide," recalled Houghton. "I was greatly astonished, remembering my absent bayonet, it seemed a hundred thoughts flashed over me in the brief instant of time I looked into the face of my foe." Houghton recovered his composure first. With his rifle at his hip, he squeezed off a shot that sent the Yankee tumbling over backwards.[58]

Captain Estep blasted the Georgians at a range of just ninety yards. Although he could see little, Estep was sure he "did the enemy serious injury." Even so, "his musketry fire became so heavy, terrible, and galling that to remain there longer was only to insure me that I would not have a horse left." Estep gave the command to limber to the rear. His teams scarcely had brought the limbers up to the guns "when the infantry began to fall back, being charged by the enemy en masse, who came yelling like devils." Estep got away, less four cannons left behind on the rise.[59]

Farther out in the field, the remnants of Carlin's brigade, seeking their former position, were instead overwhelmed in a matter of moments. So abrupt was their retreat that the Twenty-first Illinois left its colors on the field, still clenched in the hands of the dead color sergeant. Down too went the colors of the One Hundred First Ohio, but Lieutenant Colonel John Messer snatched them up. His gallantry helped keep the regiment together, though it cost Messer a bullet wound.[60]

Although they had been under fire only a few minutes, Benning's Georgians were parched. A member of the Second Georgia noticed a canteen dangling from what he took to be a dead Yankee. He laid his gun against a tree and crawled twenty feet to where the man lay. Loosening the strap, he began to slip the canteen from under the body when the Yankee sprang to his feet, unhurt. "The Yankee was a lot bigger," recalled the Georgian, "but he was too scared to do anything but run."[61]

The tall Yankee had plenty of company. Once again the Federal line broke, drifting across the road and up the slope of the west Viniard field. And again Colonel Heg rode among his men, trying to steady them by his example. "Throughout all those hours of severe danger and exposure, Colonel Heg was ever prompt at his post, always courageous and self-possessed . . . constantly exposed to the fearful fire of the enemy," recalled Captain Albert Skofstad of the Fifteenth Wisconsin with deep admiration. "Do not feel uneasy for me. I am well and in good spirits and trusting to my usual good luck," Heg had written his beloved Gunild the evening before. Less than twenty-four hours later, as the shadows lengthened across the west Viniard field, a Rebel bullet put an end to their romance. It pierced Heg's bowels, but the Norwegian kept in the saddle. He rode with his troops as they fell back into the woods, still begging them to rally.[62]

It was a tragic waste of the dying colonel's final moments. His men had done all that could be expected of them, and more. Their valor had cost them dearly. The Fifteenth Wisconsin had gone into battle 176 strong; now only 65 remained. Nearly half the men were down in the Eighth Kansas and Thirty-fifth Illinois, and in the Twenty-fifth Illinois almost two-thirds had been hit.[63]

Sergeant McGee watched the last of Heg and Carlin's brigades dissolve into the woods behind him. He recalled:

> We notice the utter demoralization of the troops who have just been defeated. We have never seen the like before. Although the Rebels have fallen back the poor fellows are so utterly demoralized with fear that it is painful to witness the efforts of the officers to rally them. In vain the officers entreat and point to our line, which is in perfect order, and tell them that the enemy have been driven back by us; in vain they draw their swords, and threaten, and kick and cuff them. The men with the utmost stolidity and with no show of resentment take it all, but at the first opportunity slip by the officers and move on to the rear.[64]

Reeling from loss of blood, Heg slipped from his saddle and was carried to a hospital in the rear. Colonel John Martin of the Eighth Kansas took command of what he was still calling a brigade. He and some of his regimental commanders claimed to have recrossed the field and held on until dark, but if they did, it was with so few troops as to attract the notice of no one but themselves.[65]

Carlin had somewhat better luck. Enough of the One Hundred First Ohio remained by the colors to be recognizable as a regiment, even though Company A now consisted only of a lieutenant and four men. Miraculously, the brigade problem-child, the Eighty-first Indiana, was still on the east side of the road in the southwest corner of the east Viniard field, pricking the left flank of Robertson's line as it passed by.[66]

Colonel Buell was standing atop the barricade, waving his hat and begging his men to stand their ground. Most darted by him and jogged off into the woods. Major Joseph Moore of the Fifty-eighth Indiana was there to intercept them. He drove the regimental colors into the ground and hauled in a few of his men; the little group became the nucleus around which the regiment soon rallied. General Wood was there as well, riding about and boosting morale with a few well-chosen words.[67]

Behind the breastworks, Wilder's Spencers were blazing and Lilly's cannons spewing canister. General Benning had his horse killed and his clothing riddled with bullets crossing the road. Now he was in the ditch with his Georgians, hanging on because someone apparently had told him help was on the way. "The place we held was much exposed to the enemy's fire, but . . . I thought I could hold it till the re-enforcements (every minute expected) should arrive, when a general advance might be made and the enemy swept from the opposite wood," he reported, pathetically. In vain did he look, as had Robertson before him, for artillery support to silence the Federal guns that were shattering his ranks.

By now Lilly and his gunners had their task mastered. They fired over two hundred rounds of double-shotted canister at ranges from seventy-five to two hundred yards that afternoon. "Each discharge would open out great gaps" in the massed Rebel ranks, marveled Henry Campbell. "The ditch was literally full of killed and wounded and proved to be a self-made grave for hundreds of them." Seventeen of twenty-three officers in the Twentieth Georgia were cut down; the enlisted men suffered about as much. That anyone survived in the ravine is a miracle. When Benning refused to budge, Lilly ran two guns forward along the edge of the timbered hollow that ran perpendicular to the ditch, unlimbering near enough to "rake the ditch from end to end" with canister. Benning's personal defiance meant little now; nobody could withstand such punishment. As the sun touched the treetops west of the Viniard fields, his Georgians began spilling out of the ditch toward the road.[68]

As long as there was light, there was time for fighting. At the Widow Glenn house, Rosecrans and his staff were able to turn their attention from the see-saw struggle between Van Cleve and Stewart to their immediate front long enough to advise McCook that he was needed at the Viniard farm. Information on the fighting, however, continued to be sketchy. At 2:42 P.M., Garfield wrote McCook in vague terms: "The tide of battle sweeps to the right. The general commanding thinks you can now move the two brigades of Sheridan's up to this place. Leave the one brigade posted at Gordon's Mills. . . . If the right is secure, come forward and direct your forces now fighting." Fifteen minutes later, more specific instructions came. "The general commanding directs me to say that he thinks you had better send one brigade from Sheridan to support Davis, who is hardly [sic] pressed," Major Bond wrote McCook. (Bond had trouble making himself understood in written orders, a shortcoming that was to have catastrophic consequences the next morning.) At 3:40 P.M., Bond corrected his earlier message: Davis was *hard* pressed.

McCook was at Lee and Gordon's Mill with Sheridan, who had relieved Wood there. Lytle's brigade brushed away a small force of Confederates from Breckinridge's division who were preparing to seize the ford; after that, all was quiet around the mill. Consequently, McCook felt comfortable dispatching Sheridan to the aid of Davis and Wood with two of his three brigades. A little after 4:00 P.M., the fiery Irishman started up the road with Bradley and Laiboldt.[69]

Colonel Luther Bradley's Illinoisans had gotten off to a rocky start. While watching his brigade come into a line near the mill an hour or so earlier, Bradley noticed the men of the Twenty-second Illinois break ranks. They danced about idiotically. Bradley pulled aside their commander. "What's the matter here?" he demanded. "Yellow jackets, sir," Lieutenant Colonel Francis Swanwick answered sheepishly. "We've got into a yellow jacket's nest." "Damn the yellow jackets," replied Bradley. "Get your men into line, we may move any minute." Try as they might, the two colonels were no match for the bees, who had the full attention of the soldiers. "We couldn't get them into line. They were hopping about like a lot of lunatics, swinging their hats, and slapping their legs, without regard to orders or anything else. We had to form four companies some rods to the rear before they would stand quietly," he recalled.[70]

Bradley reached the southwest corner of the west Viniard field at about 5:00 P.M. and rapidly deployed his brigade in double-line of battle behind the Seventy-second Indiana. The bee-stung Twenty-second Illinois lined up as the left regiment on the front line, the Twenty-seventh Illinois took its place on the right. The Fifty-first and Forty-second Illinois composed the second line. Bradley did not like the look of things. A good number of Buell and Carlin's men were still wandering in the woods, creating a nuisance as his regimental commanders tried to form their lines. Glancing to his left, Bradley noticed Crittenden. He was no help. "It impressed me that his manner was unfortunate under the circumstances," said Bradley. The strain of three hours at the Viniard farm was beginning to tell on the Kentuckian.[71]

Sheridan gave Bradley his orders: Drive back Benning and Robertson and retake Estep's battery. The Illinoisans swept into the west Viniard field "at double quick with a wild and clear shout of defiance," according to Lieutenant Henry Weiss of the Twenty-seventh. On their left, Buell went forward with the Fifty-eighth Indiana and bits and pieces of his other regiments. Carlin tried to join the charge with what men he could gather around him. His little band made it to the road, "but the want of regimental organizations prevented me from getting them farther," he admitted.[72]

Across the La Fayette road and onto the rise charged the Illinoisans, driving Robertson's skirmishers before them. The sun had nearly set, but even in the smoke and uncertain light the Yankees silhouetted on the rise were an easy target for Robertson's Texans in the east Viniard field and Benning's Georgians in the woods near the schoolhouse. "A perfect rain of bullets and balls of all kinds pour on us," wrote Lieutenant Weiss; "a most withering fire of musketry," agreed Colonel Nathan Walworth of the Forty-second Illinois. Bradley sat on his horse, filled with admiration for the Twenty-second Illinois, which lost ninety-five men in ten minutes, most from Benning's flanking fire. "They didn't mind being shot," he mused, "but wouldn't stand being stung by hornets." Just then two bullets struck Bradley in rapid succession. Lieutenant Otis Moody, his acting assistant adjutant general, fell beside him in the same volley. The Twenty-second

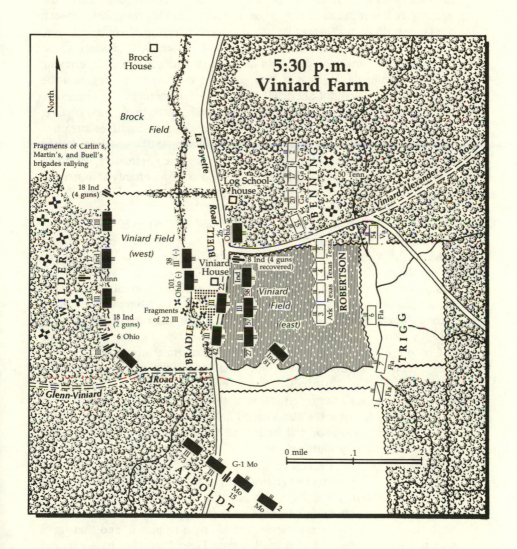

North

Brock
House

Brock
Field

La Fayette

5:30 p.m.
Viniard Farm

Fragments of Carlin's,
Martin's, and Buell's
brigades rallying

18 Ind
(4 guns)

Log School-
house

2

17

Ga

Ga

BENNING

50 Tenn

Road

20

Ga

Ga

Viniard Field
(west)

25
Ohio

15

Viniard-Alexander

Road

54
Va

38

8 Ind (4 guns
recovered)

5

4

101
Ohio (-)

Viniard
House

22

Ind

58

1

Ark Texas Texas Texas

ROBERTSON

2 Minn

Fragments
of 22 Ill

57

Viniard
Field
(east)

3

Ark Texas Texas

6
Fla

18 Ind
(2 guns)

6 Ohio

C-1 Ill

BRADLEY

42

27

Ind

7
Fla

TRIGG

Road

Glenn-Viniard

1
Fla

0 mile   .1   .2

73

LAIBOLDT

44

G-1 Mo

Mo
15

Mo
2

WILDER

17

123

1

recoiled and staggered off the rise. Most rallied behind the second line, which Colonel Walworth, now in command, had tucked safely in a ditch behind the ridge. A few, however, kept on running across the road toward the breastworks. Sheridan was out in the west Viniard field watching the fighting. A few minutes earlier, Sergeant McGee and his comrades had seen the famous division commander ride confidently forward. "We hear a commotion to our right rear, and looking around we see General Sheridan on his black horse coming, and in front of him a staff officer or orderly, carrying the General's battle flag, and as he approaches the rear of our regiment he calls out, 'Make way for Sheridan! Make way for Sheridan!' Of course we gladly open ranks and let the general and his staff pass through," said McGee. As the Twenty-second Illinois fell back and the first fugitives streamed toward him, Sheridan momentarily lost his nerve, to the absolute delight of Wilder's Hoosiers. "When Sheridan sees his men retreating, he turns and comes back—having exposed his person in a fool-hardy manner. As he approaches our line we begin to shout, with a spike of irony, 'Make way for Sheridan! Make way for Sheridan!' "[73]

Walworth had matters fairly well in hand. He replaced the Twenty-second Illinois with the Fifty-first. They too lost men in windrows—ninety-three in thirty minutes, according to one reckoning—but held on.[74] Aided by the oblique fire of the Eighty-first Indiana to its right, the Twenty-seventh Illinois on the brigade right suffered far less, losing just two killed and forty-eight wounded in thirty minutes' fighting before being relieved by the Forty-second Illinois. With less to occupy their attention, the men of the Twenty-seventh were able to help the Fifty-eighth Indiana pull Estep's guns off the rise onto the road, where the Indiana lieutenant gratefully took custody of them. Under the cover of the Eighty-first Indiana's fire, Lieutenant John Behm of the Fifty-eighth Indiana was even able to dash out into the field long enough to grab the fallen colors of the Twenty-first Illinois.[75]

As darkness fell over the east Viniard field, Walworth withdrew his men across the road, Robertson fell back into the woods east of the field, and the firing mercifully sputtered out.

For General Carlin, the end came not a moment too soon. The Illinoisan was on the brink of nervous exhaustion. His horse had been shot through the body earlier in the fight, and when the animal sank down into the dust of the La Fayette road and died, Carlin fell apart. "Removing the saddle with the help of one of my men, I seated myself upon it, and then gave way to a long, hysterical crying spell, which I could no more have checked than I could have checked the setting sun," he admitted. "I felt ashamed of what may have seemed to others a childish weakness, but could not stop till I had it out."[76]

Propped up by a member of his staff, Colonel Bradley hobbled over the field toward Wilder's lines, "faint and a little shaky." They stepped over the breastworks and walked toward the rear. Bradley ran into Crittenden. The Kentuckian was nearly exhausted, his composure unsettled. "When we got well back toward the ambulances a horseman dashed up and called out, 'What are you doing here sir? What are you doing, a colonel helping off a wounded man?' I looked up, and there was Crittenden. He recognized me, and apologizing hastily, he rode off," remembered Bradley.[77]

Nearly everyone seemed content merely to see the bloodshed end. The troops of Carlin's and Martin's shattered brigades huddled in the woods a few hundred yards behind Wilder and went into bivouac. Buell was pleased to have regained his battery and his original position; Crittenden, Davis, and Wood were relieved merely to have saved the army's right. Only Phil Sheridan, still fairly fresh to the fight, seemed intent on continuing the contest. He had Laiboldt's brigade up now on the right of Walworth. Tracking down Crittenden, he suggested the two launch a coordinated attack; despite the darkness, Sheridan felt certain he could roll up the Rebel left and start a stampede that would win the battle. The Kentuckian declined—his men had fought all day and were in no condition to attack. There the matter died, and the low moans of wounded soldiers replaced the clamor of battle in the forest and fields around the Viniard farm.[78]

CHAPTER TWELVE

THEY SKEDADDLED IN FINE STYLE

THE AFTERNOON fighting around the Brotherton farm, which by 3:00 P.M. on 19 September was the fulcrum of the Federal center, had much in common with the simultaneous struggle at the Viniard farm. In both cases, there was an overabundance of generals on the field—at least on the Union side—with no one firmly in control. At Viniard's, Davis and Wood had done as they pleased, paying scant attention to Crittenden's wishes. By late afternoon, Wood himself was little more than a supernumerary to Buell, who commanded the Kentuckian's only brigade on that part of the field, and Crittenden kept himself busy placing artillery batteries in the wood line.

Crowded along a half-mile line in the Union center were parts of the divisions of Van Cleve, Reynolds, and Palmer. His troops appropriated by Palmer and Van Cleve, Reynolds had taken upon himself the task of organizing an artillery reserve along the Brotherton ridge. Although Thomas was nominally in overall command, he had to split his attention between the left, where Johnson's division was still locked in battle with Cheatham and Liddell, and the troubled center, which meant that there really was no one in charge. On the Confederate side, it was largely "Old Straight" Stewart's show. Being a stranger both to that part of the field and to Stewart's division, Polk allowed the Tennessean to deploy his forces largely as he saw fit. Bushrod Johnson was nearing Stewart's left with Fulton and a portion of McNair's brigade, but communication between the two division commanders was minimal, and their actions, though complementary, were uncoordinated.

Like the slaughter at the Viniard farm, the combat around the Brotherton farm quickly degenerated into a struggle of brigades—and sometimes of regiments—operating largely on their own. Fortunate indeed was the brigade commander who knew the location of all his regiments.

By 2:30 P.M., Henry Clayton's Alabama brigade was showing signs of weakening in its unequal contest with Grose, Sam Beatty, and Dick. On the brigade right, the Thirty-eighth Alabama fought in two directions simultaneously. Grose had thrown forward his reserve—consisting of the Sixth Ohio Infantry and two twelve-pounder howitzers of Battery H, Fourth United States Artillery, under the supervision of the battery commander, Lieutenant Harry Cushing—to extend his line to the right when the Alabamians came up. While the right companies of the Thirty-eighth fired uphill at the Ohioans, the remainder of the regiment engaged the Seventy-ninth Indiana of Beatty's brigade. The Eighteenth and Thirty-sixth Alabama were similarly overmatched, fighting the balance of Beatty's and all of Dick's brigade, which had come up just as they were about to flank Beatty's right.[1]

Clayton was nothing if not energetic. He rode back and forth along his line, as if his mere presence would compensate for the disparity in numbers. He took his first ride at 2:30 P.M. and admonished his regimental commanders to fire only if they could see the enemy clearly. Colonel J. T. Holtzclaw took Clayton at his word. Lying as they were in some of the thickest underbrush on the battlefield, the soldiers of his Eighteenth Alabama could not see beyond the vines in front of their faces, and Holtzclaw ordered them to cease firing. For the next thirty minutes, they suffered in silence as the Federals poured a brutal fire of musketry and solid shot into their ranks. Holtzclaw was thrown from his horse and carried to their rear, badly injured, and 210 officers and men were killed or wounded holding the line. Meanwhile, the Thirty-eighth and Thirty-sixth Alabama were firing as quickly as the men could load to discourage attacks on the brigade's vulnerable flanks.

Now troubled by the random nature of the firing from his brigade, for which he was responsible, Clayton took a second ride at 3:00 P.M. For want of a better idea, Clayton decided to charge. He sent his staff ahead to brief the regimental commanders, then followed on yet another pass of the line. As he rode by, his colonels waved Clayton down to warn him that their ammunition was expended and their ranks badly thinned. "I therefore reconsidered my first intention to charge the enemy, being unable on account of the thick undergrowth to form a satisfactory idea of his strength, and withdrew for the purpose of replenishing ammunition," Clayton reported. Four hundred Alabamians remained behind, killed or wounded in about an hour.[2]

Beatty and Dick began a tentative pursuit through the underbrush, primarily to bring in the cannons of Carnes's battery, which lay between the opposing lines. After the Federals had passed over the battery a second time, a detail from the Seventy-ninth Indiana dragged the guns back to the La Fayette road, where they assumed their prize would be safe. Grose availed himself of the brief lull to pull the Sixth Ohio out of the line and send it to the rear to draw ammunition.[3]

Stewart now took the only course of action open to him. For the past hour, Brigadier General John C. Brown's Tennessee brigade had lain in support of Clayton, so near the fighting that bullets passing over the Alabamians had peppered its ranks. While Van Cleve's Federals trudged toward them, Stewart ordered Brown to conduct a passage of lines with Clayton and engage the enemy. For a moment, it looked as if the Yankees might be spared a struggle with the Tennesseans. Riding past Brown's lines, Stewart and his staff stumbled into a clump of yellow jackets' nests. While their horses kicked and stomped about madly, the nearby infantrymen broke ranks to avoid being trampled. In a few minutes order was restored, however, and Brown pushed forward.[4]

In the meantime, King had come up on Dick's right with the Sixty-eighth Indiana, One Hundred Fifth Ohio, and One Hundred First Indiana. Groping through the brush, neither King nor his staff knew quite where they were or precisely where they were needed. King initially faced his three regiments toward the northeast. The men sensed the uncertainty plaguing their commanders. "Confusion reigned even before the battle began," wrote Lieutenant Albion Tourgee of the One Hundred Fifth Ohio with the sharp power of observation that was to make him an acclaimed writer of novels, essays, and nonfiction on conditions in the South during Reconstruction. "Communications between the flanks was almost impossible. The winding roads were full of lost staff officers. The commander of a regiment rarely saw both flanks of his command at once. Soldiers are quick to note such things, and one . . . seeing a group of officers in consultation, said he guessed they were pitching pennies to decide which way the brigade should front. The enemy determined our movements for us," concluded Tourgee. The left company of the Sixty-eighth Indiana caught sight of the Rebels first. Advancing steadily in line of battle through the forest and toward the northwest was the Twenty-sixth Tennessee, the left flank regiment of Brown's brigade. The Hoosiers bent low in the brush, and the Tennesseans kept coming, unaware of the Yankees who lay in wait. At two hundred yards, Captain Harvey Espy ordered the Sixty-eighth to its feet. The Indianians let go a volley, and when the smoke cleared the Rebels were gone.[5]

While the startled Tennesseans fell back to regroup, King hurriedly changed front directly to the east. Nevertheless, his line still did not connect with that of Dick. Although less than two hundred yards lay between the brigades, Lieutenant Colonel Granville Frambes, commanding the Fifty-ninth Ohio on Dick's right flank, neither saw nor heard King's men; in his after-action report, he maintained that there were no friendly troops nearer his right than those of Heg, a half mile away at Viniard's.[6]

Frambes's fear became King's reality. His change of front accomplished nothing; six hundred yards still separated his right from Heg's left. Shortly after 3:00 P.M., Bushrod Johnson found the gap. Fulton initially struck King in front, and for a time the contest was equal. From the Brotherton ridge, Harris's battery opened a horrific fire of spherical case over the heads of King's infantrymen and into the ranks of the Forty-fourth Tennessee, slowing Fulton's advance to a crawl. King cautioned his men to hold their fire until certain of their targets. "A look of eager expectancy was seen on the faces of the men, many of them having cartridges between their teeth, awaiting the order 'Fire!'" remembered a Yankee eyewitness. At fifty yards King gave the word, and the Butternut line recoiled. Fulton's Tennesseans recovered and returned the fire, and for the next forty-five minutes the two lines were lost in smoke.[7]

King was punishing the enemy to his front, but his flanks were about to prove his undoing. On his left, Brown's Twenty-sixth Tennessee was pouring a murderous fire into the left companies of the Sixty-eighth Indiana. The bullets flew so thick and the men fell so rapidly that one terrified Indianian swore he saw 150 drop in fifteen minutes. That young Frank Wilkinson and others of the regiment should exaggerate their losses is no surprise, when all around them comrades fell. Wilkinson saw a minie ball tear through the shirt of Robert Price, his closest friend in the regiment. Another skinned his left shoulder. "Look at this, will you," Price said to a sergeant behind him, turning his head and pointing to the wound. Hardly had the words left his mouth when a third bullet plowed into the side of Price's head and he dropped forward onto his face, dead.[8]

The situation was even more critical on the brigade right. There Johnson was able to slip the Third and Forty-first Tennessee of Gregg's brigade past the One Hundred First Indiana, which "bent from the right like a willow," in the words of Albion Tourgee. As the regiment buckled, King sent his aide-de-camp, Captain F. M. Wilkinson, to appeal to Reynolds for help. None came. In a few minutes the One Hundred First broke, leaving Tourgee's regiment in the same predicament as that faced by the Sixty-eighth Indiana a few minutes earlier. When the Seventeenth Tennessee stepped into the interval opened by the collapse of the Indianians, the One Hundred Fifth Ohio refused its right wing. The Tennesseans pressed forward, and the line kept bending. Seeing the hopelessness of their stand, King ordered the One Hundred Fifth Ohio and the Sixty-eighth Indiana to retreat to avoid capture. "About face! Forward, guide center," yelled Major George Perkins to his Ohioans. "Double quick," added King over the din; then, recalled a veteran, "leaning his head upon the horse's neck, he spurred hardly faster than the blueclad mass he led to the rear."[9]

King's troops poured out of the woods and across the road. Up and over the Brotherton ridge they swarmed, passing just south of the guns of Harris's battery. For six hundred yards they kept it up—past the Tan Yard, over the Glenn-Kelly road, and up the slope of what is known today as Lytle Hill. There, safely in the rear, they halted to catch their breath. King was among them, working feverishly to restore order. He was in an ugly mood. While King was on foot conferring with his regimental commanders, a mounted officer galloped up the hill and tried to give orders to the brigade. King reminded the officer that he was in command, but the interloper persisted nonetheless. King repeated his warning in more colorful language. To demonstrate his sincerity, King drew his sword and advanced on the officer, who got the point and bid a hasty retreat. The men gave King a hearty three cheers, and the Indianian returned to the work of reforming his command.[10]

Captain Wilkinson found Reynolds and delivered King's message, but the reinforcements he brought came too late to be of any use. Wilkinson had located Reynolds at about 3:30 P.M., sitting beside Harris's battery. The general was very sorry, but he had no troops left to give; Palmer had taken the Seventy-fifth Indiana from him a few minutes earlier. As the captain turned and started back down the ridge, Reynolds reconsidered and called him back. Wilkinson could have the Ninety-second Illinois, which had hitched its horses to trees in the rear and was then resting behind the ridge; he would keep their two mountain howitzers. Reynolds passed the word to Colonel Atkins, and the Illinoisans climbed over the ridge and jogged toward the La Fayette road in line of battle. They scaled a high fence that bordered the Brotherton field on the east, and at the road faced to the right. With Wilkinson in the lead, the regiment started down the road. They had not gone twenty yards when King's men began streaming out of the timber to their left front. Things unraveled pretty quickly after that. Wilkinson told Atkins to keep his command on the road while he rode into the timber to find King. No sooner had the captain left than bullets began cutting through Atkins's ranks from the direction of the woods. The colonel started his regiment off the road by the right flank. He had two companies off and tucked behind the fence when an officer galloped up and shouted at him to clear the road immediately. Meanwhile, the pluckier of King's men had paused on the ridge to fire back at the enemy. While their intentions were admirable, their aim was atrocious. When their bullets began striking his men from behind, Atkins gave up his notion of forming along the fence and waved his regiment back to the ridge. They pushed their way angrily past King's men, reformed on the ridge to the right of Harris's battery, and lay down to await the appearance of the enemy.[11]

All this time, Van Cleve had been taking a terrific pounding of his own east of the La Fayette road. Brown had struck him hard, more by chance than design. "I encountered the enemy in an unbroken forest, rendered the more difficult of passage by the dense undergrowth which for more than two hundred yards extended along my entire line; and the difficulties were still further enhanced by the smoke of battle and the burning of the woods, rendering it impossible to distinguish objects twenty paces in advance," the general reported. Yet another of the numerous Tennessee attorneys holding general's commissions in the army, Brown, in a display of humility befitting a gentleman, had enlisted as a private at the outbreak of the war; three weeks later he was appointed colonel of the Third Tennessee Infantry.[12]

Brown had performed creditably in every engagement to date and now was about to improve on that record, although his advance began inauspiciously. Cushing's two-gun section and Battery M, Fourth United States Artillery, battered his right flank and the four smoothbore pieces of Battery B, Twenty-sixth Pennsylvania Light Artillery, that Captain Alanson Stevens had insisted on bringing into the woods boomed their greeting from in front. As was the case in almost every Confederate attack that day, Brown's own artillery could not find a suitable firing position in the forest and so was left behind. The Yankee batteries, reported Brown, "filled the air with grape, canister, shells, and solid shot, while volley after volley of musketry in quick succession swept my men by scores at every discharge." Still his men groped on blindly through the timber. Even the wounded refused to quit. Private W. H. Mayfield of the Thirty-second Tennessee was simultaneously shocked by an exploding shell and struck in the thigh by a minie ball. He was rolled onto a litter and carried toward the rear. As he recovered from the shock, Mayfield sprang from the litter, remarking: "This will not do for me." The young soldier hobbled back to his company, found a rifle, and fought on.[13]

For fifteen minutes that seemed an eternity, the Tennesseans struggled on until, after they had covered four hundred yards, the barrage lifted and they caught sight of the Yankees. Remembered Major J. P. McGuire of the Thirty-second Tennessee: "We were now within easy rifle-range of their line of battle, which poured upon us volley after volley of musketry and artillery. The double-quick was ordered, and then the charge, when our men raised the rebel yell, and pressing on in fine order soon found ourselves on the ground which had just been occupied by the enemy."[14]

Beatty's brigade gave ground steadily but in good order. On its right, Dick retired his frontline regiments onto his reserve and similarly managed to form a single line. Both brigades came to rest along a slight ridge three hundred yards east of the La Fayette road. There they momentarily checked the advance of Brown's Tennesseans, whose very success had thrown them into confusion.[15]

It looked as though Van Cleve had a better than even chance of holding his ground. The Federal batteries continued to wreak havoc on the Tennesseans, who were tired, badly cut up, and without artillery support of their own. Although they had given ground, none of Van Cleve's regiments had broken.

In an instant, the entire calculation changed. King broke just as Brown was reforming for a rush at the Yankees, starting a tremor that shook apart Van Cleve's entire line. Lieutenant Colonel Frambes of the Fifty-ninth Ohio felt it first. The retreat of King enabled Fulton to slip behind him and Brown's Twenty-sixth Tennessee to strike his right flank. The Ohioans broke like a thaw, cracking and melting into the tangle of vines and weeds. Frambes managed to halt most of them in a deep ravine at the base of the Brotherton ridge, just across the road. In the meantime, Dick had sent his inspector general to rally "the crumbling ranks" on his right. A bullet knocked the officer from his saddle, mortally wounding him before he reached the Forty-fourth Indiana, the next regiment in line, but his contribution would have changed nothing; the Indianians were too far gone to be rallied. Conditions were equally bleak on the brigade left. There Lieutenant Colonel Elhannon Mast already had been killed and Major Joseph Snider badly wounded while encouraging the men of the Thirteenth Ohio, leaving a captain in command of the regiment. As the Thirteenth was flung from the field, Brown renewed his attack in front, and the rest of Dick's line dissolved. "I was now under fire from my front, right, and rear, and was compelled to fall back, this time, more rapidly and in more confusion than at first," Dick reported with refreshing candor.[16]

Beatty laid the blame for his own collapse squarely on Dick. The Ohioan euphemistically described his retreat as follows: "The enemy continued to extend his lines past our right, and the falling back of the Second Brigade exposed my right to a galling and destructive fire, under which I caused a change of front to the rear." As his men fell back they were hit by friendly artillery fire from the ridge (for which Beatty held Captain Harris's Nineteenth Indiana Battery responsible), and the brigade disintegrated.

In the panic, Captain Stevens's battery was forgotten. The Seventeenth Kentucky rushed through the battery, and the Pennsylvanians, left without infantry protection, hurried to limber their cannons. By the time they had the guns hitched up, all the horses of three pieces were down and one limber had exploded. The right section managed to get away, but the two cannons of the left section were abandoned near the road.[17]

General Palmer was riding along his lines when Van Cleve's division finally broke. For the past thirty minutes, his own front had been strangely quiet. Not a single Rebel had shown himself in the Brock field opposite Turchin and Cruft, and Grose's men were simply resting while their batteries pulverized Brown's right. When he heard the firing recede from beyond his own right, Palmer correctly surmised that Van Cleve had given way and that the Rebels were making for the La Fayette road. The Illinoisan galloped down the Brotherton road to the La Fayette road, reaching it just as Beatty's troops began pouring across. The white-bearded, bespectacled Van Cleve was in front of the Brotherton ridge. There, with tears streaming down his cheeks, he begged his men to slow down.

"Feeling the necessity of prompt action," Palmer looked about anxiously for some unit with which to check the Confederate advance. Just south of the Brotherton house he caught sight of a familiar face. There, at the head of the largest regiment in the army—the more than seven-hundred-man Seventy-fifth Indiana—sat Colonel Milton Robinson, who had served under Palmer earlier in the war. Palmer rode to Robinson and ordered him to charge the enemy. Robinson reminded Palmer that his regiment belonged to another division but added that he would obey the command anyway. Palmer personally guided Robinson a short distance up the Brotherton road, then watched the Hoosiers disappear into the forest "with shouts that made the woods ring."[18]

The Seventy-fifth Indiana was three times the size of most regiments in the army because it had never before been in combat. None knew what to expect in their first encounter with the enemy; none, that is, but Private Henry Wildunner of Company I. Twice that morning he had told his commanding officer, Captain M. H. Floyd, that he would be the first in the company to die.

The Seventy-fifth struck the right flank of Brown's brigade like a whirlwind, hitting the Eighteenth Tennessee first. The Tennesseans never had a chance. A bullet ripped through the right shoulder of their commander, Colonel Joseph B. Palmer, and he fell from his horse with blood spurting from a torn artery. After ten months he recovered from a wound that all at first thought mortal, but his right arm was partially paralyzed for life. Lieutenant Colonel William Butler was shot down at about the same time, and command devolved on Captain Gideon Lowe, who prudently turned and ran with his Tennesseans. The Forty-fifth Tennessee folded next, and Brown hastily ordered a retreat of the entire brigade. Although badly surprised by the Indianians, he could take consolation in the knowledge that he had driven an enemy superior in strength and had retaken, for good, the thrice-fought-over cannons of Carnes's battery.[19]

Somehow the Thirty-second Tennessee had not gotten the word to fall back and was still advancing. Major J. P. McGuire, commanding the right companies of the regiment, discovered that the right wing of the brigade had disappeared. McGuire suggested to Colonel Edmund Cook that the regiment had best withdraw before it was captured. "The Thirty-second Tennessee will never leave the field until ordered to do so," Cook barked.

Then he looked toward his flanks and, thinking the better of it, consented to withdraw, just a few yards shy of the abandoned guns of Stevens's battery.[20]

The Seventy-fifth Indiana had acquitted itself well in its first action. Few lives were lost, but, for the survivors, the memories of those first casualties were to prove lifelong. Private Wildunner was hit in the first and probably only volley the Eighteenth Tennessee fired before giving way. "Cap, I told you I would be the first man killed," Wildunner said to Floyd, then started for the rear, dragging his rifle. Floyd found him later that afternoon. "I saw him lying upon his face dead, with his gun clutched in his hand and all his accoutrements on, as they were when he received the bullet. It shows what tenacity of life the poor fellow had, to endure a march of half a mile after receiving his death wound."

James Essington ducked instinctively as the first bullets whistled past the regiment. Feeling a touch upon his right shoulder, Essington turned to see his brother Wally by his side. "Are you hurt?" Wally asked. No, answered James. As Wally stepped back to his place in line, a bullet cut him down. "Not a murmur fell from his lips," remembered James, "but walking back a few feet he sat down by a tree and tried to stop the flow of blood." The passage of time did not lessen the loss James felt. Long after the war, in a little article for his local newspaper entitled "A Touch on the Shoulder," he paid tribute to the memory of his brother. "Tonight as I sit surrounded by my family, I imagine I can feel the same touch and hear a still voice asking me, 'Are you hurt?' My answer is, 'Yes, I am hurt.' He who was my brother, and is yet, has gone to that army where the question 'Are you hurt?' is never asked. I am here, and I see one by one all those who stood beside him at Chickamauga passing over."[21]

Colonel Robinson halted his regiment on the right of Grose a few minutes before 4:00 P.M. General Palmer rode up with some sobering words of advice for Robinson. "The men we had driven before us were good soldiers, who were for the moment surprised by the rush of this large regiment. I told Robinson that they would return and that his raw troops could not withstand them, but advised him to keep up appearances as long as he could, and rode to the left to reach my own two brigades," Palmer wrote.

His prediction was about to come true. As he galloped toward Cruft, Palmer glanced down a hollow to his right. There he saw a powerful Rebel line of battle advancing in the direction of Cruft's brigade, its approach masked from the Federal infantry. "I increased my speed and shouted as I reached the right of the line to call attention to the coming Rebels, and they reached the plateau a moment afterwards."[22]

The troops Palmer had spotted belonged to the Alabama brigade of Colonel James Sheffield. Since splitting off from the brigades of Robertson and Benning two hours earlier, Sheffield had drifted about, or, as one Alabama captain put it, "reconnoitered different parts of the field—gradually gaining ground toward the north." Sheffield slipped past the rear of William Bate's brigade, which Stewart was just sending into the fray to replace Brown, and struck the wooded hollow just west of the Brock field, where Palmer spied his advance.[23]

Sheffield's attack on Cruft a few minutes before 4:00 P.M. was completely unintentional. Sheffield apparently was in contact with no one of higher rank, as neither Bate nor Stewart make mention of coordinating their attacks with the Alabamian. Sheffield ordered a charge simply because he happened to have stumbled on a line of Federals. Nonetheless, his Alabamians struck hard. "They charged us at once, and were received with a volley which did not check them," Palmer observed. "On they came, and then followed one of those noisy scenes that sometimes occur on a well-fought battlefield. As they pressed us our lines were pushed back, and there seemed imminent danger that my line would break, and then I knew demoralization would follow."[24]

Palmer was hardly guilty of overstatement. Cruft's right-flank regiment, the Second Kentucky, fell into complete disorder and retreated nearly two hundred yards. "They skedaddled in fine style," wrote Captain Jacob Goodson of the Forty-fourth Alabama. So closely did the Alabamians pursue that a few intrepid Federals were able to pause in their retreat and pull in fifteen Rebels as prisoners. Palmer was so near the action that he got off a pistol shot at a Rebel officer who had ventured ahead of his own line. The Thirty-first Indiana tried to hold its ground but was swept away in the retreat of the Kentuckians.

That left Cruft with only Battery B of the First Ohio Light Artillery and the Ninetieth Ohio infantry. As the stampede reached the battery, the gunners limbered up and bounced through the Ninetieth, breaking its ranks and throwing it momentarily into disorder. "The moment was critical. Soldiers and officers ran to the rear, mingled with guns and caissons in much disorder, and the whole plateau was rapidly being commanded by the enemy's musketry," Cruft admitted. He saw no chance of saving his last regiment except by retreat, and so started back with the Ninetieth toward the Brotherton road.[25]

Help came most opportunely, thanks to the quick thinking of the "Mad Cossack," John Turchin. As the first volleys rattled through the timber from the direction of Cruft, Turchin ordered his frontline regiments, the Eleventh and Thirty-sixth Ohio, to change front to the right. The Ohioans wheeled to the west through the Brock field, forming line of battle near the edge of the forest. The Eighteenth Kentucky, which had been drawing ammunition near the road, hurried into line behind the Thirty-sixth Ohio. The Ninety-second Ohio, similarly engaged, fell in behind the Eleventh Ohio.[26]

Turchin's men advancing ran into Cruft's retreating. A shoving match ensued as each tried to pass the other. "Damn you, get out of our way. If you can't fight, give them a chance that can," screamed the troops of Turchin's brigade. Colonel William Jones of the Thirty-sixth Ohio shared their fury. Drawing his sword, he waved it aloft, crying to the fleeing soldiers of the Ninetieth Ohio: "Here are men who don't know how to run!" Those were his last words. The first Confederate volley cut him down with a mortal wound. His regiment kept on and struck Sheffield's line at an acute angle. The Rebel left extended beyond their right flank, and the Ohioans instinctively halted and fell to the ground before the Alabamians opened an enfilading fire on the right companies. Private R. C. J. Adney of the Thirty-sixth stuffed a handful of cartridges into his jacket pocket, stuck some caps in his mouth, and took aim. He could see nothing through the smoke, but went ahead and began firing anyway. Adney happened to glance back at his brother, Major William Adney, the instant a minie ball struck his hip. The major fell, but the bullet had hit his revolver and split before burrowing into his flesh, and he was not seriously wounded.[27]

Lieutenant Colonel Hiram Devol was now the only field officer left in the Thirty-sixth Ohio. As the fighting wore on with no sign of a resolution, he left his place on the right and rode to the center of the regiment to get instructions from Colonel Jones. Unaware that Jones had been hit, he kept on in search of Turchin. While Devol was gone, word of Jones's mortal wounding spread rapidly down the line. The men began yelling to one another that somebody should end the pointless exchange of volleys and order a charge. Devol had the same thought, although no one yet had bothered to tell him that Jones was down. "Returning to my position in line, and still seeing the destruction going on, I again sought the colonel; not finding him or any one else in command, I ordered the line to rise and charge." Colonel Lane ordered the Eleventh Ohio forward beside them. The Ninety-second Ohio followed. Cruft's Ninetieth Ohio rallied in time to join in, and the four Ohio regiments started into the forest toward the Alabamians.[28]

Their charge was a rousing success. Perhaps because Sheffield's Alabamians were fighting alone with no idea what lay beyond their flanks, they gave way rapidly. Sheffield's horse threw him and he injured his back, forcing him to quit the field. Brigade command technically devolved onto Colonel William Perry of the Forty-fourth Alabama, but before he could act, the Federal charge bore through the center of the brigade, carrying Perry, his regiment, and the Fourth Alabama away toward the south. Colonel William C. Oates of the Fifteenth Alabama took charge of what remained of the brigade but was able to do little to keep it together. By the time Turchin sent an aide to Lieutenant Colonel Devol to break off the pursuit, Oates's contingent had been thrown back some four hundred yards into the rear of Bate's brigade. Squads, companies, and disorganized bits of regiments wandered through the forest in search of their commands. Some attached themselves to regiments of Bate's brigade. Oates, with his own Fifteenth Alabama and whatever other troops he could rally, faced about and marched off in the direction of the La Fayette road, and Sheffield's brigade ceased to exist as an organized force.[29]

Turchin met his returning Ohioans in the Brock field. Although he had missed the charge, Turchin's men were still happy to see the general. John Booth recalled the reception the Thirty-sixth Ohio gave him:

> General Turchin, in full dress uniform, astride his white Arabian, reined up near the center of our regiment, now glancing up the line, now down the line of the regiments, with a smile of satisfaction illuminating his countenance, raising his left hand, with it grasped his chapeau-bras at the base of the plume, lifting it from his head, while in broken English he shouted: "Bully for mine brigade!" Some smiled quietly at first at the general's enthusiasm, others laughed outright; almost instantly the brigade became infected with the spirit of their general, and the men of that gallant brigade, one and all, as moved by a single impulse, gave vent to their feelings in such a happy, hearty, ringing cheer as to make those old Georgia hills reverberate its echo.[30]

As the cheers died down, Turchin and Cruft reformed their brigades in essentially the position they had occupied before "this lively little affair," as Palmer called the fight with Sheffield. The Illinoisan, however, was fated to get no rest. "As soon as the excitement . . . was over, I heard firing to my right rear, by which I knew the enemy were pushing our troops who were in that direction."[31]

Palmer was right. Stewart had decided to commit his last brigade to the fight for the La Fayette road. It was a hard decision for the Tennessean, outnumbered as he was. Perhaps Stewart felt that he had sacrificed too much to break off the fight. Whatever his reason, he summoned Bate a little after 3:30 P.M. to relieve Brown.[32]

Brigadier General William B. Bate was a gifted man with an ego to match his talents. Born in 1826 to a Tennessee family of modest means, Bate had had little formal schooling. He worked first as a clerk on a steamboat and rose steadily from there. Bate fought in the Mexican War, edited a newspaper, studied law in Nashville, was elected to the Tennessee legislature, and served as a Breckinridge elector in the 1860 election. Bate cut an odd figure, with dark hair, a swarthy complexion, a sharp nose, and a shrill voice. Behind piercing gray eyes burned "excessive ambition, and for reputation [he] would have attempted the most unreasonable projects," asserted R. M. Gray, a soldier in the Thirty-seventh Georgia. "Always on the alert, he never missed an opportunity to engage an enemy let the odds be as they might. For this he was dubbed 'Fighting Billy' by the boys." The nickname implied no affection, continued Gray. Bate "could not command the love of his troops but he did have their strict obedience, and as this was about all he seemed to care for . . . 'twas doubtless as much as was necessary. He had too little of the milk of human kindness in his composition to make an officer for whom men would cheerfully sacrifice life and limb, his management and idea seemed to be that soldiers were mere machines to dance when he worked the wires." As is often the case with martinets, his "command stood high A, number one at head quarters," said Gray.[33]

In fairness to Bate, Gray admitted that he would not send his men where he was unwilling to go himself. At Shiloh, he had ridden far in front of his regiment at a critical moment in the battle. Mounted on his coal-black stallion Black Hawk, a celebrated race horse, with a snow-white saddle, Bate was an easy target. A bullet pierced his leg and ripped the saddle, passing entirely through his horse. Faint from loss of blood, Bate dropped the reins and braced his hands on the pommel of the saddle. Black Hawk turned and found his way to the colonel's proper place behind the regiment. Bate was lifted from the saddle and carried to a cabin out of danger. The horse followed, so the story went, put his head in the door and whinnied, then walked away and lay slowly down to die.

Bate was horribly wounded. The bullet had shattered his leg, and after prolonged consultations, the attending surgeons all agreed that amputation was imperative. Bate objected. When his plea went unheeded, he took his pistols from his servant and told the surgeons that he meant to "protect that leg." He saved the leg at the cost of a pronounced and permanent limp.[34]

Here at Chickamauga, Bate received Stewart's order with characteristic enthusiasm. W. J. McMurray, an officer in the Twentieth Tennessee, was chatting with its commander, Colonel Thomas Smith, when he was distracted by a rider galloping toward them from the left of line. It was Bate. "Now, Smith, now Smith, I want you to sail on those fellows like you were a wildcat," commanded Bate, then spurred his horse on to the next regiment. "At once Colonel Smith gave the command, 'Attention, Battalion! Fix bayonets! Forward! Double-quick! March!' and the whole brigade moved as one man," recalled McMurray.[35]

While Bate hastily assembled his brigade to relieve Brown, Van Cleve and his brigade commanders worked just as intently to patch together a line with which to halt the Confederate drive against the La Fayette road. The time was a little after 3:30 P.M. The Union center still assumed the shape of an "L" along the Brotherton and La Fayette roads, albeit on the west rather than the east side of the latter. Turchin was in the Brock field fronting to the southeast and Cruft was on his right in the woods, the positions to which both returned after the repulse of Sheffield. Grose still held the same little knoll, although with considerably fewer troops than he had when he first occupied it nearly three hours earlier. The Sixth Ohio had retired after the fight with Clayton to draw ammunition and had not yet returned. During the lull after the Seventy-fifth Indiana swept Brown from the field, Lieutenant Cushing withdrew his Battery H, Fourth United States Artillery, to refill its limbers. Grose had his remaining four regiments deployed in a semicircle around the knoll, fronting generally to the southeast. The Twenty-third Kentucky held the left, the Twenty-fourth Ohio lay a hundred yards in front of and slightly to its right, and the Thirty-sixth Indiana rounded out the convex-shaped front line. All three regiments were dangerously low on ammunition. Only the Eighty-fourth Illinois, which lay in reserve, had enough cartridges for any but the briefest of engagements. Lieutenant Francis Russell was on the west side of the road in close support with the four Napoleons and two twenty-four-pounder howitzers of his Battery M, Fourth United States Artillery. To the right of Grose, the Seventy-fifth Indiana fronted east, forming an acute angle with his brigade.[36] Hazen's brigade lay just across the road in the woods south of the Poe house, drawing ammunition and resting. Lieutenant Giles Cockerill's Battery F, First Ohio Light Artillery, stood behind the brigade.[37]

Three hundred yards south of Hazen everything was a confused whirl of activity. At the vortex sat Reynolds, grounded like a statue beside Harris's battery. As he watched Van Cleve rally his infantry around the cannons, Reynolds was accosted by a bright-eyed little artillery officer. "Can you tell me where I can find a general officer," the subaltern asked. Reynolds replied that he was a general. The officer straightened up and announced that he was Lieutenant Harry Cushing. He had been drawn to the ridge by the sound of Brown's attack and now that he was here "would like to find something to do" with his battery. Reynolds was pleased to oblige him. He told the lieutenant to line up his four howitzers on the ridge to the left of Harris. Farther north, Captain Stevens had in the meantime rolled his remaining two six-pounders up beside the two James rifles that had not gone into the forest with Beatty. Reynolds now had an imposing total of twenty guns arrayed along the Brotherton ridge.[38]

The Kentuckian's batteries were a natural rallying point for Dick's infantry, but even they were not enough to check the panic. The men of the Fifty-ninth Ohio pushed their way past Harris's cannoneers and kept on running into the woods west of the field; only a handful rallied with Lieutenant Colonel Frambes behind the battery. Captain Horatio Cosgrove gathered a portion of his Thirteenth Ohio to the right of Frambes. Most of the Eighty-sixth Indiana rallied on the ridge to the left of Swallow's

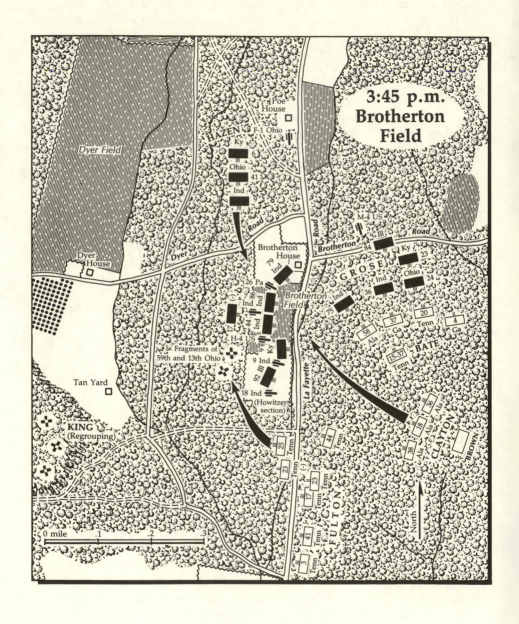

3:45 p.m. Brotherton Field

Poe House

HAZEN · F-1 Ohio

Ky · 6

Ohio · 41

Ind · 9

Dyer Field

M-4 US

Brotherton House

79 Ind

GROSE · Ky

Ohio · 24

Ind · 36

Road

Brotherton · Road · La Fayette

Brotherton Field

26 Pa

(-) · 7 · 8 · Ind

Ind · Ind

17

H-4 US

9 · Ky

Dyer House

Fragments of 59th and 13th Ohio

9 Ind

92 · Ind

18 Ind (Howitzer section)

Tan Yard

75

58 · Ala · Ind · Ga · Tenn · 4 · Ga · 20

BATE

15-37 · Tenn

36 · Ala

18 · Ala

KING (Regrouping)

25 · Tenn

23 · Tenn (-)

44 · Tenn

38 · Ala

CLAYTON · BROWN

17 · Tenn · 23 · Tenn

FULTON

41 · Tenn

3 · Tenn

0 mile · .1 · .2 · .3

North

battery, however, and a like number from the Forty-fourth Indiana fell in on the battery's right, giving Dick the semblance of a line of a battle.[39]

Sam Beatty had no idea where to find the regiments of his brigade, which had scattered like chaff on coming out of the forest. Colonel George Cram formed a scratch line with his Ninth Kentucky on the east slope just in front of Cushing's battery. A portion of the Seventeenth Kentucky rallied behind Swallow's battery, and the Seventy-ninth Indiana reformed in tolerably good order between the Brotherton cabin and Stevens's battery. The Nineteenth Ohio never recovered from its accidental shelling by Harris, and most of its members quietly sneaked off into the timber west of the Brotherton field. By 4:00 P.M. there were eight regimental flags waving along Brotherton ridge to complement Reynolds's twenty cannons. It was a formidable force, but the men were tired, thirsty, and dazed. Of greater concern to Reynolds, the ridge was barren save for a bit of stubble, leaving the artillerymen dangerously silhouetted as they served their pieces. No one dared venture a guess how long the line might hold.[40]

CHAPTER THIRTEEN

WE BURY OUR DEAD

THE MEN of Bate's brigade had a long wait before going into action. "We were exposed to a very heavy fire of artillery for two or more hours. We were lying down in the grass, and numbers of the men actually went to sleep, while the shells were bursting all around them," recalled James Cooper of the Twentieth Tennessee. But now, at 3:45 P.M., they were on their feet and rushing toward the enemy. "In five minutes," said Cooper, "all the horrors of war that a soldier ever witnessed were there."[1]

Bate struck the Federal line in the angle formed by Grose's brigade and the Seventy-fifth Indiana, and his brigade split to compensate. On the left, Colonel Bushrod Jones led the Fifty-eighth Alabama against the Seventy-fifth Indiana, while the Thirty-seventh Georgia, Twentieth Tennessee, and Fourth Georgia Battalion of Sharpshooters veered to the north to confront Grose. Colonel R. C. Tyler, in reserve with the Fifteenth and Thirty-seventh Tennessee, had no idea what was happening on the front line and so simply ordered his men to lie down.[2]

Colonel Robinson's Seventy-fifth Indiana confounded General Palmer's prediction that it would break when confronted with seasoned troops. The Indianians brought the Fifty-eighth Alabama to an abrupt halt, forcing it to settle for a bloody exchange of volleys. More impressive still, the Seventy-fifth apparently was fighting without its leaders. A rumor swept through the ranks that Colonel Robinson and Lieutenant Colonel William O'Brien had shown "the white feather" and were cowering somewhere in the rear. The regimental adjutant took command in their absence. He walked coolly along the line, admonishing the men to "fire low" and "take good aim." His encouragement was appreciated but not really needed—the enemy was so close that there was no need to aim; just shoot low into the smoke and you were sure to hit something, recalled Sergeant John Kane.[3]

It was Palmer's own veterans, ironically, who faltered first. The Twenty-fourth Ohio, in Grose's first line, bore the brunt of Bate's attack. In the second line, Lieutenant Colonel James Foy had ordered the soldiers of his Twenty-third Kentucky to lie down the instant the Confederates appeared. To Foy's front, where the Ohioans put up a gallant stand against the Twentieth Tennessee, the fighting raged with a fury unmatched that afternoon. The Twenty-fourth "stood as if every man was a hero for the space of half an hour," Foy reported, until only a handful of cartridges remained in their boxes. Only then did they give ground.

The Twentieth Tennessee was in no condition to push them. Lieutenant Russell's battery was ripping the Rebel line apart with every discharge. When Company E met the Federals it numbered twenty-three men; before it could fire a volley of its own, Russell's cannons had cut that number to just six. Somehow, despite the "murderous discharges of their howitzers, loaded with canister and grape,"[4] the soldiers of the Twentieth eventually found the courage to continue, only to come up against Lieutenant Colonel Foy's Kentuckians. "The fire was now very hot," Foy reported. "It appeared to be as though every third man in the regiment was struck. I was struck on the right breast, the bullet going through the lapels of my overcoat, and struck a large button, glancing off, doing no injury."

Foy was keeping a weather eye on his right, where the Thirty-sixth Indiana was falling back steadily before the Thirty-seventh Georgia. The Indianians were doing their best, but they too were fast running out of cartridges. Gradually the Georgians worked their way around Foy's right, which was protected by only a few companies of the Twenty-fourth Ohio that had rallied. "One or two of the captains had suggested to me that we had better retire. I thought we would have to, but hesitated about giving the command," said Foy. "Finally, seeing we were outnumbered, as I thought by the length of their line of battle . . . I very reluctantly gave the command to retire."[5]

Bate's men had not quite seen the last of Grose's Federals, who were clinging to the knoll with uncommon tenacity. As the Twenty-third Kentucky retired across the Brotherton road, Grose called up his reserve regiment, the Eighty-fourth Illinois, to replace it.

The Illinoisans never had a chance. Obsessed with silencing Lieutenant Russell's battery, the commanders of the Thirty-seventh Georgia and Twentieth Tennessee were working in concert to clear Grose off the knoll so that they could make a rush for the guns. The Twentieth and the Fourth Georgia Battalion of Sharpshooters swept around the left flank of the Eighty-fourth Illinois, while the Thirty-seventh Georgia forced its way around the right of the Thirty-sixth Indiana. The Hoosiers fired off their last cartridges and fled. Left alone, the Illinoisans were caught in a murderous cross fire. Nearly a quarter of the men fell before the regiment broke apart and scattered toward the road.[6]

The Rebels swept up the knoll behind them. "Here occurred the prettiest fighting during the whole war," James Cooper reminisced years later. "We rushed up a little hill, and the enemy were just below us, all crowded together in a deep hollow. Our rifles were in prime condition and our ammunition so good that I really enjoyed the fight."[7]

It was 4:15 P.M. After thirty minutes of dogged resistance, Grose finally was pried off a position he had held for three and a half hours. The Thirty-seventh Georgia paused to reform after some wayward men from one of Sheffield's regiments wandered into its lines, then charged ahead with the Twentieth Tennessee toward Russell's battery. Lieutenant Russell fired off one last blast of canister at fifty yards' range, then drew off his guns toward the Poe farm, where Cockerill's battery began playing on the luckless Confederates.[8]

The Seventy-fifth Indiana was in grave danger. With no mounted officer present to detect the collapse of Grose, the Indianians fought on until the Rebels were across Brotherton road. Only then, apparently, did someone notice that they were flanked. The regiment broke contact with the Fifty-eighth Alabama, faced about, and started for the rear in good order. When they ran into a cedar thicket near the road, however, the men panicked, and by the time they reached the Brotherton field the Indianians were a leaderless mob. Bate's Georgians opened fire on them from the woods to their right. No longer a unit but merely several hundred frightened men each hoping to find a way past the enemy, the Indianians were powerless to respond. Seven members of Company A were shot in the head in the space of a few yards. The color guard was decimated. The bearer of the regimental colors, Corporal James Stewart, tumbled over with a bullet in the right hip. As he fell, Color Sergeant Jacob Lair, who bore the national standard, grabbed the regimental colors. A powerful man, Lair laid the flags down long enough to throw Stewart over his back, then, gripping both colors in one hand and Stewart's shirt in the other, he started for the protection of the woods. Sadly, his effort was wasted. A minie ball plowed through Stewart as he hung bleeding on Lair's back, and when the sergeant laid him down he was dead.[9]

While running the gauntlet of minie balls, Sergeant John Kane caught sight of Colonel Robinson; the colonel, he said, was hiding behind a stack of straw in the field. There was no sign of Lieutenant Colonel O'Brien, who showed his face only after the regiment had bivouacked for the night. The next day, Kane maintained, O'Brien "left the field with a scratch on the arm and had two men help him to Chattanooga."[10]

Palmer ran into Robinson a half hour later. "He had about fifty men with him, and told me most mournfully that his entire regiment, with the exception of the few men around him, was destroyed," related Palmer. "I knew from the composition of his regiment that the majority of them, all new men, had taken care of themselves, and I tried to comfort him with that assurance. He, however, said that he knew them better than I did, and that they were all brave men, and had either fallen or were then in the hands of the enemy. I laughingly offered to bet him ten dollars that when he issued rations the next morning, he would not miss twenty-five men. He looked vexed at my offer. I rode off; but when we met again, he said I was 'nearer right than he was.' "[11]

That September afternoon was to haunt Robinson a long time. Nine autumns later, as governor of Illinois, Palmer traveled to Anderson, Indiana, the home of Colonel Robinson, to make a speech on behalf of Horace Greeley, whom Palmer supported in his run against Grant for the presidency in the campaign of 1872. While in town, Palmer learned that Robinson was running for Congress on the Grant ticket and that his opponent was making effective use of charges that Robinson had proven a coward at Chickamauga. While addressing a large gathering at the county fairgrounds, Palmer noticed Robinson in the crowd, "one of my most attentive listeners." Robinson sought Palmer out after the rally to implore him to refute the charges during an address he was to give on the public square that evening. As he had during the battle, Palmer found a chance for a little good-natured fun at the colonel's expense. "Though I liked him very much, I bantered him by saying with gravity that, inasmuch as he was a candidate on the Grant ticket, it seemed that I could hardly offer to help him until after the election, but as I made him a kind of conditional promise to refer to the subject, he left me, obviously not well satisfied with the rather unsatisfactory assurance." Palmer arrived that evening to find Robinson seated impatiently on the stand from which he was to speak. Palmer teased him mercilessly: "He sat and listened with great patience to a speech of an hour and a half, and as I intentionally acted as if about to close, he plucked me and reminded me of my promise." Palmer came to the point. He told the audience that he understood Robinson to be a candidate for Congress and that some supporters of their—the Greeley—candidate had charged Robinson with cowardice at Chickamauga. In the darkness, a score of voices responded that the charge had been made and proven; just as many denounced it as false, and the rally degenerated into a shouting match. As soon he could make himself heard, Palmer asked if any men of the Seventy-fifth Indiana had so accused Robinson. Hearty shouts of "Yes, yes" followed. Palmer then called upon any accuser from the Seventy-fifth to step forward to the stand to repeat the charge; not surprisingly, none accepted the governor's public challenge. Palmer recited the enthusiasm with which Robinson had placed his green troops under his command on the nineteenth, how he had charged into the woods, and how he had mourned the loss of his command later that afternoon. That clinched it. The accusation was dropped and Robinson was elected to Congress. "I have had some reason since that time, in my own case, to observe that false charges of military misconduct are easily made, and that some soldiers who know the truth are mean enough to be silent when the charge is intended to serve partisan purposes," Palmer recalled.[12]

No one could accuse General Hazen of neglecting his duty, so long as the Ohioan was master of his own fate. The army was his life. A man of real talent, Hazen was also a consummate careerist. He sought out challenges with an eye toward promotion. This afternoon was no different. The uproar near the Brotherton and La Fayette roads told Hazen where to find the fighting, and he started his command (less the One Hundred Twenty-fourth Ohio, which had not yet returned from the Brock field) for the Brotherton farm a few minutes before 4:00 P.M., just as Grose was losing control of his brigade.[13]

Unaware that Grose was on the verge of collapse, General Stewart agonized over Bate's stalled attack. Two drives against the La Fayette road had ended in bloody failure. To forestall a third repulse, the Tennessean gambled and threw Clayton's battered brigade back into the fight to support Bate at the same time Hazen was hurrying into position behind Sam Beatty in the Brotherton field. Not realizing that Bate had deviated to the northwest, Clayton led his brigade due west toward the La Fayette road over a path well-marked with his own dead and wounded.[14]

Fortune favored the Confederates. Purely by chance, John Fulton's brigade had crossed the La Fayette road and moved against Van Cleve's right flank on the south end of the Brotherton ridge at the very moment Clayton was nearing the road from the east. Although Stewart and Bushrod Johnson were operating independently of one another, their movements at this juncture were perfectly complementary. While Bate moved against Hazen and the left flank of the Brotherton ridge line, Clayton applied pressure from the front and Fulton positioned his command to roll up the Federal right. Four batteries, Hazen's brigade of infantry, and the dazed and frightened survivors of Van Cleve's eight regiments were all that remained to block the Confederate punch against the Union center. During the whole day, the Rebel army had never been closer to cutting the Federal army in two.

At the Widow Glenn house, Rosecrans was too distracted by events to his immediate front to give much thought to the predicament of Reynolds and Van Cleve, if he was even aware of it. About the time Van Cleve's infantry was pouring across the La Fayette road twelve hundred yards northeast of army headquarters, McNair's two Rebel regiments were moving on the Glenn house through the Brock field, less than six hundred yards away. Stragglers from Heg's left were streaming across the Glenn field just ahead of the Confederates. Minie balls sang around the cabin, and shells burst just outside. It was "the most terrific scene man could witness," wrote Colonel Sanderson, growing "so terrible and so near us that orders were given to mount with a view of falling back to a less dangerous place." A little later, as Heg's entire brigade was borne back over the La Fayette road, Rosecrans rode forward with a detachment from the Fifteenth Pennsylvania Cavalry, his headquarters escort, to try to rally those infantrymen nearest the Glenn house. His exhortations were ignored. The flat sides of the Pennsylvanians' sabres were of no more use in steadying the panicked soldiers, and Rosecrans and his party returned to the cabin. There the general sent orders to McCook to hurry Negley's division from Glass's Mill to headquarters, to be held in reserve for use as the situation might dictate.[15]

Rosecrans's timely decision to call up his last uncommitted division from the far right would prove of great value to the defense of the Union center, but when he gave the order to Negley, Rosecrans was thinking only of the visible crisis on Davis's front. Meanwhile, Reynolds had appealed to Thomas for reinforcements, and the Virginian ordered Brannan to move to his support. Although Brannan had his division on the road by 4:30 P.M., it was a march of nearly a mile and a half to the Brotherton farm. For the moment at least, Reynolds and Van Cleve were on their own.[16]

Thanks to the opportune arrival of Hazen a few minutes after 4:00 P.M., it looked as if the wobbly Federal line on the Brotherton ridge might hold. The "Bloody Ninth" Indiana, as its members proudly labeled their regiment, waded through the flotsam of the Seventy-fifth Indiana and lined up behind the fence along the La Fayette road, just east of the Brotherton cabin, at the very moment Bate's left regiment, the Fifty-eighth Alabama, emerged from the woods on the other side of the road. The Hoosiers' opening volley sent the Confederates scampering for cover. Separated from the remainder of the brigade, the Alabamians were content to shoot at the Ninth Indiana from the relative safety of the woods.

Reynolds was on hand to greet the Ninth. "What regiment is this?" he asked as the Indianians deployed. The "Bloody Ninth," was the instant response. "That is all right," he said loud enough for the men to hear, then added a few words of encouragement before riding away.[17]

Reynolds was very much in control of himself and, to the extent possible, the situation around him. Sadly, it was far different with Van Cleve. As the remnants of his two brigades tottered on the crest of Brotherton ridge, the old man lost what was left of his composure. Coming on the field with the Ninth Indiana, Hazen caught a glimpse of Van Cleve riding "wildly up the road, with tears running down his cheeks." He "asked if I had any troops, as they were wanted badly 'just down there' — pointing in the direction I was going — saying he had not a man he could control. He was an elderly, grey-haired man . . . his distress was not feigned," remembered Hazen.[18]

At the southern end of the Brotherton field, the situation looked far more grim for the Federals. That they were able to hold on at all was due to the confusion into which Fulton's Tennessee brigade had been thrown by its relatively easy success against King. Fulton's left regiment, the Seventeenth Tennessee, reached the La Fayette road at the same time the Forty-fourth Tennessee, on the brigade right, was still prying the last of Dick's Yankees from the woods.

For the time being, the regimental commanders were left to their own devices. Lieutenant Colonel Watt Floyd decided to halt the Seventeenth short of the road, opposite a fringe of open timber at the southern edge of the Brotherton field. The Twenty-fifth Tennessee was the first to cross the road, more by accident than design. Moving "step by step through a dense thicket," Lieutenant Colonel Robert Snowden had brought his regiment to within a few feet of the road before discovering that his command had become separated from the Forty-fourth Tennessee on its right. As the native New Yorker surveyed the scene before him, the cause of his predicament became clear. Silhouetted on the southern edge of the Brotherton ridge, which lay a couple hundred yards to his right and front, were the six guns of Harris's battery and Lilly's two mountain howitzers. It was evident to Snowden that their fire had pinned down the Forty-fourth back in the forest. Snowden hesitated, uncertain whether to push on with a single regiment. A few rounds thrown his way by Harris's gunners made the decision for him, as his Tennesseans, joined on their left by a few companies of the Twenty-third, ducked across the road and into the fringe of timber to escape the shelling.[19]

Once across, Snowden found himself on the right flank of the batteries and the Ninety-second Illinois. His men were ideally situated in the timbered hollow, just out of reach of the Yankee cannons, which were still trained to the front. Snowden wheeled his line of battle to the right, bringing it into position behind a fence that bordered the field on the south, and then opened fire.

Snowden's first volleys caught the Federals by surprise. Captain Harris tried to turn his right section toward the Tennesseans, but his orders were lost in the din. While trying to make himself understood, Harris was knocked from his horse by a spent ball. By the time Harris regained his senses, his infantry support had disappeared. As Snowden's Tennesseans jumped over the fence and made for his guns, Harris limbered the battery and hurried off the ridge, less one cannon abandoned to the cheering Confederates.

Smith Atkins put up a good fight for a few minutes. He pulled in his right companies to meet the threat from Snowden, but he quickly found that even his Spencer repeating rifles could not compensate for the lack of cover on the bare ridge. When word reached him that stragglers from Dick's brigade were stealing the regiment's horses, which had been left without a guard, Atkins abandoned any thought of holding his position and hurried his men back to the Brotherton woods to retrieve their mounts. Atkins was shocked by what he found there. Most of the horses were where his men had left them, but all around were "thousands of Union troops in disorder floating off through the woods toward Chattanooga."[20]

Atkins exaggerated the numbers, but the rout was real. Van Cleve's infantry had withstood a tentative advance by Clayton to their front, but the flanking fire from Snowden's Tennesseans was too much for them. The Eighty-sixth Indiana, Ninth Kentucky, Forty-fourth Indiana, and Seventeenth Kentucky all gave way, falling back to the left and rear to escape the volleys from the right. With his supply of canister exhausted, Captain Swallow could do nothing to loosen Snowden's grip on the ridge. He pulled his battery out of action and led it north toward the Poe house. A few minutes earlier, Lieutenant Cushing had withdrawn his guns in the same direction.

The ridge was now clear of Federals as far as Battery B, Twenty-sixth Pennsylvania Artillery, which was masked from the fire of Snowden's Twenty-fifth Tennessee by a roll in the Brotherton field. In the absence of support from the rest of Fulton's brigade, which was only then crossing the La Fayette road behind him, Snowden dared not press his attack farther north. He halted his men where Harris's battery had stood, and waited while Clayton's Alabamians crept across the road, seemingly in doubt that the Federals had been so easily beaten.[21]

All this happened while Van Cleve was unburdening himself to General Hazen. After the old man rode away, Hazen finished positioning his brigade. He deployed the Sixth Kentucky on the right of the Ninth Indiana, then rode south along the crest to search for some sign of Van Cleve's infantry. Instead, he saw only the Twenty-fifth Tennessee. "At this instant," recalled Hazen, "I was in the same condition Van Cleve reported himself in a few minutes earlier." Unlike Van Cleve, however, the thirty-two-year-old Ohioan kept his composure. Taking a broader view of the situation than could normally be expected of one his rank, Hazen chose to sacrifice his brigade if necessary to buy time for him to piece together a line of artillery near the Poe house capable of stopping the inevitable Confederate advance. Although many in the brigade criticized Hazen for abandoning them, Captain D. B. McConnell understood his general's action: "Hazen was at that time, like a true soldier, letting his brigade go to the dogs, if need be, while he seized the means within his reach to defeat the enemy."[22]

And to the dogs it went. Without Hazen there to guide him, Colonel Aquila Wiley led his Forty-first Ohio too far to the right of the Sixth Kentucky, opening a gap of perhaps a hundred yards. Wiley lined his men up in the timber west of the Brotherton field just as Van Cleve's men tumbled off the ridge and into his ranks. The Ohioan soon had his hands full just holding his command together.[23]

Meanwhile, the Sixth Kentucky and Ninth Indiana were coming under heavy pressure as the Confederates, sensing victory, ventured across the road. Colonel Bushrod Jones's patience had paid off. During the twenty minutes his Fifty-eighth Alabama waited in the woods, the Fifteenth and Thirty-seventh Tennessee had come up from its position in reserve and joined the Fifty-eighth on its right. A few minutes later, the Thirty-sixth Alabama of Clayton's brigade passed over Jones's left and across the road to take the Sixth Kentucky in the flank. In a matter of moments, the Kentuckians vanished. Wiley's Forty-first Ohio offered little more resistance when the Alabamians came over the ridge to its front.[24]

In the Ninth Indiana, pandemonium reigned. The Thirty-sixth Alabama poured a withering fire into its right flank from atop the Brotherton ridge, while the Fifteenth and Thirty-seventh Tennessee slipped past its left. Nevertheless, absent of orders from Hazen, Colonel Isaac Suman refused to budge. Mercifully, General Reynolds galloped up and took the decision away from him, directing Suman to fall back before his regiment was captured and to regroup behind a fence along the northwest edge of the field.

By then, the Confederates were everywhere. In the commotion, Captain McConnell of Company K never heard the order to withdraw. He was absorbed in watching the attempts of one of his privates to "plug" a large Alabamian who had darted ahead of his regiment and was waving his rifle conspicuously over his head. A plea from a frightened soldier reminded McConnell of his responsibilities. "Cap, what is the use of staying here? The brigade is gone." McConnell glanced around and saw only jubilant Confederates where the rest of the regiment had stood, then watched helplessly as his own men scurried past him "like a flock of frightened partridges." The captain wisely followed. "The Rebels opened on us . . . and I could see the poor fellows drop before me. I could see from time to time the blood start from a wound in the thigh, body, or arm, and stain the old uniform as it ran down, but the gallant fellows would keep up. One of my men was shot through the arm. He stopped, looked around, saw me coming on behind, and came back to me with the question 'What shall I do with my gun?'" recalled McConnell, who was himself in too great a hurry to offer an answer.[25]

The Indianians were met at the fence by the Sixth Ohio, which had escaped destruction despite the idiotic single-mindedness of its commander, Colonel Nicholas Anderson. Anderson either was unaware of or chose to disregard Palmer's promise to Reynolds to leave him the Sixth Ohio to support Harris's battery on the ridge. As soon as his men had replenished their cartridge boxes, Anderson started for the front. Reynolds begged him not to go, pointing out that he had no other infantry with which to defend the guns. But Anderson went on his way, adamant in his desire to rejoin Grose.

Anderson never found the brigade. He was barely across the La Fayette road when Clayton burst forth from the forest. Anderson ordered his men back to Harris's battery at the double-quick. By the time they returned, Harris was busy limbering his cannons. Anxious to contribute something to the defense of the battery he had so callously abandoned, Anderson instructed his men to lie down on the east slope of the ridge and engage Clayton's advancing Alabamians.

Their efforts were wasted. The real threat to Harris came from the Twenty-fifth Tennessee to the south, and Anderson became aware of them only after the Tennesseans opened fire on his right flank. By then Harris's battery was gone, and the Sixth Ohio found itself nearly surrounded. "Things looked desperate and I began to think of Libby [Prison]," mused a regimental officer. But the ubiquitous General Reynolds was with the Sixth, and he helped lead the regiment out of the field to the fence at the tree line, before riding forward to retrieve the equally beleaguered Ninth Indiana.[26]

The Ninth Indiana and Sixth Ohio held the fence only briefly. After a short hand-to-hand struggle, the Fifty-eighth Alabama and Thirty-sixth Alabama, by now hopelessly intermingled, dislodged the Federals, and Brotherton field was theirs. The men were elated. Ignoring Colonel Bushrod Jones's orders to halt, they crossed the Dyer road and disappeared into the woods. Jones followed his regiment reluctantly, convinced that further pursuit was both "fruitless and hazardous."[27]

He was right. Clayton and Bate had broken the Federal center, but without reinforcements to follow up the penetration, their triumph was as hollow as every other brief advantage gained by one side or the other that day. And General Stewart could do nothing to help them. Brown's brigade, reduced to fewer than eight hundred men after its brutal fight with Van Cleve, was still drawing ammunition. Stewart had no idea where to turn for troops to exploit the breach; indeed, he reported bitterly after the battle that he had seen no general officer of higher rank than he on the field since leaving Bragg at 1:00 P.M.[28]

Bate and Clayton continued on as best they could. Neither, however, had a firm hold on his forces. In Clayton's brigade, the regimental commanders were acting largely on their own, and even they were having trouble keeping their enthusiastic troops in line. From the La Fayette road, Captain John Humphreys of the First Arkansas Battery watched Clayton's infantry crest the Brotherton ridge. "Our own men were much scattered, their ranks much broken," he noted in his report. An exasperated Colonel Lewis Woodruff of the Thirty-sixth Alabama could only watch as his two left companies veered away to chase an elusive Federal flag through the Brotherton woods and out into the Dyer field. With the remainder of the regiment, Woodruff continued along the course pursued by Bushrod Jones's Fifty-eighth Alabama. Clayton's center regiment, the Eighteenth Alabama, conducted a pursuit west toward the Dyer field "somewhat in confusion," as its commander confessed. On the brigade left, the Thirty-eighth Alabama chased Dick's fugitives into the field and past the Tan Yard.[29]

The absence of Federal resistance spared Clayton from bloody embarrassment. Not so Bate. When his brigade split, the glory-seeking Tennessean stayed with his right regiments. At 4:30 P.M., he led them north toward the Poe farm in reckless pursuit.

North of the Poe house, Hazen was working frantically to justify the sacrifices of his brigade. He ordered Lieutenant Cockerill, whose battery rested on the La Fayette road, to unlimber his cannons and train them southeast into the Poe field. Lieutenant Cushing reported his battery present a few minutes later, and Hazen directed him to set up his guns on Cockerill's left. Next came Lieutenant Russell at the head of his battery, and Hazen wedged his six pieces between Cushing and Cockerill. Two guns from Battery B, First Ohio Artillery, apparently joined the line. Hazen halted enough runaways from Grose's brigade and the Seventy-fifth Indiana to form a stragglers' line in support of the guns, and Reynolds fell back with the Sixth Ohio and Ninth Indiana to their right. The infantry was welcome but superfluous. Twenty cannons, loaded with canister, were aimed and ready to sweep a field just two hundred yards wide and six hundred yards long.[30]

At 5:00 P.M., Bate led the six hundred men of the Thirty-seventh Georgia, Twentieth Tennessee, and Fourth Georgia Battalion of Sharpshooters into the Poe field. For an instant, perhaps, the Confederates could see in the fading daylight the black outline of cannon barrels trained on them from across the field. Then came the brilliant orange flashes, followed by the report of twenty guns thundering simultaneously, and the field was blanketed in smoke and blood. Bate's horse was torn to pieces by canister. The Tennessean mounted another and kept on. It too was cut down. Both regimental commanders were struck and Major T. D. Caswell fell at the head of his sharpshooters, nearly half of whom were killed or wounded. For three, maybe four minutes, the Confederates withstood the pounding. Men fell at the rate of nearly one every second. Finally, after 180 had been hit, Bate led the rest back into the woods.[31]

Ambrose Bierce watched the slaughter from behind the batteries: "Nothing could be heard but the infernal din of their discharge, and nothing seen through the smoke but a great ascension of dust from the smitten soil. When all was over and the dust cloud had lifted, the spectacle was too dreadful to describe. The Confederates were still there—all of them, it seemed—some almost under the muzzles of the guns. But not a man of all those brave fellows was on his feet, and so thickly were all covered with dust that they looked as if they had been reclothed in yellow. 'We bury our dead,' said a gunner, grimly."[32]

A few days after the battle, so the story goes, while riding over the battlefield with some officers from Bragg's staff, President Davis spied a dead sorrel adorned with the trappings of an officer's saddle at the southern edge of the Poe field. He asked whose horse it was. General Bate's of Tennessee, he was told. The president and his party rode another three hundred yards into the field. There they saw a little black mare lying dead. Again, the president inquired as to the owner. General Bate, of Tennessee, came the reply. They went a little farther before coming upon a dead artillery horse. A third time, the officers told Davis that the rider had been Bate. "This man Bate must be a gallant fellow," mused Davis aloud. Bate's impetuosity paid off. Shortly after his return to Richmond, Davis commissioned Bate a major general, though during the battle the Tennessean had been the junior brigadier in the army.[33]

Alone and uncertain of the fate of the brigade, Colonel Tyler withdrew his Fifteenth and Thirty-seventh Tennessee to the east side of the La Fayette road. Colonel Jones waited some thirty minutes for his left companies, which twice had bolted ahead without orders, to return, then he too fell back in search of Bate. The colonel found him among the traumatized victims of the Poe field assault. Jones tried to explain his own decision to retreat, but Bate cut him off with an understanding nod. "You have done right; I take off my hat to your regiment," said Bate.[34]

It was now nearly 5:30 P.M. Forty minutes remained before sunset, but already the forest, draped in smoke, was growing dark. At the Widow Glenn house, Rosecrans waited impatiently for Negley's division. As the fighting around the Viniard farm subsided, Rosecrans turned his attention to the crisis at Brotherton's. For the rest of the afternoon, the Ohioan was at his best. He badgered Thomas, who had been slow to send in reports, for information and sent staff officers over the field, so that when Negley arrived, Rosecrans knew exactly where he wanted him. He personally ordered Negley forward, pointing northeast in the direction of the Dyer field with the admonition: "You will find the enemy right in there." Rose-

crans dismounted to watch the long column of infantry tramp past headquarters, here and there offering words of encouragement. "As each company
gained his front, arms were brought to shoulder as a salute, which in each
case was returned by the general," remembered a soldier of the Eleventh
Michigan. "As the colors passed by him they were dipped in his honor,
and on returning the salute, he said: 'Make it warm for them, Michigan
boys.' This was answered by a cheer from the men, and the general added:
'I know you will.' "[35]

Negley had with him Stanley's brigade and three regiments of Sirwell's
brigade. John Beatty had been left behind to defend Glass's Mill, which
Breckinridge had threatened in an early-morning demonstration, and the
Seventy-eighth Pennsylvania of Sirwell's brigade was guarding a ford farther
south. On the west side of what is today Lytle Hill, Negley deployed his
two brigades in line of battle, with Stanley on the left and Sirwell on the
right, and sent orders to Captains Alexander Marshall and Frederick Schultz
to set up their batteries on the rise as soon as the infantry secured it. The
long line of blue started up the slope, every man certain that the opposite
side would reveal a multitude of horrors. "The firing was very heavy and
it appeared that we would be very heavily engaged," Lieutenant Colonel
William Ward of the Thirty-seventh Indiana remembered. Lieutenant Eben
Sturgis of Schultz's battery agreed: "[It] was the hottest fire of small arms
unattended by that of artillery I ever heard."[36]

As his infantry crested the ridge and Clayton's Alabamians became visible
on the far side of the Dyer field, Negley momentarily faltered. He sent an
aide back to Rosecrans. He had found the enemy but saw no sign of friendly
forces; was this where Rosecrans wanted him to fight? "That is right, fight
there, right there, push them hard," Rosecrans told the messenger.[37]

While Negley fretted, Brannan neared the Dyer field from the north.
Suddenly, there were Federals everywhere. Clayton was not about to wait
to be driven in. As the last rays of sunlight receded from the field, he
recalled his infantry. Negley's Federals followed them into the Brotherton
woods, and a few shots were exchanged in the twilight before Clayton, as
he himself put it, "fell back across the road at a leisurely pace." By sunset,
Negley had established himself along the western edge of the Brotherton
field, restoring the center of the Union line at a cost of just two killed and
three wounded.[38]

Clayton minimized the confused state of his brigade; his Alabamians
may have retired at a "leisurely pace," but they did so by companies and
squads, rather than as a cohesive body of men guided by a firm hand. The
experience of Captain John Humphreys is ample proof of the disorder. Left
alone on the La Fayette road with two disabled limbers and no infantry
support to help drag off his guns, Humphreys rode 150 yards to his right,

where Colonel Woodruff was busy rallying his Alabamians, to beg assistance. Woodruff was a wreck. He truly wanted to help, but his regiment was scattered over a mile. "See, these are all the men I have," he told Humphreys, pointing to a panting and dusty handful assembled around him.[39]

The late-afternoon hours had passed as if a dream for "Little Charlie" Harker and the men of his brigade. From the moment they set off up the La Fayette road on their ill-defined mission to protect Davis's left, the forest seemed to transform combat from the mundane to the surreal. No one was quite sure where they were going or why, or whom or where they were fighting. The reports of Harker and his subordinates reflect a groping uncertainty, a struggle to deal with events for which none were prepared. The instant Harker passed beyond the left of Heg's brigade, the woods came alive with Confederates. "It appeared now that we were attacked on both front and flank, and so fiercely that it required the utmost care to prevent confusion in my own troops, which existed among those around me," reported Harker. Colonel H. C. Dunlap of the Third Kentucky agreed: "Soon found the foe on every front; fought at every point of the compass." "The rebels seemed to be all around us and it was difficult to tell which was the front and which was the rear — in fact it was front in two or three directions at the same time," asserted the brigade historian.[40]

Harker had happened upon four equally confused Confederate commands in his advance up the road. First, he encountered the Thirty-ninth North Carolina and Twenty-fifth Arkansas of McNair's brigade, recoiling from their foray across the Brock field. After brushing aside these Confederates, who wanted only to be left alone, Harker collided with the left regiments of Gregg's brigade, which were struggling to maintain some semblance of unit integrity as they themselves tried to turn Heg's flank. Gregg's Confederates were no less surprised by the appearance of Harker than were the Yankees at having to fight in several directions at once. Once the initial shock of the strange encounter wore off, Harker acquitted himself commendably. He placed the brigade in a single line and split it into two informal task forces, entrusting the One Hundred Twenty-fifth and Sixty-fourth Ohio regiments on the east side of the La Fayette road to Colonel Emerson Opdycke, while himself moving with the Sixty-fifth Ohio and Third Kentucky on the west side.

Harker continued to fight northward. Before he got word of his new assignment, Opdycke headed off on his own with the One Hundred Twenty-fifth Ohio, northeast through timber "so dense we could see but a few rods in any direction" and squarely into the midst of Gregg's exhausted Tennesseans. The Sixty-fourth Ohio inclined even farther east of the road.[41]

Opdycke's two regiments consequently engaged the Tennesseans independently of one another. Both enjoyed easy success against an enemy weary of fighting. The Sixty-fourth Ohio gobbled up twenty prisoners at a cost of only five wounded, and the One Hundred Twenty-fifth captured nine while losing one man killed and eleven wounded.[42]

As the woods fell into an uncertain silence, General Gregg imprudently chose to ride forward and reconnoiter the Yankee forces that had disturbed his soldiers. The Texan and his staff groped through the smoke and tangle until they stumbled upon the skirmish line of the Sixty-fourth Ohio. Called upon to surrender, Gregg instead jerked his horse around and tried to ride to safety. Shots rang out, and Gregg toppled from his horse with a bullet through the neck. Thinking his wound mortal, the Federal skirmishers gathered around the general to scavenge his valuables. They pulled off his spurs — said to be of great value — and removed his sword, which they later presented to their regimental commander. Their pilfering was interrupted by the charge of some outraged Texans from Robertson's brigade, who drove away the Yankee ghouls and carried the unconscious Gregg back into friendly lines. Their audacity paid off — Gregg recovered and returned to active duty a few months later. With Gregg down, brigade command passed to Colonel Cyrus Sugg of the Fiftieth Tennessee.[43]

Meanwhile, while continuing north with his half of the brigade, Harker had engaged yet a third Confederate force. The Third Kentucky had stumbled upon the remaining three Arkansas regiments of McNair's brigade, which were resting along the La Fayette road in the interval between Gregg and Fulton, awaiting orders. McNair slashed at the left flank of the Third Kentucky. Harker countered with a thrust against McNair's right flank with the Sixty-fifth Ohio. As the Arkansans dropped back deeper into the deep forest east of the road, the Sixty-fifth pushed on due north.

Farther up the La Fayette road, unaware of the Ohioans' approach, Fulton was using the lull that followed Colonel Snowden's charge up the Brotherton ridge to reorganize his fragmented command. To recapitulate, Snowden's Twenty-fifth Tennessee and several companies of the Twenty-third sat atop the ridge, fronting north. Behind them, Lieutenant Colonel Watt Floyd's Seventeenth Tennessee and the remaining companies of the Twenty-third had edged their way across the La Fayette road and into the fringe of open timber, where they lay down, facing west. Gregg's Forty-first and Third Tennessee regiments crossed a few minutes later and formed on the left of the Seventeenth, leading both Floyd and Fulton to the mistaken conclusion that Gregg's entire brigade was beside them.

Colonel Calvin Walker, commander of the Third Tennessee, was the first to discover the advance of Harker. He responded to the unexpected appearance of Yankees on his left flank by withdrawing across the road to the shelter of the forest. Lieutenant Colonel James Tillman sent his Forty-first Tennessee in the same direction, but at least had the presence of mind to ride over to the Seventeenth Tennessee to warn Colonel Floyd of the approaching danger.

That could not be, Floyd told Tillman, as Gregg was in line on their left with his entire brigade. No, Tillman replied politely, only his regiment and the Third Tennessee had kept pace with Fulton, and at the moment, they were running for their lives. Alarmed now, Floyd called to Fulton. His reaction was the same. "Doubting the report, I suggested that our lines were connected on our left and that a flank or rear movement could not therefore be made by the enemy," admitted Fulton. Tillman repeated his story. Fulton took the point and rode at once down the road with Tillman and Floyd to confirm the presence of the Federals. The three had scarcely started when they discovered a long line of blue advancing under the forest canopy, just thirty yards from the left flank of Floyd's Seventeenth Tennessee. "I heard distinctly the commands 'Halt,' 'Front,' and immediately their fire was pouring upon our flank and rear, reported Fulton. Floyd heard the commands too, and he glanced over his shoulder toward his regiment just as the Sixty-fifth Ohio let go its first volley: "A general stampede of our men ensued. So sudden and unexpected was the attack from our rear that every man seemed to act for himself, regardless of orders. I was too far from my regiment to give any directions or render any assistance at the time."[44]

Floyd rode clear of the Yankees just as they rushed his regiment with a yell. A few company officers coerced their men into firing a round or two before retreating, but for the most part the Tennesseans simply ran into the woods across the road as fast as they could. Most made it, but eleven officers and sixty men were gathered up as prisoners by the Sixty-fifth Ohio.

Out on the Brotherton ridge, Colonel Snowden had not a clue what was happening until he heard the crackle of a Yankee volley forty yards behind him. Hit squarely from behind, Snowden could do nothing but get his men out of the open at the double-quick. To its credit, only one member of the Twenty-fifth Tennessee was taken prisoner.

Harker was elated, and with reason. Nine months earlier, these same Tennesseans had mauled his brigade on the first day of battle at Stones River. More important, Harker's determined drive up the La Fayette road had eliminated Bushrod Johnson's division from the fight. The Ohioan could not have known, but his bizarre series of encounters had cleared away the one Rebel unit capable of challenging Negley's advance into the Broth-erton field and perhaps forestalling the restoration of the Federal center.[45]

Harker knew enough, however, not to press his good fortune. Already, the routed Rebels were showing signs of life. Across the road, Bushrod Johnson was with Fulton, helping him rally his line, and Captain Blakemore of his staff was preparing the Third and Forty-first Tennessee regiments to counterattack. Harker sent word to Colonel Opdycke to rejoin him, then braced for the shock.

The Third and Forty-first Tennessee regiments struck hard. Every mounted Federal officer except the adjutant of the Third Kentucky was unhorsed by the fire, and Harker himself had two horses shot out from under him. The brunt of the attack fell upon the Sixty-fifth Ohio. Its officers dropped at a dizzying pace. Lieutenant Colonel Horatio Whitbeck tumbled to the ground, dangerously wounded. Five officers of the line fell in rapid succession. Still, the regiment held. "In this position there was some of the most brilliant fighting that it has ever been my fortune to witness . . . its grandeur surpasses description," Harker averred. The Tennesseans broke off the encounter, and Harker gradually withdrew to the Viniard farm. The Third Kentucky took with it 118 prisoners, captured during its fight with McNair and Gregg.

Among the troops taken by Harker's brigade that afternoon were several from Longstreet's corps, probably Texans of Robertson's brigade. "It was easy to distinguish them from the soldiers of Bragg's army by their clothing," noted the brigade historian, Lieutenant Wilbur Hinman. "Most of them wore the regular Confederate uniform, while the dress of the western man was a 'go as you please' matter, with every imaginable variety of garments and head covering. Scarcely any two of the latter were clothed alike."

"How does Longstreet like the western Yankees?" Harker's Ohioans chided their captives.

"You'll get enough of Longstreet before tomorrow night!" was the prophetic reply.[46]

CHAPTER FOURTEEN

THE NIGHT SEEMED TO QUAKE AND TREMBLE

PAT CLEBURNE'S division had crossed Thedford's Ford shortly after 4:00 P.M. with a chance to change the course of the battle. A mile and a half to the west, Hood was driving Davis relentlessly across the La Fayette road. Behind Hood lay the uncommitted brigades of Gracie and Kelly. In their rear was Hindman, who had crossed the creek as ordered an hour earlier and, lacking further instructions, had placed his division in reserve. With Cleburne at hand, Bragg had a force more than ample to crush Davis, Wood, and whatever other Federal units might find their way to the Viniard farm.

Although certainly aware of the general situation on that part of the field, Bragg was no more inclined then to alter his plans than he had been three hours earlier when he dismissed Hill's proposal to launch a direct attack on Lee and Gordon's Mill. He still clung to his original plan of turning the Federal left, and that meant reinforcing Polk on the extreme right. So, while Cleburne's men shed their shoes, socks, and trousers and stepped into the icy waters at the ford, Bragg urged their commander to press on toward Polk at the double-quick. A splendid opportunity to crush two divisions and roll up Rosecrans's right while Stewart thrust at his center slipped quietly away.[1]

Footsore and wet, Cleburne's men ended their eight-mile march at the Youngblood farm, behind the reformed lines of Cheatham and Liddell. They arrived at 5:30 P.M. Already the woods were eerily dark, enveloped in the settling smoke of battle. A cold wind blew up from the north, and the shivering soldiers broke ranks in search of kindling for campfires. Fighting Yankees was the last thing on their minds. "The sun was nearly down," wrote Captain Coleman of the Fifteenth Mississippi Battalion Sharpshooters. "I had no idea of meeting the enemy that evening."[2]

St. John Liddell was of a different mind. He sought out Cleburne and impatiently led him through the murky light to the edge of the Winfrey field. Pointing to the enemy lines in the woods beyond, Liddell tried his best to convince Cleburne to attack. "I pressed Cleburne to move . . . at once, with his fresh troops and drive the enemy back, as they must be greatly exhausted from our constant fighting. If Cleburne's attack was delayed till morning, the enemy would be found entrenched and fully prepared," he argued. Cleburne demurred. He would await orders from Hill.

Cleburne had good reason for hesitating. A night attack under any circumstances was a risky undertaking; over unfamiliar ground with no time to prepare, it might very well prove suicidal. And, as the historian Thomas Hay has observed, "any great success would have been difficult to follow up in the darkness and over the rugged, wooded ground."[3]

Hill rode up a few minutes later, and Liddell redoubled his efforts. "Our opportunities were fast slipping away . . . and I appealed to him, adding that Cheatham and I were too much exhausted to repeat the attempt, and all we could do until rested was to retard the enemy." Hill told Cleburne to get ready. Elated with his apparent influence over Cleburne's commander, Liddell began lecturing the Irishman. "General, I hope you will be quick, for a minute now will be worth an hour tomorrow."[4]

Liddell had no right to be smug. The decision to attack had not been Hill's to make. In a rare burst of energy, Bishop Polk had determined to continue the battle long before Cleburne made his appearance. By 4:00 P.M., "both sides seemed willing to stop. Not so your father, who commanded in person," the bishop's son-in-law and aide, William Gale, wrote his wife after the battle. As the survivors of Liddell's ill-conceived attack on the Winfrey field stumbled past him, Polk sent a messenger to Thedford's Ford to hurry Cleburne along so that he might renew the assault.[5]

Nothing occurred to change the bishop's thinking during the ninety minutes before Cleburne arrived. When Hill reported the division present, Polk directed him to deploy Cleburne in line behind Cheatham and Liddell. As soon he was ready, Polk explained, Cleburne was to advance over the latter divisions. Cheatham would follow in support. Liddell's men would be spectators; after their poor showing in the Winfrey field two hours earlier, Polk knew better than to send them in again. Turning to Captain Wheless, the bishop dictated a message informing army headquarters of his intentions. "I feel certain from the prisoners captured we have been fighting Rosecrans's entire army," he said. "I am now placing Cleburne in position on the right. [I] will advance and expect to drive them before us. Present my compliments to General Bragg and assure him that I feel confident of success tomorrow."

Wheless left a few minutes before 6:00 P.M., as Cleburne's veterans raised their chilled, aching bodies from fires just kindled and retrieved their stacked arms. Fifteen minutes later, Wheless found Bragg. He repeated the message verbatim. Bragg agreed that they had been fighting the whole Federal army. He had no objection to Polk's proposed night attack, nor did he have any instructions for the captain to take back. Bragg asked only that Wheless tell the bishop that he wished all corps commanders to attend a council of war later that evening. Wheless saluted and turned his horse just as the first shots from the Winfrey field split the evening twilight.[6]

Cleburne's attack was ill conceived and tragic, the more so because it was entirely unnecessary. The Confederates could have achieved their objective without ever leaving their campfires. Thomas had already concluded to withdraw Johnson and Baird.

Rushing toward the Poe field with his brigade to reinforce the shattered Union center, Colonel John Connell ran into General Brannan at 5:30 P.M., just as Thomas rode away. What was Thomas's opinion of the day's fight, Connell asked. Thomas, Brannan said, had just told him it was "all sixes and sevens and we were merely holding our ground on the left without any movement ordered, or any known future definite object or purpose." Thomas knew as little of the commanding general's intentions as they did, Brannan added.[7]

It did not take an order from Rosecrans, however, to convince Thomas that the advanced positions of Baird and Johnson near the Winfrey field were untenable. Thomas decided to concentrate their commands near the La Fayette road, along a ridge just east of the Kelly field. As soon as the Union center was restored, the Virginian rode out personally to show Johnson and Baird the ground they were to occupy. The position Thomas had settled on was a half mile west of the Winfrey field — just about the distance Bishop Polk hoped to push the Federals.

Thomas found Johnson and Baird conferring behind Willich's brigade. The brigades of Starkweather and Scribner were just that moment feeling their way into position on the left of Baldwin. King's decimated Regular brigade remained in the rear, near the McDonald house. Before accompanying Thomas on the reconnaissance, Johnson scribbled out written orders for the withdrawal and handed them to staff officers to deliver to his brigade commanders; tragically, Baird chose to wait until after his ride with Thomas to inform Starkweather and Scribner.[8]

Absalom Baird was a popular commander who balanced a deep concern for his troops, especially the wounded, with exacting standards of discipline. Generally cool and collected in battle, Baird seldom lost his composure and generally could be counted on to make the right decision. But as he left Thomas and Johnson near the Kelly farm and started back to his command to pass along the order to withdraw, his heart must have sunk. "I was returning when, just as the light of day began to disappear, I heard the sounds of a fierce battle in front," Baird wrote.[9]

Cleburne had formed his command for the attack with as much care as the receding twilight would permit. With his right flank resting beside Jay's Mill, Cleburne arrayed his brigades in a single line of battle three hundred yards behind Liddell's division and Jackson's brigade of Cheatham's division. Thirty-year-old Brigadier General Lucius Polk, the competent nephew of the bishop, held the right; S. A. M. Wood, another lawyer general, commanded in the center; and Brigadier General James Deshler, an Alabama-born graduate of West Point in the class of 1854, led his brigade, composed largely of dismounted Texas cavalry, on the left. Cleburne told Polk and Deshler to guide on the center (Wood's) brigade and move as quickly as the broken ground would allow — any battery encountered should be charged at once. Meanwhile, Cleburne's chief of artillery, Major T. R. Hotchkiss, ordered his own batteries to come together and follow Wood's brigade.[10]

Bragg, who would find it hard to praise his own mother, called Cleburne "one of the best and truest officers in our cause." The commanding general could have learned much from Cleburne. "While he was a strict disciplinarian, he always looked to the comfort of his men, and was dearly beloved by them," remembered J. M. Berry of the Eighth Arkansas long after the war. "His quiet, kindly humor was so blended with reproof to both officers and men as to take away the sting." Berry recalled a summer afternoon in camp at Wartrace, where his regiment drilled under the admiring eye of Cleburne. After maneuvering awhile, the regiment halted. Cleburne rode forward, calling "Attention, battalion! by the right of companies—" He hesitated an instant, and the captain of Company C sprang forward and commanded "Company, right face!" "Hold on there, captain," Cleburne interjected. "You don't know but that I was going to say by the right of companies to the moon." As the laughter subsided, Cleburne smiled and finished the order: "To the rear into column."[11]

Thirty minutes were consumed in dressing ranks and correcting alignment before Cleburne judged his command ready to advance. It was 6:00 P.M. Ten minutes of sunlight remained. St. John Liddell chafed at the delay, but his troops, grateful to be mere spectators, raised a hearty cheer when Cleburne's men at last passed by. Amid the applause, Wiley Washburn of the First Arkansas heard the sincere if inarticulate warning of a private from Govan's brigade, who obviously spoke from experience: "Boys, we're glad to see you, but there is more fighting Yankees right up there than a little."[12]

Wood struck the enemy first. It was his misfortune to have to cross the Winfrey field. The forest was quite dark, but out in the open there was enough light for Baldwin's Federals to challenge his advance. Levi Wagner

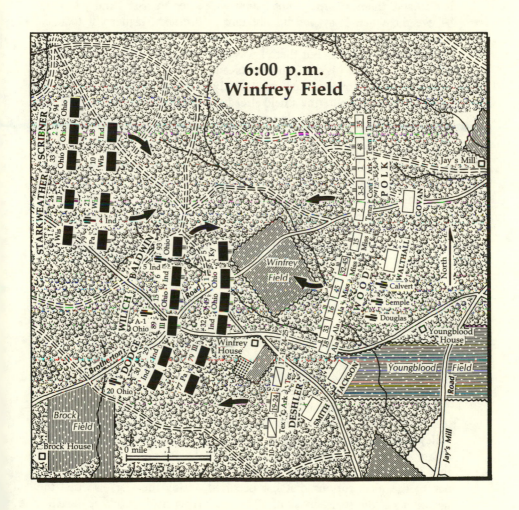

6:00 p.m.
Winfrey Field

and his comrades of Company A, First Ohio, had just entered the field from the west and were in the act of deploying as skirmishers when they saw their Rebel counterparts dart out of the woods on the far side. One hundred yards behind the enemy skirmishers, barely visible, was Wood's main line. "We knew at once that there was no chance for a skirmish line, yet we had to give them a parting shot before we retired in haste, and you may believe me when I say we did not tarry," admitted Wagner. "It took us perhaps about five minutes to get back and over the fence. I never could tell just how I got over, but there I was sound as ever." Wagner was lucky; fifteen members of his company lay bleeding amid the stubble.[13]

Wood's Confederates paused instinctively at the forest's edge, wary, even in the gloaming, of entering a field already carpeted with their countrymen. Baldwin's Federals were equally jumpy. No one knew quite what to expect from a night fight.

As soon as Wagner and his fellow skirmishers cleared the fence, which had been strengthened with rocks and tree limbs into crude breastworks, the First Ohio opened a spontaneous and ragged file fire, even though the Rebel main line had not yet showed itself in the field. Lieutenant Colonel Bassett Langdon was furious. He had intended to reserve the first volley for short range, the only chance he saw to do any damage in the dark. Langdon yelled himself hoarse trying to stop the firing and call his regiment to attention.[14]

Steadied by their officers, Wood's men pushed apart the worm rail fence bordering their side of the field and stepped into the open. The Federal fire intensified into a steady roll as the Fifth Kentucky and Willich's Thirty-second Indiana contributed their volleys to those of the First Ohio. Smoke rolled forward from the Yankee side, cloaking the twilight in gray. In the dark, the Federals overshot their foe. It was fighting by feel. Wood's regimental commanders guided on the orange musket flashes and pressed forward toward the far side of the Winfrey field.

The darkness heightened the tension. Imaginations ran wild. Unable to see, the combatants became more attuned to the sounds of battle. Every volley of musketry and exploding shell seemed to reverberate with extraordinary intensity, and everyone, from the general to the private, was convinced they had never heard the like. "Probably the conflict that now ensued was one of the most furious that has occurred during the war," asserted the historian of Johnson's division. "The enemy opened with the heaviest musketry and artillery fire the division had ever encountered. It far surpassed in intensity Shiloh or Stones River." There "burst upon us one of the most furious assaults of this or any other battle," agreed Colonel William Berry of the Fifth Kentucky. It seemed just as terrific from the other side. "The somber woods were lit up by the flashing guns and the night seemed to quake and tremble in the frayed peals," an awed Rebel artilleryman remembered. "For half an hour the firing was the heaviest I had ever heard," reported Cleburne, adding that "accurate shooting was impossible. Each party aimed at the flashes of the other's guns, and few of the shots from either side took effect."[15]

For some, the terror was too great to confront sober. A soldier of the Eighteenth Alabama Battalion said he saw one of his field officers tip a bottle to his lips. The Alabamian assumed it was whiskey; "I further thought he was trying to steady his nerve." It came as no surprise to the soldier to learn that the officer's horse had fallen, disabling him so seriously that he had to go at once to the rear.[16]

Mistakes, often tragic, were inevitable. The darkness was an invitation to the fainthearted to fall behind. Stragglers from the Thirty-third Alabama began shooting into the rear of their regiment as it crossed the Winfrey field. Through curses and screams those in the front line were able to convince them to stop, but not before a bullet cut through the neck of the adjutant, A. M. Moore, killing this son of an ex-governor and the best-loved officer in the regiment.[17]

The Thirty-third Alabama groped on with the rest of the brigade. To the Confederate soldiers standing exposed in the open field, it must have seemed as if they would never reach the enemy on the opposite side. Major John McGauhy halted the Sixteenth Alabama halfway across for no apparent reason. On his left, Colonel Sam Adams stopped the Thirty-third, waiting ten minutes until McGauhy found the nerve to continue on. Colonel E. B. Breedlove's Forty-fifth Alabama shivered as shells from the Fifth Indiana Light Artillery found their mark in its ranks, but kept on toward the fence and breastworks, behind which crouched the Fifth Kentucky. However, the Thirty-second and Forty-fifth Mississippi failed to keep pace and soon fell seventy-five yards behind the Alabamians. Mistaking them for the enemy, the Mississippians unleashed a volley into the rear rank of Breedlove's right wing. His lieutenant colonel called a halt. The company commanders of the left wing never heard the order. They led their men to within a few yards of the fence before they discovered their error and fell back.[18]

Wood was spared the humiliation of a general retreat thanks to Major Hotchkiss's decision to consolidate his batteries behind the Alabamian's brigade. When the infantry faltered, Captain Henry Semple guided his Alabama Battery through the wavering ranks. Unlimbering in front of the Thirty-second and Forty-fifth Mississippi, he opened fire on an enemy scarcely sixty yards away. Calvert's Arkansas Battery came up on Semple's right, and together they blasted the Yankee breastworks. It was the first and only instance of effective close artillery support provided attacking Confederate infantry that day.[19]

Meanwhile, the Thirty-third and Sixteenth Alabama regiments were getting timely help from Jackson's brigade, which had advanced soon after the Alabamians cleared their lines and was now sweeping the Winfrey field clear of Willich's two frontline regiments. Thoroughly distracted by the defeat of Willich, which left the right flank of his own First Ohio dangerously exposed, Lieutenant Colonel Langdon had lost all interest in the enemy to his front. "The regiment on my right was broken and running to the rear in great confusion and while I was striking my men (who were lying down) with the flat of my sword to get their attention, the rebel line was seen within forty yards of my right flank moving rapidly up perpendicular to it. I was barely able to get my men to their feet in time to see the rebel colors flaunted almost in their faces, and their guns being mostly unloaded, I directed them to retire."[20]

Colonel Adams led the Thirty-third Alabama over the breastworks and into the woods in pursuit. Not so Major McGauhy of the Sixteenth, who completely lost his nerve at the very moment victory was his. McGauhy's right companies had just bagged some thirty prisoners from the First Ohio, and his left was pushing the Federals handily, when he barked out the order to retreat. It was "obeyed in bad order, the regiment retreating in confusion," the senior captain, Frederick Ashford, recalled in disgust. Most of the regiment rallied and returned to the fight, but two companies quit the field altogether. The commander of Company G ignored Ashford's admonition to halt and let his men spill back to the rear. The officers of Company E similarly made no attempt to rally their men, and one frightened lieutenant was not seen again for two days.[21]

In the forest, all was blackness and bedlam, said Private Wagner. "We had to fall back through heavy timber, and the gloom of the forest and impenetrable pall of smoke from the firing caused such a darkness that nothing could be seen but the flash from the rebel guns. . . . I could not distinguish the blue from the gray."[22]

Colonel Baldwin was with the Sixth Indiana in the second line of the brigade, trying to steady the Indianians, as Wagner and his comrades of the First Ohio rushed through its ranks. Just minutes before the Confederate attack, Baldwin had been handed Johnson's order to retire. Any hope he may have had of an orderly withdrawal had vanished with the first ragged volleys in the Winfrey field, and now Baldwin was trying simply to hold together what remained of his brigade. Galloping to the front of the wavering Sixth, his old regiment, Baldwin grabbed the regimental colors. Shouting "Follow me!" the colonel jerked his horse to face the enemy, paused a moment, then rolled off his horse, dead. The Sixth held its ground as the spectral forms of Colonel Adams's Alabamians rushed toward them. Bayonets crossed, and for several agonizing minutes the two lines mingled in hand-to-hand combat.[23]

The confusion was complete. Lieutenant S. P. Hanley, an aide-de-camp to Cleburne, accidentally rode into the midst of the Sixth Indiana while searching for his own front line. He realized his mistake only after he heard the Yankee officers call the regiment to order by name. As Hanley slipped away in the dark, Colonel Adams faced a danger equally acute. The right companies of Jackson's brigade had come up behind him and were firing into his rear, those of Deshler's brigade had lapped his left wing, and the Sixteenth Alabama had disappeared from his right. Fearing that the Sixteenth Alabama would appear and begin firing into his right, Adams called a halt, and the Sixth Indiana broke contact and sneaked off some two hundred yards deeper into the forest. Adams's troubles were not quite over, though. "Shortly after halting I perceived from the flash of the arms that there was a fire in my front directed toward the enemy. This I afterward learned from some prisoners taken at this point, was one of the enemy's lines firing into another. While I was investigating this matter some of my center companies fell back about one hundred yards," reported Adams. "This was caused, as I learned from the officers commanding the companies, by some person giving the command to fall back and stating that it was my order." The Alabamian rode back into the Winfrey field and retrieved the wayward companies. As he prepared to plunge in again after the retreating Federals, a courier from General Wood came up and mercifully ordered him to break contact and rejoin the Sixteenth Alabama in the field.[24]

With the death of Baldwin, the mantle of brigade command passed to Colonel William Berry of the Fifth Kentucky. The Kentuckian, however, knew nothing of Baldwin's fate, nor could he have done much had he been aware of it. At the very moment Baldwin was exhorting the Sixth Indiana with his dying words, Berry was struggling to extricate his own regiment from behind the fence along the Winfrey field. Yelling to his men that the position must be maintained at any cost, Berry had repelled the first attack on his position. For an instant all was quiet. The Kentuckians peered through the dark, looking for moving shadows. Someone spoke up, pointing out that something that looked very much like a Rebel line of battle now held the ground where the First Ohio had stood and was floating past Berry's right flank.

The Forty-fifth Alabama and Thirty-second and Forty-fifth Mississippi chose that moment to renew their attack across the field. "I was completely cut off," reported Berry. The Kentuckian shouted to his company commanders to quit the fence and make for the woods. Most got the word and escaped with their commands, but somewhere in the din the command was lost, and thirty-two members of the Fifth threw up their hands in surrender as Colonel Mark Lowrey's Mississippians crossed the fence, telling their captors that their only orders had been to "hold the fence at all hazards."[25]

Berry's men were not yet out of danger. The ghostly enemy force on their flank, thinking the Kentuckians were part of their own line, held their fire, but the Seventy-ninth Pennsylvania of Starkweather's brigade, coming up from the rear, poured a volley into Berry's ranks that dropped men by the dozen. "We not stopping, they ran away, fortunately for us," reported Berry. Somehow Berry found the Sixth Indiana and succeeded in rallying his regiment on their left. By his own estimate, he had lost seven officers and one hundred men in thirty minutes of meaningless combat. The Ninety-third Ohio now came forward on Berry's left, the First Ohio rallied on the right of the Sixth Indiana, and Captain Simonson reformed his battery, less one gun lost when its limber crashed into a tree, behind the infantry.

The brigade staff accosted Berry in the dark, telling him of the loss of Baldwin and asking the Kentuckian for orders. "I had none to give except to hold the lines till I could communicate with General Johnson," he admitted. A few minutes later General Baird stumbled into his lines, and after conferring briefly, the two agreed to withdraw their commands toward the Kelly farm.

After clearing the fence at the edge of the Winfrey field, "I discovered that our whole line, so far as I could see, was so deranged that it ought to have been regulated before we advanced farther," commented Colonel Lowrey, who ordered his Mississippians to halt and cease fire. The Forty-fifth Alabama continued on to test Berry's new line but was repulsed handily. A few minutes later, D. H. Hill, never far from the shooting, rode up and told Lowrey to stay where he was, pending orders from Cleburne. For all the blood and terror, Wood's brigade had succeeded in pushing the Federals back just three hundred yards.[26]

Lucius Polk enjoyed greater success on the division right, largely because of Yankee blundering. At dusk, Starkweather had formed his brigade on the very hilltop from which he had been so ingloriously driven seven hours earlier. For his men, it was a nightmare revisited. All around lay the dead and dying from the morning's fight. Lieutenant Johnston of the Seventy-ninth Pennsylvania vividly recalled the scene:

> We stacked arms and took a survey of the battlefield, while the dead and wounded were being carried away by men detailed for that purpose. Poor Charlie Stiles was there, smiling as pleasantly in death as he was wont to smile in life. . . . There lay a poor fellow, terribly mangled, who had been struck by a cannon ball as he lay flat on the ground; his one leg, hip, and the small of his back had been entirely carried away, while his other leg

and foot was split completely open through and through. Here was a poor fellow whose skull had been fractured, his eyes rolling madly and imploringly, but his voice was speechless. I took him by the wrist; his pulse was strong and rapid, and his grasp so firm I could scarcely release his hold of me. I tried to have him carried off on a stretcher, but the surgeon, looking at his horribly crushed skull, glaring eyes and gurgling breathing, said nothing, but passed on. He knew the man was dying. And all around us were lying the dead in every variety of position. Some horribly mangled and some whose wounds could scarcely be seen; some with horribly distorted and terrified countenances and others as placid and serene as if they were taking a sweet nap.[27]

Benjamin Scribner, the gentle Hoosier colonel, was on the left of Starkweather. He too was near the scene of his morning's rout, and his men likewise began the tragic work of identifying their dead and carrying off the wounded. Just after dusk, the sound of sharp and rapid firing from their right brought the soldiers of both brigades to their feet. They grabbed their stacked rifles and hastily formed line of battle, while the firing grew heavier and nearer.

Then the problems began. As Baldwin's brigade reeled before Wood's attack, Richard Johnson groped about for some means to support his wavering left. He appealed to Baird to advance Starkweather to Baldwin's left. At the same time, he personally requested Scribner to move forward and conduct a half-wheel to the right, apparently hoping the Indianian might take the attacking Confederates in the flank.[28]

Sergeant Henry Perry of the Thirty-eighth Indiana felt a sense of impending doom as his command tramped toward the fighting. "Marching upon a concealed foe of unknown strength in the recesses of that gloomy forest, where there was not even the song of a bird or the chirp of a cricket, had a depressing effect upon the Union soldiers," he wrote. "Tree tops, limbs, and twigs were clipped off our heads and fell all around us. It was a display of fireworks that one does not care to see more than once in a lifetime."[29]

On the right of Starkweather's brigade, Lieutenant Johnston shared Perry's dread. His regiment crested the hill, then advanced sixty yards more before being ordered to lie down in rear of the Fifth Kentucky. "We order our men to hug the ground as closely as possible to escape the shot and shell that hiss and screams so wickedly over us," remembered the Pennsylvanian. "Just now a shell bursts near our colors, killing two or three men and wounding some others. This creates confusion and excitement in that part of the line, and some of the men fire their pieces and run to the rear." Those around Johnston likewise panicked and discharged their weapons. This was the fire that greeted Colonel Berry's Fifth Kentucky when it fled from the Winfrey field. While Lieutenant Johnston and his fellow officers tried to make their men understand that they were firing into friendly troops, the Fifth Kentucky returned the volley. "We could do nothing but lie still and take it, hoping that they would speedily find out their mistake," Johnston wrote. But they kept on coming, firing all the while, and the Seventy-ninth Pennsylvania disintegrated around the flustered lieutenant and the half dozen members of his company who stayed by his side. Johnston and his little party joined the retreat. Johnston paused beside a tree at the top of the hill to catch his breath. Just then, a shell struck it, showering the lieutenant with splinters and sawdust. That was the last time Johnston stopped until he was safely in the rear. Years later, Johnston wrote bitterly of the imbecility that had almost led to the destruction of his regiment: "I could not help thinking that there had been very bad generalship displayed. . . . No more stupid move could have been made than to lead men right into range of the enemy's fire when no possible good could result from it, and not a single shot could be fired."[30]

The fumbling had been greater than Johnston imagined. Realizing that the Seventy-ninth Pennsylvania was masked by the Fifth Kentucky to its front, Starkweather ordered his brigade to conduct a half-wheel to the left, so as to bring it clear of Colonel Berry's Kentuckians. Colonel Scribner chose precisely that moment to execute his half-wheel to the right. In the gloom, the result was painfully predictable. Scribner's brigade opened fire on Starkweather's men, who just as promptly returned it. Lucius Polk's Confederates put a quick end to the affair, striking both brigades simultaneously and sending them reeling in confusion back over the hill for good. Neither Scribner nor Starkweather was able to rally his broken command until they reached the ridge east of the Kelly farm, exactly where Thomas had wanted them three hours earlier.[31]

Losses in Polk's brigade were negligible. At a cost of sixty men, most of whom were only slightly wounded, the brigade took fifty prisoners and recaptured three cannons and their caissons, which had remained on the field since their loss by Van Pelt's battery that morning. Polk did not pursue the enemy. His success had been so rapid that the left flank of his brigade now masked Wood's right, which still lay in the Winfrey field. Concerned that his troops might be subjected to misdirected friendly fire, Polk sensibly called a halt for the night. Hill was on hand to confirm his decision.[32]

The success of Lucius Polk was the only bright spot in his uncle's night assault. Elsewhere, the folly of Bishop Polk's decision was becoming painfully apparent. Actually, the attack had nearly unraveled before it began. Cleburne had instructed Polk and Deshler to dress their lines on those of Wood as they moved to the attack. Polk had done so, but Deshler had lost sight of Wood when the brigades left the Youngblood field. While Wood wheeled northwest toward the Winfrey field, Deshler marched due west, opening a five-hundred-yard interval between the two commands.

Brigadier General John Jackson unwittingly stepped into the gap, confident that his brigade was tucked safely behind Cleburne. Even the rattle of small-arms fire to his front and exploding shells overhead did not unduly concern him at first. Unable to see through the twilight haze, Jackson assumed the firing meant that Cleburne was in contact ahead of his brigade; that is, until men began dropping in his front rank. Stunned by the severity of the unexpected volleys, his left regiment began to break up. Jackson responded by ordering a charge of the whole line. It was effective. Willich's two front regiments were "swept back to the second line," to use the Prussian's own words. Willich ordered up the Fifteenth Ohio to the left of and the Eighty-ninth Illinois to the right of the shattered regiments, then rode calmly among his stunned troops until they responded to his order to "Dress on your colors."

Willich had his brigade in a semicircle, its flanks tucked in to fend off an enemy that seemed to be everywhere. The combat was personal and desperate. Said a Federal eyewitness: "At one time there was a lull in the storm, and a rebel in a lusty tone called out 'Surrender boys and you're safe.' One instantaneous response of 'Never' and the crash of battle again resounded." Willich's line held, three hundred yards in the rear of his original position, and at length Jackson's Confederates broke off the assault and sullenly withdrew into the depths of the forest. In a fitting end to the fighting on that part of the field, Jackson's aide-de-camp and inspector general accidentally rode into the Federal lines and were captured.[33]

For sheer poignancy, nothing matched the struggle that ensued on the Confederate left, where contact was not made until after nightfall. Portending the chaos to come, nearly all of Deshler's skirmishers stumbled into Dodge's Federal brigade and were swiftly and quietly captured. Uncertain of both his own location and that of Wood, and troubled by Goodspeed's Federal battery, which had begun shelling his right flank, Deshler called a halt a good two hundred yards shy of the Federal lines. Although no one had fired on them, many of Deshler's men lost their nerve and stole back toward the brigade of Preston Smith. The burly Tennessee attorney ordered his own command forward to catch them. The skulkers returned to the front, and for a few minutes Deshler's line held. When it wavered a second time, Smith rode forward and personally urged the men back into their ranks. Again the line steadied, and Smith returned to his own brigade. Unbeknownst to Smith, however, Deshler, in an effort to evade the fire of Goodspeed's battery, now led his command toward the left, which unmasked the two right regiments of Smith's brigade as they moved forward.[34]

A third time Smith spied a line of troops standing in the darkness to his immediate front. He rode forward with his aide-de-camp, Captain Thomas King, and inspector general, Lieutenant J. W. Harris, to get the presumed stragglers moving. Imperiously he guided his horse into their midst. Demanding to know who was in command, the Tennessean leaned forward in his saddle to smack what he thought was another of Deshler's skulkers with the flat of his sword. The soldier dodged the blow, aimed his rifle, and fired. Smith fell to the ground, killed by Sergeant George Bryson of the Seventy-seventh Pennsylvania. In an instant, some thirty rifles were turned on King and Harris. King was killed in the volley, but Harris made good his escape.[35]

Colonel A. J. Vaughan, commanding the Thirteenth and One Hundred Fifty-fourth Tennessee Consolidated, repeated Smith's mistake. With Captain John Donelson of the brigade staff, he rode up to the front of the Seventy-seventh Pennsylvania at the very instant Smith brandished his sword at Sergeant Bryson. Bending over toward a nearby soldier, Vaughan insisted on knowing why he and his comrades were not advancing on the Federals. The startled Pennsylvanian responded with a rifle shot that narrowly missed Vaughan, killing Captain Donelson. Vaughan yelled at some troops from the Twelfth Tennessee, who had come up behind him, to shoot the impetuous Federal. Shots rang out and the Yankee fell dead. His comrades panicked. "Don't shoot, we surrender," they cried to Vaughan while grounding their arms.

Turning to them, Vaughan noticed a stand of colors unfurled before him. "Who has those colors," he demanded.

"The color-bearer," came the answer.

"Sir, to what command do you belong?" Vaughan asked.

"To the Seventy-seventh Pennsylvania Regiment," replied the color-bearer. Vaughan snatched the colors from his grasp and handed them to a captain of the Forty-seventh Tennessee, which had advanced through the woods and was standing smartly beside Colonel Vaughan, near enough to shake hands with their Yankee captives.

Elsewhere along the line the Pennsylvanians put up a brief struggle. Here and there bayonets crossed in frenetic bursts of hand-to-hand fighting until a regiment of dismounted Texas cavalry from Deshler's brigade, drawn toward the commotion, poured a volley into the right flank of the Seventy-seventh Pennsylvania that effectively ended its resistance. Most of the Yankees sneaked off in the dark, but their commander, Colonel Thomas Rose, was taken prisoner along with his field officers, seven line officers, and seventy-three of his men. Suffering from an acute case of gout, Rose had entered the battle wearing just one boot. He was a man of indefatigable spirit, however, and several months later he engineered one of the most

"Who has those colors?" Colonel Alfred Vaughan takes the standard
of the Seventy-seventh Pennsylvania.

celebrated prison escapes of the war, leading a group of Federal officers through a tunnel out of the notorious Libby Prison in Richmond.[36]

The dispersal of the Seventy-seventh Pennsylvania brought the battle to Colonel Buckner's Seventy-ninth Illinois. Lieutenant Montraville Reeves remarked to a friend that "it would be a rebel trick to attack us at dark. . . . [I] had hardly got the word out when they poured a volley into our ranks." As the Seventy-ninth returned the fire of a Confederate line to its front, a regiment drifted through the forest toward its right. Assuming it to be their relief coming up, Reeves's major told the lieutenant to go out with him to instruct the regiment where to form. The two walked to within twenty yards of the unknown line before an officer from the Seventy-seventh Pennsylvania warned them away. It was a Rebel unit, he said, and they had just called on his own regiment to surrender. A moment later, "I heard their guns come together in a hand to hand fight," recalled Reeves. As the lieutenant turned to run back to the Seventy-ninth, the top of an oak tree came crashing down onto his head. He was lucky. "Coming top foremost, it did not hurt me much. I crawled out with the loss of my hat and a blanket that I had taken from a dead Reb." By the time Reeves got back on his feet, the shooting had stopped. Somehow he eluded the enemy and found his regiment, huddled in a thicket. With his fellow officers he took count of the men. Ninety-one men were missing, captured by Vaughan's Tennesseans.[37]

Colonel Dodge could offer his troubled brigade no help. Unaware of the disaster that had befallen his frontline regiments, he had strayed into Confederate lines while trying to bring the Thirtieth Indiana into the fight. Confused and disgusted with himself, the colonel sat down on a tree stump. Two unarmed and credulous Confederates, presuming Dodge to be wounded, kindly offered to help him off the field. Dodge saw an opening. Drawing his revolver, he whispered: "If you do not conduct me through your lines and into ours you are dead men on the spot." The Rebels complied. Dodge rejoined the brigade, and his would-be benefactors found themselves on their way to Yankee prison camps.[38]

Meanwhile, in Dodge's absence, Colonel Buckner was trying to hold the brigade together. As his own regiment scattered, the preacher grabbed the flag of the Thirtieth Indiana and exhorted its members to stand fast around the colors. Bullets tore the banner to ribbons as he waved it over his head, but Buckner's appeal had the desired effect. The regiment fell back a short distance but kept together, and the Confederates broke off the attack. Buckner's faith had seen him through another clash: "Had it not been for special Providence, I should have been riddled with minie balls."[39]

In truth, the Confederates were in no condition to continue the fight. With their brigades dangerously intermingled, Vaughan and Deshler realized that they stood about as good a chance of firing upon one another as on the Yankees. They called a halt. Vaughan's Tennesseans escorted their prisoners to the rear and freed some of Deshler's captured skirmishers. Colonel Buckner marched Dodge's brigade away from the enemy, and a hush fell over the forest.[40]

CHAPTER FIFTEEN

IF I COULD ONLY DROWN
THIS TERRIBLE SOUND

THE END of the fighting offered no respite from the suffering. When night at last drew a curtain on the killing, it offered up in its place new, more subtle terrors to torment the soldiers. With the setting of the sun, the temperature plummeted. A cold north wind whistled through the forest. Frost formed. The day had been warm, the sun unrelenting. Uniforms, soaked with sweat, offered no protection from the chill of the night. In frontline units, where opposing picket lines often were only a hundred yards apart, campfires were strictly prohibited. "We were forbidden to . . . even unroll our woolen blankets. Our rubber ponchos we might use, but, while they were truly impervious to water, they were as comfortless as the smooth side of a tombstone in January," complained Lieutenant Wilson Vance of the Twenty-first Ohio. Sleep was impossible. "A dozen would lie down close together with the command 'by the right flank spoon' and three or four ponchos covered the squad," explained Sergeant Charles Partridge of the Ninety-sixth Illinois. "For a time everything was alright, but after a while the outside ones began to freeze out, and by midnight all were up."[1]

Being lightly clothed in cotton homespun, the Confederates suffered more acutely from the cold. "More than seventy-five per cent of the clothing the soldiers wore was sent them from home by their families. . . . The clothing of our soldiers was of cotton fabric and one thin blanket to the man," recalled Confederate Private B. W. Green. "I do not now remember ever having seen a gray overcoat in our army worn by officer or man (there may have been a few), but I do remember quite a number of blue coats which were taken from dead Yankees. Shoes were sometimes issued, but usually we got them from home or from dead Yankees." Scavenging is precisely what Green set out to do, but as he combed the battlefield, he found he had come too late. "I spent two hours walking over the field of

Chickamauga to get a pair of shoes from a dead Yankee, but they were in such demand that I found none."[2]

Harder to take than the cold was the lack of water. Virtually no rain had fallen for over a month, and the many streams and rivulets that normally flowed down from Missionary Ridge to water the valley were bone dry. The Confederates had Chickamauga Creek from which to draw water, but within the Federal lines, the only source of water was a small cattle pond near the Widow Glenn house. So many wounded had crawled to it during the course of the fighting that the water was now fetid, its surface streaked with blood. Veterans aptly christened the pool "Bloody Pond." Beyond the right flank of the Union infantry, opposite the large Federal hospital at the Gordon-Lee mansion, bubbled the clear and abundant waters of Crawfish Springs. Moved by the thirst of parched soldiers, especially the rapidly dehydrating wounded who lay everywhere, Colonel Thomas Harrison quietly instructed the men of his Thirty-ninth Indiana Mounted Infantry to gather all the canteens they could and fill them at the springs. By midnight, his troopers had delivered over one thousand canteens of cool springwater to grateful infantrymen.[3]

Few could recall a night so dark. The moon was in its first quarter. Thin moonbeams knifed their way through the clouds only to be blunted by the smoke that hung low over forest and fields. Scouting parties and pickets collided in the gloom. Couriers lost their way and were captured.[4]

As the shooting sputtered and died, Colonel Scribner left his brigade in search of General Baird for orders. Before riding off with Lieutenant George Devol, the lone staff officer still at his side, Scribner told his only remaining orderly to stay put, in case he lost his bearing. The colonel groped a short distance through the trees before coming upon Baird, who happened to be out looking for him. Together they retraced the path to Scribner's command, but when they came to where it had stood, they found only forest. Baird began to fret; they were lost and had wandered into enemy lines, he moaned. Scribner took a chance. "Orderly," he yelled. "Sir," came the reply through the blackness. The young soldier was sitting precisely where Scribner had left him, but he was alone. Scribner's men had fallen back by order of Colonel Berry, whose brigade had rested on their right, "but you told me to stay here, and I stayed," explained the orderly.

The four rode to the Kelly field, where they found the division encamped. The orderly rode off on an errand, Baird to find his staff. "Our movements in the night had so confused me that I did not even know the points of the compass," remembered Scribner. He asked Lieutenant Devol to find out where they were, "whether the house off yonder was Kelly's where we halted in the morning before the battle began." Scribner gave Devol two empty canteens to fill, enjoined him to learn all he could of the events of the day, then sat down in the dark, his hand firmly gripping his horse's reins to keep him from wandering off. The minutes slipped by. Scribner waited — waited and wallowed in self-pity:

> My condition was indeed forlorn and miserable. A cup of coffee that morning was my only nourishment since the evening before at Stevens's Gap; my inflamed eyes itched and burned, asthmatic coughing and breathing and all the discomforts of hay fever added to my sorry plight. At length pity for my poor horse, who had fared no better, diverted my mind from my own privations to his. A rail fence was found to which he was hitched, but in removing the saddle, my pistols fell from the holsters, and with all my groping about I was unable to find them. Observing a light in the woods at some distance off, I called out and found that it was the bivouac of Simonson's battery. They knew me at Perryville and a party of them hastened to my assistance. They found my pistols, made my fire and spread my blanket before it, and would have shared their supper with me, had I permitted them to rob themselves.[5]

Scribner was more fortunate than he realized. Lieutenant Henry Freeman of the Regular Brigade was alone in the woods on an errand when night fell. Like Scribner, he chanced upon General Baird, who asked him to tell King to close up a bit on the rest of the division. Freeman rode about looking for his command, all the while expecting to run into the enemy. At last he came upon three men from his battalion out searching for water, who pointed out for him the general direction toward the unit. Freeman rode on. "By this time it was quite dark, the smoke of the day's battle began to settle upon the trees." Stragglers and wounded from Scribner's and Stark-weather's brigades streamed past. None seemed to know where the Regulars were.

Freeman pressed on. The next troops he met were Confederates. Upon announcing his name and rank, the lieutenant was hurried rearward and ushered into the presence of General Cleburne, whom he found seated by a low fire that his orderlies were fanning into a blaze. "He was surrounded by members of his staff, some of whom were just setting out with orders to his brigade commanders. Others were giving details of the late fight and explaining the dispositions of the troops." After a time, Cleburne turned to the lieutenant and began interrogating him about Federal dispositions. Finding Freeman unresponsive, Cleburne dismissed him. "He was very polite and in a few moments directed one of his staff to take charge of me." Had he had supper, the Rebel officer wondered? Yes, replied Freeman. Well, then he was lucky, sighed the Confederate, who had not eaten all day. Freeman offered him the hardtack and coffee in his saddle bags. The famished officer dashed off to Freeman's horse. As he grabbed the saddle bags, the soldiers who had captured Freeman stepped forward angrily, announcing that the spoils were theirs. A heated exchange followed. Hearing the commotion, Cleburne left his campfire to mediate. A prisoner may dispose of his personal property as he chose, the general announced. Seeing that there was not enough to go around, Freeman decided to keep the food. Cleburne congratulated him on the wisdom of his decision, and the gathering broke up. Later, Freeman shared his rations with the hungry staff officer, to whom he also gave his sword. Freeman kept his boots, despite the Southerner's offer to buy them, and was glad he had, because he got no shoes during his long stay in Southern prisons.[6]

Of all the horrors endured that night, none made a more lasting impression on the soldiers than the wails of the wounded. "The roar of the battle's bloody storm has ceased, and all is still save the waves that sob upon the shore — those waves are the shrieks of the wounded and dying — and these are more horrible and trying to our hearts than was the storm of battle. In that storm manly courage bore us up; in this storm of groans and cries for help that come on the black night air, manly sympathy for comrades and enemy makes our hearts bleed," wrote Sergeant McGee of the Seventy-second Indiana. Fellow Hoosier Alva Griest of Company B was similarly moved. "The thunder of battle has ceased . . . but, oh, a worse, more heart-rending sound breaks upon the night air. The groans from thousands of wounded in our front crying in anguish and pain, some for death to relieve them, others for water. Oh, if I could only drown this terrible sound, and yet I may also lie thus ere tomorrow's sun crosses the heavens. Who can tell? I must sleep in spite of it all," he scribbled in his journal.[7]

"All night we could hear the wounded between ours and the Federal lines calling some of their comrades by name and begging for water. The night was cold and crisp, and the dense woodland was dark and gloomy; the bright stars above us and flickering light from some old dead pine trees that were burning in an old field on our left and in front, giving everything a weird, ghostly appearance," recorded Lieutenant R. M. Collins of the Fifteenth Texas Dismounted Cavalry. "At three o'clock we are allowed to make fires and take rest . . . as all our clothes are wet from wading the Chickamauga last evening, the fire is thankfully received," wrote William Heartsill of the same regiment. Less welcome was the spectacle the flames revealed. "We have literally walked on dead men all night, and now while campfires are casting their flickering rays over the battlefield, the scene looks horrible, hundreds of ghastly corpses mangled and torn are scattered around us. I can sit here by my little glimmering light and count a score of Federals, dead and dying. . . . It is now nearly day-light and I have not had a particle of sleep; nor do I want any while this bloody work is going on."[8]

The darkness spared most the lurid scenes of gore. Many, however, were oddly drawn to the grotesque display, with a curiosity they could neither suppress nor explain. As the black of night melted into the mist of morning twilight, Lieutenant Terry Cahal, acting inspector general on General Stewart's staff, took a ride over the ground where the division had done its heaviest fighting the afternoon before. He found more than he bargained for:

Here was one of our gallant boys who seemed to have fallen in the moment of victory, who with cap in hand and sword unsheathed seemed to have been cheering on his men to victory when he had fallen pierced through the heart; so instantaneous was his death that the fire in his eye and the flush on his cheek had not yet died out. Here was another gallant one who seemed not to have been instantly killed, but with dogged determination had fallen upon his knees and resting himself against a tree had half drawn his rammer, seemingly with the determination to avenge his own death, and then kneeling upon one knee, with the other knee bent and foot upon the ground, he seemed to be the very personification of grim determination and stern resolve. And here was one of my friends whom I had known long years before; he had fallen, so I learned, in attempting to rally his comrades when they were broken and driven back on the evening before. I had parted from him just as he went into the fight, and as he clasped my hand and bid me adieu, he repeated his motto to me, which he said should animate him in the coming fight. It was the last six lines of Lochul's reply to the seer before going into the battle of Culloden. I buried him and marked the sacred spot with a piece of board, writing his name and company upon it, and beneath the epitaph of "Dead upon the Field of Honor." And as I laid him in his last resting place I made an oath above his grave to avenge his death.[9]

Many soldiers, touched by the suffering all around them, tried to do more than simply gawk at the dying. All too often, however, attempts to give succor to the wounded brought only volleys from the enemy's nervous pickets.[10] At dusk, Colonel Sidney Barnes ordered a detail from the Eighth Kentucky to carry a white flag into the east Viniard field and bring in their wounded. "A shower of bullets was the response," noted Lieutenant Thomas Wright angrily. Still, Wright and his comrades were able to pull most of the regiment's wounded out of the cornfield. But the thought that he could have done more, had the Rebels permitted, troubled him deeply:

By this inhumanity, the poor, suffering wounded of friend and foe continued their piteous cries and groans within easy hearing distance of both lines throughout the cold, frosty night. Never before did the horrors of war seem to us so cruel. We could distinctly hear their lamentable cries, "O, water, water!" and occasionally some poor, half-frantic sufferer calling the name of some familiar comrade or friend to come there. Considering the intense cold night, with our great coats and blankets far in the rear, our scant, poor rations, and being so near so much suffering humanity, without the privilege of giving any assistance, this certainly was the most miserable night the Eighth experienced during the war.[11]

Sergeant McGee of the Seventy-second Indiana heard the same sobs from behind his breastworks on the edge of the Viniard field. One voice, clear and loud, called out above the rest, repeating the same doleful refrain hour after hour: "O, for God's sake come and help me!" Some of the men, unable to stand it any longer, inched toward the La Fayette road to help the caller, but a hail of bullets from the timber drove them back.

Later that night, volunteers were sought to man the picket line, which lay in the ditch behind the Viniard house. "As this was the second night without eating or sleeping, the men were so overcome with exhaustion that the skirmishers would go to sleep in spite of themselves and their critical and horrible surroundings," wrote McGee. "The men, too, feeling the responsibility of the position, refused to go because they could not keep awake." When not a single private accepted the duty, Sergeant McGee and a corporal volunteered to go out. It was nearly 3:00 A.M. They crept forward and slipped into the ditch. There they heard the same mournful plea, grown faint: "For God's sake come and help me!" "And to this day," recalled McGee, "that dying, wailing petition is still ringing in our ears."[12]

The incessant cries of the wounded for water were more than Theodore Petzoldt of the Seventeenth Indiana could bear. "We had orders not to move from our places, not to strike a match, not to go to sleep or make any unnecessary noise," he wrote. Orders notwithstanding, Petzoldt felt he had to help. Quietly, he slipped over the breastworks and into the west Viniard field. His canteen was empty, but the Indianian felt certain he could find water among the dead. It was so dark that Petzoldt could but dimly make out the outlines of those lying on the ground. Petzoldt crawled to a motionless form lying near the ditch. Shaking it by the shoulder, he whispered "Partner." There was no answer. Petzoldt raised the shoulders of the corpse and slipped the canteen strap off — the canteen was full. Petzoldt crawled to the nearest wounded man and gave him water. Others saw him and begged for a drink. Petzoldt went from soldier to soldier, giving each a sip, until the canteen was dry. He looked, but found no more. "How horrible it all was. Some of the water I gave to a poor fellow shot through the lungs and whose blood was slowly oozing from his mouth. He had crawled into the gully to be protected from the flying bullets during the day," remembered Petzoldt. "I would have liked to have taken [the] men back to our lines, but it would have done them no good for we could not have taken care of them there if I had. So I left them in their terrible pain and misery and went back to our lines."[13]

In the forest east of the Viniard fields, Lieutenant Colonel Benjamin Sawyer of the Twenty-fourth Alabama shared the frustration of Lieutenant Wright and Sergeant McGee over the plight of the wounded. The great dread of many, recalled Sawyer, was that the battle would rage over them in the morning. "Please have me moved from here. I don't want to be killed tomorrow and by my own people," was the appeal he heard most often. "Of course we could not help them, but we assured them the best we could that there would be no danger to them from the morrow."

Something in the plight of one wounded Yankee particularly moved Sawyer. This "brave fellow"—Lieutenant David Baker of the Eighth Kansas, grievously wounded in the thigh—pleaded to be carried to a place of safety. When told this was not possible, Baker faced his fate "like a man." He handed Sawyer $117 and asked that it be sent, if possible, with his dying message to his wife. Sawyer suggested that Baker keep a few dollars, in case he survived, then carefully wrapped the balance in a page torn from Baker's pocket notebook. By the struggling moonlight, the lieutenant colonel wrote: "This is the property of David Baker, Company B, Eighth Kansas Regiment, to be forwarded to his wife, Mrs. Elizabeth Baker, at Lafayette, Indiana." This Sawyer did in case he himself should be killed before he could mail it.

Sawyer survived the battle. Afterwards, he sent the packet through the lines under a flag of truce and soon forgot the incident. Twenty years later, a newspaper account of his wartime service brought Sawyer a letter from Baker. The lieutenant had lived. His leg had been amputated, and he now wore an artificial limb. Baker's wife had never received the money he had entrusted to Sawyer. "Being in very moderate circumstances, with a large family to support, I would be very grateful to you, indeed, if you will remit the amount," the lieutenant closed his letter. Sawyer was mortified. He wrote everyone still living who might possibly know the whereabouts of the packet he had sent through the lines and even contributed a long article in the Philadelphia *Weekly Times* calling attention to Baker's plight. "I have my fears, though, that nothing can be done at this late date toward successfully tracing the money," he wrote sadly.[14]

There were many similar instances of kindness shown the wounded that night. W. C. Brown of the Ninety-third Ohio fell during the fight near the Winfrey field, his leg broken by a minie ball. He listened as his comrades fell back in the darkness and the Confederates edged their way forward to establish their picket posts for the night. A squad passed by near where he lay. Brown called to them. He told them he was a wounded Federal and asked only that they shift him into a position that might ease his pain. "They came to me promptly and assisted me as gently as if I had been one of their own men or a brother," the Ohioan recalled. One removed his woolen blanket and spread it on the ground for Brown to lie upon, another placed Brown's cartridge box under his head for a pillow, and a third spread his poncho over him. The unexpected tenderness moved Brown. "Boys, an hour or two ago we were engaged in shooting each other, and now you are treating me with the greatest kindness. I hardly know how to thank you for it in return," he said. "Well, old fellow, we are doing to you as we should like to be done by. It may come our turn next," replied one of the Rebels. With that, they passed on to the front. Brown drifted into a fevered sleep; when he awoke the next morning, he found that one of the Southerners had returned to spread a calico quilt over him. The Ohioan never forgot the kindness of the unknown Confederates. Thirty-two years later, he paid tribute to them in the pages of *Confederate Veteran* magazine: "Was there ever a more beautiful type of chivalry and Christian charity than this? This incident grows brighter to me as the years go by. God bless you boys, wherever you may be. I would love to have you for my neighbors."[15]

William Burton of the Thirty-sixth Ohio had a brother in the Ninety-second. During the afternoon, someone told him that his brother had been killed. After dark, Burton walked out into the Brock field to search for him. He found his brother, unconscious but not yet dead, with a bullet in his head. Burton lifted him off the ground and carried him into the lines of the Thirty-sixth. He laid his brother down, then sat beside him to wait for him to die. Alfred Phillips of Company E watched Burton keep his sorrowful vigil:

> The frosty air was heavy with fog and the darkness was intense. Through the long hours of the night he sat by his dying brother alone, listening to his labored breathing, till near morning he was quiet. He pressed his ear close to his heart to hear it beating; held his cheek close to his mouth in the darkness to catch the faintest breath, but he was dead. Then he borrowed a shovel from the battery and dug a grave at the foot of a large tree. He gathered twigs of pine and lined it carefully, sides and bottom. Then he wrapped him in his blanket, a man from the battery assisted him to lower the body into the grave and he covered it with twigs of pine and earth.[16]

The proximity of the dying reminded the living of their own mortality. Many who had come out of the first day's fight unscathed were now visited with premonitions of impending death. Johnny Green of the Orphan Brigade considered his fate sealed:

> It is the only time in the war that I thought I had a presentiment, but fatigued and worn as I was, I did not drop off immediately to sleep; I knew the next day would bring us into one of the bloodiest battles the world had ever witnessed. I remembered that the men at my elbows on each side of me had both been killed by the same shot . . . and I could not shake off the conviction that I would meet my death in the next day's battle. I offered

up a prayer that the Lord would guide me and strengthen me and that when death came to me it would find me gallantly doing my duty, that my first desire should not be that I might escape death but that my death should help the cause of right to triumph.[17]

Lying on the frosty ground, unable to sleep, Major Samuel Brown of the Sixty-fifth Ohio whispered to a friend beside him: "Tomorrow I shall die. This is my last quiet talk on earth. I praise God that no human being is dependent upon me for support and that he permits me to die for my country."[18]

The poet general, William Lytle, was miserable. His cold had gotten worse, and he hardly had the strength to move about. While changing uniforms in the early morning hours of Sunday, 20 September, Lytle told his orderly that he was completely exhausted. The orderly begged him not to go into battle, but the general was insistent. He had never shrunk from duty and would not do so now. But, Lytle added, should he fall, he hoped the orderly would see to it that his body was carried from the field and his beloved little sorrel horse was well cared for.[19]

While Green, Brown, Lytle, and thousands of others brooded over what the morning might bring, the wounded struggled simply to survive the night. Grass fires, ignited during the day by bursting artillery shells, continued to burn out of control. Those who could crawled out of their path, but many spent their final moments in helpless agony, watching the flames lick over their bodies.[20]

Those who were able to walk made their way to the field hospitals. Of course, there was no guarantee that those who reached the hospitals would fare any better in the long run than those on the field—there were simply too many wounded and too few surgeons. The Gordon-Lee mansion and all its outbuildings had been appropriated as the principal field hospital of the Twentieth Corps. Many wounded from the Fourteenth Corps found their way there as well, drawn to the waters of Crawfish Springs. Tents were thrown up to accommodate the overflow. By 8:00 P.M. every bit of available shelter was occupied, yet hundreds remained unattended and without protection from the cold. Bonfires were lit for those left outdoors, straw was gathered up as bedding, and beef soup and coffee were ladled out. The stately library of the Gordon family was transformed into the primary operating room. Harried surgeons tossed amputated limbs out the glass doors into waiting wagons, to be carted away and buried. By the battle's end, nearly forty wagon loads had been drawn off.[21]

For the most part, the surgeons had neither the time, the resources, nor the skill to provide more than the most rudimentary attention to a patient. Occasionally, they effected a cure in spite of themselves. Doctor William

Graham, surgeon of the One Hundred First Indiana, came upon a member of his regiment at the Crawfish Springs hospital. He had been shot through the right lung, and with every breath blood bubbled from the wound. "Doc, for God's sake do something for me, for I cannot stand it much longer," the soldier begged. "I thought so too," admitted Graham. "I studied a moment and thought nothing would do him much good, but decided to give him a drink of whiskey. I procured a half teacup full and held up his head and he swallowed it. I then dressed his wound and left him thinking he would be dead in the morning, but I found him better, and he said then, and many times to me since the war, that the whiskey saved his life."[22]

George Stormont of the Fifty-eighth Indiana was on duty as a hospital steward at Crawfish Springs. All night long he watched as one after another of his regiment were brought in from the field. There was William Robinson, fully aware that his wound was mortal, who passed his final hours with gentle dignity. His comrades brought him to the hospital, but Robinson told them not to put him in the tent, as space was needed for those who might live. He asked only to be placed in a comfortable position and given a little water. He died quietly during the night. "Robinson was a great big, large hearted fellow," said Stormont. "I remember that he once came to my gate, while I was pastor of the church at Princeton, and gave me five dollars toward repairing the church. This was as much as the leading members could be persuaded to give. In giving his life for his country he showed himself a better man than many whose professions are much more loud." Next to Robinson lay a soldier named Carnahan, shot through the stomach and in intense agony. His wound was also mortal, but unlike Robinson, he could not understand why he was not put in the tent nor his wounds dressed. All through the night and into the next morning he appealed to the surgeons; by noon he too was dead.[23]

In one of the tents lay Hans Heg, clinging desperately to life. A steady procession of officers from the brigade came to visit him. The Norwegian impressed them to the very end. Through his misery, he spoke of duty and of his love for "my boys of the Fifteenth" Wisconsin.

Heg died Sunday morning. "I am very sorry to hear that Heg has fallen," said Rosecrans on hearing the news. "He was a brave officer, and I intended to promote him to be general." None was more affected than Stephen Himoe, surgeon of the Fifteenth Wisconsin. Married to Heg's sister, the thirty-one-year-old Himoe also had emigrated to America from Norway as a boy and settled in Wisconsin. He and Heg were the closest of friends. When war broke out, Himoe's wife and two children went to live with Mrs. Heg, and he and the colonel became tentmates. Through the long, chill night, Himoe never left Heg's side. "It was agonizing to stand beside the colonel and see him suffer and die. Colonel La Grange of the First Wisconsin Cavalry and other friends who called to see him wept like children. Everybody who knew him loved him." Profoundly shaken, Himoe submitted his resignation and went home to Wisconsin.[24]

Lieutenant Wilbur Hinman, later the historian of Harker's brigade and author of popular works of fiction on the war, walked three miles down the La Fayette road to Crawfish Springs after he was shot through the right elbow during the afternoon. He reached the springs at dusk and reported to the hospital tent of his division. "Hello, Lieutenant, they've winged you too, have they? I'll attend to you in a few minutes," the brigade surgeon cheerfully called to him while binding the stump of an amputated arm. Hinman took a seat and contemplated his surroundings:

> A field hospital just after a battle is the most grewsome and harrowing picture presented by the changing panorama of war. Words seem to have no meaning when one attempts to portray the awful scenes of suffering and death. All through the hours of that long night, by the light of blazing fires, the surgeons and their assistants moved about among the hundreds that lay upon cots or upon the ground around the tents, stanching the wounds and administering food and cordials and water to the sufferers. Often a pulseless, motionless form was borne away and laid in the fast lengthening row of those to whom death had come. I cannot dwell upon the painful subject. It was more than thirty years ago, but even while I write my eyes moisten as the picture of unutterable woe rises before me in all its vividness.[25]

Conditions were no better six miles up the road at the Cloud church, where surgeons of Brannan's division had set up their field hospital in the sanctuary and in a nearby cooper's shop. "All day countless ambulances arrived loaded with wounded. At 11:00 P.M. those buildings were overfilled," Dr. Konrad Sollheim, regimental physician of the German-American Ninth Ohio remembered. "The scene was indescribable, so touching as to stir even the physicians (who were accustomed to them) and especially so because we could see we must overcome supreme hardship in order to do a few of our duties correctly, if able to do any at all."[26]

The unsavory Texas private, William Fletcher, was dropped off at a Confederate field hospital at dusk. Stewards laid him on a bed of straw about fifty feet from the operating table. A long row of wounded lay between him and it. Since his wound was not critical, Fletcher was left alone to slowly bleed the night away. He took in his surroundings with a ghoulish fascination. "Near the table, but not in line, was a stout young man who was shot through the head. From the sides the brain could be seen oozing out. He seemed to be suffering greatly and would rise, make a step or two, and fall. He repeated this time and time again for quite a while after daylight." Fletcher noticed a member of his own company passing through the tent who had been shot in the side of his face. "He looked so disfigured by the shot and swelling that he looked funny," delighted Fletcher. The soldier sat down beside Fletcher, and the two traded stories of their wounding. "I then commenced joking him, telling him he would make better success courting when he got back, with his back to the girls." But the joke was on Fletcher. "That will be better than you," the soldier retorted, "as you can't turn any way to hide your wooden leg." It had not occurred to Fletcher that he might lose his foot, and the thought troubled him until morning, when it came his turn on the table. "Fletcher, I want to examine your wound," the doctor said, jabbing his finger into the bloody hole as he spoke. Screaming with pain, Fletcher kicked the surgeon across the tent with his sound foot. The doctor was livid. "I will leave you alone, without treatment," he snarled. "Doc, that is what I want," rejoined Fletcher. That evening, the Texan was put aboard a train for Augusta, Georgia, with both feet intact. He recovered nicely.[27]

Somewhere out on the Brotherton road, Jacob Miller of the Ninth Indiana staggered along in the dark. His gored eye was completely clotted with blood, the other swollen shut. Miller pried open his eyelid and tried to walk, but shock and loss of blood soon compelled him to give up. He sat down beside a tree, resigned to spending the night on the field. "After it seemed to me ages I imagined I heard someone coming my way. I pulled my eye open and saw, to my great joy, that it was two men with a stretcher." At the field hospital, surgeons dismissed Miller's wound as mortal, bandaged his eyes simply to ease his suffering, then placed him in a corner of the tent to die.

Miller lay still. The wet cloths soothed his burning eyes. Fatigue touched every fiber of his being, yet sleep eluded him. "My mind raced back to the line of battle. It seemed the word was yelled by someone to give them hell, and that I was hit." Over and over he replayed the moment of his wounding until, near dawn, he fell into a deep and dreamless sleep.[28]

CHAPTER SIXTEEN

GOD GRANT IT MAY BE SO

"U PON THE whole, today's work has been a terrible one, and yet there is everything to cheer us," Colonel Sanderson wrote in his journal that night. "The enemy attacked us and meant to turn our flanks and rear and possess Chattanooga. Without possessing it, the battle is of no use to them, and yet in this they failed. We are as strong in our confidence of holding as we were this morning, yea stronger."[1]

Not everyone shared the colonel's hopeful view of the situation. After a hasty supper, General Palmer left his command in search of "some superior officer, to obtain information and orders for the next day." Coming upon army headquarters, Palmer stepped inside the Glenn cabin in the hope of speaking with Rosecrans or Crittenden, who had been there since dusk. Palmer was in a foul mood, having been without sleep for forty-eight hours. When told that he could see neither Rosecrans nor his own corps commander, the Illinoisan lost his temper. Turning to the war correspondent William Shanks, who was sitting beside the military telegraphers in the hope of snatching some scrap of information, Palmer vented his spleen. "Since I saw you this morning," Palmer said, "I have got my troops together again. They are in good spirits, and ready for another fight. I have no hesitation in saying to you" — at that moment Palmer noticed the despised Dana at the other end of the table; his better judgment seemed to tell him to stop talking, but he was too tired and angry to care, and he turned to address Dana — "and I have no hesitation in saying to you, Mr. Dana, that this battle has been lost because we had no supreme head to the army on the field to direct it." With that, Palmer turned on his heel and stomped out of the cabin.[2]

Phil Sheridan shared Palmer's anger and frustration. "There did not seem to be any well-defined plan of action in the fighting, and this led to much independence of judgment in construing orders among some of the subordinate generals. It also gave rise to much license in issuing orders; too many people were giving important directions, affecting the whole army, without authority from its head."[3]

What Palmer and Sheridan described were the consequences of Rosecrans's growing exhaustion. A week earlier, Rosecrans had plummeted from the euphoria of a seemingly easy pursuit to a dread that his own badly divided army would be destroyed in detail. The tension that accompanied the reassembling of his corps had taken a severe toll on the general. "Rosecrans habitually used himself up badly in time of excitement," General Stanley observed with uncommon perspicacity. "He never slept, he overworked himself, he smoked incessantly. At Iuka and Stone River, the stress of excitement did not exceed a week. His strong constitution could stand that, but at Chickamauga this strain lasted a month, and Rosecrans's health was badly broken." To make matters worse, the general had had nothing to eat since gulping down a handful of biscuits and some coffee at daybreak.[4]

At times during the day, Rosecrans had reacted skillfully to Confederate thrusts against the La Fayette road, feeding units into precisely those points of the line most threatened. For the most part, he had done all that could have been reasonably expected of a commanding general fighting a defensive action on unfamiliar and heavily forested ground. What was missing, however, was the old aggressiveness. Rosecrans's demeanor was largely passive, his orders discretionary. Appeals to subordinates for information were often frenetic. The signs of fatigue were unmistakable.

That night, Rosecrans thought only of defense. The initiative would rest solely with Bragg. "We were greatly outnumbered, and . . . the battle the next day must be for the safety of the army and the possession of Chattanooga," he explained in his report of the campaign. Prisoners had been taken from so many regiments that Rosecrans believed the enemy numbered in excess of ninety thousand. Interrogation of captives confirmed the presence of Longstreet's corps and part of Johnston's army—perhaps even his entire force. Rosecrans did not understand that several Confederate regiments existed in name only—they had been consolidated to form one unit of regimental strength while retaining their former designations, as, for example, the Seventeenth, Eighteenth, Twenty-fourth, and Twenty-fifth Texas Dismounted Cavalry of Deshler's brigade—or that many that continued to operate alone were sadly depleted, as was the Fiftieth Tennessee, which had entered the battle with only 102 present for duty.[5]

Rosecrans was not alone in his fear of a numerically superior foe. "This seems to be conceded by all our officers, that the force encountered under Longstreet today, is a more formidable foe than heretofore encountered by this army, and there is this danger now to us, that our enemy may be tomorrow reinforced by more of the same kind of fighting men. In fact, there is now a general impression here that Lee's army is being transferred to Georgia, and that it will be henceforth the field of action," wrote Colonel Sanderson, who remained optimistic nonetheless.[6]

Bragg indeed had the greater force at hand, though not nearly in the numbers Rosecrans feared. The last troops from Virginia arrived during the night, swelling the Confederate ranks to 68,000—perhaps 72,000, less the first day's losses. Against these, Rosecrans had some 57,000 troops, minus losses. Casualties for the first day are impossible to calculate. An estimate of between 6,000 and 9,000 Confederates and perhaps 7,000 Federals seems reasonable.[7] Although the fighting had badly disrupted the command structures of both armies, the disorder was less acute in the Army of Tennessee. Confederate divisions generally retained their integrity, whereas on the Union side, brigades had been detached all over the field. Bragg also had the advantage in fresh units. The divisions of Hindman and Breckinridge had seen no serious action, and in Preston's division, only the brigade of Trigg had been engaged. The arrival of Kershaw's and Humphreys's brigades from Virginia and Colquitt's brigade from Mississippi during the night would give Bragg eleven fresh brigades. Rosecrans, on the other hand, could muster only eight: Granger at the McAfee church, on the Ringgold road, with the three brigades of his reserve corps; Negley's division, which had marched considerably but fought little; and Lytle's and Laiboldt's brigades of Sheridan's division, which had missed the fight altogether. Philip Sidney Post's brigade of Davis's division remained at Stevens's Gap guarding the mountain passes, too far off to be of use.

Rosecrans summoned his corps and division commanders to headquarters at 8:00 P.M., evidently after Palmer left in a huff. Dana estimated that twelve of nineteen showed up, including all four infantry corps commanders. While McCook and Crittenden explained the disposition of their commands and the assembled generals debated possible improvements, Thomas drowsed in a chair. Like Palmer, the Virginian had not slept in two days. He had been adjusting his forces (which consisted of the divisions of Baird, Johnson, Palmer, Reynolds, and Brannan) when he received the call to headquarters. Thomas reported that he had drawn in his lines to cover both the La Fayette and Reed's Bridge roads. He insisted that the next Confederate attack would be directed against his left flank, near the McDonald house, from the direction of Reed's Bridge. In order to extend his line northward to meet this threat and to compensate for the confused state of Johnson's division following Cleburne's night attack, Thomas requested reinforcements. Having said his piece, he went to sleep.[8]

Each time Rosecrans posed a question to him, Thomas awoke, straightened up, and announced, "I would strengthen the left," then drifted back to sleep. Rosecrans's reply was always the same: "Where are we going to take it from?" That of, course, was for him alone to decide. Apparently the question was left open; shortly after 10:00 P.M. the discussion drew to a close and Garfield sat down to draft written orders for the morning.[9]

In brief, it was Rosecrans's intention to protect both the La Fayette road to his front and the Dry Valley road behind him, while contracting his lines to offset the presumed disparity in numbers between the two armies. At the same time, Rosecrans hoped to maintain a strong general reserve on the eastern slope of Missionary Ridge for use as the situation might dictate. He instructed McCook to close the divisions of Davis and Sheridan on Thomas's right. In so doing, McCook was to refuse his own right in order to protect both the Widow Glenn house and the Dry Valley road. McCook was expected to hold a line a mile long with only five brigades, two of which—those of Carlin and Martin—numbered only eight hundred men between them. Wilder was to withdraw from the Viniard farm at dawn and extend McCook's line to the south. Rosecrans hoped that Mitchell would have his cavalry in position near Glass's Mill by daylight, in order to cover the vulnerable Federal hospital at Crawfish Springs. Thomas, meanwhile, was to maintain his present position, fronting generally east in what resembled a backward "C." His line would run from the McDonald house on the left, then cross the La Fayette road and follow the trace of the Kelly farm southward before bending back and recrossing the road near the Poe farm. Thomas was ordered to take Brannan's division out of the front line and retain it as a reserve. Crittenden was told simply to withdraw the divisions of Van Cleve and Wood to the eastern slope of Missionary Ridge behind Thomas's right. The precise locations he and McCook were to occupy were left to their discretion. To Gordon Granger, Rosecrans gave orders even more vague, directing him merely to place his corps in reserve where it might support either McCook or Thomas. Rosecrans's state of mind can be inferred from closing sentences of his orders to Thomas. "You will defend your position with the utmost stubbornness. In case our army should be overwhelmed it will retire on Rossville and Chattanooga. Send your trains back to the latter place." A commanding general who on the eve of battle speaks of being overwhelmed is not one to inspire confidence.[10]

Garfield read the written orders to each corps commander in the presence of all. It was midnight before the business of war was concluded. As was his habit, Rosecrans kept his weary generals a bit longer to socialize. Troopers from the Fifteenth Pennsylvania Cavalry brought in hot coffee, bacon, and a handful of crackers—the first food most had seen all day. Rosecrans enjoined McCook to entertain the group with a rendition of "The Hebrew Maiden's Lament," a plaintive ballad that had been popular for nearly fifteen years. As the wind whistled through the puncheons of the tiny cabin and the telegraph clicked its accompaniment, McCook sang to his fellow generals:

"Bitter tears I shed for thee." General McCook sings to General
Rosecrans and his lieutenants.

In that sombre chamber yonder,
Father's taper still burns bright;
Bending to his breast his aged,
Care-worn face he prays tonight.

Open wide before the righteous
Lies the Talmud which he reads,
And his child e'en is forgotten,
'Fore his God, and Israel's deeds.

List'ning then a few short moments,
I may by this lattice stand,
And may watch yon little window
Of our neighbor's nigh at hand.

Oh! in yonder friendly chamber,
Whence the light now peepeth forth,
Lives of Christian youths the fairest,
Live my life, my all on earth.

Dearest youth whose care-worn image,
Graven in my heart will be,
Ah thou seest not the bitter,
Bitter tears I shed for thee.[11]

The generals filed out of the cabin and returned to their commands. The telegraph fell silent. Staff officers tried to snatch a couple of hours' rest on the floor, drawing together for warmth. Dana lay down next to Horace Porter. "There were cracks in the floor of the Widow Glenn House, and the wind blew up under us," wrote Dana. "We would go to sleep, and then the wind would come up so cold through the cracks that it would wake us up."[12]

Rosecrans was not among them, although none needed rest more than he. Stuffing some hardtack in the pocket of his old army overcoat and slinging a canteen of cold tea over his shoulder, the general had stepped outdoors. Back and forth Rosecrans paced in front of the cabin, munching crackers and sipping tea as he walked.[13]

It was 2:00 A.M. before Thomas returned to his headquarters. There, a report awaited him from General Baird, who held the extreme left of the army. His left not only did not reach the McDonald house, Baird told Thomas, but it ended some four hundred yards east of the La Fayette road. Baird explained that he could not cover the ground demanded without severely attenuating his line. Left out of his report, but certainly on his mind as well as Thomas's, was the fact that the troops responsible for that sector were the badly demoralized Regulars of King's brigade. Thomas scribbled a note to Rosecrans, renewing his call for reinforcements to extend his left. This time, he asked specifically for Negley's division of his own corps. Rosecrans replied in writing that Negley would be sent to him at once.

Sometime during the night, Thomas told his commanders to build breast-works along the Kelly field salient. The soldiers used what they could scavenge in the dark: fence rails, rocks, fallen trees—anything that offered even a remote possibility of stopping a bullet. They built their breastworks just high enough to squat or lie behind; none was more than three feet high. The clatter of axes echoed through the forest. "We heard the enemy all Saturday night felling trees and getting artillery into position, so we knew we had a hot day's work before us," recalled a Rebel lieutenant.[14]

Convinced that he had done all he could for the night, Thomas lay down under a large oak tree near the Snodgrass place to sleep. A protruding root pillowed his head.[15]

McCook's singing had done nothing to improve Phil Sheridan's mood. Depressed himself, the Irishman had sensed only fear and anxiety at the Widow Glenn house. Sheridan found fault with Rosecrans's plan but was hard pressed to suggest an alternative. With the benefit of hindsight, he wrote years later:

> The necessity of protecting our left was most apparent, and the next day the drifting in that direction was to be continued. This movement in the presence of the enemy . . . was most dangerous. But the necessity for shifting the army to the left was obvious, hence only the method by which it was undertaken is open to question. The movement was made by the flank in the face of an exultant foe superior in numbers, and was a violation of a simple and fundamental military principle. Under such circumstances col-umns naturally stretch out into attenuated lines, organizations become sep-arated, and intervals occur, all of which we experienced; and properly I doubt if it could have been executed without serious danger. Necessity knows no law, however, and when all the circumstances of this battle are fully con-sidered it is possible that justification may be found for the maneuvers by which the army thus drifted to the left. We were in a bad spirit unques-tionably, and under such conditions possibly the exception had to be applied rather than the rule.[16]

Sheridan made known his displeasure to all who cared to listen. In the early morning hours, Crittenden and McCook joined him at his headquarters tent to coordinate the withdrawal of Wood's division from the line and the movements of his own command. The discussion grew animated. Sheridan wanted it known that he was disgusted with the rough reception Bradley's brigade had received the previous afternoon, and from the plan agreed upon at the Widow Glenn house he feared equally for his remaining brigades. A corporal standing guard outside the tent watched the generals depart, then listened as Sheridan paced back and forth alone inside, bewailing aloud "the situation, past, present and prospective, especially prospective, using language more emphatic than elegant, as General Sheridan only could do."[17]

General Longstreet's ego was bruised. His train had pulled up "with jerks and bangs" to Catoosa Station, outside of Ringgold, at 2:00 P.M. on the nineteenth. Longstreet and Lieutenant Colonels Moxley Sorrel and P. T. Manning of his personal staff stepped off the train onto the platform expecting a warm personal greeting from members of Bragg's staff. But there was no one there to meet them, not even a guide to lead them to the battlefield. "It would appear that if Bragg wanted to see anybody, Longstreet was the man," reasoned Sorrel. "But we were left to shift for ourselves." It was a sorry reception for the celebrated second-in-command of the Army of Northern Virginia.[18]

Longstreet and the lieutenant colonels passed the afternoon on the platform, waiting for their horses to arrive on a later train. It chugged into the station at 4:00 P.M., and the three quickly saddled up and started out on the Ringgold road in the general direction of Chickamauga Creek. A growing stream of stragglers and wounded filed by as they neared the creek. Wagons hurried past in both directions, and the roar of battle continued unabated ahead of them. Shortly before sunset, the trio apparently turned off the main road, to wander "by various roads and across a small stream through the growing darkness of the Georgia forest," said Sorrel. It was well after nightfall when they came to the east bank of Chickamauga Creek. A picket challenged them from the opposite side. "Whom comes there?" "Friends," Longstreet replied ambiguously. The pickets were skeptical. After a brief parley, one of the lieutenant colonels requested the pickets to identify their command. They replied with the number of their brigade and division. "As Southern brigades were called for their commanders more than by their numbers, we concluded that these friends were the enemy," wrote Longstreet. The general tried to bluff his way out of danger. "Let us ride down a little way to find a better crossing," he said loud enough for the pickets to hear. The trio galloped off, trailed by a poorly aimed volley from the startled pickets. "Another road was taken for Bragg," said Sorrel, "about whom by this time some hard words were passing."[19] There would be many more hard words spoken in the next twenty-four hours, both by and about the commanding general.

General Polk was the first of Bragg's corps commanders to report to headquarters for the council of war, riding up at about 9:00 P.M. Polk was entirely unprepared for what he was about to hear. While brooding beside his campfire in the early hours of the evening, Bragg had decided to completely reorganize his army in the face of the enemy, a move that only compounded the existing confusion. The army was to fight as two grand wings, Bragg told the bishop. Polk was to command the Right Wing, where Cheatham's division of his own corps, Cleburne's division of Hill's corps, and Walker's entire corps were then drawn up. Breckinridge would report to him during the course of the night. Command of the Left Wing would be Longstreet's, whenever he happened to show up. His force would consist of Buckner's corps, Hindman's division of Polk's corps, Bushrod Johnson's provisional division, his own corps commanded by Hood, and the artillery battalions of Eldridge, Williams, and Robertson.[20]

Such a restructuring midway through a battle not only was imprudent, but was also bound to create further ill will in the high command. Polk and Hill were both lieutenant generals; the arrival of Longstreet, for whom a place obviously had to be made, would add a third. Dividing the army into two wings relegated Hill to service as a corps commander under Polk, which was tantamount to no job at all.

No satisfactory explanation has ever been offered for Bragg's decision to pass over Hill for wing command. Polk's son claimed that Bragg launched into a tirade against Hill during his conversation with the bishop. According to William Polk's account, Bragg was disgusted with Hill for his failure to cooperate with Hindman in McLemore's Cove and for what he termed his "querulous and insubordinate spirit in general," leaving the bishop with the impression that he would save himself the trouble of contending with Hill's fragile ego by ignoring him. Most contemporary accounts, however, including a letter from Bishop Polk's son-in-law, William Gale, suggest that Bragg had not yet hit upon Hill as a scapegoat for McLemore's Cove but was angry only with Hindman.[21]

Bragg's actual plan of battle, although less bizarre than his organizational reshuffling, showed a singular lack of creativity on the general's part. He gave Polk oral instructions to attack the enemy at daylight on the extreme right. Because the heavy forest reduced visibility to something less than a regimental front, the advance could not be simultaneous; therefore, each brigade commander was to move only after the left flank of the unit to his right started forward. As Bragg explained in his report of the battle, "The left wing was to await the attack by the right, take it up promptly when made, and the whole line was then to be pushed vigorously and persistently against the enemy throughout its extent." Wheeler was ordered to concentrate his cavalry opposite Glass's Mill and demonstrate against that and nearby fords. In effect, Bragg was sticking to his original plan of turning the Federal left and pushing Rosecrans south into McLemore's Cove.[22]

Polk remonstrated with Bragg. The day's fighting clearly showed that Rosecrans had gathered a sizeable force in front of the Confederate right, he argued. Moreover, Granger's Reserve Corps, which Polk assumed to be at Rossville, was in a position to fall on the flank and rear of whatever force he himself might throw against the Federal left. It was thus imperative that the right wing be strengthened. Bragg dismissed the bishop's fears. He asked Polk if he fully understood the order to attack at dawn, then sent him on his way.[23]

Bragg's lackadaisical approach to the entire situation is painfully apparent from his discussion with Polk. That he gave the bishop only oral orders is incredible; no written instructions were ever prepared, nor was the adjutant general's office even aware of Bragg's intentions, said Brent.[24]

John Bell Hood showed up at headquarters a few minutes before Polk departed. He had not received Bragg's summons, choosing instead to ride to Thedford's Ford because in Virginia it was customary for subordinate commanders personally to report the status of their units to General Lee after a day's battle. The visit gave Hood a chance to meet many of the principal officers of the Western army. "To my surprise, not one spoke in a sanguine tone regarding the result of the battle in which we were then engaged," he recalled. Hood noticed Breckinridge, whom he had known since childhood, sitting on the root of a tree with a heavy black slouch hat hiding his face. Hood tried to strike up a conversation, but the Kentuckian just sat there, listless. Hood rambled on alone. Offhandedly, he expressed his personal belief that they would rout the Yankees in the morning. At that, Breckinridge sprang to his feet. "My dear Hood, I am delighted to hear you say so. You give me renewed hope; God grant it may be so." Breckinridge rode off with Polk, and Hood walked over to Bragg for his orders.

Hood faced the prospect of a bleak night on the field. "I had nothing with me save that which I had brought from the train upon my horse. Nor did my men have a single wagon, or even ambulance in which to convey the wounded. They were destitute of almost everything, I might say, except pride, spirit, and forty rounds of ammunition to the man."[25] A chance meeting with Colonel J. Stoddard Johnston of Buckner's staff, who invited Hood to their bivouac, at least spared the general the discomfort of sleeping alone in the biting air. Conditions were little better in Buckner's camp, but at least the company was good. After a late supper and some pleasant conversation, Hood went to sleep on a pile of leaves beside Johnston, whose blanket he shared.[26]

Longstreet stumbled upon headquarters at 11:00 P.M. He found Bragg asleep in an ambulance. Incredibly, the commanding general had retired without having notified D. H. Hill of his diminished role in the new command structure, nor had he taken any steps to ensure that his staff monitored Polk's preparations for battle. The most charitable explanation for Bragg's lassitude is that his old maladies had won out over his better judgment.

Bragg was awakened, and he and Longstreet conferred in private. They talked for nearly an hour. Bragg gave Longstreet a crude map depicting the primary roads and streams between Lookout Mountain and Chickamauga Creek, pointed out the general positions of the two armies, and explained the plan of battle and Longstreet's responsibilities. The generals parted shortly after midnight. Exhausted from his travels, Longstreet made no effort to find his command or to communicate with Hood or Buckner that night. A few leafy branches were gathered together and covered with blankets for his comfort and that of his lieutenant colonels, and the trio was soon fast asleep.

Lieutenant Colonel Sorrel implies that Longstreet found his interview with Bragg satisfactory, that "nothing could be simpler than the operation proposed for Rosecrans's destruction." Perhaps, but the general must have been uneasy over his complete ignorance of the terrain and unfamiliarity with the operating procedures of the Army of Tennessee. At least, however, Longstreet knew some of the key personalities on both sides. He and Buckner were old friends, D. H. Hill had served with him in Virginia in happier times, and, many years before, he had shared a room at West Point with fellow cadet William Starke Rosecrans.[27]

Now only Hill remained unaccounted for. He apparently had lingered on Cleburne's front until nearly 11:00 P.M., helping him rearrange his lines and then conferring individually with each brigade commander in the division. Finally, his larger responsibilities dawned on him. "It was near five miles to the ford [Thedford's], but as I had no orders for the next day, I deemed it necessary to find the commanding general," he reported. En route, Hill learned from stragglers that Breckinridge had come up from Lee and Gordon's Mill. Hill dispatched an aide to find and conduct him into position on Cleburne's right. Hill continued on with a single staff officer, Captain T. Coleman.

The two promptly lost their way, crossing Chickamauga Creek at Lambert's Ford a mile north of headquarters. It was midnight by the time they reached Thedford's Ford. Hill later insisted that Bragg's headquarters was not there. Perhaps Bragg and Longstreet had already retired, but it seems incredible that Hill did not at least chance upon a staff officer or a member of the headquarters guard.[28]

Meanwhile, Polk had settled in for the night at his bivouac on the east side of the creek, which was anywhere from a hundred yards to a half mile up the road from Alexander's Bridge, depending on whose account one accepts. In either case, it was too far from his command. On the return ride from Thedford's Ford, he had run into Colonel Archer Anderson, Hill's chief of staff. What was said is unclear. In a letter to Hill written shortly after the battle, Polk claimed to have passed on the order to attack at daylight to Anderson, who told the bishop that Hill was then at Thedford's Ford.

Polk told Anderson he wanted to see Hill at his headquarters; he would have couriers posted near the bridge to guide the general to his bivouac. The bishop added that Hill should post Breckinridge in support of Cleburne. Anderson replied that Hill preferred to place the Kentuckian on Cleburne's right. "Then tell General Hill he may post his troops as he pleases," Polk retorted, and the two parted company.[29]

The comedy of errors continued. Anderson reported to Hill a few minutes after he and Coleman arrived at Thedford's Ford. Anderson told Hill that his corps had been placed under the command of Polk, who wanted to see him at Alexander's Bridge, but "said not a word . . . about an attack at daylight," Hill maintained. Two other staff officers who were present attested to this, and Breckinridge, who had overheard Polk's conversation with Anderson, later assured Hill that the subject of a daylight attack never arose.[30]

Bragg's apathy was infectious. Instead of riding to Polk's headquarters, Hill lay down to catch a few hours' sleep.[31]

Polk was only marginally more attentive to his duties. He could just as easily have scribbled written instructions on the spot (to be followed by more formal orders) for Anderson to carry back, or gone on to Thedford's Ford with him.[32] Instead, he chose to return to his own headquarters, where he dictated orders for the twentieth. They read:

> Hdqrs. Right Wing, Army of Tenn.,
> Near Alexander's Bridge, September 19, 1863 — 11:30 P.M.
>
> 1. Lieutenant-General Hill, on the right, will attack the enemy with his corps to-morrow morning at daylight.
> 2. Major-General Cheatham, on Hill's left, will make a simultaneous attack.
> 3. Major-General Walker's corps will act as reserve.
> 4. Corps and division commanders will see that their troops are amply supplied with ammunition before daylight.
>
> By command of Lieutenant General Polk:
>
> [Thomas M. Jack]
> Assistant Adjutant General[33]

Remarkably, Polk said nothing to Breckinridge about the daylight attack, even though they shared a campfire during the night. According to the Kentuckian, Polk mentioned only that he was expected to prolong the line of battle on Cleburne's right.[34]

General Walker stopped by Polk's headquarters and received his orders personally. Lieutenant Colonel Jack dispatched a copy to Cheatham, who received it at 1:00 A.M. John Fisher, an enlisted member of the Orleans Light Horse Troop, Polk's headquarters escort, was selected to bear the copy to Hill.

Fisher dutifully set out for Thedford's Ford. There he found no sign of the elusive lieutenant general, nor could anyone tell him where he might be. The trooper met both Cheatham and Breckinridge, neither of whom could help. Fisher claimed he searched for four hours; "after going in every direction and inquiring of all the soldiers I met of his and other commands, I returned to headquarters." Rather than report his failure to find Hill, however, Fisher followed the example of his generals and went to bed.[35]

Trooper J. A. Perkins of the Orleans Light Horse sat beside Alexander's Bridge, stirring a fire as a thick fog settled over the creek. Perkins was under orders to keep the fire burning to alert passersby that Polk's headquarters was near and to escort Hill personally to the bishop's headquarters wagon. His instructions were vague; he was directed simply to remain by the bridge "for an hour or so." By 2:00 A.M. he had grown tired of his vigil. Throwing a few branches on the fire, Perkins left for the night, and a group of chilled infantrymen eagerly took his place by the blaze.[36]

Hill awoke an hour later. With one or two aides, he started for Polk's headquarters. At Alexander's Bridge, Hill found no courier to lead him to Polk's headquarters, as no one had relieved Perkins, nor did he take the trouble to search for it himself. The sensitive North Carolinian must have been beside himself — not only had he been cast aside in Bragg's reorganization, but his wing commander apparently had not even bothered to extend him the courtesy of a guide to his bivouac. Hill ordered an aide to find the bishop and tell him he would be on his line of battle if needed, then rode back across the creek.[37]

As the early morning hours slipped away, Breckinridge slept soundly beside Polk's campfire, blissfully unaware that he was expected to initiate the attack at daylight. Cleburne of course had heard nothing and so did nothing, neglecting even to ensure that his men had three days' cooked rations on hand, despite standing orders from corps headquarters to that effect. Longstreet passed the night at Thedford's Ford, and Hood and Buckner bivouacked together, unaware that their wing commander was even on the field. Thus did the high command pass one of the most critical nights in the history of the Army of Tennessee.[38]

CHAPTER SEVENTEEN

IF THEY BEGIN IT, WE WILL END IT

SUNDAY morning came. The sun rose early in the Georgia autumn, at 5:47 A.M. Frost blanketed the ground, heavy enough to kill crops not yet ripened for harvest. Smoke lingered in the forests. Brushfires smoldered. A dense fog descended upon Chickamauga Creek. It rolled across the low-lands, drawing a white veil of melancholy over the cold and weary soldiers. Nevertheless, mused an anxious Tennessean, "the world never seemed half so attractive before, now that there was a good chance for leaving it soon."[1]

Bishop Polk awoke at dawn, about the time Bragg expected him to open the battle against the Federal left. The bishop listened for the boom of cannon that would herald the onset of Hill's attack, but heard nothing. Only then did he seem truly concerned about the Right Wing. A call went out for John Fisher, whom everyone assumed had delivered the attack order to Hill during the night. Private Y. R. LeMonnier of the Orleans Light Horse found Fisher warming his hands over a fire near Alexander's Bridge. "Fisher, the General wants you," cried LeMonnier. "You are going to catch hell."[2]

Captain Wheless was burying the embers of the fire beside which he and Polk had slept, when the general, visibly agitated, interrupted him. "I have just learned that the messenger sent last night to General Hill with orders for renewing the fight at daylight this morning has returned without being able to find him. He was to have been here last night and I had a courier placed at the bridge to show him the way but he can't be found and there is not a moment to be lost," said Polk. "See that your horse is ready immediately. Major Jack is now preparing orders for Cleburne and Breckinridge to attack at once. I wish you to take the orders, find those officers as quickly as possible, and explain to them why the orders were not sent through their corps commander. As you pass by Cheatham, inform him that you are going to order an immediate advance of the divisions of Cleburne and Breckinridge and instruct him to have his line ready to conform to the movement." So Wheless recalled the bishop's words.[3]

The orders Lieutenant Colonel Jack handed the captain were marvelously simple, a reflection of Polk's ignorance of the situation on his front. They read:

> Headquarters, Right Wing
> Near Alexander's Bridge, September 20, 1863 — 5:30 A.M.
> Major General Cleburne,
> Major General Breckinridge:
>
> Generals: The Lieutenant General commanding, having sought in vain for Lieutenant General Hill, gives you directly the following orders:
> Move upon and attack the enemy as soon as you are in position.
> Major General Cheatham, on our left, has been ordered to make a simultaneous attack.
> Respectfully, generals, your obedient servant,
> [Thomas] M. Jack
> Assistant Adjutant General[4]

Wheless took the orders and mounted his horse. "Go, Wheless, in a hurry and don't spare your horse," Polk called as the captain rode off. Wheless galloped across the rickety planks of Alexander's Bridge into a fog "so dense it was quite impossible to distinguish objects ten paces distant." There he halted, fearful of stumbling into enemy lines. At that moment the rising sun burned a hole in the fabric of the fog, and Wheless rode toward the woods, now visible, that he knew sheltered Cheatham's command.

He found the Tennessean three or four minutes later, completely mystified by the delay in the attack. Cheatham, at least, had his men in line and ready to advance. Wheless gave him a copy of the modified orders and continued on.[5]

Polk, meanwhile, was taking no chances this time. Minutes after Wheless left, he told Lieutenant Colonel Jack to draft duplicate orders and give them to a second staff officer, Captain J. Minnick Williams, to take carry to Cheatham, Breckinridge, and Cleburne. The bishop then sat down to a hasty breakfast. As he was eating, Major Pollock Lee of Bragg's staff rode up, sent by the commanding general to find out why the attack had not begun. He did not know the reason, Polk told Lee between bites, since he had not had a chance to ride to the front.

The bishop's demeanor, breakfasting when he should have been attacking the Yankees, made quite an impression on Lee. Like most of Bragg's staff, Lee was a sycophant intent on giving the commanding general whatever he wanted. Knowing Bragg's need for scapegoats, Lee decided to distort the truth to help create one. He reported to Bragg that he had found Polk three miles behind the lines, sitting placidly on the front porch of a farmhouse reading a newspaper while awaiting his breakfast. Understandably, Bragg was enraged. Calling his staff to attention, he mounted up and galloped off to find Polk himself.[6]

Captain Wheless came upon Hill, Breckinridge, and Cleburne seated around a campfire two hundred yards behind Cleburne's line of battle a few minutes after 6:00 A.M. (Hill claimed that Wheless arrived at 7:25 A.M., but the evidence is against him.) The last of Breckinridge's troops were just then filing into position. Wheless dismounted and announced that he bore orders from General Polk. Hill reached for them, but Wheless pulled back the envelope. "These orders are for Generals Breckinridge and Cleburne," he said, handing the orders to Breckinridge. Turning to Hill, Wheless declared smugly: "In explanation, General, why these orders were not sent through you it is proper to say that General Polk has had a staff officer hunting for you since twelve last night."[7]

Cleburne handed the orders to Hill. Since his men were distributing rations, he suggested that it might be better to wait the hour it would take to complete the task before advancing. Hill agreed, not particularly impressed with the urgency of Polk's order, which, after all, said nothing about an attack at daylight but rather as soon as the troops were in position. And to Hill's way of thinking, his command was unready. He had found that Cheatham's right lay perpendicular to Cleburne's left, making a coordinated advance impossible. Presumably because Cheatham's division was not part of his command, Hill took no action to correct the alignment but simply passed the problem on to the bishop.

Hill sat down to pen his rebuttal to Polk. "He wrote the note upon a slip of paper not exceeding five inches square and consumed not less than ten to fifteen minutes in doing so, having stopped several times to engage in the conversation going on which in the main was of a most commonplace nature," fumed Wheless. "I became exceedingly impatient at the delay and was about to call his attention to it when he rose and handed me the note."[8] It read:

General: I could find no courier at Alexander's Bridge, and therefore I could not find you. My divisions are getting their rations and will not be ready to move for an hour or more. Breckinridge's wagons seem to have got lost between Thedford's Ford and this place. It will be well for you to examine the line from one end to the other before starting. Brigadier General Jackson is running from east to west. My line is from north to south. General Cleburne reports that the Yankees were felling trees all night, and consequently now occupy a position too strong to be taken by assault. What shall be done when this point is reached?

Respectfully,

D. H. Hill,
Lieutenant General.[9]

On his way back to Alexander's Bridge, Wheless met Captain Williams bearing the duplicate orders. Wheless related his conversation with Hill and suggested that Williams ride to Cheatham to let the Tennessean know there would be further delays. A few minutes later, at about 6:45 A.M., Wheless ran into Polk on his way to the front. At the bishop's request, Wheless read him Hill's note. "Allow me to suggest that unless you go and in person give General Hill positive orders to make the attack he will not begin it in three hours," the captain added earnestly. According to Wheless, Polk seemed surprised and asked him the reason for his doubts. "General Hill seems to me perfectly indifferent and certainly does not appreciate the urgent necessity of attacking immediately," answered Wheless. "Well sir, well sir. I must go and see to this myself," said Polk. He hastened down the Alexander's Bridge road, leaving Wheless behind to set up headquarters.[10]

The dust from Polk's hasty departure scarcely had settled when Bragg rode up. His "manner betrayed considerable impatience," observed Wheless with delightful understatement. The captain swallowed hard and tried to explain the delay—carefully tailoring his story to protect his commander. "General, in case you should not find General Polk I will tell you what has been done this morning: General Polk sent orders to General Hill in time for the attack to have been made by daylight if General Hill could have been found; but this was impossible, and when General Polk learned this he sent orders by me to Generals Breckinridge and Cleburne to make an immediate attack," began Wheless. Hill would not be ready to attack for at least two hours, he added, although he should have done so at daylight.

"How can you expect an officer to act before he gets orders?" asked Bragg.

The captain reminded Bragg of their meeting the night before, when he had told Wheless of his intention to hold a council of war with the corps commanders; Wheless presumed Hill would have attended and learned what was expected of him, making the orders from Polk a mere formality. An excellent argument in Polk's defense, it must have struck Bragg a bit too close to home, because Wheless quickly changed the subject. "General, General Cleburne reported to General Hill this morning while I was there that the enemy were felling trees on his front all night."

"Well, sir, is this not another important reason why the attack should be made at once," asked Bragg, rhetorically.

"Yes sir; it does certainly seem so to me; but it did not seem to impress General Hill in that way." Bragg galloped on after Polk.[11]

Polk found Hill at 7:15 A.M. The two conferred briefly. Hill said that Polk not only "made no objection" to the delay but also said nothing of the daylight attack.[12] Private LeMonnier of the Orleans Light Horse gives a different account of their exchange.

"General, why have you not attacked?" Polk demanded when they met.

"General, my men are drawing rations," answered Hill.

"Sir, this is not the time for eating; this is the time for fighting. Attack immediately; attack immediately." Without waiting for an answer, claimed LeMonnier, Polk whirled his horse and galloped off. Where Polk went next is a mystery. LeMonnier claims he rode along his line of battle ordering each division commander to attack at once, but none of those commanders mentions receiving any such orders in their reports of the battle.[13]

Bragg reached Hill's campfire at about 8:00 A.M. In his hand he waved a dispatch from Polk, written at 7:00 A.M., that said Hill had not attacked because his troops were drawing rations and his wagons had been lost; Polk had made no mention of the dangerous angle between Cleburne and Cheatham or of the evidence that the Federals were entrenched. Bragg demanded to know why Hill had not attacked at dawn. Hill replied that this was the first he had heard of an order for a daylight attack. Bragg launched into a tirade against the absent Polk, relating Major Lee's account of the bishop's leisurely breakfast, then gave Hill peremptory orders to attack as soon as possible.[14]

The delays continued. Polk evidently took no action to correct the flaw in the line between Cheatham and Cleburne, so after conferring with Bragg, Hill took the matter upon himself and rode to Cleburne's left to verify the problem. By then, however, the matter was largely academic. Cheatham had discovered in the interim that his front was partly covered by the division of Stewart. Apparently unable to locate Polk, he informed Bragg of the problem. Bragg directed him not to participate in the attack but rather to hold his command in reserve. When he learned that Cheatham would not be attacking, Polk shifted Walker's reserve corps northward to support Cleburne. At the same time, Hill took the initiative of calling on Forrest to send up cavalry to protect Breckinridge's right, thereby correcting another of the bishop's oversights. Forrest responded with his characteristic energy, and soon the division of Brigadier General Frank Armstrong was in line on the Kentuckian's flank.[15]

So concluded one of the sorriest nights and mornings in the annals of the high command of the Army of Tennessee. It is hard to affix blame with any degree of precision, thanks largely to the acrimony that engendered so many self-serving and distorted accounts of what transpired. A few general conclusions can be drawn that seem beyond dispute. Bragg erred both in giving Polk only oral attack orders on the night of the nineteenth and then in failing to see that they were implemented. Once again, Bragg's tendency to disengage himself from the details of battle was endangering his army. Polk's behavior throughout the entire affair can most charitably be described as cavalier. His failure to ensure that Hill got his orders during the night and then to reconnoiter his front in the morning represents a censurable dereliction of duty. That he did not bother to mention the daylight attack to Breckinridge during their long hours together beside his campfire is even more damning. We are left to conclude that Polk, having no faith in Bragg's plan of battle, was doing his best to subvert it through malignant neglect. And then there was Hill, who, wrote General Manigault, "had always borne the unenviable reputation, in a military phase, of having his own way and doing things only as pleased him, and were it otherwise, throwing obstacles in the way." The moment he learned that he had been cast aside in Bragg's ill-conceived, eleventh-hour reorganization of the army, Hill began to sulk. Until confronted by Bragg, he moved about with the energy of a sloth.

Union General John Palmer best summed up the consequences of Confederate delay. "Bragg claims that he ordered General Polk to attack us at daybreak," the Illinoisan wrote. "If he had done so, with the force and energy with which the Rebel attack was [eventually] made, the battle would not have lasted an hour; we would have gone to Chattanooga on the run."[16]

General Rosecrans was up early, if he had slept at all. He heard Mass, then stepped out of the Glenn cabin into the gathering light of dawn "without having a mouthful to eat or drink," said Colonel John Sanderson.[17] William D. Bickham, correspondent of the Cincinnati *Commercial* and a close friend and unabashed admirer of the general, caught a glimpse of Rosecrans as he emerged from headquarters. What Bickham saw troubled him deeply.

> He was enveloped in a blue army overcoat, his pantaloons stuffed in his boots, and a light brown felt hat, of uncertain shape, was drawn over his head. A cigar, unlit, was held between his teeth, and his mouth was tightly compressed as if he were sharply biting it. He stalked to a heap of embers where I was standing, and stood a moment silently by my side. An orderly brought a rawboned, muscular, dappled grey horse to him, and mounting without a word, he rode down the lane towards the road, his staff clattering after him, and understanding his mood, perhaps as silent as himself.
>
> I knew, for I had seen Rosecrans often under widely differing circumstances, that he was filled with apprehension for the issue of that day's fight. I recognized a change instantly, although I could hardly say in what it consisted. Rosecrans is usually brisk, nervous, powerful of presence, and to see him silent or absorbed in what looked like gloomy contemplation, filled me with indefinable dread. Remember, this was just for an instant, and when the leader thought he was entirely unobserved.[18]

Rosecrans and his party cantered north along the Dry Valley road in search of high ground nearer the left on which to establish army headquarters for the day. After riding three-quarters of a mile, they turned off the road and into a meadow about three hundred yards southwest of the Dyer farm. There, on a gentle rise, Rosecrans called a halt. It was a good site from which to observe the activity of the Union center and was within a mile of Thomas's salient in the Kelly field. Looking northeast from the knoll, Rosecrans and his staff had an unimpeded view across the Dyer field to the woods in which were posted the divisions of Negley, Reynolds, and Brannan, who had been ordered into the front line sometime before dawn. To the east, they could see past the Tan Yard as far as the timber west of the Brotherton field, and to the southeast visibility was relatively good as far as the Glenn-Kelly road, near where Davis's decimated division rested. "The sky was red and sultry and the atmosphere and woods enveloped in fog and smoke," recalled Rosecrans. Nevertheless, with the aid of field glasses he and his staff could discern clouds of dust rising above the trees that suggested a gathering of Confederate forces to strike at the Federal left.[19]

A message from Thomas confirmed their fears. The Virginian also had risen early to take a predawn ride along his lines. In the twilight he could see that Baird's left indeed fell nearly four hundred yards short of the La Fayette road. Baird had done what he could to compensate, refusing the left flank of King's Regular brigade until it faced due north. Just two hundred yards northwest of King's left began the expansive fields of John McDonald. Picked up by Wilder before the battle and turned over to Rosecrans, McDonald was now with the commanding general on the rise near the Dyer farm, a most reluctant guide. The McDonald fields, beyond the reach of Baird's Federals, were an ideal location for advancing Confederates to regroup before pressing home an attack south down the La Fayette road. Baird understood this but had no troops with which to cover the fields; now his skirmishers were sending back troubling reports that the enemy was moving toward their left. Most upsetting to Thomas was the absence of Negley, whom he had expected hours ago. The Virginian summed up his concerns to Rosecrans: "Since my return this morning I have found it necessary to concentrate my lines more. My left does not now extend to the road that branches off at McDonald's house to Reed's Bridge. I earnestly request that Negley's division be placed on my left immediately. . . . General Baird has just reported to me that the enemy are moving toward our left."[20]

Negley had not reported because no one had told him to. Rosecrans apparently had forgotten his promise to Thomas to order Negley to the left. The Virginian's latest request reached him as he and his staff were on their way to the left to begin an inspection of the lines. Rosecrans arrived at Thomas's headquarters at about 6:30 A.M. A hasty look at Baird's position convinced him that Negley was indeed needed there—and soon. While Rosecrans and Thomas conferred, Garfield scribbled orders to Negley to bring his division to the left "at once." At the same time, he informed McCook of Negley's detachment and directed him to fill the vacancy this would create "if practicable." At 7:00 A.M., for good measure, Thomas dispatched Captain J. P. Willard of his staff to personally guide Negley into position.[21]

Rosecrans's fatigue was clouding his judgment. It was not practicable for McCook to fill the gap with his depleted force, and Rosecrans should have understood this. Already McCook's line was stretched dangerously thin; to cover Negley's position would at the very least oblige McCook to leave the Widow Glenn house undefended. Clearly, Rosecrans should have refused Thomas's specific request for Negley's division when any division would have sufficed. Thomas was thinking only of himself: he wanted Negley because he was accustomed to working with him and because he wanted to reunite his corps. Rosecrans could just as well have dispatched either Wood or Van Cleve from their positions in reserve without creating even a momentary gap in his front line. With the jumbled state of units then existing on the battlefield, the detaching of one more division from its proper corps was of little import.

The commanding general was on the verge of collapse. Nervous exhaustion was written all over his face. Corporal Hannaford of the Sixth Ohio watched Rosecrans as he rode by his regiment on the way to see Thomas. "Fight today as well as you did yesterday, and we shall whip them," he told the Ohioans. His admonitions rang hollow. The commanding general appeared worn and very weary. "I did not like the way he looked," remembered Hannaford. Two Illinois soldiers likewise saw through Rosecrans's bravado. "By and by Rosecrans came around. He was in bad plight, but his voice was ringing and cheery. 'Boys,' he said, 'I never fight Sundays, but if they begin it, we will end it.' "[22]

Withal, Thomas was in good spirits—even excited, recalled a surprised William Shanks. When asked about the events of the day before, Thomas exclaimed to Rosecrans: "Whenever I touched their flanks they broke, general, they broke." "I was listening with great eagerness and looking squarely at the general, when he caught my eye, and, as if ashamed of his momentary enthusiasm, the blood mounted in his cheeks and he blushed like a woman," Shanks wrote. "His eyes were bent immediately on the ground, and the rest of his remarks were confined to a few brief replies to the questions addressed to him."[23]

Rosecrans and Thomas rode across the Kelly field to inspect Palmer's line. Rosecrans suggested that the Illinoisan's division be closed up to make it more compact. Thomas issued the necessary orders, and the two parted company.[24]

Rosecrans continued to fidget and fine-tune. He paused to tell Crittenden to shift the divisions of Van Cleve and Wood a bit closer to the left, then rode on to check on Negley's progress.[25]

He found the Pennsylvanian and his division concentrated in route column along the Glenn-Kelly road, ready to march to Thomas. Captain Willard had arrived a few minutes before Rosecrans to hurry Negley along. It was the first he had heard that he was wanted on the left, but Negley moved swiftly to comply, showing more alacrity than prudence. In the woods west of the Brotherton field, his skirmishers had caught sight of the massed columns of Longstreet's Left Wing. The pop-pop of rifle fire told of sporadic contact, but Negley nevertheless had ordered Colonels Timothy Stanley and William Sirwell to pull their brigades out of the line and assemble on the road.

Had McCook relieved his troops in the front line, Rosecrans asked? No, there was no sign of him, Negley replied. Rosecrans exploded. He upbraided Negley harshly for leaving a gap — especially with his skirmishers engaged — and told him to send Sirwell and Stanley back into line at once. Turning to Captain Willard, Rosecrans told him he could take John Beatty's brigade, which lay in reserve, to Thomas to shore up the left for the time being. Before riding on to the right to hear McCook's excuse, Rosecrans sent Crittenden urgent instructions to bring forward Wood's division, reinforced by a brigade from Van Cleve, to replace Negley, so that the Pennsylvanian might get to the left with the rest of his division before the blow fell in that sector. With his remaining two brigades, Van Cleve was to support Wood.[26]

The last thing Negley needed just then was a reprimand from Rosecrans. The near obliteration of his division at McLemore's Cove the week before had taken a terrible toll on him. By the time his troops were safely out of the cove, Negley was near collapse. Constant abdominal cramping and severe diarrhea plagued him day and night. When his division left Bailey's Cross Roads on the seventeenth, Negley was so ill that his medical director and staff officers begged him to relinquish command or at least to ride in an ambulance. Sustained by the excitement of the moment and the magnitude of his responsibilities, Negley refused. He stayed in the saddle, sharing the rigors of the march with his men. The night of the nineteenth found him so reduced by diarrhea and dehydration that it was all he could do to attend Rosecrans's conference before slipping off into a fevered sleep.[27]

Rosecrans left Negley to find McCook a little after 8:00 A.M. Now it was the genial Ohioan's turn to feel his commander's wrath. Why had he not relieved Negley and why had he permitted his line to become so elongated that "it was a mere thread"? He must close up his line to the left at once. McCook tried to remind Rosecrans of his earlier orders that Sheridan hold the Dry Valley road, but the commanding general cut him off, rebuking him bitterly for all to hear. "It is indispensable to close to the left; we cannot afford to have another Stones River," were his parting words.[28]

Rosecrans was coming apart. McCook was slow to respond to his orders to relieve Negley, there can be no doubt, but he had formed his line as directed the night before. Any blame for its tenuousness must fall squarely on Rosecrans's shoulders.

Now it was back to Negley. He was still in line of battle, awaiting a relief force that had halted tantalizingly near. Wood, it seems, was up to his old tricks. Crittenden apparently had misconstrued Rosecrans's orders for Wood to relieve Negley, because Wood had advanced his division only as far as the ridge west of the Dyer field. No one could convince the captious Kentuckian to go farther.

Negley sent Captain Alfred Hough of his staff across the Dyer field to urge Wood forward. When he refused to budge, Hough tried to circumvent Wood and convince brigade commander George Buell to come along. "I asked him if he was not going to relieve Negley, who was one quarter or one third of a mile to the front. He answered that he had orders to take the top of the hill, and took it." Captain Willard tried his hand, but with no more success. "I am ordered to post my troops on this ridge," Wood told the captain. "Sir," Willard remonstrated, "General Rosecrans promised to send one of the divisions of General Crittenden's corps to relieve General Negley that he might go to the relief of General Thomas's left." "I am ordered to post my troops on this ridge," Wood repeated.[29]

Captain Willard saved Negley from another scolding by the commanding general. He intercepted Rosecrans as the general was returning to Negley's position and explained Wood's recalcitrance. Rosecrans galloped across the Dyer field. He demanded to know why Wood had halted along the ridge. Because Crittenden had directed him to form there, Wood explained. Rosecrans dismissed his excuse and let fly a volley of profanity at Wood. "By no means, you are to replace Negley's division on the line, and I want you to do it as soon as the Lord will let you," barked Rosecrans, then rode away. Wood seethed. "Blind obedience to orders . . ."[30]

Down from the ridge and into the Dyer field came Wood a few minutes before 9:30 A.M., just as the first sounds of scattered firing rolled down from the north. Negley and his staff heard the shots too. To them, the meaning was clear — the Confederate attack against the extreme left, which they had been charged to protect, had begun. Staff officers crisscrossed the field to shepherd Wood's Federals along, but they "advanced very leisurely across the open field, having skirmishers deployed," recalled an exasperated Lieutenant William Moody of Negley's staff.

Sick and impatient, Negley started up the Glenn-Kelly road with the division artillery and Stanley's brigade as soon as it was relieved by the brigades of Barnes and Harker, leaving Sirwell to come along with his brigade as soon as he had drawn in his skirmishers and turned over his breastworks to Buell. By now the firing from the far left had become a thunderous crescendo. Ominously, Wood's skirmishers were engaged the instant they stepped over the breastworks into the Brotherton field.[31]

Rosecrans continued to shift forces in a frantic effort to consolidate his lines before the Confederate attack became general. Van Cleve crossed the Dry Valley road and occupied the ridge a few minutes after Wood left it. He was scarcely in position before Rosecrans appeared and bade him continue across the field to the edge of the timber at the double-quick. There he was to form the brigades of Dick and Beatty, "ready for any emergency."[32]

Satisfied with the deployment of his center, Rosecrans returned to the knoll. At that moment, General Davis crossed the Dry Valley road with his division just 150 yards from where Rosecrans and his staff had gathered. In compliance with orders from McCook, Davis was advancing from the position he had held in reserve behind Sheridan during the early morning. Not certain where he was needed, Davis rode to Rosecrans, who ordered him forward to extend Wood's right flank in the direction of the Viniard farm. McCook ran into Davis as his division passed by the Tan Yard. Learning of Rosecrans's plans, McCook ordered Sheridan to move Laiboldt's brigade forward to protect Davis's right and rear. Lytle remained on the Widow Glenn hill, and Walworth's brigade formed on his right, just west of the Dry Valley road. Wilder's brigade completed the line on Sheridan's right. By 10:00 A.M., nearly half the units in the Federal army were in motion. Rosecrans had violated a fundamental dictum of war — the one advising a commander not to shuffle forces unnecessarily in the presence of the enemy, particularly one about to attack.[33]

In the forest east of the Brotherton farm, General Longstreet went about preparing his command for action, looking considerably more at ease than Rosecrans. Gazing upon the general as he puffed calmly on a meerschaum pipe, the picture of composure, his veterans from the Army of Northern Virginia gave Longstreet a new nickname. They called him the "Bull of the Woods."[34]

Longstreet's placidity is admirable. He had reached the front at daybreak to conditions that can only be described as chaotic. In his first line were the divisions of Stewart, Johnson, Hindman, and Preston. Hood's division lay behind Johnson. Four major problems and a hundred smaller irritants greeted Longstreet. First, his senior corps commander, Simon Buckner, was little more than a supernumerary because his two divisions lay on opposite flanks of the Left Wing; with the attack set to begin at any moment, there was no time to reunite the corps. Second, although he had at his disposal nineteen batteries, Longstreet could find no one to serve as chief of artillery. Third, the brigades of Kershaw and Humphreys had not yet reported. After a grueling night march from Ringgold, they had bivouacked at Alexander's Bridge at 1:00 A.M. for a few hours' badly needed rest and were just now forming up. Most of the officers in these brigades — Kershaw and Humphreys included — were without horses, making command and control difficult. Finally, a gap of indeterminate width separated the right of the army from his wing.[35]

As his first order of business, Longstreet undertook to locate the Right Wing. He ordered Stewart to march north by the right flank until he made contact with Polk's left. The Tennessean moved his division five hundred yards, across the Brotherton road and onto a slight rise east of the Poe field, where his column came under fire from Federal skirmishers in the field. There Stewart halted, faced his command to the front, and directed his troops to throw up hasty breastworks. To his embarrassment, Stewart discovered that, far from joining with Polk's flank, his division now rested a quarter of a mile in front of Cleburne's division, completely masking the brigades of Deshler and Wood. Couriers were dispatched to Cleburne, and Bate bent back his right flank to make room for the Irishman's troops.[36]

While Stewart and Cleburne sorted out their difficulties, Longstreet organized his remaining units with refreshing vigor. From his frontline commanders he learned that the bulk of the Federal forces opposite his wing were concentrated in the Brotherton woods. Longstreet determined to mass his command opposite this point. To explain the topography, Longstreet had at his side young Tom Brotherton, who had left his father's farm to enlist in the Confederate Army. In the forest some three hundred yards east of the Brotherton cabin, Longstreet concentrated an attacking column of unprecedented depth. Bushrod Johnson would lead the way with two brigades up and one in reserve. Behind him, Hood also deployed his own division, still commanded by Evander Law, with two brigades forward and one back. Orders went out to Kershaw to place his own brigade and that of Humphreys behind Hood at soon as they reported. In all, Longstreet would have a massed column five brigades deep occupying a front of just over a quarter mile, aimed at precisely the spot that Negley was trying so desperately to vacate. Hindman's division, with two brigades up and one in reserve, and Preston's division, which was to be the pivot for the wheeling movement to the left once the wing advanced, completed the line of battle.[37]

One of Longstreet's first acts on reaching the front had been to pay a visit to his old friend Hood. It proved the ideal tonic for both. Recalled Hood:

> He inquired concerning the formation of my lines, the spirit of our troops, and the effect produced upon the enemy by our assault. I informed him that the feeling of officers and men was never better, that we had driven the enemy fully one mile the day before, and that we would rout him before sunset. This distinguished general instantly responded with that confidence which had so often contributed to his extraordinary success, that we would *of course* whip and drive him from the field. I could but exclaim that I was rejoiced to hear him so express himself, as he was the first general I had met since my arrival who talked of victory.[38]

Out on the Federal left, General Thomas passed the hours after sunrise waiting for Negley. That he did nothing more is odd. As Colonel Aquila Wiley of the Forty-first Ohio later pointed out in a well-reasoned article in the *National Tribune,* Thomas actually had the means at hand to extend his threatened left flank across the La Fayette road. Units were so tightly packed in the Kelly field salient that Johnson was compelled to leave the brigades of Willich and Dodge in reserve and Palmer to do the same with the brigade of Grose; even Joseph Reynolds, on the right of the line, admitted that he retained nearly half his infantry in reserve.

When, in the early hours of the morning, Thomas first discovered that his left was in the air, he should promptly have called upon at least two of these brigades to strengthen it, argued Wiley. If he was unaware that these brigades were being held in reserve, continued Wiley, then Thomas must be censured for not having informed himself of the formations his division commanders had adopted. A persuasive argument. Given that the Federals enjoyed the advantage of interior lines, Thomas would have risked little by shifting these two brigades six hundred yards across the Kelly field. Perhaps even the Virginian was feeling the effects of fatigue.[39]

John Beatty reported his brigade to Thomas at 8:00 A.M. Pointing to the woods bordering the Kelly field on the north, Thomas waved the Ohioan on toward Baird's left. Beatty became a bit confused in the timber, mistaking the direction of the line occupied by King's Regulars. Nevertheless, he took up a strong position on their left, fronting north. Beatty placed the six guns of Captain Lyman Bridges's Illinois Light Artillery squarely astride the La Fayette road and shook his skirmishers out into the southernmost field of the McDonald farm. Beatty was contemplating his line with satisfaction when, after fifteen minutes, Captain W. B. Gaw of the corps staff handed him an order from Thomas to advance his entire line four hundred yards to a "ridge or low hill" near the McDonald house. Evidently Thomas was still loath to surrender the Reed's Bridge road without a fight. Beatty was incredulous. "I represented to him that my line was long;

that in advancing it I would necessarily leave a long interval between my right and General Baird's left, and also that I was already in the position indicated to me by General Thomas." The order to advance was imperative, replied Gaw; besides, Negley would soon come up and support Beatty with the rest of the division. "I could not urge objections further, and advanced my line as rapidly as possible toward the point indicated," sighed Beatty.[40]

Baird watched dumbfounded as Beatty's line marched off toward the McDonald house. "This arrangement gave General Beatty a long, thin line, easily brushed away, and at the same time left an important gap between him and King," Baird reported. The Pennsylvanian flagged down the Seventy-ninth Illinois, which was wandering across the Kelly field toward the left with no particular instructions, and induced its commander to fall in on the left of King. Colonel Dodge followed with the Twenty-ninth and Thirtieth Indiana a few minutes later—presumably under orders from Thomas to help close the gap—but the pitiful remnant of his brigade, perhaps five hundred men in all, made no appreciable difference. And time had run out. From deep in the forest to his front, Baird heard the irregular pop-pop of rifle fire that heralded the approach of Confederate skirmishers.[41]

CHAPTER EIGHTEEN

THE LEFT MUST BE HELD

IT WAS 9:00 A.M., three hours after dawn. The rising sun had burned away the fog, and now forests and fields basked under its warming rays.[1] The men of the Orphan Brigade lay in line of battle, "cracking jokes as usual . . . in the finest spirits," observed John Jackman of the Ninth Kentucky. General Breckinridge rode back and forth along the brigade line, unable to mask his deep concern for his beloved Kentuckians. General Forrest was at his side. Brigadier General Ben Hardin Helm walked among the men, quietly offering words of encouragement. His words were deeply appreciated. No brigade in the Army of Tennessee loved its commander more. Lieutenant Lot D. Young spoke for the entire command when he called Helm "one of the kindest-hearted and best men" he ever knew.[2]

Helm was perhaps the only Confederate general whose fate was of personal concern to Abraham Lincoln. He and the thirty-two-year-old Kentuckian were brothers-in-law. While a member of the State Assembly representing Hardin County, Helm met and married Emilie Paret Todd, sister of Mary Todd Lincoln. Helm was a young gentleman of many talents whose father twice served as governor of Kentucky. He had entered West Point in 1847 at age sixteen and graduated ninth in a class of forty-two. Helm was assigned to duty with the Second Cavalry at Fort Lincoln, Texas. Before he could report, however, he contracted inflammatory rheumatism and was granted a six-month leave of absence. The illness proved a blessing. While recuperating, Helm decided a career of slow promotions and dreary frontier duty in a peacetime army was not for him. He resigned his commission and attended law school at the University of Louisville and at Harvard. Starting out in his father's lucrative practice in Elizabethtown, the younger Helm soon established himself as a fine attorney in his own right.

Lincoln last saw his brother-in-law in April 1861. He had personally invited the Kentuckian to Washington. Although Helm was an ardent

Southern-rights Democrat, the president hoped to induce him to cast his lot with the Union. Handing Helm a sealed envelope, Lincoln said, "Ben, here is something for you. Think it over by yourself and let me know what you will do." The envelope contained a paymaster's commission in the Union Army with the rank of major. Helm returned it and went south. The two remained on cordial terms, and at least twice during the war Helm sent friendly messages through the lines to the president.[3]

At about 9:15 A.M., Major James Wilson of the division staff rode up to Helm, who was sitting under a tree behind the Ninth Kentucky chatting with its colonel, and gave him oral orders from Breckinridge to advance in fifteen minutes, guiding on the brigade of Marcellus Stovall to his right. "The general got up and mounted his horse, laughing and talking as though he were going on parade," recalled John Jackman, who stood nearby.[4]

Helm took his place at the center of the brigade. It was arrayed in a single line, with the Second Kentucky on the left, followed by the Ninth Kentucky, Forty-first Alabama, Fourth Kentucky, and Sixth Kentucky. Captain Robert Cobb prepared to advance his Kentucky battery on the brigade left. Skirmishers had been deployed two hundred yards in advance nearly an hour earlier and had kept up a steady racket ever since. On Helm's right, also deployed in single line, were the brigades of Stovall and Dan Adams. At 9:30 A.M., the signal was given to advance.[5]

For seven hundred yards the Kentuckians tramped through tangled forest without seeing a single Yankee. Up a long wooded ridge they marched. Helm brought them to an abrupt halt along the crest. Two hundred yards away, just across the Alexander's Bridge road in a clearing of mossy grass, was a long line of Federals crouching behind breastworks of logs and stone.

Helm had come upon Thomas's salient at the point where his line veered sharply from its northerly course and began to run west toward the La Fayette road. The Forty-first Alabama, occupying the brigade center, stood precisely opposite the apex of the angle. Behind the breastworks were the brigades of Scribner and King.

With mixed admiration and horror, Scribner watched the Confederates prepare for their assault. Skirmishers had fallen back to the Rebel main line. Battle flags were planted along the crest. Company officers turned their backs on the enemy and coolly dressed their lines. Captain Cobb unlimbered his guns. General Helm sat astride his horse, silhouetted on the ridge in plain view, but not a shot was fired. An eerie hush fell over the field. Scribner told his frontline regimental commanders to reserve their fire while the Rebels formed, then hurried off to bring up his reserve regiments.[6]

With a yell the Rebels came pouring off the ridge toward the road. The guns of the Fourth Indiana Light Artillery roared from behind the breastworks, knocking Cobb's Kentucky Battery off the ridge before it could fire a shot in response. Scribner gave the command and his infantrymen opened fire. Confederates fell by the score amidst what an aide to General Helm called a "perfect tornado of bullets."[7]

The brigade split as it neared the breastworks. On the right, the Sixth Kentucky, Fourth Kentucky, and six companies of the Forty-first Alabama missed the breastworks and drove west toward the La Fayette road, their officers unaware that they had left the rest of the brigade behind. King's Regulars opened a largely ineffective fire through the timber against the Rebel left flank as it glided past.

General Helm pressed on against the breastworks with the Second Kentucky, Ninth Kentucky, and remaining companies of the Forty-first Alabama. They never had a chance. Cleburne had not attacked on Helm's left, leaving the Federals free to concentrate all their fire against the Kentuckian's six hundred Confederates. All four regiments of Scribner's brigade engaged Helms from in front, the right battalions of the Regular Brigade contributed an enfilading fire against his right flank, and the left regiments and Fourth Indiana Light Artillery of Starkweather's brigade pounded his left. No one could live long in the mossy clearing between the breastworks and the road. Desperate to escape the turbulence, wounded soldiers from the Ninth Kentucky crawled over the Federal breastworks and surrendered.[8]

Remarkably, Helm kept up the fight for at least thirty minutes, perhaps even an hour. Twice his men fell back across the road to the ridge, only to regroup and return to the charge with Helm at their head. At one point, the Second Kentucky closed to within forty yards of Scribner's line, its advance screened by a brushfire that threatened to engulf the breastworks in front of the Thirty-eighth Indiana. But the Hoosiers' tossed the last, precious drops of water from their canteens onto the flames, extinguishing the blaze in time to drive off the impetuous Kentuckians.

While their men caught their breath behind the ridge, the commanders of the Second and Ninth Kentucky conferred. With Helm nowhere in sight, the two discussed the wisdom of a third push at the Federal salient. The decision was taken out of their hands. Galloping up behind them, Colonel Leon von Zincken of Breckinridge's staff yelled that the right regiments of the brigade were desperately engaged and that the two must therefore attack to relieve the pressure on their comrades.

The Kentuckians and Alabamians charged across the road a third time. The results were the same. This charge, however, cost the life of their brigade commander. A bullet tore into Helm's right side as he galloped pell-mell toward the Federal breastworks, and he spun off his horse. Lieutenants Herr and Pirtle of his staff ran forward through the rain of bullets, lifted him off the ground and carried him back over the ridge. A cursory glance at the wound was enough to convince the surgeons that Helm would die.

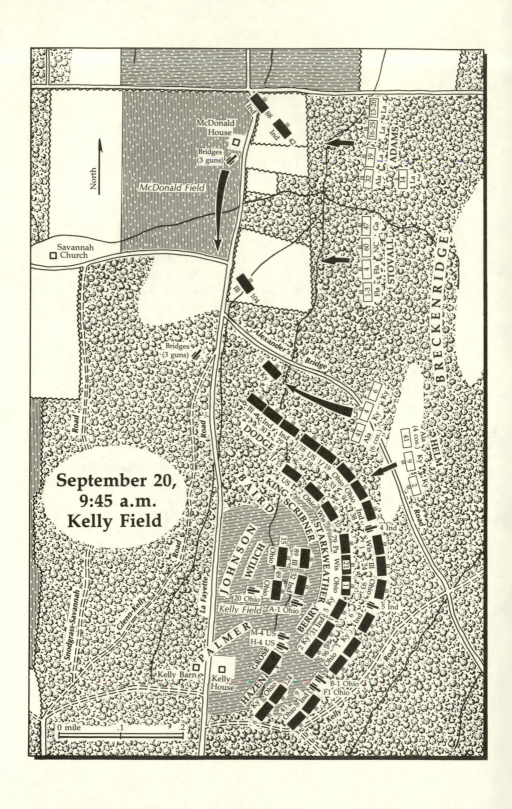

McDonald
House

Bridges
(3 guns)

McDonald Field

North

Savannah
Church

Bridges
(3 guns)

Alexander
Bridge

September 20,
9:45 a.m.
Kelly Field

88 Ind

Ind 42

III 104

15 Ky

4 Ind
30 Ind
29 Ind

1/18 US
2/18 US
1/19 US

Ohio

DODGE

BAIRD

KING

SCRIBNER

STARKWEATHER

JOHNSON

WILICH

15 Ohio
89 Ill
49 Ohio
32 Ind
20 Ohio

Kelly Field

A-1 Ohio

M-4 US
H-4 US

Kelly Barn

Kelly
House

0 mile   .1   .2

Snodgrass-Savannah Road

Glenn-Kelly Road

La Fayette Road

PALMER

GROSE

HAZEN

BERRY

6 Ky
41 Ohio
9 Ind
124 Ohio

6 Ky
6 Ky
9 Ind
5 Ky
96 Ohio

B-1 Ohio
F1 Ohio

Kelly

Wis
21
1
5 Ind
63 Ohio
24 Ill
38 Ind

10 Wis
94 Ohio
2 Ohio
21 Wis
79 Pa
1 Wis
4 Ind

2 Ky
41 Ala
4 Ky
6

STOVALL

ADAMS

BRECKENRIDGE

HELM

32 Ala
19 La
[16-25] La
[13-20] La

14 La

47 Ga
60 NC
4 Fla
1-3 Fla

41 (4 cos.) Ala
9 Ky
2 Ky

41 (6 cos.) Ala

Breckinridge had been watching the fight from the ridge, the picture of gallant aplomb. Word of Helm's wounding stunned him. "Helm has been killed," he told his staff in a voice trembling with grief. As he regained his composure, Breckinridge drafted a hasty order assigning Colonel Joseph Lewis of the Sixth Kentucky to brigade command and instructing him to somehow reunite its two wings. Breckinridge sent his young nephew, Cabell, to deliver the orders. Having done all he could for Helm's brigade, Breckinridge moved off to the right to see how Stovall and Adams were faring.[9]

Breckinridge had faith in Lewis. The son of wealthy and highly respectable members of the Bluegrass aristocracy, Joseph Horace Lewis was just a month shy of his thirty-ninth birthday. He had had a distinguished antebellum career. Originally a Whig, Lewis narrowly missed a seat in Congress in the elections of 1857. Like Helm, Lewis was an attorney who gradually and somewhat reluctantly came to espouse the cause of states' rights. He was also a natural soldier. At Shiloh he had had three horses shot out from under him while leading his regiment with uncommon skill; eight months later at Stones River, he was among the last to quit the field after Breckinridge's attack on the Federal left collapsed.[10]

Here at Chickamauga, Lewis was performing equally well, helped a bit by John Beatty's misfortune. The Ohioan had advanced his brigade north toward the McDonald farm in a single line, with the Eighty-eighth Indiana on the left, the Fifteenth Kentucky on the right, and the Forty-second Indiana and One Hundred Fourth Illinois in between. As Beatty cleared the forest and entered the southern limit of the McDonald farm, he swung his brigade gradually toward the east to confront the skirmishers of Adams, Stovall, and Lewis. At some point he lost control of the movement, and the brigade divided. The Eighty-eighth Indiana, encountering no opposition, settled easily into position on the high ground around the McDonald house with three guns of Bridges's battery. On its right, the Forty-second Indiana fell behind when its skirmishers ran into those of the Fourth Florida, which was on skirmish duty for Stovall's brigade. Gradually, the Hoosiers swept their front clear and were able to come up alongside the Eighty-eighth Indiana. The skirmishers of the One Hundred Fourth Illinois were less successful. They recoiled when confronted by the Floridians, which threw the entire regiment momentarily into confusion. By the time Lieutenant Colonel Douglas Hapeman restored order, a space of 250 yards had opened between his Illinoisans and the right flank of the Forty-second Indiana. Hapeman wheeled his regiment toward the north at the double-quick time in an effort to catch up with the Indianians, but in so doing he only created a second, equally dangerous gap between himself and the Fifteenth Kentucky on his right. Beatty sent an aide to Baird to implore the general to advance his line to cover the right flank of the Fifteenth Kentucky, then tried to close the interval between the Forty-second Indiana and One Hundred Fourth Illinois. Captain Bridges, meanwhile, recalled his three-gun section from the McDonald house.[11]

At that moment, Colonel Lewis's Confederates came crashing through the forest with a ferocity that Beatty's jumbled regiments could not resist. The Fifteenth Kentucky was hit first. While the Forty-first Alabama poured a withering volley into its right flank, the Fourth Kentucky charged it from in front, and for an instant Kentuckian met Kentuckian in a vicious hand-to-hand struggle. As the Yankee Kentuckians fell back toward the road, the pressure mounted against the One Hundred Fourth Illinois, which was also struck in front and flank. All Beatty could do was attempt to bring the two regiments closer together as they recoiled toward the La Fayette road.[12]

At the junction of the La Fayette and Alexander's Bridge roads, Captain Bridges waited impatiently with his reunited battery for the infantry to clear his front so that he might open on the Confederates. In the timber on the right side of the La Fayette road Lieutenant William Bishop stood ready with his three-gun section; Bridges was across the road with the remaining pieces.

The officers of the One Hundred Fourth Illinois shared Bridges's frustration. George Marsh, first sergeant of Company D, recalled their efforts, often comical, to keep the men together: "At the road there was more or less excitement. Colonel Hapeman was doing his best, as also Major Widmer, to hold his regiment firm. Lieutenant Rood, of Company G, said 'They are just as tired of this as you are.' Lieutenant Clark was disgusted because his revolver would not go off. Lieutenant William Ross, of Company B, who was a giant in stature, had hold of a sapling with his left hand, and waving his sword with his right, shouted, 'Come on; I am enough for a whole regiment of you myself.' "[13]

The Fourth Kentucky denied the Yankee cannoneers a role in the fight. At a hundred-yard range it delivered a volley that decimated Bishop's section. The lieutenant fell dead, and every man and horse was hit. As his frightened infantrymen streamed through the battery, Beatty shouted to Bridges the rather superfluous command to withdraw his guns. The captain managed to limber up the cannons on the left side of the road and convinced a detail from the One Hundred Fourth to drag a gun from Bridges's other section out from under the noses of the Confederates, who had closed to within fifty yards.[14]

Lieutenant Lot Young of the Fourth Kentucky grabbed the trunnion of one of the abandoned pieces and, with the help of his troops, swung it around to fire on the fleeing Federals. But the cannon was empty, and the Yankees faded into the timber unmolested. Just then, Young saw something wholly unexpected. Back out of the trees came Captain Bridges. "He dashed into the road and past us, lifting his hat and waving us a salute that would have put to shame a Chesterfield," recalled Young. "The act was almost paralyzing and not a man of the fifty or more who fired at him point blank touched him or his horse. If there is such a thing as a charmed life, this captain must have possessed it on that occasion. If living I would gladly travel miles to shake his hand."[15]

As his jubilant Kentuckians closed on the cannons, Colonel Lewis "discovered for the first time what the thicker growth of timber had prevented me from before observing, that the left of the brigade was considerably in rear." Lewis knew better than to try to stop his men just then. "Neither a halt or retreat at this juncture was, in my judgment, proper or allowable; so the command was given to take the battery, and it was done," he reported.

Lewis gave the order to regroup along the west side of the road. He looked back to see Captain G. W. McCawley, the brigade adjutant, hailing him. Helm was mortally wounded; Lewis must take command and rally the brigade, the captain shouted. Fine, said Lewis, but he would need a mount. Through a mix-up his own horse had been grazing far in the rear when the advance began, forcing Lewis to lead on foot. Lewis turned the right wing over to Lieutenant Colonel Martin Cofer of the Sixth Kentucky. Grabbing McCawley's horse, the colonel retraced his route through the timber. For a moment he lost his way and headed toward the Federal breastworks. The Yankees held their fire in the hope of an easy capture. When he was seventy yards from the breastworks, Lewis saw his error. Spinning his horse around, he rode away amid a shower of bullets.[16]

Little remained of the left wing of the brigade when Lewis finally found it. Of the 302 officers and men of the Second Kentucky who charged the breastworks, 146 had been killed, wounded, or were missing. Losses were just as severe in the Ninth Kentucky, where 102 fell out of an initial strength of 230. And when finally reunited, only half of the Forty-first Alabama would be left to answer roll call. Lewis gathered the men together and marched them off by the right flank until they met Lieutenant Colonel Cofer with the right wing, which at Breckinridge's command had retired from its exposed position along the La Fayette road. For the Orphan Brigade, the battle was over.[17]

Adams and Stovall had run into Beatty's left regiments near the McDonald house a few minutes after Lewis struck the Ohioan's right. So feeble was the Federal resistance that both thought they were fighting a mere skirmish line. In Adams's brigade, only Colonel Randall Gibson's Thirteenth and Twentieth Louisiana, which entered the McDonald field directly in front of the Forty-second Indiana, had anything like a real fight. As they emerged from the forest, the Louisianians were greeted with a cheer and a volley from the Hoosiers, who lay behind a low ridge south of the McDonald house. As the Forty-second engaged the Louisianians to its front, Adams's left regiments and Stovall's entire brigade slipped through the gap between it and the One Hundred Fourth Illinois. By the time the Indianians realized what had happened, the Rebels were two hundred yards behind them. In the commotion the bugle call to retreat was lost, but it made little difference; most of the men already had abandoned the firing line.[18]

Gibson chose that instant to order a charge. "We fell upon him with such impetuosity that he broke in confusion, the men throwing away their arms and equipment, and about eighty were so closely pressed that they surrendered," he reported proudly.[19]

Most of the Forty-second Indiana adhered to the Eighty-eighth Indiana, which had hastily changed front to the south to meet Gibson's Louisianians. The two regiments held for a few minutes, until the hopelessness of their predicament became apparent. Two Confederate brigades were between them and the left of Baird's division. At the same time, Armstrong's cavalry division was crossing the La Fayette road a half mile to the north, wreaking havoc on the Federal field hospital at the Cloud church. The Indianians took the only course open to them and withdrew into the forest west of the McDonald farm. For the rest of the day they drifted over the foothills of Missionary Ridge, lost and confused.[20]

At the road, Adams and Stovall paused to regroup. There Breckinridge joined them. The Kentuckian saw at once the opportunity presented him. "It was now evident, from the comparatively slight resistance they had encountered and the fact that they were not threatened in front, that our line had extended beyond the enemy's left." Breckinridge sent word to Hill that he intended to wheel the brigades to the left, then advance south along the road against Thomas's left flank. Without waiting for permission, Breckinridge set about realigning the brigades in the McDonald field. Marcellus Stovall filed his command off the road by the left flank. He herded the brigade into a single line on the east side of the road, about four hundred yards north of the Federal breastworks. Adams recalled his brigade from the western edge of the McDonald farm and formed on Stovall's right along the west side of the road, also in a single line. Breckinridge posted Captain C. H. Slocumb's Louisiana Battery on a slight rise along the southern edge of the McDonald field to support the advance. At 10:30 A.M., he sent the two brigades forward.[21]

The Kelly field was alive with generals and staff officers galloping to and fro. Thomas was making certain Rosecrans did not forget him; in fact, he was making a nuisance of himself. When Helm's Kentuckians appeared before his breastworks, he sent two aides rushing to headquarters within minutes of one another to renew the call for the rest of Negley's division.

The first found Rosecrans at 10:00 A.M. "Tell General Thomas that Wood's division is probably in place and Negley's on the way there," Rosecrans said. "There it goes," he added, pointing across the Dyer field at Stanley's brigade, which had just come out of the woods and was getting itself into route column on the Glenn-Kelly road.

Thomas was unduly concerned. Rosecrans was not about to neglect his sector. The commanding general was prepared to pay any price to save the left and keep the roads to Chattanooga open. At 10:10 A.M., after reassuring Thomas's first courier, Rosecrans laid out his intentions in a warning order to McCook. It read: "General Thomas is being heavily pressed on the left. The general commanding directs you to make immediate disposition to withdraw the right, so as to spare as much force as possible to re-enforce Thomas. The left must be held at all hazards—even if the right is drawn wholly back to the present left. . . . Be ready to start re-enforcements to Thomas at a moment's warning."[22]

The rout of Beatty's brigade sharpened Thomas's anxiety. As he saw the situation, Confederate units of indeterminate strength had cut communications with Rossville via the La Fayette road and were now threatening to close off the McFarland's Gap road as well. The loss of both routes of retreat was unthinkable. Unaware of Rosecrans's designs and despairing of ever seeing Negley, the Virginian at last began to draw on his own reserves to prolong the left, as Colonel Wiley maintained he should have done in the first place. By now, Cleburne had begun his assault against the center and right of the Kelly field salient. Although his lines were holding, Thomas dared not draw off all the reserves from that sector. He chose, therefore, to leave Willich in support of Johnson and call on Palmer to dispatch Grose's brigade to Baird's support.

Thomas next summoned Brannan's division, which he thought was his mobile reserve. No one had bothered to tell him that Brannan had moved into the front line opposite the Poe field earlier in the morning, so Thomas assumed the division still lay on the far side of the Snodgrass hill. He sent the forty-four-year-old Mexican War veteran orders to come to the left at once. Brannan was baffled. He rode down the line to General Reynolds for advice. "I am ordered to the left with my division," Brannan announced. "That is all very well, but you can't go," Reynolds rejoined while his own men battled Cleburne's attacking Confederates. "We are now hotly engaged and all that can be expected of us is to fight hard in one place at a time, and Heavens knows we have got our hands full right here for the present."

"Oh! I am not going but who will take the responsibility if there should be a hereafter to this apparent disobedience of orders, for that is what it amounts to?" asked Brannan.

"Of course I will take the responsibility," said Reynolds, who was senior in rank. "You send word to Thomas what the state of affairs is here and we need have no anxiety as to any hereafter to your not moving now."

A much-relieved Brannan then suggested that he could perhaps spare Van Derveer's brigade, which was not then engaged. Reynolds agreed, and Van Derveer started up the La Fayette road at 10:30 A.M.[23]

Thomas's subordinates on the left were also trying with mixed success to bolster the threatened flank themselves. After the repulse of Helm, Baird rode into the Kelly field in search of idle units. He noticed Willich's brigade resting behind breastworks in the far corner of the meadow. The Prussian was elsewhere, so Baird asked the regimental commanders to come to the aid of his troops if at any time they appeared to falter.

He was wasting his breath. "As all had different orders, I received no satisfactory reply." Baird persisted. He sought out General Johnson and convinced him to withhold at least one regiment of Willich's brigade to reinforce the left as needed. Orders accordingly went out to the Forty-ninth Ohio to form in close column and stand ready to move.[24]

John Beatty had availed himself of the lull following the withdrawal of Lewis's Confederates to rally his One Hundred Fourth Illinois and Fifteenth Kentucky. Having no other orders, Beatty marched them back to the junction of the La Fayette and Alexander's Bridge roads. Finding that he was the only officer in the brigade still mounted, Beatty turned command over to Colonel Marion Taylor of the Fifteenth, then galloped down the La Fayette road to report to Thomas or Negley his urgent need for help. On the way he met Colonel Timothy Stanley at the head of his brigade. Thomas had anticipated Beatty's request and sent Stanley's brigade up the road at the double-quick.

Negley was not with Stanley. On the way to the left, he had run into Captain W. B. Gaw, the corps topographical engineer. According to Negley, the captain directed him to take his own as well as any idle artillery batteries he might find and mass them on a high, lightly wooded knoll south of the Snodgrass hill. As Negley understood his orders, he was to face the batteries south, into the Dyer field. Telling Stanley to continue on with his brigade, Negley left the road with Batteries G and M of the First Ohio Light Artillery and led them across the field. He placed Battery M on the top of the knoll, instructing its commander, Captain Frederick Shultz, to train his guns back into the field. He then rode north with Battery G, skirting the eastern slope of the Snodgrass hill, to the next piece of high ground—an open ridge, or spur, that ran east from the Snodgrass house for some three hundred yards. There he ordered Captain Alexander Marshall to place his battery into action, fronting to the southeast. While he was thus engaged, Lieutenant Morris Temple came out of the woods from the direction of the Kelly field with the four remaining guns of Bridges's battery. In the turmoil following the loss of his right section, Bridges had ordered Temple to take the battery to the first good firing position he could find, which happened to be the Snodgrass spur. Temple reported to Negley, who asked him to continue on to the wooded knoll and go into battery beside Captain Shultz.

More artillery came Negley's way. When Battery I, Fourth United States Artillery, thundered up the La Fayette road after Van Derveer's brigade a short while later, the Pennsylvanian snatched it for duty on the ridge. Lieutenant Frank Smith placed his four twelve-pounders on the left side of the Snodgrass house, near the tree where Thomas had slept the night before, and trained them toward the Kelly field, a half mile to the northeast.

This is precisely the direction Thomas had intended all the batteries to face. When he sent Captain Gaw to brief Negley, Thomas had meant for the general to concentrate his artillery so as to sweep Baird's left and rear. Negley had misunderstood his instructions. He was tired and sick and getting sicker.[25]

In Negley's absence, then, Beatty was in command of the extreme left of the army. Fortunately for Thomas, he was up to the task. The Ohioan directed Colonel Stanley to file his column into the woods west of the Kelly field and there go into line of battle, facing north. Beatty retrieved his two regiments and tucked them behind Stanley's brigade amid a growing patter of bullets that heralded the approach of Dan Adams's Louisianians. Ahead of the Confederates came a handful of frightened Yankees, tripping through the underbrush and screaming for their comrades not to fire on them. They were the skirmishers of the One Hundred Fourth Illinois and Fifteenth Kentucky, whom Beatty had forgotten to recall in his haste to get the regiments safely behind Stanley.[26]

In Stanley's front line, the men of the Eleventh Michigan and Nineteenth Illinois hurriedly cut away the saplings and underbrush that blocked their fields of fire, then piled them in a row and laid down behind. Their line was now invisible to anyone more than a few yards away. Colonel William Stoughton understood the advantage this gave his Michiganders. He ordered the colors dropped to the ground. Jumping off his horse, Stoughton ran along the line yelling at the men to keep their heads down. "Boys, we've got them. Let every man take aim as if he were shooting a target, and be sure and not waste a bullet. Aim at their legs and you will drop their front rank."[27]

Private John King witnessed the lethal result of his colonel's admonition. "The enemy were driving the skirmishers in swiftly, firing as they came. When within two or three rods of our brigade line the regimental flags were raised suddenly, a sheet of flame went from the muzzles of our guns, and a windrow of dead and wounded Confederate lay on the ground," he recalled.[28]

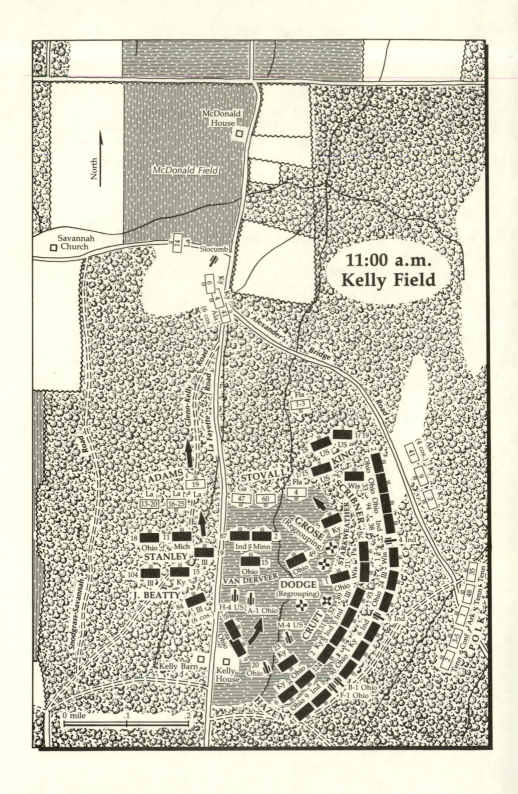

**11:00 a.m.
Kelly Field**

McDonald House

McDonald Field

North

Savannah Church

Slocumb

14 La

Ky 6 4 Ky 47 Ala (6 cos.)

Alexander's Bridge

Glenn-Kelly Road

La Fayette Road

Road

Fla 1-3

ADAMS 19

La La La 13-20 16-25

STOVALL Ga NC 47 60

Fla 1/15 US 4

1/15 US

KING 17 19 US US Ohio

2 Ohio Ohio Ind 33 94 38

Wis Ky 79 Pa

SCRIBNER STARKWEATHER

GROSE (Regrouping)

18 Ohio 11 Mich

STANLEY

87 2

19 Ind Minn Ohio 15

Ohio 49 Ky Ohio 24 Ill Wis Ind

4 Ind

4 (4 cos.) Ala Ky Ky 9 2

104 III 15 Ky

J. BEATTY

VAN DERVEER

DODGE (Regrouping)

H-4 US A-1 Ohio

(6 cos.)

CRUFT

Ohio 2 Ky Ind 31 32 89 Ind 93 Ind 6 Ohio 5 Ind

Ill 35

Ohio

M-4 US

Ky 23

Ky 6 Ind

POLK Tenn Tenn Ark Conf

Ill 48

Kelly Barn

Kelly House

9 Ohio 20 Ohio

Ky Ohio 9 Ind

B-1 Ohio F-1 Ohio

HAZEN

Ill 3-5 Ill 2

0 mile .1 .2

Adams's men were stunned. The easy dispersal of Beatty's skirmishers had instilled a false confidence in them, and they plunged through the forest at the charge, each regiment trying to outrun the other. Units broke up into excited mobs. "The men . . . while thus disordered received a terrific and unbroken volley from a line that suddenly came up, flanking us on the right. . . . The whole line was checked," reported Colonel Gibson of the Thirteenth and Twentieth Louisiana. "Some began to seek cover, and in a few minutes the command gave way in spite of every exertion." Gibson grabbed the colors and got his Louisianians back in line. Colonel Daniel Gober reformed his Sixteenth and Twenty-fifth Louisiana on Gibson's left, and together the two regiments started back toward the Yankees.[29]

The initial Federal fire had done more damage than Gibson imagined. It killed Major Loudon Butler of the Nineteenth Louisiana and dropped nearly 150 of his men. The rest fled back through the forest with their company officers chasing after them. Among those who escaped was J. W. Allen, the first sergeant of Company H, nicknamed the "Creole Company." As the first shots rang out, Allen ducked behind a tree. He chose an awkward moment to make a run for it. "On leaving the tree it seemed that they fired a peck of balls at me, only one striking my knapsack on my back, passing through my blanket . . . through two company books, clothing, and entered my Testament, breaking through the back and mashing itself nearly flat. It is in the book now, just where it struck thirty-four years ago. My compliments to the boys in blue, whose aim was so bad," Allen wrote. Sadly, the poverty of old age compelled Allen to advertise his New Testament for sale as a curiosity of the war.[30]

Among the wounded also was General Adams. A minie ball shattered the humerus bone of his left arm. Adams trailed behind his troops on foot until loss of blood forced him to sit down under a tree and rest.[31]

Like Adams's Louisianians, the soldiers of Stovall's brigade found the early going easy. Marcellus Stovall took with him into action only 897 men— his was by far the smallest brigade in the Army of Tennessee—but they enjoyed a measure of success far stronger units would be hard pressed to equal. They encountered the western tip of Baird's breastworks. The First and Third Florida was on the brigade left, the Sixtieth North Carolina was in the center, and the Forty-seventh Georgia held the right. The Fourth Florida, which had been temporarily retained by Major Rice Graves, Breckinridge's chief of artillery, to support Slocumb's battery, was then hurrying forward to rejoin the brigade.[32]

The First and Third Florida hit the Yankee breastworks first. Its commander, Colonel W. S. Dilworth, did not like what he saw. "It became apparent that the right of the enemy extended considerably beyond my left, and as there was no support for my left I feared that the enemy would turn my flank; but the order to advance was positive, and we advanced up a hill at a double-quick under a galling fire from the enemy." It was the Floridians' good fortune to have struck the line defended by King's Regulars, who, after Saturday's drubbing, had little fight left in them. The First Battalion, Eighteenth United States, stood its ground long enough for the Second Battalion to come up to its assistance, then both gave way, retreating to a second line of breastworks just a few steps ahead of the Confederates.

On Dilworth's right, the Sixtieth North Carolina had run up against Dodge's brigade, which gave an even poorer account of itself, crumbling at virtually the first fire. The Yankees scattered into the Kelly field with the North Carolinians on their heels.

The Forty-seventh Georgia was the first of Stovall's regiments to step into the Kelly field, having glided past the left extremity of the Federal breastworks. Their stay in the field was brief. When the Georgians came into the open a few minutes before 11:00 A.M., they were met by a blast of grape and canister from Goodspeed's battery, which had set up in the field just north of the Kelly farmhouse. The Georgians raised the Rebel yell and charged. Goodspeed ordered his guns double-shotted with canister. A second blast stopped the Forty-seventh just fifty yards short of the muzzles. The Rebels came no closer. With the rest of the brigade still fighting its way over the breastworks, Captain William Phillips ordered his men to lie down. A grapeshot gored Phillips's hip. Captain Joseph Cone acceded to command. His first order was to retreat. The Georgians ran back into the woods, where they settled into a ragged line behind the trees. Although they had pushed just one hundred yards into the field, Cone's Georgians nevertheless were the first Confederates to gain the Union rear.[33]

The Kelly field was a bedlam of blue. The Federal response to the Rebel penetration was little better than a disjointed series of countermeasures by brigade, regimental, and battery commanders. Colonel Grose was the first to challenge Stovall. Under an annoying fire from the Georgians in the woods, the Indianian tried to form his brigade in the open field. It was an act of valiant desperation. His men refused to stand up to a fire they could not accurately answer. Regiments intermingled and troops began trickling rearward across the field. In a well-intentioned gesture of support, a friendly battery—perhaps Battery M, First Ohio—aimed their guns too low and fired grapeshot into the backs of the soldiers of the Sixth Ohio, killing several. Their colonel agonized over what to do: "It was a trying position, the enemy's fire in our front and our own in the rear, and more danger in retiring than in remaining." Finally the battery ceased firing, and the Sixth escaped by the right flank into a little hollow at the eastern edge of the field. With his two frontline regiments, the Thirty-sixth Indiana and Eighty-fourth Illinois, Grose attempted to charge Stovall's left. Although numbers were about equal, the Federals were too disorganized to accomplish much. As Grose advanced, the six left companies of the Eighty-fourth veered to the left and fell in behind Stanley's line on the west side of the road. From there, they eventually drifted all the way back to the Snodgrass hill, where Negley set them to work guarding his batteries. With excusable hyperbole, the commander of the Thirty-sixth Indiana reported: "The men of my regiment, with one hundred men of the Eighty-fourth Illinois attaching themselves to our left, rushed vigorously to the assault, but it was like the ocean spray beating against the rock bound coast. We were utterly powerless to check the surging and powerful columns of a foe outnumbering us three to one." Captain Ebenezer Wells of General Johnson's staff offered a less flattering account of Grose's "charge." "In the second day's battle I myself saw a brigade which, being ordered to reinforce the extreme left, was changing front forward in the open ground about the Kelly house dissolve like a rope of sand under the fire of the skirmish line, which had penetrated to our rear."[34]

Grose was saved further humiliation by the timely arrival of Van Derveer's brigade, which had struggled toward the fighting through forest so "densely overgrown with small trees and underbrush and so matted as to make a passage through it impossible," said Captain Donahower of the Second Minnesota. As the Minnesotans hacked and tore their way forward, they met a steady stream of "cowardly skulkers" toiling just as hard to get clear of the battle. "One party of six emerged from the woods, carrying a blanket in which lay a man with face covered," observed Lieutenant Colonel Bishop. "These men all carried their guns also, and we set them down as a guard detailed to carry back some general officer, desperately wounded . . . who could he be? Directly a shell came howling through the woods and burst on the ground near them, when they dropped the blanket and their guns and took off at the double-quick to the rear, and the man in the blanket got up and ran after them. Out of this we got some diversion."[35]

The laughter ended when the Minnesotans stepped across the La Fayette road into the Kelly field in line of battle, fronting east. A panorama of tumult and horror unfolded before them. The Kelly house and barn were ablaze. Stunned and bleeding soldiers lurched toward them. A dozen more huddled behind the remains of a caved-in well, seeking shelter from the rain of bullets. Units mingled and broke. The roar of gunfire cascaded out of the woods into the field from the north, east, and south simultaneously, and for an instant Lieutenant Colonel Bishop was at a loss which direction to face. Then he saw the smoke from the rifles of the Sixtieth North Carolina near the woods to the north, at right angles to his line. The Rebels were clinging to the edge of the field, rising to their feet, firing, and dropping back down into the grass.

Bishop ordered the regiment to wheel to the left to meet the Confederates head on as Colonel George, tired and ill, looked on approvingly. Hardly had Bishop uttered the command when a bullet struck his mare, Betty, in the breast. Down she went, sending Bishop in a somersault over her head. "Before my horse was shot, I had one bullet through my pants near my ankle and two had struck the scabbard of my sabre. It seemed as if by holding up my hand I could have caught it full of bullets in a moment, such was the singing they made," Bishop later told his sister. The regiment had been in the field only three minutes, yet every mounted officer except Colonel George had lost his horse. Bishop left his mare, which had been a gift to him from the officers of the Second, and jogged on behind the regiment. Happily, the two would be reunited. A wounded soldier came across Betty roaming about the Kelly field later that day. Together, they helped one another to Rossville, where Bishop found the soldier and his horse at midnight. "After several weeks in the hospital both recovered and served to the end of the war," he recalled.[36]

As the only mounted officer left in the regiment, Colonel George now took a more active role in leading it. He ordered his men to begin firing by file from the right. Captain Donahower, whose company was on the extreme left of the line, was too far away to hear the order, so he yelled at his men to open up as soon as they found a target. For five or ten minutes—"every minute seeming an hour," wrote Bishop—Minnesotans and North Carolinians slugged it out. Forced to stand to load, Bishop's men clearly were getting the worst of the exchange; nearly seventy men already had been hit.

But help was on the way. The Eighty-seventh Indiana came up on the Minnesotans' left and engaged the Forty-seventh Georgia in front while at the same time pouring volleys into what remained of the Nineteenth Louisiana of Adams's brigade. Colonel Van Derveer brought the Ninth Ohio and Thirty-fifth Ohio up from the Kelly house into line behind his frontline regiments.[37]

Other Federal units found their way to the fight with Stovall. The Forty-ninth Ohio, which General Johnson had earlier agreed to place at Baird's disposal, now charged into the field from the right rear of the Second Minnesota to confront the Fourth Florida. To the right of the Forty-ninth, the Fifth Kentucky of Berry's brigade broke out of the forest squarely opposite the left flank of the Floridians. General Willich sent the Fifteenth Ohio to support Goodspeed's battery, which continued to rake the Rebels with grape and canister. Meanwhile, Baird and King had succeeded in rallying enough of the Regular Brigade to halt the First and Third Florida back in the woods along the second line of breastworks. "The colors were not more than a dozen steps from the enemy, and in another minute we would have driven them from their works, but . . . the enemy was getting in my rear and pouring a destructive fire on my left flank," reported Colonel Dilworth, who ordered the regiment to withdraw.[38]

The rest of Stovall's brigade was not far behind. The Forty-seventh Georgia crumbled around Captain Cone after taking a few rounds from the Eighty-seventh Indiana. Cone begged and beat the men, but they just dodged his blows and ran off. Cone gave up the fight and chased after his unruly Georgians.

Colonel Kammerling was at it again. His Ninth Ohio passed over the Eighty-seventh Indiana into the front line just as Cone's Georgians snapped. Captain Donahower listened to some unintelligible commands in German, then watched the Ohioans charge toward the forest. Donahower's first sergeant ran to the front of the company. "Don't let the Ninth Ohio charge alone," he yelled. Off went Company E behind him. Colonel George galloped up and demanded Donahower tell him where his men thought they were going. Donahower looked at the colonel, shrugged his shoulders, and then sprinted on after his soldiers. George waved the rest of the regiment forward, and the Sixtieth North Carolina gave way.[39]

Hit in front and on the flank, the Fourth Florida also broke apart. "As they faltered we charged on them and hurled them back as fast as they had come in this charge," wrote a member of the Forty-ninth Ohio. "Many of the Rebels threw down their arms and surrendered as we pressed them so close." The Fifth Kentucky took its share of prisoners as well, but not before its commander, Captain John W. Huston, saw his son, Lieutenant John W. Huston, Jr., shot down. "He died like a soldier, with sword in hand, in the midst of a victorious charge upon a fleeing enemy," the captain proudly reported.[40]

The defeat of Stovall's brigade at about 11:15 A.M. left Adams's Louisianians dangerously isolated on the west side of the La Fayette road. It was only then that Colonel Randall Gibson learned he was in command of the brigade. "I had observed General Adams in rear of the Sixteenth and Twenty-fifth Louisiana on foot and looking at his arm as we were advancing, but I presumed he was slightly wounded and remained with my regiment." Glancing to his left now, Gibson saw that the Nineteenth Louisiana had vanished and that Van Derveer's Federals were gaining his rear. His first act as brigade commander was to order a retreat to the McDonald farm, where he hoped to reform behind the guns of Slocumb's battery.[41]

Stanley and Beatty ordered a pursuit. Captain James Campbell of the Nineteenth Illinois recalled the chaos of victory: "At such a time it is difficult to preserve anything like organization. There are some anxious and able to advance rapidly, while others are neither anxious nor able, and, between the two extremes there are all grades of celerity. In the scattered condition produced by these causes, the Nineteenth, with portions of the other two regiments that had also joined in the pursuit, was scattered over a quarter of a mile through open woods, the advance getting as far as [McDonald's] field."[42]

Colonel Stanley came upon General Adams, who asked him to send up a stretcher. Stanley, anxious to keep up with his men, apologized that he could not comply and rode on. Now the helpless Adams became a prize claimed by every Yankee regiment on that part of the field. Captain Preston Guthrie of the Nineteenth Illinois swore that Adams surrendered to him, whatever that meant. Captain Borden Hicks of the Eleventh Michigan said his regiment captured the general and that he himself took Adams's sword. "I carried his sword on the charge we now made to the McDonald field, going into this charge with a sword in each hand, and looking savage as a meat ax." Everyone seemed to have time to plunder Adams, but none to see that he was removed from the field. Late that afternoon, Lieutenant Albion Tourgee of the One Hundred Fifth Ohio, sent to the rear in charge of his regiment's wounded, found Adams, still sitting against the same tree. Three Federal soldiers were circling him like buzzards. Adams called out to Tourgee that he was being robbed, then cursed loudly at the Yankee prowlers, who skulked away when they saw the lieutenant approach. Tourgee tried to lift him up, but Adams screamed with pain and swore that it would be murder to move him. Glancing at the general's arm, which looked well-bandaged, Tourgee concluded that Adams was bluffing in the hope that the Rebels would win the battle and rescue him. Tourgee persisted and lifted him onto a horse. His ruse discovered, Adams quickly got over his anger. He wanted to give the lieutenant a token of his gratitude, but the "damned rascals had not left him even a sleeve button." Adams thought for a moment, then told Tourgee to cut a button from his coat. If the lieutenant ever found himself in a similar plight at the hands of the Confederates, Adams said, he should send the button to him, and he would see that Tourgee was well treated. Tourgee pocketed the button, then handed Adams his own knife to keep so that he could slice tobacco from his plug, "which he seemed freely to indulge."[43]

Union surgeons operated on Adams three days later. They pulled six bone fragments and the smashed minie ball from his arm. Four weeks later they splinted it and sent him through the lines under a flag of truce at the earnest appeal of General Bragg. "He will without doubt have a good arm," noted the head surgeon with satisfaction. Adams did indeed survive the war, arm intact.[44]

General Breckinridge looked on in bitter silence as the survivors of Stovall's and Adams's brigades streamed back into the McDonald field. At Stones River, his division had battered itself almost into oblivion in a doomed charge on the last day of the battle. Here at Chickamauga, it had come close to victory, only to be repelled at a cost of nearly a third its numbers and two of three brigade commanders. The folly of sending the division forward without reserves was now horribly apparent. Breckinridge neatly summarized his disgust in his report of the battle. "Stovall had gained a point beyond the angle of the enemy's main line of works. Adams had advanced still farther, being actually in rear of his entrenchments," he noted. "A good supporting line to my division at this moment would probably have produced decisive results."[45]

CHAPTER NINETEEN

TO FIRE AT THOSE BREASTWORKS
SEEMED FOOLISH

THE FEAR that had driven Baird and his commanders on the extreme left to keep their men up all night building breastworks stood in sharp contrast to the almost serene indifference that prevailed among the Federal generals along the rest of the Kelly field line. Dawn came, and not a tree had been felled nor a stone gathered by the men of Johnson's or Palmer's divisions. At sunrise, Colonel Isaac Suman of the Ninth Indiana strolled over to General Hazen and suggested the brigade raise a line of breastworks. It was a notion "which no one before seemed to have thought of," admitted Hazen, who at first objected to the idea. He feared that Rebel artillery shells striking the works would splinter logs into lethal missiles. Suman persisted. He would put the heaviest logs and rails in front to absorb the impact of incoming shells. Hazen consented and urged Cruft to have his brigade likewise throw up breastworks.[1]

General Johnson called on Hazen a few minutes later to urge him to desist—the clatter would attract the attention of the enemy, he complained. Thoroughly persuaded by Suman's arguments himself, Hazen soon prevailed on Johnson to start his division to work as well. By then, the sun had risen above the treetops, but Johnson was unconcerned. As he helped his comrades put the finishing touches on their breastworks, Private Albert Kern of the First Ohio listened to Johnson converse with his major. "I don't think there will be much fighting today," remarked Johnson. "I hope the Lord will be on the side of the defensive," replied Major Joab Stafford, in the spirit of the Sabbath.

Suddenly the forest trembled. Five Federal batteries opened fire into the woods. The Rebel yell split the air and Union infantrymen scrambled for their rifles. Johnson was amazed. "I have not heard heavier musketry during the war than we had for one hour," he confessed.[2]

Cleburne's attack had been a long time coming. It was 10:00 A.M. before a courier handed him the order from Hill to advance, the Irishman claimed. Cleburne immediately sent staff officers hurrying to his brigade commanders with instructions for them to dress on the right, preserve their distances, and move forward. Wood got his orders quickly; not so Polk. "Owing to some mistake, I did not receive the order to advance until a few moments after General Breckinridge's division had been put in motion," he reported.

Now the real trouble began. Without bothering to notify anyone, Polk moved his brigade obliquely to the right in a futile attempt to restore his connection with Helm's left before the Kentuckian ran into the enemy. Wood, for his part, insisted that Polk first veered to the left, crowding out his own brigade and forcing him to move obliquely to the left to make room. No sooner had he done this, said Wood, then Polk obliqued sharply to the right, opening a huge gap between the two brigades. Both Polk and Wood came under heavy artillery fire before they could rectify their alignment.

Meanwhile, Deshler had advanced past Jackson's brigade, with which he had earlier lain at right angles, only to find his troops similarly blocked by Vaughan's Tennesseans. Precious minutes were lost straightening out the two lines of battle, which crossed badly nonetheless when Deshler continued his advance. All went well for the next few hundred yards, until Deshler found himself squarely and unexpectedly in the rear of Stewart's division. There he halted to await further orders from Cleburne.[3]

Lucius Polk ran into the Federal breastworks first, opposite the tightly packed brigades of Berry, Cruft, and Hazen. After enduring a heavy artillery pounding for five hundred yards, his Confederates crested a ridge just 125 yards from the Yankee works, which were so completely camouflaged with bushes as to be almost invisible. The Federals opened fire. With so many guns trained on so few, the slaughter was terrific. None who survived could find the words to express the horror. "Their position was naturally strong, and, with these works, almost impregnable," attested Colonel George Nixon, commander of the Forty-eighth Tennessee. "The enemy opened with artillery and small-arms from behind these works one of the most destructive fires ever witnessed by any troops during the war. Perfect lanes were made through the timber by the enemy's artillery," he continued. Colonel J. A. Smith of the Third and Fifth Confederate agreed: "The strife at this point was fearful. Such showers of grape, canister, and small-arms I have never before witnessed." Colonel William Robison was knocked flat by a minie ball smashing into his sword belt. In an instant he was back on his feet, exhorting the men of his Second Tennessee. His words were of little use to the Tennesseans, who were falling in windrows. In one company alone, thirty-three of forty-four soldiers were cut down in a matter of minutes.[4]

Polk galloped along the ridge shouting at his commanders to get their regiments behind the crest. Colonel Benjamin Hill of the Thirty-fifth Tennessee had anticipated the order and was clutching the earth himself when Polk rode by. "Hold this position and the day [is] ours," yelled Polk, an entreaty that must have caused Hill to reflect on the young general's sanity.[5]

For the Federals, it was a turkey shoot. Berry, Cruft, and Hazen combined the fire of their four thousand rifles against Polk's eleven hundred men, and Starkweather's Twenty-fourth Illinois contributed flanking volleys. Five Federal batteries pounded the ridge. It was almost too easy. Hazen had his regiments firing by volleys with parade-ground precision. So strict was fire discipline in his brigade that the men still had about forty rounds each after ninety minutes of fighting. The Federals crouched to shoot and lay down to reload, and their losses were remarkably light. Where Polk lost 350 men, most in the first assault, not a single enlisted man was killed in Cruft's brigade and only thirteen were wounded in Hazen's command. Berry's casualties were about as light, and the only fatality in Starkweather's brigade was an infantryman hit in the back of the head by a stray fragment of canister casing from a friendly battery.[6]

Captain Henry Richards of the Ninety-third Ohio actually had trouble staying awake during Polk's attack. He had been sick for several days in August and would have checked himself into the hospital, had he not feared what people might think of him. So he marched off with the regiment. He had ridden in an ambulance the last three days, but the prospect of battle gave him strength. Adrenalin carried him through the first day's action, but now his energy deserted him, and Richards nodded off repeatedly during the shooting.[7]

With little fear of dying, the Federals had time to notice the small oddities of battle. "A white dove bewildered by the noise of the firing flew in and out amid the smoke clouds of the battle, and at last flew down upon the wheel of a gun carriage," related the historian of the First Ohio. "It was a strange place for an emblem of purity and peace. An artilleryman captured it, with his hands blackened by powder, caressed it for a moment and then gave it wing to get away. In an instant it was lost in the storm."[8]

"To stand off at a distance of one hundred fifty yards and fire at those breastworks, without inflicting any loss of any consequence upon their defenders, seemed . . . very foolish," mused Colonel Wiley. Nevertheless, Polk's Confederates hung on behind the crest "like bull dogs," in the words of one Federal eyewitness, and for the next three hours kept up the futile contest with a hollow tenacity.[9]

They were getting little help from Wood, who lost control of his brigade when Polk moved off to the right and never regained it. His four regiments and battalion of sharpshooters were scattered across a half-mile front, holding on in ravines or behind ridges in the face of an unrelenting hammering by Federal artillery.

On the brigade right, Colonel Mark Lowrey, commanding the Thirty-second and Forty-fifth Mississippi, had done his best to preserve the connection with Polk's left when it veered away. By the time his own skirmishers ascended the ridge, Lowrey's main line had broken into a run in an effort to keep up with Polk. Realizing that he could keep aligned with Polk only at the risk of losing touch with his own brigade, Lowrey called a halt in the movement to the right and instead ordered the regiment to march due west up the ridge. At the crest, his Mississippians were met with the same greeting that had awaited Polk's brigade. Lowrey faced the angle where the breastworks turned sharply to the west, a point defended by Turchin's brigade and the Twenty-first Indiana Battery. Its six twelve-pounder Napoleons opened with rapid volleys of grapeshot that tore gaping holes in the ranks of Mississippians. Before Lowrey could fully grasp the situation, nearly a quarter of the regiment had fallen. His major was dead, shot through the heart, and nineteen men lay dead in a heap around the regimental colors. "I would have caused my men to fall back over the crest of the hill and cease firing, but having had orders to go forward and engage the enemy and none to fall back, I supposed it was my duty to keep up the fire, and that a movement was going on the enemy's right flank that would soon remove them from their stronghold," Lowrey reasoned. With that lone hope, he clung to the crest.[10]

Lowrey could count on his men to obey his orders, no matter how quixotic they might seem. The Thirty-second and Forty-fifth Mississippi was a crack regiment. At Tullahoma that spring, General Hardee had judged it the best-drilled regiment in the brigade and complimented the Mississippians in a general order. Lowrey himself was a man of tremendous personal magnetism. He radiated self-assurance. At the age of twenty-four, after "a long struggle with my almost unconquerable resolution to become rich — struggle between worldly interest and Christian duty — I yielded to the call of my church." Lowrey became a Baptist minister, deeply loved by his congregation in the little Mississippi village of Kossuth. Lowrey continued his ministry in the army, preaching actively to his men. They dutifully yielded to his ministrations, and Lowrey baptized fifty members of the regiment in one two-week revival alone.[11]

Captain John Sloan of Company G obeyed Lowrey's orders, and it cost him dearly. As he stood exhorting his troops, a shell fragment ripped away his upper set of teeth and a chunk of his tongue, leaving his chin and jaw dangling against his chest, a bloody pulp. Deep gashes ran from the corner of his right eye to what had been his mouth, completing the mutilation of his face. He was carried to the rear, where surgeons dismissed his case as hopeless. Like Private Miller of the Ninth Indiana, Sloan was laid in a corner to die; no one bothered even to try to give him water. And as with Miller, Sloan's long ordeal had just begun.[12]

The movement to which Lowrey had attached such hope was merely the scurrying for cover of the regiments to his left. Colonel E. B. Breedlove, with less concern for the letter of Wood's orders and possessed of more common sense than Lowrey, had ordered his Forty-fifth Alabama to take cover behind the ridge beyond Lowrey's left. The nearest Yankee breastworks were across the La Fayette road, nearly four hundred yards away, completely invisible to the Alabamians. "My men had been strictly charged not to fire without orders, and then only when they could see the foe. They were not ordered to fire and did not," reported Breedlove.

Breedlove had lost sight of the regiments on his left—the Sixteenth Alabama and Thirty-third Alabama—which were advancing in a gradual half-wheel to the left under the personal supervision of Wood. He led them forward nearly a half mile under a heavy fire of artillery, over the prone soldiers of Bate's brigade to within five hundred yards of the enemy. There they halted, seeking cover in a narrow ravine that split the long ridge in front of the Federal breastworks opposite the Poe field. To their left were Brown's Tennesseans of Stewart's division, awaiting orders to advance from behind their own log-and-rail breastworks.[13]

Wood was at a loss what to do next. Lieutenant Richard Goldthwaite, acting commander of Semple's battery, found the Alabamian in the ravine, obviously perplexed. Goldthwaite had unlimbered his guns behind the Forty-fifth Alabama and was looking for further instructions. Wood had none to give, but he promised to let Goldthwaite know before he moved from the hollow, a pledge he quickly forgot. Cleburne came upon Wood next. Wood blurted out his problems: Polk had crowded him out, forcing him to advance over Bate's front, and Deshler was stuck behind Clayton. Cleburne, interested only in restarting the stalled attack, told Wood to get his left regiments moving at once; he would see to Deshler. The Irishman was clearly annoyed with Wood. While he praised Polk and Deshler lavishly in his report of the battle, Cleburne offered not a single kind word on behalf of the Alabamian, who resigned shortly thereafter.[14]

Cleburne's desire to press the attack is laudable, but it presented Wood with a painful dilemma. For him to lead his two regiments into the Poe field, where they would be subject to both frontal and flanking fire, without a simultaneous advance by Stewart on their left would be tantamount to suicide. Yet the general plan of battle required that he move before the units to his left took up the assault. Fortunately, Bragg himself had begun to realize the impracticality of this directive. Angered by the erratic nature of the assaults against the Federal left, he instructed Major Pollock Lee to pass along the line and give orders directly to every division commander to move on the enemy at once. Ironically, Longstreet only moments earlier had sent a messenger to Bragg informing him that he had completed his own preparations and was ready to attack.[15]

Lee found Stewart a little before 11:00 A.M., about the same time Cleburne was upbraiding Wood, and gave him the oral order to attack. The Tennessean demurred. He understood that he was to take his instructions from Long-street, who had told him that he should move only after the assault had been taken up by the division to his right. Lee insisted the order to attack was peremptory. Stewart acquiesced and rode off to confer with Wood. Stewart agreed to send Brown forward simultaneously on Wood's left and to support the assault with the brigades of Bate and Clayton.[16]

Wood's Alabamians scampered from the ravine and Brown's Tennesseans jumped over their breastworks. Together they swept into the Poe field with a yell "under the most terrible fire it has ever been my fortune to witness," marveled Stewart.

Wood was in trouble from the start. The Forty-fifth Alabama, which tried to join the attack, was driven back in a matter of minutes by the fire of Turchin's bluecoats, who crouched unseen in the forest to its right. "I gave the order to retreat, and fell back to the first cover, without regard to the preservation of the line," Colonel Breedlove confessed. "For the length of time exposed at this point the casualties were much greater than in any other engagement I have ever been in. Here again we could not see the enemy, and did not return his fire."[17]

The Sixteenth Alabama was also subjected to a murderous flanking fire from Turchin's line when it approached the Poe field; nevertheless, it pressed on through the dry cornstalks to within 150 yards of King's breastworks, which lay just across the La Fayette road. When their commander, Major John McGauhy, fell, the Alabamians began to waver. Captain Frederick Ashford, the senior officer standing, ordered them to take what cover they could and keep up the fight. Albion Tourgee, whose One Hundred Fifth Ohio was opposite the Alabamians, watched the drama unfold: "First came pattering shots that cut the trees above us or made a little eddy in the dry autumn leaves. Then it came nearer and we could see the gray ranks advancing through the open wood, halting now and then to fire. Our men were lying down; but when the enemy came in range, Turchin's regiments rose and gave them a thunderous volley. When they came nearer our brigade took up the battle. The enemy halted; the men lay down in the shelter of the trees and for a time the fight went on, Indian fashion."[18]

The Thirty-third Alabama, meanwhile, had charged on a direct course for the Poe house. Somewhere in the field, the regiment collapsed under a converging fire from Battery M of the Fourth United States Artillery and

Battery C, First Ohio. With the few men who remained, perhaps seventy in all, Colonel Sam Adams made it to the house, which by then was engulfed in flames from exploding shells. Around the house, Adams gathered up a few Tennesseans from Brown's brigade who had ventured across the road. By sheer force of will, he drove them on toward the Yankee breastworks, just seventy-five yards away. Raising the Rebel yell, Adams and his followers pushed apart a rail fence that stood between them and the Yankees and dashed forward in a wild attempt to reach the breastworks. It was a moment of madness, recalled W. E. Preston of Company B. Men moved instinctively, and, not surprisingly, their instincts sometimes failed them. "Some men on each side in their excitement had failed to remove their iron ramrods from their guns after reloading and had shot them away, sticking them in trees and saplings. Some ramrods caught twenty feet high or more, and all were usually bent," wrote Preston. At forty yards the Rebels halted. Adams grabbed the colors and waved them about in a desperate bid to spur the men on, but they understood the hopelessness of their predicament even if he did not, and as one they broke and ran back across the Poe field into the woods.[19]

Brown had little more success. Like Adams, he was guiding on the Poe house, his brigade advancing in a single line of battle with the Twenty-sixth Tennessee on the left. The Twenty-third Tennessee Battalion and the Thirty-second, Forty-fifth, and Eighteenth Tennessee regiments completed the line to the right.

The Forty-fifth and Eighteenth Tennessee regiments closed on the burning Poe house at the same time as Adams's little band. The Tennesseans moved "in good order but rather too fast; it seemed to be impossible to restrain them," reported Colonel Anderson Searcy of the Forty-fifth. (Understandably, the men were anxious to clear the open field as quickly as possible.) The two regiments pressed on across the La Fayette road toward the Federal breastworks, where the Seventy-fifth and One Hundred First Indiana of King's Brigade were withholding their fire for close range. At fifty yards, the Federals delivered their volley, and the Tennesseans recoiled. Searcy and the commander of the Eighteenth Tennessee lost control of their regiments, allegedly because the breakup of Adams's Thirty-third Alabama had exposed their right flank. A panic seized the men, said Lieutenant Cahal of the division staff, and in falling back they threw Clayton's supporting line into confusion as well. Kneeling behind the breastworks with his comrades of the Seventy-fifth Indiana, Sergeant David Floyd watched the Southerners depart: "Officers with drawn swords and pistols threw themselves in front of the retiring crowd, and by every device which physical and mental nature for the moment could invent, they tried to rally and reform the column of men from the broken mass of humanity that was retreating over the Poe field."[20]

Brown's left regiments drove against Connell's breastworks south of the Poe house. After ten minutes of bitter fighting, with the two lines a stone's throw apart, the Tennesseans actually succeeded in breaching the works. However, a severe enfilading fire of canister from Battery C, First Ohio, soon brought the Thirty-second Tennessee to a standstill. The Thirty-second hurriedly withdrew, exposing the flank of the Twenty-third Tennessee, which in turn fell back, followed by the Twenty-sixth Tennessee.[21]

Brown was out in the Poe field, riding about trying to rally his broken brigade, when a spent grapeshot knocked him off his horse. As Clayton struggled to extricate his brigade from Brown's confused ranks and move on into the assault, a spent shot struck him as well. With both commanders temporarily disabled, the two brigades continued to intermingle in the field under a continuous pounding from the Yankee artillery. To compound the problem, Clayton had ordered his men to break into a charge at least two hundred yards east of the field, so that by the time they emerged from the woods most were exhausted. Clayton's attack never really got started, and the two brigades retreated together shortly before 11:30 A.M.[22]

"Fighting Billy" Bate took his brigade into the Poe field at about the same time as Clayton. Lieutenant Cahal, studying the fight from the comparative safety of the woods, said the men went into action deeply troubled by the apparent futility of their task. Certainly that was the feeling of R. M. Gray of the Thirty-seventh Georgia. "We were ordered to carry the enemy's works directly in our front. The position being exceedingly well-fortified and defended by a half dozen batteries did not offer a very inviting prospect to the rank and file nor to any one save Fighting Billy. He knew as well as we and much better that a major general's baton lay in his success, and he would have sacrificed every member of his brigade to attain it," Gray remembered bitterly. "We were lying down behind a hasty breastwork of old logs when he rode up and gave the order 'Forward.' He had his fighting cap on certain. And we arose quickly and leaping the logs advanced at the double quick. Of course we caught it."[23]

Caught it they did as they entered the Poe field for the second time in as many days. "Shot, shell, grape, and minie balls came tearing through our columns by the hatful," averred Gray. Bate had yet another horse shot out from under him. At the forest's edge, Lieutenant Colonel Dudley Frayser ordered his Fifteenth and Thirty-seventh Tennessee from the double-quick into the charge. The Tennesseans raised a cheer and ran into the field. Halfway across, Frayser took a minie ball below his left knee that paralyzed the leg temporarily. Lying among the furrows with "many of my companions wounded and dead around me," conscious but unable to rise, he watched the colors continue forward.

Nearing the road, the Tennesseans came up behind the Sixteenth Alabama, which was still clinging to its hard-won foothold in the field. As the commander of the Sixteenth tells it, the leaderless Tennesseans fired just one volley before turning on their heels and running, less the colors of the Fifteenth Tennessee, which lay beside the body of the color-bearer. An intrepid young Alabama private named J. J. Alexander, so the story goes, scrambled out under a heavy fire to grab the flag, which he later returned to its less than deserving owners.

Meanwhile, the flames of a nearby grassfire had edged dangerously near to where Lieutenant Colonel Frayser lay. Before the flames could claim him, his regiment streamed past. Frayser was helped to his feet and handed the colors of the Thirty-seventh Tennessee, which its young color-bearer had dropped as he fell. Propped up by a couple of soldiers, Frayser hopped off the field with his command.[24]

The retreat of Frayser's Tennesseans might have been less precipitate had the regiment to their right played a more active role in the attack. But Colonel Bushrod Jones elected to stop his Fifty-eighth Alabama at the fringe of the forest rather than risk a charge across the field, which he believed "would have been the extreme of rashness." Jones maintained that his decision stemmed from a lack of support to his right and his inability to locate Bate. Whatever the reason, his troops took cover and engaged the enemy from behind trees while their comrades died out in the Poe field.[25]

Jones was unsupported because the regiments on his right, the Thirty-seventh Georgia and Twentieth Tennessee, were already in the field. Like Wood's Alabamians before them, these Confederates of Bate's brigade were caught in a blistering cross fire from the brigades of King and Turchin as they came into the open. Once again, King's Federals held their fire until the enemy was at virtually point-blank range. At fifty yards they opened up. "Here the smoke from the enemy's guns was so dense I could only see my command at intervals," said Lieutenant Colonel Joseph Smith of the Thirty-seventh Georgia. "On we went filling up the great gaps made in our ranks quickly, reaching the line almost feeling the flash of their pieces in our faces. Blinded, bleeding, almost annihilated, we gave way and got back as quickly as possible to our starting point," Private Gray admitted.[26]

It was about 11:30 A.M. when the last Confederate backed out of the Poe field. A writhing mass of Butternuts overlay the cornfield. Casualties had been staggering. In the Sixteenth Alabama, the last unit to quit the fight, 124 of the 285 who answered muster that morning had fallen. Add to this the 119 lost in the Winfrey field the night before, and the Sixteenth came out of the battle with casualties of 59 percent. Colonel Sam Adams left 149 soldiers of his Thirty-third Alabama lying in the Poe field. In Bate's brigade, losses for the two days amounted to four of the general's horses and 634 of his men, or 57 percent of the total strength. Brown's brigade had been reduced by a third.[27]

The inestimable value of field fortifications of even the crudest sort had been vividly demonstrated. General Reynolds had been able to repel the attacks of Wood, Bate, and Brown without the need to call on his second line. Although just two or three feet high, the log, rail, and stone breastworks in front of Reynolds's line had limited his losses to fewer than two dozen.[28]

Perhaps because so few fell, veterans were able to recall with uncommon clarity those unfortunate soldiers who were hit. In the Thirty-sixth Ohio, one of those struck was a Corporal Wood of Company E. Rather foolishly, Wood "was standing, with his head well above the works, coolly looking for a good shot," when a bullet drilled through his cheek below the left eye and passed out the back of his neck. Wood collapsed, dead. Or so Sergeant John Booth assumed. In a few minutes, Wood came to. Staring down at him was Lieutenant Colonel Devol. "Colonel, I guess they have given it to me this time," Wood said, then got up on his hands and knees and crawled off toward the rear. After a few yards he blacked out. That afternoon, some kindly field musicians found Wood. Placing him in a blanket, they carried the Ohioan nearly two miles before depositing him in an ambulance. Wood survived. Twenty-seven years later, he wrote Sergeant Booth that the "wound, although nearly killing me at the time by the shock, has never caused me any inconvenience."[29]

And then there were those, like Private Elijah Moore of the Seventy-fifth Indiana, whose wounds should not have killed them but did. A "brawny-armed woodchopper," Moore was "crooked, awkward, and slow," an embarrassment on the parade ground who was forever out of step. During the first months of the regiment's existence, the company sergeants had made Moore their special project, drilling him individually for half an hour every day until Moore could no longer stand it. "Captain, I wish you would excuse me from drill, I can't learn — it's all foolishness anyhow. I enlisted to fight," he pleaded.

Moore never did learn. Even in battle he was an oddity. "He always loaded down his pockets with cartridges, because he could not get them out of his cartridge box," remembered Sergeant Floyd. "He loaded his gun in battle with the coolness and style of a squirrel hunter, and in taking aim always raised his piece to his left shoulder. If the other boys had been as slow reloading as he, Stewart's column would undoubtedly have swept over the barricades."

In the heat of the fight, Moore turned and handed Floyd his rifle. "Sergeant, just hold my gun," he asked. Floyd watched him with amazement: "Apparently unconscious of the awful situation, and as if he were about retiring for the night in his peaceful home in Indiana, he deliberately sat down on the logs that were piled up for breastworks and, with his back to the advancing enemy, coolly pulled off his boot and shook out a bullet that had lodged therein." Ten weeks later, Moore was dead from the effects of that wound to his foot.[30]

In one of his rare opportunities to give an order on the field of Chickamauga, General Buckner appeared just as Stewart was reforming his division and forbade him from attempting another attack across the Poe field. That might have been the end of the slaughter on that part of the line, had Cleburne not been intent on continuing the struggle. As Wood's men poured back out of the Poe field, Cleburne waved them to the rear to regroup. In their place, he brought up Deshler's brigade from its position behind Stewart's division to close the gap with Polk's left occasioned by Wood's withdrawal.

A good-natured rivalry existed between the Mississippians of Wood's brigade and Deshler's Texans, who now saw a chance to gain the upper hand on their comrades. "We were moved to the right under fire in this sort of hot haste to fill a gap caused by Wood's Mississippi brigade giving way. This was the outfit that had poked so much fun at us Texas fellows, and the boys seemed to enjoy it as a good joke on the mud-heads," Lieutenant Collins of the Fifteenth Texas Dismounted Cavalry reminisced. But the joke turned sour when the Texans came up against the breastworks of Turchin and Hazen. Wrote Collins: "As we reached the crest of the hill in our front, we struck the same sawyer that had knocked Wood's brigade out at the first round. The rain of lead that the Federals poured into our line was simply terrific. Our loss in officers and men for the first few minutes was alarming in the extreme. . . . We were ordered to lie flat down and hold it."[31]

Like Colonel Lowrey's Mississippians before them, all Deshler and his Texans could do was dig in behind the crest and try to return the Yankee fire. Cleburne was beginning to see the futility of his mission. Finding it "a useless sacrifice of life for Polk to retain his position," he directed the young brigadier to pull his men out from behind the ridge and fall back three hundred yards into the forest to where Wood was reforming. To cover their withdrawal, Cleburne told Deshler to hold on as long as he possibly could.[32]

Deshler hastened along the ridge to inform his regimental commanders of Cleburne's wishes. Colonel Roger Mills, commander of the Sixth, Tenth, and Fifteenth Texas, was laboring to keep his men in the fight. Two Federal batteries were raking his line and already the men were crying out for more ammunition. A little before noon, Mills sent a courier to Deshler to ask how he might resupply. "A few minutes after I saw [Deshler] coming toward my right, some forty paces from me, when he was struck by a shell in the chest and his heart literally torn from his bosom," wrote Mills, who now found himself in command of the brigade. The circumstances could hardly have been less auspicious. In what had become a familiar pattern with Confederate artillery units, Douglas's battery had been unable to get into action in support of the brigade. A messenger from the Twenty-fourth Texas Dismounted Cavalry reported its colonel down, struck in the right leg by a piece of shrapnel. Couriers from other regiments now brought their requests for ammunition to Mills. His own lieutenant colonel told him that his four left companies had not fired a shot because they could not see the enemy. Ordering bayonets fixed, ammunition redistributed, and the cartridge boxes of the dead and wounded to be scavenged, Mills happily turned command over to his lieutenant colonel and then started off with some men to hunt up ammunition.

They returned with a generous supply. While Mills supervised its distribution, a staff officer from division headquarters arrived to remind the Texan that the ridge must be held at all hazards. It was nearly 2:00 P.M. For two and a half hours Mills's Texans had clung to the crest, yet all they had to show for their steadfastness were hundreds of dead and wounded. In the Seventeenth, Eighteenth, Twenty-fourth, Twenty-fifth Texas Dismounted Cavalry alone, two hundred had been hit. Good men were dying for no good reason. The death of one young soldier, a Private William McCann, particularly moved Colonel Mills:

> . . . He stood upright, cheerful, and self-possessed in the very hail of deadly missiles; cheered up his comrades around him and after he had expended all his ammunition, gathered up the cartridge boxes of the dead and wounded and distributed them to his comrades. He bore himself up like a hero through the entire contest, and fell mortally wounded by the last volleys of the enemy. I promised him during the engagement that I would mention his good conduct, and as he was borne dying from the field he turned his boyish face upon me and, with a light and pleasant smile, reminded me of my promise.

Enough was enough, reasoned Mills. Leaving a thin line of sharpshooters along the crest to keep up appearances, he pulled the remainder of the brigade back twenty yards, out of the hail of Federal bullets. The desperate assaults of Cleburne and Stewart at last were over.[33]

Breckinridge was blameless for the failure of his attack against the Federal left. That no supporting line came up to exploit the gains of Adams and Stovall was a consequence of the laxity, acrimony, and incompetence that characterized the direction of the Confederate Right Wing. Polk and Hill must bear responsibility for this sorry state of affairs.

Hill at least understood the vulnerability of Breckinridge and Cleburne as they advanced to the attack. "As soon as the movement began, a staff officer was sent to Polk with a note reminding him that the corps was in single line without reserves, and if broken at one point was broken at all," he reported.

Polk was with Walker, who was moving his reserve corps into position behind Cleburne, when he was handed the reminder from Hill. In response, Polk ordered Walker to continue north until he was within supporting distance of Breckinridge.[34]

Meanwhile, Helm's attack had been repelled and Breckinridge had begun his sweep around the Federal left with the brigades of Stovall and Adams. By his own account, Hill gave formal approval to the Kentuckian's flank attack, yet he failed to grasp the opportunity it presented to roll up the enemy's flank and cut off his lines of retreat to Chattanooga. Instead, Hill became fixated on filling the gap in his lines created by the repulse of Helm.

By the time Polk and Walker arrived at 11:00 A.M., Hill could talk of nothing else. Someone had told him that Brigadier General States Rights Gist had crossed Chickamauga Creek earlier in the morning with his brigade and was then a short distance to Hill's rear. Hill sent a staff officer to bring him forward, intending to use his brigade to take the place of Helm.

Gist had not yet reported when Polk and Walker showed up with the four brigades of the Reserve Corps. Here were troops enough for Hill to both replace Helm and support the attack of Stovall and Adams, yet the thought seems never to have crossed his mind. Indeed, Hill actually complained to Polk and Walker that he had requested only a single brigade, not two divisions. Fine, replied Walker, there was one coming up right behind him. Hill declined Walker's offer; he wanted Gist's brigade, of which he had heard glowing reports, and none other. Incredibly, Polk and Walker acceded to Hill's bizarre request. The three sat and waited for Gist, while a half mile to the west, Adams and Stovall were beginning to lose their foothold in the Union rear.[35]

The gallant and gifted Gist, a graduate of Harvard Law School, rode up at about 11:30. Gist and 980 men of his brigade had arrived at Catoosa Station from Mississippi on the afternoon of the nineteenth. Six companies of the Forty-sixth Georgia were left behind at Rome for want of sufficient railroad cars, and the entire Sixteenth South Carolina was at Kingston, Georgia, awaiting transportation. At Catoosa Station, Gist found orders from Bragg directing him to escort to the army a large ordnance train that was then being assembled at Ringgold. Unfortunately, the train was not ready until 10:00 P.M., so it was sunrise before the brigade reached Alexander's Bridge. After "a most fatiguing march during the entire night," said Gist, the men hardly were in any condition to launch an attack.[36]

But Hill was adamant. He wanted Gist's brigade to continue the assault on Baird's breastworks. Walker protested. Why not allow him to take his

entire corps and attack toward the La Fayette road? Tempers flared. The two
fell into what St. John Liddell called a "miserable dispute" in which Walker
"severely criticized and loudly found fault with the propriety of Hill's plan
of attack." Liddell claims to have tried to play the part of peacemaker—an
unlikely role, given his own explosive temperament. Said Liddell:

> I rode up to General Hill and told him I regretted these disputes. Something
> must be done, and I was ready to obey his orders, no matter what they were.
> Hill, however, walked off toward the skirmish line, apparently angry at
> something said by Walker. Walker saw this and remarked, "This man is
> mad, and in a mad fit will expose himself to sharpshooters and will get
> killed." He then loudly called Hill to come back, apparently much troubled.
> Hill shortly afterwards returned, reserved and tired of discussion.[37]

What of Polk's role in all this? Among those present, only he possessed
the authority to override Hill's proposed piecemeal deployment of Walker's
brigades. Whether he even tried to do so is unclear. Polk's son asserts that
he gave Hill orders to take Walker's entire command and "attack the enemy
to his front," then turned over the operation to Hill while he left to supervise
affairs on Cleburne's front. The younger Polk suggests that Polk intended
Walker's troops to be committed "en masse and at once into the interval
left by the repulse of Helm" in order to "properly support Breckinridge."
If this is true, then Polk also failed to grasp the significance of the turning
movement of Stovall and Adams. And his own actions before he left belie
the spirit of his supposed order to Hill. Concerned about Cleburne, he directed
Walker to detach Walthall's brigade and send it forward in support of Lucius
Polk's brigade. It proved a waste. Walthall lost his way in the thickets and
ran up against Starkweather's breastworks while trying to find the bishop's
nephew. His regiments milled about in confusion for a few minutes before
Walthall yanked them out of range.[38]

Even Polk's limited instructions to Hill caused friction and ultimately
were disregarded by the contentious North Carolinian. Captain William
Carnes, who had attached himself to Polk's staff after losing his battery,
witnessed what probably was Polk's attempt to give Hill his instructions.
Recalled Carnes:

> I had been sent by General Polk with an order to another commander, and
> on returning I found him and General Hill dismounted and sitting on a
> fallen tree. As I approached within a respectful distance I dismounted and
> awaited the end of their conference. At its conclusion General Polk arose
> and said to General Hill that he regretted that General Hill could not agree
> with him, but that he was so well convinced of the correctness of his views
> that he had to insist on compliance with them. With that he turned away
> from General Hill, and as he approached me I heard him say, "That is the
> most pig-headed general officer I have ever had to deal with."[39]

Polk rode away. Walker assigned Gist to command the division containing his own brigade and those of Wilson and Ector, which had been reduced by losses to about five hundred men each. Gist turned his brigade over to its senior colonel, Peyton H. Colquitt of the Forty-sixth Georgia. Colquitt arrayed his demi-brigade with the Twenty-fourth South Carolina on the left, the Eighth Georgia Battalion in the center, and the four companies present from the Forty-sixth Georgia on the right. A few minutes before noon, he led them forward through the same thick forest traversed by Helm's Kentuckians two hours earlier. Seemingly as an afterthought, Hill told Gist to send Wilson and Ector in behind Colquitt to support his advance. Walker seethed. The Georgian foresaw disaster. "My command being thus disposed of, my only occupation was to help form the detached portions of my command as they came out from a position I felt certain they would have to leave when they were sent in."[40]

Colquitt was about to strike a line even stronger than the one that had repelled Helm so handily. General Palmer had helped Grose rally his brigade after the repulse of Stovall and Adams. It now stood behind the breastworks to the left of King, together with the remnants of Dodge's brigade. The presence of Grose allowed King to contract and thus strengthen his front while at the same time boosting the confidence of his shaky Regulars.[41]

Colquitt ran up against the Federal breastworks at about 11:45 A.M. In negotiating the thick forest, his brigade had inclined too far to the right, so that only the Twenty-fourth South Carolina on the left actually fronted the works; the rest of the brigade drifted beyond the angle held by King and was raked by an enfilading fire from an enemy they could not see. Colquitt succeeded in wheeling the Forty-sixth Georgia and Eighth Georgia Battalion to the left so that they were at least able to return the fire.[42]

Meanwhile, the Twenty-fourth South Carolina was being decimated. Its commander, Colonel Clement Stevens, was on the right of the regiment when the Federals opened fire. Lieutenant Colonel Elison Capers, over on the left, looked his way for orders. "Stevens gallops down on his blooded stallion, sword in hand, and rings out 'Change front forward on tenth company, by companies left half wheel.' The command was given as if he was on parade," wrote Capers, who set about to implement it. Together with the regiment's major and the commander of the left company, Capers tried to bring the company into the new line. But Major Palmer was shot dead and the captain fell, badly wounded, leaving Capers to cope by himself. Frightened and confused soldiers began crowding around him. At length, Capers got the two left companies into line in the mossy glade opposite the breastworks. Up came Colonel Stevens with the rest of the brigade. As he neared, a bullet killed his horse. The colonel mounted the dead major's horse, but as he swung into the saddle a minie ball knocked Stevens to the ground, grievously wounded. "My heart sank," Capers recalled. Capers rode among the men to steady them as well as himself. His sword was shot out of his hand. A soldier handed it back to him, and as Capers sheathed it a grapeshot struck it. An instant later a bullet gored his left thigh. Capers dismounted and turned the command over to the senior captain, who also was wounded. In a few minutes, the captain passed out from loss of blood.[43]

Colquitt was alert to the trouble in the Twenty-fourth. He left the Forty-sixth Georgia and dashed down the line to encourage the South Carolinians, but was shot dead the moment he reached their position. That kind of encouragement the South Carolinians did not need, and they broke for the rear, completely unnerved. After twenty-five minutes of one-sided combat, nearly half the regiment had been hit. The rest of the brigade fell back about five minutes later, their withdrawal covered by Ector and Wilson, who maintained a harassing fire from the timber for another ten minutes.[44]

The ruin of Colquitt's brigade at last convinced Hill that Breckinridge had been right to try to outflank the Federals rather than charge them head on. Sadly, his awareness came too late. He decided to send Walker's only remaining brigade, that of Govan, to the support of Colquitt on the Georgian's right, which would have the effect of turning the left flank of the Yankee works.

Govan's brigade had performed poorly the previous afternoon and, in any event, was far too small a force to be of much use. Nevertheless, Hill ordered Govan to try his luck at turning the Federal left. Liddell decided to accompany the Arkansans, and the brigade moved out at noon, with a half mile of forest and fields between it and the La Fayette road.[45]

Govan's route of advance, similar to that followed by Stovall during the morning, took him across the front of the Fifteenth and Forty-ninth Ohio regiments of Willich's brigade, which had remained in the forest beyond Baird's breastworks after taking part in the pursuit of Stovall. As Govan's Confederates entered the open field southeast of the McDonald house, the Ohioans opened on them from the woods along the field's southern fringe. With Liddell's concurrence, Govan wheeled the brigade to the left through the field. The Sixth and Seventh Arkansas Consolidated charged, pursuing the Ohioans through the woods toward the breastworks.[46]

Van Derveer was in the woods to the left of and slightly behind Willich's Ohioans when Govan conducted his wheeling movement. Captain Donahower was busily engaged with a detail from the Second Minnesota in rounding up and disarming some two dozen prisoners from Stovall's Sixtieth North Carolina when he spied Govan's Arkansans nearing his little band. They were only fifty yards away, deployed in two lines. A mounted officer rode between the lines. When he shouted "Ready, Aim," Donahower yelled at his men and the North Carolinians to hit the ground. Several Confederates were hit by the friendly fire, and a few made good their escape amidst the confusion. Donahower, his detail, and the remaining prisoners ran in the opposite direction. As he was retreating through the woods, Donahower noticed the Eighty-seventh Indiana move off on his right to engage the enemy. A few minutes later, while his detail caught their breath in the relative safety of the Kelly field, Donahower saw soldiers from the Eighty-seventh trickle out of the timber, their colonel among them, carrying the national colors.[47]

The brunt of Govan's assault was directed south along the La Fayette road, where John Beatty had been doing everything possible to meet another attack in this sector. When the smoke cleared from the fight with Adams, Beatty had discovered that his last two regiments, the One Hundred Fourth Illinois and Fifteenth Kentucky, had disappeared. He rode around for a time looking for them, but no one knew where they had gone; not until that night did Beatty learn that a division staff officer had ordered the regiments to fall back to the Snodgrass hill to sustain Negley's batteries.

On his ride, Beatty came upon Dick's brigade, which Rosecrans had shunted to the left. Beatty placed Dick behind Stanley's brigade, which was still in the woods on the west side of the road.[48]

As pressing as his duties were, Beatty was too sensitive a man not to be moved by the misery around him:

> A Confederate boy, who should have been at home with his mother, and whose leg had been fearfully torn by a minie ball, hailed me as I was galloping by. . . . He was bleeding to death, and crying bitterly. I gave him my handkerchief, and shouted back to him, as I hurried on, "Bind up the leg tight!"
>
> The adjutant of the rebel General Adams called to me as I passed him. He wanted help, but I could not help him — could not even help our own poor boys who lay bleeding near him.
>
> Sammy Snyder lay on the field wounded; as I handed him my canteen he said, "General. I did my duty." "I know that, Sammy; I never doubted that you would do your duty." The most painful recollection to one who has gone through a battle, is that of the friends lying wounded and dying and who needed help so much when you were utterly powerless to aid them.[49]

Beatty next ran into his adjutant, Captain James Wilson, who was returning from the Snodgrass hill, where he had spoken with Negley. Wilson brought disturbing orders. Negley wanted Beatty and Stanley to withdraw immediately to the Snodgrass hill. The Pennsylvanian had retained Sirwell's brigade there in support of the batteries, and now, with a third of the army crumbling before him out in the Dyer field, he was anxious to reunite the division. Unaware that the Confederates had pierced the Federal center, Beatty chose to disregard the order. He recalled, "Convinced that the withdrawal of the troops at this time from the position occupied would endanger the whole left wing of the army, I thought it best to defer the execution of this order until I could see General Negley and explain to him the necessity of maintaining the line and reenforcing it."

Beatty was interrupted in his search for Negley by the sound of rapid firing coming from the direction of Stanley's brigade. He turned his horse and galloped back up the road.[50]

Stovall's under-strength brigade had looked like a leviathan to the Federals when it burst into the Kelly field. So it was with Govan's tiny command, which overwhelmed Stanley in a matter of minutes. While Stanley's men engaged the Fifth and Thirteenth Arkansas and the First Louisiana to their front, the rest of Govan's line moved to outflank the Yankees on the left. What happened next is anyone's guess. "Being hard pressed I gave the order, after firing a number of rounds, to fall back to the support. Upon looking around however, I found the support had disappeared and we were left to our own resources." So says Stanley. Beatty agreed that Dick's brigade "retired hastily without firing a shot." Dick tells a very different story: "Colonel Stanley's brigade . . . being soon hard pressed, I went to his support, but after firing a short time his line gave way in confusion, and retreated in disorder over my command lying on the ground. This uncovered my line and caused it to become somewhat confused, but having partially recovered, I gave the enemy a galling fire for more than fifteen minutes." So read the reports of officers with reputations to protect.[51]

Regardless of who broke when, Stanley clearly gave a better account of himself than did Dick. He managed to hold his brigade together, and with it fall back in the direction of the Snodgrass hill. Beatty rode at his side. Dick, on the other hand, completely lost control of his brigade, which ceased to exist as a recognizable command. The lieutenant colonel of the Forty-fourth Indiana and a few of his men followed Stanley; the Eighty-sixth Indiana, after having suffered just one killed and thirteen wounded, scattered and was lost for the day; the Fifty-ninth Ohio retreated southwest toward the Dry Valley road and out of the battle after losing just six men; and the Thirteenth Ohio fragmented into squads, a few of which found their way to the Snodgrass hill.[52]

Enough of Dick's panic-stricken soldiers fled into the Kelly field to draw the attention of Colonel Sidney Barnes, who had just reported the Fifty-first Ohio and Eighth Kentucky to General Baird in the northeast corner of the field. His remaining regiments, the Ninety-ninth Ohio and Thirty-fifth Indiana, had gotten lost during the march to the left and were then wandering about in the woods west of the Kelly field.

Baird acted quickly to counter this second threat to his rear. He directed Barnes to face his regiments to attack westward across the field, then ordered

Scribner to face his second line to the rear to provide a covering fire. Other units hastened to help. Willich sent the Thirty-second Indiana and Eighty-ninth Illinois out into the field to support Goodspeed's battery, which was booming away at Govan's Confederates. There Lieutenant Colonel Duncan Hall, commanding the Eighty-ninth, fell, shot through the bowels. His major dismounted and cradled the dying Hall in his arms. Hall whispered his last words: "Tell my parents I died for my flag and my country; tell my regiment to stand by their flag and their country."[53]

Barnes struck the Sixth and Seventh Arkansas as it entered the field. The Arkansans had fallen some three hundred yards behind the rest of the brigade and were now hopelessly isolated. Van Derveer's infantrymen blocked their advance, Goodspeed's cannons frowned at them from their left front, and Barnes's Federals were just twenty yards from their left flank, bayonets fixed and yelling wildly. Not surprisingly, the Arkansans fled; "in great confusion," according to a Federal eyewitness, "throwing away their arms and accoutrements."[54]

Barnes chased them into the woods. The path of his pursuit cut directly across the rear of Govan's remaining regiments, which were still pushing south. Their capture appeared imminent. Govan was uncertain how to proceed. Only the quick thinking of Lieutenant Colonel John Murray, commanding the Fifth and Thirteenth Arkansas on the right of the line, saved the brigade. "As I had the enemy in my front so badly whipped as to render it improbable that they would attempt to follow me, I proposed to turn upon the enemy in rear, but finding that the men were opposed to this, and somewhat demoralized on account of the enemy's being behind them, and thinking if I attempted to cut my way through I might be fired upon, after cutting through the enemy, by our friends, I concluded it was best to move by the right flank and endeavor to get out in that way." Murray offered his suggestion to the other regimental commanders, who agreed to follow him. Together they moved their commands west into the expansive fields of the Mullis farm, where they chanced upon a scout from Forrest's cavalry, who offered to guide them into friendly lines. For ninety minutes the Arkansans and Louisianians tramped over unknown fields and through obscure forests until, at 2:00 P.M., they heard the welcome challenges of friendly pickets.[55]

CHAPTER TWENTY

GENTLEMEN, I HOLD THE FATAL
ORDER OF THE DAY

ROSECRANS was thoroughly committed to the salvation of his imperiled left. To the second of Thomas's two aides, who reached him at about 10:15 A.M., Rosecrans promised to send Van Cleve immediately to the Kelly field. Since the departure of Van Cleve would leave him without a reserve for either the center or right, Rosecrans decided to draw in his right even more; in other words, to shift that part of the army to the north. To forestall further calls for help from Thomas, Rosecrans concluded to transfer two brigades from Sheridan's division to the left as well, with the third to follow as soon as McCook was able to draw in his lines, which would then consist only of Wood's division, Davis's two weakened brigades and Wilder's mounted infantry. Once all this was accomplished, Rosecrans's line of battle would terminate in front and slightly to the left of the Widow Glenn house. An unavoidable gap of nearly two miles would exist between the right of the army and the hospital at Crawfish Springs, which for the time being was screened by Edward McCook's cavalry brigade. A mile further to the south, Long's cavalry brigade kept up its vigil at the fords near Glass's Mill.

Rosecrans may have had a clear understanding of what he expected to come out of all this, but he did a poor job of communicating his intentions to his staff. There were far too many orders for Garfield to write all of them himself, so Major Frank Bond, the senior aide-de-camp, was enlisted to help. The former railroad executive was loyal and capable, but his primary responsibility since joining the army staff had been the keeping of its ciphers. Bond had little experience in preparing orders and lacked the intuitive understanding of the nuances of Rosecrans's often poorly phrased oral instructions that Garfield possessed. Garfield was too busy to supervise Bond; even he was having a hard time making clear Rosecrans's intent. Rosecrans expected too much to happen in too short a time, and the resultant written orders issued between 10:30 A.M. and 10:45 A.M. were cloudy, complicated, and even contradictory.[1]

The first went to McCook at 10:30 A.M. The product of Garfield's pen, it read: "The general commanding directs you to send two brigades, General Sheridan's division, at once and with all dispatch to support General Thomas, and send the third brigade as soon as the line can be drawn up sufficiently. March them as rapidly as you can without exhausting the men. Report to these headquarters as soon as your orders are given in regard to Sheridan's movement." Rosecrans evidently intended to explain to McCook in person precisely where the brigades were to go.[2]

McCook received the order at 10:55 A.M. and obeyed it without question. He sent word to Wilder, who was then about four hundred yards south of Sheridan on the west side of the Dry Valley road, to "close up on his right, and keep the line connected, and occupy the ground left by him, as he was going to move to the left." Wilder started for the Glenn field at once.[3]

Sheridan was at the Widow Glenn house talking with Lytle when McCook's chief of staff, Gates Thruston, galloped up a little after 11:00 A.M. with the order for him to start for the left. Sheridan had just come from Laiboldt, having posted him on the open east slope of the rise now known as Lytle Hill behind Davis in column of regiments to protect the right flank of his decimated division, and was about to accompany his poet brigadier on an inspection of his lines. The Irishman was incredulous. Thruston repeated the order: He was to move Lytle and Walworth to Thomas's support at once; speed was of the essence. Sheridan nodded and, turning to Lytle, told him to get his brigade out onto the Glenn-Kelly road. Lytle looked crestfallen; it was hard to abandon a position as naturally strong as the Widow Glenn hill. The Ohioan set his command in motion and in a few minutes led it down the hill in route column. Walworth started his brigade at the same time. Their route of march would take them past Laiboldt and along the road directly behind Davis.[4]

Lytle had another reason to regret leaving the Widow Glenn hill, one that had nothing to do with mundane considerations of tactics or position. When he marched off the hill, the Ohioan seemed to know that he was marching to his death.

At least that is the impression Lieutenant Pirtle got. Earlier that morning, after finishing breakfast, Lytle had spread out a piece of canvas beneath a tree and sat down on it to rest. His cold had gotten worse. As exhausted as he was, Lytle could not nap. He called Pirtle over to his side. As Pirtle sat down, Lytle put his arm around him and asked, in a quiet, fatherly way: "My boy, do you know we are going to fight two to one today?" Pirtle was shaken. Lytle explained further. Longstreet had joined Bragg with a huge force, so that the Army of the Cumberland would be fighting at a tremendous disadvantage. Never before had Lytle seemed so troubled on the eve of battle. He made Pirtle promise to "stick to him to the last." Pirtle gave his word, and Lytle lapsed into silent reverie.

Doubts were teasing Rosecrans's tired mind as he dictated the orders that were to put nearly half his army in motion. Should he really be stripping his center and right in the face of the enemy? Five minutes after instructing McCook to send away Sheridan, he had Bond write this oddly inconsistent admonition to Thomas: "The general commanding directs me to say, if possible, refuse your left, sending in your reserves to the northward, as he would prefer having Crittenden and McCook on your right." And to Granger went a simple query that revealed the depth of his uncertainty: "Is Missionary Ridge available, supposing we should fall back?"[5]

Garfield wrote out the movement orders for Van Cleve at 10:45 A.M. They were addressed to Crittenden. A few minutes earlier, the Kentuckian had begged Rosecrans to allow him to accompany Van Cleve into battle. Rosecrans assented, and Crittenden rode out into the Dyer field with the only division of his corps left to him.

Reading Garfield's dispatch a few minutes before 11:00 A.M., Crittenden realized that he was fated to go through another day of battle without a command. As he had the day before, the Kentuckian now looked about for ways to make himself useful. A message from Wood provided an opportunity. In bringing forward the Sixth Ohio and Eighth Indiana batteries, Wood had found the forest in which his line of battle was formed too dense for artillery to be of much use; better to leave his remaining battery, the Third Wisconsin, out in the Dyer field, advised Wood.

Scanning the field for an effective firing position, Crittenden's gaze settled on a four-hundred-yard-long open ridge that rose abruptly out of the western limit of the Dyer field. The ridge offered clear fields of fire east as far as the Brotherton woods and south to the Dyer road, which would allow the artillery to cover a retreat, should the infantry be forced from its breastworks. From the crest of the ridge, cannoneers could also range their pieces into the woods east of the La Fayette road.

Crittenden ordered Major Mendenhall to gather all the artillery he could find. Mendenhall started the Third Wisconsin toward the ridge, then rode to the commanders of Van Cleve's batteries, the Twenty-sixth Pennsylvania and Seventh Indiana, with the same instructions.[6]

Captain Sanford C. Kellogg was a man with a mission. As aide-de-camp and nephew of General Thomas, he was both duty bound and personally committed to seeing that the general's wishes were fulfilled. And at the moment, what Thomas most desired was reinforcements; specifically, John Brannan and his division.

When Thomas sent Kellogg galloping for Brannan at about 10:15, Van Derveer had not yet arrived in the Kelly field nor, apparently, had Thomas heard from the staff officer he had earlier sent directly to Brannan. Thomas and Kellogg were still under the impression that Brannan was somewhere in the vicinity of Horseshoe Ridge or the Dyer field, a mobile reserve, not to be "put in line of battle at the opening of the battle, and to be held subject to Thomas' call whenever he might want him," as General Reynolds later explained it. This had been the agreement the night before at the Widow Glenn house.[7]

Reynolds was on horseback behind his breastworks when Brannan came to him a second time for advice. "I am again ordered to the left with my command," he announced. "Do you think you can maintain your position without me? Kellogg is here and says the call is urgent."

It was then quiet on Reynolds's front. "Well, perhaps Thomas needs you more than I do, and I believe I can hold my own here. So go along and good luck to you," replied Reynolds.

Brannan left and Kellogg rode up. Brannan was not to have been in line in the first place, but was to have been held in reserve for Thomas, Kellogg offered by way of explanation for ordering him away. Reynolds understood. In defense of Brannan, Reynolds told the captain that Brannan had come forward to fill a gap that had existed on his (Reynolds's) right; it was a move Reynolds said he had endorsed wholeheartedly.

With Brannan about to leave, Reynolds was again concerned for his right. He was unaware that Wood had replaced Negley and thus assumed his flank to be exposed. Reynolds shared his fears with the captain:

> I explained to Kellogg that my right flank had been in the air during all the previous day's fighting and although I believed I could maintain myself there after Brannan should go to the left; still I would like for him to say to the people up there, meaning of course Thomas or Rosecrans, that my right flank was entirely exposed, and although I felt as above stated, if they had any troops lying around loose and would be kind enough to send them my way I would welcome them and probably be able to give them a job. I had not then the least idea of the actual condition of affairs "up there." I am very glad indeed that I did not know the actual state of affairs on the right of our army about, or not long after, that time.[8]

As Kellogg rode off, Reynolds noticed, "with some satisfaction I freely confess, that Brannan had not moved out hastily from my right." Apparently Brannan was having second thoughts about pulling out of the line. According to Colonel Connell, Brannan issued movement orders to the brigade commanders, only to countermand them moments later.[9]

After noticing that Brannan had not left, Reynolds claimed to have "paid no further attention to him, except to turn over in my own mind how, most prudently, to throw back my right after he had gone and occupy with the range of my fire, as best I could, the space no longer covered by his command." Colonel Connell, however, later insisted that Reynolds's adjutant, speaking on the general's behalf, implored him to stay where he was. Regardless of who made the decision to disobey Kellogg, the bottom line is that Brannan remained on Reynolds's right.[10]

Kellogg found Rosecrans shortly after 10:30 A.M. Conditions were ripe for a misunderstanding. The captain, excited and anxious to accomplish his mission quickly, probably did not waste his breath on lengthy explanations. Rosecrans, exhausted and preoccupied with the risky movement to the left he was trying to orchestrate, probably gave Kellogg only his partial attention and asked few if any questions. Garfield, who might have been able to clarify the situation, was busy writing the movement orders for Sheridan and Van Cleve.

"Thomas is heavily pressed," Kellogg blurted out breathlessly. What precisely he said after this is uncertain, but it seems to have run something like this: Thomas had requested Brannan, who already was moving out of line to comply, leaving Reynolds's right flank was exposed. Could Thomas have Brannan?[11]

"Tell General Thomas our line is closing towards him and to hold his ground at all hazards, and I will reinforce him with the entire army if necessary. Tell General Brannan to obey General Thomas's orders," Rosecrans said to Kellogg. He looked to Garfield.[12] The Ohioan was still busy writing orders. Turning to Major Bond, Rosecrans said: "If Brannan goes out, Wood must fill his place. Write him that the commanding general directs him to close to the left on Reynolds and support him."[13]

What Bond wrote was this:

Headquarters Department of the Cumberland
September 20 — 10:45 A.M.
Brigadier-General Wood, Commanding Division:
The general commanding directs that you close up on Reynolds as fast as possible, and support him.
Respectfully, etc.

Frank S. Bond, Major and Aide-de-Camp[14]

Bond marked the order "Gallop" to emphasize its urgency.

Rosecrans neglected to read the order — if he had he certainly would have rendered it conditional upon Brannan's having left the line — but merely gave it to Lieutenant Colonel Starling, who happened to be present, and asked him to deliver it. Rosecrans told Starling that the written order directed Wood to "close to the *left* on Reynolds and support him." Crittenden was there too. He had not yet ridden off to join Van Cleve, so there was no need to route the order through him.[15]

Starling hesitated. "There was no firing, and no evident need of support for any one," he later testified. Garfield, who had finished writing the order to Van Cleve and rejoined the party, told Starling that "the object of the order was that General Wood should occupy the vacancy made by the removal of Brannan's division, Brannan having been ordered to General Thomas's left." Starling saluted and galloped off the knoll a few minutes before 11:00 A.M.[16]

Crouched behind their breastworks, the soldiers of Wood's division peered anxiously across the Brotherton field into the forest beyond, waiting for the Rebels to appear. "We well knew that the enemy was immediately in our front ready to take advantage of any false step that we might make," recalled Colonel Harker.[17] A foolhardy Illinois colonel had confirmed their presence, in strength, beyond any doubt.

Frederick Bartleson was a hard fighter with more courage than common sense. As the men of his One Hundredth Illinois Infantry settled in behind the breastworks they had inherited from Negley a little after 9:30 A.M., Colonel Bartleson glimpsed a row of Confederate skirmishers hiding behind the fence along the La Fayette road, near the Brotherton house. Pausing neither for permission nor to think the situation through, Bartleson ordered a charge. Over the breastworks and into the Brotherton field ran the Illinoisans, while Colonel Buell and the other officers of the brigade looked on in stunned silence. The Rebel skirmishers scattered into the forest. Bartleson, out in front on horseback, and his 230 men went in after them. The Illinoisans made it another hundred yards before running into what must have seemed like half the Confederate Army. A masked battery, camouflaged in the underbrush, raked their ranks with canister. Rifle volleys blazed from their front and on both flanks. The regiment dispersed. Most turned and ran until they were safely behind the breastworks, but Bartleson managed to hold onto a few poor souls for a pointless stand behind the picket fence bordering the Brotherton house. The Southern skirmishers, reinforced by the remainder of their regiment, counterattacked. Bartleson fell, badly wounded, and his little company broke up. A couple of his men paused long enough to drag the colonel into the house, where they dropped him. The Confederate skirmishers stopped at the fence along the road, and all was as it had been, save a few score more dead and wounded Federals.[18]

Bartleson had run dead center into Longstreet's massed column. The skirmishers he chased belonged to the Forty-fourth Tennessee of Fulton's brigade; the masked artillery that put an abrupt halt to his charge was Everett's Georgia Battery, supported by Culpeper's South Carolina Battery.[19]

Once he overcame his astonishment at Bartleson's stupidity, Buell ordered the Twenty-sixth Ohio forward to Brotherton Ridge to cover him. When the Illinoisans returned, Buell left four companies of the Twenty-sixth on the ridge, and from that moment on his line was animated by the rattle of skirmish fire.[20]

The clatter from the skirmish line greeted Lieutenant Colonel Lyne Starling as he approached the rear of Wood's low breastworks. He found the Kentuckian standing beside a tree behind Buell's brigade. General McCook was with him. Starling leaned over in the saddle and handed Wood the order. It was 11:00 A.M. While Wood read the order, Starling began to explain its intent. Wood interrupted. Brannan was in position, he said, there was no vacancy between Reynolds's division and his own. "Then there is no order," retorted Starling.[21]

There the matter should have ended.

And with anyone but Tom Wood, it most assuredly would have. Rosecrans had upbraided Wood twice for failing to obey orders promptly. First there had been the abortive reconnaissance of Lookout Mountain and the written reprimand sent over the telegraph for all to see. Then there was the dressing down just ninety minutes earlier in front of Wood's entire staff. The barbs of Rosecrans's invective pained the Kentuckian. Anger clouded his reason. No, he told Starling, the order was quite imperative, he would move at once.

Starling was dumbfounded. Could Wood at least wait ten minutes while he relayed the general's concerns to Rosecrans? No, he intended to move. Brannan indeed was in place, but to Wood the meaning of the order "was clear and undoubted. It clearly told me I was to withdraw my division from the line, and passing northward and eastward immediately in rear of the line of battle, to find General Reynolds's position, to close upon him and support him." Remarking that he "was glad the order was in writing, as it was a good thing to have for future reference," Wood carefully placed the order in his pocket notebook. Before he did, some say he waved it before his staff with the words: "Gentlemen, I hold the fatal order of the day in my hand and would not part with it for five thousand dollars."[22]

Whether Wood actually uttered those words is irrelevant. That they accurately reflect his sentiments there can be no doubt. After Starling left to tell Rosecrans of Wood's plan to quit the line, Wood asked McCook to fill the gap in the line that would result when he pulled out, which he intended to do immediately. Wood forever maintained that McCook promised to do so, but the Ohioan just as strongly denied it. "There was not only no time to fill the space, but I had no troops to fill it with, unless a small brigade could cover a division interval," McCook later wrote. To his credit, McCook tried to close as much of the interval as he could. Leaving

"Gentlemen, I hold the fatal order of the day." General Wood
brandishes the order to pull out of the line.

Wood, he galloped off to order Davis to bring Martin's tiny brigade into the breastworks on Carlin's left the instant Buell abandoned them.[23]

The debate over the propriety of Wood's action raged until the last of the parties to the affair were dead, and interest in it continues unabated to this day. Opinions among participants in the battle varied widely, often according to their loyalties. Chaplain Thomas Van Horne, biographer and confidant of Thomas, absolved Wood of blame, writing: "The fact that this order was not sent through Crittenden, the corps commander, emphasized the requirement to make the movement as fast as possible."[24] (Van Horne overlooked the fact that Crittenden was with Rosecrans at the time.) Henry Cist, an admirer of Rosecrans, held a very different view:

If Reynolds's division was posted on the left of Brannan's division, then there was no gap, and no place for Wood to place his division as ordered, and he knew it. He could support Reynolds, but to do this he was compelled to disobey the first part of the order, which in its spirit and intent was to keep him on the line of battle, simply moving his division to the left. No wonder he wanted to keep his order safe where he could produce it if occasion required. Wood, irritated at the reprimand of Rosecrans earlier in the day, intent on maintaining his dignity, chose ... to undertake to carry out an order in the execution of which he felt safe, so long as he had it in writing.[25]

John Turchin expressed essentially the same argument as Cist, albeit dispassionately. Dissecting the order, he found it internally inconsistent from the strict standpoint of military parlance, which made it imperative that Wood seek clarification before acting. Said Turchin:

The way things stood at the time, the order contradicted itself. The first part of it meant for General Wood to move his division to the left in the line and join Reynolds, and the second meant to move it out of the line and place it in the rear of Reynolds. According to the phraseology accepted in military language the order had no sense; one part of it was contradicting the other part. Why then not to ascertain the meaning of it from the person who wrote the order before moving? The idea of implicitly obeying orders by such officers as commanders of divisions, without reasoning about them, is absurd.[26]

When all the venom is skimmed away, the facts of the situation can be distilled rather easily. Rosecrans erred in not checking the written order to see that it expressed his intent. He was tired and it showed. Wood let petty bitterness get the better of him. The order was an impossible one. Reynolds's front was quiet, while Wood's was alive with skirmish fire. Wood unquestionably should have held his position until he was able to clarify the order. A true professional would have considered another reprimand a small price to pay where so much was at stake.

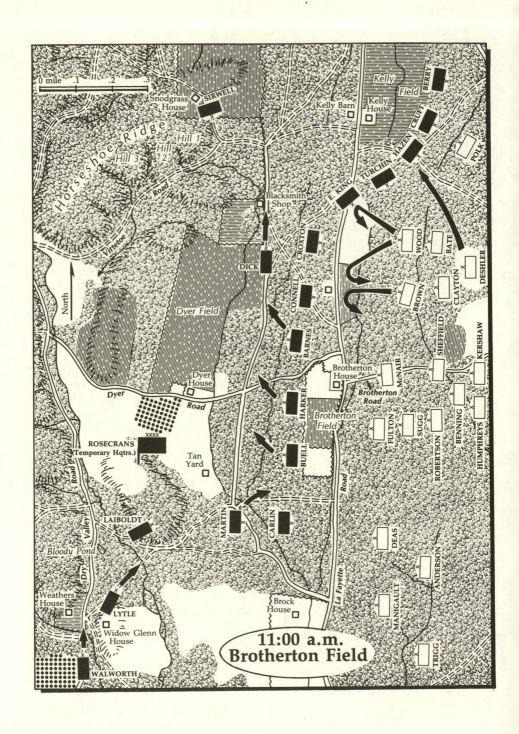

0 mile   .1   .2   .3

Snodgrass
House
SIRWELL

Kelly
Field
Kelly Barn
Kelly
House
BERRY
CRUFT
POLK

Horseshoe Ridge

Hill 1
Hill 3   Hill 2

Road

HAZEN

Vitteloe

TURCHIN

E. KING

WOOD
BATE
DESHLER

Blacksmith
Shop

CROXTON

BROWN
CLAYTON

North

DICK

CONNELL

Dyer Field

BARNES

KERSHAW

SHEFFIELD

Brotherton
House
McNAIR

Dyer
House

Dyer

HARKER

*Brotherton
Road*

Road

FULTON

SUGG

*Brotherton
Field*

BENNING

HUMPHREYS

ROSECRANS
(Temporary Hqtrs.)

XXXX

BUELL

ROBERTSON

Tan
Yard

Road

MARTI

DEAS

LAIBOLDT

CARLI

La Fayette

ANDERSON

Bloody Pond

Dry Valley

MANIGAULT

Weathers
House

Brock
House

LYTLE

Widow Glenn
House

TRIGG

**11:00 a.m.
Brotherton Field**

WALWORTH

Just six hundred yards separated Rosecrans from Wood—a five-minute ride at most—but it may as well have been six hundred miles. Wood had no intention of going to Rosecrans to confirm the order. Instead, he sent staff officers to tell Barnes, Harker, and Buell to move at once.[27]

Barnes faced his command about, marched out of the woods, and started up the Glenn-Kelly road. Harker shrugged and did the same. Only Buell balked. "Tell the general that my skirmishers are actively engaged, and I cannot safely make the move," he told Wood's messenger. "The enemy was making bold demonstrations in my front, so much so that whenever one of my skirmishers moved or rose to his feet he was shot at. . . . I was fearful of making the movement, with the enemy not over two hundred yards distant, closing watching every maneuver," Buell explained in his report. Major Charles Hammond, who had succeeded Colonel Bartleson in command of the One Hundredth Illinois, was more emphatic. He told Buell he would face a court-martial before he would obey such a ludicrous command.

The messenger returned. The order to move was imperative. Buell calmed Hammond, ordered his skirmishers to hold on until relieved, and then reluctantly pulled his troops out from behind their breastworks.[28]

ALL WAS A SICKENING CONFUSION

GENERAL Longstreet had grown impatient with delay. Although Breckinridge's attack had begun before the Left Wing was in position, Longstreet and his subordinates had spent the morning readying their units for battle with a diligence that their colleagues on the Right Wing would have done well to emulate. Kershaw arrived with his and Humphreys's brigade at 10:00 A.M. They took their place as the fifth and final line of Longstreet's massed column.

For the next sixty minutes, nearly eleven thousand Confederates waited in the deep woods east of the Brotherton farm for the order to advance. To recapitulate, Longstreet had eight brigades packed into just under seventy acres of forest. The first line lay six hundred yards east of the La Fayette road and was composed, from left to right, of the Seventh Texas Infantry, First Tennessee Battalion, and Fiftieth Tennessee Infantry of Gregg's brigade (the latter two units having been consolidated due to their severe losses the day before), Fulton's Tennessee brigade, and McNair's brigade. They occupied a front of five hundred yards, approximately the width of the Brotherton field. Colonel Cyrus Sugg formed the second line with the remaining regiments of Gregg's brigade. As commander of this provisional division, Bushrod Johnson would be responsible for the early stages of the attack.

Robertson's Texas brigade and Sheffield's Alabama brigade comprised the third line, Benning's Georgians the fourth. General Law retained command of the division. The brigades of Kershaw and Humphreys made up the fifth line.

It was now 11:00 A.M. Wood was reading the order from Rosecrans. A half mile to the east, Longstreet was awaiting the return of the messenger he had sent to Bragg requesting permission to begin his attack. Major Pollock Lee had just ordered Stewart forward at Bragg's behest and was on his way to Hood to deliver the same message.

The sound of rapid firing from the direction of the Poe field startled Longstreet. He was unable to divine its meaning until someone told him that Major Lee was giving orders directly to his division commanders. Longstreet sent his own staff officers to Hood and Johnson. They arrived before Lee, allowing Longstreet the dignity of ordering his wing into action himself. At 11:10 A.M., he gave the command to advance.[1]

Through the forest tramped Fulton's and McNair's Confederates, bowing their heads before an annoying fire from Buell's skirmishers, who were still out in the Brotherton field waiting for somebody to relieve them. Raising the Rebel yell at the edge of the timber, the Southerners swept across the La Fayette road and into the field. Federal skirmishers dropped by the dozen. Those not hit surrendered or took their chances and made for the breastworks.

Johnson's division sheered as it struck the Brotherton farmhouse and barn. A zigzag rail fence that ran from the barn to the woods on the west side of the field cut the Rebel line in two. McNair passed north of the house, driving west along both sides of the Dyer road. Fulton swarmed around and south of the house. Peeking inside, a squad from the Twenty-fifth Tennessee found the wounded Colonel Bartleson and several of his officers. Its commander, Colonel Snowden, was delighted. From the hapless Illinoisans, Snowden was able to supply himself and his officers with new swords, belts, and pistols.[2]

In the timber west of the field, Colonel Martin was frantically beckoning his regiments into line behind Buell's abandoned breastworks. He was too late. Scarcely had the men of the Eighth Kansas come into line when from the weeds to their front arose the Seventeenth Tennessee. Two or three volleys were enough to send the Kansans reeling from the breastworks. On their right, the pitiful remnant of the Fifteenth Wisconsin faced off against the equally decimated Fiftieth Tennessee and First Tennessee Battalion. For a moment the contest was equal. Then the Seventeenth Tennessee worked its way onto the Federals' flank. Lieutenant Colonel Ole Johnson fell in the cross fire, and the ninety-odd soldiers still standing in the Fifteenth dispersed. When Deas's brigade joined the attack on Bushrod Johnson's left a few minutes later, Martin's remaining regiment, the Twenty-fifth Illinois, crumbled and the rout was complete. General Davis held Martin and his men blameless. Speaking of both his brigades, the Hoosier reported: "The sudden withdrawal of troops from my left and the absence of any support on my right made my position little better than an outpost and perfectly untenable against the overwhelming force coming against it. Nothing but precipitate flight could save my command from annihilation or capture."[3]

Only Martin's brigade, opposite his left flank, had stood between Fulton and the Brotherton woods. Now his Tennesseans leapt over the empty breastworks and headed into the woods, pausing just long enough to rifle the cartridge boxes of dead Yankees for extra rounds. Only twenty minutes after stepping off from their line of departure, Fulton's men were on the edge of the Dyer field, with nothing but stubble and sedge standing between them and the Yankee rear.[4]

McNair's men found the going a little tougher when they entered the woods. There they ran into the right flank of Buell's moving column. The Federals had hardly gotten started. "Before I had marched a regimental front, stray shots came whistling through the trees," recalled Lieutenant Colonel Young of the Twenty-sixth Ohio, whose regiment was struck first. Young galloped to the left side of his regiment, hoping to face it about to meet the Rebels. Before he could issue an order his men broke, carrying him with them some seventy-five yards back into the Dyer field. With its morale already shattered, the One Hundredth Illinois disintegrated in the wink of an eye. In fact, admitted Buell, "my little brigade seemed as if it were swept from the field." Riding at the head of his column, Buell was cut off from most of the brigade and borne away in the tide of stunned soldiers. He even lost his brigade headquarters flag, which was captured along with the orderly who carried it. Buell managed to extricate himself from the panicked mass in the Dyer field. There he rode about for a few minutes, trying to rally what was left of his brigade. Only the Fifty-eighth Indiana and a few stragglers from other commands answered his plea. With these, he fell back toward the ridge from which Mendenhall's batteries already were booming.[5]

Although beyond Buell's reach, the Thirteenth Michigan was putting up a good fight. Being out in the Dyer field on the left of the brigade column when the Confederates struck, the Michiganders had had a few extra moments to absorb the shock. The instant the Twenty-sixth Ohio broke, Major Willard Eaton ordered his men to lie down in the field. As soon as the Ohioans cleared his ranks, Eaton opened with a volley that brought McNair's Rebels to an abrupt halt at the wood line. Fired by his success, Eaton ordered a charge. His impetuosity paid off. "We charged them with the bayonet, and ran them back into the woods, from where we soon drove them," recorded the regimental historian proudly. Meanwhile, Lieutenant Colonel Young had used the time bought by the Thirteenth to rally his own regiment. He started after the Michiganders. A volley from Fulton's Tennesseans cut through his right companies. That was enough for Young. Facing his men about, he withdrew them across the Dyer field toward Mendenhall's batteries, which were fast becoming a magnet for fleeing Federals.[6]

The Thirteenth Michigan plunged into the Rebel column and chased McNair all the way back to the Brotherton field. There McNair bumped into Colonel Sugg, who offered to pass through his brigade and take up the attack. McNair agreed, and Sugg led his four reserve regiments forward.

The Michiganders' luck ran out. "We had learned something in battle experience; so we fell flat to the ground until the Yankees emptied their guns, when we rose up and with the Rebel yell, in which the brigade had become proficient, we charged the breastworks and drove the enemy pell-mell through the woods," recalled one of Sugg's Tennesseans.[7]

As Bushrod Johnson drove due west toward the Dyer field, General Hood brought his own division forward to extend the Ohioan's right and silence the troublesome enfilading fire from Connell's Federals. Hood's decision was a tactical necessity, but it did contravene the plan of battle, which called for a general wheel to the left, or south.

Sheffield's brigade led the way, trailed by Benning's Georgians and the Texas Brigade. As they crossed the La Fayette road south of the Poe field, the Alabamians kicked up a cloud of dust that completely screened their movements from Connell's nervous Federals, who from the beginning had had little inclination to resist.

When Buell forsook the breastworks to his right, Connell, though he knew himself doomed, went through the motions of defending his position. He sent his adjutant to warn Brannan of the danger, then threw out several companies from the Eighty-second Indiana to the south to watch for the enemy's approach, "where I knew it would be sure to come." Connell ordered his right flank regiment, the Seventeenth Ohio, to change front to the south as well, but it was too late. Sheffield caught the Ohioans on the move, and before his Alabamians were seventy-five yards from the breast-works, the Seventeenth broke apart.[8]

Captain Josiah Church rammed double-shotted canister into the six guns of his Battery D, First Michigan Light Artillery, and blasted the Confederates, who had closed to less than fifty yards. The slaughter was terrific, but the Alabamians came on. The Thirty-first Ohio panicked and ran, leaving the Michigan cannoneers unsupported. Captain Church made a gallant attempt at saving his battery. (Battery commanders had to think fast at Chickamauga to survive.) He ordered one section to hold its ground and cover the withdrawal of the rest of the battery. Cannoneers dragged the four pieces fifty yards through the weeds and vines. There the limbers joined them, and the Michiganders rushed to affix the guns as the Alabamians swarmed over the breastworks and around the two guns left behind. They took aim at the horses and opened fire. The chilling screams of animals in agony split the air, and six horses fell dead in the harness, dragging down their limber with them. Enough survived from the other teams to enable Church to haul away three guns. With these, he headed across the Dyer field to join Mendenhall.[9]

Connell scrambled to restore his line. He ordered the remaining companies of the Eighty-second Indiana to retake the breastworks. Colonel Morton

Hunter waited until his front was clear, then ordered his men to stand up and fire. The Rebels backed away from the breastworks, and Hunter called for a charge. By the time the Indianians reached the works, the enemy was nowhere to be seen. Neither was "a single man in the Union army, outside of the Eighty Second Indiana," remembered Hunter. When Sheffield's men realized they were not being pursued, they reformed and counterattacked. Hunter ordered his regiment to fall back firing.

Not all the Yankees were anxious to leave the breastworks. Lieutenant Jacob Ruffner, the acting brigade provost marshal, stood behind the breastworks in plain view of the enemy, holding the colors of the Eighty-second in one hand and coolly squeezing off shots from his revolver with the other, until a bullet in the neck sent him spinning to the ground.[10]

Sam Beatty's men were lying along the edge of the forest just behind Connell's brigade, waiting to take their turn on the Glenn-Kelly road, when that command folded. Pandemonium ensued. "Had a sufficient space intervened, a stand could have been promptly made, but under the circumstances it was impossible to do anything," lamented Colonel Frederick Knefler of the Seventy-ninth Indiana, who saw his men trampled by Connell's Ohioans. "The enemy in overwhelming numbers were advancing and firing rapidly, and at the same time turning our right. Our retreating forces in our front were running over us; we were between the enemy and open ground, while they were concealed by a dense cover of underbrush," reported Colonel Alexander Stout of the Seventeenth Kentucky. Just as Stout tried to change front to meet the enemy, Estep's Eighth Indiana Battery came crashing through his lines, crushing several of his men and scattering most of the rest. Stout could do nothing: "The uproar was so great, and the dust and smoke so dense, that the officers could scarcely be seen or heard." His lieutenant colonel collapsed with a shattered knee, then his sergeant major fell, shot through both legs. With the major, adjutant, the colors, and about one hundred men, Stout started for the Snodgrass hill. Sam Beatty, meanwhile, had been separated from his brigade and carried off the field in the panic.[11]

General Crittenden was on horseback out in the Dyer field, midway between the ridge and Beatty's brigade, when the breakthrough came. "Looking at the artillery which Major Mendenhall had just put in position, and not knowing exactly what to do with it under my last order [i.e., to move Van Cleve north], my difficulty was suddenly removed by the enemy. . . . Upon turning from the batteries and looking at the troops I was astounded to see them suddenly and unaccountably thrown into great confusion." Suddenly the mob was surging all around him. Crittenden forced his horse through the throng and spurred it up the ridge, hoping to gather the infantry around his cannons. Van Cleve was also in the Dyer field. The old general was crying again. No one was listening to him. His aide was captured less than twenty yards from his side. Van Cleve gave up and let himself be carried away with the tide of defeat. "All was a sickening confusion," he mourned.[12]

General Brannan, at least, was keeping a grip on himself and the little that remained of his division. As Connell broke to the rear, pursued by Sheffield, Brannan ordered Croxton to pull in his right flank and change front to face south. For good measure, he sent a staff officer to the Snodgrass hill to ask Negley to have his batteries ready to cover his withdrawal in that direction, should the need arise.

The "gallant and dashing" Croxton, as Brannan called the young Kentuckian, responded well to the crisis. Under the cover of Lieutenant Marco Gary's Battery C, First Ohio Light Artillery, which threw shell and spherical case into the right flank of the Confederates, Croxton shepherded his brigade into line. The Tenth Kentucky filed to the right and advanced from its position in reserve to the right side of the Gary's battery. The Tenth Indiana and Seventy-fourth Indiana regiments, which only twenty minutes earlier had repelled the attack of Brown's Tennesseans across the Poe field, came up on the left of the battery. Brannan now at least had his troops facing the right direction.[13]

Sheffield's Alabamians paid no attention to Croxton but headed due west for the Dyer field. Benning's Georgians, who trailed Sheffield, likewise ignored Croxton until Gary's cannoneers got their attention with a blast to their right flank.

"Old Rock" Benning wheeled his brigade to the right. Two hundred to three hundred yards separated the two sides. Benning formed a single line of battle in the timber along the southern edge of the Poe field, west of the road, and accepted Croxton's challenge a few minutes after noon.[14]

The Kentuckian was ready for him. "A volcano of fire burst out in our front and a hail of grape shot and bullets whizzed through our ranks," wrote a stunned Benjamin Abbott, adjutant and close personal friend of Benning. The Georgians staggered. A few men ducked out of line to find cover. The story was told that Benning angrily confronted a squad cowering in the timber. "God damn you, men, get from behind those trees and rocks, and give 'em hell!" A shell exploded a few feet away, killing his horse. Benning tumbled to the ground. When he stood up, dazed but unhurt, Benning's perspective had changed. "God damn you, men, stay behind those trees and give 'em hell," he yelled.[15]

Captain Abbott lost his horse as well. He and Benning jogged after their troops, who had closed to within forty yards of the Yankee breastworks.

Croxton was with the Tenth Kentucky, shouting words of encouragement to his fellow Kentuckians, when a bullet struck him in the leg. It was a serious wound, and as Croxton reeled in the saddle the Tenth lost faith and broke up. That left Gary's battery on its own. The lieutenant waited ten minutes after the Kentuckians abandoned him, hoping they might return, while his gunners kept the Rebels at bay. Finally, with thirteen men and twenty-five horses down, Gary limbered up and fell back. Brannan intercepted him and ordered the lieutenant to join Negley's batteries on the Snodgrass hill.[16]

With Croxton hit, command passed to Colonel William Hays. The brigade split, half going west and the rest heading north. The Fourteenth Ohio and Fourth Kentucky regiments streamed out of the fight into the Dyer field, ignoring Hays's attempts to stay them. Lieutenant Colonel Marsh Taylor, as the senior officer on the left, took charge of the Tenth and Seventy-fourth Indiana regiments and calmly led them in an orderly withdrawal into the lines of Reynolds's division.[17]

In the confused retreat of the brigade right, Company E of the Tenth Kentucky was forgotten. Sergeant Richard Boyle and some forty of his comrades were left hanging on "behind friendly trees. All others were gone. There we stood, loaded and fired . . . as if we were a thousand. Some brave Confederates passed . . . to our rear, but were called back by a staff officer, who rapidly rode after them. Suddenly there appeared to our sight in our rear an officer on a gaily caparisoned horse who commanded us to cease firing, as the supposed enemy were really our own men. I looked around and said: 'I'll be damned if I don't know what I'm doing.' He wheeled, remarking that he would report me, and was gone. I then knew he was a Confederate." Boyle also knew then that it was time to leave.[18]

Benning halted at the breastworks to regroup and hunt up another horse. He found one, a Federal artillery horse still wearing a bridle. Benning slid onto the animal. Riding bareback, he again led his men forward, this time north through the forest toward Reynolds's division.

While the men were regrouping, Captain Abbott wandered over to a stack of Yankee knapsacks heaped beside the breastworks. The Georgian sat down and absentmindedly picked through them, until one particular ream of stationery caught his eye. He smiled at its irony: "The letter paper contained captions of pictures of valiant Federals in magnificent array, carrying the Stars-and-Stripes grandly over their heads, storming Confederate earthworks and fortifications."[19]

Out of the woods and into the Dyer field charged the brigades of Fulton, Sugg, McNair, Sheffield, and Robertson at 11:45 A.M. It was a triumph of rare splendor. All who witnessed the moment were deeply moved, but none captured the thrill better than Bushrod Johnson:

Our lines now emerged from the forest into open ground on the border of long, open fields, over which the enemy were retreating. . . . The scene now presented was unspeakably grand. The resolute and impetuous charge, the rush of our heavy columns sweeping out from the shadow and gloom of the forest into the open fields flooded with sunlight, the glitter of arms, the onward dash of artillery and mounted men, the retreat of the foe, the shouts of the hosts of our army, the dust, the smoke, the noise of fire-arms — of whistling balls and grape-shot and of bursting shell — made up a battle scene of unsurpassed grandeur.[20]

Johnson's contemplation of the battlefield was interrupted by General Hood. It was too early for self-congratulation; much remained to be done. From the knoll that had been Rosecrans's temporary headquarters, the Sixth Ohio Battery barked and fumed at Fulton's Tennesseans, as if to dare them to come on. More menacing was Mendenhall's long line of cannons on the ridge one thousand yards away, around which pockets of Yankee infantry were beginning to form. Clearly these guns had to be silenced — and quickly. Johnson saluted Hood. Did the general have any orders? He did. "Go ahead, and keep ahead of everything," said Hood. That was all Johnson needed to hear.[21]

NO MORE SHOW THAN
A BROKEN-BACKED CAT

LIEUTENANT James Fraser of the Fiftieth Alabama stood with his regiment in a snarled thicket east of the La Fayette road, waiting for the command to advance. It was 11:15 A.M. "There was but little or no skirmishing in our immediate front, but up on the right of the brigade they were cracking away at each other frequently," remembered Fraser. He and every other soldier of Brigadier General Zachariah Deas's Alabama brigade knew that it was only a matter of minutes before they would have their first taste of combat at Chickamauga.

A pounding of hooves caused Fraser to look to his right. Down the line rode Generals Longstreet and Buckner. The lieutenant was impressed: "Longstreet is the boldest and bravest looking man I ever saw. I don't think he would dodge if a shell were to burst under his chin." The two generals drew rein beside Deas, a jolly-looking, forty-three-year-old former cotton broker with a broad face and barrel chest. "General Longstreet, I presume," smiled Deas. "Yes, sir," replied the general. Deas told Longstreet his name and announced his brigade. Longstreet pointed into the forest to their front. The enemy was somewhere in there, he said. Deas called the Alabamians to attention, and Longstreet and Buckner rode on to find Arthur Manigault, commander of the next brigade in line.

At 11:20 A.M., Deas and Manigault moved to the attack. Patton Anderson trailed two hundred yards behind in reserve. Six hundred yards of dense timber and undergrowth lay between Deas's Alabamians and the Federal breastworks. "We moved along, first at slow time, then quick, then double quick, and as we came in sight the boys all took the run, and every one shouted and shot as fast as he could," said Fraser.[1]

General Carlin was returning from an inspection of his skirmish line when the attack came. A moment earlier, said Carlin, "not the least sign of an enemy could be seen." Now everything was chaos. Deas had chosen to advance without skirmishers of his own, so Carlin's skirmishers knew nothing of the Rebel approach until Deas's main line was on top of them. The Yankees bolted, the Confederates charged, and it was a race for the breastworks among Carlin, his skirmishers, and the Alabamians.[2]

In his front line, Carlin had the One Hundred First Ohio, the Eighty-first Indiana, and the Twenty-first Illinois. In their decimated state they covered a front barely two hundred yards wide. Tucked in a thicket a short distance to the rear was the Thirty-eighth Illinois. It was to the Thirty-eighth that Carlin rode as the last of his skirmishers hopped over the breastworks and the front line opened fire. The Alabamians recoiled. Just as quickly, they recovered and resumed their advance. Deas's line lapped Carlin's, a fact not lost on the Illinoisan, who could see the Twenty-second and Fiftieth Alabama regiments feeling their away around his right flank.

Carlin yelled at Lieutenant Colonel Daniel Gilmer to get the Thirty-eighth Illinois into line on the right of the Twenty-first before it was too late. "From some cause not now ascertainable he hesitated," reported an exasperated Carlin, "but finally succeeded in giving an order to his men to rise." Carlin would never know why Gilmer faltered; a bullet cut the colonel down almost instantly. The Confederates reached the breastworks before the Thirty-eighth, which managed just one ragged volley before it broke, less seventy-nine men who threw down their rifles and surrendered.[3]

The rest of the brigade was doomed. Without support on its flank, the Twenty-first Illinois was easily rolled up. Its colonel, John Alexander, was killed and nearly half the regiment was taken prisoner. "They scattered to the four winds," said Lieutenant Fraser, whose regiment hit the Twenty-first in front. "A great many of them were so cowardly that they did not shoot as we advanced on them but stuck their heads behind logs and waited for us to pass them. It was the quickest and prettiest fight I ever saw."

The fight swept to the Eighty-first Indiana, command of which Carlin had handed over to Major James Calloway the previous afternoon in the Viniard fields. The Illinoisan had led his adopted regiment brilliantly then, but there was nothing he could do now. His men had fired about seven rounds apiece into the enemy in their front, when the major's attention was drawn to his right. "I saw to my inexpressible surprise and horror the right of the Twenty-first Illinois was breaking and rapidly melting away. After a second and more careful observation I noticed the enemy was actually crossing the breastworks on the right and extending his left flank in our rear, completely flanking our position." Having no orders and seeing no chance to get any, Calloway wisely yelled to his men to retreat as best they could. Most got away, and only twenty were captured.[4]

That left the One Hundred First Ohio, alone and nearly surrounded.

Deas's Alabamians poured past the regiment's right flank and, after Martin's brigade broke apart, Sugg's Texans turned their fire against its left flank. For Sergeant Benjamin Strong of Company A, the order to withdraw came a moment too late. He got up and began running, but a bullet crushed his left elbow before he had gone thirty yards. Strong fell, his arm numb. "Almost directly a Rebel line of soldiers passed over me. One grabbed for my new white felt hat, but was going so fast he missed it. Another line passed by, and one of the Confederates offered me a drink of water, the third line went by and I was ordered to get up and go to the rear." There Strong joined a procession of Yankee wounded winding its way through the woods toward a field hospital. On the way, some kindly Confederates fashioned him a sling from a handkerchief. At the hospital near Reed's Bridge, surgeons told Strong the arm would have to be amputated, but not just then; they had no time for Northern wounded. Strong wandered off and sat down in a corner of the tent. No one came to his assistance, and Strong was left to treat his wound himself. He made it a point of walking down to the creek to wash his arm and change the dressing daily, until finally he was put aboard a train for Libby Prison. There, thirteen days after the battle, a surgeon at last saw him. Strong was laid on a filthy table. Without ether or chloroform to dull his senses, Strong watched the surgeon cut a four-inch incision below the elbow, reach in with his fingers, and pull out fragments of bone. When the wound healed, Strong's left arm was an inch shorter than his right.[5]

Out on the open, forward slope of Lytle Hill, the soldiers of Colonel Bernard Laiboldt's brigade peered toward the forest five hundred yards to their front, where the brigades of Martin and Carlin were being punished, and looked for clues that might tell them how the fight was going. At first all they could see was a soft pillow of smoke rising from the trees. Then the signs became more definite, and more ominous. Dazed and bleeding soldiers stumbled out of the pines and across the field toward the brigade. "Riderless, frightened horses were galloping about, their heads swaying from side to side; the bridle reins and saddle stirrups flying. First there were few of them, but soon they became quite numerous," observed Sergeant Henry Castle of the Seventy-third Illinois with growing alarm.[6]

All doubt was removed when General Davis came galloping wild-eyed up the slope in search of Laiboldt. Pulling up beside the Missourian, he warned: "If you're here to support me, [you'd better] do it immediately." Laiboldt balked. His brigade occupied what he called a "very favorable" defensive position, the four regiments being deployed in column of regiments at company distance on the hillside. In other words, they were stacked one behind the other, each in line of battle. Behind them were the six guns of Battery C, First Illinois Artillery. The incline and absence of any vegetation permitted each regiment and the battery a clear field of fire all the way to the woods where Davis's division was fighting. Laiboldt thus had the rare opportunity to bring every rifle in his brigade to bear simultaneously. His men shared the colonel's delight with their surroundings. "It was a position without fortifications but one which we thought we could hold until doom's day against all attacks from the front," averred Sergeant Maurice Marcoot of the Fifteenth Missouri.[7]

Although well positioned to meet an attack, the brigade was ill prepared to advance. Coming off the slope, Laiboldt would be able to bring only his lead regiment effectively into action against an enemy line of battle of indeterminate length, and in coming off the hill his men would run into the Tan Yard, an obstacle course of shacks, ash-hoppers, tanning pits, and nitre vats. So Laiboldt understandably declined to move. Lieutenant Colonel Horace Fisher, the corps inspector general, lent his support to Davis's plea. Fisher had been riding behind Buell's brigade when the breakthrough occurred and knew what it portended, if unchecked. Still Laiboldt objected. Finally McCook rode up and resolved the impasse with a direct order: The colonel must attack at once to ease the pressure on Davis. Laiboldt meekly suggested that he be allowed to deploy from column into line of battle, but McCook cut him off—the order was peremptory, he must charge at once.[8]

The idea of going into action with their flanks unprotected chilled Sergeant Castle, and his comrades in the Seventy-third Illinois did not like their prospects. Theirs was the lead regiment, and with both flanks unsupported they feared the worst. Nor did the Illinoisans have much faith in the regiments behind them. The Seventy-third had joined the brigade a year earlier, a collection of naive, newly recruited Illinois farm boys thrown into the company of three veteran regiments of German immigrants. The Illinoisans must have struck the old soldiers as an odd lot. Their colonel, lieutenant colonel, major, six of ten captains, and several lieutenants were Methodist preachers. Many of the enlisted men were the sons of prominent Methodist families, and the Seventy-third became known throughout the army as the "Preacher Regiment." As raw recruits, the Illinoisans held prayer meetings after morning and evening roll calls. That practice was abandoned soon after they joined their present brigade, however, when the men discovered that the Germans had been cleaning out their tents of blankets, canteens, and anything else of value while the regiment was engaged in prayer.[9]

With their larcenous comrades formed behind them, the Illinoisans fixed bayonets, raised a yell to disguise their disquiet, and started down the hill.[10]

The rigors of active campaigning were taking a toll on Assistant Secretary Dana. For the past two days he had eaten little and slept less. He had passed the long night hours listening to the cold wind whistle through the drafty puncheons and cracked floorboards of the Widow Glenn cabin. Now, sitting on his horse under the warm morning sun on the knoll with Rosecrans and his staff, a gentle breeze stroking his face, Dana began to nod. All was quiet in the fields before him, only the low rumble of fire from the direction of the Kelly field disturbed an otherwise idyllic morning. By 11:00 A.M., Dana could no longer take it. He dismounted, handed his reins to an orderly, and lay down in the grass, where he fell into a deep sleep.

Dana sat up with a start. "I was awakened by the most infernal noise I ever heard. Never in any battle I had witnessed was there such a discharge of cannon and musketry. . . . The first thing I saw was General Rosecrans crossing himself. . . . 'Hello!' I said to myself, 'if the general is crossing himself, we are in a desperate situation.' " Dana jumped on his horse. "I had no sooner collected my thoughts and looked around toward the front, where all this din came from, than I saw our lines break and melt away like leaves before the wind."[11]

Bullets began to fall on the knoll. A minie ball ripped open James St. Clair Morton's hand as he stood beside Rosecrans. Shells burst among the trees. The shock of unexpected combat confused the senses. "Instantly the word 'mount' was given, and as quickly we were on horse," wrote Colonel Sanderson. "All this occurred so quickly, and in that brief moment so many things occurred, that it is impossible to describe with any kind of accuracy."

Rosecrans drew on the last of his emotional reserves. As the first fugitives from Buell's brigade came running out of the woods east of the Dyer house, he yelled at the commander of his cavalry escort, Colonel William Palmer, to throw out a line and stop the stragglers. Then, with his staff strung out behind him, Rosecrans galloped off the knoll toward the reverse slope of Lytle Hill, some four hundred yards away. "His powerful gray horse ran off and no one could keep up with him," Captain Porter told his sister after the battle. "Horses were falling at every point. Mine suddenly was found going on three legs. I jumped off to see what was the matter, and found he was not shot but had run a nail in his foot. I worked it out with my sabre, and found fortunately he was not lame. There was no time to lose, I assure you."[12]

Rosecrans ducked behind the hill to escape the fire. There he met McCook, who was oddly confident. He had just ordered in Laiboldt, McCook told Rosecrans, which "would soon set the matter to rights." Somewhat reassured, Rosecrans ordered McCook to hurry along Sheridan's remaining brigades, which were then coming up the Glenn-Kelly road, about six hundred yards to the southwest and immediately behind the southern end of Lytle Hill. With these brigades, Rosecrans hoped to strike the Confederates in the left flank while Laiboldt and Davis held them in check in front.[13]

Neither Rosecrans nor McCook had the vaguest notion of the magnitude of the disaster that had befallen the center and right of the army in the roughly fifteen minutes that had elapsed since Longstreet's column came crashing across the Brotherton field. Neither did they appreciate the length of the Confederate lines. Rosecrans had seen only the destruction of Buell's brigade and heard the firing from Davis's front. From this, he concluded that Bragg's left flank lay somewhere opposite the right of Davis.

Rosecrans, of course, was tragically misinformed, as events were rapidly to demonstrate. While he and McCook conferred, Manigault's brigade was moving as yet undetected into the Glenn field, at least seven hundred yards beyond the right flank of Sheridan's moving brigades. Anderson trailed close behind, ready to support either Deas or Manigault as circumstances might dictate. Hoping to turn the Confederate left, Rosecrans was instead about to see his own right rolled up like tissue.[14]

The reception his brigade received at the base of the hill was about what Colonel Laiboldt had expected. Colonel Jaquess's Illinoisans advancing met Carlin's frightened soldiers retreating, and in the ensuing shoving match, regimental integrity disappeared. Some dove for cover in the Tan Yard, others took advantage of the confusion to sneak away to the rear with Carlin's men. Enough, however, stood by the colors to deliver a respectable volley into the forest. Then Deas's Alabamians returned the fire, hitting the Seventy-third from the left, the front, and the right. Down went the color sergeant. While Jaquess's men struggled to reload, the Confederates surged forward "without a moment's faltering," reported General Deas proudly.[15]

In the Seventy-third it was now every man for himself. Sergeant Castle could make no sense of the fight. "I saw my friends falling dead or wounded all about and near me. Dan Foster and his brother John fell within my reach. I could not observe what was going on at any distance." Then Castle was hit, first in the right leg and then in the left. "As I struggled to my feet . . . I saw that all those who could were falling back. I determined to try it, although the bullets from the muskets of the enemy were puffing up the earth over that open field which I should have to cross, much as large drops of rain at the beginning of a thunder shower puff up the dust upon a dry road." As Castle took his first painful steps, an Alabamian yelled at him to surrender. Castle ignored him, and the Rebel fired, cutting two fingers off his left hand. "I crippled along across that field without any further hurt, much to my surprise, and was even able to assist, with three others, in removing from the field a comrade who fell with a broken thigh a few yards in front of me, just as I reached the timber, and who pleaded piteously to be saved from going to prison."[16]

The remaining regiments of Laiboldt's brigade fell like dominoes behind the Seventy-third. The Forty-fourth Illinois tried to file to the right to engage the Confederates lapping around the right flank of Jaquess's fast-disintegrating command. A few companies made the adjustment, sending a ragged volley into the ranks of the Twenty-second Alabama that killed its color-bearer. But when the soldiers of the Seventy-third and the survivors of Carlin's brigade stampeded its front, the Forty-fourth collapsed. The mass of retreating Federals grew as it neared the summit. Colonel Joseph Conrad could do nothing. His Fifteenth Missouri was carried off in the panic, the men easy targets for the Rebel bullets that "swept the hill from three sides." Deas's Confederates pursued so closely that Missourian Maurice Marcoot could hear plainly their demands of "Surrender, you Yankee son-of-a-bitch."

At the height of Yankee desperation, the pendulum swung briefly to the north. Halfway up the slope, Deas's men were struck by a blistering volley from a Union regiment that suddenly appeared on the tree-covered summit. Deas momentarily lost his grasp on his brigade. Another color-bearer fell in the Twenty-second Alabama. Lieutenant Colonel John Weedon seized the colors in a desperate bid to keep his men moving. Weedon "rushed to the front [and] stood under its folds, thus making himself a target; and while drawing the fire of the enemy, a ball struck him in the temple. He fell enveloped in the folds of the flag." With their colonel down, the Alabamians backed away a few yards and fell to the ground. The Fiftieth Alabama stopped alongside them, hit in the rear by a misdirected volley from the Thirty-ninth Alabama, which had lagged behind. Gradually Deas's entire brigade came to a halt along the slope.[17]

Deas had run into the Eighty-eighth Illinois of Lytle's brigade. Phil Sheridan had reached the summit just as Laiboldt's command collapsed on itself. He was incensed. The day before, Crittenden had ordered Bradley into the east Viniard field to be chopped up, and now McCook had sent Laiboldt to a similar fate. Sheridan called on Lytle, whose brigade was on the Glenn-Kelly road near the base of the hill, to come up on the double-quick and try to save Laiboldt. "While Sheridan was not there to put us in, he was there to help us out, and he was reported to have expressed himself on the following day in language more forcible than polite regarding the matter of our going in," quipped an appreciative Sergeant Castle.[18]

Lieutenant Pirtle watched Lytle bring the brigade into action. The Ohioan led the lead regiment, the Eighty-eighth Illinois, up the wooded slope. Pirtle could make out the forms of Deas's skirmishers gliding from tree to tree in front of the Eighty-eighth. Men began to fall. "Forward into line," shouted Lytle, and with a cheer the Illinoisans followed him to the crest, sending the Rebels scurrying down the opposite slope. Lytle positioned the regiment and then wheeled his horse back down the hill to fetch the Thirty-sixth Illinois. Back up the hill he rode, waving the Thirty-sixth into line on the right of the Eighty-eighth. Then came the Twenty-fourth Wisconsin. At

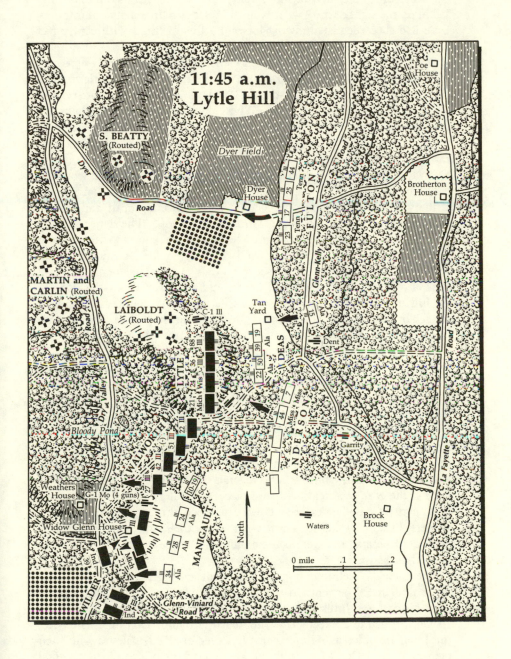

**11:45 a.m.
Lytle Hill**

the same time, the men of the Twenty-first Michigan raised a cheer and
fell in on the right of the Twenty-fourth Wisconsin. In a matter of minutes,
Lytle had succeeded in throwing forward a line of battle within fifty feet
of the lead elements of Deas's brigade.[19]

Pirtle was about to join Lytle when General McCook suddenly appeared.
He pointed to a spot in the woods just off the road and told Pirtle to place
the Eleventh Indiana Battery there. The lieutenant got the battery into
position, then rode toward Lytle. "The combined sounds of battle are so
overpowering that although I am but a few paces distant I cannot hear
what General Lytle is saying but I know he is encouraging the boys for I
can see his emphatic gestures with his sabre."[20]

On the summit the spectacle defied description. The dead and wounded
of Laiboldt's brigade lay everywhere. Terrified soldiers mingled about. An
artillery wagon swung into the side of a tree, breaking apart and raining
limbs down on the soldiers of the Thirty-sixth Illinois. "The sight was truly
appalling," marveled one Illinoisan. "The ground was covered with dry grass
and old logs which the bursting shells had set on fire. A thick cloud of
smoke had risen about as high as our heads and seemed hanging like a
funeral pall in the air. Under this we could see, away down the slope of
the hill and across the little valley just as far as the eye could reach, moving
masses of men hurrying toward us. In our front, not more than seventy
or seventy-five yards distant, the enemy's front line lay secreted."[21]

Laiboldt may have been wrecked, but Deas was also in trouble. That
much, at least, was perfectly clear to Colonel William Oates. Commanding
the left-flank regiment of Sheffield's brigade, Oates had lost his way in the
cloud of dust raised by the brigade when it crossed the La Fayette road.
When the dust settled, there was no sign of his own or any other friendly
brigade. Oates edged through the Brotherton field and into the woods. He
steered too far to the left, and his Fifteenth Alabama exited the forest into
the Dyer field, north of the Tan Yard. "Looking around I saw away to my
left and front a fight going on; the Federals in solid phalanx along the pine
ridge at the edge of a field, with two pieces of artillery in their midst, were
beating the Confederates back down the slope through the open field,"
witnessed Oates. "I did not know what troops they were, except that they
were Confederates and were being beaten, and without orders I resolved to
go to their assistance."[22]

The colonel's well-intentioned effort went awry. As his regiment came
up behind the Nineteenth Alabama, a shell exploded near Oates, ripping
apart his coat and bruising his left hip. Oates fell, but his men pressed on.
As he struggled to his feet, Oates shouted after them: "Don't fire, Fifteenth,
until you are ordered!" Limping along, his leg numbed, Oates saw his men
prepare to fire. "Don't fire until you are ordered, men," he yelled a second

time. Oates was too far away to be heard. The regiment opened fire into the back of the Nineteenth Alabama. Its commander, Colonel Samuel McSpadden, spun around in the saddle, grabbed the colors and by frantically waving them convinced the Fifteenth to cease fire. Oates hobbled up and brought his regiment into line on the right of the Nineteenth.[23]

Fortunately, Deas received better-coordinated assistance on his left. While Deas's brigade stalled on the slope of Lytle Hill, Manigault continued due west through the Glenn field. A yawning gap several hundred yards wide opened between the two brigades, stretching through the timber from the Glenn-Kelly road to the northern edge of the Glenn field. Colonel Walworth's Illinois brigade was coming into position opposite the interval, with his right anchored on the Widow Glenn hill.

General Hindman reacted promptly to the threat, ordering Patton Anderson's brigade up from the second line to fill the space between Deas and Manigault. One of Bragg's few real friends and supporters in the army, the forty-one-year-old Tennessean was a talented officer who had had a varied antebellum career. While a young country doctor in Mississippi, Anderson had raised an infantry battalion for service in the Mexican War. Elected lieutenant colonel, he served conspicuously at the head of his First Mississippi Rifles, gaining favorable notice by fellow officers Braxton Bragg and Jefferson Davis. Anderson came home to serve a term in the state legislature, then went west as united states marshal for the Washington Territory, which he later represented in Congress. The outbreak of hostilities found him in Florida, where he was appointed colonel of the First Florida Infantry. His initial service was at Pensacola with Bragg, who developed a genuine — and rare — affection for Anderson that lasted through the war. Anderson, Bragg later wrote, was "as noble and true a soldier as any age can boast."[24]

Anderson's actions at Chickamauga confirmed the commanding general's faith in the ability of his loyal subordinate. Quickly appraising the situation, Anderson saw that Deas's left regiment, the Twenty-second Alabama, was being chewed up by an enfilading fire from the Eleventh Indiana Artillery, posted partway up the wooded incline. At the same time, the Parrott section of Battery G, First Missouri Light Artillery, had trained its pieces into the Glenn field against the right flank of Manigault; in support of the rifled guns were the Twenty-second and Fifty-first Illinois regiments of Walworth's brigade.

Anderson split his brigade to deal with the dual threat. He ordered the Seventh and Forty-fourth Mississippi (his two right regiments) to move against the Indiana battery, retaining the remainder of the brigade for use against the Parrott rifles and their infantry supports. Meanwhile, Manigault renewed his assault against the Widow Glenn hill, where the two Napoleon sections of the Missouri battery were posted, along with the Twenty-seventh

Illinois and a small detachment of the Twenty-first Michigan, left behind on the skirmish line when Lytle was ordered away.[25] The Seventh and Forty-fourth Mississippi regiments sprinted toward the Indiana battery, each anxious to be the first unit to the guns. Caught off-guard by this sudden advance of the enemy, Captain Sutermeister hollered for his section commanders to limber their pieces. A volley from the Mississippians wiped out the horses of the rifled section, toppled five drivers, and wounded the section commander. Sutermeister abandoned his two rifled cannons to the Seventh Mississippi, which lost only twelve men in the charge, and toiled up the hill with the rest of his battery.[26]

Directly up the slope from the abandoned cannons stood the Twenty-fourth Wisconsin. Moments earlier, Lytle had told the men: "Boys, if we whip them today we will all eat our Christmas dinner at home." Now the Wisconsin farm boys were barely hanging on against a confident enemy only sixty feet away.[27]

Lytle's entire position was in jeopardy. The wild charge of Anderson had heartened Deas's Alabamians, who renewed their drive up the hill. With Confederates converging on it from three sides, Lytle's brigade began to break up. The Thirty-sixth Illinois gave ground first, allowing the Alabamians to claw their way through the timber to within pistol range of the left flank of the Twenty-fourth Wisconsin. Major Carl von Baumbach swung his two left companies around to meet the threat. Then the Twenty-first Michigan on his right began to falter. The pressure on the Twenty-fourth became unbearable. Lytle was right there, a wild look in eyes, his mustache twisted and curled from the work of nervous and impatient fingers. Pirtle was beside him. "The noise of the battle, the shouting and reports of the musketry are so dreadful that no conversation can be carried on," wrote the lieutenant.

Lytle leaned over toward Pirtle. "I bend to catch what he is saying. He calmly says with a firm voice 'Pirtle, I am hit.' For an instant I cannot speak; my heart almost ceases to beat, but I say 'Are you hit hard, General?' 'In the spine—if I have to leave the field you stay here and see that all goes right.' 'I will, General.'"

Pirtle watched Lytle intently to see if he would go, but the general sat still. Only the added fervor with which he chewed his tobacco betrayed his agony. The Rebel volleys rose in pitch. Looking to Lieutenant Charles Boal, his topographical engineer, Lytle yelled: "For God's sake, bring up another regiment." Boal did not hear him. Lytle looked to Pirtle, who reluctantly left his side and galloped down the reverse slope of the hill to where Colonel Silas Miller was trying to reassemble his Thirty-sixth Illinois.[28]

Captain Howard Green of the brigade staff took Pirtle's place at the general's side. Lytle turned to give Green an order. As he did, a minie ball

"Carry him or we will be taken prisoner." The death of Brigadier
General William Lytle.

smashed his left cheek, splattering blood on the captain's coat. Lytle reeled. Green leapt to the ground and caught the general by the head and shoulder, laying him down carefully as both their horses galloped away. "He recognized me as I caught him and tried to speak, but failing to do so, he spoke to me with his eyes — giving me a look that spoke volumes of thanks for my efforts to assist him," recalled Green, who hastily examined the wound. "The ball struck him in the left corner of the mouth, passed through his head and came out near the right temple so that the blood welled up into his mouth so rapidly that he was unable to speak."

Green summoned two of the general's orderlies, and together they carried Lytle away. As they started, Colonel Thomas Harrison rode up, having come over to coordinate the deployment of his Thirty-ninth Indiana Mounted Infantry with Lytle's brigade. Harrison dismounted to help. Suddenly four shells exploded on the right flank of the Twenty-fourth Wisconsin, and the regiment gave way. One of the orderlies was hit. "It was just at this time that Lytle opened his eyes, and I could see by his expression that he was trying to speak, but could not. I asked him if he wished to lie down, and he said yes (by nodding his head)." Green told Harrison to lay the general down. "No, carry him or we will be taken prisoner," urged Harrison, as the last of the Twenty-fourth streamed past. Again Lytle tried to speak. "Finding it impossible, he threw his arms out convulsively and catching hold of my knees, he gave me one embrace, which I think was his death struggle, for his limbs immediately relaxed, his eyes rolled up into his head and he fell over limp and lifeless," said Green. Harrison got back on his horse and rode away to his own regiment, the orderly ran off to save himself, and Green was left alone with the body. He knelt over Lytle just long enough to be sure he was dead, then started off the field.[29]

Running forward, shoving his way through the crowd, was Lieutenant Pirtle. He had been helping Colonel Miller rally his regiment below the hill when the general's horse galloped by. Pirtle's only thought now was of his commander, whose side he had vowed not to leave. Nearing the spot where he had left Lytle, Pirtle now saw only a swarm of jubilant Confederates. Blinded by tears, he turned and made his way rearward.[30]

It was a strange twist of fate that the bullet that killed the beloved Ohioan should have come from a rifle fired by one of Patton Anderson's Mississippians. Anderson and Lytle had been warm friends and political allies before the war, and had last seen one another in Charleston, South Carolina, during the portentous final weeks of 1860. "As they bade each other farewell there they promised that nothing should ever interfere with their friendship, and if either should ever be in trouble the other was to assist him in every way practicable," wrote Anderson's widow years later.[31]

Lytle had many friends in gray. Oddly drawn to the hill, one after another now passed his body, a battlefield parade of mourners from the ranks of the enemy. First came Anderson. Overcome with grief, he dismounted and took Lytle's wedding band, several cartes de visite from his pockets, and a lock of his hair, intending to send them through the lines to the Ohioan's family. Anderson posted a guard over the corpse and continued on with his brigade. Major William Miller Owen, General Preston's chief of artillery, found Lytle later that afternoon. Lytle and Owen too had been friends before the war, as had their fathers before them. General Preston happened by while Owen stood gazing on the body. "What have you here," he asked offhandedly. "General Lytle of Cincinnati," replied Owen. "Ah! General Lytle, the son of my old friend, Bob Lytle. I am sorry it is so," said Preston, who also dismounted to pay his respects. The last to come upon the scene was E. W. Thomasson, a surgeon who had served with Lytle in the Mexican War. He too clipped off a lock of the poet's hair, which he mailed on to Lytle's sister, along with his pocket notebook. Lytle was "as good a man as ever lived, [even] if he did have on Yankee clothes," Thomasson remarked to the guard, whom he ordered to take the body back to his tent for a decent burial.[32]

In a stand no less poignant than that of Lytle, Colonel Walworth had fought the left regiments of Anderson's brigade and the right regiments of Manigault's brigade to a standstill for nearly twenty minutes until, flanked on both the left and right, he was forced from the field. Nearly half the brigade had fallen; the rest retreated through the woods toward the Dry Valley road, which lay three hundred yards behind them.[33]

The rout of Sheridan's division was nearly complete. Contemplating the disaster, Colonel Silas Miller, who succeeded the fallen Lytle to brigade command, wrote angrily: "Sheridan's division through no fault of his went into the fight on Sunday with no more show than a broken-backed cat in hell without claws . . . with both flanks exposed and receiving fire from three directions. He held his position till he would have been a murderer to have asked even to try to do so longer."[34]

It was noon. Just forty minutes had elapsed since Hindman started across the La Fayette road, yet already he had stampeded two Federal divisions and advanced the brigades of Deas and Anderson to within three hundred yards of the Dry Valley road. Ahead of the Rebels surged a stunned rabble of blue, intent only on putting as much distance between themselves and their pursuers as possible. Along the road and atop the ridge immediately east of it, amid the human wreckage and uncertainty, Union generals were making the decisions of their careers.

Rosecrans was there. He had seen Lytle's riderless and blood-streaked horse come down from the hill, followed closely by the survivors of Lytle's and Laiboldt's brigades, and concluded that the right was lost. Flagging down

Laiboldt in the chaos, he told him to reform behind the first ridge west of the Dry Valley road, then sent a messenger in search of Sheridan, hoping to confer with him in person. While he waited for the Irishman, Rosecrans joined his staff in a recklessly courageous effort to rally stragglers along the ridge. "Here General Rosecrans threw himself into the very thickest of the fight," attested correspondent William Sumner Dodge.

Sheridan got the message, but he adjudged "affairs too critical" to permit him to go to the commanding general just then.

Rosecrans waited a few minutes for Sheridan. When he did not come, Rosecrans decided to leave. Confident that he had done all he could there on the right, Rosecrans left a handful of staff officers to see that his orders to Sheridan were carried out; then, accompanied by Garfield, Major Bond, and two or three others, he pushed his way up the Dry Valley road, intent on joining Thomas.[35]

Captains Horace Porter and J. P. Drouillard were two of those left behind. They were on a low ridge between Lytle Hill and the Dry Valley road. Porter was determined to stay there "as long as we could hold ten men together."

That proved harder than Porter imagined. No sooner did the two captains scrape together about one hundred men than a Rebel shell burst among them, and their "line vanished in an instant," rued Porter. Still they kept at it. Assistant Secretary Dana, determined, so he later said, to reach Sheridan, paused a moment to watch Porter and Drouillard: "They would halt a few of them, get them into some sort of a line, and make a beginning of order among them, and then there would come a few rounds of cannon shot through the tree tops over their heads and the men would break and run. I saw Porter and Drouillard plant themselves in front of a body of these stampeding men and command them to halt. One man charged with his bayonet, menacing Porter; but Porter held his ground, and the man gave in."[36]

So, after twenty minutes, did Porter and Drouillard. By then the Rebels were so near that the commands of their officers could be heard clearly. Most of the men who had stood by the captains were dead or wounded. Porter's horse had been hit and was stomping about, almost unmanageable; a moment later a minie cut the captain's scabbard in two. Porter and Drouillard joined the blue tide ebbing across the Dry Valley road and over the innumerable foothills and ravines toward the base of Missionary Ridge, looming two miles to the west. For his actions, which held off Hindman's Confederates long enough for several wagons and most of Sheridan's artillery to make good their escape, Porter was later awarded the Medal of Honor.[37]

The two young captains had accomplished far more than any general officer on that part of the field. Davis had been separated from his division early in the fight. Neither Martin nor Carlin had any notion of his whereabouts, nor apparently had Davis's staff, who delivered the division flag to Carlin. Gathering what troops they could, the two brigade commanders fell in behind Sheridan, who was leading a ragged column of his own toward Missionary Ridge.[38]

Sheridan had concluded further resistance was futile. That was apparent to Corporal Charles Brough of the Fifteenth Pennsylvania Cavalry, whom Rosecrans had dispatched with a message to Davis nearly an hour earlier. After an aimless search for the Indianian that took him over half the battlefield, Brough found Sheridan. The young trooper waved the message in the air and asked the general where he might find Davis. "I don't know, my boy; but it's too late. Let me see it," counseled Sheridan. He tore open the envelope and read the order. "Too late! Too late!" was all he could say. Sheridan turned away, grabbed the division standard from his orderly, and rode among the troops, "begging his men to halt and re-form; but it availed nothing, and turning to everybody around him, said: 'It's time for all of us to get away from here.' " Maurice Marcoot heard a similar admission of defeat. The Missourian had run into a cordon of brigade officers while trying to escape the battle. Just then Sheridan rode up and told the officers to let the men pass. "Let them go," he shouted. "Let them go for their lives."[39]

The only life General McCook cared about at that moment was his own. In the confusion, McCook and his staff ran into part of Rosecrans's cavalry escort. With the troopers was the local farmer, John McDonald, whom Rosecrans had impressed into duty as a guide. Now McCook was anxious for the old man to lead him off the field. As trooper John Davis recalled, the general expressed himself quite clearly. Sticking his revolver under McDonald's nose, McCook warned: "If you guide us into the rebel lines I will blow your head off." "The general used some additional adjectives," recalled Davis.[40] In what can only be a reference to McCook, Colonel Sanderson said he saw a general with his staff "turning his back to the battle, and running away from it like a scared hare, never stopping until he had safely reached" Chattanooga.[41]

As McDonald led him over the hills beyond the Dry Valley road and away from the fighting, McCook regained his composure. Obviously embarrassed over his behavior, McCook tried to restore his tarnished image. He weakly announced that he should like to find Thomas but doubted the chances of success. He made a tentative movement in that direction and ran into the wounded James St. Clair Morton. Doubtless to McCook's relief, Morton confirmed the impossibility of reaching Thomas. Forever clearheaded and methodical, even when in pain, Morton pulled out his prismatic compass to try to locate the rolling sounds of battle and clouds of dust rising on the horizon. It was all too clear, he told McCook—the whole army was in retreat toward Chattanooga. The engineer's estimate was good enough for McCook. With farmer McDonald leading the way, the general and his party continued on over the hills toward the Rossville Gap. At various intervals McCook repeated a desire to go to Thomas, but his protestations fooled few. Even Major John Levering of General Reynolds's staff, so sick with fever that General Thomas had ordered him off the battlefield in an ambulance that morning, could see that McCook was not quite right. "I had proceeded about halfway to Chattanooga when we were overtaken by General McCook and staff on a rapid retreat," Levering recorded in his diary. "They reported to me: 'Our whole force [is] cut to pieces and flying in all directions.' After McCook, his staff, and escort passed us, no more seemed to be following. They galloped ahead out of sight. It looked very much like a run on the part of McCook."[42]

Even as Rosecrans, McCook, and Sheridan turned their backs on the crumbling right wing, a glimmer of hope arose. Alone and apparently forgotten, a tiny remnant of Sheridan's division, consisting of the Twenty-seventh Illinois, the pickets of the Twenty-first Michigan, a handful of men from the Fifty-first Illinois under the command of Lieutenant James Boyd, and the Napoleon smoothbore section of Battery G, First Missouri, was holding Manigault's brigade at bay from atop the Widow Glenn hill.[43]

That they could do so for long, however, was in grave doubt. Already Manigault's left-flank regiment, the Thirty-fourth Alabama, had slipped past the Yankee defenders and was regrouping in a ditch along the Glenn-Viniard road. His right regiment, the Tenth and Nineteenth South Carolina, had dislodged the Forty-second Illinois from the woods north of the Glenn field and was feeling its way toward the hill. And while the Missouri gunners had managed to keep the rest of the Southerners pinned down in the field, they were running dangerously low on ammunition.[44]

When the artillery fire slackened, Manigault ordered the Twenty-eighth and Twenty-fourth Alabama regiments to charge. Up the open slope they swarmed, just as an exploding shell set the Widow Glenn cabin afire. The Missourians abandoned their guns and ran behind the hill. Their infantry support covered them with a few broken volleys before they too ducked behind the reverse slope. The elated Alabamians sprinted forward to take possession of the cannons.[45]

In an instant, the entire equation changed. Over the west side of the hill came Colonel Harrison's Thirty-ninth Indiana Mounted Infantry, fighting on foot. A volley from the Hoosiers' Spencers sent a shiver through the ranks of the Twenty-fourth Alabama. The Thirty-ninth came up beside the burning cabin, and a vicious fight ensued for possession of the battery. "The heat was so intense that it scorched our clothing," recalled a Yankee.

"Ammunition had been left in the house, and the shells began to burst, throwing fire and shingles one hundred feet high."[46]

The appearance of the Thirty-ninth Indiana was due to the quick thinking of Lieutenant Colonel Gates Thruston, assistant adjutant general to McCook. When first told by Rosecrans to close up on the left, McCook had sent Thruston to Crawfish Springs to order Mitchell's cavalry to fill the gap on the right that this movement would create. Thruston delivered the order just after Longstreet burst through the Federal center. Heading back up the Dry Valley road, Thruston ran into Colonel Harrison and his regiment coming from a cross road. "The storm of battle was sweeping over the ground" where he had left McCook, recalled Thruston. Harrison agreed to help, and together they led the regiment up the road at a gallop.[47]

While Manigault tried to cope with the challenge posed to his front by the Thirty-ninth Indiana, a far greater threat was developing against his left flank. From the timber southwest of the hill, just across the Glenn-Viniard road, came the sudden crash of volley on top of volley. The Rebels had never heard the like. Stunned and bleeding, they began to falter.

The unexpected fire came from the Spencers of Wilder's brigade, which had been on the way up from the south to close the gap with Sheridan when Hindman's attack came. Wilder was in sight of the Glenn hill when Manigault reached it, his brigade deployed on foot in column of regiments. With no time to bring up the horses for a mounted charge, which some of the men expected, the Hoosier motioned his lead regiment, the Ninety-eighth Illinois, into the field against the Confederate flank. Their colonel, John Funkhouser, fell badly wounded in the early firing, but the Illinoisans kept on. They caught the Thirty-fourth Alabama practically from behind. The Alabamians offered no resistance, but broke and ran helter-skelter across the meadows toward the La Fayette road. Twenty-eight were caught in the melee. Wilder threw his next regiment, the Seventy-second Indiana, into action on the left of the Ninety-eighth, extending the line to the Glenn hill. The One Hundred Twenty-third Illinois and Seventeenth Indiana came up to fill out the line on the right. Colonel Smith Atkins reported with his Ninety-second Illinois, which had spent the morning on detached service watching the enemy from west Viniard field, and fell in behind the brigade.[48]

Manigault knew enough to quit. "As far to the left as I could see, the enemy overlapped us, and there were no troops opposing or attacking him," he wrote. "What had become of the troops on my left, I could not imagine." Manigault sent a staff officer to find out where Preston was, then withdrew.

So heavy was the fire from Wilder's Spencers that Longstreet, hearing the clatter from nearly a half mile off, thought for a moment that a fresh Federal corps had come crashing down on his left. Caught in the cross fire, Manigault felt the ferocity of the Federal volleys. A minie ball pierced his horse under the saddle, coming out through one of the general's pant legs and cutting his sword in two. As Manigault dismounted, bullets peppered his clothing.[49]

Manigault's withdrawal rapidly degenerated into a rout. Wilder charged and drove the Thirty-fourth and Twenty-eighth Alabama regiments all the way back to the La Fayette road. The Thirty-ninth Indiana, Twenty-seventh Illinois, and Lieutenant Boyd's tiny detachment from the Fifty-first Illinois bounded down the hill and chased away the Twenty-fourth Alabama. Eli Lilly unhitched a section on the Glenn hill and threw a few rounds at the retreating Rebels for good measure.[50]

Manigault had been caught in the flank because Preston had not advanced. Only the ardent plea of Manigault's staff officer caused him to move Trigg as far forward as the La Fayette road. Gracie and Kelly remained in their jump-off positions east of the Viniard fields. No explanation was ever given for Preston's failure to play his part in the wheeling movement. Neither, however, was he censured, so it may be assumed that either Longstreet or Buckner had decided to hold the Kentuckian's division in reserve.

Upon the appearance of Trigg's brigade, Wilder halted the pursuit and recalled his brigade to the Glenn hill. The men returned to find their horses had been brought up; it was the first they had seen of the animals in over forty-eight hours. "Never were soldiers more delighted than we were with meeting the horses then and there. We were almost famished with hunger, worn out with fatigue, and the reaction, after such intense excitement, left us limber as rags. We clutched at our horses like a drowning man at a root or limb of a tree, and like a drowning man had scarcely strength to pull ourselves upon their backs," remembered Sergeant Magee. "Those of us who had left our haversacks tied on our horses, explored their utmost recesses in the hope of finding at least a hardtack. Not a crumb was left." The designated horse guards, or "number fours" as they were called, had eaten every last biscuit.[51]

While he planned his next move, Wilder permitted his men to refill their canteens and water their horses in nearby Bloody Pond. The men flocked eagerly to its fetid water. "Neither the men nor horses had had water for hours and neither dead men and dead horses nor the blood and mud of Bloody Pond detained them from quenching their agonizing thirst in the pond," said Wilder. "Some of them waded into the pond. Others knelt at the edge and drank beside men who had fallen dead of wounds while drinking."[52]

Wilder surveyed the field from the Glenn hill. He could see little through the trees, but both the rattle of rifle fire and the smoke of battle were receding to the west, a good indication that Anderson and Deas had driven well across the Dry Valley road. A half mile to the north, the same telltale signs suggested a bitter fight was raging between the Dyer field and the long spur that would become known as Horseshoe Ridge.

Accompanied by Colonel Atkins, Wilder edged forward to Lytle Hill to better reconnoiter the situation. There, said Atkins, they could clearly see wide Butternut columns charging across the Dyer field. Wilder announced to Atkins that he intended on "charging with his brigade through the center of the Confederate column, taking regiments in flank and pushing for Thomas on the left," then asked the Illinoisan for his opinion of the scheme. "I replied to him that it was a desperate and bold movement, but that Wilder's brigade of Spencer rifles could do it."

The two rode back to the Glenn hill, intending to roll up Hindman and Johnson. The time of day is uncertain; it may have been as late as 1:00 P.M. and certainly it was well after noon. Wilder said he drew up the command in column of regiments, five lines deep. Atkins recalled that the formation was a hollow square with two regiments in the front line and openings for Lilly's battery. In either case, Wilder was certain that he could rout the whole of Longstreet's wing, if need be. Most of his men seem to have shared his confidence; with a faith bordering on reverence for their commander and their Spencers, they at least were willing to try.

Wilder and his men would never know whether they might have turned the tide of battle. Before they had gone a hundred yards down the northern slope of the Glenn hill, Wilder and Atkins spied a hatless, red-haired man in civilian clothing riding madly for them. Drawing rein beside Wilder, the nearly hysterical rider demanded to know what unit the colonel commanded. "First Brigade, Fourth Division, of the Fourteenth Corps, Wilder's Brigade of Mounted Infantry," Wilder calmly replied. The civilian introduced himself, nervously repeating his name and title three times: "Charles A. Dana, Assistant Secretary of War." All was lost, declared Dana. In rapid succession he told Wilder and Atkins that "our troops had fled in utter panic; that it was a worse rout than Bull Run; that General Rosecrans was probably killed or captured." Wilder explained his intention of taking his brigade to Thomas. Absolutely not, snapped Dana. He categorically forbade Wilder from making any attempt to cut his way through to the left and insisted that he withdraw at once. Dana also demanded an escort to Chattanooga.

In issuing an order to a unit commander on the field of battle, Dana was going far beyond the mandate from Stanton that had brought him to the army. The entire notion was preposterous. But Wilder was a mere colonel, uncertain of the extent of Dana's authority and probably wary of the ramifications should he choose to defy Stanton's lapdog. So he yielded—to a point. Wilder agreed to call off the attack and he detailed some scouts to see the assistant secretary off safely. He did not, however, abandon the field.

After Dana left, Wilder set his troops to work gathering up the hundreds of stragglers and scores of wagons milling about. He brought in the guns of Battery G, First Missouri, and some one hundred ambulances of wounded that were rocking north along the road from Crawfish Springs. Sergeant Magee was among those dispatched to comb the forest west of the Dry Valley road, where "caissons, limber-chests, guns, ambulances and men were wandering in confusion over the hills and knobs like sheep without a shepherd." It was 3:00 P.M. before Wilder started slowly up the Dry Valley road toward McFarland's Gap, screening McCook's reformed wagon train and ambulance corps as he went.

To his dying day, Wilder believed he could have reached Thomas and shattered Longstreet's wing in the bargain. "I would have struck them in flank and rear with five lines of Spencer rifles in the hands of the steadiest body of men I ever saw, and am satisfied we would have gone through them like an avalanche," he wrote thirty years later. "I have lived at Chattanooga for eighteen years and have gone over the Chickamauga field with a great many ex-rebels, who all admit that if I had been allowed to attack as I wished, it would have been fatal to Bragg's army." Atkins agreed and years later offered his measure of the two parties to the affair: "Wilder was daring and desperate; Dana, a coward and an imbecile."[53]

THE SIGNS GREW RAPIDLY WORSE

MAJOR Mendenhall had done his job well. On the long, narrow ridge that marked the western limit of the Dyer farm, he had concentrated sixteen guns from the Seventh Indiana, Twenty-sixth Pennsylvania, and Third Wisconsin batteries, which comprised the artillery of Van Cleve's division. When Van Cleve received orders to march to the left just before the breakthrough, Mendenhall moved the batteries laterally along the top of the ridge to parallel the expected movement of the infantry. It never came, of course, and the batteries stopped on the crest of a two-hundred-yard-long extension of the ridge that rose half a mile north of the Dyer house.

It was a natural position of great strength, offering the Yankee cannoneers a panoramic view of the whole of the Dyer field. Just northeast of the ridge there arose a lightly wooded knoll that commanded the field from the north and blocked any approach to the Snodgrass hill through the field from the south. On the bald crest of the knoll were deployed the two three-inch rifles and four James rifled cannons of Battery M, First Ohio Light Artillery, which Negley had placed there earlier in the morning.

Back on the open spur east of the Snodgrass farmhouse, the Pennsylvanian was dividing the fire of his batteries between Govan's attacking Confederates in the Kelly field and Longstreet's forces in the Dyer field.[1]

After the breakthrough, Mendenhall's position acted as a magnet for Federal batteries chased out of the Dyer field. Lieutenant Cushing brought his Battery H, Fourth United States Artillery, into position on the right of the Third Wisconsin. After untangling itself from Buell's disordered brigade, the Eighth Indiana Battery came onto the ridge to the right of Cushing. A few minutes later, Captain Church showed up with the three remaining guns of his Battery D, First Michigan Artillery, bringing the total number of Federal cannons on the ridge to twenty-nine.[2]

General Crittenden and his staff were with the batteries. If they could only rally some infantry to support the guns, the Kentuckian said, he was certain they would "yet drive those fellows back or hold them in check." The Kentuckian was doing everything he could think of to make it so. It was Crittenden who personally placed Cushing's battery into the line. Reaching the ridge at the head of his limbers, the lieutenant had asked Crittenden which way he should retire. "You are not to retire at all, but hold your position," the general barked.

Halting the retreating infantry proved infinitely more difficult. Crittenden, Lieutenant Colonel Starling, and the general's staff fanned out along the ridge, imploring the broken units of Buell and Beatty to plant their colors and gather around the guns. Most ignored the pleas and kept on running into the woods behind the ridge. But there were exceptions. Lieutenant Colonel James Embree held part of the Fifty-eighth Indiana together in front of the Seventh Indiana Battery. Lieutenant Colonel William Young got most of the Twenty-sixth Ohio into line behind a fence at the base of the ridge in front of the Third Wisconsin Battery, and Major Willard Eaton hastily drew up a few companies of the Thirteenth Michigan about a hundred yards forward of the Eighth Indiana Battery.[3]

The Confederates were taking a terrific pounding. The converging fire of Mendenhall's artillery and Battery M, First Ohio, threatened to limit their penetration to the eastern edge of the Dyer field. Clearly the Yankee guns had to be silenced. Their presence, combined with the failure of Polk to crack the Kelly field salient, convinced Longstreet that a wheel to the left, as prescribed in the plan of battle, was no longer tactically sound. To do so would expose his right and rear to the Federal artillery and a possible counterattack by whatever infantry might rally around them. Longstreet therefore approved Hood's decision to send both Bushrod Johnson and Law against Mendenhall's guns. When he learned of Manigault's setback on the far left, Longstreet ordered Hindman to break off his pursuit of Sheridan, consolidate his forces in place, and then bring them north to connect with Johnson's left. He also dispatched a messenger to Wheeler at Glass's Mill, directing him to force a crossing and then ride north to join up with the infantry on its left flank.[4]

Johnson and Law plunged into the Dyer field at 11:40 A.M. On the left, Fulton led his brigade due west along the Dyer road. Next came Sugg, who wheeled his brigade to the northwest against the southern tip of the ridge in an attempt to take Mendenhall's batteries in the flank. McNair, who in destroying Buell's brigade had fallen behind Sugg, now moved obliquely to the right into the front line, intending to advance directly against the ridge. In Law's division, Sheffield moved diagonally across the Dyer field against the northern tip of the ridge, opening a gap of perhaps two hundred yards

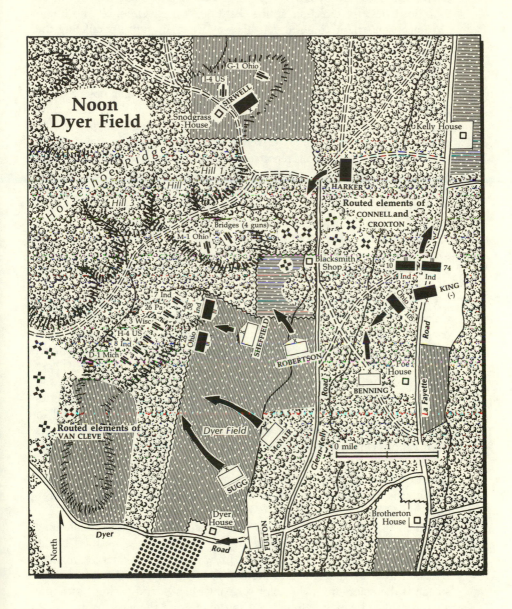

**Noon
Dyer Field**

G-1 Ohio
1-4 US
SIRWELL
Snodgrass
House
Kelly House

Horseshoe Ridge

Hill 1
Hill 2
Hill 3

HARKER

Routed elements of
CONNELL and
CROXTON

Bridges (4 guns)
M-1 Ohio

Blacksmith
Shop

10
Ind
Ind 74
Ind
Ind

KING
(-)

Ind
26 Pa
3 Wisc
H-4 US
8 Ind
D-1 Mich

26 Ohio 58 Ind

SHEFFIELD

ROBERTSON

Poe
House

BENNING

Routed elements of
VAN CLEVE

Dyer Field

McNAIR

0 mile   1

SUGG

North

Dyer
Road

FULTON

Dyer
House

Brotherton
House

Glenn Kelly Road

La Fayette Road

between his brigade and that of McNair. Robertson, who had been trailing Sheffield, moved now by the right flank to clear his front, and then advanced in a northwesterly direction against Battery M, First Ohio, on the knoll. On Robertson's right, Benning felt his way generally north paralleling the La Fayette road toward King's Federal brigade, his left regiments marching through the heavy timber west of the road.[5]

Tension gripped the ridge. Most infantrymen were still ignoring orders to rally. The acrid smoke of twenty-nine booming cannons obscured the Dyer field, effectively cloaking the advancing Confederates. "It was a time of painful anxiety," admitted Crittenden. "I still hoped that support would come from somewhere or be driven on me. But the signs grew rapidly worse." Lieutenant Cushing reported that the enemy had worked its way around the ridge and was now behind them. At first, Crittenden was incredulous. Then from the right, bullets whizzed out of the smoke, felling battery horses by the dozen. While Crittenden looked on, all the horses attached to one limber were killed simultaneously. Crittenden and Starling rode to the next ridge, about a hundred yards in their rear, hoping to find some infantry to bring forward. But they met only Van Cleve, who had scraped together a pitiful detachment of one hundred dazed soldiers. With these, they started back to the batteries.[6]

Out in the Dyer field, the situation was growing desperate for Lieutenant Colonel Young and the Twenty-sixth Ohio. To the front, Sheffield's Alabamians were closing fast, their line of battle stretching far beyond the left of Young's tiny command. Peering over his shoulder through the smoke, Young saw the artillerymen scrambling to hitch up their pieces. "There was no support anywhere in sight; every man in the command saw and felt the hopelessness of attempting a stand at this point, and as the batteries were already moving off, finding it impossible to rally my command in any force, I fell back into the woods, [which] were filled with fugitives from various commands, utterly disordered." Young's disingenuous apology for leaving the field begs the truth. The Third Wisconsin Battery, which lay directly up the slope from his regiment, was going nowhere. Thirty-two of the battery's thirty-six limber horses were dead. When Young's Ohioans deserted the battery, they doomed it to capture.[7]

Captain Lee Terrell of Sheffield's staff understood this clearly. Galloping along the front of the brigade, he drew rein at the Forty-seventh Alabama, which had paused in the field a stone's throw from the ridge, its commander reluctant to charge straight into the barrels of the Yankee cannons. Terrell snatched the colors from the color sergeant's hands, and without speaking a word yanked his horse around and spurred toward the guns. With a yell, the Forty-seventh followed. The Wisconsin cannoneers frantically depressed their pieces, "hoping to wipe the entire line out with one volley," wrote

Captain Joseph Burton of Company D. Burton and his men steeled themselves for the blast, but the Yankees aimed too low, and their rounds burrowed
into the dirt or bounced harmlessly over the heads of the Alabamians. "In
much less time than it takes to tell it," continued Burton, "the men of the
Forty-seventh, with clubbed guns, were fighting the artillerists for possession
of their pieces. These fellows fought valiantly, but unavailingly." Eleven
cannoneers were captured, along with five of the battery's six guns.

The men of the Forty-seventh now turned their fire against the right
flank of the Twenty-sixth Pennsylvania Light Artillery, which had managed
to hold off the approach of the rest of the brigade to its front and left. They
killed the battery commander, Captain Alanson Stevens, along with every
horse but one in the right section. The Pennsylvanians tried to drag the
pieces away by hand, but, as one survivor put it, "underbrush and woods
is not good ground for batteries to maneuver in." They got off with the
left section but had to abandon the two guns of the right section. The
Seventh Indiana Battery, with more time to react, lost only one piece to
the Alabamians.[8]

On Sheffield's left, McNair and his men found the going tougher. In the
open field, the mounted officers were easy targets. A shell fragment ripped
into McNair's thigh, wounding him seriously. Colonel Robert Harper took
over and was mortally wounded a moment later. Command devolved upon
Colonel David Coleman of the Thirty-ninth North Carolina, whose regiment
had gotten out ahead of the rest of the brigade and was taking a terrible
beating from the Eighth Indiana Battery and Church's Battery D, First
Michigan. Realizing he had to either silence the guns or retreat, Coleman
chose the former course and spurred his horse forward. His regiment followed, scattering handily the detachment of the Thirteenth Michigan that
stood between them and the ridge.

Sugg's brigade closed on the batteries from the south at the same time,
sending a volley up the slope that caught the Federal cannoneers in the
flank. The artillery began pulling back, and Sugg and Coleman converged
on the ridge with a rush. Captain Church had horses enough to draw off
only one of the three cannons he had brought across the Dyer field. In the
Eighth Indiana Battery, every horse lay dead or mangled in the harness.
The gunners depressed their guns and let go one final, defiant blast of double-
shotted canister, then fled into the woods, leaving behind all six guns.
Lieutenant Cushing's Regulars, on their left, were more fortunate, losing
only one piece.[9]

Members of the Thirty-ninth North Carolina steadfastly maintained that
theirs was the first regiment to ascend the ridge and touch the barrels of
Yankee cannons; decades later they even sent a delegation of veterans, headed
by a former Yankee, to the battlefield park to confirm their contention.

Sugg and his regimental commanders insisted in their reports that the honor of capturing the Eighth Indiana Battery and the guns of Cushing and Church belonged to them. Regardless of who got there first, the soldiers of McNair's brigade had nothing of which to be ashamed. Indeed, they would soon have cause to gloat. Back in Mississippi, General Walker had derided them as a poorly disciplined mob of misfits who ought to be discharged. After the battle, upon hearing of the brigade's action in the Dyer field, Walker apologized profusely to the wounded McNair for his earlier slurs.[10]

Riding toward the ridge from the reverse slope at the head of Van Cleve's little detachment, Crittenden met Mendenhall, who told him that the batteries had been captured. Though stunned and disappointed, the Kentuckian was not yet ready to give up. With Van Cleve, Mendenhall, and Starling, he changed course and headed for the first ridge west of the Dry Valley road. There he shook his one hundred troops into a skirmish line to try and net stragglers. For thirty minutes Crittenden waited there, hoping to meet an officer from Davis's or Sheridan's division who could brief him on the fate of the right. None passed by.

Crittenden was fresh out of ideas. The Kentuckian called his staff around him. It looked to him like Rosecrans and McCook were either dead or captured and the army routed. "I believe I have done all I can. Can any of you make a suggestion?" he asked. If Crittenden cared anything about public opinion or newspaper accounts, he had better try to reach Thomas, advised Lieutenant Colonel Starling. "You know I care for nothing of that kind. My whole object is to do my duty as an officer," answered Crittenden. In that case, suggested Starling, if Rosecrans and McCook were lost, Crittenden's place was in Chattanooga to reorganize the scattered troops. Crittenden agreed, and with his small coterie started along the crowded Dry Valley road toward Rossville.[11]

Somewhere on the road north of Crittenden were Rosecrans and Garfield. After leaving the right, Rosecrans, accompanied by Garfield, Major Bond, and a small escort, had ridden back to the knoll that had been his temporary headquarters. He found it swarming with demoralized soldiers. Everett's Georgia Battery was playing on the knoll from the far side of the Dyer field, and Fulton's brigade was rapidly closing on it. "Under a shower of grape, canister, and musketry," Rosecrans forced his way through the mob north across the Dyer road in a tentative attempt to go to Thomas. There Lieutenant William Moody, aide-de-camp to General Negley, intercepted him. Negley — ill, exhausted, and overwhelmed by the disaster that evidently had befallen the center — had sent Moody and Captain Alfred Hough on a desperate ride to army headquarters to solicit reinforcements to protect his batteries. Moody and Hough split up to improve their chances of getting through. With Confederates swarming over the Dyer field, they followed a circuitous route west along Horseshoe Ridge, and then south along the ridge bordering the Dyer field. Moody rode along the left side of the elevations, Hough the right.

Moody was on the ridge west of the Dyer house when he caught sight of the commanding general. "Across the open field I could see General Rosecrans, alone, his staff and escort, with drawn sabers, endeavoring to check the avalanche of panic-stricken men who were fleeing before the desperate onslaught of the enemy," Moody reported. He rode into the field to deliver Negley's request. Rosecrans must have thought the captain mad; did he not have eyes to see the panic all around him? "I can't help him, it's too late," replied Rosecrans.

Hough buttonholed Rosecrans a few minutes later. Hough repeated Negley's request, and Rosecrans just as adamantly repeated that he could offer no help. The captain saluted and rode off, only to find the way back blocked by Bushrod Johnson's infantry, which had just seized Mendenhall's batteries.[12]

It was then, at noon, that Rosecrans decided to quit the field. As he explained in his report: "I [had] . . . attempted to rejoin General Thomas and the troops sent to his support, but found the routed troops far toward the left, and hearing the enemy's advancing musketry and cheers, I became doubtful whether the left had held its ground and started for Rossville." There he hoped to learn definitively the state of affairs on the left, at which point he would decide whether to join Thomas on the battlefield or continue on to Chattanooga to begin preparations for its defense.[13]

Rosecrans and his staff forced their way through the human wall onto the Dry Valley road. There, stretched out along the road as far north as the eye could see, was the wreckage of an army in retreat. Frightened and leaderless soldiers, angry officers on horseback, the walking wounded, scores of wagons, caissons, limbers, and ambulances clogged the road, proof positive of the worst rout sustained by a Union army since Bull Run.

As he drifted north with the mob, Rosecrans fell into silent contemplation. To Garfield, the general appeared "abstracted, as if he neither saw nor heard. With the conviction that nothing more could be done, mental and physical weakness seemed to overcome" him.[14]

What was going through Rosecrans's mind? True to character, he was dipping into the deep well of his faith for strength. "It was possibly one of the most trying and anxious periods of my life," he wrote his brother after the battle. "I could hear the roar of the battle and knew the swarming rebel host were surging against our brave men. But in the midst of it all I prostrated myself in spirit at the feet of our Crucified Lord and implored His most

Sacred Heart to pity us[,] and [I] repeated to our Holy Lady the prayer of the Church very often[,] 'Monstra te esse Matra.' "[15]

At McFarland's Gap, according to Lieutenant Cist, Rosecrans met a detachment from Negley's division. Probably survivors of Beatty's brigade who had been swatted off the battlefield by the attack of Stovall and Adams, they told a lurid tale of defeat and despair. Negley, they said, was near Rossville "rallying stragglers"; the entire division had been "knocked all to pieces." Rosecrans's fear deepened as he passed through the gap and turned up the valley road toward Rossville. The last time he saw Negley, that general had been on his way to the extreme left. Hough and Moody had confirmed his presence there less than two hours ago. If the story these soldiers told was true, then Thomas must have been routed. The whole army would soon be in Chattanooga, a "broken mass."

By the time Rosecrans's party reached Rossville, recalled Cist, the firing from the front had subsided. Rosecrans and Garfield dismounted and put their ears to the ground, hoping to divine from the vibrations the nature of the combat. Hearing no artillery firing, and catching only a hint of what seemed to be a scattering fire of musketry, Rosecrans began to believe that the reported rout of the left was real, asserted Cist. He conferred with Garfield.[16]

What passed between them remains a matter of conjecture. Here is Rosecrans's own version of their discussion, as related in a magazine article twenty-four years later:

> In view of all the interests at stake I decided what must be done. I said to General Garfield and Major Bond: "By the sound of the battle over to the southeast, we hold our ground. Our greatest danger is that Longstreet will follow us up the Dry Valley Road. Post, with all of our commissary stores, is over the ridge, not more than two or three miles from the Dry Valley Road. If Longstreet advances and finds that out, he may capture them. This would be fatal to us. To provide against what may happen: First, Sheridan and Davis must have renewed orders to resist the enemy's advance on the Dry Valley Road. Second, Post must be ordered to push all our trains into Chattanooga and securely park them there. Third, orders must go to Mitchell to extend his cavalry line obliquely across that ridge, connect with the right of Sheridan's position on this valley, and cover Post's train from the enemy until they are out of danger. Fourth, orders must go to Spear's brigade, now arrived near there, to take possession of the Rolling-Mill bridge across Chattanooga Creek, put it in good order, hold it until Post arrives with his trains, then turn the bridge over to him and march out on the Rossville Road and await orders. Fifth, Wagner in Chattanooga must have orders to park our reserve artillery defensively, guard our pontoon bridge across the Tennessee, north of the town, and have his men under arms ready to move as may be required. Sixth, General Thomas must be seen as to the conditions of the

battle and be informed of these dispositions. General Garfield, can you not give these orders?" I asked. Garfield answered:

"General, there are so many of them I fear I may make some mistakes, but I can go to General Thomas for you, see how things are, tell him what you will do, and report to you."

"Very well, I will take Major Bond and give the orders myself. I will be in Chattanooga as soon as possible. The telegraph line reaches Rossville, and we have an office there. Go by Sheridan and Davis and tell them what I wish, then go to Thomas, and telegraph me the situation."[17]

It is doubtful that Rosecrans actually rattled off to Garfield all the intricate orders he claimed to have. Nevertheless, his version of events probably is closer to the truth than that of Garfield. In a "private" discussion a few weeks later with his close friend and political ally, Major General Jacob Cox, Garfield said he had to beg Rosecrans to allow him to make his way to Thomas, a plea to which the commanding general "assented listlessly and mechanically." That Rosecrans was teetering on the edge of nervous collapse there can be no doubt, but the testimony of others present suggests that he still had a fair grasp of the situation. Lieutenant Cist maintained that Garfield convinced Rosecrans his place was in Chattanooga to "receive and reorganize" the army. Major Bond corroborated Rosecrans's claim to have asked Garfield to issue a series of orders in his name, a request with which the chief of staff was reluctant to comply. Said Bond: "General Garfield asked a number of questions, and evinced a hesitancy in undertaking the great responsibility of issuing such important orders in Rosecrans's absence, when finally the general said to him, 'Very well, I will go to Chattanooga myself. You go to Thomas. . . . Report to me at Chattanooga as to the condition of affairs with Thomas.' "[18]

The two parted company at about 2:00 P.M. Accompanied by Captain Gaw and two orderlies, Garfield started down the La Fayette road toward the battlefield. Rosecrans took the road to Chattanooga. "The reverse should have been done," lamented Cist. "Rosecrans should at once have gone to the front, and by his presence there aided, as he did at Stone's River, more than any other thing to retrieve the fortunes of the day. . . . That was the turning point, and his hour had arrived."[19]

THEY CAN KILL US, BUT
WHIP US NEVER

FROM daybreak until noon, General Thomas had had time for nothing but the defense of the Kelly field line and the protection of the McFarland Gap and La Fayette roads. Although the battle for the left still raged, Thomas could no longer ignore the racket on the far side of the Snodgrass hill, opposite his right and rear. When the volleys seemed suddenly to draw closer, Thomas started toward the hill to have a look for himself.

As he was leaving the Kelly field, Thomas ran into Captain Kellogg. His nephew brought disturbing news. While riding down the Glenn-Kelly road in search of Sheridan, whom Thomas had been expecting for some time, Kellogg had spotted a large body of troops in an open cornfield to the rear of Reynolds's position advancing cautiously with skirmishers deployed. When he rode closer they fired on him before he was able to make out their uniforms or flags.[1]

Thomas rode on. He next met General Wood, who was coming up the La Fayette road at the head of Barnes's brigade. Wood had his own tale of woe for Thomas. He had been looking for Reynolds without success (in truth, he had inadvertently marched right past his rear) and was growing nervous. His anxiety increased markedly when Thomas told him that Reynolds did not then, nor did he ever, need support. Baird and Beatty, however, needed reinforcements desperately to repel Liddell's attack on the left, Thomas added.

Wood saw an opening. Showing Thomas the fateful order from Rosecrans, the cagey Kentuckian asked him if he would accept responsibility for changing it. Thomas agreed, and Wood hurried Barnes's brigade to the left, his dignity intact and his decision to abandon the line shielded, if not vindicated.[2]

Wood's next tactical decision proved nearly as fortunate as his decision to quit the center had been disastrous. The Kentuckian had left Harker's command in route column in the woods near the intersection of the Vittetoe and Glenn-Kelly roads while he went on ahead with Barnes. He returned just as the brigade began to take fire from its rear and right. Reconnoitering the source of the shooting, Wood came to the edge of a small meadow north of the Dyer farm. A worm rail fence bounded the field on the north, the Glenn-Kelly road marked its eastern limit, and the knoll from which Captain Schultz's Battery M, First Ohio, was booming away at Law's division dominated its western edge.[3]

Entering the field from the south was Robertson's Texas Brigade—the unknown force that had fired on Captain Kellogg a few minutes earlier. Kellogg had been misled by the odd appearance of the enemy. En route to Georgia, the soldiers of Hood's and McLaw's (Kershaw's) divisions had had the rare pleasure of drawing new uniforms, which consisted of dark blue shell jackets and light blue trousers. It was smart-looking attire, but hardly appropriate. "Our first impression on seeing them was that they were Yankees," recalled a soldier from Strahl's brigade. "This impression was caused partly by the color of their uniform, but more by its uniformity, and the superior style of their equipment, in haversacks, canteens and knapsacks. The contrast between them and General Bragg's motley, ragged troops was striking in the extreme. . . . They were certainly superior to the troops of the Army of Tennessee in dress."[4]

Wood was not deceived, either by the identity of the troops or their purpose. "When I discovered the enemy in force in the valley south of my command, I at once divined his intention, and appreciated the terrible hazard to our army and the necessity for prompt action. His object was clear. Having turned our right and separated a portion of our forces from the main body, he was seeking the rear of our solid line of battle, to attack it in reverse, hoping thus to cut our communication with Chattanooga and capture and destroy the bulk of our army."[5]

Robertson's immediate objective was the knoll. Seize that, and the way was open to Negley's batteries and the Snodgrass hill. Seize the Snodgrass hill, and Thomas's entire Kelly field line would be compromised. As the brigade stepped into the cornfield, Robertson ordered it to wheel to the left to take the knoll from the flank. Robertson's right flank swung around to within three hundred yards of Wood, who galloped back to bring Harker forward to check the Texans' advance. "A new line was rapidly formed at right angles to the old, and Harker's brigade was thrown out to check the enemy as one throws a piece of meat to a savage dog to gain time," quipped First Sergeant Samuel Snider of the Sixty-fifth Ohio.[6]

Wood was at his best. Robertson was "in full and plain view in the open fields, and it was evident his force far outnumbered mine," he reported with a bit of hyperbole. "But I felt that this was no time for comparing numbers. The enemy at all hazards must be checked." The Sixty-fourth Ohio double-quicked by the right flank into line of battle in an oak brake north of the field, fronting south. Colonel Emerson Opdycke's One Hundred Twenty-fifth Ohio came into position next on its right. The rest of the brigade was in motion behind the Ohioans, hurrying to extend the line farther to the right. Wood chose not to wait for them but to fight with what he had. Drawing rein behind the One Hundred Twenty-fifth, he told Opdycke to charge and seize the fence along the northern edge of the field. Opdycke was a martinet with a surly personality, but he could fight. "Forward, double-quick," he barked. While the company commanders repeated the order and the men fixed bayonets, Opdycke pushed his horse forward through the line. "Open a way, let me pass," snapped the Ohioan. His troops stepped aside, Opdycke passed to the front, raised his hat, and completed the order: "March."[7]

Together the Sixty-fourth and One Hundred Twenty-fifth Ohio passed through the skirt of woods that lay between them and the fence. They reached it, tore it apart, piled the rails as breastworks, lay down, and opened fire into the right flank of the Fourth Texas, all before Robertson's men knew what had happened. "That was the meanest, most unsatisfactory place I struck during the whole war. With ... men staggering and stumbling to the rear covered with blood, some swearing and some calling on God to protect them in their blind endeavor to find shelter from the storm of iron hail, [it] made me feel like the world was coming to an end then and there," Sergeant Val Giles remembered. Among those hit was a lovesick young lieutenant. He had a beautiful sweetheart in Texas, said Giles. "They kept up a regular correspondence and he cherished those letters above everything else and carried them with him wherever he went. With a blue ribbon tied around them he placed them in a black morocco notebook, securely fastened in the inside pocket of his uniform coat." The lieutenant was an odd sort — in the heat of the noonday Georgia sun, he was wearing his coat buttoned to the chin — but he was brave. "He urged the men forward and exposed himself recklessly," recalled Giles. "A minie ball struck him on the left breast above the heart. His sword flew from his hand and he fell heavily to the ground, apparently dead. But he was not killed. The bullet never entered his body, but embedded itself in his bundle of love letters. When the battle was over he took pride in showing his mutilated letters to his intimate friends, prouder of them than ever because they had saved his life."[8]

The Fourth Texas recoiled in disorder, having absorbed the brunt of the flanking fire. The Third Arkansas and First Texas clawed their way to the crest of the knoll, only to find that Captain Schultz had pulled his battery off just ahead of them.[9]

There were still Confederates to be cleared out, however. As soon as Harker came into line with the Third Kentucky and Sixty-fifth Ohio, Wood ordered Opdycke to "advance, firing" to a large copse of trees and a second fence that bordered the field on the south side. The One Hundred Twenty-fifth and Sixty-fourth Ohio reached it handily. Settling in behind the fence amid the cover of the trees, they opened a deadly flanking fire on the Fifth Texas, which was sprinting across their front in an effort to catch up with the rest of its brigade. The Texans wheeled to the right and opened fire on the Federals for a short time before withdrawing across the field toward the timber south of the copse.[10]

Charging with the Third Kentucky and Sixty-fifth Ohio, Harker brushed the remainder of Robertson's brigade off the knoll with surprising ease. In this the Ohioan received help from an unexpected quarter. Mistaking Robertson's well-dressed troops for Federals, McNair's ragged veterans fired into their left flank and rear just as Harker opened on their right. Robertson's brigade came apart. In explaining the breakdown of his Third Arkansas, Colonel Van Manning revealed how unexpected success on the battlefield could often be as disruptive as defeat. "The distance and speed with which we were required to move before engaging the enemy, together with the annoyance and confusion consequent upon our moving so closely in rear of other troops [Sheffield's], threw us into battle under serious disadvantages. The fatigue of the men and the deranged condition of the line are some of the prominent evils invariably and unavoidably experienced under the above circumstances," he wrote. Sergeant Giles described the problem from the viewpoint of the common soldier: "The smoke from fifty cannon and ten thousand muskets so completely enveloped the Texas Brigade . . . that at times a man could not recognize his file leader. . . . of course our lines were broken and irregular . . . causing companies and even regiments to lap over each other, which created any amount of confusion." Then Harker struck, before Robertson was able to restore order.

As the Rebels poured back down the southern slope of the knoll into the Dyer field, Harker brought the Third Kentucky into line behind the fence in a bit of open ground that lay between the copse of trees and the knoll—a horribly exposed position. On the crest he placed the Sixty-fifth Ohio. Just west of that regiment, on a slightly higher ridge, Lieutenant Colonel Embree had rallied his Fifty-eighth Indiana after its retreat in the face of Sheffield's attack on Mendenhall's batteries.[11]

By defeating Robertson and reoccupying the knoll, Harker now effectively enfiladed Sheffield's line. The Alabamian realized this, and he fell back across the Dyer field after only a brief stay on the ridge among the captured Federal cannons. Both Robertson's and Sheffield's brigades streamed south-eastward toward the safety of the timber, hurried along by the fire of Harker's Federals.

The significance of Wood's and Harker's actions to the preservation of the Union left was incalculable. Not only did their counterattack neutralize two Confederate brigades, but, as Sergeant Snider observed, it bought time — time that General Brannan was putting to good use, rallying a scratch line along Horseshoe Ridge from the broken commands of Croxton and Connell.

Wood was delighted. "That was a glorious charge and if I live it shall be made official and go into history," he yelled to Opdycke's Ohioans. The general kept his word and praised the One Hundred Twenty-fifth lavishly in his report of the battle. He was heard to boast that the regiment had fought like tigers, giving rise to a nickname that the Ohioans carried proudly through the rest of the war. They had become "Opdycke's Tigers."[12]

Harker's Federals were helped in their work by the poor showing of Benning's Georgia brigade. While Sheffield and Robertson wheeled toward the Federal batteries northwest of the Dyer field, Benning had continued on the seemingly easier course of pushing Brannan's shattered division due north through the forest east of the Glenn-Kelly road and taking Reynolds's division in the flank.

Things did not work out as the Georgian hoped. Before Benning was able to roll up King's brigade, General Reynolds delivered an unexpected counterstroke — he went after the Georgian. Galloping to Major George Perkins, whose One Hundred Fifth Ohio lay in reserve, Reynolds pointed off into the woods to the southwest and yelled out: "Have your men fix bayonets and charge right down through there."

Lieutenant Tourgee and every other member of the regiment who heard the order took it as their death sentence. Their lives were to be traded for time.

The commands were given — "Attention! Fix bayonets! Right wheel! Charge bayonets! Double-quick!" — and the regiment surged forward. As the Ohioans disappeared into the forest, Reynolds withdrew the rest of the brigade into position beside Turchin, who pulled a portion of his command out from behind the breastworks to make room for King's men.[13]

Benning had grown reckless in the pursuit. He had neglected to deploy flank guards, so was caught completely by surprise when the 250 Ohioans came crashing down onto his right flank. His brigade evaporated into the forest. Tourgee and his comrades were astounded. The Georgians "evidently thought us the advance of a heavy column," reasoned the Ohioan. "Some fell upon their faces and after we had passed rose and fired upon us. One of these sent a bullet through the major's thigh." Few of the Rebels were so plucky; most simply fled. The Ohioans knew better than to press their luck. "It was now our turn to run, and we ran as fast as the nature of the ground permitted," joked Tourgee. Major Perkins limped along with them.[14]

The sudden setback was too much for Benning, whose only thought was to report the disaster to Longstreet. "I was sitting on my horse, when he came back in a sadly demoralized condition," recalled Longstreet. "He was riding an old artillery horse and urging it along with a piece of rope which he used for a whip. His hat was gone. He was greatly excited and the very picture of despair."

"General, I am ruined; my brigade was suddenly attacked and every man killed; not one is to be found," blurted Benning. "Please give me orders where I can do some fighting."

Longstreet glanced impassively at his frantic subordinate. "Nonsense, General, you are not so badly hurt," he replied. "Look about you. I know you will find at least one man, and with him on his feet report your brigade to me, and you two shall have a place in the fighting line."

Longstreet's impassivity restored Benning's balance, and the Georgian rode off to piece his brigade back together.[15]

It would take far more than a facetious order to solve the crisis in the Dyer field. Where thirty minutes earlier the brigades of Sheffield and Robertson had moved smartly to the attack, a confused rabble now surged blindly toward the rear. Hood was there, trying through sheer force of will to restore a semblance of discipline. He tried to make light of Harker's Federals. "Move up, men; those fellows are shooting in the tops of the trees," he shouted. Perhaps Hood believed his mere presence would suffice to rally at least the soldiers of his old brigade. If so, he was disappointed. Neither his Texans nor Sheffield's Alabamians would halt until they reached the timber. Hood kept at it nonetheless and was still in the field when Brigadier General Joseph Kershaw arrived on foot with his brigade a little after noon.[16]

Kershaw's timing was superb. His South Carolinians crossed the Glenn-Kelly road and entered the southeast corner of the Dyer field as the last of Law's troops melted back into the forest. Kershaw needed no orders. A quick look about the field was enough to tell him where he was needed. From the copse of trees four hundred yards to the north, Harker's rifles blazed. And from atop the knoll, seven hundred yards to the northwest, the Federals were vigorously waving their flags, as if to say "Here we are, come on Rebels."[17]

Hood was eager to oblige them. Leaving his Texans in the timber, he started back into the field under a shower of bullets to hurry Kershaw into action. "Aunt Pollie" Robertson caught sight of Hood. Anxious for orders, he rode forward to intercept him. Robertson saluted and was about to speak when, to his horror, a minie ball crushed Hood's right leg just below the hip, splintering the bone. Hood dropped his reins and slid out of the saddle into the outstretched arms of his courier, Abner Wilkins, who eased him to the ground with the help of some soldiers from the Texas brigade. Through his anguish, Hood muttered his standing order of the afternoon: "Go ahead, and keep ahead of everything." Wilkins summoned a stretcher, and the general was borne from the field. Dr. T. G. Richardson, then chief medical officer of the Army of Tennessee and later president of the Medical Association of the United States, pronounced the leg beyond saving and performed the amputation. Hood's recovery was miraculous. Four months later he was up and about. Although he returned to active duty, this afternoon in the Dyer field was the last time he would fight with his old brigade.[18]

Hood's wounding was an incalculable loss to the Confederate effort at Chickamauga. His presence on the field at the height of the breakthrough, when total success depended on a rapid exploitation of the breach, was critical; no other field commander in Bragg's army had the sort of reckless, self-assured aggressiveness so appropriate to the moment. His absence threw the command structure on this part of the field into chaos.

As Hood was carried to the rear, his subordinates tried to muddle along. Kershaw had his brigade facing north in a single line of battle and was ready to move against Harker when a staff officer from Law brought word of Hood's wounding and suggested that, as the ranking brigadier, he assume command of Robertson's and Benning's brigades. At that moment, Bushrod Johnson rode up and, hearing the suggestion, demanded a comparison of dates of rank—this while they and the troops stood in the open under a murderous fire. Kershaw, who had no interest in the command, indulged Johnson, only to find that he was indeed the ranking officer. While Kershaw contemplated how, being a newcomer to the fight and without a horse, he was going to exercise his new responsibilities effectively, Major J. H. Cunningham "made the opportune suggestion" that the decision be bucked to Longstreet. "Relieved by this, I requested him to direct General Humphreys to move up and support me on my right, he having been thrown in my rear by my change of front," reported Kershaw. The gathering broke up. Cunningham rode off to find Humphreys, Johnson returned to his division, and Kershaw started forward with his brigade. Inexplicably, the Federals had ceased fire.[19]

The odd behavior of the Yankees—first the "ostentatious display" of their colors along the line and then the pause in their fire at the very moment it should have reached a crescendo—stemmed from a combination of befuddlement and false hope on the part of their commanders. From the knoll, the new uniforms of Kershaw's South Carolinians looked as blue as that of any Federal unit. Harker ordered his men to hold their fire and had the color-bearers wave the colors from the crest. Down in the field itself,

Wood and Opdycke were equally confused. As Kershaw's men stepped forward into the attack, a cry went along the line of the One Hundred Twenty-fifth Ohio: "Those are McCook's troops," and then, recalled Lieutenant Charles Clark of Company H, "just when we ought to have poured the entire contents of our cartridge boxes into those moving battalions as rapidly as possible . . . orders were given to cease firing and keep the flags well up." Clark was as deceived as his commanders. "Those moving battalions did appear to wear blue, dusty blue. . . . We had never seen a Confederate clothed otherwise than in butternut or gray. And their battle flags, both in color and size, appeared in the distance to resemble the brigade and division headquarter flags of McCook's corps."[20]

"I could not conceive it possible that our troops had been so suddenly routed," said Harker in defense of his inaction. "I was therefore in the most painful state of uncertainty that it is possible to conceive a commander to be placed in. The idea of firing upon our own troops was a most horrible one to me, yet if perchance they should be rebels, valuable time was being lost to me, and they would take advantage of it."

Thomas relieved Harker of his dilemma. The Virginian shared the Ohioan's uncertainty; he had been expecting Sheridan from that direction and hoped the approaching Confederates were actually the leading elements of his division. Nonetheless, Thomas told Harker that, if they opened on him after seeing the colors, he must return the fire. Thomas repeated his sensible order to Wood and Opdycke.[21]

The suspense was short-lived. Kershaw's skirmishers happily trained their rifles on the exposed Federal color-bearers. The color sergeant of the One Hundred Twenty-fifth was hit and the standard shot in two. Sergeant George Harlan, the twenty-one-year-old color-bearer of the Sixty-fifth Ohio, was shot in the left arm while brandishing the colors on the open crest. Harlan survived his wound and returned home to his Ohio farm a hero. By a strange twist of fate, he was killed in a threshing-machine accident there exactly two years later.[22]

Kershaw made good use of the opportunity handed him. While the rest of the brigade fixed bayonets and moved north through the field of stubble to confront Harker head on, Kershaw sent Lieutenant Colonel Franklin Gaillard and his Second South Carolina out of the line with orders to find and envelop the Federal right flank. Gaillard's men moved off to the northwest at the double-quick, through the field and across the front of Harker's perplexed troops on the knoll, who initially held their fire. On the extreme summit of the knoll, to Harker's right and rear, was the Fifty-eighth Indiana. Lieutenant Colonel Embree and his officers fell into a passionate debate over the identity of the troops who were fast coming up "in good order, bayonets fixed, and guns at right shoulder shift."

"Keep the flags well up." Sergeant George Harlan waves the colors
of the Sixty-fifth Ohio atop the knoll.

While the Hoosier officers agonized, Lieutenant Colonel Gaillard led his men toward a ravine just south of the Vittetoe road that ran up behind the knoll held by Embree and Harker. Gaillard had found the key to turning the entire Federal line. Pointing to the ravine, he yelled: "Let us get behind those fellows up there and capture them."

It took a volley in their right flank to settle the argument among the officers of the Fifty-eighth. The Indianians responded with a few scattered shots, then stumbled down the northern slope and across the Vittetoe road toward Horseshoe Ridge.[23]

The rout of the Fifty-eighth Indiana doomed Harker's brigade, a fact that was not lost on Lieutenant Colonel Gaillard. Reforming his regiment atop the knoll, the South Carolinian moved quickly to press his advantage. He changed front to the southeast and poured a withering volley into the right flank of the Sixty-fifth Ohio that toppled both its commander and senior captain. Captain Thomas Powell, a line officer whose real aspiration was to be regimental chaplain, assumed command. With the regiment completely absorbed in a fight to its front with both the Third South Carolina Battalion, which had fought its way to within a hundred yards of his position, and the Third South Carolina Regiment, Powell could do nothing to meet the threat to his flank. He prudently ordered the regiment to break contact and abandon the knoll. The Ohioans withdrew all the way to the Snodgrass house. Over one-third their number were back on the knoll, dead or wounded.[24]

Among the dead on the knoll was one young Confederate lieutenant whose death, had Harker's men known of his humanity, would certainly have caused them the deepest regret. Nine months earlier at Fredericksburg, while still a sergeant, Joseph Kirkland had left the protection of the stone wall on Marye's Heights to give water to the Federal wounded. It was bitingly cold, and the Yankees were begging for water. Kirkland could not bear their suffering. Seeking out Kershaw, he moaned: "General, I can't stand this!" "You can't stand what, Kirkland?" replied Kershaw. "Those poor fellows out there are our enemies, it is true; but they are wounded and dying, and they are helpless! I have come to ask leave to carry water to them," announced Kirkland. Kershaw tried to dissuade him, pointing out the obvious danger, but when that failed, he bade the sergeant go. Kirkland gathered and filled all the canteens he could, then slipped over the wall. A smattering of sharpshooter's bullets greeted him. Kirkland bent low and moved among the wounded who, discovering his purpose, began to sit up and call to him. The Yankee skirmishers ceased firing, and the "Angel of Fredericksburg" went about his mission of conscience unmolested.

As his comrades swarmed over the knoll and past him here at Chickamauga, Kirkland gasped to a friend: "Tell Pa good-by. I did my duty. I died at my post."[25]

With the way now clear, the men of the Third South Carolina Battalion scampered forward to join Gaillard's command on top of the knoll. Together they turned their fire on the right flank of the Third Kentucky, which lay exposed below them in the open ground between the base of the knoll and the copse of trees. Colonel Henry Dunlap tried to meet their volleys by ordering his right companies to file to the right at the double-quick, but this desperate maneuver served only to encourage the enemy to his front. Caught in a cross fire, eighty Kentuckians fell in a matter of minutes before Dunlap gave the order to retreat.[26]

General Wood was watching the action from near the blacksmith shop when the Third Kentucky gave way. As a Kentuckian, Wood took a special interest in the fate of the Third. He rode among its crumbling ranks, trying to steady the men, until a Rebel bullet knocked down his horse. That was enough to convince Wood to join his fellow Kentuckians in a run for the Snodgrass hill.[27]

Harker had come off the knoll early in the fight and was now with the One Hundred Twenty-fifth and Sixty-fourth Ohio regiments in the copse of trees. There a vicious struggle had been going on independent of the fight for the knoll. The Ohioans had checked the Confederate advance across the field, but at a severe cost. "The terrible splendor of this advance is beyond the reach of my pen," wrote Colonel Opdycke. "The whole line seemed perfect and as if moved by a single mind. The musketry became severe and my losses heavy." Line officers and noncommissioned officers were dropping at an alarming rate on the Federal side, and the enemy had closed to within seventy-five yards. Over the din, Lieutenant Clark shouted to Opdycke: "They can kill us, but whip us never."

A commendable sentiment, but Harker knew the time had come to quit the field. It was a foregone conclusion that, given the chance, the South Carolinians would push down from the knoll and cut off his line of retreat. With no relief in sight, Harker at 12:50 P.M. ordered his two remaining regiments to fall back northward to the next piece of defensible terrain, the open spur nearly a half mile in his rear that crowned the cornfield of the Snodgrass farm.[28]

GIVE US A POSITION TO HOLD

GEORGE Washington Snodgrass and his family had come to northern Georgia from their native Virginia in 1848, long after the best of the Cherokee "lottery tracts" were gone. Perhaps that explains why Snodgrass built their home on a spur of Missionary Ridge, a most unpromising piece of land on which to start a farm. Snodgrass raised his log cabin about a half mile west of the La Fayette road, on the northern slope of a lightly wooded knoll that was known, appropriately enough, as the Snodgrass hill. The Snodgrass cabin was nestled thirty yards back from the crest. It measured a mere twenty by eighteen feet, with a chimney on the east side and a front door that opened to a gravel walk on the south side. The back door opened into a shed, which in turn connected with a kitchen. Behind the kitchen was a small smokehouse. The gravel path in front of the house ran some thirty feet to a rough-hewn picket gate, which was part of a split-rail oak fence that surrounded the house and its outbuildings. On the west side of the house was a small peach orchard. A dirt lane known locally as the Snodgrass road ran north from the Vittetoe road, past the house, and on to the Mullis-Vittetoe road. Such was the homestead where Snodgrass, a vigorous sixty years old at the time of the battle, lived with his third wife and seven of his nine children—the eldest a soldier in the Army of Tennessee, the youngest just four years old.[1]

The cultivated portion of the Snodgrass farm consisted of an irregularly planted field of corn that began 150 yards southeast of the house and stretched some 600 yards north, where it met up with the cornfield of the Mullis family. The ground between the southern border of the cornfield and the Vittetoe road appears to have been a lightly wooded pasture. From the house, a gentle ridge ran slightly north of east 200 yards into the Snodgrass cornfield. This was the open spur to which Harker had ordered his men.

From the Snodgrass hill west to the Dry Valley road was a series of hills and ridges that after the battle became known collectively as Horseshoe Ridge. As Glenn Tucker pointed out, this spur of Missionary Ridge "is in no manner shaped like a horseshoe, nor is it possible while the trees are in foliage . . . to gain a very clear conception of the outlines of the elevation, which would more closely resemble an octopus with shortened tentacles, or an irregularly shaped starfish, than a horseshoe."[2] Near the Snodgrass farm, Horseshoe Ridge consists of three distinct hills. The first of these, which for want of a better name we will call Hill One, began practically at the doorstep of the Snodgrass house and crested about three hundred feet south of it. The second, which we will label Hill Two, was slightly higher and crested four hundred feet west of the top of Hill One. A third hill — Hill Three — had a less clearly defined crest and began about three hundred feet west of the top of Hill Two. All three hills were heavily timbered and in most places covered with underbrush, which by mid-afternoon on the second day of the battle would be largely shot away or trampled under foot. Visibility along the ridge varied from a few feet to nearly one hundred yards.[3]

The hills were separated from one another by ravines. A relatively wide and shallow ravine running north from the Vittetoe road defined the west slope of Hill One and the east slope of Hill Two; a narrow and deeper draw similarly separated the west slope of Hill Two from Hill Three.

A narrow plateau with extremely steep slopes ran west from Hill Three for about four hundred yards. Horseshoe Ridge itself, however, ran southwest from Hill Three and ended abruptly on the north side of the Vittetoe road. Nearby, tucked in a little meadow between the Vittetoe and Dry Valley roads, was the home of Hiram Vittetoe, his wife, and their three daughters.

Unlike the Vittetoes, the Snodgrass family was not at home to witness the grand drama that was about to unfold on their property. George Snodgrass was a stubborn old man, but he was no fool. He had refused to leave when the first Yankee foragers showed up at his doorstep on 18 September, but when bullets began to drop around his house and through the ceiling the next afternoon, Snodgrass packed up his family and retreated to a ravine deep in the woods northwest of the farm. There he met the Poes, Brothertons, Kellys, McDonalds, Brocks, and Mullises, all driven from their homes by the fighting. For eight days and nights the band of neighbors camped under the stars. Thanks to the thoroughness of Union foragers they had little food or water. By night they huddled around a heap of burning logs, by day, the men in the group combed the woods and nearby fields for food. All they found were a few field peas, which they fed raw to their hungry children.[4]

For the moment, the Snodgrass farm and Horseshoe Ridge belonged to the Federals. Whether they remained in their hands would depend on how

Generals Brannan and Negley and a handful of other officers made use of the sixty minutes of time that Harker's men were buying with their blood out in the Dyer field.

Brannan reached Hill One at noon, driven from the Dyer field with the fugitives of Connell's and Hays's brigades. While regimental officers tried to halt the panic and rally their commands, Brannan galloped over to the open spur east of the house, where he found Negley with Sirwell's brigade, Bridges's Illinois Battery, and Battery I, Fourth United States Artillery. The batteries of Schultz and Marshall had pulled off the knoll and were then on Hill Three.

Brannan and Negley conferred briefly. What passed between them was clouded by post-battle criminations and self-serving testimony. Evidently Brannan asked Negley to dispatch a regiment to Hill Two to extend his right, a request to which Negley responded by placing at Brannan's disposal the best regiment in his division, the 539-strong Twenty-first Ohio Volunteer Infantry, seven companies of which were armed with a five-shot, cylinder-fed, .56 caliber Colt revolving rifle. It was an odd weapon, incorporating the revolving action Samuel Colt had used in his famous pistols and adapting it to a long-barreled rifle with a full stock. Although slow and awkward to load, it could deliver five rounds just as fast as a soldier could cock the hammer and pull the trigger, nine seconds for a veteran. And the men of the Twenty-first had plenty of rounds to fire. At daybreak, their enterprising ordnance sergeant had ridden over to the division ordnance train and scrounged all the .56 caliber ammunition he could lay his hands on, so that each man now went into the fight loaded down with ninety-five rounds.[5]

Worn down by diarrhea and fatigue, Negley was finding it hard to concentrate. By the time Brannan met him at noon, Negley had just about lost his stomach for the fight. He had seen Robertson's Texans approach to within a few hundred yards of his batteries and was anxious to remove them to a safer location. The Pennsylvanian also was concerned about the welfare of Schultz's and Marshall's batteries. A few minutes earlier, he had sent Colonel Sirwell with the Seventy-fourth Ohio out onto the ridge to find and support the artillerymen. Now he concluded to move the remainder of the brigade and artillery in the same direction. That suited Brannan. Extracting a promise from Negley to cover his right from Hill Two with Sirwell's brigade, Brannan galloped back to help rally what remained of his division on Hill One. Negley ordered the Thirty-seventh Indiana to face to the right and, with the artillery, moved off behind the northern slope of Horseshoe Ridge toward Hill Two.[6]

The Pennsylvanian was growing careless. In his haste to get out from the open, Negley neglected to tell Lieutenant Frank Smith, commander of Battery I, Fourth United States Artillery, that he was leaving. Although his four guns stood alone and unsupported beside the Snodgrass house, Smith prudently decided to hold his position. Negley also forgot to notify Colonel Archibald Blakely, who with his Seventy-eighth Pennsylvania was out in the cornfield in support of Bridges's battery. Blakely rode around the Snodgrass farm awhile, looking for some sign of Negley or the brigade, then gave up and ordered his regiment out of the cornfield. Purely by chance, he moved off in the same direction Negley had taken.[7]

Lieutenant Colonel Dwella Stoughton, commander of the Twenty-first Ohio, was the next of Negley's subordinates to feel abandoned. Neither Negley nor Brannan had told him where to take his regiment. Leaving his men in the Snodgrass peach orchard, Stoughton ventured out onto Horseshoe Ridge to find some answers. On Hill One he ran into Colonel Moses Walker, a fellow Ohioan and old friend of the Twenty-first who had lived before the war in the town where the regiment had been organized. Walker was quite a sight, "as brave a man as ever displayed a sturdy person, carefully attired in full uniform, and with an expansive white waistcoat, as if he were going to a ball — as a great, big attractive target for the sharpshooters," recalled a member of the regiment.

Happy to see a familiar face amidst the bedlam, Stoughton told Walker that he "wished to join his regiment in any movement that Walker's brigade attempted to make on the hills." Stoughton was being charitable. Walker had no brigade at the moment. He had been placed under arrest for some minor infraction of military discipline before the battle and the lackluster John Connell put in his place. Technically, he was prohibited from giving orders to anyone. But with Connell nowhere to be found and his old brigade milling about in confusion, Walker acted. Waving his hand in the direction of Hill Two, he told Stoughton to take his regiment off to the right.[8]

Stoughton returned to the orchard and led the Twenty-first out onto Horseshoe Ridge under a steady fire from Kershaw's skirmishers, who were crossing the Vittetoe road to the south. The Ohioan still was not clear where Walker wanted him. He marched and countermarched his troops past Hill Two to Hill Three, at one point halting them with their backs toward the fire. The men became panicky. Captain Silas Canfield, the senior company commander, lost his temper. "If we maneuver these men much longer under fire, I fear we will lose control of them," he barked at Stoughton. "Give us a position to hold and we will hold it, give us an enemy to charge and we will charge them, but men will not stand fire from the rear." Stoughton took the point. He faced the regiment about and brought it into line across Hill Three, its left touching the top of the ravine, at about 12:40 P.M.[9]

Meanwhile, Brannan and Walker were bringing a semblance of order to Hill One. From fragments of regiments they molded a line of battle. Colonel

Morton Hunter brought about half his Eighty-second Indiana out of the Dyer field in good order and settled in on the southern edge of the hilltop. Lieutenant Colonel Durbin Ward fell in with a corporal's guard from the Seventeenth Ohio on Hunter's right. Colonel Alexander Stout somehow made it to the hill with fifty members of his Seventeenth Kentucky, which Walker threw into the line with Ward's Ohioans. A few soldiers belonging to the Thirty-first Ohio took position on the hill as well. All told, Walker had assembled about 210 bewildered but reasonably resolute men by the time Brannan rode up at about 12:30 P.M. Brannan had the good sense to release Walker from arrest and told him to assume command of the scratch line on Hill One.[10]

When Lieutenant Colonel Gabriel Wharton turned up with his Tenth Kentucky, most of the Fourteenth Ohio, and about forty-five men from the Fourth Kentucky—all that was left of Hays's brigade—Brannan and Walker diverted them to Hill Two to fill the gap created when Stoughton overshot his position. A detachment from the Fifty-eighth Indiana fell in at the same time. Colonel George Dick's brigade, which had given such a poor account of itself in the fight against Govan, was represented by a hundred men from the Thirteenth Ohio under the command of Captain Horatio Cosgrove and by a few squads from the Forty-fourth and Eighty-sixth Indiana regiments that found their way into the Snodgrass cornfield at about the same time, where they took position on the open spur.[11]

John Beatty rode into the chaos in search of the Fifteenth Kentucky and One Hundred Fourth Illinois, missing since the fight with Govan. There was no sign of his errant regiments. Nevertheless, "I found abundant opportunity to make myself useful," recalled Beatty, who set to work helping Walker on Hill One.[12]

It was 12:45 P.M. when Brannan, Walker, and Beatty completed their patchwork line along Horseshoe Ridge. To their left, Harker's men were coming out of the Dyer field and rallying on the Snodgrass spur. Captain Powell hastily formed most of the survivors of the Sixty-fifth Ohio, along with two companies from the Third Kentucky, in the timber on the eastern slope of Hill One, just south of the Snodgrass house. To the left of the house, near Smith's battery, Captain Charles Tannehill herded together a few men who had become separated from their companies. The Sixty-fourth Ohio, which had retired from the Dyer field in good order, halted on the spur to Tannehill's left. Colonel Dunlap, meanwhile, rallied his badly roughed-up Third Kentucky on the reverse slope behind the Sixty-fourth Ohio. Colonel Opdycke's One Hundred Twenty-fifth Ohio, the last to quit the fight with Kershaw, marched smartly up the slope and formed on the left of the Sixty-fourth at 1:00 P.M. The survivors of Dick's Eighty-sixth and Forty-fourth Indiana regiments that had congregated on the ridge—perhaps sixty men in all—fell in and extended the line a few yards farther to the east. There were now some twelve hundred Federals arrayed along or near the open spur.[13]

General Wood was pleased with Harker's new position. "Troops holding it could load and fire behind it out of reach of the enemy's fire, and then advance to the crest of it to deliver a plunging fire on the advancing foe," he reported. "In addition there was a moral effect in its command over the ground south of it which inspired the courage of the troops holding it. General Brannan formed on my right and higher up on the main ridge, thus giving to our united lines something of the shape of an irregular crescent, with the concavity toward the enemy."[14]

Thomas shared Wood's regard for the position, and he had confidence enough in Harker to make his headquarters behind the Ohioan's brigade. A few minutes after Wood and Harker completed their line, General Thomas rode up with a retinue that included Ambrose Bierce and the correspondent William Shanks and set up headquarters under a large oak tree beside the Snodgrass road, just behind the crest held by the Sixty-fourth Ohio. Visibility was mixed. Although five hundred yards of forest blocked Thomas's view of the Kelly field, he could see north and northeast through the Mullis fields as far as the McFarland's Gap road.[15]

The presence of Thomas was electrifying. Nearly every soldier in Harker's brigade who left a record of his experiences in the battle mentions having seen Thomas, sitting stolidly amid the noise and confusion, and of the uplifting effect this had on morale. To Harker, Thomas said simply: "This hill must be held and I trust you to do it."

"We will hold it or die here," Harker promised.

To Colonel Opdycke, Thomas repeated the command. "You must hold this position at all hazards."

"We will hold this ground or go to Heaven from it," was the colonel's lyrical reply.[16]

That was a sentiment Thomas appreciated. It accorded precisely with his notions of combat. During a staff call one day before the Tullahoma campaign, Thomas had laid out his theory of training and fighting. "Put a plank six inches wide five feet above the ground and a thousand men will walk it easily," he began. "Raise it five hundred feet and one man out of a thousand will walk it safely. It is a question of nerve we have to solve, not dexterity. It is not to touch elbows and fire a gun but how to do them under fire," continued Thomas, his enthusiasm growing. "We are all cowards in the presence of immediate death. We can overcome that fear in war through familiarity. Southerners are more accustomed to violence and therefore more familiar with death." Thomas grew animated. "What we have to do is to make veterans. McClellan's great error was in his avoidance of fighting. His congratulatory report was 'All Quiet along the Potomac.' The result was a loss in morale. His troops came to have a mysterious fear of the enemy."

Thomas paused a moment and looked at his staff, who were watching their general's fervent presentation with mild surprise. His normal shyness returned. "Well, Gentlemen, we will defer bragging until we capture Bragg."[17]

Word of Thomas's presence spread quickly down the line, giving peace of mind and added determination to the soldiers who were about to defend Horseshoe Ridge. "It is strange what an effect the appearance of Old Pap, as they familiarly called General Thomas, at any point of danger had upon his men," averred Lieutenant Colonel Ward of the Thirty-seventh Indiana. "It always restored confidence. Indeed his old corps believed they could not be whipped when he commanded them."[18]

The same could not be said for Negley. His troops loved him and counted themselves fortunate to be under his command, not because he possessed a rock-solid resolve under fire but rather because of his deep concern for their welfare, which made him reluctant to commit them to battle in fluid situations where the risks were great.[19]

Now was one such time. Somewhere between the Snodgrass hill and the ridge west of Hill Three, Negley lost his will to fight. As he passed the latter hill he ordered off the batteries of Schultz and Marshall. Any lingering notion he may have entertained about staying to fight vanished when he saw the Dry Valley road. It was a scene of unbridled hysteria and crazy rumors, best described by Lieutenant Colonel Ward of the Thirty-seventh Indiana: "Many of the officers of all ranks showed by their wild commands and still wilder actions that they had completely lost their heads and were as badly demoralized as the private soldiers. Many of these had thrown away their arms evidently thinking only of saving themselves by flight."[20]

Negley and Sirwell and their staffs made a halfhearted attempt at turning them around, but their efforts were wasted. "As soon as a detachment brought to the front to support the batteries heard the sound of the enemy's muskets in their front, they disappeared like smoke. They were soon all gone," recalled Negley's adjutant.[21]

Five hundred yards to the southeast, Bushrod Johnson's Confederates were consolidating their position around Mendenhall's captured guns. Word of their imminent approach reached Negley. "Reliable information," which proved completely spurious, was passed of a Rebel cavalry force pounding down the Dry Valley road from his right to his rear. "Finding it impossible to organize any of the passing troops, and unable to communicate with General Thomas, and being informed by a staff officer [Lieutenant Moody] that Generals Rosecrans, McCook, and Crittenden had left the field, I deemed it vitally important to secure the safety of the artillery, which appeared to be threatened with immediate capture," Negley explained.[22]

With seven hundred men of Sirwell's brigade and four batteries of artillery, Negley started for Rossville. Not only did he march off the field with twenty-two cannons desperately needed by the defenders of Horseshoe Ridge, but he picked up straggling infantry that might otherwise have rallied with Brannan. To his column came Beatty's two missing regiments, portions of the One Hundredth Illinois and Thirteenth Michigan from Buell's brigade, and Colonel Connell with a few score men he had gathered from his brigade.[23]

When Negley's column finally came off the hills onto the Dry Valley road, the men faced a panic even greater than that which they had left back on Horseshoe Ridge. Recalled Lieutenant Colonel Ward: "At one point we found cannon and wagons blocked by an accident in a narrow defile, and could not for a short time pass through. A badly demoralized colonel rode up to them and in a loud and badly frightened tone called out, 'Get out of here at once! The Rebel cavalry are right on you!' This may have been intended for good, but the effect was to cause teamsters and artillerymen to jump from their horses and start off on the run, and the demoralized soldiers to increase their speed." Negley did what he could to inject some order into the flight, sustained by the conviction that his decision to leave the field had been correct.[24]

At 1:00 P.M. Kershaw delivered the first of what would prove a series of poorly coordinated Confederate assaults on the Snodgrass spur–Horseshoe Ridge defenses. The South Carolinian's first effort was less an attack, really, than the culmination of his pursuit of Harker.

Kershaw's brigade was ill prepared to overcome the unexpected resistance it met along the ridge. The regiments had scattered badly during the chase, so that they hit the new Federal line piecemeal across a front far too wide for Kershaw to control on foot.

On the left, Lieutenant Colonel Gaillard's Second South Carolina charged recklessly up the ravine between the second and third hills, expecting to meet no more resistance than they had in turning Harker's flank thirty minutes before. Instead, they found the Twenty-first Ohio waiting for them behind hastily formed breastworks of fallen timber. Colt rifles blazed and the South Carolinians recoiled off the hill all the way back down to the Vittetoe road. There, recalled John Coxe, "protected from the terrific fire from the top of the hill, we lay down . . . and for awhile enjoyed a nice breeze passing through the woods, now and then blowing from the trees bunches of yellow leaves, which gently sailed down and settled on the ground among us. And I recollect that in my mind I compared these falling leaves to the falling men on that battlefield."[25]

So rapidly had the Second South Carolina vanished that the officers of the Twenty-first thought they had encountered nothing more than a reinforced skirmish line. On that assumption, Stoughton ordered his men to their feet and down the slope in pursuit. It was a bad idea. At the base of the hill the Ohioans were as vulnerable as the Second South Carolina had been a few minutes earlier. "We had sufficient notice of their coming to be ready for them," remembered Coxe. "Our officers commanded us to hold our fire till they got in short range and then 'give it to them.' Here they came armed with Colt repeating rifles and a shout. They were allowed to get within twenty yards of our position in the thick undergrowth along the road, then, before they visualized our presence, we rose up as one man and poured into them such a volley from our faithful Enfields as to make many of them bite the dust for the last time." Back up the hill went the Ohioans.[26]

The Third South Carolina Battalion and the Third South Carolina, meanwhile, had come at Hill Two by way of the knoll in the Dyer field. Obliquing to the northwest, they moved along the ridge toward the knoll from which the Fifty-eighth Indiana had been driven a half hour before. Coming up on its crest, the South Carolinians were exposed to a heavy fire from Brannan's Federals on Hill Two, which lay two hundred yards to the north. Hurrying down the knoll, over a fence, and through a deep ravine, they crossed the Vittetoe road and pushed on another one hundred yards before meeting Kershaw, who halted them at the base of the hill and waved them back to the ravine, there to wait until he could organize the brigade for a concerted assault with Humphreys, whose appearance he anxiously awaited.[27]

Kershaw was in no position to press the attack on his own. His brigade was dispersed along the foot of Horseshoe Ridge over a front that, taking into account the twists and turns of the terrain, was nearly half a mile wide. The Seventh and Fifteenth South Carolina regiments had drifted at least three hundred yards to the right of the Third South Carolina. After a halfhearted probing attack against the southeastern slope of Hill One and Harker's line on the spur, they fell back into the woods just south of the Vittetoe road, the center of their line bisected by the Snodgrass road. Two hundred yards to the right of the Seventh and Fifteenth South Carolina was the Eighth South Carolina, which had fought its way to the edge of the Snodgrass cornfield independent of the brigade.[28]

Brigadier General Benjamin Humphreys was not the man for the moment. The fifty-five-year-old Mississippian had succeeded to brigade command following the death at Gettysburg of William Barksdale, one of the most talented brigadiers in the Army of Northern Virginia. Barksdale had loomed as a figure of almost heroic stature in an army filled with larger-than-life heroes. Many, Humphreys included, believed him irreplaceable. Capable but timid, Humphreys accepted his promotion reluctantly. "A humiliating sense of my incompetency and the great responsibility painfully oppressed me in taking command of a brigade that had signalised its valor on so many bloody fields," he later admitted. "My appointment changed the name from 'Barksdale' to 'Humphreys's Brigade.' Though the name of Barksdale disappears from the army roll, no other name will be more fondly cherished as a bright ornament in the Confederate army, or more affectionately remembered."[29]

As he led his brigade north through the Dyer field, Humphreys met General Longstreet. "I never saw him wear so bright and jubilant a countenance," recalled Humphreys. The two exchanged salutes. "Drive them, General, these western men can't stand it any better than the Yankees we left in Virginia," laughed Longstreet. Humphreys continued cautiously on past the blacksmith shop toward the Snodgrass cornfield. If Longstreet's optimistic admonition had any effect on Humphreys, it was not evident in his behavior.[30]

While he waited for Humphreys, Kershaw was joined by Colonel Oates and his Fifteenth Alabama. No other regiment saw more of the battlefield or caused more problems than the Fifteenth, thanks to its imperious commander. After the defeat of Lytle, Oates broke away from Deas's brigade and wandered north across the Dyer field. As he watched his regiment march to its next adventure, Oates noticed a young boy of about fifteen years of age, a member of Company G, lagging in the rear and crying. Oates approached him. In a fatherly voice, Oates told the little soldier not to cry, that "he had not yet been hurt and he might live through the battle, and not to be so unmanly as to become frightened and go to crying." "Afraid, hell! that ain't it," retorted the boy. "I am so damn tired I can't keep up with my company."[31]

Oates moved his regiment east around the knoll and into the deep ravine just south of the Vittetoe road. There he found Kershaw's brigade. Without bothering to inform Kershaw of his presence or seek his permission, Oates advanced his Alabamians into the wide gap between the Third and Seventh South Carolina regiments. Once there, Oates began to throw his weight around. Noticing the gathering of Federals atop Hill One and concerned by the space that still existed between his left and the right of the Third South Carolina, Oates jogged over to Colonel Nance and asked him to close up on the Fifteenth and then join Oates in an assault on the hill. Nance declined. Oates, claiming to be the senior colonel present, even though his commission had not yet come through, then tried to order him to comply.

Again Nance refused. "I bestowed upon him a few encomiums and returned to my regiment and extended my line by placing the men in one rank," said Oates. He then tried his luck with the commander of the Seventh South Carolina, which lay deeper in the ravine to the right and rear of the Fifteenth. Lieutenant Colonel Elbert Bland and Major John Hard had been killed in the fight with Harker, leaving the regiment in the hands of its senior captain, E. J. Goggans. Goggans was no more inclined to cooperate than Nance. He refused to move up on Oates's right, saying that Kershaw personally had placed the regiment where it was. Oates ordered him forward. Goggans neither replied nor moved. Oates tried a different approach. "I got up on a log and made an appeal to the State pride of the regiment and asked the men not to go where I directed merely, but to follow me," boasted Oates. "One captain said, 'Colonel, I will follow you with my company.' As he started the whole regiment moved, and I led them into action."[32]

Out of the ravine and across the road charged the South Carolinians, obliquing to the left across the pasture toward the eastern slope of Hill One. The Fifteenth South Carolina took up the assault to their right, advancing into the cornfield toward Smith's battery on the spur. To their left, Oates's own regiment scampered directly up the southern slope of Hill One.

Kershaw was over on the left of the brigade, oblivious to Oates's meddling on the right. When he heard the firing begin in that direction, Kershaw assumed Humphreys had come up and gone directly into the attack against Harker. Consequently, he now ordered the Second South Carolina Regiment, the Third South Carolina Battalion, and the Third South Carolina Regiment to press the assault on their front. It was about 1:15 P.M.[33]

Colonel Morton Hunter called what followed "the most determined and furious attack . . . that I ever saw or heard of." For a moment, it appeared as if Oates's impetuosity would carry the day. His Alabamians clawed their way up the south face of Hill One to within a few yards of the Union lines. To their left, Nance's Third South Carolina drove up the western slope of the hill. To their right, the Seventh South Carolina had gained the crest and was driving in the handful of Federals holding the eastern side.

The tide quickly turned. Up the northern side of the Snodgrass hill came Timothy Stanley at the head of his brigade, which he had pieced back together after its losing fight with Govan. Stanley had fewer than five hundred men, but he deployed them precisely where they were most needed. With no time to form line of battle, he sent the Nineteenth Illinois, now down to about 160 men, forward from the Snodgrass house and out onto Hill One in column of companies. As soon as the Eleventh Michigan came up, he waved it into action on the left of the Nineteenth to protect a two-gun section of Smith's Battery I, Fourth United States Artillery, that Walker had ordered forward to support his tiny command on the hill. Stanley held

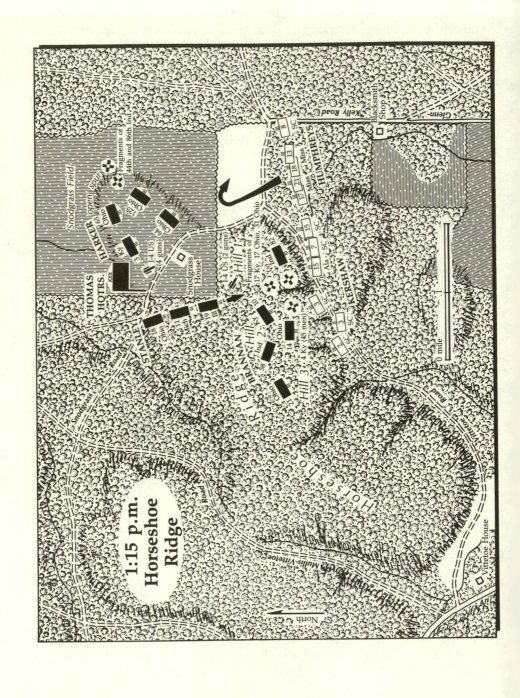

1:15 p.m.
Horseshoe
Ridge

the Eighteenth Ohio, reduced to a hundred men, in reserve beside Smith's other section at the Snodgrass house.[34]

Stanley was knocked off his horse with a bullet in the shoulder the instant he showed himself on the hill, but there were enough field officers on the hill that he was not missed. Colonel William Stoughton took command, and John Beatty was there to help guide the brigade.[35]

It was, in any case, a soldier's fight. No orders were needed—the enemy was on the hill and had to be pushed off; that was clear to the lowest private. The struggle was brief but desperate. So close were the two lines that Colonel Oates recalled one frightened Federal who threw down his rifle and ran through the ranks of the Fifteenth Alabama for protection. The men of the Eleventh Michigan cursed as they tried to engage the enemy; their rifles already were so corroded with powder that they were becoming hard to load, and the regiment's supply of ammunition was running dangerously low. But the intensity of their volleys was not crucial, the mere shock of their appearance was enough to break the Seventh South Carolina's hold on the crest, and Rebels began trickling back down the slope.[36]

Alfred Clark, the color-bearer of the Seventh, was not among them. He had run a few paces ahead of the regiment when it gained the crest and now stood virtually alone a few yards from Stanley's Federals. A Union field officer yelled that he would give a captain's commission to the man who captured the colors. Several sprang forward just as Clark was hit. Clark turned, threw the colors down off the hill, where they landed safely among his comrades, then fell over dead. It was an act of courage that survivors on both sides would talk about for years to come.[37]

Colonel Oates was livid at the Seventh for having "ingloriously fled," as he put it. He ran among the South Carolinians, trying to rally them, but only a captain with a handful of his men responded. Then Oates looked toward his own men. They too were starting down the hill. By the time Oates caught up with them, his Alabamians were across the Vittetoe road. Stanley's Federals had come off the hill and were in close pursuit. "Halt, halt men!" Oates screamed. "Is there no officer who will set the example?" A lone lieutenant heeded the call. Rallying his men, he joined Oates behind a line of crude breastworks the regiment had built at the edge of the ravine from logs and the rails of a nearby fence before going into action. A few volleys were enough to send the Yankees back up the hill.[38]

Among the other regiments of Kershaw's brigade the results were similar. The Second South Carolina advanced up the draw between the second and third hill to the ridge, only to be thrown off once again by the Colt rifles of the Twenty-first Ohio. The Third South Carolina Battalion and the Third South Carolina Regiment gained a toehold on the crest of Hill Two, which they held until an enfilading fire from Smith's section on the first hill drove them away. Out in the Snodgrass cornfield, the Fifteenth South Carolina had been cut to pieces by the disciplined volley firing of Harker's Federals.[39]

Kershaw had had enough for the moment. He ran from regiment to regiment, ordering them back under the cover of the ravine. There they followed the example of Oates's Alabamians, stripping apart the worm rail fence at the northern edge of the Dyer field for breastworks while Kershaw sent staff officers off to look for reinforcements.[40]

And what of Humphreys? Timidity had paralyzed him at the edge of the cornfield a few minutes after 1:00 P.M. Looking up the slope of stunted cornstalks, Humphreys was chilled by the sight of Smith's cannons and Harker's long blue line. "My brave boys wanted to charge on, but I had seen too many lines repulsed from just such looking places. . . . A very slight reconnaissance satisfied me that to attempt to attack would be the loss of one half of my brigade," he wrote later by way of an apology for his failure to support Kershaw. Captain J. S. McNeily of the Twenty-first Mississippi saw things differently. With thinly veiled disgust, he later wrote:

> The two right regiments were very little exposed. The left regiment was the most exposed and returned the fire. The left center, to which I belonged, had not, I think, fired a volley, for we were all expecting the order to charge at double-quick — but it never came. Ordering a halt, General Humphreys rode through our ranks and out into the open in the face of the enemy. Here, after a moment of close scrutiny, he turned and shouted the order " 'Bout face," and we marched from under fire. . . . In . . . conversation with General Humphreys . . . I expressed the disappointment of the whole command at his order to retire, telling him the men were keyed up to the highest tension, and would have gone over the enemy's line as we did at Gettysburg.[41]

While his men grumbled, Humphreys sent word to Longstreet that he had "engaged and reconnoitered" the enemy's position but "found it impossible to drive him from it." Longstreet took the Mississippian at his word and told him to take up a defensive position near the blacksmith shop. So ended Humphreys's brief contribution to the assault on the Snodgrass hill.[42]

A hush fell now over the field, punctuated only by the inevitable moans of the wounded and the occasional crack of a sharpshooter's rifle. Sharpshooting, the Civil War equivalent of sniper fire, was a distinctly Confederate specialty. Many brigades contained battalions of sharpshooters that acted as skirmishers in an advance and snipers in a static situation. In other commands, the best shots were selected to climb trees or creep close to the enemy to pick off mounted officers.

Kershaw's sharpshooters availed themselves of the lull to practice their insidious art. The whiz of their bullets caused every field officer in Harker's brigade except the reckless Opdycke to dismount or stay behind the spur, and it attracted the notice of Thomas. Riding up behind the Third Kentucky, the Virginian inquired if there were any good squirrel hunters in the regiment. Of course, the Kentuckians replied. Thomas then asked the nearest company officer, Captain George McClure, to take a small detail out and shoot down some of the sharpshooters. With six men from his Company K, McClure crept around the eastern slope of Hill One down to the Vittetoe road, where he spotted a sharpshooter in a tall oak. The entire detail fired into the tree, and as the Rebel fell to the ground dead, another dozen or so hopped down from trees and ran off.[43]

Lieutenant Colonel Stoughton of the Twenty-first Ohio was slow to appreciate the threat. While his men hugged the ground behind a scattering of logs, the colonel sat placidly on his horse, adorned in a bright cloak that made him the target of choice for every Rebel sharpshooter on that part of the field. Captain Canfield stood beside him. Several bullets zipped past. Glancing toward a tree from which the last shot came, Stoughton remarked to Canfield, as if surprised: "The damn cuss is firing at me." The captain suggested he move about to present a less inviting target. Stoughton sat still. "I guess they won't hurt anybody," he replied absently. The next shot came from the same tree and killed his horse. Stoughton picked himself up off the ground and looked through his field glass for the sharpshooter. Another shot rang out from the tree. It ripped through Stoughton's right arm and came out beneath the shoulder. "I think this will use me up," Stoughton moaned as he sank to the ground. Canfield cradled the colonel in his arms. "These joint wounds are dangerous," Stoughton went on. He cautioned Canfield to say nothing of his wound to the men. Before he was carried off to the field hospital at the Snodgrass house, Stoughton asked Canfield to help Major Arnold McMahan with the regiment. "I want you to see that the men do their duty, for they have a hard fight before them."[44]

THOMAS IS HAVING A HELL
OF A FIGHT

BUSHROD Johnson had trouble comprehending the completeness of his victory over Crittenden. When at noon he suddenly found himself in possession of the ridge west of the Dyer field, along with nine Federal cannons, Johnson's first instinct was to dispose his forces defensively to fend off what he assumed would be an inevitable counterattack. Accordingly, he deployed Sugg's brigade in line of battle on the northwestern slope of the ridge and brought Fulton up on his left. Colonel Coleman had fallen back off the ridge for want of ammunition and was now in the woods south of the field alongside Robertson's brigade.

Johnson pushed his skirmishers off the ridge and into the Vittetoe corn-field. To their relief, they kicked up nothing but panic-stricken Federals swarming north. Along the road in both directions as far as the Confederates could see, everything was chaos. North of the Vittetoe house, the road passed through a gorge—a natural choke point toward which swearing and frightened Yankee teamsters were struggling to drive the wagons of McCook's ammunition train.[1]

It was an opportunity not lost on Johnson. He called Everett's battery to the ridge to shell the wagons and ordered his skirmishers to open fire on the teamsters. At the first boom of the cannons, the train broke up. Teams ran wild. Wagons overturned and crashed into trees. In a matter of minutes the gorge was blocked. Teamsters jumped from their seats and abandoned their wagons amid rumors that Confederate cavalry were charging down the road. Caissons, limbers, and guns were left behind. This was the panic that had convinced Negley the day was lost.

Johnson's skirmishers dashed across the Vittetoe cornfield to count their spoils. They laid claim to four cannons, seven caissons, and thirty wagons, most of which were fully laden with ammunition that would supply the needs of Johnson's division for the remainder of the battle.[2]

Now Johnson was ready to consider a further advance. He ordered Sugg and Fulton to reform in the Vittetoe field and draw ammunition. A staff officer brought up Dent's battery from Hindman's division, which he had found wandering about near Lytle Hill, and Johnson placed it on the ridge east of the cornfield. There it opened a harassing fire on the retreating Federals. Despite the overwhelming evidence of a Union rout, Johnson hesitated, and with reason. He had heard nothing from Longstreet since beginning the assault, and Hood's admonition to "keep ahead of everything" no longer seemed quite sufficient. Moreover, his was a division in name only. Fulton's brigade had numbered only 556 at the start of the day's action, Sugg's 848. Coleman had over a thousand men but was still back in the Dyer woods. "No general officer or re-enforcements having come up, and seeing no troops in my vicinity, I became impatient at the delay," explained the Ohioan. "Giving orders that our position should be held at all hazards, I galloped off in person in search of support."[3]

Johnson's first inclination was to advance northwest toward McFarland's Gap. Had he done so, and succeeded in seizing the gap, only the La Fayette road would have remained as a line of retreat for the Federals. To reach the Rossville Gap by that route would have meant retiring across the front of Bragg's right wing, a risky proposition to say the least.[4]

What Johnson saw when he rode back into the Dyer field at about 12:15 P.M. determined the course of his movements for the rest of the day. There, as related earlier, he found Kershaw's brigade preparing to move toward Harker on the knoll "near to which we had captured the battery of nine guns in our advance, and where I saw the United States flag now floating." Johnson met Kershaw and, learning that Hood had been wounded, tried to cajole the South Carolinian into coming to his support. When that failed, he tried to assume command of the corps by challenging Kershaw's date of rank. Major E. H. Cunningham of Hood's staff put a stop to the unseemly contest. He told Johnson that Kershaw's mission was to drive off Harker and that he had best look elsewhere for help. Longstreet, who could have halted this slide toward anarchy among his subordinates, was somewhere back in the forest near the Brotherton farm and out of touch for the moment. Consequently, Johnson and Kershaw went their separate ways, each to attack Horseshoe Ridge independently of the other; or, as Archibald Gracie, Jr., put it, to "pull in opposite directions."[5]

Johnson accepted Cunningham's arbitration. Sending Captain Blakemore off to find and bring up Coleman's brigade, Johnson turned and rode west down the Dyer road. Near the Dyer house he ran into Hindman and

Anderson, who, having driven off Davis and Sheridan, were riding north to investigate the state of affairs beyond their own right flank. Blakemore had gotten there ahead of Johnson and had asked Hindman to move to the support of his division, an appeal that Johnson now passionately endorsed.

Hindman agreed and immediately placed Anderson at Johnson's disposal. The Ohioan explained his plan. He would march north past the Vittetoe house and across the southern plateau of Horseshoe Ridge, then wheel his division to the right in an effort to take the Federals in the flank. Anderson was to fill the vacancy between his right and the left of Kershaw. He wished Deas's brigade, which was out of ammunition, to fall in on his left after it had drawn a resupply from the captured train. Hindman concurred and also promised to send along Manigault as soon as possible.[6]

As he rode back to his division, Johnson had second thoughts about waiting for Hindman: "More than an hour had now been spent in this position, and I resolved to press forward my line even before support reached me." Neither would he wait any longer for Coleman. Forming line of battle facing north across the Vittetoe cornfield, with Fulton on the left and Sugg on the right, Johnson sent his command forward toward the heights at about 1:30 P.M.[7]

Through the cracks in the boards of his windowless, one-room cabin, Hiram Vittetoe, a staunch Rebel sympathizer, watched the line of battle draw near. In a hole beneath the kitchen floor, covered with boards, were his wife and three teenage daughters. For two days they hid out from the Yankees. "The Rebels have the field," Vittetoe shouted when he realized the soldiers were Confederates. His wife and daughters threw off the floorboards and ran out of the cabin. Fulton's Tennesseans were delighted with the surprise appearance. Colonel Watt Floyd of the Seventeenth Tennessee was moved to relate the incident in his report: "Just as we passed the house . . . four very nice looking ladies . . . came bounding toward us, clapping their hands, and shouting as I had never seen women shout before. The tear of joyful sympathy started from many a soldier's eye, and you might have read in their countenances, 'We will save you or die.' " "The ladies came out . . . waving their aprons and bonnets," one of Floyd's men remembered fondly. "We were almost worn out, but managed to give them a few cheers."[8]

Johnson's men pushed on across the Vittetoe road and up the tangled slope. At the brow of the southernmost hill of Horseshoe Ridge they paused to correct alignment and wait for the artillery limbers to catch up. During the pause, Anderson's Mississippians came up on their right. Anderson reported his brigade to Johnson and then galloped down the Vittetoe road and into the ravine to coordinate his movements with Kershaw. The South Carolinian briefed him on the Federal dispositions and suggested he move against Hill Three with an eye toward rolling up the Yankee right, but offered only to play a supporting role himself. He would engage the enemy along his front sufficiently to hold them in place, but was unwilling to order his men up the ridge a third time.[9]

Anderson acquiesced, reluctantly. His misgivings were well founded; no more than 350 yards separated Johnson's right from Kershaw's left, barely enough space for the Mississippian to deploy two regiments on line. Returning to his command, Anderson selected the Tenth and Forty-fourth Mississippi regiments to make the assault. The Ninth, Forty-first, and Seventh Mississippi he would hold in reserve, ready to exploit any breach.[10]

Laid out along the slope of Hill Three for the Mississippians to contemplate as they formed line of battle was a chilling vista of gore. The Colt rifles of the Twenty-first had begun to overheat and foul during Kershaw's second attack, so rapidly did the Ohioans empty the cylinders. Each discharge sent a flash of fire into the dry leaves and undergrowth, igniting brushfires along the path taken by the Twenty-first when it pursued the South Carolinians down the hill. Seventeen-year-old Wilson Vance, a second lieutenant in Company D, described the scene as it appeared from the crest:

> Scattered over the burning and smoking hillside lay a number of wounded men belonging to the regiment, who had fallen in our swift advance or slow and stubborn retreat to the old position, and soon their cries for relief became fairly appalling, as the agony of being roasted was added to the pain of their wounds. Volunteers rushed forward and drew the poor fellows back; but some of them were piteously burned, the white, cooked flesh peeling back from their charred finger-bones, and in the case of an old school-mate of mine, great flakes falling off his cheeks. And so they died.[11]

Johnson continued his deliberate preparations. Four Napoleon guns from Dent's battery were wheeled through the underbrush into place in front of Fulton's waiting Tennesseans. The three howitzers of Everett's Georgia battery were brought up beside Dent. The remaining section of Dent's battery took position in front of Sugg's brigade. At 1:45 P.M., the artillery opened fire on the woods to their front. A few minutes before 2:00 P.M., the infantry stepped forward at the quick-time. They advanced cautiously toward their immediate objective, the ridge west of Hill Three. The men were "well-nigh worn-out" from the excitement of the morning, recalled a soldier of the Seventeenth Tennessee, and Johnson was taking care to pace them.[12]

No such considerations troubled Anderson. He threw the Tenth and Forty-fourth Mississippi up Hill Three with an almost reckless abandon. Dent's right section blasted the crest to cover the advancing Mississippians. Few Ohioans were hit, but the exploding shells ignited more brushfires, and in a few minutes their entire front was blanketed in smoke. Out of the smoke emerged the Mississippians, just a few yards from the crest. The Twenty-first Ohio opened fire and the Rebel line shivered. Still the Mississippians pressed on. They came within thirty feet of the Twenty-first before the overwhelming firepower of the Colt rifles forced them to yield. One terrified Mississippian dropped his rifle and darted into the ranks of Company C to surrender. As he regained his composure, the Rebel examined his surroundings. Seeing only a single line of Yankees, he asked in astonishment: "Where are your men?" "Here they are," replied his captor, waving his hand along the rapidly thinning line of Ohioans. "My God!" said the Rebel. "I thought you had a whole division here."[13]

Anderson was at the foot of the hill to greet his Mississippians as they stumbled down the slope in retreat after just ten minutes in action. He immediately sent forward his reserve regiments. Again the Colt rifles halted the enemy. This time, however, the Mississippians held their ground and returned the fire, inching nearer the crest after each volley.

The Federal fire began to slacken. Colt cylinders, choked from rapid use, refused to revolve. Desperate soldiers urinated on the cylinders to cool the steel. Many had nearly exhausted their ninety-five rounds. Sergeant John Bolton, the quick-thinking regimental ordnance sergeant, organized a detail to rummage the cartridge boxes of the dead and wounded. With ammunition running low, some experimented. A few shoved .57 caliber cartridges into the cylinders, only to have the rifles burst in their faces when they tried to fire. Then someone discovered that by attaching the bayonet to the end of the rifle the slightly larger Enfield ball could be used without splitting the muzzle. Those armed with Enfields exchanged their weapons for Colt rifles dropped by fallen comrades. Enfield cartridges were redistributed, and for the moment the ammunition shortage was eased.[14]

The strain of ninety minutes of nearly continuous Confederate attacks was beginning to tell on the Twenty-first. In Company D, Captain Charles Allen had been shot in the stomach, leaving the youthful Lieutenant Vance in command. Unable to accept the burden, Vance at first merely watched in open-mouthed amazement as good soldiers snapped under the stress of combat:

> The first man to manifest this queer frenzy was . . . apparently well balanced and cool at ordinary times, and as brave as any man in the corps. He had not been under fire more than half an hour till he became a raving maniac. There was method in his madness, however, since he never ceased to fight — only he ceased to fight intelligently. He ran far out in advance of the line, and taking his position by the side of a tree, loaded and fired furiously, all the time shouting and yelling, and turning to taunt his comrades with vile profanity . . . calling them cowards because they would not come forward to join him. Neither commands, threats, nor coaxing availed to bring

him back to his place, and at last his madness became such a painful exhibition of gibbering apishness that his death was a welcome relief to us all — if one may say such a thing. Another man had two or three fingers shot off his right hand, and he instantly flashed into temporary insanity. He cursed and reviled the Johnnies with the most horrible and grotesque profanity that ever came from man's worst imagination, dancing and gyrating almost comically. Then he sought a wounded comrade, who, lying upon the ground and unable to stand upright, could still load his rifle. Thus aided, the crazy man kept on firing and shouting and cursing till the loss of blood made him faint, when he was persuaded to go to the rear.[15]

When one of his best men succumbed, Vance found the courage to act. The soldier in question was a "great, tall, strong fellow... of perhaps forty-five, sober, steady and reliable as the sun, whose absence made an ominous hole in the ranks." Vance found him lying face down behind a tree in the rear of the firing line.

"What is the matter with you?" he asked. The soldier raised his face. "It was pallid and sickening as he looked at me with a wild, almost crazed expression," recalled Vance.

"I'm wounded, I'm wounded," babbled the soldier.

"Where?"

"Right here-here-here," he cried, beating a tattoo on his forehead. The skin was neither broken nor bruised.

"What do you mean by telling me such a lie? You're not wounded; you're not hurt — get back to your place, sir!" snapped Vance.

The soldier refused to budge. "I can't, lieutenant, I can't. I tell you I'm wounded — right here — right here."

Vance lost his temper. He struck the man with his sword, again and again, all the while thinking how the soldier, who was old enough to be his father, could have "picked me up and thrown me down the hill at the enemy." Vance beat him to his feet and then drove him back to his place. With each blow, the soldier cried: "Oh, lieutenant, for God's sake, don't, for God's sake, don't. I'm wounded — I'm wounded."

"Get to work, sir, and let me hear no more of your crazy notions," commanded Vance. With a look of abject despair, the soldier sulked into line and began firing. Vance went about his duty. "Ten minutes later I went to the head of the company line, and in my heedless haste stumbled over a dead body. Looking down, the stony, staring gaze of a dead man's eyes met mine." It was the distressed soldier. "He was dead — shot through the forehead."

Vance was stunned. "As I knelt by the body and searched his pockets for the little trinkets that should be sent to his family, and found there the pictures of the wife and the chubby children, and the locks of hair and soiled and worn letters from home, I felt like a murderer. The scene swam before my eyes, and I fairly reeled."[16]

An unexpected fire beyond the right flank of the regiment restored Vance's balance. Standing up, he saw Confederate skirmishers scurry over the ridge west of Hill Three and disappear into the timber behind the Twenty-first. Along the brow, a line of Rebels was hastily forming to deliver a volley into the flank company. Captain Henry Alban, the senior officer present on the right, swung companies A and F a few paces to the rear and opened fire in time to drive them off, but when the smoke cleared they were back in greater numbers. Alban shook the men out in a single line and kept up a steady fire.

The Confederates belonged to the Forty-first Tennessee of Sugg's brigade. They had trod gingerly through the woods for fifteen minutes while Anderson's brigade struggled to hold on against the Twenty-first, expecting with each step to meet a blast of musketry. But the ridge was empty. Now, at 2:15 P.M., Sugg had only to wait a few short minutes for Fulton to come up on his left. Then, together, they would wheel to the right and sweep the Federals off the field.

In the meantime, he threw his right regiment against Alban's Ohioans. "Our assailants seemed to understand that our frail line was all they had to overcome to reach the rear and very heart of the horseshoe formation," wrote Vance. "There was that peculiar fierceness in the manner of the assault that men show when they realize that the supreme opportunity has presented itself, and are determined not to let it slip. And our boys could do nothing but set their teeth and fight, as for their lives."[17]

At the McAfee church, the fifty-four hundred men of the Reserve Corps passed a quiet Sabbath morning. They fried bacon and boiled coffee with no particular haste. After breakfast, they cleaned their weapons and drew extra ammunition, then fell in around the church. No orders came, and the men were allowed to rest in the ranks. Lounging in the meadows, they wrote letters, read the Bible, or speculated among themselves on what the day might bring. A few habitual card players, fearing the worst, tossed away their decks rather than risk having them sent home with their corpses.[18]

Gordon Granger knew no more than his soldiers what to expect. He had heard virtually nothing from army headquarters. The evening before, Rosecrans had largely ignored the Reserve Corps in his planning. Prior to the council of war, which Granger apparently did not attend, Garfield sent Granger a brief telegram updating him on the day's fighting. He closed it with the following general admonition: "You must help us in the fight tomorrow by supporting Thomas." During the meeting, Granger's role was modified slightly. The resultant order, sent by Garfield at 10:20 P.M., was short on specifics: "The general [commanding] places your corps in reserve to-morrow, and directs you to post it on the eastern slope of Missionary Ridge to support McCook or Thomas. Leave the grand guards from your command out, with instructions to hold their ground until driven in, and then to return slowly, contesting the ground stubbornly."

To be in a position to support either wing of the army, Granger would have had to move his corps at least as far south as the McFarland's Gap road. Instead, he concentrated his command on the Ringgold road in the neighborhood of the McAfee church, a mile and a half east of the foothills of Missionary Ridge and a good three miles north of the extreme left of Thomas's line. Perhaps a dispatch, since lost to the record, was sent him later that night revising his instructions. In any event, dawn found Granger located where he could certainly do McCook no good and with his most expeditious route to Thomas the highly vulnerable La Fayette road. All he was in a position to do with any degree of certainty was protect Rossville Gap.[19]

At 8:00 A.M., Thomas wired Granger to ask if he was within supporting distance and to suggest that he let Rosecrans know at once if he was not. From sunrise until he left the field shortly after noon, Rosecrans communicated with Granger only twice. Both messages were sent to Rossville, where Granger had had his headquarters until that morning, when he advanced them to the McAfee church. They were puzzling inquiries that suggested trouble but said nothing of how the battle was actually progressing nor expressed any desire that Granger close up on Thomas. Neither was dated as to time. The first asked: "Is Missionary Ridge available, supposing we should fall back?" The second: "Do the ridges in front and left of Rossville admit of placing artillery in position with any possibility of commanding the valley and road?" From these telegrams, Granger might infer that he was to remain close to Rossville.[20]

Granger was still at the McAfee church at 10:30 A.M., when the first sounds of heavy firing drifted his way from the direction of Thomas's left. He fretted and spoke frequently to his staff of his desire to go to Thomas, but for nearly an hour he made no move in that direction. Granger apparently was unable to reconcile his orders to support Thomas with his implied mission of covering Rossville, so he waited at the McAfee church for explicit instructions from Rosecrans or a direct appeal from Thomas to reinforce the left. Three staff officers rode off in different directions in the hope of intercepting any messenger who might be in search of the Reserve Corps with orders. Meanwhile, Granger and Steedman conducted a personal reconnaissance nearly a mile beyond their front. They found it clear of Confederates. Granger and Steedman returned to their respective headquarter tents, which were about three hundred yards apart.[21]

Still Granger worried. He climbed atop a haystack and tried to make some sense out of the clouds of dust rising on the horizon. Both the dust and the sounds of battle seemed to be sweeping from Thomas's left toward his rear, but no one could be certain. By 11:30 A.M., all three staff officers had returned empty handed. Colonel James Thompson, the corps chief of artillery, remarked offhandedly: "Thomas is having a hell of a fight over there."

That did it. Granger stopped his nervous pacing. "I can't stand this any longer. We are needed over there and if we don't hurry up it will be too late," he proclaimed.

That was how J. Gordon Taylor, an aide-de-camp to the general, remembered Granger's decision to move to the relief of Thomas.[22] His chief of staff, Major J. S. Fullerton, had a somewhat different recollection of the decisive moment. He climbed on the haystack with Granger. "We sat there for ten minutes listening and watching," said Fullerton. "Then Granger jumped up, thrust his glass into its case, and exclaimed with an oath: 'I am going to Thomas, orders or no orders!' 'And if you go,' I replied, 'it may bring disaster to the army and you to a court-martial.' 'There's nothing in our front now but ragtag, bobtail cavalry,' he replied. 'Don't you see Bragg is piling his whole army on Thomas? I am going to his assistance.' "[23]

Taylor's version has a more authentic ring to it, but regardless of which story is true, the key point is that Granger—and not Steedman, as that general and his cronies tried to claim after the war—made the decision to go to the relief of Thomas. Some have argued that there really was no decision to make, that Granger's orders clearly spelled out his responsibility to support the left. That may have been true at the time the orders were written, but the situation had become muddied as a result of Rosecrans's two vague expressions of concern about the safety of the Rossville Gap. By mid-morning, Granger's role was no longer clear.[24]

Neither Granger nor Steedman were attractive personalities. Granger's reputation as a martinet with a decidedly sadistic streak was well deserved. His brutal treatment of foragers a few days earlier had confirmed that. Steedman was little better. Declared the commander of his second brigade, Colonel John Mitchell: "Save for the . . . fight, no more worthless man ever commanded men than General Steedman. He had no idea of the needs of his men, no thought of their food and clothing or comforts, 'no more than [of] a hog.' His devotion to cards and whiskey and women filled the measure of his delight except when under fire and then he was a lion."[25]

Granger concluded to go to Thomas with Steedman's two brigades and leave Dan McCook behind to cover the Ringgold road. He sent Captain Taylor to tell the impetuous Ohioan that "under no circumstances was he to be driven from his position. If attacked, he was to fight his command to the last extremity." McCook's reply was true to character: "Tell General Granger when my brigade retreats he can report Dan McCook among the killed."[26]

Steedman was ready to fight. He wholeheartedly endorsed Granger's decision and had his men on their feet and ready to march in a matter of minutes. Granger and his staff rode to the head of the column. A courier was sent ahead with a note to Thomas's chief of staff announcing that "General Granger is moving Steedman with two brigades to General Thomas's assistance." At noon the march began. The division moved at the quick time with regiments arrayed in columns of four. Whitaker's brigade took the lead.[27]

Most of the soldiers were green. None of Whitaker's four regiments had seen more than a picket clash since their organization; neither had the Eighty-ninth Ohio nor Twenty-second Michigan, which were temporarily brigaded with Whitaker. Only the Ninety-eighth and One Hundred Twenty-first Ohio regiments of Mitchell's brigade, which fought at Perryville, had tasted real combat.

The early signs were hardly encouraging to men not accustomed to the varied texture of battle. Cartridge boxes, muskets, knapsacks — all manner of equipment littered the road and fields. Stragglers and wounded soldiers greeted the column with lurid tales of defeat which only they had survived.[28]

Pickets from Davidson's cavalry brigade caught sight of the Federals entering the long cornfield a mile and a half north of the Cloud church. Since mid-morning, Forrest had held the church, which had been converted into a Union field hospital. With the approach of Granger, he pulled his cavalry back across the La Fayette road. He massed the batteries of Morton, Huggins, and Huwald, reinforced by a section from Cobb's battery sent over by Breckinridge, on a grassy ridge about six hundred yards east of the McDonald farm, and made ready to shell the column when it passed. Arrayed in a cornfield in front of the batteries was Davidson's cavalry.[29]

At the Cloud church the untested soldiers came upon long rows of dead Federals. Steedman reclaimed the hospital, and the column pushed on into a snarl of vines and briars. For several barefoot soldiers in the Ninety-sixth Illinois, the thorns were a reprieve. They were permitted to return to the McAfee church.[30]

The Rebel artillery belched and fumed. Steedman halted and began to form line of battle. Granger galloped to the nearest artillery, which happened to be Battery M, First Illinois, and ordered it to follow him. He led it onto a low rise at the west edge of the cornfield. The Illinoisans returned the fire, but they clearly were getting the worst of it. Shells burst just in front of the battery. Solid shot ricocheted off the knoll. Granger's passion for cannons got the better of him. He dismounted, pushed aside the crew chief from one of the pieces, then sighted the gun himself. "At one time a shell passed so near his head as to make him dodge very suddenly," recalled a surprised member of the crew. After a few rounds, Granger calmed down. "Seeing we could do nothing more, he ordered us to limber up and to follow him, for 'he had work for us to do,'" said the artilleryman.[31]

Granger found Steedman in the act of deploying his infantry to move against Forrest. Granger called him off. "They are nothing but rag-a-muffin cavalry," he sneered. Steedman put his division back into column. With the La Fayette road now too dangerous to traverse, the two generals agreed that the best course lay through the open fields southwest of the Cloud church. To keep an eye on Forrest, Granger sent Major Fullerton back to the McAfee church to bring up Dan McCook's brigade and place it on an open ridge northwest of the McDonald farm.[32]

Steedman pushed his men at double-quick time into and through the McDonald fields. Here the evidence of battle was unmistakable and graphic. "The whole country was on fire — fences, woods, haystacks, houses and everything almost that would burn. It was a mingling of smoke and powder, burning pines, and the exhalations of dead bodies," wrote one soldier. Sergeant Isaac Doan of the Fortieth Ohio, one of the untried regiments, recalled the strain:

> We soon came across signs of recent conflict. Many of the dead were torn and blackened and burned by bursting shell until the ghastly fragments were indescribably shocking. The hardest part of a battle is going into it. . . . I think any thoughtful man upon going into battle, must go with deadly sadness in his heart. I have seen the thoughtless and foolhardy go in with a laugh and jest upon their lips, but they were not nearly so apt to stand fire as those who advanced with pale cheeks and serious aspect for these had anticipated the danger and braced their nerves to meet it, and the shock of battle did not come to them as a surprise.[33]

For Edward Robbins, a young hospital orderly with the Seventy-eighth Illinois, the suffering was too great to pass by. As he crossed a fence near the McDonald house, a voice called to him: "Hello Yank. Have you got any water?"

"Yes, what's the matter with you, Johnny," asked Robbins.

"I am wounded and waiting to die," answered the Rebel, who had been shot through the bowels.

Robbins went to him. He raked away the dry leaves so that the little fires that smoldered all around would not touch the Rebel, then gave him a drink. The column kept on, and Robbins was soon alone amid a score of wounded Confederates. He passed among them, giving each a drink until his canteen was empty, then started off through the brush to find his command. The dying soldier called Robbins back. He was going the wrong way; the Confederates were "thicker than hell just beyond those bushes." The Rebel pointed out the right direction, and Robbins was soon safely back with his regiment.[34]

Steedman's men entered the Mullis cornfield. Dust rose in great billows from the dry furrows. Sunlight glinted off polished rifle barrels. The pace accelerated to a run.

At the Snodgrass house, all eyes were fixed on the approaching column. The courier sent ahead by Granger had lost his way or fallen captive, so neither Thomas nor his staff knew whether the huge force was friend or foe. Someone guessed it to be Rebel cavalry. No, chimed in General Wood, it could not be cavalry, "for don't you see the dust rising above them ascends in thick misty clouds, not in spiral columns, as it would if the force was cavalry."

Thomas's renowned self-control was failing him under the stress. Any large enemy force coming from the north, be it cavalry or infantry, spelled certain defeat. He fussed with his beard until it stood out from his face at every angle. He tried to peer through his field glasses but his hands shook. Sensing the tension of its rider, Thomas's horse began to jump about. "Take my glass, some of you whose horse stands steady — tell me what you can see," barked Thomas. William Shanks stood beside Thomas's horse. Peering through a field glass himself, Shanks was sure he could see the United States flag. "Do you think so? Do you think so?" Thomas asked nervously.

Finally, unable to bear the tension, Thomas told Captain Gilbert Johnson, a member of Negley's staff, to ride into the cornfield to get a better look. Confederate sharpshooters took aim at him, but Johnson made it to the column and back again. When he returned with news of Granger's approach, said Shanks, "the relaxation which followed was a positive relief." Thomas mumbled a curse at Bragg, smoothed his whiskers, and was once again his taciturn self.[35]

Granger rode up at 1:45 P.M., during a lull in the fighting. Kershaw had just fallen back, and Johnson and Anderson had not yet begun their assault. Steedman rested his troops along the northern slope of the open spur behind Harker's men, then joined the gathering of generals and staff.

Thomas ordered Steedman to move his division into line on the left of Harker. Since the fight began, Thomas had been troubled by the gap of nearly one half mile that existed between the Kelly field salient and the Horseshoe Ridge–Snodgrass spur line, but until now he had had no troops with which to fill it.[36]

As Steedman prepared to move, the roar of heavy musketry arose from the direction of Hill Three. A courier from Brannan brought word of Anderson's attack and the approach of Bushrod Johnson beyond the Union right. The Twenty-first Ohio was holding on, he said, but in time would be outflanked.

Thomas faced a critical challenge. He had to push an enemy of undetermined strength off his right flank and fill the gap between the Snodgrass hill and the Kelly field before the enemy discovered and exploited it. Steedman's division he correctly adjudged too weak to split between the two threatened points.[37]

Thomas chose to meet the threat of the moment. He ordered Steedman to move at once to the right of Brannan and throw the Confederates off Horseshoe Ridge.[38]

Whitaker's brigade lay in double line of battle on the northern slope of the Snodgrass spur. Mitchell was similarly deployed in two lines behind Whitaker. The men were brought to their feet and hurried off by the right flank at the double-quick time. They moved along the base of Horseshoe Ridge, following the trace of a deep, heavily overgrown ravine. Steedman halted Whitaker's column in the midst of an oak forest behind Hill Three and the long ridge running west from it. Here the soil was poor and graveled and the underbrush sparse. The command "Left Flank" echoed down the column, and a simple facing movement brought the brigade into line of battle. While Whitaker's men dressed ranks and checked their rifles, Mitchell pushed his command on at a run to clear the rear of Whitaker's brigade.

In Whitaker's first line, from left to right, were the Twenty-second Michigan, One Hundred Fifteenth Illinois, and Ninety-sixth Illinois, all untested. The Eighteenth Ohio Battery trailed behind the center. The second line consisted of the Eighty-ninth Ohio, Eighty-fourth Indiana, and Fortieth Ohio.[39]

The men were thoroughly winded. As soon as lines were dressed and weapons capped, regimental commanders allowed their troops to lie down pending the order to move forward. Skirmishers deployed. "It was certainly a serious moment," remembered Lieutenant Isaac Royse of the One Hundred Fifteenth Illinois, "but there was never a time so serious as to prevent John Darmer of Company E having a little fun. While his comrades were trying to rest, he was making grimaces to show how 'scared' he was."[40]

Three hundred yards of forest lay between Whitaker's Federals and Horseshoe Ridge. Rebel skirmishers fired a few scattered shots from the summit and scampered out of sight. "But they had fired to some purpose, for there was a dull thud as a bullet struck a man in the Fortieth Ohio and a sickening sensation came over those who heard it," an eyewitness recalled. "There is a Reb on the hill," yelled a skirmisher just in front of the Ninety-sixth Illinois. "Why don't you shoot him then?" replied Colonel Thomas Champion calmly. The skirmisher fired and the Rebel rolled down the slope.[41]

At 2:15 P.M., bugles blared the commands "Attention, Fix bayonets, For-

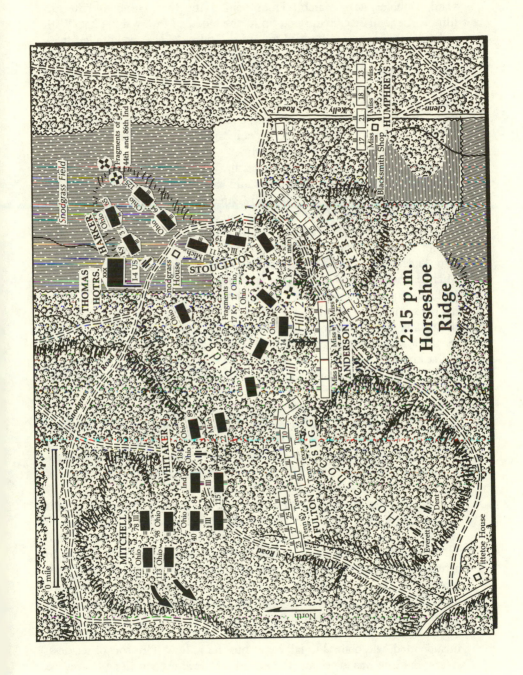

2:15 p.m.
Horseshoe Ridge

ward, Double-quick, March." From behind the One Hundred Fifteenth Illinois, General Steedman stood up in the saddle and waved his hat. With a cheer, the line surged forward toward the ridge. "There were fallen trees, which served to break up the lines somewhat, but the movement was, in the main, admirably executed," said Sergeant Charles Partridge of the Ninety-sixth Illinois. "A series of little ravines were passed, and the soldiers broke into a double-quick. Ascending a longer ridge, there came a pattering of shots, like the first drops of a shower; then the ragged, tearing report of an irregular skirmish volley; then the constant, deafening roar as regiment after regiment took up the deadly work."[42]

First to meet the shock of battle was the Twenty-second Michigan. With eighty rounds in their cartridge boxes and bayonets fixed, the Michiganders rushed up the northern slope of Hill Three and over the crest. Ahead of them was the Twenty-first Ohio, its ranks so depleted and its front so attenuated that it impressed one Michigander as little more than a "thin line of men." Raising a yell, they charged through the Twenty-first and into Anderson's stunned Mississippians. The Confederates reeled, and the Michiganders followed in headlong, spontaneous pursuit. Lieutenant Colonel William Sanborn yelled himself hoarse trying to stop his regiment. Leaving his place in rear of the line, he galloped forward and by a combination of shouts and gestures, succeeded in bringing the Twenty-second to a halt in the hollow at the foot of the hill. Hardly had he restored order when a bullet knocked him from the saddle. A blistering fire of grape and canister from Everett's battery on the ridge to the Michiganders' right raked their line. The color sergeant fell dead, his chest ripped open by grapeshot. A corporal pried the colors from the dead man's grasp. As he stood up to wave them, a bullet passed through his head. Another member of the color guard raised the flag, only to have his left arm taken off by a solid shot. Not only was the color guard decimated, but casualties throughout the regiment were staggering. Nearly one hundred men fell in this, the first two minutes of real combat the Twenty-second had ever seen.[43]

Amid the confusion, Kershaw launched a counterattack against Hills Two and Three to cover the retreat of Anderson. The Second South Carolina struck the Twenty-second and forced it back up the hill. At the top, the Michiganders were rallied by Colonel Heber Le Favour. Le Favour, who actually commanded the Twenty-second, had been given responsibility both for his own regiment and the Eighty-ninth Ohio when they were attached to Whitaker's brigade. Consequently, he had remained atop the ridge to better coordinate the movements of the regiments.

The Second South Carolina reached the crest of Hill Three but, being unsupported, was obliged to fall back into the hollow. This sort of reckless, seesaw fighting was to become the pattern of the afternoon along Horseshoe

Ridge. "When the men were ordered to advance they kept their lines pretty well, but there were many whose eagerness carried them ahead of it, and some where timidity kept them in rear of it," explained a Union participant. "In retreating, the men paid little attention to keeping their lines well-dressed, and had the appearance of a mass rather than a line."[44]

Meanwhile, on the ridge west of Hill Three, the Ninety-sixth and One Hundred Fifteenth Illinois regiments had grappled with Sugg's Tennesseans. The first casualty of the encounter was the Eighteenth Ohio Battery. When the cannoneers took fire on the crest, the battery commander, Captain Charles Aleshire, lost his nerve. Aleshire turned his limbers around and came crashing back down the northern slope, straight at the Eighty-ninth Ohio, which lay at the base of the ridge in support of the front line. Colonel Caleb Carlton got his men to their feet and hastily moved them to the right to dodge the battery. Carlton's maneuver, necessary though it was, masked the Eighty-fourth Indiana and left the Twenty-second Michigan without a supporting line.

Carlton was perhaps the best regimental commander in the brigade. A career soldier, he was a member of the West Point class of 1854. Promotions had come slowly to Carlton, who began the war as a second lieutenant in the Fourth United States Infantry. Typhoid fever struck him down after Second Bull Run, and the start of the Tullahoma campaign found him in Pennsylvania on recruiting duty, still convalescing. In July, his lifelong friend, General Crook, secured for him an appointment as colonel of the Eighty-ninth. Although still unwell, Carlton hastened to the front. He quickly won the respect and affection of his new command. Said Captain Joseph Foraker of Company E: "Colonel Carlton was one of the most capable officers it was my fortune to meet during all my experience in the service." Foraker never forgot Carlton. Thirty years later, as a senator from Ohio, Foraker obtained for his old colonel a promotion to brigadier general in the Regular Army. With so many green troops in the brigade, Carlton was a good man to have on hand.

Captain Aleshire took his battery all the way back to the Snodgrass house. There Colonel Thompson, the corps chief of artillery, placed it in action in support of Harker. Thomas approved this disposition, since Aleshire's battery could now be called upon to cover the gap on Harker's left with fire if need be.[45]

On the ridge, the slaughter was terrific. Every member of Whitaker's staff was hit in the first minutes of fighting. Whitaker himself took a spent bullet in the stomach. The wound was painful but not serious. Nonetheless, Whitaker rode off the field, apparently without notifying the ranking colonel, Thomas Champion of the Ninety-sixth Illinois, of his departure. Steedman by his mere presence did much to maintain order in the brigade but, for the most part, the six regiments were left to fight on their own.

What drove Whitaker to abandon his brigade in its first moments in battle was not his bruised stomach but his need for liquor. Whitaker was a gallant officer who had distinguished himself in battle on several occasions, most notably at Shiloh. But like so many senior officers of the day, he had a weakness for the bottle. When he returned thirty minutes later, it was all the Kentuckian could do just to keep his balance in the saddle.[46]

Like the Twenty-second Michigan on its left, the One Hundred Fifteenth Illinois initially succeeded in sweeping the Confederates off the ridge. The Illinoisans chased the Forty-first Tennessee of Sugg's brigade down the southern slope and reformed their line at the base of the hill. And like the Michiganders, the One Hundred Fifteenth lost heavily in its first charge. Lieutenant Colonel William Kinman took a bullet through the body on the way up the ridge. A second round hit him in the forehead as he lay on the ground, killing him instantly. John Darmer, the regimental jokester, was struck twice in rapid succession. Darmer "threw down his gun and began dancing around and swinging his hands, much as he had done in pretense of fear just before the assault began," recalled Lieutenant Royse. "So well did he imitate his ordinary fun-making pranks that [I] thought he was at his old tricks, and sharply ordered him to take up his gun and go to work."[47]

Just as quickly as they had been forced off the ridge, Sugg's Tennesseans regrouped and counterattacked, pushing the One Hundred Fifteenth back to the brow. There the regiment steadied, and for a few minutes kept the Southerners at bay. Lieutenant Royse's description of the action on his front applies with equal validity to any point along Steedman's line:

> The men loaded and fired at will. Each man handled his gun, in his own way, getting in as many and as effective shots as possible. Sometimes the whole line lay close to the ground, loading and firing without rising, in this way doing very destructive work without being exposed to the shower of bullets passing overhead. At other times, the men would step back a few paces from the crest, load their pieces, and then step briskly forward till a good aim would be secured, fire, and as quickly repeat the operation. There was such a constant shower of bullets passing over our heads, mostly from ten to fifty feet above us, that at almost any moment, leaves, twigs, and pieces of bark would be seen falling from the trees.[48]

Gradually Sugg's Tennesseans worked their way up the slope, forcing the raw troops of the One Hundred Fifteenth off the crest. Colonel Carlton waited for the Illinoisans to pass over his Eighty-ninth Ohio, then ordered his men forward in a bayonet charge over the same ground. With its commander, Lieutenant Colonel J. D. Tillman, down with a bad shoulder wound, the Forty-first Tennessee surrendered the top of the ridge after only a brief struggle. The Eighty-ninth Ohio came into line beside the Twenty-second Michigan and settled into an exchange of volleys with the Third Tennessee. No more than fifteen minutes had elapsed since Whitaker had launched his first charge on the ridge.[49]

Carlton had succeeded in stabilizing the left of his line against Sugg's right regiments. At the same time, however, a more serious threat developed to his right. There the Ninety-sixth Illinois was breaking up in the face of stubborn resistance from the Seventh Texas and portions of the Fiftieth Tennessee and Seventh Texas regiments of Sugg's brigade to its front and growing pressure from Fulton's brigade, which extended perhaps two hundred yards behind its right flank. A heavy fire from the Rebel batteries of Dent and Everett was turning the ridge into a living hell. Casualties were immense and, as among the other regiments of Whitaker's brigade, the officers of the Ninety-sixth were especially hard hit. Lieutenant Colonel Isaac Clarke was shot in the chest on the left of the regiment while calmly surveying the scene on horseback. On the right, Colonel Champion had two horses shot out from under him in rapid succession. There were no more horses to be had, so the colonel ran to the rear of the center of the regiment to direct the fight. There he was accosted by Captain Moe of the division staff, who suggested he refuse his right companies to meet the approach of Fulton on his flank. Champion tried, but his men had run out of fight. Slowly at first, the Illinoisans backed up the southern slope of the ridge. Here and there, soldiers stopped to kneel and fire. But as they neared the crest, a panic set in and the regiment fled down the reverse slope in disorder. The Ninety-sixth had lost one hundred men in twenty minutes.[50]

The collapse of the Ninety-sixth Illinois was no more than a momentary setback. By now, Mitchell's brigade had cleared the rear of Whitaker and was on the way up the ridge to take on Fulton. The incline here was sharp and the men tired quickly. As Mitchell neared the crest, he called up his rear regiments, the Seventy-eighth Illinois and One Hundred Twenty-first Ohio, to extend his line to the right.

The fight with Fulton was short and savage. Frightened fugitives from the Ninety-sixth Illinois crying "Retreat! Retreat!" ran through Mitchell's left regiment, the One Hundred Thirteenth Ohio, as it struggled up the slope. "Then and there I wished I could die," remembered Lieutenant Colonel Darius Warner, the regimental commander. "My men wavered and fell back half way down the hill."

Warner was in no real danger. Mitchell's front extended well beyond the left of Fulton's brigade. As soon as the commanders of Fulton's left regiments saw the Federals on their flank, they broke contact and withdrew toward the safety of their own batteries. The rest of the brigade followed. Those troops from Sugg's brigade still clinging to the ridge fell back a few moments later.[51]

When Thomas asked Granger if his men could clear Bushrod Johnson's Tennesseans off Horseshoe Ridge, Granger purportedly replied: "Yes. My men are fresh, and they are just the fellows for that work. They are raw troops, and they don't know any better than to charge up there." He was right. As the historian Francis McKinney so ably expressed it: "This storming of [Horseshoe] Ridge by Steedman's men was the most spectacular and profitable counterattack of the day from the Union point of view. It accomplished in twenty minutes what Longstreet tried for six hours to do. The Army of Tennessee lost its elan on the south slope of [the] ridge while, on the north slope, the Army of the Cumberland discovered its own latent power."[52]

Granger was not present to witness the triumph of his "raw troops." After delivering his troops to Thomas, Granger remained at the Snodgrass house to indulge in his favorite battlefield activity — sighting cannons. For a time he helped work the guns of Smith's Regular battery. When Captain Aleshire reported with the Eighteenth Ohio Battery, Granger helped him place his pieces and then set to work aiming and firing them.

It took the death of his beloved adjutant, Captain William Russell, to remind Granger of his larger duties. Russell was killed on the ridge while encouraging the Eighty-ninth Ohio, and his horse took a bullet in the hip. Bleeding and riderless, the animal galloped through the forest to the Snodgrass farm. An incredulous William Shanks watched the animal go to where Granger was firing a cannon. Reported Shanks:

> The horse singled Granger out in the crowd and excitement, ran up to him, fondled about him with his head, and did everything that a dumb brute could do to attract attention. At first, Granger, busy at the guns, did not notice the horse, until the animal grew troublesome. His own horse and that of Captain Russell were very much alike, and, mistaking the animal for his own, Granger called to his orderly to take him away. The orderly explained that it was not his horse, and Granger then saw that it was Russell's, and noticed that it had been wounded. The truth flashed across his mind at once, and he sent several of his body-guard in search of the body of his adjutant. . . . When the orderlies returned with the dead body of the captain, Granger gave himself up to grief. At last his great sorrow vented itself in an exclamation addressed to General Thomas —
> "By God, general, he was the best soldier I ever knew!"
> After this, the fountain of his tears seemed to dry up.

Granger ordered the body taken to the rear, and then lost himself in his cannons.[53]

Lieutenant Colonel Warner returned to the crest of Horseshoe Ridge with the One Hundred Thirteenth Ohio just as the last of Fulton's Tennesseans scrambled off it. This time there was no pursuit. "My men lay down on their faces and rested," admitted Warner, who knew better than to push his regiment too hard in the early stages of what everyone suspected would be a long and bitter struggle for the ridge. While the men gulped water from their canteens or gobbled down hardtack, Steedman, Mitchell, and Champion set about to restore order to the jumbled lines of the division.[54]

Captain Borden Hicks of the Ninety-sixth Illinois was busy redistributing ammunition among the men of his company when a staff officer galloped up and yelled: "Captain, why in thunder don't you form this regiment?"

"I am forming my company, sir. Where's Colonel Champion?" replied Hicks.

"He's taken command of the brigade, Whitaker's wounded."

"Well, where's Colonel Clarke?"

"Why, don't you know, Clarke was killed in the first fire," answered the staff officer.

Hicks walked over to the colors. He thrust them in the dirt and around them gradually reassembled what was once a regiment. Perhaps 150 men were left. One hundred had fallen, and two or three companies had attached themselves to the One Hundred Thirteenth Ohio and were thus lost to Hicks for the rest of the day. Then he stepped forward to try his hand at speechmaking. "Comrades, you have made one charge — a gallant charge. On yonder hillside lie the bodies of your fallen comrades. Forward to avenge their deaths," Hicks announced. Captain Moe intercepted the Illinoisans as they started back up the slope and told Hicks to move to the far right to extend the line in that direction.[55]

Steedman had entered the battle with some thirty-nine hundred men. Perhaps six hundred were lost in the twenty or twenty-five minutes it had taken to repel Bushrod Johnson. He thus still had a formidable force with which to hold both Horseshoe Ridge and the long ridge northwest of it. At 3:00 P.M., Steedman's line of battle stood as follows. On the left, the Twenty-second Michigan had regrouped on the summit of Hill Three, allowing Major McMahan to consolidate the Twenty-first Ohio along the saddle between Hills Two and Three. The Eighty-ninth Ohio shared the hilltop with the Michiganders. Hill Three dropped off rather abruptly on its west side beyond the right flank of the Ohioans. On the lower ridge was the Eighty-fourth Indiana of Whitaker's brigade. Next came the stray companies of the Ninety-sixth Illinois, followed along the ridge in a generally northwest direction by the One Hundred Thirteenth Ohio, Ninety-eighth Ohio, Seventy-eighth Illinois, One Hundred Twenty-first Ohio, and the portion of the Ninety-sixth Illinois under Captain Hicks. On Hicks's right, Lieutenant Thomas Burton unlimbered four guns from his Battery M, First

Illinois Light Artillery. The remaining section he wedged into line on the brigade left. After regrouping, the One Hundred Fifteenth Illinois rested at the base of the ridge in support of the Eighty-fourth Indiana. To its right, the Fortieth Ohio lay in reserve to Mitchell. Thus formed, Steedman's line ran approximately five hundred yards and commanded both the southern plateau of Horseshoe Ridge and the taller hill to its west.[56]

No one understood better than Thomas how close the Union forces on Horseshoe Ridge had come to disaster. As the last shots from Steedman's front died down at about 2:45 P.M., Thomas turned to Granger and, grasping his hand, confessed: "Fifteen minutes more, General, might have been too late."[57]

The situation was growing a bit brighter for the Federals. Sometime between 2:30 and 3:00 P.M., Colonel Van Derveer rode into the Snodgrass cornfield at the head of his brigade. Thomas rode out to meet the column. He told Van Derveer to take his men to Hills Two and Three and there relieve Brannan's tired troops. Thomas paused a moment to greet the Second Minnesota, which had made a timely charge to win the Battle of Mill Springs for him nearly two years before. "Colonel, I want you to hold the hill," he told the rheumatic James George. "We will, general, until we are ordered away or are mustered out of service," replied George. To Lieutenant Colonel Bishop, the de facto commander of the Second, Thomas spoke a few words of encouragement and complimented him on the "good order" of his men.[58]

Van Derveer formed a single line with its center astride Hill Two. There he relieved the few hundred men of the Fourth Kentucky, Tenth Kentucky, and Fourteenth Ohio who had been in action against Kershaw and Anderson under the supervision of Colonel Walker since 1:00 P.M. Walker allowed them to retire two hundred yards to rest and draw ammunition from the fast-dwindling stores brought along by Steedman.[59]

Colonel Morton Hunter was delighted to see the Ninth Ohio coming into line on his right. Riding over to Colonel Kammerling, Hunter suggested he halt along the saddle between Hills One and Two and throw up breastworks. The irrepressible German, however, was no more prepared to listen to advice than he had been that morning or the day before. While Hunter and his Indianians looked on in wonder, Kammerling led his men over the brow and down the draw in a mad dash toward the enemy. The rattle of musketry split the air. Five minutes later, they were back, their colonel chastened at last. The Rebels were too damned thick down there, snarled Kammerling.[60]

The Eighty-seventh Indiana formed on Kammerling's right behind the breastworks built by Croxton's men. The Second Minnesota lay down a few yards behind and slightly above the Twenty-first Ohio, and the Thirty-fifth Ohio rounded out the line to its right and rear.[61]

The timely arrival of Van Derveer's brigade unquestionably strengthened the Union line on Horseshoe Ridge, but it had by no means solved Thomas's most pressing concern of the moment: ammunition. The ammunition train of the Fourteenth Corps had been one of the first casualties of Longstreet's breakthrough. Some of the wagons were lost along the Dry Valley road, others simply drifted off into the foothills of Missionary Ridge. Steedman brought with him nearly ninety-five thousand spare cartridges, but these were quickly used up in resupplying Harker and Brannan. Harker's men were down to two or three rounds each, so that the cartridges they drew now did not go far. Most men returned to the firing line with no more than ten rounds in their cartridge boxes.

None of the cartridges Steedman brought were suitable for the Colt rifles of the Twenty-first Ohio, which was down to a handful of rounds per man. The dead and wounded of the regiment on the field had been stripped clean, and now Sergeant Bolton hurried off with a detail to the Snodgrass house to rummage the boxes of the wounded there. Van Derveer's men were only a little better off. Lieutenant Colonel Bishop estimated that his troops averaged fifteen rounds apiece when they arrived from the Kelly field. Even Steedman's regimental commanders complained of having exhausted over half their basic load in repelling Johnson.[62]

Thomas sent two of his aides off to look for his or anyone else's ammunition train that might be nearby. More than that he could not do. However deep his anxiety might have run, Thomas took care to disguise it. To a courier from Brannan, who brought word that the men were burning up rounds faster than they could be resupplied, Thomas said: "Tell General Brannan that his is my old division and that they will hold their position." Another time he called back an aide who was dashing off with a message and told him to ride leisurely so as not to alarm the troops. A staff officer about to leave Thomas on an errand, doubting whether the line would hold, paused to ask: "General, after delivering your order, where shall I report to you."

"Here, Sir, here," came the impatient reply.[63]

A FEW ARE HOLDING OUT
UP YONDER

LONGSTREET was directing the battle in the same manner General Lee managed battles back east — making careful preparations and entrusting the details of the engagement to his subordinates.[1] Such a style might serve in an army in which generals were accustomed to working with one another and in which the lines of authority were clearly understood. However, it was bound to fail when applied to the schismatic command structure of the Army of Tennessee, the fabric of which had been further weakened by Bragg's eleventh-hour decision to divide the army into wings.

From 1:00 to 2:30 P.M., Longstreet was content to play the role of bystander. He issued no orders of consequence to his generals, who were left to muddle through as best they could. Not surprisingly, there was a good deal of confusion and a decided lack of coordination. Longstreet apparently neglected even to spell out who was in command on the far left. Bushrod Johnson thought he was in charge, which in fact seems to have been Longstreet's intention. Hindman, however, believed he was responsible for both his own and Johnson's divisions.

The question was still open when Longstreet at last awoke to the dramatically changed circumstances on his front. Far from continuing the grand left wheel that Bragg had expected, the divisions of the Left Wing had turned right after the breakthrough and butted up against unexpectedly heavy opposition. It took the bloody repulse of Johnson on Horseshoe Ridge to convince Longstreet that new instructions were needed. At about 2:45 P.M. he ordered Johnson to reorganize his own brigades and to deploy those of Hindman's division as soon as they arrived for a renewed assault on the ridge. Longstreet claimed that he then repeated his earlier oral orders to Wheeler to bring forward his cavalry to pursue the fragments of Rosecrans's army then in retreat toward the gaps. However, Thomas Claiborne, formerly chief of cavalry for the Department of East Tennessee and now a member of Buckner's staff, later said that Longstreet did not believe he had the authority to send for Wheeler and, in any case, gave the matter no thought until later in the day, after the chance for a meaningful pursuit had all but vanished.[2]

While waiting for his lunch to be brought up, Longstreet set out on a belated inspection of his lines, as he put it, to "view the changed conditions of the battle." General Buckner accompanied him. They rode west to east, from the Vittetoe house toward the blacksmith shop. "I could see but little of the enemy's line, and only knew of it by the occasional exchange of fire between the lines of skirmishers," recalled Longstreet. Passing the right flank of Humphreys's brigade, Longstreet and Buckner rode across the Glenn-Kelly road and into the forest west of the Poe field. Near the La Fayette road, they came under fire from concealed Yankee skirmishers.

Longstreet and Buckner had run into the breastworks of King's brigade, which they correctly interpreted as the right flank of Thomas's line in the Kelly field. Cutting short their tour, the two galloped south to the protection of Law's division. Longstreet asked Buckner to see that the reserve artillery of the Left Wing was placed near the charred remains of the Poe house so as to sweep north along the La Fayette road and deter any attempt by Thomas to reinforce Horseshoe Ridge with troops from the Kelly field. Then he invited the Kentuckian to join him for lunch.[3]

How Longstreet failed to appreciate the half-mile gap in the Federal lines is something of a mystery. Unquestionably, the heavy woods between the blacksmith shop and the La Fayette road limited visibility. Still, by his own admission, Longstreet's brush with King's skirmishers had fixed to his satisfaction the limit of the Federal breastworks surrounding the Kelly field. From Humphreys he must have learned of the position of Harker in the Snodgrass cornfield. That left six hundred yards unaccounted for. At a minimum, a reconnaissance in that direction should have been ordered. There were ample forces at hand for such a movement. Humphreys's brigade lay idle near the blacksmith shop. Law had his three brigades reformed and in line between the Poe house and the Dyer field. Buckner had advanced Preston's division to the Brotherton house, ready to commit it wherever and whenever Longstreet deemed appropriate.

But Longstreet did nothing. Perhaps he felt one concerted push by Johnson, Hindman, and Kershaw would suffice to knock the Federals off Horseshoe Ridge. Clearly this is the impression Major William Owen, acting chief of artillery of Preston's division, got when he found Longstreet and Buckner at lunch a little after 3:00 P.M. Owen had served with the Army of Northern Virginia and was someone with whom Longstreet felt at ease.

Longstreet interrupted his meal of Nassau bacon and Georgia sweet potatoes to hail Owen. Did the major happen to have any tobacco? Owen drew out his little bag, and Longstreet filled his meerschaum pipe. The general was enjoying himself immensely. "We were not accustomed to potatoes of any kind in Virginia, and thought we had a luxury," remembered Longstreet.

Owen asked Longstreet how the battle was progressing; was the enemy beaten? "Yes," Longstreet answered. "All along his line; a few are holding out upon the ridge up yonder, not many though. If we had had our Virginia army here, we could have whipped them in half the time. By the by," Longstreet added with a smile, "don't you want some guns for your command? I think my men must have captured fifty today." By all means, Owen said. "Well, you can have as many as you want." "General, hadn't you better put that in writing," suggested Owen. Longstreet laughed and told his adjutant to write Owen an order for the guns.[4]

A courier from army headquarters rode up while Longstreet was still eating. General Bragg wished to see him at once.

Longstreet found Bragg at his temporary headquarters near Jay's Mill some time after 3:00 P.M. He sketched the situation on the field for the commanding general. Two Federal corps were in full retreat toward Chattanooga. Large numbers of cannons and prisoners had been seized. Johnson was about to renew the attack on Horseshoe Ridge, where a small contingent of Federals had delayed the advance of the Left Wing. Buckner was massing artillery near the Poe house to prevent Union reinforcements from reaching the ridge.

Longstreet claimed that he then suggested that Bragg loan him some of Polk's troops, which had not been engaged since noon. With these, he could pursue the enemy along the Dry Valley road and perhaps seize the McFarland and Rossville gaps, thereby cutting off the Federals from Chattanooga.

According to Longstreet and others present, Bragg refused to accept that a great victory had been won. He knew only that his plan for rolling up the Federal left had failed. For this he blamed Bishop Polk. "There is not a man in the right wing who has any fight in him," snarled Bragg. Request denied.

Longstreet was astounded. "From accounts of [Bragg's] former operations I was prepared for halting work, but this, when the battle was at its tide and in partial success, was a little surprising. His humor, however, was such that [I] was at a loss for a reopening of the discussion. He did not wait, nor did he express approval or disapproval of the left wing, but rode for his headquarters at Reed's Bridge. There was nothing for the left wing to do but work along as best it could."[5]

Johnson renewed the attack at 3:30 P.M. Manigault was in line of battle on Fulton's left at the foot of a deep gorge that ran up to the saddle held by Steedman. Deas was on the high hill immediately west of the gorge. Coleman had come up and taken a position in support of Fulton. Starting with Deas, Johnson rode along the entire line, personally putting each brigade in motion toward the ridge. With the exception of the Second South Carolina, which moved with Anderson, Kershaw's brigade was engaged only to the extent of keeping Brannan on Hill One and Harker in the Snodgrass cornfield occupied with a harassing fire.[6]

Privates Thomas J. Doughman and W. S. Thacker of the Eighty-ninth Ohio had left the ranks and crawled forward of the crest to get a better look at what the enemy was up to.

They got it. Just a few dozen yards ahead of them were Sugg's Tennesseans, stepping deliberately through the brush in line of battle, "their colors bright as when they were unfurled for the first time." His curiosity satisfied, Thacker got up and scampered back to the regiment. Doughman decided to stay awhile. "Thinking that now was my chance to get a color bearer, I got up on my feet right by a small sapling and went to firing at the color bearer, supposing that my regiment would raise, but they did not—still remained firing while lying down."

Doughman was the sole target of the first Rebel volley. A minie ball drilled his canteen. Another pierced his haversack. A third struck him in the left hip, cut the nerves to his leg, passed through his torso, and came to rest in his right hip. Doughman spun around and fell to his hands and knees, facing his company. His left foot went numb. "Jeff, you wounded?" asked a friend as Doughman crawled through the ranks. "Yes, the sons of bitches, go after them."

Doughman kept on crawling, convinced that he had suffered nothing worse than a foot wound. But after a few yards, he grew oddly nauseated and faint. Bullets began to pepper the dirt around him. The young Ohioan crawled behind a stump to rest. "Jeff, can you walk?" asked a sergeant from his company. "I don't know, I'll try." The sergeant helped Doughman to his feet. "Not until then did I discover where I was wounded," he recalled. "I then saw the blood coming down my left pants leg and could feel the ball just under the skin under my right hip." Together they struggled down the ridge and through the forest, all the way to the farmhouse of the tiny Cooper farm, over a half mile behind the firing line. Mrs. Cooper was there to help Doughman to the floor. The kindly sergeant returned to the battle. Doughman was only the second wounded man to find the house. A third came in a few minutes later, shot through the groin. Then a straggler from an Indiana regiment wandered in. He closed the door. The cabin fell dark, and Doughman soon drifted into a deep sleep.[7]

Private John Dillman of Company D was less fortunate than Doughman.

Just eighteen years old, Dillman was "always full of life and mischief." His sergeant, William McKell, remembered how the young Ohioan threw away his deck of cards before leaving the McAfee church. Dillman felt certain he would be killed in the initial volley and did not want his parents to know of the bad habits he had acquired in the army. When the Eighty-ninth came onto the ridge for the first time, Dillman lost his nerve. He sprinted back down the slope and disappeared into the forest. During the lull he returned, "so ashamed . . . that he could look no one in the face." When the Rebels attacked a second time, McKell watched him for any sign of faltering. But Dillman's only thought was of making right with his comrades. Recalled McKell: "He took his place in line, using no caution to protect himself, but standing out in open view of the rebels, loading and firing his gun. A ball struck him in the center of the forehead with a dull thud. He raised his eyes, looking wildly about, and fell like a log."[8]

Cowardice, be it fleeting or chronic, was not limited to the rank and file. Captain Moe came upon Lieutenant Colonel William Jones, the commander of the Fortieth Ohio, cowering behind a tree a hundred yards in rear of the regimental firing line. Moe dismounted, drew his pistol, and coolly marched the colonel to Steedman, who ordered him off the field with a string of curses.[9]

Jones was not missed. "There was very little reporting done or orders given by anybody that afternoon. Every man's duty was plain and he did it without much instruction or interference," admitted a Yankee field officer. Most officers took their diminished role in stride, picking up rifles and cartridge boxes from the wounded and joining the firing line. Colonel Champion of the Ninety-sixth Illinois grabbed a gun and helped repel Manigault's attack from the ranks.[10]

Casualties among officers continued to be catastrophic. Particularly hard hit was the Ninety-eighth Ohio. Captain Moses Urquhart, who took the regiment into battle, was shot from his horse in the first fire. Captain Armstrong Thomas acceded to command. He mounted the animal and was killed a moment later. During the lull, Captain John Lochry took over. He was shot dead from Urquhart's horse early on in the second attack. Command now devolved on the senior lieutenant, a young man named Milliner. Next in line, should he fall, was a lieutenant named Roach. Between the two had grown some bad feelings based on a trivial misunderstanding, so that they were no longer on speaking terms. Before assuming command, Milliner stepped hastily over to Roach and pleaded: "Roach, had we not better make friends? It may be this is the last opportunity we will ever have to do it." "With all my heart," said Roach, extending his hand. Much relieved, Milliner mounted the jinxed horse. A few minutes later, a minie ball shattered his arm from wrist to elbow. He was carried to the rear and Roach took his place in the saddle.[11]

It was a seesaw fight. Charge and countercharge, up and down the slopes of Horseshoe Ridge. John Patton of the Ninety-eighth Ohio explained the fighting best: "There were places on the summit of the ridge wrested from the enemy that was so swept by their artillery that a line of infantry could not remain there, and would consequently fall a little back out of its range. This would give to that part of the line the appearance of giving way and losing ground, but it was only apparently so—there was no real giving. When the enemy's infantry would appear on the summit and at such places and endeavor to come over they were in every case driven back." Occasionally one side or the other would cling to the crest a bit too long, and then the fighting became hand-to-hand.[12]

The raw troops of Steedman's division marveled at the racket. "The firing of the musketry was so incessant that the ear could not distinguish the separate discharges," said Isaac Doan of the Fortieth Ohio. Overwhelmed by the noise, tension, and their own fear, men made foolish mistakes. In Battery M, First Illinois Light Artillery, a cannoneer was thrown through the air and his back sprained by the recoil of his gun; he had been clutching the trail when the gun went off. Another neglected to step aside when the lanyard was pulled, and the trail slid over his foot, crushing it.

No creature was untouched by the frenzy. " 'Battery,' our dog, who had been doing his fighting in connection with gun number one, would charge out from under the gun after the rebels as they neared us," the historian of Battery M wrote. "When they came for the last time, he charged too soon and was severely scorched on the back by the fire of the gun. He immediately reported at the line of caissons, making no more charges that day." Sergeant Doan expected to meet a similar fate: "I fired eighty rounds from my breech-loading carbine, and the cartridge chamber became so hot that I could not bear my hand upon it, and I was actually afraid the thing would shoot back in my face when I would put in a new cartridge."[13]

Steedman was in his element. When the One Hundred Fifteenth Illinois, which had returned to the ridge on the right of the Eighty-ninth Ohio, again gave way, he rode straight into the swarm of tired and frightened men and confronted their colonel, Jesse Moore. "This is all a mistake. I have given no orders to fall back," he barked. "Move at once up the slope to your position." Moore demurred. His regiment had suffered terribly; he did not think he could get his men to go back up there. Steedman lost his temper. He grabbed the regimental standard from the color-bearer, told Moore he was free to leave the field in disgrace, then commanded the men to follow him up the ridge. They did. At the crest, the general's horse was hit. Over the head of the falling animal went Steedman. Stunned a moment, he bound up his bleeding hands, then began walking behind his regiments along the summit.[14]

Steedman got a bit carried away with his histrionics. Coming up behind Thomas Edmundson, the color sergeant of the Seventy-eighth Illinois, Steedman demanded the banner so that he might steady the regiment. Edmundson refused. He could carry the colors anywhere the general could. To demonstrate, he stepped forward two paces, rammed the standard in the dirt, and told the men to come up and rally around the colors. The Illinoisans did so at once, and Steedman went on his way.[15]

For thirty minutes the two lines battled for the ridge. Fatigue was taking its toll on the Confederates. Individually at first, then by squads, the Tennesseans of Fulton and Sugg trickled down the slope and collapsed behind trees. Neither oaths nor blows from the swords of their officers could drive them back into the fight.[16] To their left, the brigades of Deas and Manigault intermingled badly. "The different regiments became mixed with each other, and here and there the faint-hearted were stealing to safer positions in the rear," admitted Manigault. "Men fought from behind trees and coverts [sic], loading and firing while they dodged from point to point. . . . In short, the character of the battle at this juncture was that of skirmishing on a grand scale."[17]

Deas's brigade broke first. The Alabamians had suffered heavily in the fight against Laiboldt and Lytle that morning and so had little energy left for the struggle on Horseshoe Ridge. Try as they might, they could not penetrate Mitchell's line. Three times the brigade charged. The Twenty-second Alabama was the most persistent, and paid a commensurate price. Two hundred five of the 371 men who went into action that morning were dead or wounded by sunset, a loss of more than 55 percent. The color-bearer was shot and killed a few feet from the line of the One Hundred Twenty-first Ohio, and the colors lost.[18]

Manigault's brigade split in two. The Thirty-fourth and Twenty-eighth Alabama regiments fell back with Deas and refused to rally. Major John Slaughter, commander of the Thirty-fourth, sympathized with his men. They somehow had lost their canteens during the night and thus went through the day without a drop of water. By late afternoon, their tongues were swollen and their lips sore from biting off cartridges. Speech was painful, and the words came out garbled.[19] The remainder of the brigade kept up the fight with Fulton on its right.

Johnson sent Lieutenant George Marchbanks of his staff to bring Deas's brigade back into action. The lieutenant found the Alabamians milling about in the Vittetoe cornfield. With Deas and his regimental commanders, Marchbanks reformed the brigade and herded it into the gorge along the Dry Valley road. Further than that the men could not be driven.[20]

To compensate for the loss of Deas, Johnson called on Coleman's brigade. Galloping along the brigade line, he yelled: "Arkansas boys, forward!" He drew rein ten feet from J. C. Moore of the Twenty-fifth Arkansas. "Just then I saw a picture that will be with me as long as life lasts. General Johnson's horse was standing up on its hind feet. Johnson, with his hat off and sword elevated, cried: 'Arkansas, go for them!'" Coleman's brigade drove to within a few yards of the summit. "We fought them nearly hand-to-hand, using [the] dead for breastworks and their cartridges and guns when ours would become heated," recalled Moore.[21]

The number of skulkers continued to grow at an alarming rate. Colonel Oates was watching his men trade fire with the Federals atop Hill One when young Jack Cariker, a sixteen-year-old private of Company D, approached, "his little freckled face aglow with excitement." "Colonel, there is one of our men down there behind a tree who refuses to come up and fight," panted Cariker.

"Jack, go and bring him to me," answered Oates.

"Colonel, he is a great big man," protested Cariker.

"Well, Jack, bring him, though he be as big as an elephant, and if he refuses to come stave your bayonet through him," Oates responded firmly.

Away went the little private. In less than a minute he was back, driving before him one of the largest men in the regiment. "Here he is, Colonel," grinned Cariker. The soldier darted behind a tree. Oates upbraided him: He was a good soldier — why did he not fight? The big soldier lamely replied that he was sick. "I saw at once, from the way he clung to that pine and covered himself with it, that he was demoralized through fear instead of being sick." Oates yanked him into the open. Just as quickly, the man sprang back behind the tree. "I again pulled him out, and struck him over the head with my sword and knocked him down, cutting his head a little, which satisfied him that the safest place for him was with his company. . . . I heard no more of his sickness," Oates recalled.[22]

Anderson's brigade gave way next. Once again, its men had clawed their way to within a few yards of the Twenty-first Ohio, only to wilt before the Colt rifles.

The Yankee fire, however, was noticeably weaker. McMahan's men were squeezing off their last rounds deliberately, trying to make them count. When a man had fired his last cartridge, he stepped out of the firing line and moved to the rear. McMahan probably had no more than two hundred men still actively in the fight. Behind the Twenty-first, the Second Minnesota opened with a volley right into the backs of the Ohioans. Captain Cusac yelled at Lieutenant Colonel Bishop to cease firing or aim higher.[23]

After two hours of combat, Anderson's Mississippians were in no condition to exploit the obvious weakness of the enemy line. They too were running low on ammunition. In the Tenth Mississippi, which had been issued inferior arms, the rifles had become so choked that "the men were compelled to force the balls home by hammering the ends of their ramrods against trees," reported their commander. At 4:00 P.M., Anderson ordered his regiments off the hill and back into the ravine to rest and redistribute ammunition.[24]

Johnson's division collapsed a few minutes later. The retreat, when it came, was precipitate, said Johnson. It took every effort on the part of the officers simply to rally enough men to support the batteries of Dent and Everett, which raked the ridge with canister to discourage any possible Federal pursuit. Slowly, Johnson pieced his command back together along the southern tip of Horseshoe Ridge. Like Steedman, Johnson was undaunted in his resolve to continue the battle. "I ordered that the hill should be held at all hazards, and determined that all should be lost before I would abandon it. I felt that this position on the extreme left was one of the utmost importance and might determine the fate of the day."[25]

I NEVER SAW BETTER FIGHTING

BRIGADIER General Robert Mitchell had chosen to ignore Gates Thruston's oral order that he close up his cavalry on McCook's right. Nor did he respond to Thruston's warning that the Confederates appeared to be gaining the upper hand in the battle. The night before, Rosecrans had instructed Mitchell to hold Crawfish Springs at all costs. Absent written orders to the contrary, that was what he intended to do.[1]

Only after his own staff officers confirmed that Confederate infantry stood where army headquarters had been and that everything on the right was retreating toward Chattanooga did Mitchell realize the grave danger, not only to his cavalry but to the field hospital at the Gordon-Lee house and to the trains of the Twentieth Corps, which had come down from the mountains early that morning and were now his responsibility. Sometime after noon, Mitchell gave orders for the trains to assemble and for the ambulances to load up all the wounded able to ride. The First Tennessee Cavalry and Fourth Indiana Cavalry regiments were detailed to help evacuate the hospital.

It was not a duty the troopers relished. "The scene around the hospital . . . was one of peculiar sadness, and to be seen was never to be forgotten," remembered William Carter of the First Tennessee. "Hundreds of our men who had been taken from the battlefield badly wounded had answered the last roll-call amid the boom of cannon, and as the living demanded all the time and attention of those in charge, the dead, for the time being, were laid out in rows, side by side, awaiting the burial party."[2]

Scores of ambulances were loaded. E. H. Bowman, the chief surgeon of Laiboldt's brigade, took charge of some sixty wagons himself. Nevertheless, hundreds of wounded otherwise able to travel were left in the tents for want of wagons. Unable to bear the thought of abandoning them, Carter and his comrades dismounted and lifted wounded soldiers onto their horses, intending themselves to walk alongside. Their colonel checked the humanitarian impulses of the Tennesseans. He ordered the wounded to dismount and return to the hospital, pointing out quite correctly that, in the event the regiment was attacked, the troopers would be unable to hold their own on foot.[3]

The possibility of an assault on the trains was very real. At noon, the divisions of Martin and Wharton had splashed across the ford at Glass's Mill. Wheeler had been charged with guarding the fords of Chickamauga Creek down to the flank of the Left Wing; to this mission were appended discretionary orders enjoining him to "attack the enemy at every opportunity which presented itself." When he found the ford unguarded, Wheeler decided the time was ripe for an attack. He hurried his troopers along the road from the mill until they came to the edge of a large open field, five hundred yards west of the ford. In the woods beyond was drawn up the Federal cavalry brigade of Colonel Eli Long. Wheeler ordered his men to dismount and form line of battle. White's Tennessee battery opened fire on the Yankees.[4]

Long was completely deceived by the Rebel activity across the field. When Wheeler's troopers stepped into the open, the colonel thought they were a division of infantry. So did the men of the First Ohio Cavalry, who speculated that the "perfect lines of battle" were Longstreet's troops from Virginia. Thus they were understandably stunned when a lieutenant from General Crook's staff galloped up to the regiment and yelled out: "The orders from the general are 'Prepare to Charge.'" Lieutenant Colonel Valentine Cupp offered no objections. He ordered his men to sling carbines and draw their sabers. The Rebel line was now just three hundred yards distant and closing at the quick time. "In this position we waited, every moment expecting to hear the command that would move us into the jaws of death at a gallop," remembered John Chapin of the First Ohio. "Three lines of rebel infantry with loaded guns before us and coming our way, and we were to charge those bristling walls of steel. I said to Sergeant Irwin, on my left: 'If this charge is made not a man can come out alive.'"

At that moment, General Crook himself appeared. "The order was, prepare to *resist* the charge!" he shouted. "That was quite different, and I for one felt much easier," sighed Chapin.[5]

The troopers hurriedly dismounted to support a two-gun section of the Chicago Board of Trade Battery that was belching canister into the field, but the clarification of their duty had come too late. The enemy was only fifty yards away and coming on at the charge. The cannoneers limbered up and left at a gallop, and the Ohioans remounted. Colonel Cupp called out "Fours, left about, march," then spilled off his horse, shot through the bowels. Chapin had just swung his horse around when a bullet caught him behind the right shoulder. It punctured his right lung before lodging against a rib. "I can't say that the shot hurt; it was only a sting, but served to cut my breathing short and bring me off my horse," wrote Chapin. With one leg still in the stirrup, Chapin tried to remount. But the horse bucked and started, shoving the Ohioan into a tree. "I concluded that my only salvation was to leave my horse, or rather, to allow my horse to leave me, and to try walking. I therefore rolled to the ground while the horse was on the run, with as much ease and grace as a drunken man might roll off a log." Chapin laid aside his rifle and sabre, took off his belt, and tried to walk. His breath came short and labored. Staggering to a tree, Chapin sat down and watched the battle swirl around him.[6]

It was all over in a matter of minutes. Outnumbered and intimidated, the Federal troopers offered only token resistance. Eighty-six men were lost, most of them captured.[7]

Wheeler recalled his men from the forest to remount. As he retraced his steps back to his horse, Private J. K. Womack of the Fourth Tennessee Cavalry came upon a wounded Yankee whose gentle aspect touched him. "What can I do for you?" asked Womack.

"Nothing, for I think I will soon be dead," the Federal answered.

Womack looked him over. The soldier had only a flesh wound and had not lost much blood. "Friend, you are not hurt much, and you can get well if you will try. You are just sick from the wound," Womack assured him.

Just then a member of Womack's company approached. "I am going to take his boots," he cried out greedily. Womack stopped him. "This is my prisoner, and I will see that his boots are not taken from him." The covetous Confederate persisted. Womack settled the question with a threat: "This is my prisoner, and as long as I have a load in my gun you are not going to take them." He placed the wounded man under a shade tree and then bade him goodbye. "I shall never forget the kind expression and evidence of confidence he had in me," remembered Womack.[8]

Few were the wounded lucky enough to find champions among the enemy. Far more typical was the scene John Wyeth of the Fourth Alabama Cavalry witnessed. A captured Union officer who had been shot through the foot came limping along toward him with a group of enlisted prisoners. One of his captors, a surly Texas Ranger, announced that he wanted the officer's boots, which Wyeth noticed were especially fine. Realizing the futility of a protest, the officer sat down while the Texan yanked off the boot from his sound foot. It fit. The Ranger motioned for the other. The Federal begged him to cut it off so as to lessen the pain of removing it. "You reckon I'm going to spoil that boot?" snickered the Texan. With a hard tug he pulled it off, unaffected by the anguished screams of the Federal. Wyeth turned away in disgust. By way of apology, he later wrote: "Earlier in the war this incident would not have been possible, but men had become callous and indifferent, and then the necessities of the Southern troops, half-starved and poorly clad as they were, justified to some extent the wholesale appropriation of all the belongings of their prisoners."[9]

Wheeler intended to pursue cross-country toward the Gordon-Lee house. Before he could begin, however, he received an order to move to Lee and Gordon's Mill and attack the enemy there. Who the order came from is unclear. Wyeth, the only member of Wheeler's command to leave a reliable account of the day's action, said Wheeler knew nothing of Longstreet's success nor had heard a word from him. Otherwise, Wyeth insisted, he never would have adopted the course he did—that is to say, recross Chickamauga Creek after he was already over, move down its eastern bank, and ford its waters opposite the mill.[10]

It was 3:00 P.M. before Wheeler was again across the creek and ready to advance. By then Mitchell had drawn up the brigades of Colonels Ray and Campbell at the edge of a large pasture that lay between the mill and Crawfish Springs. Colonel P. Sidney Post had joined him with his brigade of infantry after four days of screening McCook's trains as they labored over the mountains toward McLemore's Cove. Mitchell held out against repeated attacks by Wheeler until nearly 5:00 P.M., when with Post's brigade he fell back toward Missionary Ridge, covering the withdrawal of the trains and ambulances. Despite his best efforts, over one thousand wounded Federals were left behind and some twenty wagons laden with ordnance stores were captured. Such losses were trifling, however, compared to the damage Wheeler might have wrought had he been made aware early in the afternoon of the precipitate retreat of the Federal army two miles to the north.[11]

By 3:00 P.M. the hysteria along the Dry Valley road had subsided. As they passed through McFarland's Gap, the Federals felt a sense of relief. No longer fearful of Rebel cavalry, they sat down to rest amid the spacious fields of the McFarland farm. They were tired and thirsty but willing to be led. Generals and colonels rode about the fields, identifying and piecing together the fragments of their commands. Here Davis was reunited with Carlin and Martin. He placed Hotchkiss's battery to cover the gap and in less than half an hour had rallied about a thousand men from his division. Sheridan was nearby with fifteen hundred troops of his own.[12]

Gates Thruston had met Davis and Sheridan, whom he found to be "furious . . . swearing mad," just before they passed through the gap. The three conferred briefly. Thruston agreed to ride toward the left to see if a possibility still existed for reaching Thomas. A few troopers from the Second Kentucky Cavalry accompanied him.

The lieutenant colonel and his escort picked their way past overturned wagons and abandoned caissons. Somewhere west of the Vittetoe cabin they stumbled upon a line of skirmishers from Deas's brigade, who fortunately had their gazes fixed in another direction. Thruston led his escort off the road and around the northern slope of Horseshoe Ridge. Near the Snodgrass house they came upon Federal wounded awaiting treatment. "Galloping through the wounded as best we could, I checked my horse before the form of an officer borne in the arms of his comrades to find it was an old home friend, Lieutenant Colonel Durbin Ward, a moment before severely wounded. Time was pressing; I could offer but a word of sympathy," wrote Thruston. Another hundred yards or so and he found Thomas. It was about 3:30 P.M. and Longstreet had just begun his concerted attack against the ridge. "Thomas was intently watching the conflict near the crest, a few steps in rear of the battle-line. His face was anxious but defiant," Thruston recalled.

Thruston briefed Thomas on the state of affairs near McFarland's Gap. Thomas thanked him and asked the lieutenant colonel to try to bring up Sheridan and Davis to reinforce Steedman. Impressed with the import of his mission, Thruston galloped the entire way back to the spot on the Dry Valley road where he had left Davis and Sheridan. There was no sign of either the generals or their staffs, only a road clogged with troops trudging toward the gap. Thruston had no choice but to plunge forward. "The miseries of a mounted officer trying to pass marching infantry on a narrow roadway can be well imagined," he wrote. "Time was precious. I rode furiously through the thicket, alongside, and appealed to officers. 'See Jeff, Colonel?' they said; 'See Phil?' Some old trudger in the ranks called out: 'We'll talk to you my son, when we get to the Ohio River.' " Thruston lost half an hour squeezing through the defile. At the head of the column he spotted Sheridan and Davis.[13]

Thruston returned to a changed situation. Negley had arrived shortly after Thruston left. Somewhere between Horseshoe Ridge and McFarland Gap, the Pennsylvanian had found some of his old strength. Or perhaps he had begun to realize the terrible mistake he had made in leaving the field in the first place. In either case, he wanted very much to go back, but he could not quite bring himself to do it alone. Near the gap he spotted Carlin at the head of his brigade. Sword in hand, Negley rode to the brigadier general and suggested they go to Thomas. "If you will go to his relief I will support," Negley promised. Carlin merely shrugged his shoulders and advised the general to talk to Sheridan.

Negley missed Sheridan but found Davis. With him was Captain Joseph Hill of the army staff. "I will report to General Thomas, inform him of the position here, and tell him that we can assist him," announced Negley. Davis offered no objection, and Negley and Hill started along the route taken by Thruston a few minutes earlier. They ran into the same Rebel skirmishers, and Negley lost his nerve; perhaps it would be better to go back to talk things over with Davis again, he reasoned.[14]

Sheridan was with Davis when Negley slunk back at about 4:00 P.M. Also present was Lieutenant Colonel Arthur Ducat, an aide-de-camp to Rosecrans. The four fell into a heated discussion over what course of action to pursue. No one seemed to agree later on what they decided. Negley said that Davis agreed to march at once for Thomas's right via the Dry Valley road and that Sheridan offered take his column to Rossville and from there march down the La Fayette road toward Thomas's left. He volunteered to stay behind and help rally stragglers as they came in. Captain Hill later testified to the correctness of Negley's recollection. Ducat, however, understood that Davis was not to go to Thomas but rather remain on the Dry Valley road to cover the retreat of the trains and artillery and to prevent any Rebel force from descending on Rossville by way of McFarland Gap. Captain Hough, who eavesdropped on the discussion, maintained that the four could not agree upon a plan and concluded simply to go their separate ways.[15]

That was certainly the impression Thruston got when he rode up just as the meeting was breaking up. Davis, he said, was full of fight and ordered "a right-about" at once. Sheridan seemed "without faith" and intent on going to Rossville with his division. Negley appeared to be vacillating.[16]

The gathering concluded. Davis allowed time to refill canteens and then led his column of twenty-five hundred men through the gap at about 4:30 P.M. It was just under two miles to Horseshoe Ridge. If Davis succeeded and stayed on the road, he would come up directly against the left flank of Deas's exhausted brigade.[17]

Garfield's six-mile ride from Rossville to the Snodgrass house was the highlight of his military career; apart from his assassination, it was perhaps the most memorable moment of his life. During the presidential campaign of 1880, Garfield's supporters inflated it into an event second only to Paul Revere's ride in its importance and unsurpassed in its danger. In truth, as Garfield's first serious biographer admitted, "this ride . . . although a creditable display of courage, involved no unusual risk." What it did accomplish was to give Thomas his first reliable news of the disaster that had befallen the rest of the army.[18]

Accompanying Garfield on his ride were two orderlies from the Fifteenth Pennsylvania Cavalry. Along the way he met up with Captains Gaw and Barker, the two aides Thomas had sent to the rear in search of ammunition. The two parties banded together. Their journey along the La Fayette road was uneventful until they passed the Cloud church. From the pasture on the east side of the road came rifle fire. How much is uncertain. Garfield told Thomas that an entire battalion had opened on them. Sergeant T. J.

McCall, an orderly with no reputation to preserve, later wrote that a lone Rebel skirmisher fired just one shot at them. Whether a volley or a single bullet, the unexpected fire was enough to cause the four horsemen to leave the road. "We jumped our horses up the bank and over the fence," remembered McCall. "Captain Gaw's horse fell on the bank. The captain thought the horse was shot, and hopped over the fence and pretty nearly outran the horses. He commanded me to give him my horse. I appealed to General Garfield, and he told me to let him have the horse and go and get the captain's horse, which had run back toward the Cloud house."[19]

Garfield was now safely inside Dan McCook's skirmish line. From there, he rode unmolested across the Mullis field to the Snodgrass farm. By his own estimate, Garfield reached Thomas at 3:35 P.M.[20]

"I shall never forget my amazement and admiration when I beheld Thomas holding his own with utter defeat on each side and wild confusion in the rear," wrote Garfield.

"We have repulsed every attack so far," Thomas told him, "and we can hold our ground if the enemy can be kept from our rear."[21]

Garfield brought with him only bad tidings. Not only had Alexander McCook and Crittenden been routed, but he knew of no ammunition closer than Chattanooga. No reinforcements could be expected from Rossville, he added. (Garfield was unaware of the plans made by Davis, Sheridan, and Negley; in fact, he incorrectly assumed Sheridan to be fighting somewhere on Horseshoe Ridge with Thomas.) Worse yet, he had run into at least a battalion of Confederates during his ride. The only thing positive Garfield had to offer was a little ammunition that Gaw and Barker had rounded up along the way.

Garfield sat down on a log and began a message to Rosecrans. Granger, Wood, and a handful of other officers gathered around him to fill in the details. A few minutes before 4:00, Garfield handed the completed dispatch to a telegrapher to wire to Chattanooga.[22] It read:

> General Thomas' Headquarters
> Battlefield, Five Miles South of Rossville
> September 20, 1863 — 3:45 P.M.

General Rosecrans:

I arrived here ten minutes ago, via Rossville. General Thomas has Brannan's, Baird's, Reynolds's, Wood's, Palmer's, and Johnson's divisions still intact after terrible fighting. Granger is here, closed up with Thomas, and is fighting terribly on the right. Sheridan is in with the bulk of his division, but in ragged shape, though plucky and fighting [where Garfield heard this is unclear]. General Thomas holds nearly his old ground of this morning. Negley was coming down on Rossville from the road leading from where we saw the trains in our route, and I sent word to him to cover the retreat of trains through Rossville. I also met the Fourth U.S. Battery at that place, and posted it as a reserve in case of need. As I turned in from the Rossville [La Fayette] road to General Thomas' line I was opened upon by a rebel battalion. One orderly killed; Captain Gaw's horse killed and my own wounded.

The hardest fighting I have seen to-day is now going on here. I hope General Thomas will be able to hold on here till night, and will not need to fall back farther than Rossville; perhaps not any. All fighting men should be stopped there, and the Dry Valley and Lookout roads held by them. I think we may in the main retrieve our morning disaster. I never saw better fighting than our men are now doing. The rebel ammunition must be nearly exhausted. Ours is fast failing. If we can hold out an hour more it will be all right. Granger thinks we can defeat them badly to-morrow if all our forces come in. I think you had better come to Rossville tonight and bring ammunition.

Very truly, yours.
J. A. Garfield[23]

Rosecrans's ride ended between 3:30 and 4:00 P.M. at the headquarters of General Wagner in Chattanooga. Lieutenant Cist watched as he was helped from his horse into the house. "He had the appearance of one broken in spirit, and as if he were bearing up as best he could under a terrible blow, the full force and effect of which he himself did not at that time clearly perceive and only partly felt."

For a time, Rosecrans managed to work through his exhaustion. All the matters he originally had wanted Garfield to attend to he dispatched in the first thirty minutes following his arrival.[24] Then he sat down to write out instructions to Thomas, wherever he might then be. Rosecrans had not yet heard from Garfield and, in his melancholy state of mind, assumed the worst. Had Rosecrans waited until he received word from Garfield, the course of the battle might have been altered. As it was, he wrote out the following at 4:15 P.M.:

> Headquarters[,] Department of the Cumberland,
> Chattanooga, September 20, 1863 — 12:15 P.M. [sic]
>
> Major-General Thomas:
> Assume command of all the forces, and with Crittenden and McCook take a strong position and assume a threatening attitude at Rossville. Send all the unorganized force to this place for re-organization. I will examine the ground here and make such dispositions for defense as the case may require and join you. Have sent ammunition and rations.
>
> W. S. Rosecrans,
> Major-General[25]

Crittenden reported to headquarters a few minutes later. Rosecrans had nothing to tell Crittenden just then, so the Kentuckian took a seat and waited with him for news from the front.[26]

Longstreet had gradually come to appreciate both the importance of Horse-shoe Ridge and the stubbornness of the Yankee defenders. "It was evident that with this position gained I should be complete master of the field," he reported. When the combined attack of Hindman, Johnson, and Anderson petered out around 4:00 P.M., Longstreet decided the time had come to commit Preston's division, his only unbloodied reserve. He asked Buckner to see that the twelve guns of Major Samuel Williams's reserve artillery battalion at the Poe farm intensified their fire in the direction of the Kelly field to forestall any effort by Thomas to draw reinforcements from his left. Stewart was ordered to attack any such force in the flank.[27]

Preston commanded a powerful division that on 20 September numbered 4,078 officers and men. Of these, 2,003 belonged to Gracie's brigade. Trigg's brigade, which had seen limited action in Viniard's field the day before, counted 1,199 of all ranks. Kelly's brigade was down to 876 troops, the Sixty-fifth Georgia Infantry having been placed on detached service that morning.[28]

Much was expected of Preston's division, although it had never been under fire before Chickamauga. Especially promising was thirty-year-old Archibald Gracie, Jr., widely regarded within the army as a "rising young general." Gracie was a native of New York City. Born to a wealthy merchant family, he was educated in Heidelberg, Germany, and at West Point, where he graduated in 1854. Two years later, he resigned from the military to join his father, who had moved his business concerns to Mobile, Alabama. When war came, Gracie's father returned with the family to New York; only young Archibald chose to stay and give his allegiance to the Confederacy. None doubted his loyalty to the cause. "It was a great privilege to know General Gracie as I did," reminisced Bishop Quintard. "He was a character that old Froissart would have delighted to paint. Chivalrous as a Bayard, he had all the tenderness of a woman. A warrior by nature . . . he had a horror of shedding blood and would almost shed tears in the hour of victory over the thin ranks of his brigade." Major Owen watched the brigade march through the Dyer field toward the front. "Gracie is . . . devoted to his profession. . . . He is justly proud of his brigade of young soldiers, most of whom have never been under fire. They will do good work."[29]

Gracie halted to the left of Humphreys and behind Kershaw. Colonel John Kelly began to form his brigade in line of battle to the left of Gracie. Trigg had been left behind to support Williams's artillery. Preston rode up the knoll overlooking the Dyer field to confer with Hindman, who had established his headquarters on the summit. Though his neck was bruised and bloodied from a shrapnel wound, Hindman had elected to stay in the saddle. He was delighted to see Preston and began at once to brief him on the Federal defenses. John Dyer, whose father owned the largest farm on the battlefield, was present as a courier for Preston to fill in the details of the topography of Horseshoe Ridge.[30]

Preston left the knoll to help Kelly get his brigade into line. Suddenly, Gracie's brigade stepped forward and disappeared into the woods. Preston sent an aide galloping off after the New Yorker to find out by what authority he had moved.

By the time the aide reached Gracie, the young brigadier had cleared Kershaw's line in the ravine and was moving across the Vittetoe road toward Hill One and the open spur. Kershaw, it seems, had taken it upon himself to order Gracie forward. To improve Gracie's chances, Kershaw agreed to send the Second South Carolina in on his left and the Fifteenth and Eighth South Carolina regiments in on his right. The remaining regiments of his brigade and Oates's Fifteenth Alabama had nearly exhausted their ammunition and so stayed in the ravine.

Being new to the fight, Preston was unprepared for the haphazard nature of the Confederate attacks on Horseshoe Ridge. Although angry that Gracie had been ordered in prematurely and without his concurrence, Preston realized it was too late to call him back. Instead, he directed Kelly, whose brigade was only partly formed, to advance at once.[31]

Gracie attacked in a single line of battle. The Forty-third Alabama Infantry was on the brigade left. Next came the Third Alabama Battalion, then the Fourth, First, and Second Alabama battalions. The Sixty-third Tennessee regiment was on the right. "At length ... the banner of the Legion was unfurled for the first time in battle, the command, 'Forward — double-quick!' was given by the gallant Gracie, and the brigade rushed impetuously into action," wrote the historian of the First Alabama Battalion. "The first volley of the enemy, who were lying in wait behind a fortification of logs in an excellent position, bore with fatal precision upon our line, and created many a gap in our heretofore intact ranks; but it was responded to by an answering volley and a rousing cheer, which rose high above the din of conflict," he continued. "I shall attempt no recital of what followed — the heart grows sick at the memory."[32]

The linear tactics of the time caused Gracie's brigade to split apart when it came up against the curved slope of Hill One. On the left, the Forty-third Alabama ran into the rear of Anderson's brigade and was forced to mark time behind the ravine. The Third Alabama Battalion kept on and butted up against the southern edge of the hill.

To its right, the Fourth Alabama Battalion was hit by an enfilading fire from Stoughton's Yankees on the crest. The Alabamians began shooting wildly. Things went from bad to worse for the scared and inexperienced Butternuts. As they neared the cornfield, they ran into the disciplined volley firing of Harker's veterans on the open spur. "A heavy fire pouring upon

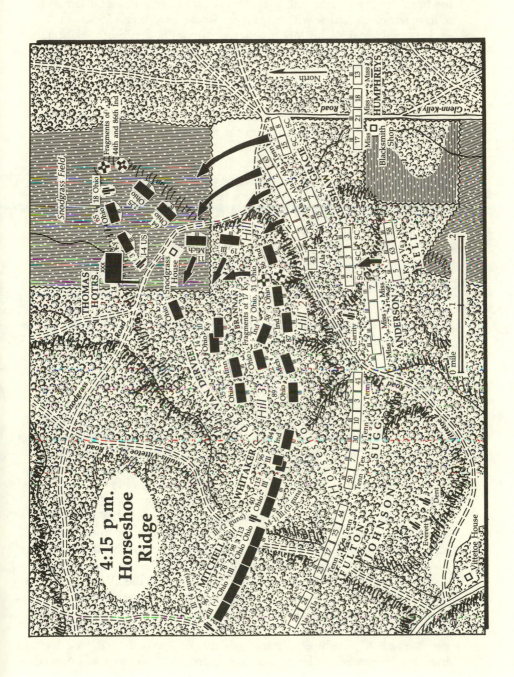

4:15 p.m. Horseshoe Ridge

me from the front, right, and left, and my ranks being almost decimated, to have advanced farther without support would have been reckless in the extreme," said Major John McLennon, commander of the Fourth Alabama. He obliqued the battalion to the left and told the company commanders to have their men take what cover they could find at the base of the hill. From there, they kept up a steady fire against the Federals on the slope until their ammunition ran out.[33]

Lieutenant Colonel John Holt of the First Alabama Battalion was not so easily deterred. He urged his men up the slope until a bullet shattered his knee. Captain George Huguley took charge and kept at it. Casualties were terrific, but the Alabamians persisted. "Our officers and men all seamed to view with each other in their deades of novel daring," wrote a survivor. "General Gracey flue from wing to wing between the fire . . . giving comand and encerageing his men to more despert deads. He had too horses killd under him and meney shot went throu his clothing. I had seven shot in throu my coat but non more than grained the skin."[34]

From the crest, the mad advance of the First Alabama Battalion looked inexorable. Said Henry Haynie of the Nineteenth Illinois: "Again the foe comes on in renewed assault; they come so swiftly that we can hardly count their volleying. The reports of their guns and our own are blended in a dirge of destruction, and the smoke of musketry and of cannon is so thickly spread over and about us that we can hardly see aught save those who are next to us. . . . Through the thick smoke suddenly we see a swarm of men in gray, not in battle-line, but an on-coming mass of soldiers bent on burying their bullets in resisting flesh."[35]

The Second Alabama Battalion charged with equal ferocity. A few yards from the breastworks, its commander was shot down. The color-bearer was hit three times and the flag staff twice shot away, but both bearer and colors kept on. Along the works, which were held by the Eleventh Michigan, the fighting was hand-to-hand. Colonel Stoughton had never seen anything like it: "A contest ensued, which in its fierceness and duration has few parallels. The enemy was in heavy force, and fought with the most determined obstinacy. As fast as their ranks were thinned by our fire they were filled up by fresh troops. A dense cloud of smoke enveloped our lines, and in some places the position of the foe could only be known by the flash of his guns." Kershaw agreed. "This was one of the heaviest attacks of the war on a single point," he reported. Said a member of the Eleventh: "The slope in our front was strewn with the enemy's dead, so thick you could almost walk on them, our men's faces were black with powder smoke, their tongues fairly hung out for want of water." The Michiganders could not stand such punishment from fresh troops. Gradually they fell back from the breastworks. The Alabamians hopped over the logs and opened

"One of the heaviest attacks of the war on a single point." The Second Alabama Battalion and the Eleventh Michigan Infantry grapple on Hill One.

fire into the backs of the Federals, who fled to the cover of the northern slope of the hill. Now outflanked, the Nineteenth Illinois gave way, and the First Alabama Battalion entered the works. Moses Walker's Federals retreated next, allowing the Third Alabama Battalion to take a place on the crest as well.

The Alabamians were too few and too low on ammunition to press their advantage. Already over two-thirds of the 239 officers and men of the First Alabama Battalion lay dead or wounded, including seven members of the color guard heaped together a few yards in front of the breastworks. The two sides glared at one another from across the hilltop. The receding daylight and dense smoke masked the weakness of the Rebel ranks, and so for the time being, neither Beatty nor Stoughton gave any thought to a counterattack to regain the crest.[36]

Out in the Snodgrass cornfield, the Sixty-third Tennessee was butchered. The regiment had become separated from the brigade during the initial advance, and it drifted due north against the open spur while the rest of the command obliqued to the left. Gracie brought the Forty-third Alabama over from where it stood idle behind Anderson to fill the resultant gap. The extra troops were of no use against Harker; neither were the Eighth nor Fifteenth South Carolina, which supported the Tennesseans on their right. The Federal volleys were simply too well-timed and precise to permit an advance, and the dried cornstalks were too low to offer any cover.[37]

The way Harker's troops fought — showing their heads above the crest of the spur just long enough to deliver their volleys — was driving Major John Stackhouse of the Eighth South Carolina to distraction. According to a member of Kershaw's brigade, Stackhouse was "a pure Christian gentleman and a churchman of the straightest sect. It is doubtful if he ever had an evil thought, and . . . he was always sincere and his language chosen and chaste." Until now. Peering through the smoke and cornstalks on his hands and knees for a sign of the enemy, Stackhouse would yell out when they appeared: "There they are, boys, give them hell!" Then under his breath he would add: "May God forgive me for that." The Federals disappeared before his men could fire. Growing more frustrated, he cried out, a bit louder: "Boys, give it to them, give them hell," once again adding quietly, "May God forgive me for that!" Again the South Carolinians missed their mark. Stackhouse lost his temper. Springing to his feet, he shouted at the top of his voice: "Give them hell; give them hell, I tell you, boys; give them hell, God Damn their souls!"[38]

Thomas was not present to witness the capture of Hill One by Gracie at 5:00 P.M. Thirty minutes earlier, a telegrapher had passed him the dispatch from Rosecrans ordering a withdrawal to Rossville. As Thomas and Garfield would tell it, the Virginian balked at the thought of leaving the field. "It will ruin the army to withdraw it now. This position must be held until night," Thomas allegedly told Garfield. Garfield later said that he not only agreed but insisted that Thomas not withdraw at all. He construed Rosecrans's order as discretionary. Granger said he added his voice in support of a continued stand and expressed his opinion that morning would find them masters of the field. No, said Thomas, he would obey the order, but not while his position was under attack. Thomas told Captains Gaw and Barker to deliver the last of the available ammunition to Harker and Stoughton. He asked Colonel Walker to tell Brannan to be prepared to withdraw on order and sent Captain Willard with a similar message to Palmer, Johnson, and Baird. So goes the traditional version of what happened.[39]

If Thomas really did have any doubts about obeying Rosecrans's order, they were fleeting. Every division and brigade commander on the left reported receiving orders from Thomas to fall back at about 5:00 P.M.—an hour before sunset and nearly two and a half hours before dark. But to admit that Thomas complied with his instructions immediately is not to cast aspersions on his performance. By 4:30 P.M., the chronic shortage of ammunition and the ferocity with which Gracie sustained his attack were enough to convince any rational commander that the Horseshoe Ridge–Snodgrass spur line could not be held much longer.

Thomas chose to begin the movement on the Kelly field line, commencing with Reynolds's division on the right, to be taken up in turn by Palmer, Johnson, and Baird. At about 4:30 P.M., Thomas sent Captain Barker to notify Reynolds to start his withdrawal. Next, similar orders were drafted and sent to Baird, Johnson, and Palmer. A few minutes later, Thomas turned command of the forces on Horseshoe Ridge over to Granger and rode off the Snodgrass hill toward the La Fayette road to show Reynolds where to form to cover the retirement of the remaining divisions from the Kelly field. The heroic stand was drawing to a close.[40]

CHAPTER TWENTY-NINE

Don't Waste Any Cartridges
Now, Boys

ROSECRANS moved about Wagner's headquarters as if in a dream. He
seemed only to half-understand what he read or what was said to him.
A few minutes before 5:00 P.M., Rosecrans was given Garfield's encouraging
dispatch of 3:45 P.M. He scribbled out a terse, ambiguous reply that read:
"Your dispatch of 3:45 received. What you propose is correct. . . . I trust
General Thomas has been able to hold his position. Ammunition will be
sent up."[1]

With which proposal was Rosecrans agreeing? That the retreat be halted
at Rossville? That the routed portions of the army be returned to the
battlefield to renew the battle in the morning? That Rosecrans come to
Rossville and personally take charge? Perhaps Rosecrans himself was not
sure. One thing is certain, however: he did not have the strength to go
anywhere. Had he intended to act on any part of Garfield's advice, Rosecrans
at a minimum should have sent McCook and Crittenden to Rossville to
reform their commands. Instead, after reading Garfield's dispatch, he told
Crittenden and McCook, who had just wandered in, to lie down and get
some rest, adding: "I am nearly worn out and want someone with me to
take command, if necessary to assist me." Nothing more.[2]

That Rosecrans's reply was ambiguous made no difference. Neither Garfield nor Thomas was on the Snodgrass hill to receive it, if indeed the field
telegraph was still operating there after Gracie seized Hill One.

Garfield's dispatch did nothing to lift Rosecrans's spirits. After writing
out his answer, Rosecrans composed a telegram to Halleck in Washington
apprising him of the defeat. Uncharacteristically passive in tone, it revealed
nothing less than the utter despair of its author.[3] The telegram read:

Chattanooga, Tenn., September 20, 1863 — 5 P.M.

Maj. Gen. H. W. Halleck,
General-in-Chief:

We have met with a serious disaster; extent not yet ascertained. Enemy overwhelmed us, drove our right, pierced our center, and scattered troops everywhere. Thomas, who had seven divisions, remained intact at last news. Granger, with two brigades, had gone to support Thomas on the left. Every available reserve was used when the men stampeded. Burnside will be notified of the state of things at once, and you will be informed. Troops from Charleston, Florida, Virginia, and all along the seaboard are found among the prisoners. It seems that every available man was thrown against us.

W. S. Rosecrans,
Major-General, Commanding[4]

Washington knew of the defeat even before Rosecrans composed his gloomy telegram. Far worse tidings had already reached the War Department. On arriving at Chattanooga at 4:00 P.M., fresh from the battlefield and still seized with fear, Assistant Secretary Dana had penned a frantic message to Stanton. Dana knew nothing of Thomas's stand and presumed the entire army to be in abject flight. His telegram read, in part: "My report today is of deplorable importance. Chickamauga is as fatal a name in our history as Bull Run. . . . Our soldiers turned and fled. It was wholesale panic. Vain were all attempts to rally them. Our wounded are all left behind. . . . Enemy not yet arrived before Chattanooga." Dana acted as his own cipher clerk and sent the message in the War Department secret code. The operator at Nashville broke it and spread the news. An Associated Press stringer in Louisville picked up the story and filed a report quoting Dana's statement that "Chickamauga is as fatal a name in our history as Bull Run." Criminations would follow apace.[5]

In the Kelly field, Generals Palmer and Johnson listened intently to the crash of musketry coming from the direction of the Snodgrass hill. All afternoon they had heard it, but now the firing seemed to rise in a crescendo. Palmer was worried. Defeat there would place the enemy squarely in the rear of the Kelly field salient. He suggested that they send a brigade to help Thomas. Johnson agreed.[6]

Hazen's brigade drew the assignment, largely because it was the only brigade that still had a fair supply of ammunition, nearly forty rounds per man by Hazen's own count. At 4:30 P.M., he pulled his troops from behind their breastworks and started them at the double-quick across the La Fayette road and into the forest. It was a grueling hike. Like most of the Federals still on the field, the soldiers of Hazen's brigade had had no water since the night before. Details sent to find water during the day had been captured, and now "pangs of hunger seemed mild in comparison" to the driving thirst, recalled a veteran. "Before night, men's tongues were swollen and their lips blackened and cracked until the power of speech was gone."[7]

Hazen reached the Snodgrass cornfield in rear of Harker's line at 5:30 P.M. The first face Hazen saw was a familiar one, that of Colonel Opdycke, who had once been a company officer in the Forty-first Ohio, his old regiment. Thinking he was doing the colonel a favor, Hazen immediately ordered his lead regiment, the Ninth Indiana, to relieve the One Hundred Twenty-fifth Ohio on the crest. But Opdycke would have none of it. His troops were doing fine on their own, he bristled. If Colonel Suman wished, he could form his Hoosiers behind the men of the One Hundred Twenty-fifth and alternate volleys with them from the crest. Suman acquiesced, adding the three hundred rifles of his regiment to the line on the spur.

Some thirty minutes later, Brannan asked Hazen to detach a regiment to Hill Two to help repel an attack by Kelly. Hazen sent the Ninth Indiana and replaced it on the firing line with the Forty-first Ohio. The men recognized Opdycke as they came up behind him. They raised three hearty cheers on their way to the crest and then opened fire on Major Stackhouse and his luckless South Carolinians. "The bullets rattled through the corn in a very uncanny way," recalled Hazen.[8]

The added firepower of Hazen's brigade was welcome but not crucial. By 5:30 P.M., the Confederates in the cornfield had taken all the pounding they could stand and had fired off most of their ammunition. They broke off the pointless contest, during which hardly a man in Harker's brigade had been struck, and withdrew across the Vittetoe road. In the Sixty-third Tennessee, which had held on the longest, two hundred men had fallen out of about four hundred engaged.[9]

On the crest of Hill One, the toehold of Gracie's three Alabama battalions had grown precarious. The men were running low on cartridges, and rifles were fouling. Brushfires crackled along the slopes, scorching the wounded and covering the hilltop with a smoke that not only masked their own position but hid that of the enemy as well. The sun would not set for another ten or fifteen minutes—at 6:01 P.M. to be precise—but amid the tall trees and smoke it was already murky twilight.

Gracie gave the command to withdraw just as Beatty and Stoughton launched a counterattack with the Eighteenth Ohio, which had passed most of the afternoon in reserve beside Smith's battery. The Ohioans charged up the northern slope and across the hilltop with a yell, bayonets fixed. The Alabamians fired their last rounds and then stumbled down the southern slope. As Stoughton's Federals settled back into their breastworks, someone struck up the "Battle Cry of Freedom." The whole line took up the strain, recalled a Yankee veteran, "and when they came to the words 'Down with the traitors, up with the Stars,' every fellow emphasized them with a vim that made the woods and rocky hills sing."[10]

Colonel John Kelly's brigade had moved to the attack with the same ferocity that Gracie's had shown. Like Gracie, Kelly was considered one of the most promising young officers in the Army of Tennessee; just twenty-three years old, he was also the youngest brigade commander in the army. Preston intended for Kelly to guide his brigade against the western slope of Hill One to support Gracie, but the deep draw that ran from the center of Anderson's line up to the saddle between Hills Two and Three channeled his attack in that direction. Preston's two brigades thus operated independently of one another.[11]

Kelly launched his attack ten minutes after Gracie. The Fifty-eighth North Carolina ascended the southern slope of Hill Two, the Sixty-third Virginia marched up the draw, and the Fifth Kentucky, on the brigade left, moved against Hill Three. Brushfires laced the slopes. A thick cloud of smoke hung over the woods, hurrying the onset of twilight. The marching soldiers cast long shadows. The instant they crossed the Vittetoe road, Kelly's men came under a withering fire. But Kelly refused to halt to return it; instead, he sent his line forward at the double-quick. For some reason, he believed the troops on the hill to be Confederates.

The Federal volleys took a terrible toll. In the Fifty-eighth North Carolina, the major, adjutant, senior captain, and three lieutenants fell in the first few minutes of combat. Twenty-two of thirty-four men in the right-flank company were struck by a cross fire from the Ninth Ohio while the regiment moved against the Eighty-seventh Indiana to its front. The Tenth Kentucky came up on Van Derveer's left and added its rifles to the flanking fire. The right wing of the Fifty-eighth began to unravel, just twelve feet from the Yankee breastworks. Lieutenant Colonel Edmund Kirby galloped down the line to rally it, crying "Push them, men, push them." Four bullets hit him simultaneously. Three young enlisted men named Childs, Sherwood, and Phifer, all sons of wealthy planters, rushed to Lieutenant Colonel Kirby's body. The three had all been close friends of Kirby before the war. One by one, they were shot down. Later that evening, the regimental commander, Colonel John Palmer, found the bodies of all four piled together.[12]

Convinced that Kelly was wrong about the identity of the troops that were tearing apart his regiment, Palmer ordered his left and center companies to return the fire while he rode down the slope to rally the right-wing companies. He got them partway up again before noticing that the rest of the brigade had halted behind him. Palmer first motioned his men to lie down and fire, then recalled them from the hilltop.[13]

Kelly's unwarranted caution had cost the Sixty-third Virginia dearly as well. Major J. M. French drove his men to within fifteen paces of the Federal works before he allowed them to stop and fire. Their first volley was enough to send the Yankees reeling. French was prepared to pursue over the ridge, but a courier from Kelly called him off, saying that they had fired on friendly troops. The Virginian ordered a cease-fire, which the Federals used to reoccupy their breastworks. French moved his line back a bit before settling for an exchange of volleys with an enemy he could barely see in the receding light.[14]

The story was the same with the Fifth Kentucky. A relatively inexperienced regiment, the Fifth was the target of many camp jokes told by veterans of the Orphan Brigade in the days before the battle. "There were jokes about their hurting themselves with army rifles and bayonets; they were squirrel hunters, butternuts, etc., and as most of them were from the mountain sections where ginseng at one time constituted a sort of staple of barter, they were dubbed Sang Diggers," recalled Orphan Ed Thompson.[15]

Now they were up against the Twenty-first Ohio. Major McMahan had told his company commanders to permit the men to fall back individually after they had fired their last round. By the time the Fifth Kentucky attacked at 4:45 P.M., McMahan's regiment looked like a bedraggled skirmish line. Few if any of the Ohioans had enough cartridges to fill the cylinders of their Colt rifles. When the Kentuckians had closed to within sixty yards, McMahan's line let go its final volley, then retired through the Second Minnesota to the reverse slope.[16]

The Minnesotans came forward with about ten rounds per man. "Don't waste any cartridges now, boys," yelled Lieutenant Colonel Bishop before the crash of musketry drowned him out. "The men in gray commenced falling, but they seemed to bow their heads to the storm of bullets, and picking their way among and over their fallen comrades who already encumbered the slope by hundreds, they came bravely and steadily on," wrote Bishop in admiration of the Sang Diggers' resolve. "As, however, they approached nearer, and they seemed to lose the assuring touch of elbows, and as the vacancies rapidly increased, they began to hesitate—'Now we've got 'em, see 'em wobble,' were the first words passed in our line since the firing had begun—then they halted and commenced firing wildly into the treetops, then turned and rushed madly down the slope."[17]

So it looked from the Union perspective. Colonel Kelly, on the other hand, reported that the Fifth reached the brow and hung on tenaciously for the next sixty minutes, trading fire with the Yankees across the hilltop. In either case, by 5:00 P.M., Kelly's attack had stalled.[18]

General Preston had anticipated just such a turn of events. "When the fire on Gracie and Kelly was fully developed, its great volume and extent assured me that support was indispensable." He sent for Trigg, who was supporting Williams's artillery battalion near the Poe farm against a rumored approach of Federal cavalry up the La Fayette road, then called Colonel Kelly off the firing line to assure him that help was on the way.

Trigg at first dispatched only the Fifty-fourth Virginia and Sixth Florida, choosing to remain behind with the First Florida Dismounted Cavalry and Seventh Florida to guard the artillery. When the threatened cavalry attack turned out to be merely the advance guard of Wheeler's command, Trigg hurried on to join Preston with the remainder of his brigade.[19]

Bushrod Johnson timed his third assault against Steedman to coincide with Preston's appearance on the field. It was not much of a fight. Of those in Johnson's division not dead or wounded, probably a third were hiding behind trees or bent low in ravines, far from the firing line. Lieutenant Colonel Watt Floyd of the Seventeenth Tennessee reported the woods behind his regiment were alive with skulkers. Sergeant George Dolton of Battery M, First Illinois Light Artillery, claimed the ravine behind Steedman's division was similarly filled; among the skulkers, he said, were many officers.[20]

Few men on either side had much ammunition left. In Company F of the Ninety-eighth Ohio, a quick tally between attacks had revealed that only one man had any cartridges left, and he just one. A few cartridge boxes were brought up, but the rounds turned out to be the wrong caliber.

The men of the One Hundred Fifteenth Illinois had faced that problem all afternoon. They were armed with old-fashioned .69 caliber Remington muskets—large and unwieldy but very lethal. No ammunition of that caliber was available, so the Illinoisans improvised. A veteran explained: "The boys would find a box of cartridges, and then would hunt a gun of the same caliber as the cartridges. The result was that we were fighting Indian fashion—every one doing the best he could under the circumstances, without regard to tactics or alignment."[21]

Of those who still had ammunition, many found their rifles so fouled as to be useless, the barrels too hot to touch. A few tried to fire anyway, only to have their rifles explode in their faces.

By 4:30 P.M., unit integrity in Steedman's division had evaporated. Regiments intermingled during the innumerable charges and countercharges. Nearly a third of the men were down, and several hundred others were skulking behind the ridge. Because there were no designated stretcher-bearers in the Reserve Corps, many soldiers took it upon themselves to help wounded comrades off the field, further depleting units already dangerously thinned.[22]

For what it was worth, General Whitaker was back. His answer to the shortage of artillery ammunition was novel to say the least. "When I last saw General Whitaker that day, he was under the influence of something that made him reel considerably in the saddle," recalled Sergeant George Dolton of Battery M. "I do not think, when he left my guns, that he could have told where his command lay. He wanted some of my men to fix bayonets on their cannon, when they told him they were out of ammunition."[23]

Bushrod Johnson sent Lieutenant Marchbanks a second time to Deas and Manigault to ask them to cooperate in the assault. Both frankly admitted that they no longer trusted their men under fire. Johnson decided to attack with what he had: perhaps eight hundred men still in the ranks from the brigades of Fulton and Sugg, joined on the left by the Twenty-eighth and Thirty-fourth Alabama regiments of Manigualt's brigade. Fighting under Colonel John Reid, who had more faith in the men than did his brigade commander, these two regiments gave a good account of themselves.[24]

Most of the Confederates had at least a few rounds left, and in the end, it was those cartridges that made the difference. Here and there, small pockets of Yankees resisted with the bayonet and threw the enemy off the crest. Gradually, however, all were forced back.

At about 5:30 P.M., the One Hundred Fifteenth Illinois fell off the ridge again, this time for good. The left section of Battery M covered its retreat with a volley of canister that checked Fulton's Tennesseans. In a few minutes they were back, supported by the Twenty-eighth Alabama. This time the Tennesseans drove both the guns and the Seventy-eighth Illinois from the ridge.[25]

Further west on the ridge, the One Hundred Twenty-first Ohio and Ninety-sixth Illinois were holding on in support of the right section of Battery M. At 6:00 P.M., as the sun set, a staff officer galloped along the line telling the officers to fall back to the next ridge, some three hundred yards in their rear, as soon as they heard the bugle sound retreat. In a few minutes, the call was sounded. The infantry left first. The cannoneers fired a final, defiant load of double-shotted canister to hold the enemy in check, laid their wounded across the limber chests, hitched up their guns, and left the ridge.

It was a painful moment. "When the order was given to withdraw . . . the wounded began to call pitifully and ask if they were to be left. It was very trying to hear their pleading and go away leaving them behind," said an Ohioan. "To carry them back seemed like attempting the impossible and there seemed to be no other way to get them back. Some of the boys of our company found the running gear of a light wagon on which they put wounded comrades and themselves drew it all the way to Rossville Gap. And some of the boys even carried their comrades all the way back to that place."[26]

Steedman's Federals retired in disorder to the northwest, through a wide ravine and onto the next ridge. There they threw together a breastwork of logs and boulders and waited. Johnson's Confederates felt their way up the ridge for which they had fought nearly four hours. "I could have walked two hundred yards and not stepped over eighteen inches without walking on dead Yankees," said a member of Coleman's brigade. Johnson advanced his line as far as the ravine, where he halted to give Kelly's brigade on his right a chance to catch up.[27]

Steedman claimed to have withdrawn from the ridge in compliance with orders. Even before Gracie seized Hill One, Thomas had concluded that the Horseshoe Ridge line could not be held until dark and had decided to carry out the general withdrawal from the battlefield as ordered by Rosecrans, to begin with the divisions holding the Kelly field salient. Colonel Moses Walker delivered the withdrawal order for the units on Horseshoe Ridge to Brannan and Granger. The latter in turn passed along the command to Steedman. All this implies an orderly movement off the ridge, which was not the case. Steedman retreated at about 6:00 P.M., ammunition exhausted and under heavy pressure from Johnson. With or without orders from Thomas, he could no longer have held his position.[28] So hastily was the ridge abandoned that no one bothered to tell Colonel Le Favour up on Hill Three what was going on. Whitaker was too drunk and Steedman apparently too preoccupied to have given any thought to their two adopted regiments.

Le Favour sensed trouble. When at sundown the firing on his right suddenly ceased, he rode to the western crest of the hill to have a look at the low ridge. It was empty; not a single unhurt soldier from Whitaker's brigade remained.

Le Favour was not about to be left behind. He quickly faced the Eighty-ninth Ohio and Twenty-second Michigan about and led them off Hill Three. They had gone scarcely a hundred yards when Le Favour was halted by Major Smith of the division staff, who demanded to know where he was going. "To the rear as the other troops have fallen back and we are out of ammunition," replied Le Favour. "Ammunition and reinforcements will be sent at once and the orders are that that position must be held at all hazards, with the cold steel if necessary," snapped Smith, parroting an earlier command to that effect given by Granger. Le Favour countermarched his tired troops. He placed the Eighty-ninth Ohio along the western slope to cover his now unprotected flank, and the Twenty-second Michigan retook its original position. In the deepening darkness, the men lay down with empty cartridge boxes, praying they had seen the last of the Confederates.[29]

Nearly an hour had elapsed since Kelly's attack ground to a halt along the slopes of Hills Two and Three. Since then, the two sides had kept up a desultory fire through the haze. A little after 6:00 P.M., Kelly decided to renew the assault. He pulled the Fifty-eighth North Carolina out of line and transferred it from the right of the brigade to the left. In its place, he deployed the Seventh Mississippi, on loan from Anderson. Kelly intended to take the Federals in the flank. With Steedman gone, Kelly ordered Colonel Palmer to form line of battle across the low ridge and then come at Hill Three from the west—in other words, directly at Le Favour's helpless little detachment.[30]

On the reverse slope of the saddle between Hills Two and Three, the men of the Twenty-first Ohio were enjoying their first rest since noon. Lieutenant Vance took stock of his company's supply of ammunition. The men felt around in their cartridge boxes and searched their pockets; only three or four turned up even a single cartridge. Sergeant Bolton and his detail returned from the Snodgrass house with a few pocketfuls, just enough to supply each man in the regiment with one bullet.[31]

Captain Cusac stood in front of the regiment, beside an old graveyard. Nearby, beneath a huge oak tree, Colonel Van Derveer and Lieutenant Colonel Boynton talked in low tones. Comparing notes, they found that their men had burnt off most of their ammunition in repelling Kelly. In the Second Minnesota, Lieutenant Colonel Bishop guessed he had one hundred rounds left among his 250 soldiers. Boynton claimed his Thirty-fifth Ohio was so low that he borrowed a few rounds from Bishop. Neither Van Derveer nor Boynton relished the prospect of remaining on the field with empty cartridge boxes; nor did they feel comfortable with the situation beyond their right flank, where the firing had suddenly ceased. Without bothering to confirm their misgivings with a simple reconnaissance, they decided that Le Favour had abandoned Hill Three, which the trees and twilight made invisible.[32]

Van Derveer rode over to Cusac, whom in the uncertain light he mistook for McMahan. "Move those men up on the line," he told Cusac.

"Colonel, we have no more ammunition."

"It does not make a God damned bit of difference," remonstrated Van Derveer. "Have the men fix bayonets and hold that line."

Their conversation grew loud, catching the ear of Lieutenant J. S. Mahoney of Company K. When he caught the gist of it, he walked over to give Van Derveer his opinion of the order.

"It will be the same as murder to take the men in," Mahoney insisted.

Van Derveer turned in his saddle to face the brazen lieutenant. "It must be done, sir," he snapped.

Cusac had had enough. "The language and the manner that the command was given in, stirred up my Irish blood, and I said to him, go and talk with the officer in command."

By the time he found McMahan, who was standing behind the regiment, Van Derveer had cooled down a bit. His orders, however, were unchanged. The major was to move "to the extreme right of our position and meet the enemy should he attempt to turn our flank." McMahan hesitated. "I was entirely willing to take orders from him under the circumstances," he recalled, "but I was unwilling to order the charge, though I did not permit that fact to be known to the men. It is due to Colonel Van Derveer for me to say that his manner was not imperious, but kind and encouraging. He promised, however, to support the charge with other troops, but failed to do so. . . . At that moment we moved in opposite directions and I have never seen him since." It was about 6:30 P.M.

Lieutenant Mahoney viewed the movement with misgiving. "By our advance, it would be easier to withdraw the remainder of the line, which was being done. Viewed in this light, it looks to me as if we were sacrificed to help some others off the field."[33]

The regiment split as it moved off. Captain Cusac, in command of the left wing, misunderstood the intent of Van Derveer's order and took Companies B and G back to their original position at the top of the draw. With the rest of the Twenty-first, McMahan advanced west up Hill Three. He had only a vague idea where he was going and even less what he would do when he got there. Pausing at the hilltop, he asked Colonel Carlton for suggestions. Carlton merely shrugged.

A crackle of snapping twigs from the low ridge told McMahan where he was needed. Through the smoke-choked darkness he led his men at the double-quick, down the west slope of Hill Three and straight toward the advancing line of the Fifty-eighth North Carolina. The Ohioans squeezed off their last cartridges and fell back up the slope to the right of the Eighty-ninth. Caught by surprise, the North Carolinians broke ranks and took cover behind trees. Those with ammunition engaged the Ohioans until Palmer told them to stop while he tried to figure out what was happening.[34]

An eerie stillness settled over the forest. The "shades of the evening were gathering, and in the ravines a fleecy fog was just beginning to rise," remembered Lieutenant Vance. "The roar of the day's long combat had about ceased, and a palpitating silence, surcharged with dreadful chances, hung over all the field. . . . The men lay down, almost without a word, and let the chill influence of the awful quiet about them work upon them." A slightly wounded member of Vance's company broke the silence with an odd avowal: "I love the old flag! I am willing to die for the old flag!"

"Dry up, old man; we don't need any of that! This ain't no Fourth of July, by a damned sight!" someone snapped. The old soldier sat down with a sigh to bandage his bleeding leg.[35]

CHAPTER THIRTY

THE STORM BROKE LOOSE

B RAGG had been less than candid with Longstreet during their brief mid-afternoon conversation. Apparently, he neglected to tell Longstreet why he could have no troops from the Right Wing and why he believed Polk's men had no fight left in them. Nearly ninety minutes before meeting with Longstreet, Bragg had sent orders to Polk to renew the assault against the Federal breastworks immediately. Nothing happened. Bragg sent another courier, and another, yet not a shot was heard. His patience with the bishop had thus hit a new low by the time Longstreet made his plea for reinforcements.[1]

Tempers were equally short among the generals of the Right Wing. Polk was discovering firsthand how hard it was to cajole contentious subordinates into any sort of coordinated action. At the same time that Bragg was dictating his orders for Polk to renew the assault, a messenger from Hill brought the bishop word of the march of Granger down the La Fayette road. Hill feared an attack on his right flank and requested that Polk send him reinforcements. While awaiting an answer, Hill fell into a heated argument with Walker, who asked that he be allowed to withdraw his command some two hundred yards until Granger's intentions became clearer. Hill refused, pointing that any retrograde move, no matter how slight, would simply invite a Federal attack. Walker persisted, as was his wont. Hill just as self-righteously held his ground, and by mid-afternoon the two men were no longer on speaking terms.[2]

At 2:00 P.M., Polk ordered Cheatham to the extreme right of the army to reinforce Hill. Cheatham marched his division by the right flank north as far as the Reed's Bridge road. There he faced his command to the front. Vaughan, on the right, touched the road. To his left was Strahl, followed in line by Wright and Maney. Two hundred yards in front of Cheatham's line were the brigades of Stovall and Gibson. Colonel Lewis had taken

Helm's battered brigade several hundred yards to the rear to rest after the morning attack. Gist's division was directly forward of Breckinridge. To Gist's right and front, opposite the McDonald farm, was Liddell's division.[3]

When the threat from Granger failed to materialize, Polk sat down on a log with Hill to go over the plan of attack. He intended that Hill should attack the Federal left along the La Fayette road with Walker's corps and Cheatham's division. Cleburne would demonstrate against the center of the Union line to prevent the enemy from reinforcing its left. Breckinridge, who was present, asked to be permitted to lead the attack. Polk agreed. Walker would now advance due west across the road while Breckinridge swung south against the breastworks.[4]

Hill objected to the plan. What his objections were is unclear, but Captain Carnes, who waited at a respectful distance for Polk to conclude, saw the bishop stand up abruptly and say to Hill angrily: "Well, sir, I am sorry that you do not agree with me, but my decision is made and that is the way it shall be done." Polk strode to his horse, mounted, and rode away with Carnes.[5]

Hill sulked and found reasons to drag his feet. Before the last attack that morning, Hill had sent to Bragg for a brigade to close a gap of about five hundred yards between Cleburne and Gist. Bragg had promised to dispatch Jackson at once. Jackson lost his way, and at 3:00 P.M. had yet to report. Hill refused to budge until Jackson showed up. Polk repeated his order that the advance begin immediately. When it became clear that Hill had no intention of moving, Polk sent couriers in search of Jackson to tell him to move into line on the right of Cleburne. Jackson got the message but declined to act on it, since Bragg's original instructions had been that he should report to Hill. More time was lost while Jackson searched out Hill. It was 3:30 P.M. before he found him and another thirty minutes before his brigade was in position.[6]

Jackson's brigade was too small to close the interval with Cleburne. Rather than give Hill yet another excuse for delay, Polk circumvented him and sent Captain Carnes directly to Cleburne to order him to close up on Jackson's left. Cleburne liked to see the ground he was expected to occupy before moving his men, so he and Carnes rode through the forest on an inspection of the lines. The minutes slipped away. Carnes grew impatient. "On our return, as [Cleburne] was riding along in his usual slow, imperturbable fashion across the angle between our lines, I noticed that he was getting uncomfortably near the enemy's position, and as I, feeling constrained to follow, rode in his rear, I ventured to suggest that he was within short range of their guns," wrote Carnes. Cleburne neither replied nor changed his course. "Suddenly he was startled by the 'zip' 'zip' of the minie balls and the sharp rattle of infantry fire opened on us, when he turned to the left and dashed quickly out of range in the timber," continued Carnes, "but all too slowly for my impatient desire to lengthen the distance between the enemy and the party whom official courtesy forced to be the rear man in this retreat."[7]

It took a peremptory order from Polk, delivered by Captain Carnes at about 4:45 P.M., to finally get Hill started. Liddell set his division in motion first. Walthall, advancing on the right, ran into Dan McCook's skirmishers near the McDonald house. The Yankees fell back northwest through the cornfield and into a pasture. There, on an open rise six hundred yards from the farm, McCook had deployed his brigade in double line of battle. The six guns of Battery I, Second Illinois Light Artillery, were arrayed on the weed-laced forward slope.

The tall grass in front of the battery had caught fire earlier in the afternoon. A detail from the Fifty-second Ohio had put out the flames, but the burnt grass still smoldered. A bitter cloud hung over the battery, masking it from the view of Walthall's skirmishers, who were sprinting across the field after McCook's skirmishers. Govan's skirmishers, meanwhile, moved unopposed into the forest east of the Mullis farm. As soon as McCook's skirmishers cleared the guns, Captain Charles Barnett ordered the battery to blanket the pasture with canister.

The noise and commotion was too much for "Buffalo Tom" Finnell, an excitable Irish immigrant who served as number two on one of the guns; in other words, it was his duty to take the ammunition from number five and put it into the muzzle of the cannon for number one to ram home. Somehow, Finnell failed to notice the gun being fired while he was getting another load of canister. The number one cannoneer yelled at him to shove the canister into the muzzle. Finnell refused. "There's a load in her already," he cried. The sergeant ordered him to put the canister in. Finnell laid it in gingerly, then ran off to one side and threw himself flat in the weeds. "Krist gud, boy, touch her off aizy," he screamed at the gunner holding the lanyard. "Touch her off aizy, or she'll boorst! There's two loads in her! Krist gud, touch her aizy!" The episode became a favorite story at battery reunions.[8]

Walthall's skirmishers sprinted back to the main line of their brigade, which had crossed the La Fayette road and was now two hundred yards into the cornfield. There Liddell halted Walthall while he rode back in search of his own artillery to silence Barnett's guns. Walthall had his men take cover between the rows of corn. On Walthall's left, Govan had fallen behind a bit and was not yet across the road.[9]

Liddell's presence west of the La Fayette road added another danger to an already risky undertaking. Few movements were more perilous than the withdrawal of an army while still in contact with the enemy. For Thomas,

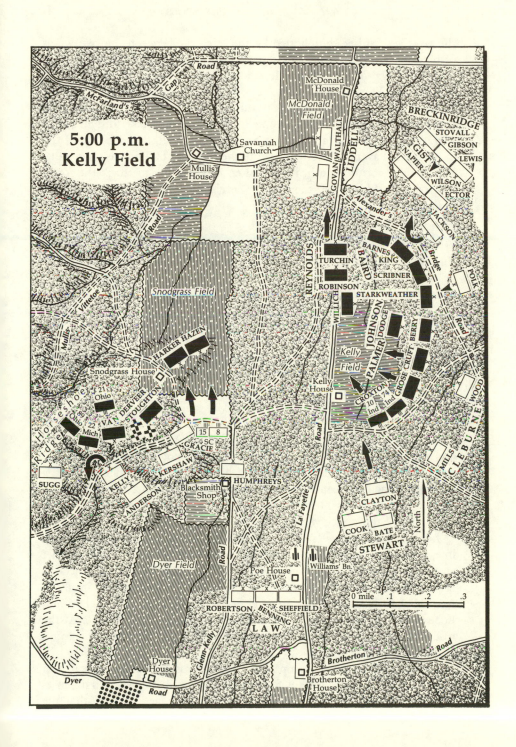

the task was further complicated by the large gap between the two wings of his command. This would effectively prevent one wing from covering the withdrawal of the other, at least at the critical moment when contact was broken. Thus each would have to withdraw independently.

There were two grave threats posed by Liddell. Should he continue to move west unopposed, Liddell's route of advance would take him along the McFarland's Gap road (also known as the Ridge road), thus closing off the only practical avenue of retreat open to the divisions of Thomas's left wing. Were Liddell to turn south, he would be in a position to attack the forces on Horseshoe Ridge from the rear. It was clearly imperative that Liddell be removed.

Reynolds, for one, was relieved at the prospect of quitting the field. Ever since the breakthrough, he had been convinced that the eventual capture of his division was a foregone conclusion, a fear he freely shared with his subordinates. Turchin was of a like mind. He worried away the afternoon beneath a tall oak tree behind the firing line. At one point, he called Lieutenant Colonel Douglas Putnam of the Ninety-second Ohio over to ask him the time. It was a little after 2:00 P.M., Putnam told him. Turchin rued the slow passage of the day; he wished only for nightfall, so that they could get out of there. Putnam asked Turchin what he intended to do in the interim. "Do!" cried the Russian. "This brigade stays right here until we are all cut to pieces, that's what we'll do!"[10]

Colonel Edward King no longer had an opinion on the matter. Thirty minutes earlier, a sharpshooter's bullet had cut him down. "I well remember our men begging Colonel King to dismount and not expose himself needlessly, as several shots had been fired at him while sitting on his horse," a member of the Nineteenth Indiana Battery lamented. King finally relented. He slid down off his horse—right into the path of an oncoming bullet. Struck above the right eye, King died instantly.[11]

Turchin left the breastworks first. Before moving out, he ran down the line, personally telling every company commander to keep his men quiet and to have them discard anything that might rattle. Turchin marched his brigade by the right flank in double line to the La Fayette road, ready to face about to repel an attack from either north or south. Colonel Milton Robinson of the Seventy-fifth Indiana followed with King's brigade. At the road, the column turned north. Reynolds rode at the head of the column to meet Thomas.[12]

A chance encounter with a pair of stragglers roaming about in search of water changed Thomas's plans for Reynolds. They hailed the Virginian as he rode through the forest west of the road and warned him that the

Confederates were in the timber to his left. They looked to be a strong force and had a battery with them, the soldiers told Thomas.[13]

Thomas galloped on until he struck the La Fayette road in rear of Baird's left. There he spotted the head of Reynolds's column marching toward him. Thomas rode closer. He shouted to Reynolds to form line of battle perpendicular to the road at once. Pointing over his shoulder in the direction of the McDonald farm, Thomas yelled: "They are there; clear them out."

To Turchin fell the task of sweeping Liddell from the Union rear. He was exactly the man to lead what the historian Glenn Tucker aptly termed the "last dying gasp of Federal offensive power" at Chickamauga.[14] With his right anchored on the road, the "Mad Cossack" led the brigade at the double-quick north through the forest. He halted at the edge of the old weed-infested field south of the McDonald farm to give his regimental commanders a moment to dress ranks. The brigade was still in double line, with the Eleventh and Ninety-second Ohio now in front. The Twenty-first Indiana Battery followed to provide covering fire. Fate had dealt Turchin a wonderful hand. Just one hundred yards away, coming into line in the tall grass, was the exposed left flank of Govan's brigade. Taking his hat off and waving it by the crown, Turchin bellowed: "My brigade, charge bayonet, give 'em Hell, God Damn 'em!" The order passed rapidly along the line. The Federals let go a volley from the woods, then burst in the open with a yell.[15]

Govan had only the briefest warning of the Yankee onslaught. Just as his men stepped onto the La Fayette road, along the precise route they had taken during their bloody morning attack, Govan was saluted by Captain J. W. Stringfellow, who had run back from the brigade skirmish line. Stringfellow breathlessly told Govan that a large body of enemy infantry supported by artillery was about to come out of the woods on his left flank. Govan hurried the brigade across the road with orders for the men to lie down in the overgrown field, but Turchin struck before the Confederates could complete the movement.[16]

On the brigade left, the Sixth and Seventh Arkansas Consolidated fired just one ragged volley before it broke and ran back across the road. The Arkansans kept on running for four hundred yards. A lucky cannon shot struck and killed Turchin's horse early in the charge, sending the general sprawling with nothing more serious than a scratched leg. The portly Russian got up and ran after his front line. Lieutenant Benjamin Stearns of the Thirty-sixth Ohio caught up with Turchin as he puffed along on foot. Rather impudently, the young lieutenant complimented Turchin on his endurance. "When in action one may lose all thought of himself, but this is a personal matter to me," huffed Turchin.[17]

Lieutenant Colonel John Murray, commanding the Fifth and Thirteenth

Arkansas Consolidated on the brigade right, was startled as he rode along the line of his regiment to see only the Eighth Arkansas remaining on his left. Murray galloped to Major Anderson Watkins, who had assumed command of the Eighth the previous afternoon, and asked him to change front to the left to meet the attack, saying he would do the same. Watkins, shaky in his new role, refused to move unless Murray ordered him to do so. This Murray was reluctant to do. By the time he tracked down and presented the dispute to a member of Liddell's staff, both regiments had been swept off the field.[18]

The sudden collapse of Govan's brigade left Walthall little time to change front to meet Turchin's attack. What time the Mississippian did have he squandered in trying to silence Battery I, Second Illinois Artillery, the Twenty-first Indiana Battery, and a friendly battery belonging to Forrest's command that had mistaken Walthall's Mississippians for Yankees. The three batteries were enfilading his line, but the more immediate threat came from Turchin's infantry. While Walthall busied himself directing the counterbattery fire of Fowler's battery, his brigade was struck and driven off the field just as precipitately as had been Govan's. Colonel James Scales of the Thirtieth Mississippi was cut off and captured along with most of the brigade's skirmishers. Fowler was forced to abandon two guns and got off with the remainder only because the men of the Ninety-second Ohio were too winded to pursue.[19]

On the verge of exhaustion himself, Turchin took it upon himself to call a halt. Running out into the field of corn stubble on the left of his brigade, Turchin motioned to his men to follow him to the open rise where Dan McCook's line of battle lay. Some of the officers got the idea, and bit by bit the brigade veered to the left. Turchin stumbled up the gentle slope gasping for air. Another lieutenant from the Thirty-sixth Ohio helped him as far as Barnett's battery, where Turchin stopped to catch his breath beside a gun. Resting in the grass behind the knoll, Turchin's men laughed and congratulated one another on their easy success. Losses had been minimal. The Ninety-second Ohio, which did the bulk of the fighting, suffered only fifteen wounded and fifteen captured in the charge. In the Thirty-sixth, however, the joviality was cut short when a hasty count revealed that both the regimental colors and the entire color company were missing.[20]

Captain E. P. Henry, the company commander, had missed the cue to turn toward the knoll and instead continued north nearly half a mile, off the McDonald farm and through the forest all the way to the Cloud church, where the sight of Forrest's cavalry in the fields east of the La Fayette road caused him to halt. Henry and his company were not alone. Colonel Philander Lane had pressed on as well with fifty men from the right companies of the Eleventh Ohio and a few soldiers from the Ninety-second.

With Lane was General Reynolds, who had been riding behind the Eleventh. Reynolds knew nothing of Turchin's decision to stop the charge. "I understood that this movement was intended to open the way to Rossville for the army, and did not then know of any other road to that point," Reynolds later explained. "I therefore pressed right on in the charge, expecting the whole division to do the same until the rebel lines and batteries were cleared and the road opened, and found myself with only about fifty men under Colonel Lane."[21]

Reynolds had no idea where he was. As he conferred with Lane about what they should do, Reynolds spotted two men in what looked like Union blue riding toward them. He went out alone to meet them while Lane, Henry, and their men looked on anxiously.

The two soldiers on horseback belonged to McCook's brigade and had been sent out to look for water. Reynolds called out for Lane and Henry to join them, and the little band found its way safely into McCook's lines.[22]

Thomas had taken charge of the division during Reynolds's absence. His first act was to deploy Robinson's brigade, which had come up too late to take part in the charge, astride the McFarland's Gap road at a point a half mile west of the La Fayette road. There the road cut through the first of several gorges on its way to McFarland's Gap. Control of the gorge was crucial to the success of the withdrawal.

Thomas placed Robinson atop the commanding hills, both over nine hundred feet high, that stood on either side of the road, with orders to "hold the ground while the troops on our right and left passed by." Turchin reassembled his brigade between those of Robinson and McCook, giving Thomas three brigades with which to guard the McFarland's Gap road. When Reynolds reported in a few minutes later, Thomas turned over the responsibility of "covering the retirement of the troops" to him.[23]

It was to prove a greater charge than either Thomas or Reynolds probably anticipated. What Thomas had hoped would be an orderly withdrawal from the Kelly field salient came very close to being a disastrous rout. As it was, the movement was disjointed. Thomas was not there to supervise it, nor did Baird, Johnson, Palmer, and Reynolds try to coordinate their departures with one another. Each acted as he thought best to preserve his own command.

Palmer, for one, was startled to see Reynolds march his troops away at about 4:45 P.M. Leaving his division, Palmer rode back into the Kelly field to intercept Reynolds and find out why he had pulled out. Near the Kelly house Palmer met Captain Kellogg, who happened to bear his copy of the withdrawal order. Palmer sent aides to Grose and Cruft with the order and then rode out onto the road to await them.[24]

The Confederates were determined to make the movement a costly one.

From the Poe house, Williams's artillery battalion opened a terrific barrage on the Kelly field. Major Felix Robertson contributed two batteries from the army's reserve artillery, raising to twenty the number of guns that were pounding the field over which the Federals would have to pass on their way rearward. Simultaneously, the batteries of Douglas, Calvert, Semple, and Scogin opened fire from the east to soften up the Yankee breastworks prior to the attack of Breckinridge, Jackson, and Cleburne.

Lieutenant Colonel Moxley Sorrel, Longstreet's efficient chief of staff, hoped to inflict a decisive defeat on the moving columns of the enemy. Catching sight of Reynolds's division as it crossed the La Fayette road, Sorrel galloped to General Stewart and ordered him to attack the Federals in the flank. Stewart politely refused. "His answer was that he was there by orders and could not move until he got others," recalled a dumbfounded Sorrel. "I explained that I was chief of staff to Longstreet and felt myself competent to give such an order as coming from my chief and that this was customary in our Virginia service." But this was not Virginia and Bragg was not Lee. Stewart understood well the risk one ran in taking the initiative or acting on anything less than unambiguous, written orders in Bragg's army. He was sorry, Stewart told Sorrel, but he must insist that the order come directly from Longstreet. To his credit, Sorrel took the rebuke in stride. "Valuable time was being lost, but I determined to have a whack at those quick-moving blue masses," he wrote. "Asking General Stewart to get ready, that I hoped to find Longstreet, I was off, and luckily did find him after an eager chase. Longstreet's thunderous tones need not to be described when, in the first words of explanation, he sent me back with orders to Stewart to fall on the column with all his power."[25]

The Tennessean waved Clayton's and Bate's brigades forward at the double-quick just as Colonel Grose prepared to abandon his breastworks. "Which way or where to retire was not an easy question to solve, the enemy fast approaching from the right and left toward our rear, their artillery fire meeting," reported Grose. Scanning the field, he decided to withdraw his command in the direction of the Kelly house. To steady the men, Grose and an aide rode with the brigade flag on the left flank of the lead regiment, the direction from which the heaviest artillery fire came.

The colonel's heroics accomplished nothing. Before Grose's column was halfway across the field, Stewart's skirmishers had climbed over the breastworks vacated by Reynolds and opened fire on the flank. Exploding shells tore through the Federal ranks. In the words of its commander, Colonel David Higgins, the Twenty-fourth Ohio, on the brigade left, was "crushed, and with other regiments of the brigade was forced to give way, torn and bleeding at every part." The survivors streamed across the road past Palmer and into the forest. They kept on running across the Snodgrass cornfield and into the foothills of Missionary Ridge.[26]

Screened by Grose, who fell back on his left, Cruft succeeded in keeping most of his brigade together across the field. Colonel Thomas Sedgewick of the Second Kentucky reported proudly that his regiment led the march through the stubble at common time with parade-ground precision. A leisurely pace might do for the head of the column, but in the rear, where the Ninetieth Ohio marched, every minute was critical. Confederates were pouring over the breastworks in force and rushing toward the Ohioans. Unable to respond, the regiment broke and the men scattered across the field. For Private Harry Sark of Company C, it was a moment of deep personal tragedy. He started toward the road with John Cahill, a close friend who had saved his life at Stones River. But Cahill tripped and fell, and before Sark could turn back to help him, two Alabamians had grabbed Cahill. Sark shot one of them, but the other yanked Cahill away. Sark was crestfallen. He had failed to save the man to whom he owed his life. After the war, Sark learned that Cahill had died at Andersonville.[27]

Palmer had moved into the woods west of the road to escape the shelling. There he watched Cruft's brigade come toward him. The fire from Williams's artillery was beginning to tell. Shells burst closer to the column. Suddenly a Rebel battery bounced over the breastworks to his right and unlimbered. It was the Eufaula Artillery, an Alabama battery. The Confederate gunners took aim at Cruft's moving limbers. "As Standart's battery passed, a Rebel shot struck between the wheels of one of his gun carriages," observed Palmer. "The axle was crushed by the shot, and the gun seemed to leap in the air and then fell to the ground, and as the Rebel fire seemed aimed at Cruft's flank, I expected that soon shot would enfilade his line with terrible slaughter," he continued. "While completely absorbed in the scene before me, and in an agony of apprehension, in view of what I supposed to be the danger to Cruft's men from the Rebel battery, my horse sank to the ground, and I fell at the foot of the tree. . . . I was at once conscious that my hat had fallen off, and that my hair, mouth, eyes, and collar were filled with some soft substance, but what it was I could not for a moment, blinded as I was, even guess." Palmer stood up and wiped his eyes. Then he saw that a rebel shot had struck a dead pine, throwing a piece onto his horse and spraying him with rotten wood. Palmer waited for Cruft to enter the timber with his men, then turned and rode toward the slope of Missionary Ridge to help rally the division.[28]

Johnson was handed the order to withdraw at 5:00 P.M., fifteen minutes after Palmer. He chose not to comply. His front line was heavily engaged with Wood's Confederates, who had opened a harassing fire on Johnson's line to support the attack of Lucius Polk and Jackson on their right. Johnson sent a staff officer to Thomas to say that he supposed that the order was based on the erroneous assumption that all was quiet on his front; he felt certain he could hold his own but feared the consequences of a withdrawal under fire. Before the staff officer returned, Palmer began his movement, Clayton's Alabamians poured into the Kelly field from the south, and Johnson suddenly found himself outflanked.

From his position in reserve on the west side of the field, near the La Fayette road, General Willich watched the brigades of Dodge and Berry unravel under the flanking fire of musketry and the unceasing barrage of artillery. "Then the storm broke loose; first in small squads, then in an unbroken stream, the defenders rushed without organization over the open field, partly over and through my brigade, which was formed in two lines," he reported. Goodspeed's battery went into action against the Eufaula Artillery, and Willich shifted his right regiments to prevent Clayton from pushing farther into the field. As soon as the last of Johnson's men reached the cover of the woods, Willich fell back under orders from Thomas to join Reynolds's covering force on the McFarland's Gap road.[29]

That left Baird's division, which had been reinforced late in the morning by two regiments of Barnes's brigade and during the afternoon by the remainder. It was upon Baird that the full fury of the Confederate attack fell. Jackson came up against King's Regulars from the north. His advance through the forest was tentative. With each step, the gap between his left and Lucius Polk's right grew, so that by the time he came in sight of the Yankee breastworks, Jackson's flank was exposed to a withering fire. He halted his command about 150 yards from the Regulars, who for a change were holding on, and wheeled up Scogin's battery to pound their line.[30]

Lucius Polk was faring no better against Scribner and Starkweather. On the brigade right, the Thirty-fifth Tennessee broke the moment it came under fire from the Yankee works. Colonel Benjamin Hill called on Lieutenant Thomas Key to send up a section of his (Calvert's) battery to silence the Fourth Indiana Battery, which was tearing apart his Tennesseans, then rode back to restore some order in the command. "During the progress of this artillery duel, my negro boy having failed to bring up my sword, I took a pole or club and with this drove up officers and men of my own command who were shielding themselves behind trees," he reported.[31]

While Colonel Hill beat some pride back into his men, Polk asked Key to bring forward his remaining section to the ridge opposite the breastworks. Key initially refused both Hill's and Polk's requests, saying that his horses could not possibly survive the Federal fire. Polk countered by ordering the guns dragged up by hand and sent some volunteers from the brigade back to get them. Through the underbrush and up the crest the infantrymen hauled the cannons. There, at a range of under two hundred yards, they opened with double-shotted canister on Starkweather's Federals and the Fourth Indiana Battery.

Captain Carnes watched the artillery duel with interest. Although the close range made grape and canister the preferred ammunition, Carnes noticed that the Federals were responding with solid shot, and then only intermittently. He also observed that their infantry fired only when forced to by an advance of Polk's infantry off the ridge. Carnes hurried to Bishop Polk with his conclusion—the Yankees were exceedingly low on all types of ammunition.

Polk agreed to test Carnes's theory with his nephew's brigade. He sent orders to Breckinridge and Cheatham to engage the enemy with fire but not to press their attack until Lucius Polk had a chance to develop the strength of the enemy defenses. The bishop sent Carnes back to his nephew with orders for him to charge at once. "Riding by the side of General Lucius Polk, I witnessed the splendid charge of the veterans of his brigade up the ridge. . . . I never witnessed a more enthusiastic and intrepid charge," said Carnes.[32]

It was at this most inopportune moment that Baird received the withdrawal order. He chose to obey it promptly, mainly because Johnson had already begun to fall back on his right. Lieutenant Johnston of the Seventy-ninth Pennsylvania overheard Starkweather bellow out the command to withdraw. He was incredulous. "We had whipped the enemy in the morning, and we felt that we were whipping him now," said Johnston. "I could scarcely credit my own eyes when I saw the regiment breaking and double-quicking to the rear. Cautioning my own men to keep together and keep with me (I had but thirteen of them all told) I started to the rear amid a still increasing tempest of lead and iron."[33]

Starkweather got his brigade off largely intact, but not so Scribner. Calvert's battery was raking his line unmercifully and Polk's infantry was forming for the charge. His own men were almost out of ammunition. "Everything assumed a discouraging aspect," rued the Indianian. Then he caught a glimpse of Palmer's division falling back into the field to the south. Still unaware of the withdrawal, Scribner assumed it to be reinforcements on the way to bolster his line, so that when a staff officer from King's brigade rode up with his copy of the withdrawal order, Scribner refused to obey, confident that help was on the way. But when he looked a second time at Palmer's column, Scribner realized that it was actually retreating in confusion. Then Starkweather moved out on his right. Still Scribner declined to yield, until a division staff officer brought the same order.

By then it was too late. Polk's Rebels jumped over the breastworks as Scribner pulled his men away, and the retreat became a rout. Yankees surrendered by the score. Colonel Oscar Moore was too far from Scribner to get the order to fall back. Lacking orders, he refused to withdraw his Thirty-third Ohio from the breastworks until completely surrounded. Moore himself made it across the Kelly field, but seventy-eight of his troops were cut off and captured. Other regiments fared even worse. The Tenth Wisconsin veered to the left as it retreated, right into the midst of Clayton's Alabamians. Its lieutenant colonel, major, and 143 of its officers and enlisted men fell captive. Another 124 belonging to the Second Ohio were taken prisoner by Polk, who intended to push on all the way to the La Fayette road. Turning to Carnes, he said: "Go back and tell the old general that we have passed two lines of breastworks, that we have got them on the jump, and I am sure of carrying the main line." Carnes rode at breakneck speed back to the bishop, whom he found waiting in a small glade with Breckinridge and Cheatham, near the Tennessean's line. Carnes presented his report. Polk turned to his generals. "Push your commands forward, gentlemen, and assault them vigorously along the whole line," he said. Cheatham passed the order on to his staff, then yelled out to his troops: "Forward, boys, and give 'em hell!" Bishop Polk, always careful to be chaste of speech, added with a smile: "Do as General Cheatham says, boys."[34]

Maney's Tennesseans charged over Jackson's prone troops toward the breastworks with a "terrific yell." Colonel Randall Gibson led Adams's brigade in on their right at the double-quick. Only Barnes's brigade and King's hapless Regulars were left to contest the Confederate advance. They fired a few ragged volleys before breaking under the combined pressure from Lucius Polk on their right and Maney and Gibson to their front. A few dozen more Regulars fell prisoner, bringing to more than five hundred the number captured during the battle. Polk's brigade claimed most of the prisoners, and Gibson's men had to content themselves with the scores of rifles that the Regulars had discarded in their flight across the Kelly field.[35]

In the forest west of the road everything was a maddening confusion. Said Baird: "As my men fell back the enemy pressed after them, and in crossing the open field very many were struck down. They reached the woods, in as good order as could be expected, but then, uncertain which direction to take, and having no landmark to guide them, many became separated from their regiments. . . . A number, doubtless, became confused at this time and marched into the lines of the rebels." Scribner was astounded. "In whatever direction we turned our gaze we beheld our men wandering about singly, or in groups, without purpose, without leaders, disorganized, but not demoralized or panic-stricken," he wrote. "Several times I approached officers of higher rank and offered them my command, as a nucleus to form upon for any undertaking they thought best to make. One officer advised me in a confidential, friendly way, to take my men off as best I could, and if I found that I could not take my battery with me, to cut loose the horses and try to save them, if possible. These words and the manner of the officer utterly amazed me. I had not imagined that we could be reduced to such straits."[36]

General Hill, who had followed the advance from behind Breckinridge's line, decided not to overextend himself. With darkness coming on, he told Gibson and Lewis to break off their pursuit at the La Fayette road and sent orders to Cleburne to stop Lucius Polk. Bishop Polk confirmed the order and sent scouts into the woods to verify the rout of the enemy. Stewart halted Clayton and Bate in the southern edge of the Kelly field. As the tired, thirsty, but exultant Confederates reformed their ranks along the road, a spontaneous cheer erupted that was picked up by every unit of the Right Wing. "The shouts of the army beat anything in that line we had ever heard or have since," said a soldier of the First Arkansas, who, like his comrades, was ready to keep going. "It was late. Rockets were going up all the time, and all knew we should have kept on, could have captured their army few now doubt." Recalled James Cooper of the Twentieth Tennessee:

> At sunset . . . everyone seemed wild with joy, from generals down to privates, all joined in the exultant cheer that rang over that blood-stained field, telling in tones as loud as "Heaven's artillery," that we were victorious. Wild shouts ran from one end of our lines to the other and even the poor wounded fellows lying about through the woods joined in.
>
> Provisions were brought up and as soon as our excitement had subsided we lay down to obtain that much needed rest, expecting ere the night was over, to start in pursuit of the retreating Yankees. We were too tired to heed the dead bodies lying all around us, so close we could almost touch them with our hands.[37]

Phil Sheridan had kept his part of the bargain purportedly struck by him, Negley, and Davis at the McFarland farm. A few minutes before sunset, the head of his fifteen-hundred-man column reached the Cloud church, having skirmished with Forrest's cavalry most of the way from Rossville. Sheridan made contact with Dan McCook's brigade and then sent to Thomas for orders. Granger saw in Sheridan's arrival a chance to make a stand until the next morning, by which time Rosecrans was certain to return. With Sheridan, McCook, Turchin, Robinson, and Willich, Thomas indeed had a strong line posted between the La Fayette and McFarland's Gap roads. Whether it was strong enough to resist a determined Confederate attack, even one coming just before nightfall, is doubtful. Thomas, at least, considered his troops too disorganized to withstand the enemy at that or any other point on the battlefield. He told Sheridan to march back up the La Fayette road and cover the Ringgold road from the vicinity of the McAfee church to prevent Confederate cavalry from slipping into Rossville from the east.

Colonel Moses Walker found Thomas behind Robinson's line. Brannan had sent him to inquire for orders. Thomas told Walker to have Brannan and Granger report to him to receive their final instructions for the withdrawal from Horseshoe Ridge. Turning to Colonel Robinson, Thomas asked if he had any regiments with enough ammunition left to cover the movement. By chance, the Sixty-eighth and One Hundred First Indiana regiments had come upon an overturned wagon along the side of the McFarland's Gap road in which were two full boxes of ammunition. It was barely enough to give each man a handful of cartridges, "yet the scramble by each for his share of it was greater than I ever saw it for rations," recalled the major of the One Hundred First. Thomas turned the two regiments over to Walker, who led them south through the Mullis cornfield toward the Snodgrass house.[38]

To Davis, who was coming down the Dry Valley road with his column, Garfield sent word that he should return to Rossville. There would be no need for his division. Thomas was withdrawing.[39]

A hush fell over Horseshoe Ridge at sunset. The acrid smoke of gunpowder blanketed the ground. It mingled with the rising smoke of burning brush and leaves, blinding the troops of both sides as completely as if it were the dark of night. Beyond six or eight paces, nothing could be distinguished with certainty — a soldier standing still at that distance might as easily be a tree.[40] It was on this ghostly stage that the final, pathetic drama of Chickamauga was about to be played out.

Colonel Trigg had come onto the field just as the firing from Bushrod Johnson's final assault on the low ridge west of Hill Three reached its peak. He had dropped the First Florida Dismounted Cavalry off near Hill One to support Gracie's battered brigade and so had with him just the Seventh Florida. Hurrying along the Vittetoe road toward the left of the line to find the Sixth Florida and Fifty-fourth Virginia, which had gone into action ahead of him, Trigg ran into General Preston, who sent him into action with the Seventh Florida on the left of Kelly. Trigg led the Floridians up and over the low ridge moments after Whitaker's Federals abandoned it. To Trigg's right, the Fifty-eighth North Carolina felt its way up the slope of Hill Three, where it ran into the Twenty-first Ohio a few minutes before sundown. In the ravine on the northern side of the ridge, Trigg found the remainder of his brigade, resting in line of battle on Johnson's right.[41]

There he also ran into Colonel Kelly, who briefed him on the situation. Kelly told Trigg that the Fifty-eighth North Carolina had just clashed briefly with what appeared to be the right flank of those Union forces still occupying

Horseshoe Ridge. Kelly was confident that, if they cooperated, the two of them could bag the Yankees. Trigg agreed. Kelly then sketched out his proposal. He suggested that Trigg wheel his brigade to the east, out of the ravine and up the northwestern slope of Hill Three. That should put it on the right flank and in the rear of the Federal defenses. Kelly would move his brigade up the southern slope of the hill simultaneously. Trigg concurred with the plan and set about putting his command in motion. Kelly rode away to rejoin his brigade. On the way, he met a courier from Preston, who again wished to confer in person with the young colonel — at once. Kelly rode off to find Preston. The movement with Trigg would have to wait.[42]

Trigg knew nothing of Kelly's detour or of the Alabamian's failure to brief his regimental commanders on the joint movement against Hill Three. Confident that Kelly would do his part, Trigg wheeled his brigade up the hill a few minutes before 7:00 P.M.[43]

"Then came the strangest, weirdest episode of the whole battle," remembered Lieutenant Vance of the Twenty-first Ohio, who with his men was lying down on the hill. "Filing in through the depths of the great ravine on our right and below us, came a long line of soldiers, carrying their muskets at a right shoulder shift, marching 'left in front,' and making no noise. The rising mist distorted them somewhat and blurred their outlines, but they seemed to be in dark uniforms, and came from the direction in which Steedman's brigades had gone. As they slowly moved along and finally came to a front, facing us, they showed up a full brigade in strength," continued Vance. "Our fellows regarded them with a curiosity that was almost listless, and calmly debated as to who they were, some maintaining that they were Confederates who . . . were about to assault us in flank, while others, from the direction from which they came, were as strongly impressed that they were Union troops. Wrapped in the fog, they looked like so many phantoms on a ghostly brigade drill, and it gave one a creepy sensation to look at them."[44]

The uncertainty was more than Captain Henry Alban of Company F could bear. He stepped over his men and jogged down the hill. As he neared the advancing line, Alban asked, "What troops are these?" An officer sprang forward, put a revolver to Alban's head, and told him to shut up. When Alban failed to return, Lieutenant Vance's first sergeant, Celestine Crochard, decided to go out and have a look. Standing up, Crochard said to his diminutive, teen-aged commander: "Boy, I think I will go and see who they are." Vance tried in vain to talk him out of it, and the sergeant walked down the hill into captivity. The line grew nearer. "The suspense was growing unendurable," said Vance. Finally, a member of the Twenty-first yelled out: "What troops are you?" "Jeff Davis's troops," came the reply through the smoke. An audible sigh of relief rose from the ranks of the

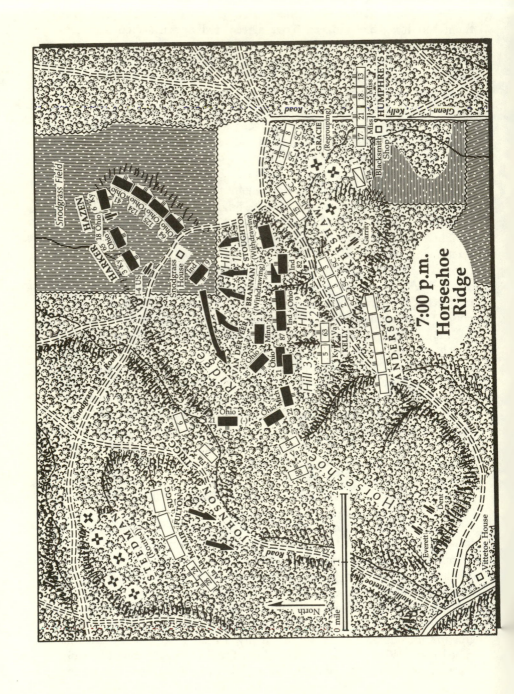

Snodgrass Field

HAZEN

HARKER

18 Ohio | 6 Ky | Ohio | 124 | 125 | 4 Ohio

65 Ohio

3 Ky

1 4 US

Snodgrass
House

3 Ind

Hill 1

Hill 2

VAN DERVEER

2 Minn

21 Ohio

9 Ohio

Ohio
21 (-)

39 Ohio

22 Ohio

54
Va

58
NC

STOUGHTON (Withdrawing)

BANNAN (Withdrawing)

2 Ind

82 Ind

87 Ind

Hill 3

Snodgrass Road

JOHNSON

SUGG

FULTON

McNair

STEEDMAN

Vittetoe Road

Vittetoe
House

Dent

Everett

Blacksmith
Shop

GRACIE

8 SC

15 SC

43 Ala

5 Va

SC 5

Va 3

KERSHAW

SC 2

SC 3

SC 7

2 Va

Garrity

ANDERSON

7 Miss | 41 Miss

KELLY

5 Ky

63 Va

Horseshoe Ridge

17 | 21 | 18 | 13

HUMPHREYS

Kelly Road

Glenn

(Regrouping)

Dry Valley Road

0 mile

North

7:00 p.m.
Horseshoe
Ridge

Twenty-first — Davis's division had come over to relieve them. A moment later, the line emerged from the twilight haze, and the Ohioans found themselves looking down the rifle barrels of the Seventh Florida. Sergeant L. E. Timmons stepped forward from the ranks of the Seventh and took the regimental colors of the Twenty-first from the color-bearer. The rest of the men laid down their empty rifles, and it was done. The six-hour stand of the Twenty-first Ohio — the most distinguished service rendered by any single regiment at Chickamauga — had ended in surrender. Years later, contemplating the perfidy that had sent his regiment to its fate, Major McMahan wrote: "If it was not for the gravity of the subject and the untold suffering and death that resulted from the most stupid as well as criminal negligence . . . I could smile through my misery."[45]

Colonel Carlton had ridden across the hill to see Le Favour and was told that he had ridden down the western slope to reconnoiter. After waiting a few minutes behind the Twenty-second Michigan, Carlton rode back over to his regiment. He found the men in the process of grounding their muskets. Private Henderson Hylton of the Fifty-fourth Virginia stepped forward to claim the regimental flag of the Eighty-ninth Ohio.[46]

Le Favour had left his regiment after some of the men in the right companies heard voices call out from the low ridge: "Don't fire! Don't hurt your friends!" Le Favour rode in the direction of the voices, and before he knew it, he was in the middle of the Fifty-fourth Virginia. Crouching behind his troops on the right flank of the Twenty-second was Lieutenant William Hamilton. "Soon a heavy line of troops swerved round from our right and front," he remembered. "It was now so dark we could not distinguish the color of the uniform. They marched towards us, guns at charge and when within two or three rods of us began to call on us to surrender." There was no resistance. "Every man perceived that we were surrounded and overwhelmingly outnumbered and leaving their guns on the ground, they sprang to their feet and became prisoners." To Private Oscar Honaker of the Fifty-fourth went the prized regimental colors. In five, perhaps ten minutes, and a cost of fewer than ten men wounded, Trigg had captured three Yankee regiments.[47]

Over on Hill Two, the soldiers of the Thirty-fifth Ohio waited anxiously, bayonets fixed, as the other regiments of Van Derveer's brigade began to move off the hill into the Snodgrass field, where General Brannan intended to assemble his command behind Harker's brigade in anticipation of the final withdrawal order from Thomas. While they awaited their turn to leave, some of Boynton's men on the right flank of the regiment heard the tramp of marching troops from the direction of Hill Three. They crept out from the ranks to the top of the draw. Peering through the thicket, the Ohioans could make out nothing on the adjoining hilltop, but down in the draw and on the eastern face, they saw the blurred forms of troops lying in line of battle. Boynton joined them. He saw the same thing (the Fifth Kentucky and Sixty-third Virginia regiments of Kelly's brigade) and knew it meant trouble. Without waiting for orders, Boynton changed the regimental front to face southwest into the draw. The Thirty-fifth scarcely had settled into its new position when a column of troops was discovered in the ravine below the northwest slope of the hill (the Sixth Florida of Trigg's brigade). Boynton bent back his right to cover the ravine, then rode off in search of Van Derveer or Brannan to warn them of the developing threat.[48]

Lieutenant Colonel Boynton found Brannan and Van Derveer near the Snodgrass cornfield. Brannan ordered the Ohioan to hold his regiment in place as flank guard and promised to send the Ninth Indiana, which Hazen had agreed to give him for the express purpose of reinforcing his right, to help Boynton cover the hill. "He [Brannan] directed its colonel to report to me, and ordered me to post it as my knowledge of the position might suggest," explained Boynton. "He called me aside to say that the regiment was commanded by a colonel, but that he would not know my rank, and he wanted me to post it at the threatened point as I was acquainted with the whole situation."[49]

Their little deception did not quite work. Meeting the Ninth Indiana as it marched up the northeastern slope of Hill Two from the cornfield, Boynton imperiously ordered its commander, Colonel Isaac Suman, to follow him with the regiment across the hilltop. Turning to his major and staff, Suman asked: "What do you think Hazen will say if we follow the order of that colonel?" "Old Hazen would be hotter than hell," answered the adjutant. "He is trying to work you, Colonel," added the major. Boynton tried a different approach. Pointing past the officers, he proclaimed: "That regiment is a lot of damned cowards!" The men took the bait. "We will go with you, colonel" they shouted. Suman gave in. "We will go," he sighed, "and what's your orders?"[50]

Boynton placed the Ninth Indiana on the left of the Thirty-fifth Ohio along the southwest slope of the hill, facing down into the draw. It was 7:10 P.M., fifteen minutes before the end of evening twilight. The Hoosiers had no idea where they were. "It was getting quite dark," recalled one. "We could not see more than six or eight paces if that far. Captain D. B. McConnell of Company K could not distinguish between the Union and Confederate dead that blanketed the slope, nor could he see the length of his own regiment. Although they could make out little in the gloom, the men assumed the worst. "Through the ranks ... passed the whisper, 'The army is retreating, and we are placed out here and left, to hold the enemy back so long as we can, to enable the army to retreat unmolested,'" said McConnell.[51]

Curiosity got the better of some of the men, and they stole down into the draw to "prospect," as the adjutant put it. They prospected straight into the ranks of the Sixty-third Virginia, which at that moment was advancing up the slope with the Fifth Kentucky on its left. After idling away the last hour of daylight at the foot of the ridge, waiting for Kelly to return, Colonel Hiram Hawkins of the Fifth Kentucky had decided to act. He assumed command of the Sixty-third Virginia, then moved both regiments across the draw and up the west side of Hill Two.[52]

The capture of the roving Hoosiers raised a commotion that attracted the attention of Colonel Suman. Riding out to investigate, Suman came face to face with an officer from the Sixty-third Virginia who, with pistol leveled, demanded his surrender. Suman replied that he had already surrendered. This seemed to satisfy the Rebel, and he soon lost interest in Suman. In the meantime, the two Confederate regiments had marched past Suman and were now parleying with the Ninth Indiana for its surrender. Suman pushed his horse through the Rebel ranks and galloped back into his own regiment. He gave the order to fire. His men responded with a scattered volley that sent the surprised Rebels scurrying down into the draw. Colonel Hawkins was furious. "My command . . . moved but a short distance, when a line of battle was discovered forty to sixty yards distant, who first announced that they were friends and then that they surrendered," he reported. "Stealing this advantage, they treacherously fired upon us, killing and wounding several of my men and officers."[53]

Suman had seen enough for one night. Though not a man in the Ninth had been hit, he faced the regiment about and started back across the hilltop. Boynton galloped over to stop him. "I am not going to surrender my regiment," Suman shouted excitedly. Boynton ordered him back into position. Suman loudly refused. His bellowing attracted the attention of every soldier within earshot, and the men of the Thirty-fifth Ohio began to jeer the Indianians for backing away from a position they themselves were prepared to hold with bayonets and empty cartridge boxes. The Hoosiers muttered among themselves, then yelled at Suman to lead them back. Boynton added a threat of court-martial. Suman relented. Back to the edge of the hill marched the Ninth.[54]

The firing on Hill Two had attracted the attention of Trigg, who was busy supervising the division of the prisoners among his three regiments. The Virginian asked his orderly, James Chenault, to ride over to the adjoining hilltop and find out the cause of the shooting. Chenault rode to within a few paces of the Thirty-fifth Ohio, which was lying in underbrush. He challenged the soldiers in the bushes, who replied with a challenge of their own. Whose troops were on their right, the Ohioans demanded. "Trigg's brigade," Chenault answered, then asked: "What troops are these?" Someone yelled out: "The Thirty-fifth Ohio. Now, you surrender." The young orderly wheeled his horse to get away, and the Ohioans opened fire. Chenault and his horse fell, casualties of the last volley fired at Chickamauga.

A few of the bullets landed among Trigg's men and their prisoners. Captors and captives pushed and shoved their way toward cover. The Fifty-fourth Virginia broke up and lost control of its prisoners. Yankees by the score broke free and ran toward the source of the volley. Lieutenant William Albertson and the young drummer boy of the Twenty-second Michigan, John Clem, feigned death and later sneaked away in the darkness. Clem, who after the war attended West Point and later rose to the rank of general, embellished his accounts of his exploits at Chickamauga to the point of claiming that he had shot a Rebel colonel on Horseshoe Ridge, although, unfortunately for his claim, no Confederate field officer fell on that part of the field.

At least half of those captured from the Twenty-first Ohio made their way through the confusion into Boynton's line. Lieutenant Vance was among the lucky ones. Major McMahan was not. He, ten of his officers, and 120 of his men stumbled into the ranks of the Sixth Florida and were recaptured.[55]

Colonel Carlton enjoyed a moment of freedom. When the shots rang out, he spurred his horse through the throng of Ohioans and Virginians, then ducked into the draw and began to feel his way east. Out of the dark a line of Confederates with bayonets fixed charged toward him, shouting "Who are you?" Carlton tried to bluff his way by, but the Rebels surrounded his horse and grabbed the bridle. In a few minutes, Carlton's men caught up with him. They too were recaptured by the Fifth Kentucky. For an instant, their fate was in doubt. Angered by the volley of the Ninth Indiana, the Kentuckians begged Colonel Hawkins to let them shoot the Yankees. Fortunately, Hawkins restored order. A head count revealed that he had netted both Carlton and Le Favour along with most of their troops. Kelly chose this moment to return. He shook hands with Carlton—the two had been classmates at West Point—assigned details to the prisoners, then ordered his men to bivouac for the night. Trigg decided against pressing on farther in the dark and went into bivouac as well.[56]

Boynton was still on Hill Two with the Thirty-fifth Ohio and the Ninth Indiana, waiting for permission to withdraw. Colonel Walker had returned to the Snodgrass field with the Sixty-eighth and One Hundred First Indiana about thirty minutes earlier. There he found Brannan, Granger, Wood, and Steedman huddled together near the Snodgrass house. Walker relayed Thomas's order to withdraw and turned the two regiments over to Brannan, who directed their commander, Lieutenant Colonel Thomas Doan, to report to Boynton out on the hill.

For nearly seven hours, Colonel Walker had not stepped down from the saddle. He had begun the day under arrest and ended it a hero. Now, his last errand run, Walker tried to dismount to relieve himself. "I found both my lower limbs in a state of partial paralysis," he recalled. "During the day I had received a buckshot or pistol ball in my right leg. My left knee had been cut by a minie ball and a piece of shell had injured my left shoulder and spine, but so great had been the excitement of the day that I was not until now aware that I was seriously hurt." Boynton told Doan to move his men quietly forward and to the right of the Thirty-fifth Ohio. In ten minutes, Walker explained, Boynton would move his regiment and the Ninth Indiana off the hill. Doan was to wait until the last troops marched out of the Snodgrass field, then withdraw his command slowly. Doan's men crawled over the backs of the Ohioans to the edge of the hill. There Major George Steele of the One Hundred First came upon James Chenault. He was just barely alive. Chenault begged Steele to move him outside of the Yankee line, so that he might die in peace. Steele beckoned to a couple of soldiers, and they carried him a few yards down the slope. Steele edged forward with them. Peering into the blackness, he saw torches flicker in the ravine behind Hill Three. Then campfires sprang up. "This was evidence to my mind that the enemy had had all the fighting they wanted for that day, at least, and I was glad to make the discovery, because we had had all we wished."[57]

GOD HELP ME TO BEAR IT ARIGHT

IT WAS 10:00 P.M. when Dan McCook's brigade filed off the open rise northwest of the McDonald farm and onto the McFarland's Gap road, the last Federal unit to leave the battlefield. McCook, who had wanted so much to open the battle at Jay's Mill, at least had the satisfaction of drawing the curtain on it.

His men brought up the rear of a retreat the likes of which the Army of the Cumberland had never seen. Never before had the army been forced from a battlefield, nor compelled to abandon its dead and wounded. The night was clear and cold. The moon was bright and the stars plentiful. "The roads in the direction of Rossville seemed to be full of Union soldiers utterly confused and bewildered, wandering about in search of their commands. Some of these were so confused that they could not tell front from rear," a veteran remembered. As the shock of battle wore off, the marching soldiers took note of their surroundings, and the impressions of that night stayed with them the rest of their lives. Wrote George Turner of the Ninety-second Ohio:

> The thunder of battle had ceased and everything was still. We were on a road over which the tide of battle had not rolled, though the fighting ground was not far off. Along this road, as we moved, as noiselessly as possible, in packed columns, I saw by the roadside more touching, affecting sights than in all the battle. Every little way was one and sometimes two soldiers bearing along or resting with and bending over in the moonlight a wounded or dead comrade or brother. I had seen men falling on every side, torn, mangled, and trampled, had passed over parts of the field where were scores of wounded and dead, but nothing was so touching as to see a soldier bearing, by manly strength, the body of a wounded or dead comrade or relative along the road, half a mile from the battlefield, or sitting by the side of a body wrapped in a blanket, as if waiting for strength to come to carry it further to a place of

safety, or expecting to see life come to the form in the pale moonlight. And I saw others sitting by lifeless and wounded forms in the dark shade of trees or rocks, as if they wished to shut out the world from themselves and their dead.[1]

Few of the wounded were lucky enough to have someone to look after them. Many had crawled or hobbled off the battlefield, only to collapse, exhausted, on the side of the road, there to die alone and forgotten. "Some were calling the names and numbers of their regiments, but many had become too weak to do this; by midnight the column had passed by," said John Beatty. "What must have been their agony, mental and physical, as they lay in the dreary woods, sensible that there was no one to comfort or to care for them, and that in a few hours more their career on earth would be ended." The general and his aide paused beside a little brook to water their horses. They raked together the remains of an old fire, and on it cooked two ears of corn for their only meal since daybreak. The sounds and sights of the battle thundered in Beatty's mind. "How many terrible scenes of the day's battle recur to us as we ride on in the darkness," he reflected. "We see again the soldier whose bowels were protruding, and hear him cry 'Jesus, have mercy on my soul!' What multitudes of thought were then crowding into the narrow half hour which he had yet to live—what regrets, what hopes, what fears! The sky was darkening, earth fading; wealth, power, fame, the prizes most esteemed of men, were as nothing."[2]

General Sheridan fell in beside Thomas just outside of Rossville. They passed through the gap and entered the little hamlet at 10:00 P.M. There they dismounted on the side of the road. Sheridan walked over to a worm fence, yanked off the top rail, and laid it into an angle of the fence to make a seat. The two sat down, and Sheridan waited expectantly for Thomas to comment on the events of the day. But the troops and the minutes marched by, and Thomas said nothing. The silence made Sheridan uneasy. "As the command was getting pretty well past, I rose to go in order to put my troops into camp," he recalled. "This roused the general, when, remarking that he had a little flask of brandy in his saddle-holster, he added that he had just stopped for the purpose of giving me a drink, as he knew I must be very tired. He requested one of his staff officers to get the flask, and after taking a sip himself, passed it to me. Refreshed by the brandy, I mounted and rode off to supervise the encamping of my division."[3]

A little later, Colonel Scribner rode into Rossville. As he waited for the fields to clear out enough to place his troops in line, Scribner noticed a large campfire burning brightly in an orchard across the road. He dismounted and walked to it. There he found Captain Willard. Sprawled around the fire were the sleeping officers of the corps staff. Willard offered Scribner a chair, and the grateful Hoosier sat down to warm himself. A hand gently touched his shoulder. It was Thomas. Scribner jumped up to salute. Thomas was a bit more talkative with Scribner. He conversed about the weather and a dozen other small topics but, as with Sheridan, said not a word about the day's fighting. Neither did he ask Scribner about the state of his command. After a few minutes of idle chatter, Scribner excused himself and returned to his troops.[4]

Thomas had much to occupy his thoughts. The fate of the army lay with him. Rosecrans had delegated to him the task of defending the gap at Rossville to prevent a Confederate advance on Chattanooga. A few wagon loads of meat and biscuits were ordered out from the city to feed the troops, and Spear's fresh brigade was on hand, but apart from this, Thomas was left to his own devices. He had to fashion an effective blocking force at once from the thousands of tired, hungry, and disorganized soldiers milling about in the fields and forests around Rossville. "Oh, how weary they were," affirmed Sergeant Partridge of the Ninety-sixth Illinois. "For two nights they had hardly slept at all. Since before daylight of that morning they had eaten nothing except an occasional bit of hardtack from their knapsacks. For hours, many had had no water. They were dusty, powder-grimed, so hoarse that they could hardly speak above a whisper; so tired that they could hardly rise after they lay down."[5] To John Beatty, the task appeared hopeless: "At this hour of the night (eleven to twelve o'clock), the army is simply a mob. There appears to be neither organization nor discipline. The various commands are mixed up in what seems to be inextricable confusion. Were a division of the enemy to pounce down upon us between this and morning, I fear the Army of the Cumberland would be blotted out."[6]

Beatty need not have worried. Pursuit was the furthest thing from Bragg's mind. Just as it had been the night before, communication within the Confederate high command was virtually nil. Bragg apparently went to bed shortly after dark, convinced that the Federals were still on the field in strength and that morning would bring a renewal of the contest. He neither issued orders to his wing commanders nor bothered to seek them out to learn the situation on their fronts.

They were equally derelict. Shortly after nightfall, Polk told Lieutenant Colonel O. B. Spence of his staff to ride along the line in order to familiarize himself with the disposition of the Right Wing and confirm that the enemy had fled the field, and then to report what he found to Bragg. Polk himself seemed less than interested in what Spence might turn up. He had his nephew, William Gale, build him a campfire and lay out his blanket. By 8:00 P.M., the bishop was fast asleep in the Kelly field, "within ten yards of a dead Yankee and one poor devil who lay sobbing out his life all night long."[7]

Longstreet was even more remiss than Polk. The one thing Bragg had asked of Longstreet during their brief afternoon meeting was to keep him informed of events on the left, but the Georgian failed to do even this. Evidently, the only message he sent Bragg was an ambiguous note at 6:15 P.M. that said "we have been entirely successful in my command today" and hoped "to be ready to renew the conflict at an early hour tomorrow." Despite his later protestations to the contrary, it is clear that Longstreet was unaware that Thomas had sneaked off Horseshoe Ridge. So strongly did he suspect that the Federals were still on the ridge that Longstreet early the next morning told Bragg's headquarters in response to a summons that he dare not leave the front. If, as he later claimed, Longstreet knew Thomas had quit the field at dark, why did he not notify Bragg immediately? To this question, Longstreet offered a weak response: "It did not occur to me on the night of the twentieth to send Bragg word of our complete success. I thought that the loud huzzas that spread over the field just at dark were a sufficient assurance and notice to any one within five miles off." In truth, the only cheers that rose from the Snodgrass hill or Horseshoe Ridge that night seem to have come from the brigades of Harker and Hazen to disguise their withdrawal. It was 10:00 P.M. before Kershaw realized they had gone. Bushrod Johnson tried to report his success, but after riding around lost in the dark for three hours, first in search of Longstreet's headquarters and then Bragg's, he gave up and returned to his command, "worn out with the toils of the day."[8]

Lieutenant Colonel Spence found Bragg sometime before midnight. In the sandy soil, he sketched out the position of the Right Wing. Bragg asked Spence to tell Polk and Longstreet to report to headquarters in person. Spence returned with the message to Polk, then rode off to find Longstreet.

The bishop was in no hurry to comply. At 11:00 P.M., presumably after Spence had relayed to him Bragg's order, Polk asked Gale to check on the well-being of his other nephew, Lucius Polk, while he waited by the campfire. Polk's brigade was only a few hundred yards away, but it might as well have been in another state. "For two hours I rode around and among our men in the search, most of the time in a dense forest of pine and oak," said Gale. "The moon was shining as clear as possible and gave a most unearthly appearance to this horrid scene. Wounded, dying, and dead men and horses were strewn around me and under me everywhere, for the field was yet hot and smoking from the last charge, and thousands were lying insensible, or in agony. . . . I can never forget the horrid indecency of death that was fixed on their agonized faces, upturned in the pale moonlight, as I spurred my mare over and around their prostrate forms." Gale gave up the search and returned to the headquarters campfire. Spence was there, having failed in his attempt to find Longstreet. Together they rode with

Polk to Bragg's headquarters a little after 1:00 A.M. According to Gale and Spence, Polk told Bragg that the Federals were "routed and flying precipitately from the field" and urged a prompt pursuit to finish the work before they had a chance to throw up defenses around Chattanooga. "Bragg could not be induced to look at it in that light and it was not done," recalled Gale. There is one gaping hole in the story told by Gale and Spence. In a letter to his wife the next morning, the bishop wrote that it was 9:00 A.M. before he himself could say with certainty that the Union army had withdrawn toward Chattanooga.[9]

Johnny Green of the Orphan Brigade called that night on the battlefield "one of the most beautiful moonlit nights I ever beheld." His sentiments seem to have been unique. Most recalled only the horror. Many of those who passed through the battle unhurt shook off their exhaustion and ventured out in search of wounded comrades, to carry them back to the field hospitals or, if they were too late, to bury their friends where they had fallen. The Army of Tennessee had never before found itself in possession of a battlefield, and so the men were unprepared for the enormity of their task.[10] Sam Watkins was on one such detail. He wrote:

> The Confederate and Federal dead, wounded, and dying were everywhere scattered over the battlefield. Men were lying where they fell, shot in every conceivable part of the body. Some with their entrails torn out and still hanging to them and piled up on the ground beside them, and they still alive. Some with their under jaw torn off, and hanging by a fragment of skin to their cheeks, with their tongues lolling from their mouth, and they trying to talk. Some with both eyes shot out, with one eye hanging down on their cheek. . . . And then to see all those dead, wounded and dying horses, their heads and tails drooping, and they seeming to be so intelligent as if they comprehended everything.
>
> One scene I now remember, that I can imperfectly relate. While a detail of us were passing over the field of death and blood, with a dim lantern . . . we came across a group of ladies, looking among the killed and wounded for their relatives, when I heard one of the ladies say, "There they come with their lanterns." I approached the ladies and asked them for whom they were looking. They told me the name, but I have forgotten it. We passed on, and coming to a pile of our slain, we had turned over several of our dead, when one of the ladies screamed out "O, there he is! Poor fellow! Dead, dead, dead!" She ran to the pile of slain and raised the dead man's head and placed it on her lap and began kissing him and saying, "O, O, they have killed my darling, my darling, my darling!" I could witness the scene no longer. I turned and walked away.[11]

Lewellyn Shaver of the First Alabama Battalion found dead friends by the dozen out on the slopes of the Snodgrass hill. "One incident of that sickening inspection I must be permitted to mention. In our search among the many prostrate forms around us, we came upon one covered carefully with a blanket. On drawing the blanket from the face I beheld one whom I well knew—a remarkably handsome youth of scarce eighteen summers. But a few short hours before, we had lain side by side on our arms, conversing of home and of our probable fate in the coming battle. I thought of his mother—whose idol he was—all unconscious of his fate, and moved on ... with feelings to which I shall attempt to give no expression." Shaver and his detail worked deep into the night, carrying off the wounded and identifying the dead. In the twilight of early morning, he found the "remnant of the First Battalion—now a mere squad—huddled around a single fire. Each face was powder-stained and haggard to the last degree." The men hardly spoke; their thoughts were of the dead, and words seemed inadequate to express the depth of their grief and shock. "As a specimen of what was spoken around that fire that night," related Shaver, "I give the following: 'Jim, poor fellow, was shot down in the first volley; he fell forward on his face, and never spoke.' 'Bird, they say, is mortally wounded, he was a good boy.' 'During the fight I passed brother Archy lying on his side, wounded. I could not stop to help him. The poor fellow smiled faintly on me, and summoning all his strength, waved his hand towards the enemy.' "[12]

Captain H. H. Dillard of the Sixteenth Tennessee watched his men bring in the wounded. "A great many fires were built all along the line, and the suffering were brought to them. Some talked of their loved wives and children, others were calling for their mothers," said Dillard. "Some were praying, some were dying; while the rough, stern soldiers, with hands and faces all black with powder, pitying, stood in groups about them." When the gloom became too heavy for him, Dillard walked off into the forest. Try as he might, Dillard could not distance himself from the agony:

I rambled about a good deal over the field where we were, and the havoc was frightful. The woods were full of branches and tops of trees, like a heavy storm had just passed through. Some trees more than a foot through were cut down by cannon balls. The underbrush was shorn off to the ground. One man was squatted by the side of a tree with his gun up, resting against it, cocked and aimed toward the log breastworks about fifty yards off. His head was leaning forward; he was shot through about the heart. He was a Confederate. Another was lying on his face with one hand grasping his gun just below the muzzle and the rammer in his other hand. Another lay on his back with both hands clinched in his long, black whiskers, all clotted with blood. He was shot in the mouth, and I think was a Federal lieutenant. About five feet off was another, with his head gone. I came across a soldier leaning down over one that was dead, and as I approached him he was in the act of spreading a handkerchief over his face. He looked up at me and said: "This is my captain, and a good one too. I want to send him home if

I can." I saw a good many looking over the dead for a comrade, and when identified would straighten him out, put a knapsack or chunk under his head, and lay a hat on his face; then perhaps cast their eyes up and around for some peculiar tree or cliff or hill by which to identify the spot in coming back.[13]

Captain Daniel Coleman, the youthful commander of the Fifteenth Mississippi Battalion Sharpshooters who had celebrated his twenty-third birthday during the retreat from Chattanooga, learned that night what he had feared since morning—that his younger brother had fallen in the first charge. Coleman located the body near the Yankee breastworks. The youth had been shot through the heart, in the groin, in the thigh, and in the leg. Coleman took his brother's sword and pocket book, then dragged himself to his campfire to give voice to his grief. "Thus it is that two of my dear brothers have fallen in this cruel war at the hands of our wicked enemies and I alone am left now. . . . Oh God help me to bear it aright and not to bear revenge or malice," he wrote in his diary. "I thought of my mother and sisters. How terrible a blow this second great affliction would be to them. I could get no peace until I turned to my Heavenly Father and committed my grief to him."[14]

Not all those who roamed the battlefield did so out of kindness or concern. For many, the lure of easy plunder was irresistible. "We were very hungry and tired, and at once went for the full haversacks and knapsacks of the Federals," said John Coxe of the Second South Carolina. "They were full of such 'goodies' as ground old government Java coffee, crackers, ham, sugar, canned beef, and other good things. We ate ravenously of everything right away." John Wyeth of Forrest's cavalry stuffed his haversack with Yankee hardtack. Val Giles of the Fourth Texas picked up a new rifle, some writing paper, a pair of woolen gloves, and a Webster spelling-book to send home to his children.[15]

Private Doughman of the Eighty-ninth Ohio almost lost his life to one of these battlefield ghouls. Just after dawn, a group of Rebel stragglers burst open the door of the Cooper house, where Doughman lay wounded. Doughman had taken off his shoes and laid them beside him. One of the Rebels asked Doughman if he would swap his new Yankee shoes for that man's beat-up old boots. Doughman declined, saying he planned to wear them again after his wound healed. "You'll never wear them again," laughed the Rebel as he snatched up the shoes and walked out the door. The next Confederate to look Doughman over for plunder was not so easily placated. "He swore a terrific oath and wanted to know where I was wounded," remembered Doughman. "I told him. He raised his gun saying 'I guess I'll knock your brains out!' and was putting his threat into execution when Old Lady Cooper catched his arm, arrested the blow and turned him around.

She remarked that he shouldn't abuse these men since they were wounded and prisoners. He left swearing."[16]

Doughman was lucky. He had a roof over his head and a compassionate woman to look after him. Few wounded Federals were so fortunate. At the Snodgrass farm, the mortally wounded were heaped in rail pens to protect them from roving animals. Wild boars helped themselves to the amputated arms and legs stacked nearby. Out on the ridge, where brushfires had been raging since mid-afternoon, those too badly wounded to walk or crawl away burned to death. [17]

Monday, 21 September, dawned cold and clear. Frost had formed again during the night. Brushfires smoldered along Horseshoe Ridge, and an acrid smoke still hung heavily over the forest. The stench was awful. Already, the bodies of those killed on the nineteenth had begun to decompose. Up and down the Confederate line, soldiers awoke to a vista of blackened and swollen corpses, shattered trees, and trampled fields. Discarded equipment lay scattered everywhere.[18]

St. John Liddell was up before daylight. During the night, his scouts had crept across the La Fayette road to feel for the enemy. They combed the McDonald farm and the forest beyond but found no sign of the Federal army. Liddell rode to Polk's campsite, which had grown to include his ambulance wagon, in the predawn twilight to report the departure of the Yankees from his front. "I found the old general in bed in his ambulance half asleep," said Liddell. "I got his orders to move in pursuit." As Liddell turned to leave, Bragg and his staff arrived. Liddell repeated the findings of his scouts for Bragg, "expecting confidently to receive my orders now directly from him to go forward." But Bragg merely listened. A moment later, Polk stuck his head out of his ambulance and fell into a private conversation with the commanding general. Liddell waited a few minutes, hoping for further instructions. When it became apparent that Bragg and Polk had none to give him, Liddell left, troubled by the apparent inability of the two to agree upon a course of action. "Surely now was the time to push hard upon the traces of the enemy, not giving him one minute's rest. The men were ready and willing and not a moment should be lost," he mused.[19]

Neither Bragg nor Polk seem to have accepted Liddell's report as conclusive proof that the Yankees had gone. Bragg ordered the bishop simply to push forward his skirmish line to "find and feel" the enemy, then rode off to consult with Longstreet sometime before 7:00 A.M.[20]

Longstreet also harbored doubts about the whereabouts of the enemy. At 6:40 A.M., as related earlier, he sent Bragg a note, begging to be excused from reporting to headquarters, since he feared to leave his line with the enemy still on his front. So Bragg rode to him. What the two discussed remains a matter of debate. Longstreet maintained that, on the assumption the enemy had quit the field, Bragg should seize the initiative and cross the Tennessee River above Chattanooga at once, so as to force Rosecrans to evacuate the city. That done, part of the army should be detached to expel Burnside from East Tennessee. Longstreet said that Bragg agreed to the plan and left his bivouac with a promise to start the Right Wing moving immediately to carry it out.[21]

Bragg recalled Longstreet's proposal a bit differently. He said Longstreet suggested a movement directly upon Nashville. Far from initially agreeing with the scheme, Bragg claimed to have dismissed it out of hand. Referring to it in his report, Bragg wrote: "The suggestion requires notice . . . only because it will find a place on the files of the department. Such a movement was utterly impossible for want of transportation. Nearly half our army consisted of re-enforcements just before the battle without a wagon or an artillery horse, and nearly, if not quite, a third of the artillery horses on the field had been lost," he explained. "The railroad bridges, too, had been destroyed to a point south of Ringgold, and on all the road from Cleveland to Knoxville. To these insurmountable difficulties were added the entire absence of means to cross the river except by crossing at a few precarious points."

Longstreet, Hill, and Polk were unrelenting in their criticism of Bragg for failing to undertake a bold offensive along the lines suggested by Longstreet. Certainly a limited pursuit as far as Chattanooga was in order once Bragg became satisfied the field was his. However, Bragg was correct in his assertion that the army was in no condition for a prolonged offensive. Food shortages were acute, due in part to breaks in the railroad to Atlanta, and many Confederates awoke Monday morning with empty haversacks. Transportation was indeed a problem. The troops from Virginia were entirely dependent upon the wagons of the Army of Tennessee to meet their needs, yet, as the historian Thomas Connelly has observed, Bragg's own transportation system had been on the verge of collapse for several months. A hundred other obstacles to a bold movement presented themselves. Pontoon bridges were nonexistent. A move across the river would expose his own lines of communication. Supply lines were tenuous. Then too there was the matter of Bragg's health. Unquestionably, the battle had sapped what little energy he might have had in reserve. Captain Jacob Goodson of Sheffield's brigade spoke with the commanding general while on an errand to headquarters just after the battle. Goodson had never seen Bragg before, and his appearance shocked him. "His countenance shows marks of deep and long continued study; he has a wild abstracted look, and pays but little attention to what is passing around him; his mind seems to be in a continued strain."

Sick and exhausted, uncertain of Rosecrans's whereabouts or intentions and faced with "insurmountable difficulties of his own," Bragg reverted to his old indecisiveness. He busied himself with trivialities, issuing orders for the army to bury its dead and gather abandoned weapons from the field.[22]

General Forrest needed no orders to guide him. He was in the saddle before dawn, riding hard up the La Fayette road to test the resolve of the defeated Federals. Near Rossville, his troopers ran into pickets from Minty's cavalry brigade. A few shots were exchanged before the Federals scattered, and a minie ball cut through the neck of Forrest's horse, severing the main artery. Forrest jammed his finger into the hole, and the horse carried him on. Forrest drew rein atop a high, wooded knoll a mile south of Rossville that overlooked the gap. He removed his finger from the wound to dismount, and the horse fell to the ground, dead. Four Federal signal officers were surprised and captured while still in their trees. Forrest took a pair of field glasses from one and climbed up an observation tree to study the enemy's dispositions.

Below him spread a scene of chaos. Confused columns of retreating infantry thronged about Rossville and snaked along the roads northwest toward Chattanooga, which Forrest could plainly see in the bright morning light. Federal pontoon bridges floated in the Tennessee. Troops and trains were crossing over the bridges and in boats. The captured signal officers said that Rosecrans was preparing to abandon the city. Forrest was elated. Pursuit would be easy; victory over the clearly demoralized enemy, certain. At 9:00 A.M., he scribbled the following note to Polk:

> On the Road
> September 21, 1863
>
> Genl
> We are in a mile of Rossville. Have been to the point of Missionary Ridge. Can see Chattanooga and everything around. The enemy's trains are leaving, going around the point of Lookout Mountain.
> The prisoners captured report two pontoons thrown across for the purpose of retreating.
> I think they are evacuating as hard as they can go. They are cutting timber down to obstruct our passage.
> I think we ought to press forward as rapidly as possible.
>
> Respectfully,
> N. B. Forrest
> Please forward to Gen. Bragg[23]

Forrest waited impatiently for an answer, but none came. As the morning wore away, he sent a second message, more urgent than the first, directly to Bragg. He could take Chattanooga with a single brigade of infantry, if it were sent at once. "Every hour is worth a thousand men," Forrest wrote. Despairing of a reply, Forrest finally rode back to the battlefield to see Bragg. He urged an immediate pursuit. Bragg resisted, citing a lack of supplies. "General Bragg, we can get all the supplies our army needs in Chattanooga," Forrest is said to have answered. Bragg still refused to authorize a pursuit, and Forrest rode away in disgust.[24]

The night of Sunday, 20 September, had been one of unsurpassed anxiety for the high command of the Army of the Cumberland. "Our army was in a sad plight that night after the battle," recalled a Union soldier. "The army seemed a mass of men rather than an organized force. Many regiments were separated in detachments; brigades were divided in the same way. All was hurry and confusion." Captain Alfred Hough agreed: "The confusion and disorder was great at Rossville, the retreating troops seeing others here stopped, and being tired and worn out threw themselves down anywhere, there was no head to, no order in, the mass. I truly believe that a charge of one regiment of cavalry suddenly made would have routed the whole mass, but thanks to General Thomas they were kept too busily occupied for any such movement."[25]

Rosecrans was in no condition to offer Thomas any help, as Captain Alfred Hough discovered. Overwhelmed by the chaos, Negley sent Captain Hough to Chattanooga for guidance from the commanding general. Hough shoved his way through the crowd and reached army headquarters at midnight. He found Rosecrans in the act of telegraphing Washington. Hough briefed the general on conditions at Rossville. Rosecrans listened, listless and distracted. "He looked worn and exhausted and was laboring under excitement," said Hough. "He heard my statement but in doing so showed want of one requisite of a great military commander, firmness and self-reliance under adverse circumstances. He was evidently crushed under the weight of his disaster." Rosecrans had nothing constructive to offer Hough. As he left headquarters, Hough looked back to see Rosecrans on his knees beside Father Treacy, weeping and imploring the priest for spiritual comfort.[26]

President Lincoln could read the despair in Rosecrans's frenetic dispatches. "Be of good cheer," he wired Rosecrans in the small hours of the morning on 21 September. "We have unabated confidence in you and in your soldiers and officers. In the main you must be the judge of what is to be done. If I was to suggest, I would say save your army by taking up strong positions until Burnside joins you, when I hope you can turn the tide. . . . We shall do our utmost to assist you."[27]

The president's message reflected an optimism he did not feel. At daybreak, he strode into the bedroom of his private secretary, John Hay. Sitting down heavily on the bed, he sighed: "Well, Rosecrans has been whipped, as I feared. I have feared it for several days. I believe I feel trouble in the air before it comes. Rosecrans says we have met with a serious disaster—extent not ascertained. Burnside, instead of obeying the orders which were given him on the fourteenth and going to Rosecrans, has gone up on a foolish affair to Jonesboro to capture a party of guerrillas who are there."[28]

Daybreak brought only slightly improved prospects for the army at Rossville. "No one seemed to think of further battle; certainly we were ill prepared to receive an attack," wrote one Illinois soldier of affairs there at about the time Forrest was peering through his field glasses. As Forrest predicted, the Federals grew stronger with each passing hour. Stragglers reported in throughout the morning. Brigade and division commanders brought together their scattered units. By noon, Thomas had shaped a fairly formidable defensive perimeter along Missionary Ridge and across the Dry Valley as far west as Chattanooga Creek. Garfield, however, lacked confidence in it as a good line from which to fight a general battle, and Thomas worried about the ease with which his flanks could be turned. Probes by Forrest's cavalry fed his anxiety, and by mid-afternoon, Thomas was advising Rosecrans that the army should retire to Chattanooga. Rosecrans concurred, asking only that Thomas hold on until dusk.[29]

The withdrawal began at 9:00 P.M. and was over before dawn. Quietly and without the loss of a man, the Army of the Cumberland slipped off Missionary Ridge and into the entrenchments around Chattanooga.[30]

DENUNCIATIONS FIERCE
AND STRONG

"DENUNCIATIONS fierce and strong are heard from all quarters against the Secretary of War for not reinforcing this army, and allowing it to contend against such fearful odds. If the demands of General Rosecrans had been granted, long since made, instead of being here we should now be upon the Atlantic seaboard." So Colonel John Sanderson wrote in his diary of the anger and frustration felt at army headquarters in the immediate aftermath of Chickamauga.[1]

Ironically, it was Stanton who now rescued the Army of the Cumberland. Dana's frenetic "disaster" telegram of Sunday afternoon galvanized the secretary into action. He called on Lincoln, aroused the cabinet, summoned Halleck, and told them that twenty thousand men should be sent immediately from the Army of the Potomac to succor the beleaguered army at Chattanooga. Stanton swore he could do it in five days; Lincoln observed with regret that it would take twice as long just to get that many troops to Washington, but in the end he gave the transfer his blessing. Stanton ordered the Eleventh Corps under O. O. Howard and the Twelfth Corps under H. W. Slocum to board trains for Tennessee. "Fighting Joe" Hooker was placed in charge of the operation.[2]

Behind its entrenchments, the Army of the Cumberland despaired of help. No more than thirty-five thousand men answered muster, the field fortifications were weak, and only ten days' rations remained. During the battle, wrote John Beatty, officers "shouted Burnside at the boys until we became hoarse. But alas, by nightfall Burnside had played out. . . . [He] is now regarded as a myth, a fictitious warrior, who is said to be coming to the relief of men sorely pressed, but who never comes." The morning after the battle, Rosecrans warned Lincoln: "We have no certainty of holding our position here. If Burnside could come immediately it would be well;

otherwise he may not be able to join us unless he comes on the west side of river."[3]

For nearly a week, Burnside had repeatedly assured both Rosecrans and the War Department that he was on his way to join the battle against Bragg. Taking Burnside at his word, Halleck gave the matter no further thought. "Nothing heard from General Burnside since the 19th. He was then sending to your aid all his available force," Halleck wired Rosecrans on 21 September, obviously surprised to learn that Burnside was still in East Tennessee.

President Lincoln added his voice to the chorus urging Burnside to move. After reading Rosecrans's first telegram announcing defeat, Lincoln telegraphed Burnside tersely: "Go to Rosecrans with your force without a moment's delay." That brought only more empty assurances. "Am now sending every man that can be spared to aid Rosecrans," Burnside replied, yet he sent no one. In the days following, Lincoln alternately tried coercion and moral suasion to prod Burnside into going to Rosecrans's relief, but nothing had any effect.

Nor could the army expect assistance from Mississippi. Oddly, the War Department's telegram of 15 September, ordering Grant to send reinforcements to Rosecrans, was delayed in transit and did not reach Grant until several days after the battle. Several weeks more would pass before a relieving column under Sherman set off for Chattanooga, causing a correspondent of the Cincinnati *Commercial* to write: "I have heard the very pertinent question asked whether it was the design to succor Rosecrans in this war or the next."[4]

Stanton could have supplied the answer. On 30 September, he wired Dana: "If Hooker's command gets safely through, all that the Army of the Cumberland can need will be a competent commander. The merit of General Thomas and the debt of gratitude the nation owes to his valor and skill is fully appreciated here and I wish you to tell him so. It is not my fault that he was not in chief command months ago."

The secretary apparently concluded that Rosecrans had to go as early as 23 September. That evening, Lincoln's private secretary, John Hay, had interrupted Stanton at his office while the secretary was waiting for military telegraphers to decipher an intricate message from Rosecrans detailing the reasons for the defeat at Chickamauga. "I know the reasons well enough," sneered Stanton. "Rosecrans ran away from his fighting men and did not stop for thirteen miles." Stanton listened awhile as the dispatch was read, then broke in. "No, they need not shuffle it off on McCook. He is not much of a soldier. I never was in favor of him for a major general. But he is not accountable for this business. He and Crittenden both made pretty good time away from the fight to Chattanooga, but Rosecrans beat them both."[5]

Stanton was not alone in believing a change in command imperative. A week after the battle, Secretary of State Seward suggested to Lincoln that he replace Rosecrans with Thomas. Secretary Chase, a longtime admirer of Rosecrans, also withdrew his support for the general. Garfield's complaints to him of Rosecrans's delaying tactics before the campaign had shaken Chase's confidence in the general. Now Garfield was writing him privately that the army had completely lost faith in Rosecrans, a feeling he apparently shared. The specific contents of the letter were never revealed, but Montgomery Blair, the postmaster general, affirmed that Garfield's correspondence "finally broke the camel's back and made even Chase consent to Rosecrans's removal." Garfield later shared his feeling in person with his close friend General Jacob Cox and, allegedly, even with Stanton and the president.[6]

Lincoln unquestionably no longer had confidence in Rosecrans, and intimated as much both to Secretary of the Navy Gideon Welles and to Hay. However, he was not yet ready to relieve him. Political considerations dictated that the president wait until after the fall gubernatorial and congressional elections before making a change. On 9 October, Ohioans were to go to the polls to choose as their next governor either the prowar Republican John Brough or the vehemently antiwar Democrat Clement Vallandigham. Rosecrans enjoyed immense political support in Ohio. He had been outspoken in his support of the Lincoln administration's war effort and in his denunciation of Vallandigham, and he was vigorously encouraging the officers and men of the army to do the same.[7]

Rosecrans did little to help his own cause. Bragg had shown no inclination to storm Chattanooga — indeed, the first Confederate troops did not appear on the outskirts of the city until 22 September — yet Rosecrans's telegrams to Washington bordered on the hysteric. That day, he wrote Lincoln: "General Burnside will be too late to help us. We are about 30,000 brave and determined men; but our fate is in the hands of God; in whom I hope." The next morning, he seemed to take a manic swing. Again he wrote the president directly: "We hold this point, and I cannot be dislodged except by very superior numbers and after a great battle."[8] Such indications of emotional instability certainly must have caused Lincoln to question Rosecrans's fitness for command. According to the journalist Henry Villard, who was at army headquarters at the time, the Ohioan sealed his fate on 3 October, when he offered Lincoln the following proposal: "If we maintain the position in such strength that the enemy are obliged to abandon their position, and the elections in the great States go favorably, would it not be well to offer a general amnesty to all officers and soldiers in the rebellion?" Rosecrans wrote with the best of intentions, offering a way to speed the collapse of the Confederacy, but he had touched a sensitive nerve. Lincoln was understandably wary of generals who tried to involve themselves in what were essentially political issues. Rosecrans's proposal, said Villard, thus "gave great offense and raised suspicions of political aspirations in his part."[9]

That Rosecrans might pose a political threat to the administration was implied in an alarming dispatch from Dana. On 11 October, he warned Stanton: "I judge from intimations that have reached me that in writing his own report of Chickamauga, General Rosecrans will elaborately show that the blame of his failure in this great battle rests on the Administration; that is, on the Secretary of War and the General-in-Chief, who did not see that Bragg would be reinforced, and who compelled him to move forward without cavalry enough, and very inadequately prepared in other respects."[10]

Since the battle, Dana had been doing his best to engineer the removal of Rosecrans and those close to him. He hung about headquarters, keeping an ear open to any expressions of dissatisfaction with the commanding general and, when those proved insufficient, supplementing them with his own conclusions about the state of the army and its high command.

A week after the battle, he had vilified McCook and Crittenden in a confidential message to Stanton. He accused them of having fled the battlefield after the rout of the right wing and then having gone directly to bed upon reaching Chattanooga. The feeling against them was widespread and intense, said Dana, and among those calling for their dismissal were Palmer, Sheridan, Johnson, Hazen, and Wood. Dana fervently endorsed their appeal. Rosecrans could not be trusted to relieve McCook or Crittenden, the assistant secretary warned. The commanding general lacked "firmness and steadiness of will" and dreaded "so heavy an alternative as is now presented." While not yet counseling the removal of Rosecrans as well, Dana offered that "if it be decided to change the chief commander also, I would take the liberty of suggesting that some Western general of high rank and great prestige, like Grant, for instance, would be preferable as his successor to anyone who has hitherto commanded in the East alone."

Stanton showed Dana's telegram to the president. As Stanton probably expected, Lincoln was deeply disturbed by it. He read it to Seward and Welles, both of whom recommended the removal of McCook and Crittenden. Lincoln assented. On 28 September, the War Department issued an order consolidating the Twentieth and Twenty-first corps into a new organization—the Fourth Corps—which would be commanded by Gordon Granger, who just happened to be a close friend of Dana. McCook and Crittenden were dismissed and ordered to stand ready to face a court of inquiry. On 10 October, they left the army for the North in disgrace. Both were eventually cleared of any misconduct, but their reputations were ruined, and for the duration of the war, neither held field commands.[11]

Gone too was Negley. Tom Wood had seen to that. To preempt criticism of his actions on the second day of the battle, he lashed out at the Pennsylvanian. Wood denounced Negley bitterly to Dana and all others who cared to listen. Wood made good on his threat, often repeated at headquarters, to publish matters in his report that would destroy Negley's reputation, and he bullied Rosecrans into taking action against him. Rosecrans relieved Negley but allowed him to prepare a special defense against the accusations of Wood and similar charges of misconduct raised by Brannan in his report. After examining the papers submitted by Negley, Rosecrans concluded in a letter to the War Department that the Pennsylvanian had "acted according to his best judgment under the circumstances of the case." Nevertheless, he sent Negley home on thirty days' leave and suggested he seek a court of inquiry to clear his name. Negley took Rosecrans's advice; however, it was June 1864 before a court was finally convened. It not only cleared Negley of any misconduct but found he had exhibited "great activity and zeal in the discharge of his duties" and reprimanded Wood for his baseless and clearly malicious allegations against the general. A cloud hung over Negley nonetheless, and he resigned from the army in January 1865. To his dying day, he maintained that he had been the victim of discrimination practiced by West Pointers against volunteer officers.[12]

After the dismissal of McCook and Crittenden, Dana stepped up his criticism of Rosecrans. His attacks became more direct. "I have never seen a public man possessing talent with less administrative power, less clearness and steadiness in difficulty, and greater practical incapacity than General Rosecrans," he wrote on 12 October. "His mind scatters, there is no system in the use of his busy days and restless nights . . . he is a feeble commander."[13]

Such accusations were damning indeed, but it was Dana's intimation that Rosecrans would seek to blame Washington for the disaster at Chickamauga that most harmed the general. The administration recognized its vulnerability to such charges. Welles, for one, lamented the imbecile management of the campaign by the War Department. "I do not find that Stanton has much to say or do. If there are facilities of combination and concentration, it is not developed," he wrote in his diary on 23 September. "No assistance has been rendered Rosecrans. For four weeks the Rebels have been operating to overwhelm him, but not a move has been made, a step taken, or an order given, that I can learn. Halleck has done nothing, proposed nothing, and is now just beginning to take measures to reinforce Rosecrans. Has he the mind, energy, or any of the qualities or capabilities for the important position assigned him?"[14]

In mid-October, the matter was concluded. Vallandigham had been soundly thrashed at the polls. Out of ten thousand votes cast by Ohioans in the Army of the Cumberland, the Copperhead had received fewer than three hundred. The administration scored significant victories nationwide, rolling back the Democratic gains of the year before. Rosecrans's utility had come to an end. The way was open for his dismissal, suggested William Shanks.[15]

The decision rested with Lincoln. Reflecting on the marked lack of cooperation between Rosecrans and Burnside throughout the campaign, Jacob Cox later wrote that there should have been an overall commander to coordinate their activities. The president obviously shared this view, because during the second week of October he decided to combine the departments of the Tennessee, the Cumberland, and the Ohio, with Grant in command of the whole. He presented his plan to the cabinet. Stanton enthusiastically recommended replacing Rosecrans with Thomas. The cabinet concurred, but Lincoln hesitated. He could not bring himself to relieve Rosecrans, so it was agreed that the decision would be left to Grant. Duplicate orders were drafted. One set left Rosecrans in charge of the Department of the Cumberland, the other gave it to Thomas. Both placed Grant in command of the three combined departments, rechristened the Military Division of Mississippi. Stanton personally carried the orders west. In Indianapolis, he met Grant and handed him both sets. Grant had no special fondness for Thomas, but he cared even less for Rosecrans. He chose to relieve the Ohioan.[16]

Monday, 19 October, dawned clear and cool, giving the promise of a stunning Indian summer day in the mountains around Chattanooga. Rosecrans left headquarters early and rode out over a pontoon bridge with General Reynolds for an inspection of his lines near Brown's Ferry. He left Granger temporarily in command. The order relieving him came while Rosecrans was out. Granger read it and laid it on Rosecrans's desk. General Daniel Butterfield, Hooker's chief of staff, dropped by headquarters during the afternoon. Granger pulled him aside. After swearing Butterfield to silence, Granger showed him the message. "Rosecrans is out on a tour of inspection," he said. "He doesn't know this himself."

Rosecrans returned to headquarters at dusk. He strode past Granger, who grabbed Reynolds and whispered: "The old man has been relieved. Thomas is in command."

Rosecrans picked up the telegram, which ordered him to go to Cincinnati and there await further orders. He sent for Thomas.

Thomas had dreaded this moment. Rumors that he was to supersede Rosecrans had been making the rounds for nearly a week. So open was the speculation that Thomas felt obliged to go to Dana to silence the stories. In a voice tremulous with emotion, he thanked the assistant secretary for Stanton's earlier expression of confidence in him, but insisted that he could never take a command "given to him at the expense of another officer, especially his commanding officer." He asked Dana to tell Stanton as much. Thomas then went to Rosecrans to reassure him of his continued fidelity and faith in the general. As Rosecrans tells it, Thomas said: "General, I asked General Garfield to speak to you about the traitors from Washington now in camp and I want now to tell you that I should consider your removal from the command of this army a national injury, and should it be done I will no longer serve with it but ask to be relieved and sent elsewhere." Touched by his sincerity, Rosecrans replied: "General, of this be sure, no cloud shall ever come between us."

Thomas reported to headquarters. Rosecrans quietly handed him the orders placing the Virginian in command of the army. "It was a tense moment," recalled Rosecrans. "Slowly and solemnly he read them, turning paler and drawing his breath harder, as he proceeded and at the conclusion."

After a moment's silence, Thomas spoke. "General, you remember what I told you some two weeks ago?"

Rosecrans read his thoughts and cut him off. "Yes, but we are in the face of the enemy. No one but you can safely take my place now; and for our country's sake you must do it. Fear no cloud of doubt ever coming into my mind as to your fidelity to friendship and honor."[17]

Turning to the few officers present, Rosecrans softly announced his intention to leave at 5:00 A.M. the next morning. To Thomas, he whispered: "I can't bear to meet my troops. I want to leave before the announcement is made, and I will start early in the morning." Thomas remonstrated with Rosecrans, as did his staff, but the Ohioan was adamant. He conferred with Thomas well into the night over the details of pending operations, and was gone before dawn.

When he left, Rosecrans seemed in good spirits. He had a smile and a kind word for every member of his staff, but inside he was grief stricken. As he traveled north, it was all Rosecrans could do just to keep on his feet. Reaching Cincinnati, he fell into bed, in agony from an acute attack of diarrhea.[18]

In the Army of Tennessee, there was no such dramatic denouement, just bickering as usual after a major battle. On this occasion, it was Bragg who instigated the trouble. At the very time his attention should have been focused on pursuing the still badly demoralized Federal army and preventing it from consolidating its defenses around Chattanooga, Bragg devoted nearly all his very limited energy to moving against his detractors. Intent on ridding the army of his enemies once and for all, Bragg unwittingly triggered an upheaval that led to a near mutiny by his senior generals and resulted in the most serious internal crisis in the troubled history of the Western army.[19]

Observing the situation from Richmond, the perceptive socialite Mary Chesnut lamented in her diary: "Bragg, thanks to Longstreet and Hood, had won Chickamauga; so we looked for results that would pay for our losses in battle. Surely they would capture Rosecrans. But no! There sat Bragg like a good dog, howling on his hind legs before Chattanooga, and some Yankee Holdfast grinning at him from his impregnable heights. Bragg always stops to quarrel with his generals."[20]

The initial targets of Bragg's intemperate, poorly timed housecleaning were Hindman and Polk. He intended to blame Hindman for the Mc-Lemore's Cove debacle, Polk for the delay in the attack on the morning of 20 September.[21]

On 22 September, Bragg ordered Wheeler's cavalry and the divisions of Cheatham and Lafayette McLaws, the latter just arrived from Virginia, to advance to within two miles of Chattanooga the following morning. The remainder of the army was directed to have three days' cooked rations on hand and to stand ready to move.[22] Having taken this tentative step toward following up his victory on the battlefield, Bragg turned to what was really on his mind. He wrote his wife for the first time since the battle, devoting a significant portion of the letter to a scathing criticism of Polk's conduct on the second day. Then he had Colonel Brent send the bishop a terse note demanding "as early as practicable" an explanation of his failure to attack at daylight on 20 September as ordered. When no reply was forthcoming, Bragg repeated the request on 25 September.[23]

Bragg was not really interested in Polk's explanation. He had already made up his mind to rid himself of Polk. That same day, he wrote President Davis of the failures of Hindman and Polk during the campaign and suggested that he might find it necessary to replace them.[24]

On 28 September Polk responded with a long account of his part in the confused events of the night of 19 September in which he laid the blame for the delay in the daylight attack squarely on the shoulders of Hill. Bragg was not convinced. Lafayette McLaws said he spoke with Bragg on the subject shortly after joining the army from Virginia. When Bragg complained about Polk not carrying out his orders, McLaws suggested that perhaps Polk had indeed given his lieutenants orders to attack, but that they had not been obeyed. "I cannot help that!" shouted Bragg. "When I give a general an order, I look to him for its execution. I cannot be hunting up excuses for him. If his subordinates do not obey his orders, he must suffer the consequences so far as I am concerned, for I must look to him. I can go no further." Bragg lost no time in telling Polk that his explanation was unsatisfactory, and on 29 September, he suspended both Polk and Hindman from their commands. In an apparent attempt to minimize any backlash, he directed them to leave the army and go to Atlanta to await further orders.[25]

President Davis was deeply saddened to learn that victory had not eased the rancor in the Western army. He had sustained Bragg in his quarrels with his generals in the past and would continue to do so, but he strongly urged him to reinstate Polk. Bragg refused, but offered Davis a compromise: Would he consider a swap of Polk for Hardee?[26]

Richmond was not interested, and Adjutant General Cooper now intervened to try to convince Bragg to back down. On 1 October, he informed Bragg that he had no authority to suspend Polk: "The power of a commanding general in such cases is limited to arrest and to the furnishing of charges in order to trial." Bragg was not deterred. The next day, he preferred formal charges against Polk: Disobedience of a direct order to attack the enemy at daylight on 20 September and a more general charge of "neglect of duty to the prejudice of good order and military discipline."[27]

Davis tried again to dissuade Bragg from his vendetta. For the sake of the army and the nation, he counseled forbearance. On 3 October, he wrote:

> When I sent you a dispatch recommending that Lt. Genl. Polk should not be placed in arrest, it was with the view of avoiding a controversy which could not heal the injury sustained, and which I feared would entail further evil. Believing that he possessed the confidence and affection of his corps, it seemed to be better that his influence in your favor should be preserved by a lenient course. . . . The opposition to you both in the army and out of it has been a public calamity, and I had hoped the great victory which you have recently achieved would tend to harmonize the army and bring to you a more just appreciation of the country. . . . It must be a rare occurrence if a battle is fought without many errors and failures . . . and the public exposure of these diminishes the credit due, impairs the public confidence, undermines the morale of the Army, and works evil to the cause for which brave men have died.[28]

Davis's admonition came too late. The suspension of Polk created an immediate uproar, both in the army and in Richmond. As he had after Stones River, Bragg once again underestimated both the influence of his enemies and the extent of the opposition to him within the army. "We are still here," General Preston wrote his nephew from atop Missionary Ridge on 3 October. "Another victory and the result nothing. All are disheartened." Bragg's own chief of staff, General William Mackall, remarked that he knew of not one contented general in the army. The bishop had loudly condemned Bragg's failure to press Rosecrans in the days immediately following the battle. Longstreet, Hill, Buckner, and Preston shared his sentiments, and after Polk was suspended, they flocked to his support. Expressions of sympathy were almost universal from the high command of the army, and a steady stream of distinguished civilians passed through Polk's Atlanta quarters to offer their condolences and support. Newspapers formerly friendly to Bragg now begged Davis to remove him for the good of the army.

"I hope you will not be uneasy about my situation," Polk wrote his daughter. "I have done my duty and I have no fears as to the result of any investigation or inquiry. I had no idea I had so many friends as I find springing up everywhere since this act of persecution has been attempted. The feeling of the army is all I could desire. My brother officers feel as I desire they should. The poor man who is the author of this trouble is I am informed as much to be pitied. . . . I certainly feel a lofty contempt for his puny efforts to inflict injury upon me."[29]

The anti-Bragg forces intensified their efforts to unseat the commanding general. In Polk's absence, they looked to Longstreet for guidance. He had already proved himself adept at the style of intrigue practiced in the Army of Tennessee. Longstreet had written Secretary of War Seddon on 26 September to apprise him of "our condition and our wants." After discoursing at length on his self-styled brilliant plan to take the offensive in Tennessee, which Bragg had spurned, Longstreet lashed out at the general: "To express my convictions in a few words, our chief has done but one thing that he ought to have done since I joined this army. That was to order the attack upon the 20th. I am convinced that nothing but the hand of God can save us or help us as long as we have our present commander," he wailed. "Now to our wants. Can't you send us General Lee?" Of course, Seddon could not, which increased Longstreet's chances for getting the command.[30]

Polk was impressed with Longstreet's letter. Assuming Longstreet to be sincere in his desire that Lee come west, Polk wrote the Virginian himself. In so doing, he temporarily ceded the mantle of leadership of the anti-Bragg clique to Longstreet.[31]

On 4 October, the corps commanders met secretly to consider an alternate commander for the army and to prepare a petition to Davis for Bragg's removal. Details of the meeting are lacking, as few of the participants wrote or spoke of it, even after the war. The culmination was a long petition that carefully avoided any reference to Bragg's military failings, which would have been construed as mutinous, and argued instead for his removal on the sole ground that "the condition of his health unfits him for the command of an army in the field." None of the twelve generals who signed the document ever admitted authorship. Most of the meager evidence on the subject suggests Buckner wrote it—as Thomas Connelly has pointed out, his signature is the first to appear on the petition, in the place where one would normally sign a letter. Longstreet lamely suggested that Hill was responsible for getting up the petition. To Lafayette McLaws, who brought his dislike of Longstreet with him from Virginia, the Georgian's motives were clear. "Longstreet's staff are very subordinate in carrying out the issues of their chief and he has no scruples," McLaws later advised Hill, adding that "you may be able to trace back Bragg's opposition to you to a probability that Longstreet excused his opposition to Bragg by quoting your judgment and sayings as having influenced him in forming his opinion." The eminent historian Thomas Robson Hay came to a similar conclusion. "Longstreet, aided and abetted by Polk, was the real troublemaker. Polk was more tolerant and more cautious than Longstreet. But Longstreet had no compunctions," he told Hill's son.[32]

In any event, Bragg got wind of the movement to unseat him, and at headquarters it was assumed that Hill, abetted by Buckner, was the instigator. Whether he knew of the secret meeting is uncertain, but Bragg at last recognized that the foment he had helped unleash had grown beyond his ability to contain it. After Stones River, Davis had come west and silenced the discordant voices in the high command. Bragg hoped he would now do the same. On 5 October, he telegraphed the president, imploring him to intercede again.[33]

Davis had already made up his mind to pay the army a visit. Although the petition for Bragg's removal had not yet been sent, Davis evidently knew of it. Even before the corps commanders met, he had sent a trusted member of his staff, Colonel James Chesnut, husband of the diarist Mary Chesnut, to look into the matter. Chesnut was overwhelmed by the intensity of feeling against Bragg, and he wired Davis to hasten to the army.[34]

Davis stopped first in Atlanta on 8 October. There he conferred with Polk. He entreated the bishop to return to the army, and even went so far as to admit that Bragg's suspension of Polk was "a great blunder which he deeply regretted." Polk refused, swearing he would resign rather than again serve under Bragg. He did, however, offer Davis a way out. He would accept a transfer to another department.[35]

Davis arrived at army headquarters the next morning. Instead of cooling tempers, his actions almost resulted in open revolt. At a minimum, the president's handling of the command crisis reflected a remarkable absence of tact. To begin with, he had brought with him John Pemberton, the New York–born lieutenant general who had lost Vicksburg, to replace Polk. Bragg approved the appointment, but Polk's corps came near to mutiny when it was announced. Neither Davis, nor Bragg, nor Pemberton himself seem to have had a clue of the low esteem in which both his fellow generals and the rank and file held the New Yorker. General Mackall broke the news to Pemberton. "I told him that there was not a division in this army that would be willing to receive him; that I was sorry to be obliged to tell him so unpleasant a truth, but so it was." Davis and Bragg yielded to popular opinion, and a mortified Pemberton was sent sadly on his way.[36]

Davis's next misstep was even more painful. From the moment Davis arrived, it was clear to everyone concerned that he had no intention of removing Bragg. Yet he called Longstreet, Buckner, Hill, and Cheatham to army headquarters for the express purpose of hearing their views on Bragg's fitness to command. As Bragg sat dumbly in a corner, the president called on each for his opinion, beginning with Longstreet. The Georgian said he stated unequivocally that Bragg had mishandled the army after Chickamauga, resulting in an incomplete victory. The other generals offered similar appraisals, and the meeting concluded. The anti-Bragg forces had played their hand and come up short.[37]

Now it was Bragg's turn. Two days after the ablutionary meeting at headquarters, he formally requested that Davis relieve Hill from duty with the Army of Tennessee. By way of justification, Bragg wrote: "Possessing some high qualifications as a commander, he still fails to such an extent in others more essential that he weakens the morale and military tone of his command. A want of prompt conformity to orders of great importance is the immediate cause of this application." Davis obliged him. "Regretting that the expectations which induced the assignment of that gallant officer to this army have not been realized, you are authorized to relieve Lt. Genl D. H. Hill from further duty with your command."[38]

Hill was outraged. He repeatedly demanded that Bragg specify his grievance. Bragg did not, because he could not. In truth, he had no complaint with Hill's performance during the campaign. As he told Major E. T. Sykes, one of his few remaining friends, after the war, he had dismissed Hill for having engaged in "mutinous assemblage." Or, as Lafayette McLaws astutely explained to Hill shortly after the fact: "You were, as you always are, open and outspoken, made no secret of your opposition to him and you were looked on as the head and front of the coalition against Bragg. I have no doubt but that all your sarcastic remarks . . . were repeated to General Bragg, and that he felt personally aggrieved at your conduct."[39]

For Hill, the war had all but come to a close. Davis compounded his humiliation by refusing to nominate Hill to the Confederate senate at the grade of lieutenant general, to which he had appointed him three months earlier, on that July afternoon when he had beseeched him to go west. Aside from a brief stint at Petersburg and as a division commander under Johnston in the closing hours of the war in North Carolina, Hill saw no further field service.[40]

Others suffered, but none as greatly. While Longstreet did not get command of the Army of Tennessee as he had once hoped, neither was he censured for his part in the sordid conspiracy. Instead, he was sent off to East Tennessee with his corps to retake Knoxville from Burnside. So, in a manner of speaking, he at last had an independent command. Buckner tried to sustain the fight against Bragg but ended up losing his corps. After Chickamauga, William Preston had written his nephew: "I have a dull future before me with Bragg. No approval or praise if I win, ruin and censure if I lose. I intend to get away if I can. I wish I could get control of Southwest

Virginia. Is it possible?" It was not. Preston went to western Virginia, but in command of a second-rate brigade under the departmental commander, General Sam Jones.[41]

The master of intrigue, Bishop Polk, once again emerged relatively un-scathed. President Davis concluded that there was nothing in Bragg's charges against him to warrant either a court-martial or a court of inquiry, and so he dismissed the entire matter. Polk went to Mississippi to take Hardee's corps, and Hardee returned to Tennessee to assume command of his corps.[42]

In the end, this reshuffling accomplished nothing. It was the same old story, only the consequences were more tragic than usual. As at Tullahoma after Stones River, Bragg's preoccupation with the enemy within led him to ignore the Federal army at Chattanooga, which day by day grew stronger. By the time Bragg realized the weakness of his lines, it was too late. Grant sprang from Chattanooga like a caged lion suddenly freed. Sixty-seven hundred more Confederate veterans were lost in the battles around the city, and the gateway to the Deep South passed forever to the Union.

Casualties at Chickamauga had been appalling. Missing reports and con-tradictory estimates make it impossible to offer up with certainty any figure for the Confederates. On the low end, John Turchin in his *Chickamauga* pronounced the losses of the Army of Tennessee to be as follows: 1,790 killed, 11,158 wounded, and 1,380 missing, for a total of 14,328. On the high end, Glenn Tucker sets forth its losses as 2,673 killed, 16,274 wounded, and 2,003 missing, for a total of 20,950 casualties. Thomas Livermore sug-gested a figure in between those of Turchin and Tucker. He set down the Confederate losses as 2,312 killed, 14,674 wounded, 1,468 missing, for a total of 18,454. Bragg himself said he lost two-fifths of his force, which had numbered about 68,000. Regardless of which estimate is closer to the actual figure, the losses were clearly staggering and, at that late date in the war, irreplaceable.

The Army of the Cumberland lost 1,656 killed, 9,749 wounded, and 4,774 missing, for a total of 16,179 casualties. Rosecrans had entered the battle with 57,840 men.[43]

No strangers to battlefield slaughter themselves, the French were never-theless astounded by the carnage at Chickamauga. Said the Paris *Figaro* of the battle: "These Americans are fighting on a military system inaugurated by the Kilkenny cats. The two armies meet and fight and slaughter each other with the utmost fury. Then they [fall] back and reorganize for another general massacre. Positively, the war will end when the last man is killed."[44]

The survivors searched for some greater meaning to the butchery they had witnessed. Few could find any. Henry Cist could write only that, "all things considered, the battle of Chickamauga was the hardest fought and bloodiest battle of the rebellion." Lieutenant Colonel Orrin Hurd of the Thirtieth Indiana agreed, but could think of nothing to justify the sacrifice. "There is no record that will show harder fighting and better behavior of men than was displayed in this battle under the most trying circumstances." Reflecting on the battle in general and the slaughter on Horseshoe Ridge in particular, General Hindman was moved to write in his report: "I have never known Federal troops to fight so well. It is just to say, also, that I never saw Confederate soldiers fight better." The worldly old Prussian, August Willich, cut through the empty adulation. "Looking back on the manner this brigade and so many others have done their duty, I cannot repress a regret to see our best troops melt away to a mere nothing. My brigade now numbers scarcely eight hundred rifles. Now the veterans day by day die out."[45]

General Hazen asked the key question from the Federal perspective: "Was the battle of Chickamauga necessary to the holding of Chattanooga?" He could find no satisfactory answer himself. Rosecrans went to his grave believing it was. Chattanooga was the object of the campaign. It had been held; ergo, Chickamauga was not a Union defeat after all, he argued. In one sense, he was right. Rosecrans really had had no alternative but to press on after Bragg vacated Chattanooga, Thomas's advice to the contrary notwithstanding. Washington had shown no patience when Rosecrans had halted after driving Bragg out of Tennessee in the relatively bloodless Tullahoma campaign, but had used threats and cajolery to nudge him on. With Meade inactive in Virginia and Grant likewise in a torpor in Mississippi, Stanton and Halleck would have shown no greater forbearance had Rosecrans paused to regroup at Chattanooga.

Not unexpectedly, Tom Wood dismissed the battle as a criminal sacrifice of life to no good end. President Lincoln, who saw the battle for the resounding defeat it was, recognized that it would be an empty victory for the South so long as the Union army held Chattanooga. In the uncertain aftermath of the battle, when Rosecrans's grasp on the city appeared tenuous at best, the president wrote Halleck: "I think it very important for General Rosecrans to hold his position at or about Chattanooga. . . . If he can only maintain this position . . . the rebellion can only eke out a short and feeble existence, as an animal sometimes may with a thorn in its vitals."[46]

Neither Hill nor Polk would have argued with Lincoln's logic. Two weeks after the battle, Polk protested in a letter to President Davis:

General Bragg . . . let down as usual, and allowed the fruits of the great but sanguinary victory to pass from him by the most criminal incapacity; for there are positions in which "weakness is wickedness."

By that victory, and its heavy expenditure of the life-blood of the Confederacy, we bought and paid for the whole of the State of Tennessee . . . at the very least; and all that was wanted was to have gone forward and taken possession of it. It was but a repetition of our old story in the battles of the West.[47]

Two decades afterward, with none of his personal bitterness mellowed by age, Hill wrote: "There was no more splendid fighting in '61, when the flower of the Southern youth was in the field, than was displayed in those bloody days of September '63. But it seems to me that the elan of the Southern soldier was never seen after Chickamauga — that brilliant dash which had distinguished him was gone forever. . . . He fought stoutly to the last, but, after Chickamauga, with the sullenness of despair and without the enthusiasm of hope. That 'barren victory' sealed the fate of the Southern Confederacy."[48]

THE OPPOSING FORCES IN THE CHICKAMAUGA CAMPAIGN

The following list was assembled from *War of the Rebellion: A Compilation of the Official Records of the Union and Confederate Armies* and John Turchin's *Chickamauga*. With respect to officer casualties, (k) signifies killed, (mw) mortally wounded, (w) wounded, and (c) captured.

Army of the Cumberland
Major General William S. Rosecrans, Commanding

Department Headquarters
1st Battalion Ohio Sharpshooters
10th Ohio Infantry (Provost Guard)
15th Pennsylvania Cavalry (Escort)

FOURTEENTH ARMY CORPS
Major General George H. Thomas, Commanding
9th Michigan Infantry (Provost Guard)[1]
1st Ohio Cavalry, Company L (Escort)

First Division
Brigadier General Absalom Baird
First Brigade
Colonel Benjamin F. Scribner
38th Indiana   94th Ohio
2d Ohio   33d Ohio
10th Wisconsin

---

1. Not engaged, on provost duty and train-guard.

Second Brigade
Brigadier General John C. Starkweather
1st Wisconsin   21st Wisconsin
24th Illinois   79th Pennsylvania
Third Brigade
Brigadier General John H. King
15th United States, 1st Battalion
16th United States, 1st Battalion
18th United States, 1st Battalion
18th United States, 2d Battalion
19th United States, 1st Battalion
Artillery
1st Michigan Light, Battery A   4th Indiana Light Battery
5th United States, Battery H

Second Division
Major General James S. Negley
First Brigade
Brigadier General John Beatty
42d Indiana   88th Indiana
104th Illinois   15th Kentucky
3d Ohio[2]
Second Brigade
Colonel Timothy R. Stanley (w)
Colonel William L. Stoughton
18th Ohio   19th Illinois
11th Michigan   69th Ohio[3]
Third Brigade
Colonel William Sirwell
78th Pennsylvania   21st Ohio
74th Ohio   37th Indiana
Artillery
Illinois Light, Bridges's Battery   1st Ohio Light, Battery M
1st Ohio Light, Battery G

Third Division
Brigadier General John M. Brannan
First Brigade
Colonel John M. Connell
17th Ohio   31st Ohio

2. Not in the battle.
3. Not in the battle.

38th Ohio[4]   82d Indiana
Second Brigade
Colonel John T. Croxton (w)
Colonel William H. Hays
4th Kentucky   10th Kentucky
10th Indiana   74th Indiana
14th Ohio
Third Brigade
Colonel Ferdinand Van Derveer
9th Ohio   35th Ohio
2d Minnesota   87th Indiana
Artillery
1st Michigan Light, Battery D   1st Ohio Light, Battery C
4th United States, Battery I

Fourth Division
Major General Joseph J. Reynolds
First Brigade[5]
Colonel John T. Wilder
17th Indiana   72d Indiana
92d Illinois   98th Illinois
123d Illinois
Second Brigade
Colonel Edward A. King (k)
Colonel Milton S. Robinson
68th Indiana   75th Indiana
101st Indiana   80th Illinois[6]
105th Ohio
Third Brigade
Brigadier General John B. Turchin
11th Ohio   36th Ohio
89th Ohio[7]   92d Ohio
18th Kentucky
Artillery
Indiana Light, 18th Battery   Indiana Light, 19th Battery
Indiana Light, 21st Battery

4. Not in battle, on train guard.
5. Mounted brigade, on detached duty throughout campaign.
6. On duty in Nashville, Tenn.
7. Detached, serving with Steedman's Division of Reserve Corps.

TWENTIETH ARMY CORPS
Major General Alexander McDowell McCook, Commanding
2d Kentucky Cavalry, Company I (Escort)

First Division
Brigadier General Jefferson C. Davis
First Brigade[8]
Colonel P. Sidney Post
22d Indiana   59th Illinois
74th Illinois   75th Illinois
Second Brigade
Brigadier General William P. Carlin
21st Illinois   38th Illinois
81st Indiana   101st Ohio
Third Brigade
Colonel Hans C. Heg (mw)
Colonel John A. Martin
15th Wisconsin   25th Illinois
35th Illinois   8th Kansas
Artillery
Wisconsin Light, 5th Battery   Minnesota Light, 2d Battery
Wisconsin Light, 8th Battery

Second Division
Brigadier General Richard W. Johnson
First Brigade
Brigadier General August Willich
49th Ohio   39th Indiana[9]
32d Indiana   15th Ohio
89th Illinois
Second Brigade
Colonel Joseph B. Dodge
77th Pennsylvania   29th Indiana
30th Indiana   79th Illinois
Third Brigade
Colonel Philemon P. Baldwin (k)
Colonel William W. Berry
6th Indiana   1st Ohio
93d Ohio   5th Kentucky

8. Left at Stevens's Gap with trains. On 20 September, acted with cavalry on the right.
9. Mounted and detached from brigade.

Artillery
1st Ohio Light, Battery A   Ohio Light, 20th Battery
Indiana Light, 5th Battery

Third Division
Major General Philip H. Sheridan
First Brigade
Brigadier General William H. Lytle (mw)
Colonel Silas Miller
88th Illinois   36th Illinois
24th Wisconsin   21st Michigan
Second Brigade
Colonel Bernard Laiboldt
2d Missouri   15th Missouri
44th Illinois   73d Illinois
Third Brigade
Colonel Luther P. Bradley (w)
Colonel Nathan H. Walworth
22d Illinois   27th Illinois
42d Illinois   51st Illinois
Artillery
Indiana Light, 11th Battery   1st Missouri Light, Battery G
1st Illinois Light, Battery C

TWENTY-FIRST ARMY CORPS
Major General Thomas L. Crittenden
15th Illinois Cavalry, Company K (Escort)

First Division
Brigadier General Thomas J. Wood
First Brigade
Colonel George P. Buell
26th Ohio   58th Indiana
13th Michigan   100th Illinois
Second Brigade[10]
Brigadier General George D. Wagner
15th Indiana   40th Indiana
51st Indiana[11]   57th Indiana
97th Ohio

10. Not engaged in battle, stationed at Chattanooga.
11. On duty in Nashville, Tenn.

Third Brigade
Colonel Charles G. Harker
3d Kentucky   64th Ohio
65th Ohio   125th Ohio
73d Indiana[12]
Artillery
Indiana Light, 8th Battery   Indiana Light, 10th Battery[13]
Ohio Light, 6th Battery

Second Division
Major General John M. Palmer
First Brigade
Brigadier General Charles Cruft
1st Kentucky[14]   2d Kentucky
31st Indiana   90th Ohio
Second Brigade
Brigadier General William B. Hazen
41st Ohio   124th Ohio
6th Kentucky   9th Indiana
Third Brigade
Colonel William Grose
36th Indiana   24th Ohio
6th Ohio   23d Kentucky
84th Illinois
Artillery
1st Ohio Light, Battery B   1st Ohio Light, Battery F
4th United States, Battery H   4th United States, Battery M

Third Division
Brigadier General Horatio P. Van Cleve
First Brigade
Brigadier General Samuel Beatty
9th Kentucky   17th Kentucky
19th Ohio   79th Indiana
Second Brigade
Colonel George F. Dick
44th Indiana   86th Indiana
13th Ohio   59th Ohio
Third Brigade
Colonel Sidney M. Barnes

12. On duty in Nashville, Tenn.
13. Not engaged, stationed at Chattanooga.
14. Five companies detached as wagon guard.

51st Ohio   99th Ohio
35th Indiana   8th Kentucky
21st Kentucky[15]
Artillery
Indiana Light, 7th Battery   Pennsylvania Light, 26th Battery
Wisconsin Light, 3d Battery

RESERVE CORPS[16]
Major General Gordon Granger, Commanding
1st Missouri Cavalry, Company F (Escort)

First Division
Brigadier General James B. Steedman
First Brigade
Brigadier General Walter C. Whitaker
40th Ohio   89th Ohio[17]
84th Indiana   96th Illinois
115th Illinois   22d Michigan[18]
Ohio Light Artillery, 18th Battery
Second Brigade
Colonel John G. Mitchell
98th Ohio   113th Ohio
121st Ohio   78th Illinois
1st Illinois Light Artillery, Battery M

Second Division
Second Brigade
Colonel Daniel McCook
85th Illinois   86th Illinois
125th Illinois   52d Ohio
69th Ohio[19]
2d Illinois Light Artillery, Battery I

CAVALRY CORPS
Major General David S. Stanley[20]
Brigadier General Robert B. Mitchell

15. Not engaged, stationed at Whiteside's.
16. The corps consisted of three divisions, but only three brigades participated in the Battle of Chickamauga; the remainder of the corps was stationed at different points in the rear.
17. Temporarily attached.
18. Temporarily attached.
19. Temporarily attached.
20. Taken ill before battle; did not participate.

First Division
Colonel Edward M. McCook
First Brigade
Colonel Archibald P. Campbell
2d Michigan   9th Pennsylvania
1st Tennessee
Second Brigade
Colonel Daniel M. Ray
2d Indiana   4th Indiana
2d Tennessee   1st Wisconsin
1st Ohio Light, Battery D (section)
Third Brigade
Colonel Louis D. Watkins
4th Kentucky   5th Kentucky
6th Kentucky

Second Division
Brigadier General George Crook
First Brigade
Colonel Robert H. G. Minty
3d Indiana (battalion)   4th Michigan
7th Pennsylvania   4th United States
Second Brigade
Colonel Eli Long
2d Kentucky   1st Ohio
3d Ohio   4th Ohio
Artillery
Chicago (Illinois) Board of Trade Battery

Army of Tennessee
General Braxton Bragg, Commanding

Headquarters
Dreux's Company Louisiana Cavalry (Escort)
Holloway's Company Alabama Cavalry (Escort)

RIGHT WING
Lieutenant General Leonidas Polk
Greenleaf's Company Louisiana Cavalry (Escort)

Cheatham's Division[21]
Major General Benjamin F. Cheatham
Jackson's Brigade
Brigadier General John K. Jackson
1st Georgia   5th Georgia
2d Georgia Battalion Sharpshooters
5th Mississippi   8th Mississippi
Smith's Brigade
Brigadier General Preston Smith (k)
Colonel Alfred J. Vaughan, Jr.
11th Tennessee   12th-47th Tennessee
13th-154th Tennessee   29th Tennessee
Dawson's Battalion Sharpshooters
Maney's Brigade
Brigadier General George Maney
1st-27th Tennessee   4th Tennessee (Provisional Army)
6th-9th Tennessee   24th Tennessee Battalion Sharpshooters
Wright's Brigade
Brigadier General Marcus J. Wright
8th Tennessee   16th Tennessee
28th Tennessee   38th Tennessee
51st-52d Tennessee
22d Tennessee Battalion
Strahl's Brigade
Brigadier General Otho F. Strahl
4th-5th Tennessee   19th Tennessee
24th Tennessee   31st Tennessee
33d Tennessee
Artillery
Major Melancthon Smith
Carnes' (Tennessee) Battery   Scogin's (Georgia) Battery
Scott's (Tennessee) Battery   Smith's (Mississippi) Battery
Stanford's (Mississippi) Battery

HILL'S CORPS
Lieutenant General Daniel H. Hill

Cleburne's Division
Major General Patrick R. Cleburne

21. Of Polk's Corps.

Escort
Sanders's Company Tennessee Cavalry
Wood's Brigade
Brigadier General S. A. M. Wood
16th Alabama   33d Alabama
45th Alabama   18th Alabama
32d-45th Mississippi
15th Mississippi Battalion Sharpshooters
Polk's Brigade
Brigadier General Lucius E. Polk
1st Arkansas   3d-5th Confederate
2d Tennessee   35th Tennessee
48th Tennessee
Deshler's Brigade
Brigadier General James Deshler (k)
Colonel Roger Q. Mills
19th-24th Arkansas
6th-10th Texas Infantry-15th Texas Cavalry (Dismounted)
17th-18th-24th-25th Texas Cavalry (Dismounted)
Artillery
Major T. R. Hotchkiss (w)
Captain Henry C. Semple
Calvert's (Arkansas) Battery
Douglas' (Texas) Battery
Semple's (Alabama) Battery

Breckinridge's Division
Major General John C. Breckinridge
Escort
Foules's Company Mississippi Cavalry
Helm's Brigade
Brigadier General Benjamin Helm (mw)
Colonel Joseph H. Lewis
41st Alabama   2d Kentucky
4th Kentucky   6th Kentucky
9th Kentucky
Adams's Brigade
Brigadier General Daniel W. Adams (w, c)
Colonel Randall L. Gibson
32d Alabama   13th-20th Louisiana
16th-25th Louisiana   19th Louisiana
14th Louisiana Battalion Sharpshooters

Stovall's Brigade
Brigadier General Marcellus A. Stovall
1st-3d Florida   4th Florida
47th Georgia   60th North Carolina
Artillery
Major Rice E. Graves (k)
Cobb's (Kentucky) Battery   Graves' (Kentucky) Battery
Mebane's (Tennessee) Battery   Slocumb's (Louisiana) Battery

RESERVE CORPS
Major General William H. T. Walker

Walker's Division
Brigadier General States R. Gist
Gist's Brigade
Brigadier General States R. Gist
Colonel Peyton Colquitt (k)
Lieutenant Colonel Leroy Napier
46th Georgia   8th Georgia Battalion
16th South Carolina[22]   24th South Carolina
Ector's Brigade
Brigadier General Matthew D. Ector
Stone's (Alabama) Battalion Sharpshooters
Pound's (Mississippi) Battalion Sharpshooters
29th North Carolina   9th Texas
10th Texas Cavalry (Dismounted)
14th Texas Cavalry (Dismounted)
32d Texas Cavalry (Dismounted)
Wilson's Brigade
Colonel Claudius C. Wilson
25th Georgia   29th Georgia
30th Georgia   1st Georgia Battalion Sharpshooters
4th Louisiana Battalion
Artillery
Ferguson's (South Carolina) Battery[23]
Howell's (Georgia) Battery

Liddell's Division
Brigadier General St. John R. Liddell

22. Not engaged; at Rome.
23. Not engaged; at Rome.

Liddell's Brigade
Colonel Daniel C. Govan
2d-15th Arkansas   5th-13th Arkansas
6th-7th Arkansas   8th Arkansas
1st Louisiana (Regulars)
Walthall's Brigade
Brigadier General Edward C. Walthall
24th Mississippi   27th Mississippi
29th Mississippi   30th Mississippi
34th Mississippi
Artillery
Captain Charles Swett
Fowler's (Alabama) Battery
Warren Light Artillery (Mississippi Battery)

LEFT WING
Lieutenant General James Longstreet

Hindman's Division[24]
Major General Thomas C. Hindman (w)
Brigadier General Patton Anderson
Escort
Lenoir's Company Alabama Cavalry
Anderson's Brigade
Brigadier General Patton Anderson
Colonel J. H. Sharp
7th Mississippi   9th Mississippi
10th Mississippi   41st Mississippi
44th Mississippi
9th Mississippi Battalion Sharpshooters
Garrity's (Alabama) Battery
Deas's Brigade
Brigadier General Zachariah C. Deas
19th Alabama   22d Alabama
25th Alabama   39th Alabama
50th Alabama   17th Alabama Battalion Sharpshooters
Dent's (Alabama) Battery
Manigault's Brigade
Brigadier General Arthur M. Manigault
24th Alabama   28th Alabama

24. Of Polk's Corps.

34th Alabama   10th-19th South Carolina
Waters's (Alabama) Battery

BUCKNER'S CORPS
Major General Simon B. Buckner
Escort
Clark's Company Tennessee Cavalry

Stewart's Division
Major General Alexander P. Stewart
Johnson's Brigade[25]
Brigadier General Bushrod R. Johnson
Colonel John S. Fulton
17th Tennessee   23d Tennessee
25th Tennessee   44th Tennessee
Bate's Brigade
Brigadier General William B. Bate
58th Alabama   37th Georgia
15th-37th Tennessee   20th Tennessee
4th Georgia Battalion Sharpshooters
Brown's Brigade
Brigadier General John C. Brown (w)
Colonel Edmund C. Cook
18th Tennessee   26th Tennessee
32d Tennessee   45th Tennessee
23d Tennessee Battalion
Clayton's Brigade
Brigadier General Henry D. Clayton
18th Alabama   36th Alabama
38th Alabama
Artillery
Major J. Wesley Eldridge
1st Arkansas Battery   T. H. Dawson's (Georgia) Battery
Eufaula Artillery (Alabama Battery)
Company E, 9th Ga. Artillery Battalion (Everett's; formerly Billington W.
York's Battery)

Preston's Division
Brigadier General William Preston
Gracie's Brigade
Brigadier General Archibald Gracie, Jr.
1st Alabama Battalion   2d Alabama Battalion

25. Part of Johnson's Provisional Division.

3d Alabama Battalion   4th Alabama Battalion
43d Alabama   63d Tennessee
Trigg's Brigade
Colonel Robert C. Trigg
1st Florida Cavalry (Dismounted)   6th Florida
7th Florida   54th Virginia
Third Brigade
Colonel John H. Kelly
65th Georgia   5th Kentucky
58th North Carolina   63d Virginia
9th Georgia Artillery Battalion
Major A. Leyden
Company C (Wolihin's Battery)
Company D (Peeples's Battery)
Jeffress's (Virginia) Battery
Reserve Corps Artillery
Major Samuel C. Williams
Baxter's (Tennessee) Battery   Darden's (Mississippi) Battery
Kolb's (Alabama) Battery   McCant's (Florida) Battery

Johnson's Division[26]
Brigadier General Bushrod R. Johnson
Gregg's Brigade
Brigadier General John Gregg (w)
Colonel Cyrus A. Sugg
3d Tennessee   10th Tennessee
30th Tennessee   41st Tennessee
50th Tennessee   7th Texas
1st Tennessee Battalion
Bledsoe's (Missouri) Battery
McNair's Brigade
Brigadier General Evander McNair (w)
Colonel David Coleman
1st Arkansas Mounted Rifles (Dismounted)
2d Arkansas Mounted Rifles (Dismounted)
25th Arkansas   39th North Carolina
4th and 31st and 4th Arkansas Battalion (Consolidated)
Culpeper's (South Carolina) Battery

26. A provisional organization, embracing Johnson's and, part of the time, Robertson's brigades, as well as Gregg's and McNair's. On 19 September, attached to Longstreet's corps, under Major General Hood.

LONGSTREET'S CORPS[27]
Major General John B. Hood (w)

McLaws's Division
Brigadier General Joseph B. Kershaw
Major General Lafayette McLaws
Kershaw's Brigade
Brigadier General Joseph B. Kershaw
2d South Carolina   3d South Carolina
7th South Carolina   8th South Carolina
15th South Carolina   3d South Carolina Battalion
Humphreys's Brigade
Brigadier General Benjamin G. Humphreys
13th Mississippi   17th Mississippi
18th Mississippi   21st Mississippi

Hood's Division
Major General John B. Hood (w)
Brigadier General E. McIver Law
Law's Brigade
Brigadier General E. McIver Law
Colonel James Sheffield
4th Alabama   15th Alabama
44th Alabama   47th Alabama
48th Alabama
Robertson's Brigade[28]
Brigadier General Jerome B. Robertson
3d Arkansas   1st Texas
4th Texas   5th Texas
Benning's Brigade
Brigadier General Henry L. Benning
2d Georgia   15th Georgia
17th Georgia   20th Georgia

RESERVE ARTILLERY
Major Felix H. Robertson
Barret's (Missouri) Battery
Le Gardeur's (Louisiana) Battery
Havis's (Georgia) Battery
Lumsden's (Alabama) Battery .
Massenburg's (Georgia) Battery

27. Army of Northern Virginia.
28. Served part of the time in Johnson's provisional division.

CAVALRY[29]

Major General Joseph Wheeler

Wharton's Division

Brigadier General John A. Wharton

First Brigade

Colonel C. C. Crews

Malone's (Alabama) Regiment

2d Georgia   3d Georgia

4th Georgia

Second Brigade

Colonel Thomas Harrison

3d Confederate   3d Kentucky

4th Tennessee   8th Texas

11th Texas

White's (Tennessee) Battery

Martin's Division

Brigadier General William T. Martin

First Brigade

Colonel John T. Morgan

1st Alabama   3d Alabama

51st Alabama   8th Confederate

Second Brigade

Colonel A. A. Russell

4th Alabama   1st Confederate

Wiggins's (Arkansas) Battery

FORREST'S CORPS

Brigadier General Nathan Bedford Forrest

Escort

Jackson's Company Tennessee Cavalry

Armstrong's Division[30]

Brigadier General Frank C. Armstrong

Armstrong's Brigade

Colonel James T. Wheeler

3d Arkansas   2d Kentucky

6th Tennessee   18th Tennessee Battalion

Forrest's Brigade

Colonel George C. Dibrell

4th Tennessee   8th Tennessee

29. From return of 31 August 1863 and reports.
30. From return of 31 August 1863 and reports.

9th Tennessee   10th Tennessee
11th Tennessee
Shaw's Battalion, O. P. Hamilton's Battalion, and
R. D. Allison's Squadron (Consolidated)
Huggins's (Tennessee) Battery
Morton's (Tennessee) Battery

Pegram's Division[31]
Brigadier General John Pegram
Davidson's Brigade
Brigadier General H. B. Davidson
1st Georgia   6th Georgia
6th North Carolina   10th Confederate[32]
Rucker's Tennessee Legion   Huwald's (Tennessee) Battery
Scott's Brigade
Colonel John S. Scott
Detachment of John H. Morgan's Command
1st Louisiana   2d Tennessee
5th Tennessee
Robinson's (Louisiana) Battery (one section)

31. Taken from Pegram's and Scott's reports and assignments, but the composition of the division is uncertain.
32. Temporarily detached from Scott's Brigade.

NOTES

ABBREVIATIONS

ADAH	Alabama Department of Archives and History
BGSU	Bowling Green State University
CCNMP	Chickamauga-Chattanooga National Military Park
CHS	Cincinnati Historical Society
CV	*Confederate Veteran*
CWC	Civil War Collection
CWTI	*Civil War Times Illustrated* Collection
DLC	Library of Congress
DU	Duke University
InHS	Indiana Historical Society
ISHL	Illinois State Historical Library
MDAH	Mississippi Department of Archives and History
MnHS	Minnesota Historical Society
MoHS	Missouri Historical Society
NCDAH	North Carolina Department of Archives and History
OHS	Ohio Historical Society
OR	*War of the Rebellion: A Compilation of the Official Records of the Union and Confederate Armies* (All references are to Series 1)
SHSP	*Southern Historical Society Papers*
TSLA	Tennessee State Library and Archives
TU	Tulane University
UNC	Southern Historical Collection, University of North Carolina
US	University of the South
USAMHI	United States Army Military History Institute
WRHS	Western Reserve Historical Society

CHAPTER ONE / YOU ARE THOROUGHLY OUTDONE

1. Daniel Harvey Hill, "Chickamauga — The Great Battle of the West," in *Battles and Leaders of the Civil War,* ed. Clarence Buell and Robert Johnson, 4 vols. (New York: Thomas Yoseloff, 1956), 3:639; Hal Bridges, *Lee's Maverick General, Daniel Harvey Hill* (New York: McGraw Hill, 1961), 190–93; William Piston, *Lee's Tarnished General: James Longstreet and His Place in Southern History* (Athens: University of Georgia Press, 1987), 62–64.

2. Quoted in Bridges, *Lee's Maverick General,* 190.

3. An unusual comment by Hill, since he actually ranked Stewart. Ezra Warner, author of *Generals in Gray,* suggested that Hill was confused in his recollections and actually was referring to Benjamin F. Cheatham, not Stewart. Cheatham was three numbers higher than Hill on the list of major generals and was then serving with the Army of Tennessee. Ezra Warner to Ken Bandy, March 1974, courtesy of Ken Bandy.

4. Hill, "Chickamauga," 638; Bridges, *Lee's Maverick General,* 181.

5. Thomas L. Connelly and Archer Jones, *The Politics of Command: Factions and Ideas in Confederate Strategy* (Baton Rouge: Louisiana State University Press, 1982), 52–55.

6. Steven E. Woodward, *Jefferson Davis and His Generals: The Failure of Confederate Command in the West* (Lawrence: University of Kansas Press, 1990), 5–6.

7. Polk to his daughter, 15 November 1863, Leonidas Polk Papers, University of the South.

8. Polk to R. W. Gibbes, 17 October 1863, Polk Papers, US.

9. William Polk, *Leonidas Polk, Bishop and General,* 2 vols. (New York: Longmans, Green, 1893), 2:287.

10. Grady McWhiney, *Braxton Bragg and the Confederate Defeat. Volume 1: Field Command* (New York: Columbia University Press, 1969), 27–28.

11. Richard Taylor, *Destruction and Reconstruction: Personal Experiences of the Late War* (New York: D. Appleton, 1879), 100.

12. Archer Anderson, *The Campaign and Battle of Chickamauga, an Address Delivered before the Virginia Division of the Army of Northern Virginia Association, at Their Annual Meeting, in the Capitol at Richmond, Virginia, October 25, 1881* (Richmond: William Ellis Jones Printers, 1881), 17.

13. Quoted in D. B. Morton, "Last Surviving Confederate Lieutenant General," *CV* 17, no. 2 (February 1909): 83.

14. Hill, "Chickamauga," 641, 643.

15. Gale to William Polk, 28 March 1882, Polk Papers, US.

16. Ferdinand Gross to Rosecrans, John Parkhurst to Rosecrans, and Arthur Ducat to Rosecrans, all written 28 February 1882; William Starke Rosecrans Papers, University of California at Los Angeles.

17. Henry Villard, *Memoirs of Henry Villard, Journalist and Financier, 1855–1900,* 2 vols. (Boston: Houghton Mifflin, 1904), 2:67; Theodore C. Smith, *The Life and Letters of James Abram Garfield,* 2 vols. (New Haven: Yale University Press, 1925), 1:282–83.

18. John P. Sanderson, letter diary, 27 September 1863, Ohio Historical Society; Hill, "Chickamauga," 638; Michael Fitch, *The Chattanooga Campaign, with Special Reference to Wisconsin's Participation Therein* (Madison: Wisconsin History Commission, 1911), 13; William D. Bickham, *Rosecrans' Campaign with the Fourteenth Army Corps, or the Army of the Cumberland: a Narrative of Personal Observations...* (Cincinnati: Moore, Wilstach, Keys, 1863), 28–29.

19. Peter Cozzens, *No Better Place to Die: The Battle of Stones River* (Urbana: University of Illinois Press, 1990), 17–18; John Fitch, *Annals of the Army of the Cumberland, Comprising Biographies, Descriptions of Departments, Accounts of Expeditions, Skirmishes, and Battles* (Philadelphia: J. B. Lippincott, 1863), 326–27.

20. William Shanks, *Personal Recollections of Distinguished Generals* (New York: Harper, 1866), 260–61; Jacob Cox, *Military Reminiscences of the Civil War*, 2 vols. (New York: Charles Scribner's Sons, 1900), 2:8–9.

21. Shanks, *Distinguished Generals*, 66–67; Sanderson, letter diary, 20 October 1863, OHS.

22. Rosecrans to Editors, *National Tribune*, 31 March 1870; Rosecrans to McCook, 8 November 1879, Rosecrans Papers, UCLA; Villard, *Memoirs*, 2:214.

23. *A Brief Historical Sketch of the "Fighting McCooks,"* Reprinted from the *Proceedings of the Scotch-Irish Society of America* (New York: Jampes Kempster Printing Company, n.d.), 1–6, 23.

24. David Lathrop, *The History of the Fifty-ninth Regiment Illinois Volunteers; or a Three Years' Campaign through Missouri, Arkansas, Mississippi, Tennessee and Kentucky, with a Description of the Country, Towns, Skirmishes and Battles...* (Indianapolis: Hall and Hutchinson, 1865), 192; Alfred Hough, *Soldier in the West: The Civil War Letters of Alfred Lacey Hough* (Philadelphia: University of Pennsylvania Press, 1957), 63.

25. Nadine Turchin, "'A Monotony Full of Sadness': The Diary of Nadine Turchin, May 1863–April 1864," ed. Mary Ellen McElligott, *Journal of the Illinois State Historical Society* 70, no. 1 (February 1977): 61; John Beatty, *The Citizen Soldier; or Memoirs of a Volunteer* (Cincinnati: Wilstach, Baldwin, 1879), 235–36; K. McCook-Knox, "Alexander McDowell McCook," unpublished biographical sketch in McCook Family Papers, DLC.

26. Shanks, *Personal Recollections*, 266; Cozzens, *No Better Place to Die*, 24.

27. Ezra Warner, *Generals in Blue: Lives of the Union Commanders* (Baton Rouge: Louisiana State University Press, 1964), 166.

28. Smith, *Life and Letters of Garfield*, 1:238–56.

29. Ibid., 268–69.

30. Ibid., 271–76.

31. Sanderson, letter diary, 15 October 1863, OHS; David Sloane Stanley, *Personal Memoirs of Major General D. S. Stanley, U.S.A.* (Cambridge: Harvard University Press, 1917), 131.

32. Smith, *Life and Letters of Garfield*, 1:276.

33. Francis McKinney, *Education in Violence: The Life of George H. Thomas and the History of the Army of the Cumberland* (Detroit: Wayne State University Press, 1961), 201–2.

34. George Wilson, "Wilder's Brigade. The Mounted Infantry in the Tullahoma-Chickamauga Campaigns," *National Tribune,* 12 October 1883.

35. Samuel C. Williams, "General John T. Wilder," *Indiana Magazine of History* 31, no. 3 (September 1935): 174–76; Arndt M. Stickles, *Simon Bolivar Buckner, Borderland Knight* (Chapel Hill: University of North Carolina Press, 1940), 201–2.

36. Wilder thus described the new rifle: "The Spencer magazine rifle, capable of firing a shot without drawing on the magazine, which held seven cartridges; the rifle carried an ounce bullet of fifty-two caliber in copper cartridge, and had a bayonet, and was a most formidable weapon, especially at short range, and would carry with accuracy a half mile." Wilder, "The Battle of Hoover's Gap. Paper of John T. Wilder . . . Read Before the Ohio Commandery of the Loyal Legion, November 4, 1908," in *Sketches of War History 1861–1865. Papers Prepared for the Commandery of the State of Ohio, Military Order of the Loyal Legion of the United States, 1903–1908* (Cincinnati: Monfort and Company, 1908), 169; Wilson, "Wilder's Brigade"; Glenn W. Sunderland, *Wilder's Lightning Brigade—And Its Spencer Repeaters* (Washington, Ill.: The Book Works, 1984), 28–29.

37. Henry M. Cist, *The Army of the Cumberland* (New York: Charles Scribner's Sons, 1882), 149–50; J. Cutler Andrews, *The North Reports the Civil War* (Pittsburgh: University of Pittsburgh Press, 1955), 438.

38. Abraham Lincoln, *The Collected Works of Abraham Lincoln,* ed. Roy P. Basler, 8 vols. (New Brunswick, N.J.: Rutgers University Press, 1953), 6:236; Herman Hattaway and Archer Jones, *How the North Won: A Military History of the Civil War* (Urbana: University of Illinois Press, 1983), 384–87.

39. Garfield to Rosecrans, 12 June 1863, James A. Garfield Papers, DLC; Rosecrans to Francis Darr, 26 November 1879, Rosecrans Papers, UCLA.

40. Chase to Garfield, 31 May 1863, and Garfield to Rosecrans, 12 June 1863, both in Garfield Papers, DLC; Rosecrans to Francis Darr, 26 November 1879, Rosecrans Papers, UCLA.

41. Quoted in Hattaway and Jones, *How the North Won,* 390–91.

42. Thomas Van Horne, *History of the Army of the Cumberland, Its Organization, Campaigns, and Battles,* 2 vols. (Cincinnati: Robert Clarke, 1875), 2:302–3; Stanley Horn, *The Army of Tennessee* (Norman: University of Oklahoma Press, 1952), 233–35.

43. Wilder, *Battle of Hoover's Gap,* 2–8; McKinney, *Education in Violence,* 211–12.

44. Polk, *Leonidas Polk,* 2:209–11; Cist, *Army of the Cumberland,* 161.

45. Polk, *Leonidas Polk,* 2:212–13; Horn, *Army of Tennessee,* 237.

46. Polk, *Leonidas Polk,* 2:214–15.

47. Charles Todd Quintard, *Doctor Quintard, Chaplain C.S.A. and Second Bishop of Tennessee, Being His Story of the War* (Sewanee, Tenn.: University Press, 1905), 87–88; Thomas Lawrence Connelly, *Autumn of Glory: The Army of Tennessee, 1862–1865* (Baton Rouge: Louisiana State University Press, 1971), 137.

48. Kate Cumming, *Gleanings from the Southland* (Birmingham, Ala.: Roberts and Son, 1896), 119.

Chapter Two / Golden Moments Are Passing

1. Cist, *Army of the Cumberland*, 170; Hattaway and Jones, *How the North Won*, 404, 426.

2. *OR*, 30, pt. 1, 50; E. T. Wells, "The Campaign and Battle of Chickamauga," *United Service* 16 (September 1896): 205; Gilbert E. Govan and James W. Livingood, *The Chattanooga Country, 1540-1976: From Tomahawks to TVA* (Knoxville: University of Tennessee Press, 1977), 167-68.

3. Govan and Livingood, *The Chattanooga Country*, 222; Robert Shackelton, "The Battlefield of Chickamauga," *Blue and Gray* 1 (1893): 488-89; *OR* 30, pt. 1, 50.

4. *Atlas of the Battlefields of Chickamauga, Chattanooga and Vicinity. Published . . . by the Chickamauga and Chattanooga National Park Commissions. Plate 1: General Topographical Map of the Theatre of Operations* (Washington: G.P.O., 1901); Rosecrans to Alexander McCook, 8 November 1879, Rosecrans Papers, UCLA; Thomas Green to Rachel Green, 30 September 1863, Civil War Miscellaneous Collection, USAMHI.

5. *OR* 30, pt. 1, 50, 169; Horn, *Army of Tennessee*, 237; McKinney, *Education in Violence*, 216-17.

6. Philip Henry Sheridan, *Personal Memoirs of P. H. Sheridan*, 2 vols. (New York: Charles L. Webster, 1888), 1:271-72.

7. Hattaway and Jones, *How the North Won*, 426, 435-36.

8. William M. Lamers, *The Edge of Glory: A Biography of General William S. Rosecrans, U.S.A.* (New York: Harcourt, Brace, and World, 1961), 295; Sanderson, letter diary, 16 and 24 August 1863, OHS.

9. Donn Piatt, *General George H. Thomas, a Critical Biography. With Concluding Chapters by Henry V. Boynton*. (Cincinnati: Robert Clarke, 1893), 370-71.

10. Ibid.

11. Rosecrans to McCook, 8 November 1879, Rosecrans Papers, UCLA; *OR* 30, pt. 1, 50; Glenn Tucker, *Chickamauga: Bloody Battle in the West* (Dayton, Ohio: Morningside, 1984), 401.

12. Quoted in Piatt, *Thomas*, 371.

13. Rosecrans to McCook, 8 November 1879, Rosecrans Papers, UCLA.

14. Andrews, *North Reports the Civil War*, 443; "Garfield – Rosecrans," *National Tribune*, 18 March 1882.

15. Society of the Army of the Cumberland, *Burial of General Rosecrans, Arlington Cemetery, May 17, 1902* (Cincinnati: Robert Clarke, 1903), 91-93.

16. John Hay, *Letters of John Hay and Extracts from Diary*, 3 vols. (Washington, D.C.: N.p., 1908), 2:77-78; Lincoln, *Collected Works*, 6:373.

17. *OR*, 30, pt. 1, 50; McKinney, *Education in Violence*, 217.

18. R. M. Collins, *Chapters from the Unwritten History of the War between the States; or, Incidents in the Life of a Confederate Soldier, in Camp, on the March, in the Great Battles, and in Prison* (St. Louis: Nixon-Jones Printing Company, 1893), 142-43; W. E. Preston, "Memoirs of the War, 1861-1865," 19-20, unpublished manuscript in the Thirty-third Alabama Infantry Papers, ADAH;

B. F. Sawyer, "Annals of the War: Chickamauga," Philadelphia *Weekly Times*, 13 March 1886.

19. St. John Richardson Liddell, *Liddell's Record*, ed. Nathaniel C. Hughes (Dayton, Ohio: Morningside, 1985), 131.

20. Connelly, *Autumn of Glory*, 148; Horn, *Army of Tennessee*, 239.

21. Liddell, *Liddell's Record*, 131.

22. Hill, "Chickamauga," 639; Thomas R. Hay to D. H. Hill, Jr., 17 June 1923, D. H. Hill, Jr., Papers, NCDAH; Statement of Archer Anderson, 16 October 1863, D. H. Hill Papers, NCDAH.

23. Hattaway and Jones, *How the North Won*, 442.

24. Longstreet to Wigfall, 18 August 1863, Louis T. Wigfall Family Papers, DLC; James Longstreet, *From Manassas to Appomattox, Memoirs of the Civil War in America* (Philadelphia: J. B. Lippincott, 1896), 433–34; Stickles, *Buckner, Borderland Knight*, 229.

25. Piston, *Lee's Tarnished General*, 65–66.

26. Polk to Hardee, 30 July 1863, Polk Papers, US; Hattaway and Jones, *How the North Won*, 442–43.

27. Horn, *Army of Tennessee*, 239–40.

28. Smith, *Life and Letters of Garfield*, 1:312.

29. OR 30, pt. 1, 50.

30. Govan and Livingood, *The Chattanooga Country*, 222; Wells, "Chickamauga," 206–7; OR 30, pt. 1, 48–49.

31. Wells, "Chickamauga," 208–9; Cist, *Army of the Cumberland*, 174.

32. Wells, "Chickamauga," 209.

33. OR 30, pt. 3, 48, 276, and pt. 4, 518–19.

34. William S. Rosecrans, "The Chattanooga Campaign," *National Tribune*, 6 March 1882.

35. Ibid.; OR 30, pt. 3, 36; Wells, "Chickamauga," 209.

36. OR 30, pt. 1, 51, and pt. 3, 36–38.

37. *Ninety-second Illinois Volunteers* (Freeport, Ill.: Journal Publishing House and Bookbindery, 1875), 95; Sunderland, *Wilder's Lightning Brigade*, 54; OR 30, pt. 3, 46.

38. Polk to Susan Rayner, 14 August 1863, Polk Papers, US; Hill, "Chickamauga," 640; Connelly, *Autumn of Glory*, 163–65.

CHAPTER THREE / GLAD TO BE A SOLDIER

1. Hay, *Letters and Extracts*, 2:82.

2. *Ninety-second Illinois*, 95–97; OR 30, pt. 1, 445; J. H. Fullerton, "Dates and Figures," 1, Historical Files, CCNMP.

3. W. M. Mercer Otey, "Operations of the Signal Corps," *CV* 8, no. 3 (March 1900): 129–30.

4. Cumming, *Gleanings from the Southland*, 119.

5. Williams, "General Wilder," 24; Robert Sparks Walker, "The Pyramids of Chickamauga: Brigadier General Preston Smith," Chattanooga *Sunday Times Magazine Section*, 2 August 1936, 5.

6. *OR* 30, pt. 1, 445, and pt. 3, 122; Arthur Middleton Manigault, *A Carolinian Goes to War: The Civil War Narrative of Arthur Middleton Manigault* (Columbia: University of South Carolina Press, 1983), 91; Henry Campbell, "Three Years in the Saddle. Journal of Events, Facts, and Incidents Connected with the Eighteenth Indiana Battery," 76–80, Henry Campbell Papers, Wabash College.

7. *OR* 30, pt. 1, 51, 445; Wells, "Chickamauga," 210.

8. *OR* 30, pt. 2, 27, and pt. 4, 560–61.

9. *OR* pt. 2, 27, 137; George Brent Journal, 21 August 1863, William J. Palmer Collection of Braxton Bragg Papers, Western Reserve Historical Society.

10. Connelly and Jones, *Politics of Command,* 135; *OR* 30, pt. 4, 529, 538, 547.

11. G. Moxley Sorrel, *Recollections of a Confederate Staff Officer* (New York: Neale, 1905), 202; Liddell, *Liddell's Record,* 134; Ezra Warner, *Generals in Gray: Lives of Confederate Commanders* (Baton Rouge: Louisiana State University Press, 1959), 203–4; Brent journal, 17 August 1863, Palmer Collection, WRHS.

12. *OR* 30, pt. 4, 531.

13. Manigault, *Carolinian Goes to War,* 123.

14. Lafayette McLaws to D. H. Hill, 25 January 1864, Hill Papers, NCDAH; J. F. Wheless, "Confederate Data: Reminiscences of the Battle of Chickamauga," 2–3, CWC, TSLA.

15. Manigault, *Carolinian Goes to War,* 92; Govan and Livingood, *The Chattanooga Country,* 219.

16. Horace Porter to his mother, 25 August 1863, Horace Porter Papers, DLC.

17. McKinney, *Education in Violence,* 220–21.

18. Ibid.; *OR* 30, pt. 3, 126–27.

19. McKinney, *Education in Violence,* 221; *OR* 30, pt. 1, 51; Alfred Pirtle, "Leaves from My Journal. A Brief Sketch of the Last Campaigns of Brigadier General William H. Lytle," 1–2, Lytle Family Papers, Cincinnati Historical Society.

20. McKinney, *Education in Violence,* 221; *OR* 30, pt. 1, 52.

21. Photograph 72.836: Pontoon Bridge, Bridgeport, Alabama, Army of the Cumberland Photograph Album, Special Collections Department, Chicago Public Library.

22. Pirtle, "Leaves from My Journal," 25, Lytle Family Papers, CHS; A. C. Kemper, "General W. H. Lytle," *National Tribune,* 5 July 1883; Whitelaw Reid, *Ohio in the War: Her Statesmen, Her Generals, and Soldiers,* 2 vols. (Cincinnati: Moore, Wilstach and Baldwin, 1868), 1:860–64.

23. Sheridan, *Memoirs,* 1:272–73; Pirtle, "Leaves from My Journal," 2, Lytle Family Papers, CHS; *OR* 30, pt. 3, 171.

24. Hans Christian Heg, *The Civil War Letters of Colonel Hans Christian Heg,* ed. Theodore C. Blegen (Northfield, Minn.: Norwegian-American Historical Association, 1936), 143–54.

25. Heg, *Civil War Letters,* 247–48; *OR* 30, pt. 1, 528–29, and pt. 3, 218; W. S. Burke, *Military History of Kansas Regiments During the War for the Suppression of the Great Rebellion* (Leavenworth, Kans.: W. S. Burke, 1868), 194–95.

26. Burke, *Military History of Kansas Regiments,* 195; *OR* 30, pt. 1, 496, pt. 3, 219, and pt. 4, 574.

27. James E. Love to Molly Wilson, 30 August 1863, James E. Love Papers, MoHS.

28. McKinney, *Education in Violence,* 222; *OR* 30, pt. 1, 246; Moses Walker, "A History of the First Brigade, Third Division, Fourteenth Army Corps during the Period in which Major General W. S. Rosecrans Commanded the Army of the Cumberland," George Thomas Papers, RG 94, National Archives.

29. *OR,* pt. 1, 52, 246, 270–71, 602.

30. *OR* 30, pt. 3, 234, 242; Smith, *Life and Letters of Garfield,* 1:316–17.

31. James P. Suiter diary, 5 September 1863, ISHL; William Bircher, *A Drummer Boy's Diary* (St. Paul: St. Paul Book and Stationery Company, 1889), 71–72; Heg, *Civil War Letters,* 243.

32. *Ninety-second Illinois,* 118; Horace Porter to his sister, 13 September 1863, Porter Papers, DLC; Heg, *Civil War Letters,* 242–43.

33. *OR* 30, pt. 1, 852, and pt. 3, 322–23; Wells, "Chickamauga," 210–11; McKinney, *Education in Violence,* 223.

34. Brent journal, 21–25 August 1863, Palmer Collection, WRHS; Connelly, *Autumn of Glory,* 158–64.

35. Brent journal, 27 August, 1863, Palmer Collection, WRHS; Bragg to E. T. Sykes, 8 February 1873, John F. H. Claiborne Papers, UNC; Breckinridge to Hill, 15 October 1863, Hill Papers, NCDAH; William C. Davis, *Breckinridge: Statesman, Soldier, Symbol* (Baton Rouge: Louisiana State University Press, 1973), 367–68; Frederick Joyce, "The Orphan Brigade at Chickamauga," *Southern Bivouac* 3 (1884/85): 29–32; John Jackman journal, 87, DLC.

36. Connelly, *Autumn of Glory,* 148; *OR* 30, pt. 2, 27.

37. Longstreet, *Manassas to Appomattox,* 433–35; Piston, *Lee's Tarnished General,* 64–68.

38. Brent journal, 27 August 1863, Palmer Collection, WRHS; *OR* 30, pt. 2, 27; Gilbert Kniffin, "On the Tennessee," Cincinnati *Commercial Gazette,* 8 September 1888.

39. Brent journal, 28 and 29 August, 1863, and Memorandum of Organization of Rosecrans's Army, 29 August 1863, both in Palmer Collection, WRHS; Liddell, *Liddell's Record,* 134–36; Manigault, *Carolinian Goes to War,* 92.

40. *OR* 30, pt. 2, 137, and pt. 4, 574; Brent journal, 29 August – 2 September, 1863, Palmer Collection, WRHS; Robert Shook, "Timely Information to General Bragg," *CV* 18, no. 7 (July 1910): 39.

41. Brent journal, 30 August–3 September 1863, Palmer Collection, WRHS; *OR* 30, pt. 4, 584.

42. Suiter diary, 7 September 1863, ISHL; F. W. Perry, "Chickamauga. Toilsome March of the Fourteenth Corps Over the Mountains," *National Tribune,* 28 June 1883; Pirtle, "Leaves from My Journal," 8–9, Lytle Family Papers, CHS; R. P. Findley, "The Story of a March," *Grand Army of the Republic War Papers, Papers Read before the Fred C. Jones Post, No. 401, Department of Ohio, G.A.R.* (Cincinnati: Fred C. Jones Post, No. 401, 1891), 362–63; Benjamin T. Smith, *Private Smith's Journal, Recollections of the Late War,* ed. Clyde Walton (Chicago: R. R. Donnelley and Sons, 1963), 86; Maurice Marcoot, *Five Years in the Sunny South, Reminiscences of Maurice Marcoot* (N.p., n.d.), 33; *OR* 30, pt. 3, 344.

43. Beatty, *Citizen Soldier*, 328; Pirtle, "Leaves from My Journal," 10, Lytle Family Papers, CHS.

44. Pirtle, "Leaves from My Journal," 10–11, Lytle Family Papers, CHS; William R. Carter, *History of the First Regiment of Tennessee Volunteer Cavalry in the Great War of the Rebellion, with the Armies of the Ohio and Cumberland, under Generals Morgan, Rosecrans, Thomas, Stanley and Wilson, 1862–1865* (Knoxville: Gaut-Ogden Company, 1902), 85–86.

45. *OR* 30, pt. 1, 602, and pt. 3, 414–16, 419–25, 455–58.

46. Ibid., pt. 1, 485, and pt. 3, 326, 345.

47. Ibid., pt. 1, 246; Wells, "Chickamauga," 212.

48. Stanley, *Memoirs*, 134–35, 158; *OR* 30, pt. 1, 53, 890–92.

49. Beatty, *Citizen Soldier*, 329–30; *OR* 30, pt. 1, 246, and pt. 3, 408–9, 444–45; William Wirt Calkins, *The History of the One Hundred and Fourth Regiment of Illinois Volunteer Infantry, War of the Great Rebellion, 1862–1865* (Chicago: Donohue and Henneberry, 1895), 314.

50. Liddell, *Liddell's Record*, 135–37; *OR* 30, pt. 4, 589.

51. Hill, "Chickamauga," 641.

52. Brent diary, 3–4 September, 1863, Palmer Collection, WRHS; *OR* 30, pt. 4, 596.

53. *OR* 30, pt. 4, 594.

54. Ibid., pt. 2, 21.

55. Ibid., pt. 4, 599–600; Andrews, *North Reports the Civil War*, 444–45.

56. *OR* 30, pt. 4, 607, 610–11 and pt. 2, 27.

57. Brent diary, 6 September 1863, Palmer Collection, WRHS; *OR* 30, pt. 4, 614.

58. Brent diary, 7 September 1863, Palmer Collection, WRHS; "Notes of Lieutenant W. B. Richmond, Aide-de-Camp to Lieutenant General Polk on Movement of the Army of Tennessee," 6 September 1863, Polk Papers, US; Connelly, *Autumn of Glory*, 172–73.

59. William W. Heartsill, *Fourteen Hundred and Ninety-one Days in the Confederate Army, a Journal Kept by W. W. Heartsill, for Four Years, One Month, and One Day* (Jackson, Tenn.: McCowat-Mercer Press, 1954), 147; Brent diary, 7 September 1863, Palmer Collection, WRHS; "Notes of W. B. Richmond," 7 September 1863, Polk Papers, US; Daniel Coleman diary, 101–2, UNC; Collins, *Unwritten History of the War*, 145.

60. Manuscript Recollections of George Washington Dillon, in Dillon Papers, TSLA; David Shires Myers Bodenhamer Memoirs, CWC, TSLA.

61. Hill, "Chickamauga," 642; Obituary of A. P. Stewart in Chattanooga *News*, 31 August 1908; "Notes of W. B. Richmond," 9 September 1863, Polk Papers, US.

62. See the account of Samuel C. Reid, *Great Battle of Chickamauga, a Concise History of Events from the Evacuation of Chattanooga to the Defeat of the Enemy* (Mobile: F. Titcomb, 1863), 3–4, for a similar appraisal. Reid was a correspondent for the Mobile *Tribune* and was with the Army of Tennessee during the campaign. For a differing view on the viability of holding Chattanooga, see Thomas Hay, "Campaign and Battle at Chickamauga," *Georgia Historical Quarterly* 7 (1923): 219–20.

63. Connelly, *Autumn of Glory,* 152–53.

64. OR 29, pt. 2, 699; Piston, *Lee's Tarnished General,* 68.

65. Harold B. Simpson, *Hood's Texas Brigade, Lee's Grenadier Guard* (Waco, Tex.: Texian Press, 1970), 297–99; Robert Clifford Black, *The Railroads of the Confederacy* (Chapel Hill: University of North Carolina Press, 1952), 187–88; D. Augustus Dickert, *History of Kershaw's Brigade, with Complete Rolls of Companies, Biographical Sketches, Incidents, Anecdotes, etc.* (Newberry, N.C.: Elbert H. Aull Company, 1899), 263–64.

66. Francis A. Burr, *The Great Battle of Chickamauga* (Memphis: Tracy Printing Company, 1883), 18–19.

67. Ibid., 19.

Chapter Four / Glimmer in the Twilight

1. Smith D. Atkins, *Chickamauga. Useless, Disastrous Battle. Talk by Smith D. Atkins, Opera House, Mendota, Illinois, February 22, 1907, at Invitation of Woman's Relief Corps, G.A.R.* (N.p., 1907), 3; *Wilder's Brigade Reunion. Effingham, Ill., September 17, 1909. Remarks by Smith D. Atkins, Late Colonel of the Ninety-second Illinois Volunteer Infantry (Mounted).* (N.p., 1909), 4–5.

2. *Ninety-second Illinois,* 100.

3. OR 30, pt. 3, 444, 459–60.

4. Ibid., 444, 479.

5. *Ninety-second Illinois,* 100.

6. OR 30, pt. 3, 482; McKinney, *Education in Violence,* 224.

7. OR 30, pt. 1, 53, and pt. 3, 481; Richard Johnson, "Chickamauga, Sketch of the Campaign and Famous Battle," *National Tribune,* 23 January 1896.

8. McKinney, *Education in Violence,* 227; James H. Wilson, "The Heros of the Great Rebellion," 225, unpublished manuscript in the James H. Wilson Papers, DLC; OR 30, pt. 3, 251, 345, 367, 479.

9. McKinney, *Education in Violence,* 227; OR 30, pt. 3, 488, 493; G. C. Kniffin to D. H. Hill, 26 August 1884, Hill Papers, Virginia State Library.

10. McKinney, *Education in Violence,* 227.

11. OR 30, pt. 3, 467–68.

12. Bircher, *A Drummer Boy's Diary,* 670–72; William H. Newlin, *A History of the Seventy-third Regiment of Illinois Infantry Volunteers, Its Services and Experiences in Camp, on the March, on the Picket and Skirmish Lines, and in Many Battles of the War, 1861–1865* (Springfield, Ill.: The Regimental Reunion Association, 1890), 205–17; Brent journal, 8–9 September 1863, Palmer Collection, WRHS.

13. *Ninety-second Illinois,* 101; Atkins, *Chickamauga,* 7; *OR,* 30, pt. 1, 629.

14. Bragg to his wife, 22 September 1863, Bragg Papers, MoHS.

15. OR 30, pt. 4, 522–23; Will T. Martin, "A Defense of Bragg's Conduct at Chickamauga," *Southern Historical Society Papers* 2 (1883): 203–4; Brent journal, 9 September 1863, Palmer Collection, WRHS.

16. OR 30, pt. 2, 27–28; Brent journal, 9 September 1863.

17. B. F. Sawyer, "Annals of the War: Chickamauga," Philadelphia *Weekly Times,*

13 March 1886; Marshall Wingfield, *General A. P. Stewart, His Life and Letters* (Memphis: Privately printed, 1954), 74.

18. Charles E. Nash, *Autobiographical Sketches of Gen. Pat Cleburne and Gen. T. C. Hindman, Together with Humorous Anecdotes and Reminiscences of the Late Civil War* (Little Rock: N.p., 1898), 7–70.

19. Manigault, *Carolinian Goes to War,* 93; OR 30, pt 2. 138, 292.

20. OR 30, pt. 2, 29, 138–39, 300.

21. Shanks, *Personal Recollections,* 293–94; Warner, *Generals in Blue,* 341–42; "In Memoriam: James Scott Negley," in *Society of the Army of the Cumberland. Thirtieth Reunion, Louisville, Kentucky, October 8, 9, 1901* (Cincinnati: Robert Clarke, 1902), 181–82.

22. OR 30, pt. 1, 271, 326, and pt. 3, 484, 509; Calkins, *One Hundred and Fourth Illinois,* 116–17; William D. Ward, "The Storm Breaks," 104, William D. Ward Recollections, DePauw University Archives.

23. McKinney, *Education in Violence,* 227; OR 30, pt. 3, 484.

24. George W. Skinner, *Pennsylvania at Chickamauga and Chattanooga. Ceremonies at the Dedication of the Monuments Erected by the Commonwealth of Pennsylvania to Mark the Positions of the Pennsylvania Commands Engaged in the Battles* (Harrisburg, Pa.: Wm. Stanley Ray, State Printer, 1900), 219.

25. Ibid.; Calkins, *One Hundred and Fourth Illinois,* 117; OR 30, pt. 1, 326, and pt. 3, 510–11; Hough, *Soldier in the West,* 138–39.

26. McKinney, *Education in Violence,* 227; OR 30, pt. 3, 510–11.

27. OR 30, pt. 3, 511; McKinney, *Education in Violence,* 227.

28. *Ninety-second Illinois,* 103; OR 30, pt. 1, 34–35.

29. Alexis Cope, *The Fifteenth Ohio Volunteers and Its Campaigns, War of 1861–1865* (Columbus, Ohio: Press of Edward T. Miller, 1916), 304–5; for an excellent discussion of the role of the "ubiquitous" Confederate deserter, see Albion Tourgee, *The Story of a Thousand, Being a History of the Service of the One Hundred Fifth Ohio Volunteer Infantry, in the War for the Union* (Buffalo: McGerald and Son, 1896), 212–13.

30. "Notes of W. B. Richmond," 10 September 1863, Polk Papers, US; OR 30, pt. 2, 29; Brent journal, 10 September 1863, Palmer Collection, WRHS.

31. Taylor Beatty diary, 10 September 1863, UNC; "Notes of W. B. Richmond," 10 September 1863, Polk Papers, US.

32. OR 30, pt. 2, 294, 300–301.

33. Martin, "Bragg's Conduct at Chickamauga," 204; Statement of Colonel David Urquhart, 22 November 1863, Palmer Collection, WRHS.

34. Beatty diary, 11 September, 1863, UNC.

35. Connelly, *Autumn of Glory,* 182–83; Beatty diary, 11 September 1863, UNC.

36. W. E. Preston, "Memoirs of the War," 20, unpublished manuscript in Thirty-third Alabama Papers, ADAH; Heartsill, *Fourteen Hundred and Ninety-one Days,* 148; Irving Buck, *Cleburne and His Command* (Dayton, Ohio: Morningside, 1982), 118.

37. Calkins, *One Hundred and Fourth Illinois,* 118–19; OR 30, pt. 1, 327.

38. OR 30, pt. 2, 295–96, 315; William M. Owen, *In Camp and Battle with*

the Washington Artillery of New Orleans, a Narrative of Events During the Late Civil War (Boston: Ticknor and Company, 1885), 271.

39. *OR* 30, pt. 2, 296, 316; Milton Preston Jarnagin Memoirs, 14–15, TSLA.

40. Jarnagin memoirs, 17, TSLA; *OR* 30, pt. 4, 636.

41. Beatty diary, 11 September 1863, UNC.

42. *OR* 30, pt. 2, 296.

43. Coleman diary, 105–7, UNC; Buck, *Cleburne and His Command*, 102; Calkins, *One Hundred and Fourth Illinois*, 120.

44. Jarnagin memoirs, TSLA 17; Martin, "Bragg's Conduct at Chickamauga," 205.

45. Beatty diary, 11 September 1863, UNC; Buck, *Cleburne and His Command*, 120; Manigault, *Carolinian Goes to War*, 94.

46. Benjamin Scribner, *How Soldiers Were Made; or, the War as I Saw It Under Buell, Rosecrans, Thomas, Grant and Sherman* (Chicago: Donohue and Henneberry, 1887), 140–41.

47. Calkins, *One Hundred and Fourth Illinois*, 121.

Chapter Five / A Ticklish Place

1. McKinney, *Education in Violence*, 227–28; *OR* 30, pt. 3, 545.

2. *OR* 30, pt. 3, 564–65.

3. Ibid., pt. 1, 53, 603, 630, 683.

4. Warner, *Generals in Blue*, 206, 626–27; W. Reid, *Ohio in the War*, 1:917.

5. *OR* 30, pt. 1, 630, 683.

6. Ibid., 53–54, and pt. 3, 543–45.

7. Luther Bradley Reminiscences, 13, Bradley Papers, USAMHI.

8. Sheridan, *Memoirs*, 1:275–76; Horace Cecil Fisher, *The Personal Experiences of Colonel Horace Newton Fisher, A Staff Officer's Story* (Boston: N.p., 1960), 79–80.

9. *OR* 30, pt. 1, 486, and pt. 3, 511.

10. Ibid. pt. 1, 54; Rosecrans, "The Chattanooga Campaign," *National Tribune*, 6 March 1882.

11. *OR* 30, pt. 3, 568, 586; Wells, "Chickamauga," 216–17.

12. *OR* 30, pt. 3, 568, 598, 602.

13. Ibid., 56, 523, 592, 840–41; Hattaway and Jones, *How the North Won*, 449; Rosecrans to the Editors, *National Tribune*, 31 March 1870.

14. Villard, *Memoirs*, 1:164; Charles A. Dana, *Recollections of the Civil War* (New York: Boughmans, 1898), 102–7; James H. Wilson, manuscript of his *Life of Dana*, 369–70, in Wilson Papers, DLC.

15. Dana, *Recollections*, 104–5.

16. Shanks, *Personal Recollections*, 263; Granger to Rosecrans, 6 June 1864, Rosecrans Papers, UCLA; Smith Atkins to Henry Cist, 18 March 1898, Abraham Lincoln Book Shop.

17. Horace Porter to his mother, 13 September 1863, Porter Papers, DLC; John Levering Recollections, Historical Files, CCNMP; Sanderson, letter diary, 12 September 1863, OHS.

18. McKinney, *Education in Violence*, 228; Dana, *Recollections*, 108–9.

19. Horn, *Army of Tennessee*, 253.

20. Connelly, *Autumn of Glory*, 186–87; "Notes of W. B. Richmond," 12 September 1863, Polk Papers, US.

21. *OR* 30, pt. 1, 711–12, 802; John M. Palmer, *Personal Recollections of John M. Palmer: The Story of an Earnest Life* (Cincinnati: Robert Clarke, 1901), 172.

22. Palmer, *Personal Recollections*, 171–72; *OR* 30, pt. 1, 711, 723–25.

23. Palmer, *Personal Recollections*, 172.

24. "Notes of W. B. Richmond," 12 September 1863, Polk Papers, US; *OR* 30, pt. 2, 30; Connelly, *Autumn of Glory*, 186–87.

25. "Notes of W. B. Richmond," 12 September 1863, Polk Papers, US; *OR* 30, pt. 1, 446–47, pt. 3, 45; Polk, *Polk*, 2:226–27; Connelly, *Autumn of Glory*, 187.

26. *OR* 30, pt. 3, 44–45.

27. Liddell, *Liddell's Record*, 139–40.

28. "Notes of W. B. Richmond," 12 September 1863, Polk Papers, US.

29. *OR* 30, pt. 2, 30–31, and pt. 3, 49–50; Hill, "Chickamauga," 644–45.

30. "Notes of W. B. Richmond," 13 September 1863, Polk Papers, US; Wheless, "Data," 3–4.

31. Wheless, "Data," 4; "Notes of W. B. Richmond," 13 September 1863, Polk Papers, US; Jefferson Davis, *Jefferson Davis, Constitutionalist: His Letters, Papers and Speeches*, ed. Dunbar Rowland, 10 vols. (Jackson, Miss.: Mississippi Department of Archives and History, 1923), 6:78.

32. Brent journal, 13 September 1863, Palmer Collection, WRHS; "Notes of W. B. Richmond," 13 September 1863, and William D. Gale to his wife, 15 September 1863, both in Polk Papers, US.

33. *OR* 30, pt. 1, 852.

34. Brent journal, 13 September 1863, Palmer Collection, WRHS; Hill, "Chickamauga," 645.

35. *OR* 30, pt. 3, 589.

36. Eugene Marshall diary, 12 November 1863, Eugene Marshall Papers, DU.

37. Carter, *First Tennessee Cavalry*, 89–90; *OR* 30, pt. 1, 918.

38. *OR* 30, pt. 1, 918.

39. Polk, *Polk*, 2:230; Brent journal, 15 September 1863, Palmer Collection of Bragg Papers, WRHS.

40. Hill, "Chickamauga," 645–46.

41. McKinney, *Education in Violence*, 229; *OR* 30, pt. 3, 599, 603; J. Hill to Rosecrans, 1 March 1882, Rosecrans Papers, UCLA.

42. *OR* 30, pt. 3, 628.

43. Newlin, *Seventy-third Illinois*, 218–19; *OR* 30, pt. 3, 629.

44. *OR* 30, pt. 3, 629.

45. Ibid., 628–29, 648; Pirtle, "Leaves from My Journal," 36–37, Lytle Family Papers, CHS; Levi Wagner Reminiscences, 274, *CWTI* Collection, USAMHI.

46. Washington L. Gammage, *The Camp, the Bivouac, and the Battlefield, Being a History of the Fourth Arkansas Regiment* (Little Rock: Southern Press, 1958), 90; John T. Goodrich, "Gregg's Brigade in the Battle of Chickamauga," *CV* 22, no. 6 (June 1914): 264; Connelly, *Autumn of Glory*, 192; *OR* 30, pt. 1, 169.

47. Hay, "Campaign and Battle at Chickamauga," 224; Brent journal, 15 September 1863, Palmer Collection of Bragg Papers, WRHS; Polk, *Polk*, 231.

48. *OR* 30, pt. 4, 657; Brent journal, 16 September 1863, Palmer Collection of Bragg Papers, WRHS.

49. *OR* 30, pt. 1, 249. Edward E. Tinney, "The Families of Chickamauga Battlefield," manuscript in Historical Files, CCNMP; Federal Writers' Project, WPA, *Georgia: A Guide to Its Towns and Countryside* (Athens: University of Georgia Press, 1940), 437–39; Davidson, *The Tennessee*, 2:151; Govan and Livingood, *The Chattanooga Country*, 75–97; James Alfred Sartrain, *History of Walker County Georgia*, *Volume 1* (Dalton, Ga.: A. J. Showalter, 1932), 3–4.

50. Sanderson, letter diary, 16 September 1863, OHS; John A. Kane, "From Chickamauga to Chattanooga, the Battlefield Account of Sergeant John M. Kane," *East Tennessee Historical Society Publications* 45 (1973): 100; Francis Arthur Green, *The Witness of a House* (Chickamauga: Gordon-Lee House, 1984), 1–2, 11, 41.

51. Brent journal, 17 September 1863, Palmer Collection of Bragg Papers, WRHS; *OR* 30, pt. 3, 660, 662.

52. Shanks, *Personal Recollections*, 271; J. T. Woods manuscript notes on Chickamauga, in Laurence M. Strayer Collection of J. T. Woods papers.

53. Rosecrans to J. T. Woods, 15 February 1882, Strayer Collection.

54. Robert M. Rogers, *The One Hundred Twenty-fifth Regiment Illinois Volunteer Infantry. Attention Battalion!* (Champaign, Ill.: Gazette Printing Company, 1882), 75–76; Nixon Stewart, *Dan McCook's Regiment, Fifty-second O.V.I., a History of the Regiment* (Alliance: Review Print., 1900), 60; Charles Partridge, *History of the Ninety-sixth Regiment Illinois Volunteer Infantry* (Chicago: Brown, Pettibone and Company, 1887), 167.

55. *OR* 30, pt. 3, 668; Sanderson, letter diary, 16 September 1863, OHS.

56. Robert Minty, *Remarks of Brevet Major General R. H. G. Minty Made September 18, 1895 at the Dedication of the Monument Erected to the Fourth Michigan Cavalry, at Reed's Bridge, Chickamauga National Park* (Ogden, Utah: Brantley Paper Company, 1896), 3; Joseph Vale, *Minty and the Cavalry, a History of Cavalry Campaigns in the Western Armies* (Harrisburg, Pa.: Edwin K. Meyers, 1886), 219–20.

57. Simpson, *Hood's Texas Brigade*, 302–4; Goodrich, "Gregg's Brigade," 264; Dickert, *History of Kershaw's Brigade*, 264; John C. West, *A Texan in Search of a Fight* (Waco, Tex.: Texiana Press, 1961), 111.

58. *OR* 30, pt. 1, 498, and pt. 3, 710–11, 725.

59. Ibid., pt. 1, 55; 248, 487, 892; Stanley, *Memoirs*, 158.

60. *OR* 30, pt. 1, 859, and pt. 2, 471, 531; John Lindsley, *The Military Annals of Tennessee. Confederate. First Series: Embracing a Review of Military Operations, with Regimental Histories and Memorial Rolls* (Nashville: J. M. Lindsley, 1886), 450; William E. Sloan diary, 46, CWC, TSLA.

61. Minty, *Remarks of Brevet Major General Minty*, 3; *OR* 30, pt. 1, 445.

62. Brent journal, 17 September 1863, Palmer Collection of Bragg Papers, WRHS; *OR* 30, pt. 4, 663.

63. The late summer and autumn of 1863 saw wild extremes of weather. In mid-August, Minnesota shivered through freezing temperatures that killed corn and left a sheet of ice over the fields. A heat wave followed in mid-September from the plains states down into northern Georgia, but temperatures began dropping rapidly from the sixteenth to the eighteenth. By 18 September, the Midwest lay under a general frost that fast worked its way south, and snow swept the plains just one month later. Tucker, *Chickamauga*, 411.

64. Louis A. Simmons, *The History of the Eighty-fourth Regiment Illinois Volunteers* (Macomb, Ill., Hampton Brothers, 1866), 82; Judson Bishop, *The Story of a Regiment, Being a Narrative of the Service of the Second Regiment, Minnesota Veteran Volunteer Infantry, in the Civil War of 1861–1865* (St. Paul: N.p., 1890), 96.

65. Anderson, *Campaign and Battle of Chickamauga*, 19.

66. Simmons, *Eighty-fourth Illinois*, 82.

CHAPTER SIX / SOUNDS OF ILL OMEN

1. See Charles M. Cummings's *Yankee Quaker, Confederate General: The Curious Career of Bushrod Rust Johnson* (Rutherford, N.J.: Fairleigh Dickinson University Press, 1971) for an excellent biography of this most unusual general officer; Tracy M. Kegley, "Bushrod Rust Johnson, Soldier and Teacher," *Tennessee Historical Quarterly* 7 (1948): 249–53.

2. OR 30, pt. 2, 451.

3. Ibid., 31.

4. Connelly, *Autumn of Glory*, 197.

5. Vale, *Minty and the Cavalry*, 224.

6. Skinner, *Pennsylvania at Chickamauga*, 303, 309.

7. Thomas Berry, *Four Years with Morgan and Forrest* (Oklahoma City: Harlow-Ratliff Company, 1914), 160; OR 30, pt. 2, 452; Skinner, *Pennsylvania at Chickamauga*, 309.

8. Skinner, *Pennsylvania at Chickamauga*, 309; OR 30, pt. 2, 452; Vale, *Minty and the Cavalry*, 226.

9. Minty, *Remarks of Brevet Major General Minty*, 276–77; Vale, *Minty and the Cavalry*, 226; OR, pt. 2, 452.

10. OR 30, pt. 1, 447, 922; Minty, *Remarks of Brevet Major General Minty*, 277; Vale, *Minty and the Cavalry*, 233–34; Richard Robbins Recollections, 4, unpublished manuscript in Michigan Historical Collections, University of Michigan.

11. OR 30, pt. 1, 923, pt. 2, 452–53, 472; Vale, *Minty and the Cavalry*, 226–27, 234.

12. Sunderland, *Wilder's Brigade*, 71; Theodore Petzoldt, *My War Story, As Told Fifty Years After the War to Tracy B. Caswell at Denver, Colorado, 1911–1913* (Portland, Ore.: N.p., 1917), 99–100.

13. Benjamin McGee, *History of the Seventy-second Indiana Volunteer Infantry* (Lafayette, Ind.: S. Vatter and Company, 1882), 168; OR 30, pt. 1, 447.

14. Liddell, *Liddell's Record*, 137.

15. Edward T. Sykes, "Walthall's Brigade, a Cursory Sketch with Personal Experiences of Walthall's Brigade, Army of Tennessee, C.S.A., 1862–1865," *Publications of the Mississippi Historical Society, Centenary Series* 1 (1916): 486–87; "General Walthall," *Illinois Central Magazine* 4, no. 8 (February 1916): 9–12; Bragg to Sykes, 8 February 1873, J. T. Claiborne Papers, UNC.

16. Alan Griest Journal, 101, Harrisburg CWRT Collection, USAMHI; J. N. Abbott, "Opening of Chickamauga Fight, *National Tribune,* 9 April 1914; John H. Freeman diary, 18 September 1863, CWC, TSLA; OR 30, pt. 2, 272, 277, 279, 285.

17. A lunette is a type of military fieldwork that has two projecting faces and parallel flanks.

18. Campbell journal, 101–2, Wabash College; OR 30, pt. 1, 447, 466, and pt. 2, 272.

19. OR, pt. 2, 281, 285.

20. John Dyer, *The Gallant Hood* (Indianapolis: Bobbs-Merrill, 1950), 200–202; John Bell Hood, *Advance and Retreat. Personal Experiences in the United States and Confederate States Armies* (Philadelphia: Press of Burke and M'Fetridge, 1880), 60–61.

21. OR 30, pt. 2, 31–32; Hood, *Advance and Retreat,* 61.

22. Robbins Recollections, 4, Michigan Historical Collections; OR, 30, pt. 1, 923, and pt. 2, 472.

23. Minty, *Remarks of Brevet Major General Minty,* 278.

24. OR 30, pt. 1, 447; Sunderland, *Wilder's Brigade,* 73; Petzoldt, *My War Story,* 99.

25. McGee, *Seventy-second Indiana,* 169–70.

26. Joseph Cumming Recollections, 44, UNC.

27. Freeman diary, 18 September 1863, CWC, TSLA; Cumming Recollections, 44, UNC; OR 30, pt. 2, 357; Bromfield L. Ridley, Jr., "Southern Side at Chickamauga, Article I," *CV* 6, no. 9 (September 1898): 408.

28. Minty, *Remarks of Brevet Major General Minty,* 278; McGee, *Seventy-second Indiana,* 170; *Indiana at Chickamauga, 1863–1900. A Report of the Indiana Commissioners, Chickamauga National Military Park* (Indianapolis: Sentinal Print Company, 1900), 205.

29. OR 30, pt. 1, 823, 832, and pt. 2, 452, 524; *Indiana at Chickamauga,* 205; Petzoldt, *My War Story,* 100.

30. McGee, *Seventy-second Indiana,* 172.

31. OR 30, pt. 1, 114, 605.

32. Ibid., 55.

33. Ibid., 114–116, 248, 328, 498, 605.

34. Ibid., 66, 860; J. T. Woods, *Steedman and His Men at Chickamauga* (Toledo: Blade Printing and Paper Company, 1876), 20–21.

35. OR 30, pt. 1, 171–72, 328, 336–37; Hough, *Soldier in the West,* 347; Palmer, *Personal Recollections,* 174–75.

36. Heg, *Civil War Letters,* 245–46.

37. Pirtle, "Leaves from My Journal," 50–52, Lytle Family Papers, CHS.

38. Chauncey A. Castle, "Comrade Castle's Address," in *Minutes of Proceedings of the Fourteenth Annual Reunion, Survivors Seventy-third Regiment Illinois Infantry Volunteers, Held Afternoon and Evening, Wednesday, September 27, 1900.* (N.d., n.p.), 11.

39. Robert L. Kimberly, *The Forty-first Ohio Veteran Volunteer Infantry in the War of the Rebellion, 1861–1865* (Cleveland: W. R. Smellie, 1897), 59; OR 30, pt. 1, 336–37.

40. Bishop, *Second Minnesota*, 97; William W. Lyle, *Lights and Shadows of Army Life; or, Pen Pictures from the Battlefield, the Camp, and the Hospital* (Cincinnati: R. W. Carroll, 1865), 287; George Lewis, *The Campaigns of the One Hundred Twenty-fourth Ohio Volunteer Infantry* (Akron: Werner, 1894), 53; Scribner, *How Soldiers Were Made*, 143.

41. Simmons, *Eighty-fourth Illinois*, 86–87.

42. Pirtle, "Leaves from My Journal," 52, Lytle Family Papers, CHS.

43. Sanderson, letter diary, 18 September 1863, OHS.

44. Connelly, *Autumn of Glory*, 199–200; Anderson, *Campaign and Battle of Chickamauga*, 403–4; OR 30, pt. 2, 31, 51, 239, 247, 357; Hill, "Chickamauga," 649.

Chapter Seven / Withdraw If Not Too Late

1. James T. Holmes, *52d O.V.I., Then and Now* (Columbus, Ohio: Berlin Print Company, 1898), 78–79.

2. OR 30, pt. 1, 122–24, 871; Allen Fahnestock to Henry Boynton, 24 February 1894, Eighty-sixth Illinois File, CCNMP.

3. G. M. Pease, "Chickamauga. The Part Taken by the Sixty-Ninth Ohio and McCook's Brigade," *National Tribune*, 3 July 1890; William Rea, "Roasted Bacon at Bridge," *National Tribune*, 15 October 1914.

4. David Magee to Henry Boynton, 23 February 1894, and William Faulkner to Boynton, 7 April 1894, both in Eighty-sixth Illinois File, CCNMP; OR 30, pt. 1, 875–78.

5. OR 30, pt. 1, 124; John Mitchell to J. T. Woods, 25 July 1876, Strayer Collection; Woods, *Steedman and His Men*, 26; J. T. Woods, "Chickamauga," unpublished manuscript dated 25 October 1883, Strayer Collection.

6. OR 30, pt. 1, 274–75, 400; "Few Survivors of Civil War Days Still Live in Vicinity of Chickamauga Battlefield," *Chattanooga News*, 22 September 1893.

7. J. T. Woods, "Chickamauga," manuscript dated 25 October 1883, and Mitchell to Woods, 25 July 1876, both in Strayer Collection; Woods, *Steedman and His Men*, 26–27; OR 30, pt. 1, 249.

8. Faulkner to Boynton, 7 April 1894; Jay Minnich, "Jay's Mill," 25, unpublished manuscript in Civil War Papers, Reminiscences: Army of Tennessee, TU; Gustave Huwald to unknown addressee, 7 October 1866, in James Nutt Papers, UNC; G. W. R. Bell, "Reminiscences of Chickamauga," CV 12, no. 2 (February 1904): 71; Rea, "Roasted Bacon at Bridge."

9. Magee to Boynton, 23 February 1894, Eighty-sixth Illinois File, CCNMP; OR 30, pt. 1, 873–80.

10. Bell, "Reminiscences of Chickamauga," 71; *OR* 30, pt. 2, 528.

11. I. B. Walker, "Chickamauga. Going into Action with Hands Full of Bacon and Coffee," *National Tribune*, 2 July 1891; John Chase, *History of the Fourteenth Ohio Regiment, O.V.V.I., from the Beginning of the War in 1861 to Its Close in 1865* (Toledo: St. John Printing House, 1881), 47.

12. "In Memoriam: General J. T. Croxton," in *Society of the Army of the Cumberland. Eighth Reunion, Columbus, 1874* (Cincinnati: Robert Clarke, 1875), 172-74.

13. I. B. Walker, "Chickamauga"; Peter B. Kellenberger to Addison A. Pollard, 15 November 1863, Peter B. Kellenberger Civil War File, InHS; *OR* 30, pt. 1, 415; Tucker, *Chickamauga*, 131.

14. Jay Minnich to J. A. Chalaron, n.d., and Minnich, "Jay's Mill," 59-61, both in Civil War Papers, Reminiscences: Army of Tennessee, TU; Curtis Green, "Sixth Georgia Cavalry at Chickamauga," *CV* 8, no. 7 (July 1900): 324.

15. *OR* 30, pt. 2, 528; Huwald to unknown addressee, 7 October 1866, Nutt Papers, UNC.

16. Jeremiah Donahower, "Narrative of the Civil War, Volume 2," 106-7, in Jeremiah Donahower Papers, MnHS; Bishop, *Second Minnesota*, 98; *OR* 30, pt. 1, 400, 428; W. Reid, *Ohio in the War*, 1:890.

17. Wells, "Chickamauga," 221; John Wyeth, "Appearance and Characteristics of Forrest, *CV* 4, no. 2 (February 1896): 43; H. B. Clay, "Concerning the Battle of Chickamauga," *CV* 13, no. 2 (February 1905): 72; Cumming Recollections, 45, UNC; *OR* 30, pt. 2, 240, 248.

18. Wheless, "Data," 5; Brent diary, 19 September 1863, Palmer Collection, WRHS.

19. Jay Minnich, "Liddell's Division at Chickamauga," *CV* 13, no. 1 (January 1905): 24; *OR* 30, pt. 1, 416, 422, pt. 2, 51, 248; John Morton, *The Artillery of Nathan Bedford Forrest, "Wizard of the Saddle"* (Nashville: Publishing House of M. E. Church, South, 1909), 117.

20. Donahower, "Narrative, Volume 2," 112-13, Donahower Papers, MnHS; Alexis H. Reed diary, 19 September 1863, Second Minnesota File, CCNMP; *OR* 30, pt. 1, 428, 432, 434, and pt. 2, 524.

21. Moses Walker, "History of the First Brigade," Thomas Papers, RG 94, National Archives; *OR* 30, pt. 1, 400, 408.

22. Minnich to Chalaron, undated letter, Civil War Papers, Reminiscences: Army of Tennessee, TU; Huwald to unknown addressee, 6 October 1866, Nutt Papers, UNC; Green, "Sixth Georgia Cavalry at Chickamauga," 324.

23. *OR* 30, pt. 1, 416, 418, 422, 571, and pt. 2, 248; Minnich, "Jay's Mill," 12-14, Civil War Papers, Reminiscences: Army of Tennessee, TU.

24. Freeman Cleaves, *Rock of Chickamauga: The Life of General George H. Thomas* (Norman: University of Oklahoma Press, 1948), 158-59.

25. Sanderson, letter diary, 19 September 1863, OHS.

26. *OR* 30, pt. 1, 124-25, 250.

27. Ibid., 124-25, 713, 982; Ebenezer Hannaford, *The Story of a Regiment, a History of the Campaigns, and Associations in the Field, of the Sixth Regiment, Ohio Volunteer Infantry* (Cincinnati: By the Author, 1868), 453-54.

28. *OR* 30, pt. 1, 73.

29. Sidney Johnson, *Texans Who Wore the Gray* (Tyler, Tex.: N.p., 1907), 73; Warner, *Generals in Gray*, 81.

30. Minnich to Chalaron, undated letter, Civil War Papers, Reminiscences: Army of Tennessee, TU; Donahower, "Narrative, Volume 2," 114, Donahower Papers, MnHS; *OR* 30, pt. 1, 407–8, 428, 432; Morton, *Artillery of Forrest*, 117; Frank Smith to Charles Boynton, 2 May 1892, Battery I, Fourth United States Artillery File, CCNMP; John Stevens, "Chickamauga: A Wartime Letter from an Indiana Boy," *National Tribune*, 28 May 1908; Morton Hunter, "Battle of Chickamauga. The Part Taken by the Eighty-Second Indiana — Address Delivered by General Morton C. Hunter at Columbus, Indiana, October 7, 1887," Bloomington *Telephone*, 14 October 1887; Judson Bishop, *Van Derveer's Brigade at Chickamauga* (St. Paul: N.p., 1903), 10–11.

31. G. W. Miller, "The Thirty-first Ohio at Chickamauga," *National Tribune*, 21 February 1907; S. A. McNeil, "At Chickamauga," *National Tribune*, 14 April 1887.

32. Lewis Hosea, "The Regular Brigade of the Army of the Cumberland," in *Sketches of War History, 1861–1865. Papers Prepared for the Ohio Commandery of the Loyal Legion of the United States*, 6 vols. (Cincinnati: Robert Clarke Company, 1903), 5:328–29.

33. *OR* 30, pt. 1, 319; Henry Freeman, "Chickamauga," 1, Henry B. Freeman Papers, Wyoming Historical Society.

34. *OR* 30, pt. 2, 248–49.

35. John M. Johnston, "At Chickamauga. A Soldier's Story of the Battle," Lancaster *New Era*, 10 September 1892; *OR* 30, pt. 1, 275, 299–300, 304–5.

36. Scribner, *How Soldiers Were Made*, 143–44; *OR* 30, pt. 1, 293, 295, 297; August Bratnober diary, 19 September 1863, Tenth Wisconsin File, CCNMP.

Chapter Eight / They Are Coming

1. Sanderson, letter diary, 19 September 1863, OHS; *OR* 30, pt. 1, 534–35; R. Johnson, "Chickamauga," *National Tribune*, 23 January 1896.

2. "Few Survivors of Civil War Days Still Live in Vicinity of Chickamauga Battlefield," Chattanooga *News*, 22 September 1893; Tinney, "Families of Chickamauga Battlefield," 28; Sanderson, letter diary, 19 September 1863, OHS; Dana, *Recollections*, 111–12.

3. *OR* 30, pt. 1, 56, 76, 487, 713, 982; Crittenden to Garfield, 11:00 A.M. 19 September 1863, Rosecrans Papers, UCLA.

4. Anderson, *Campaign and Battle of Chickamauga*, 25–26; Connelly, *Autumn of Glory*, 203; *OR* 30, pt. 2, 78.

5. *OR* 30, pt. 2, 252, 258, 261, 273, 277–81; J. D. Smith, "Walthall's Brigade at Chickamauga," *CV* 7, no. 10 (October 1904): 483.

6. Scribner, *How Soldiers Were Made*, 145–46; Bratnober diary, 19 September 1863, Tenth Wisconsin File, CCNMP; *OR* 30, pt. 1, 290.

7. *OR* 30, pt. 1, 290, and pt. 2, 263; Bratnober diary, 19 September 1863, Tenth Wisconsin File, CCNMP; Henry Perry, *History of the Thirty-eighth Regiment*

Indiana Volunteer Infantry (Palo Alto: F. A. Stuart, 1906), 88–89; John T. Rone, "First Arkansas Brigade at Chickamauga," *CV* 8, no. 4 (April 1905): 166.

8. *OR*, pt. 1, 293, 295, and pt. 2, 273, 283, 285; William H. Kell, *Military Record of Lieutenant Colonel William H. Kell* (N.p., n.d.), 19; Scribner, *How Soldiers Were Made*, 145–48, 154.

9. Johnston, "At Chickamauga. A Soldier's Story of the Battle"; *OR* 30, pt. 1, 299–300, 304–5; Rone, "First Arkansas Brigade at Chickamauga," 167.

10. *OR* 30, pt. 1, 309, 318, 324, and pt. 2, 273, 283; R. A. Jarman, "History of Company K, Twenty-Seventh Mississippi Infantry," Aberdeen *Examiner*, 28 February 1890.

11. Freeman recollections, 7–8, Wyoming Historical Society.

12. *OR* 30, pt. 1, 316, 319; A. B. Carpenter to "Dear Uncle," 29 September 1863, A. B. Carpenter Papers, Yale.

13. Bishop, *Van Derveer's Brigade*, 11–12; S. P. Zehring, "Chickamauga: The Conspicuous Gallantry of Van Derveer's Brigade," *National Tribune*, 13 October 1887; *OR* 30, pt. 1, 431, 433; Donahower, "Narrative, Volume 2," 115, Donahower Papers, MnHS.

14. Stevens, "Chickamauga: A Wartime Letter"; *OR* 30, pt. 1, 433; Morton Hunter, "Chickamauga," *National Tribune*, 21 May 1888.

15. Albert Dickennan, "The Ninth Ohio at Chickamauga," *National Tribune*, 13 October 1906.

16. H. H. Hill, "The Second Minnesota: Reminiscences of Four Years' Service at the Front," *National Tribune*, 13 July 1899; Bishop, *Van Derveer's Brigade*, 12; Donahower, "Narrative, Volume 2," 117, Donahower Papers, MnHS; *OR* 30, pt. 1, 408, 428; Bishop, *Second Minnesota*, 99–100.

17. A. H. Reed, "Chickamauga. The Fourteenth Corps' Magnificent Stand Against Overwhelming Forces," *National Tribune*, 21 September 1916.

18. *OR* 30, pt. 2, 524; Donahower, "Narrative, Volume 2," 117–19, Donahower Papers, MnHS; Bishop, *Van Derveer's Brigade*, 12; Bishop to Arnold McMahan, 10 March 1889, William J. Sullivan Collection of Twenty-first Ohio Infantry Papers, Bowling Green State University.

19. *OR* 30, pt. 1 428–29, 433; Donahower, "Narrative, Volume 2," 120–21, Donahower Papers, MnHS; Reed diary, 19 September 1863, Second Minnesota File, CCNMP.

20. *OR* 30, pt. 1, 416–19, 422, and pt. 2, 258, 261, 263, 266.

21. Ibid., pt. 1, 416–17, 422.

CHAPTER NINE / WE SHALL SOON BE IN IT

1. McKinney, *Education in Violence*, 236; *OR* 30, pt. 1, 126–27.

2. Warner, *Generals in Blue*, 254; Wells, "Chickamauga," 221; *OR* 30, pt. 1, 534–35.

3. I. K. Young, "Chickamauga. The Battle as I Saw It," *National Tribune*, 22 April 1886; *OR* 30, pt. 1, 535, 538, 543; John C. Wysong diary, 19 September 1863, Civil War File of John C. Wysong, InHS.

4. Allen Buckner, *Memoirs of Allen Buckner* (Lansing: Michigan Alcohol and Drug Information Foundation, 1982), 1–8, 18; Wells, "Chickamauga," 222.

5. *OR* 30, pt. 1, 713, and pt. 3, 741; Richard O'Connor, *Ambrose Bierce: A Biography* (Boston: Little, Brown, 1967), 1–7; quotations from his works are from *The Collected Writings of Ambrose Bierce* (New York: Citadel Press, 1946).

6. Cumming Recollections, 30–46, UNC.

7. *OR* 30, pt. 4, 240; Warner, *Generals in Gray*, 47; Marcus J. Wright, "A Sketch of the Life and Character of General Benjamin Franklin Cheatham of Tennessee," unidentified newspaper article in the Marcus Wright Papers, UNC.

8. *OR* 30, pt. 2, 78; William R. Talley autobiography, 29, Havis's Georgia Battery File, CCNMP; Anderson, *Campaign and Battle of Chickamauga*, 27–28.

9. *OR* 30, pt. 1, 417, 419, 422, and pt. 2, 84, 87, 89.

10. Charles D. Stewart, "A Bachelor General," *Wisconsin Magazine of History* 17 (1933): 131–45; Villard, *Memoirs*, 1:215.

11. Cope, *Fifteenth Ohio*, 319; Wells, "Chickamauga," 221.

12. *OR* 30, pt. 1, 538, 543, and pt. 2, 84; William Stahl diary, 19 September 1863, Richard F. Mann Collection, USAMHI.

13. William Hazen, *A Narrative of Military Service* (Boston: Ticknor, 1885), 127; *OR* 30, pt. 2, 107.

14. Lewis, *One Hundred Twenty-four Ohio*, 57–59; *OR* 30, pt. 1, 775, 778, and pt. 2, 111; John McElroy, *Chickamauga. Record of the Ohio Chickamauga and Chattanooga National Park Commission* (Cincinnati: Earhart and Richardson, 1896), 104.

15. Jacob Miller, "The History of My Wound," 1–2, Jacob Miller Papers, Civil War Miscellaneous Collection, USAMHI.

16. Samuel Keeran, "Chickamauga," *National Tribune*, 10 September 1891; *OR* 30, pt. 1, 773, 775, 778, and pt. 2, 111, 114, 115; Lewis, *One Hundred Twenty-four Ohio*, 59; Walker, "Pyramids of Chickamauga (Preston Smith)," *Chattanooga Sunday Times Magazine Section*, 2 August 1936.

17. *OR* 30, pt. 2, 114.

18. "In Memoriam: Charles Cruft," *Society of the Army of the Cumberland, Fifteenth Reunion, Cincinnati, Ohio, 1883* (Cincinnati: Robert Clarke, 1884), 233–35; *OR* 30, pt. 1, 729–30; *Indiana at Chickamauga*, 159.

19. *OR* 30, pt. 1, 780, 786, 792, 799; Hannaford, *Sixth Ohio*, 454; Suiter diary, 19 September 1863, ISHL.

20. Warner, *Generals in Gray*, 346; Lindsay, *Military Annals of Tennessee Confederate*, 344.

21. *OR* 30, pt. 2, 118, 126.

22. Carroll Henderson Clark Memoirs, 34, CWC, TSLA; *OR* 30, pt. 2, 125.

23. *OR* 30, pt. 2, 122–26.

24. "Lieutenant Colonel W. W. Carnes, Memphis, Tennessee," *CV* 6, no. 8 (August 1898): 384; William W. Carnes, "Chickamauga. A Battle of Which the Half Has Not Been Told," *Atlanta Constitution*, 8 April 1883, and "Chickamauga," *SHSP* 14 (1886): 399.

25. Richard W. Johnson, *A Soldier's Reminiscences in Peace and War* (Philadelphia: J. R. Lippincott, 1886), 230.

CHAPTER TEN / GIVE HELP WHERE NEEDED

1. Charles Kirk, *History of the Fifteenth Pennsylvania Volunteers Cavalry, which was Recruited and Known as the Anderson Cavalry in the Rebellion of 1861–1865* (Philadelphia: N.p., 1906), 233–34.

2. Atkins, *Chickamauga*, 10; Horace Porter to his sister, 3 October 1863, Porter Papers, DLC; Kirk, *Fifteenth Pennsylvania Cavalry*, 234; Lewis Day, *Story of the One Hundred and First Ohio Infantry, a Memorial Volume* (Cleveland: William Bayne, 1894), 156.

3. *OR* 30, pt. 1, 73, 497–98, 607, 838.

4. Anderson, *Campaign and Battle of Chickamauga*, 27–28.

5. *OR* 30, pt. 2, 361; Wheless, "Data," 5–6; Connelly, *Autumn of Glory*, 204–5.

6. *OR* 30, pt. 2, 140, 176, 303; Hill, "Chickamauga," 651.

7. *OR* 30, pt. 2, 107, 111, 114.

8. Ibid., 84, 87, 89, 91, 92.

9. Samuel R. Watkins, *"Co. Aytch," Maury Grays, First Tennessee Regiment; or, a Side Show of the Big Show* (Chattanooga: Times Printing Company, 1900), 103–4; *OR* 30, pt. 2, 94–95, 99.

10. *OR* 30, pt. 2, 130, 133; Edwin Reynolds diary, 19 September 1863, Fifth Tennessee File, CCNMP.

11. *OR* 30, pt. 2, 130–31.

12. Ibid., 134.

13. Ibid., 133; Reynolds diary, 19 September 1863, Fifth Tennessee File, CCNMP.

14. Davis, *Jefferson Davis, Constitutionalist*, 6:125; Ira J. Chase, "Turchin's Chickamauga," Indianapolis *Journal*, 6 May 1889.

15. Nadine Turchin, "'A Monotony Full of Sadness,'" 27–30; Joseph Warren Keifer, *Slavery and Four Years of War. A Political History of Slavery in the United States, Together with a Narrative of the Campaigns and Battles of the Civil War in Which the Author Took Part: 1861–1865*, 2 vols. (New York: G. P. Putnam's Sons, 1900): 1:277–79; Stanley, *Personal Memoirs*, 134–335.

16. *OR* 30, pt. 1, 440, 473; Libby Prison Notebook of Major Arnold McMahan, Sullivan Collection, BGSU.

17. *Society of the Army of the Cumberland, Twenty-eighth Reunion, Detroit, Michigan, September 26 and 27, 1899* (Cincinnati: Robert Clarke, 1900), 104; *OR* 30, pt. 1, 440; Nadine Turchin, "'Monotony Full of Sadness,'" 73.

18. "Statement of General J. J. Reynolds in Regard to What Occurred When He Came onto the Field Near the Poe House in the Morning," manuscript in Historical Files, CCNMP; *OR* 30, pt. 1, 440.

19. Edwin W. High, *History of the Sixty-eighth Regiment Indiana Volunteer Infantry, 1862–1865, with a Sketch of E. A. King's Brigade, Reynolds's Division, Thomas's Corps in the Battle of Chickamauga* (Metamora: Sixty-eighth Indiana Infantry Reunion Association, 1902), 62.

20. *OR* 30, pt. 1, 803, 808.

21. Ibid., 808, 811, 815, 820; *History of the Seventy-ninth Regiment Indiana Volunteer Infantry in the Civil War of 1861 in the United States* (Indianapolis:

Hollenbeck Press, 1899); C. A. Brasher, "Chickamauga," *National Tribune*, 9 May 1889; Skinner, *Pennsylvania at Chickamauga*, 222.

22. T. L. Massenberg, "Captain W. W. Carnes' Battery at Chickamauga," *CV* 12, no. 11 (November 1904): 517–18; Lindsley, *Military Annals of Tennessee. Confederate*, 822; Carnes, "Chickamauga. A Battle the Half of Which Has Not Been Told."

23. Carnes, "Chickamauga. A Battle the Half of Which Has Not Been Told"; Massenberg, "Carnes' Battery," 518; Lindsley, *Military Annals of Tennessee. Confederate*, 823.

24. Bromfield L. Ridley, Jr., "Southern Side at Chickamauga. Article II," *CV* 6, no. 11 (November 1898): 515.

25. Anderson, *Campaign and Battle of Chickamauga*, 27–28; OR 30, pt. 2, 362, 401.

26. OR 30, pt. 2, 401.

27. Ridley, "Southern Side, Article II," 515; OR 30, pt. 2, 119.

28. OR 30, pt. 1, 823, pt. 2, 401; James Carnahan, "Indiana at Chickamauga," in *War Papers, Read before the Indiana Commandery of the Loyal Legion of the United States*, vol. 1 (Indianapolis: By the Commandery, 1898), 97.

29. OR 30, pt. 2, 362.

30. Ibid., pt. 1, 555, 564, 571, and pt. 2, 94, 99, 102; A. P. Huggins to J. P. Strange, undated letter in Nutt Papers, UNC.

31. W. H. Smith, "Melanchthon Smith's Battery," *CV* 12, no. 11 (November 1904): 532; OR 30, pt. 1, 555, and pt. 2, 95, 103.

32. Watkins, *"Co. Aytch,"* 104–5; OR 30, pt. 2, 99.

33. OR 30, pt. 2, 96, 132.

34. Ibid., pt. 1, 477, 482, 768, 771, 773, and pt. 2, 132, 135; Hazen, *Narrative of Military Service*, 127; George B. Turner to his mother, 23 September 1863, George B. Turner Papers, OHS; David W. Magee diary, 104, Eighty-sixth Illinois File, CCNMP.

35. Lyle, *Lights and Shadows*, 289–90; Joshua Horton, *A History of the Eleventh Regiment (Ohio Volunteer Infantry), Containing the Military Record . . . of Each Officer and Enlisted Man of the Command* (Dayton: W. J. Shuey, 1866), 100–101; William F. Scott, *Philander P. Lane, Colonel of Volunteers in the Civil War, Eleventh Ohio Infantry* (New York: Privately Printed, 1920), 223–24.

36. Lyle, *Lights and Shadows*, 292; OR 30, pt. 1, 480.

37. Stahl diary, 27, Mann Collection, USAMHI; OR 30, pt. 1, 282, 538–39.

38. Huggins to Strange, undated letter in Nutt Papers, UNC; OR 30, pt. 1, 543–46, 558; Cope, *Fifteenth Ohio*, 310.

39. OR 30, pt. 1, 543.

40. Ibid., 474, 776, and pt. 2, 132; David W. Magee diary, 104, Eighty-sixth Illinois File, CCNMP; Hazen, *Narrative of Military Service*, 127; Reynolds diary, 19 September 1863, Fifth Tennessee File, CCNMP; Rob Adney, "Account of Battle of Chickamauga," manuscript in Thirty-sixth Ohio File, CCNMP.

41. Smith, "Smith's Battery," 532; Christopher Losson, *Tennessee's Forgotten Warriors: Frank Cheatham and His Confederate Division* (Knoxville: University of Tennessee Press, 1989), 107; OR 30, pt. 1, 535, 555, 558.

42. Smith, "Smith's Battery," 532.

43. Owen, *In Camp and Battle*, 272; Wheless "Data," 5–6.

44. OR 30, pt. 1, 564, 568, 571; Stahl diary, 26–27, Mann Collection, USAMHI; Wagner reminiscences, 75, *CWTI* Collection, USAMHI.

45. Wagner reminiscences, 75, *CWTI* Collection, USAMHI; OR 30, pt. 1, 571, and pt. 2, 274, 278, 281, 283, 285.

46. OR 30, pt. 1, 538–39, 564, 567, and pt. 2, 259, 264, 267, 268.

47. Ibid., pt. 1, 564, and pt. 2, 262, 274.

48. Ibid., pt. 1, 287, 539.

Chapter Eleven / A Bellyful of Fighting

1. Warner, *Generals in Blue*, 116, 343–44; *Society of the Army of the Cumberland. Twelfth Reunion. Toledo Ohio, 1880* (Cincinnati: Robert Clarke, 1881), 171–77; J. Montgomery Wright, "Notes of a Staff-Officer at Perryville," in *Battles and Leaders of the Civil War*, 3:60–61, and Don Carlos Buell, "East Tennessee and the Campaign of Perryville," ibid., 43; Keifer, *Slavery and Four Years of War*, 1:300–301.

2. Gordon Whitney to Peter Cozzens, 17 November 1990, author's papers.

3. Day, *One Hundred and First Ohio*, 156; Tinney, "Families of Chickamauga Battlefield," 30; OR 30, pt. 1, 498.

4. OR 30, pt. 1, 668–69; Photograph of the Lost Corner School, c. 1900, Historical Files, CCNMP; "Few Survivors of Civil War Days Still Live in Vicinity of Chickamauga Battlefield," *Chattanooga News*, 22 September 1893; Gilbert R. Stormont, *History of the Fifty-eighth Regiment of Indiana Volunteer Infantry, Its Organizations, Campaigns, and Battles, from 1861–1865* (Princeton, Ind.: Press of the Clarion, 1895), 181.

5. McGee, *Seventy-second Indiana*, 177; OR 30, pt. 1, 448; Petzoldt, *My War Story*, 102.

6. Burke, *Military History of Kansas Regiments*, 199; Lindsley, *Military Annals of Tennessee. Confederate*, 451; OR 30, pt. 1, 533.

7. Burke, *Military History of Kansas Regiments*, 199; Lindsley, *Military Annals of Tennessee. Confederate*, 451; OR 30, pt. 1, 529, pt. 2, 453.

8. Burke, *Military History of Kansas Regiments*, 200; Lindsley, *Military Annals Tennessee. Confederate*, 451; OR 30, pt. 1, 529, 533; Goodrich, "Gregg's Brigade," 264.

9. OR 30, pt. 2, 453–54, 473.

10. Ibid., pt. 1, 529; Burke, *Military History of Kansas Regiments*, 200.

11. OR 30, pt. 1, 447, 607, 608.

12. Ibid., 499, 515–16; William P. Carlin, "Military Memoirs," *National Tribune*, 16 April 1885.

13. Ibid., 521, 527; Day, *One Hundred and First Ohio*, 160; Goodrich, "Gregg's Brigade," 264.

14. OR 30, pt. 2, 510; Warner, *Generals in Gray*, 261; Angelina V. Winkler, *The Confederate Capital and Hood's Texas Brigade* (Austin: E. Von Boeckman, 1894), 151; Jerome B. Robertson, *Touched with Valor, Civil War Papers and Casualty*

Reports of Hood's Texas Brigade, Written and Collected by General Jerome B. Robertson, Commander of Hood's Texas Brigade, 1862–1864, ed. Harold B. Simpson (Hillsboro, Tex.: Hill Junior College, 1964), 14–15.

15. Robertson, *Touched with Valor,* 14; Cozzens, *No Better Place to Die,* 215.

16. D. H. Hamilton, *History of Company M, First Texas Volunteer Infantry, Hood's Brigade, Longstreet's Corps, Army of the Confederate States of America* (Kansas City, Mo.: E. L. Mendenhall, 1925), 31–32; William Andrew Fletcher, *Rebel Private, Front and Rear* (Austin: University of Texas Press, 1954), 88; Joseph Benjamin Polley, *A Soldier's Letters to Charming Nellie* (New York: Neale, 1908), 141, and *Hood's Texas Brigade, Its Marches, Its Battles, Its Achievements* (New York and Washington: Neale, 1910), 209; OR 30, pt. 2, 514.

17. OR 30, pt. 2, 510, 512.

18. Ibid., 510; Jacob Goodson to his niece, 28 September 1863, Forty-fourth Alabama File, CCNMP.

19. Polley, *Hood's Texas Brigade,* 210.

20. Winkler, *Confederate Capitol and Hood's Brigade,* 144–45; Valerius C. Giles, *Rags and Hope, the Recollections of Val C. Giles, Four Years with Hood's Brigade, Fourth Texas Infantry, 1861–1865,* ed. Mary Laswell (New York: Coward-McCann, 1961), 208; Joseph Polley, "A Battle 'above the Clouds,'" CV 5, no. 3 (March 1897): 104.

21. OR 30, pt. 1, 516, 529, and pt. 2, 511, 516.

22. Ibid., pt. 2, 413–14, 430; "Colonel Robert C. Trigg, of Virginia," CV 17, no. 2 (February 1909): 65.

23. James E. Love to Molly Wilson, 19 September 1863, Love Papers, MoHS; OR 30, pt. 1, 839, 845–46, 849; Thomas J. Wright, *History of the Eighth Regiment Kentucky Volunteer Infantry, During Its Three Years Campaigns, Embracing Organizations, Skirmishes, and Battles of the Command, with Much of the History of the Old Reliable Third Brigade, Commanded by Hon. Stanley Matthews, and Containing Many Interesting and Amusing Incidents of Army Life* (St. Joseph, Mo.: St. Joseph Steam and Printing Company, 1880), 188.

24. McGee, *Seventy-second Indiana,* 176; Day, *One Hundred and First Ohio,* 160–61; OR 30, pt. 1, 447, 527, 522, and pt. 2, 511.

25. OR 30, pt. 1, 447; *Indiana at Chickamauga,* 205.

26. OR 30, pt. 2, 430.

27. Ibid., pt. 1, 840, 851; Wright, *Eighth Kentucky,* 188–89.

28. OR 30, pt. 2, 430.

29. Ibid., pt. 1, 516, 840; Day, *One Hundred and First Ohio,* 162–63.

30. OR 30, pt. 1, 840, 845–46; Wright, *Eighth Kentucky,* 189.

31. James E. Love to Molly Wilson, 23 September 1863, Love Papers, MoHS.

32. OR 30, pt. 1, 848–49.

33. Day, *One Hundred and First Ohio,* 163; OR 30, pt. 1, 516, 527.

34. West, *Texan in Search of a Fight,* 114; Polley, *Hood's Texas Brigade,* 212.

35. West, *Texan in Search of a Fight,* 107, 114.

36. OR 30, pt. 1, 454, 499–500.

37. Ibid., pt. 2, 511, 518.

38. Ibid., pt. 1, 631; Wilbur Hinman, *The Story of the Sherman Brigade. The Camp, the March, the Bivouac, the Battle; and How the Boys Lived and Died during Four Years of Active Field Service* (Alliance, Ohio: Press of Daily Review, 1897), 420; Charles Belknap, *History of the Michigan Organizations at Chickamauga, Chattanooga and Missionary Ridge, 1863* (Lansing, Mich.: Robert Smith Printing Company, 1897), 128.

39. OR 30, pt. 1, 608, 632, 691.

40. Ibid., 632, 691.

41. Ibid., 448, and pt. 2, 500; McGee, *Seventy-second Indiana*, 178.

42. *Society of the Army of the Cumberland, Seventeenth Reunion*, 224–25; OR 30, pt. 1, 654–55.

43. OR 30, pt. 1, 523, 527, and pt. 2, 430, 433.

44. Ibid., pt. 1, 654.

45. Ibid., 670.

46. Ibid., 633, 659; P. L. Hubbard, "The Capture of the Eighth Indiana Battery," *National Tribune*, 6 June 1907; George Woodruff, *Fifteen Years Ago; Or, the Patriotism of Will County* (Joliet, Ill.: Joliet Republican Book and Job Steam Printing Company, 1876), 284. Woodruff, who was not a member of the regiment, asserts that the charge was made after the brigade had rallied behind Wilder. However, Major Charles Hammond says in his report that the charge occurred in the first moments of the fighting; the same can be inferred from Buell's report.

47. Belknap, *Michigan at Chickamauga*, 128; OR 30, pt. 1, 654.

48. Hamilton, *Company M, First Texas*, 32; Stormont, *Fifty-eighth Indiana*, 182; OR 30, pt. 1, 662.

49. OR 30, pt. 2, 435–36, 438, 440.

50. Ibid., pt. 1, 851.

51. Fletcher, *Rebel Private*, 92.

52. OR 30, pt. 1, 670.

53. McGee, *Seventy-second Indiana*, 176; OR 30, pt. 1, 448.

54. Campbell journal, 106–7, Wabash College; Petzoldt, *My War Story*, 104; OR 30, pt. 1, 466, 677.

55. Petzoldt, *My War Story*, 104.

56. Sorrel, *Recollections of a Confederate Staff Officer*, 203; Warner, *Generals in Gray*, 25–26.

57. OR 30, pt. 1, 517–18; Tucker, *Chickamauga*, 171; J. H. Martin, "Longstreet's Forces at Chickamauga," *CV* 20, no. 12 (December 1912): 564.

58. William R. and M. B. Houghton, *Two Boys in the Civil War and After* (Montgomery, Ala.: Paragon Press, 1912), 141.

59. OR 30, pt. 1, 677.

60. Ibid., 524, 527; Day, *One Hundred and First Ohio*, 164.

61. Tucker, *Chickamauga*, 171.

62. Heg, *Civil War Letters*, 160–63.

63. OR 30, pt. 1, 529; "Kansas at Chickamauga and Chattanooga," *Transactions of the Kansas State Historical Society* 8 (1904): 273.

64. McGee, *Seventy-second Indiana*, 180.

65. *OR* 30, pt. 1, 529, 533.

66. Ibid., 524; Charles R. Green, *Volunteer Service in the Army of the Cumberland* (Olathe, Kans.: N.p., 1913–14), no pagination.

67. *OR* 30, pt. 1, 655, 662; Stormont, *Fifty-eighth Indiana,* 182–83.

68. *OR* 30, pt. 1, 448, pt. 2, 518; Campbell journal, 106–7, Wabash College; John Rowell, *Yankee Artilleryman, through the Civil War with Eli Lilly's Indiana Battery* (Knoxville: University of Tennessee Press, 1975), 116–18.

69. *OR* 30, pt. 1, 67, 74, 77, 129, 132, 133, 579; Sheridan, *Memoirs,* 1:278.

70. Bradley reminiscences, 14–15, Bradley Papers, USAMHI.

71. Ibid., 17; *OR* 30, pt. 1, 594.

72. *OR* 30, pt. 1, 516, 662; Stormont, *Fifty-eighth Indiana,* 183; "Battle of Chickamauga: Excerpts of Letters from 2nd Lieut. Henry M. Weiss to His Wife in Shipman, Illinois," 2, in Twenty-seventh Illinois file, CCNMP.

73. McGee, *Seventy-second Indiana,* 177–78; "Weiss Letters," 2, Twenty-seventh Illinois File, CCNMP; Bradley reminiscences, Bradley Papers, USAMHI, 17; *OR* 30, pt. 1, 594–95.

74. Henry Hall to his father, 3 October 1863, Henry Hall Papers, Massachusetts Historical Society.

75. *OR* 30, pt. 1, 595, 662; Gene Kelly, comp., *Collection of Civil War Letters Written by Mercer County Soldiers* (N.p., n.d.), no pagination.

76. Carlin, "Military Memoirs," *National Tribune,* 16 April 1885.

77. Bradley reminiscences, Bradley Papers, USAMHI, 18; *OR* 30, pt. 1, 579, 595, 662; Stormont, *Fifty-eighth Indiana,* 183.

78. Bradley reminiscences, Bradley Papers, USAMHI, 18; Sheridan, *Memoirs,* 1:278; W. P. Carlin to Edward Ruger, 18 April 1867, Thomas Papers, RG 94, National Archives.

Chapter Twelve / They Skedaddled

1. *OR* 30, pt. 1, 780, 808, and pt. 2, 401, 404, 407; McElroy, *Chickamauga and Chatanooga,* 26; Hannaford, *Sixth Ohio,* 463.

2. *OR* 30, pt. 2, 401, 404–5.

3. Ibid., pt. 1, 808, 823; Hannaford, *Sixth Ohio,* 463.

4. *OR* 30, pt. 2, 362, 370; Bodenhamer memoirs, CWC, TSLA; Ridley, "Southern Side, Article II," 516.

5. Tourgee, *Story of a Thousand,* 218, and "A Civil War Diary of Albion W. Tourgee," ed. Dean H. Keller, *Ohio History* 74, no. 2 (Spring 1965): 101–2; High, *Sixty-eighth Indiana,* 65.

6. *OR* 30, pt. 1, 833; High, *Sixty-eighth Indiana,* 65.

7. *OR* 30, pt. 1, 471, and pt. 2, 473; High, *Sixty-eighth Indiana,* 66.

8. Frank Wilkinson to D. Price, 5 November 1863, Civil War File of Robert J. Price, InHS.

9. Tourgee, *Story of a Thousand,* 220; *OR* 30, pt. 2, 473; High, *Sixty-eighth Indiana,* 66, 79.

10. High, *Sixty-eighth Indiana,* 67.

11. Ibid., 79; "Statement of General Reynolds," 2, Thomas Papers, RG 94,

National Archives; *OR* 30, pt. 1, 440, 456; *Ninety-second Illinois*, 109; Charles E. Cort, *"Dear Friends," the Civil War Letters and Diary of Charles Edwin Cort*, ed. Helyn W. Tomlinson (Minneapolis: N.p., 1962), 105-6.

12. *OR* 30, pt. 2, 370; Warner, *Generals in Gray*, 35-36.

13. *OR* 30, pt. 2, 371, 379-80.

14. Lindsley, *Military Annals of Tennessee. Confederate*, 474.

15. *OR* 30, pt. 1, 808, 823, and pt. 2, 371.

16. Ibid., pt. 1, 823, 833.

17. *History of the Seventy-ninth Regiment Indiana Volunteer Infantry in the Civil War of 1861 in the United States* (Indianapolis: Hollenbeck Press, 1899), 90; *OR* 30, pt. 1, 808, 820.

18. Palmer, *Personal Recollections*, 11; "Statement of General Reynolds," 3, and Horatio Van Cleve to Edward Ruger, 24 May 1867, both in Thomas Papers, RG 94, National Archives; David Bittle Floyd, *History of the Seventy-fifth Regiment of Indiana Volunteers, Its Organizations, Campaigns, and Battles (1862-1865)* (Philadelphia: Lutheran Publishing Society, 1893), 137; Kane, "From Chickamauga to Chattanooga," 101.

19. Floyd, *Seventy-fifth Indiana*, 138; Robert O. Neff, *Tennessee's Battered Brigadier: The Life of General Joseph B. Palmer* (Murfreesboro, Tenn.: Historic Travellers' Rest, 1988), 85-87; *OR* 30, pt. 2, 371.

20. Lindsley, *Military Annals of Tennessee. Confederate*, 475; *OR* 30, pt. 2, 371.

21. Unidentified newspaper clipping in the Civil War File of James E. Essington, InHS; Floyd, *Seventy-fifth Indiana*, 138.

22. Palmer, *Personal Recollections*, 176-77.

23. Jacob Goodson to his niece, 28 September 1863, Forty-fourth Alabama File, CCNMP; William C. Oates, *The War between the Union and the Confederacy and Its Lost Opportunities, with a History of the Fifteenth Alabama and the Forty-eight Battles in Which It Was Engaged* (New York: Neale, 1905), 254, 261; *OR* 30, pt. 1, 474, 482. Regrettably, neither the reports of Sheffield nor those of his regimental commanders have been preserved, and the division commander, Law, did not file a report. Thus my description of the movements of Sheffield's brigade is in part speculative.

24. Palmer, *Personal Recollections*, 177; Oates, *War between the Union and the Confederacy*, 254.

25. *OR* 30, pt. 1, 730-31, 741, 757; McElroy, *Chickamauga and Chattanooga*, 82-83; Palmer, *Personal Recollections*, 12.

26. *OR* 30, pt. 1, 480, 1070; Turner to his mother, 23 September 1863, Turner Papers, OHS.

27. *OR* 30, pt. 1, 1070; R. C. J. Adney, "The Thirty-sixth at the Battle of Chickamauga," manuscript recollections in John C. Booth Papers, OHS.

28. John Booth, "Chickamauga, A Campaign Unrivaled in the Annals of War," *National Tribune*, 2 October 1890; *OR* 30, pt. 1, 480, 730, 731, 1070; John B. Turchin, *Chickamauga* (Chicago: Fergus Printing Company, 1888), 77; Turner to his mother, 23 September 1863, Turner Papers, OHS.

29. *OR* 30, pt. 1, 1070, and pt. 2, 392, 395; Adney, "Thirty-sixth at Chickamauga," Booth Papers, OHS.

30. Booth, "Chickamauga."

31. Palmer, *Personal Recollections*, 12; *OR* 30, pt. 1, 474, 731; McElroy, *Chickamauga and Chattanooga*, 83.

32. *OR* 30, pt. 2, 362.

33. R. M. Gray reminiscences, 62–63, UNC; Warner, *Generals in Gray*, 19; "General William B. Bate," *CV* 2, no. 11 (November 1894): 336.

34. "General Bate," 336–37.

35. W. J. McMurray, "The Gap of Death at Chickamauga," *CV* 2, no. 11 (November 1894): 329.

36. *OR* 30, pt. 1, 780, 786, 792, 799; *Indiana at Chickamauga*, 170.

37. *OR* 30, pt. 1, 778; Amasa Johnson, "Ninth Indiana Regiment at Chickamauga, an Address Given August 25, 1887 During the Fifth Annual Reunion of the Ninth Indiana Veterans' Association by Captain Amasa Johnson," typescript in Ninth Indiana File, CCNMP.

38. *OR* 30, pt. 1, 799; "Statement of General Reynolds," 5, Thomas Papers, RG 94, National Archives.

39. *OR* 30, pt. 1, 830, 833, 836; Carnahan, "Indiana at Chickamauga," 99.

40. *OR* 30, pt. 1, 808, 815, 816, 818–19; Carnahan, "Indiana at Chickamauga," 98.

Chapter Thirteen / We Bury Our Dead

1. McMurray, "Gap of Death," 330; James L. Cooper memoirs, 36, CWC, TSLA.

2. *OR* 30, pt. 2, 384, 389, 392, 395.

3. Kane, "From Chickamauga to Chattanooga," 103; Floyd, *Seventy-fifth Indiana*, 141.

4. Cooper memoirs, 34, CWC, TSLA; *OR* 30, pt. 1, 792; Lindsley, *Military Annals of Tennessee. Confederate*, 134.

5. *OR* 30, pt. 1, 788, 792; *Indiana at Chickamauga*, 170.

6. *OR* 30, pt. 1, 786; Suiter diary, 19 September 1863, ISHL.

7. Cooper memoirs, 64, CWC, TSLA.

8. Lindsley, *Military Annals of Tennessee. Confederate*, 134; *OR* 30, pt. 1, 801, pt. 2, 792.

9. Floyd, *Seventy-fifth Indiana*, 142.

10. Kane, "From Chickamauga to Chattanooga," 108.

11. Palmer, *Personal Recollections*, 178.

12. Ibid., 178–80.

13. Hazen, *Narrative of Military Service*, 128; Amasa Johnson, "Ninth Indiana at Chickamauga," Ninth Indiana File, CCNMP.

14. *OR* 30, pt. 2, 362, 402.

15. Sanderson, letter diary, 19 September 1863, OHS; *OR* 30, pt. 1, 56, 329; Kirk, *Fifteenth Pennsylvania Cavalry*, 213.

16. *OR* 30, pt. 1, 250.

17. Floyd, *Seventy-fifth Indiana*, 141–42; D. B. McConnell, "The Ninth Indi-

ana," *National Tribune*, 11 November 1886; A. Johnson, "Ninth Indiana at Chickamauga," Ninth Indiana File, CCNMP; OR 30, pt. 2, 389.

18. Hazen, *Narrative of Military Service*, 128; OR 30, pt. 1, 762.

19. OR 30, pt. 2, 473, 489; Joseph Vaulx, "Commander of Memphis Encampment," *CV* 14, no. 4 (April 1906): 151.

20. Atkins, *Chickamauga*, 10; *Ninety-second Illinois*, 109–10; OR 30, pt. 2, 489.

21. OR 30, pt. 1, 808, 811, 816, 823, 836, and pt. 2, 489; *Indiana at Chickamauga*, 249, 288–89; Carnahan, "Indiana at Chickamauga," 99.

22. McConnell, "Ninth Indiana"; OR 30, pt. 1, 762; A. Johnson, "Ninth Indiana at Chickamauga," Ninth Indiana File, CCNMP.

23. OR 30, pt. 1, 50.

24. Ibid., 762, 771, and pt. 2, 389; John Inzer, "Colonel Robert C. Tyler," *CV* 15, no. 5 (May 1907): 237.

25. McConnell, "Ninth Indiana"; A. Johnson, "Ninth Indiana at Chickamauga," Ninth Indiana File, CCNMP; OR 30, pt. 1, 768.

26. Hannaford, *Sixth Ohio*, 463; OR 30, pt. 1, 796.

27. Hannaford, *Sixth Ohio*, 463; OR 30, pt. 2, 389.

28. OR 30, pt. 1, 363, 372–73.

29. Ibid., pt. 2, 402, 405, 407, 409, 412.

30. Ibid., pt. 1, 762, 778, 799, 801; McElroy, *Chickamauga and Chattanooga*, 123; Hazen, *Narrative of Military Service*, 129.

31. OR 30, pt. 2, 384, 388, 392; McMurray, "Gap of Death," 330.

32. Ambrose Bierce, "Chickamauga," San Francisco *Examiner*, 24 April 1898.

33. Ibid.; Tucker, *Chickamauga*, 161.

34. OR 30, pt. 2, 389, 396.

35. Ibid., pt. 1, 360, 847; Belknap, *Michigan at Chickamauga*, 113.

36. Eben Sturgis diary, 19 September 1863, *CWTI* Collection, USAMHI; Ward, "The Storm Breaks," 11; OR 30, pt. 1, 360, 847.

37. OR 30, pt. 1, 847.

38. Ibid., 385, pt. 2, 402; Ward, "The Storm Breaks," 11; Belknap, *Michigan at Chickamauga*, 113.

39. OR 30, pt. 1, 412.

40. Hinman, *Sherman Brigade*, 420; OR 30, pt. 1, 691, 700.

41. OR 30, pt. 1, 691, 702, 707; Hinman, *Sherman Brigade*, 420.

42. OR 30, pt. 1, 702, 707.

43. Goodrich, "Gregg's Brigade," 264; Simpson, *Hood's Texas Brigade*, 220–21; Hinman, *Sherman Brigade*, 422; Charles Clark, *Opdycke Tigers, the 125th O.V.I., a History of the Regiment and the Campaigns and Battles of the Army of the Cumberland* (Columbus, Ohio: Spahr and Glenn, 1895), 97; OR 330, pt. 2, 495.

44. OR 30, pt. 2, 456, 474, 480–81.

45. Ibid., pt. 1, 692, and pt. 2, 489.

46. Hinman, *Sherman Brigade*, 420, 423; OR 30, pt. 1, 692, pt. 2, 456.

Chapter Fourteen / Quake and Tremble

1. Tucker, *Chickamauga*, 176–77; Connelly, *Autumn of Glory*, 207; OR 30, pt. 2, 140, 154; Wiley A. Washburn, "Reminiscences of Confederate Service," *Arkansas*

Historical Quarterly 35 (Spring 1976): 57; Preston, "Memoirs of the War," 20, Thirty-third Alabama Papers, ADAH.

2. Coleman diary, 19 September 1863, 110, UNC; Mark M. Boatner III, *The Civil War Dictionary* (New York: David McKay, 1959), 820; Washburn, "Reminiscences of Confederate Service," 57; Hay, "Campaign and Battle at Chickamauga," 225.

3. Hay, "Campaign and Battle at Chickamauga," 225; Liddell, *Liddell's Record,* 144.

4. Liddell, *Liddell's Record,* 143–44.

5. Gale to his wife, 21 September 1863, Gale-Polk Family Papers, UNC.

6. Wheless, "Data," 7; Wheless to Gale, 8 October 1867, Gale-Polk Family Papers, UNC.

7. Charles Develling, *History of the Seventeenth Regiment, First Brigade, Third Division, Fourteenth Corps, Army of the Cumberland, War of the Rebellion* (Zanesville, Ohio: E. R. Sullivan, 1889), 101–2.

8. OR 30, pt. 1, 250, 276–77, 310, 536, 539.

9. Ibid., 277; Richard Johnson, "Men and Events. Recollections of Distinguished Generals of the Civil War," *National Tribune,* 15 August 1895; for a biography of Baird, see John A. Baird, Jr., " 'For Gallant and Meritorious Service,' Major General Absalom Baird," *Civil War Times Illustrated* 15, no. 3 (June 1976): 4–9.

10. OR 30, pt. 2, 154, 160, 174; Warner, *Generals in Gray,* 71–72.

11. J. M. Berry, "The Quiet Humor of General Pat Cleburne," *CV* 12, no. 4 (April 1904): 176; Bragg to E. T. Sykes, 8 February 1873, John F. H. Claiborne Papers, UNC.

12. Washburn, "Reminiscences of Confederate Service," 57; Liddell, *Liddell's Record,* 144; Boatner, *Civil War Dictionary,* 820.

13. Wagner reminiscences, 76, *CWTI* Collection, USAMHI; OR 30, pt. 1, 572.

14. OR 30, pt. 1, 572; Preston, "Memoirs of the War," 20, Thirty-third Alabama Papers, ADAH.

15. OR 30, pt. 1, 565, pt. 2, 154; William Sumner Dodge, *History of the Old Second Division, Army of the Cumberland* (Chicago: Church and Goodman, 1864), 35; "William A. Brown's Book," 106, Stanford's Mississippi Battery File, CCNMP.

16. Tucker, *Chickamauga,* 183.

17. Preston, "Memoirs of the War," 20, Thirty-third Alabama Papers, ADAH.

18. OR 30, pt. 2, 163, 168, 170.

19. Ibid., 170, 174.

20. Ibid., pt. 1, 572.

21. Ibid., pt. 2, 163, 165.

22. Wagner reminiscences, 79, *CWTI* Collection, USAMHI.

23. Dodge, *Old Second Division,* 546–47.

24. OR 30, pt. 2, 166; Buck, *Cleburne and His Command,* 129.

25. OR 30, pt. 1, 569, pt. 2, 170.

26. Ibid., pt. 1, 565, 570, 577, and pt. 2, 168, 170; Dodge, *Old Second Division,* 546–47.

27. John M. Johnston, "At Chickamauga. A Soldier's Story of the Battle," Lancaster *New Era*, 10 September 1892.

28. *OR* 30, pt. 1, 287, 300; Scribner, *How Soldiers Were Made*, 149.

29. Perry, *Thirty-eighth Indiana*, 90.

30. John M. Johnston, "At Chickamauga. A Soldier's Story of the Battle," Lancaster *New Era*, 10 September 1892.

31. *OR* 30, pt. 1, 300, pt. 2, 176; John M. Johnston, "At Chickamauga. A Soldier's Story of the Battle," Lancaster *New Era*, 10 September 1892; Scribner, *How Soldiers Were Made*, 149–50; W. E. Bevens, *Reminiscences of a Private, Company "G," First Arkansas Regiment Infantry* (N.p., 1913), 42; James E. Edmonds diary, 19 September 1863, *CWTI* Collection.

32. *OR* 30, pt. 2, 176–85.

33. Ibid., pt. 1, 539, 544, and pt. 2, 84; Stahl diary, 27–28, Mann Collection, USAMHI; Cope, *Fifteenth Ohio*, 310.

34. *OR* 30, pt. 2, 108, 188.

35. J. W. Harris to his mother, John Harris letters, CWC, TSLA; *OR*, 30, pt. 2, 108; Skinner, *Pennsylvania at Chickamauga*, 207; John Obreiter, *The Seventy-seventh Pennsylvania at Shiloh. History of the Regiment* (Harrisburg, Pa., Harrisburg Publishing Company, 1908), 162–63; Carnes, "Chickamauga. A Battle of which the Half Has Not Been Told," Atlanta *Constitution*, 8 April 1883.

36. *OR* 30, pt. 2, 108, 112, 188; Obreiter, *Seventy-seventh Pennsylvania*, 164; Wells, "Chickamauga," 222.

37. Montraville Reeves to Ransom Reeves, 5 October 1863, Montraville Reeves Papers, University of Illinois Library; *OR* 30, pt. 1, 555, 558.

38. Buckner, *Memoirs*, 20; *OR* 30, pt. 1, 556.

39. Buckner, *Memoirs*, 19.

40. *OR* 30, pt. 1, 558, pt. 2, 108, 188.

Chapter Fifteen / This Terrible Sound

1. Partridge, *History of the Ninety-sixth Illinois*, 175; Wilson Vance, "On Thomas' Right at Chickamauga," *Blue and Gray* 1 (1893): 88; Newlin, *Seventy-third Illinois*, 229; Heartsill, *Fourteen Hundred and Ninety-one Days*, 153.

2. B. F. Green, "Two Armies — A Comparison," *CV* 16, no. 3 (March 1918): 101.

3. Bircher, *Drummer Boy's Diary*, 76; Simmons, *Eighty-fourth Illinois*, 93; *OR* 30, pt. 1, 634; Sunderland, *Wilder's Brigade*, 82; James Burke, "Chickamauga: The Troops that Successfully Resisted the Charge of Longstreet's Veterans," *National Tribune*, 19 May 1887.

4. Tucker, *Chickamauga*, 190; Joseph Gibson, *History of the Seventy-eighth Pennsylvania Volunteer Infantry* (Pittsburgh: Pittsburgh Printing Company, 1905), 99; Manigault, *Carolinian Goes to War*, 96; Lewellyn A. Shaver, *A History of the Sixtieth Alabama Regiment, Gracie's Alabama Brigade* (Montgomery, Ala.: Barrett and Brown, 1867), 14.

5. Scribner, *How Soldiers Were Made*, 150–51.

6. Freeman, "Chickamauga," 11–12, Henry Freeman Papers, Wyoming Historical Society.

7. Griest journal, 101, Harrisburg Civil War Round Table Collection, USAMHI; McGee, *Seventy-second Indiana*, 180.

8. Collins, *Unwritten History of the War*, 153; Heartsill, *Fourteen Hundred and Ninety-one Days*, 152.

9. Terry Cahal to Colonel Atkinson, 30 September 1863, CWC, TSLA.

10. Silas S. Canfield, *History of the Twenty-first Regiment Ohio Volunteer Infantry* (Toledo: Vrooman, Anderson, and Bateman, 1893), 110.

11. Wright, *Eighth Kentucky*, 190.

12. McGee, *Seventy-second Indiana*, 183.

13. Petzoldt, *My War Story*, 107–8.

14. B. F. Sawyer, "Annals of the War: Chickamauga," Philadelphia *Weekly Times*, 13 March 1886.

15. W. C. Brown, "How Confederates Treated a Federal," *CV* 12, no. 5 (May 1905): 228.

16. Alfred R. Phillips, *Fighting with Turchin* (N.p., n.d.), 110–11.

17. Johnny Williams Green, *Johnny Green of the Orphan Brigade: The Journal of a Confederate Soldier* (Lexington: University of Kentucky Press, 1956), 93–94.

18. S. P. Snider, "Reminiscences of the War," *Glimpses of the Nation's Struggle, Military Order of the Loyal Legion of the United States, Minnesota Commandery, Second Series* (St. Paul, Minn.: By the Commandery, 1890): 2:234–44

19. Elizabeth Lytle Broadwell to her uncle, 5 October 1863, Lytle Family Papers, CHS.

20. Sunderland, *Wilder's Brigade*, 82.

21. *OR* 30, pt. 1, 495.

22. William B. Graham, "An Account of My Capture at the Battle of Chickamauga," 2, William B. Graham Civil War File, InHS.

23. Stormont, *Fifty-eighth Indiana*, 184–85.

24. E. B. Heg, "Stephen O. Himoe, Civil War Physician," *Norwegian American Studies and Records* 11 (1940): 31, 33, 36, 55–56; Heg, *Civil War Letters*, 163–64.

25. Hinman, *Sherman Brigade*, 440.

26. Constantin Grebner, *We Were the Ninth: A History of the Ninth Regiment, Ohio Volunteer Infantry, April 17, 1861 to June 7, 1864*, ed. and trans. Frederic Trautmann (Kent, Ohio: Kent State University Press, 1987), 150.

27. Fletcher, *Rebel Private*, 93–94.

28. Miller, "The History of My Wound," 2, Civil War Miscellaneous Collection, USAMHI.

Chapter Sixteen / God Grant It May Be So

1. Sanderson, letter diary, 19 September 1863, OHS.

2. Palmer, *Personal Recollections*, 180; Shanks, *Personal Recollections*, 267; *OR* 30, pt. 1, 609.

3. Sheridan, *Memoirs*, 1:292.

4. Lamers, *Edge of Glory*, 336; Porter to his sister, 3 October 1863, Porter Papers, DLC.

5. Lamers, *Edge of Glory* 337; OR 30, pt. 1, 57; Hill, "Chickamauga," 652.

6. Sanderson, letter diary, 19 September 1863, OHS.

7. Lamers, *Edge of Glory*, 337.

8. McKinney, *Education in Violence*, 236; Van Horne, *Army of the Cumberland*, 1:342; OR 30, pt. 1, 135; Gates Thruston to Joseph Fullerton, 24 April, 1891, Historical Files, CCNMP.

9. Dana, *Recollections*, 113; Rosecrans to the Editors, *National Tribune*, 31 March 1870; Rosecrans, "The Chattanooga Campaign"; Van Horne, *Army of the Cumberland*, 1:342.

10. OR 30, pt. 1, 57, 69; McKinney, *Education in Violence*, 236.

11. Song quoted in Tucker, *Chickamauga*, 198–99; Dana, *Recollections* 114; Kirk, *Fifteenth Pennsylvania Cavalry*, 240; Johnson, *A Soldier's Reminiscences*, 227.

12. Dana, *Recollections*, 114; Gates P. Thruston, "Chickamauga," *Southern Bivouac*, no. 2 (1886/1887): 409.

13. Kirk, *Fifteenth Pennsylvania Cavalry*, 273.

14. Cahal to Atkinson, 30 September 1863, and Cooper memoirs, 35, both in CWC, TSLA; Coleman diary, 20 September 1863, 112, UNC; S. A. McNeil, "The Thirty-first Ohio at Chickamauga," *National Tribune*, 9 February 1888; James G. Essington, "Second Year's History of the Seventy-fifth Indiana Volunteer Infantry," Noblesville *Republican Ledger*, 16 October 1885.

15. OR 30, pt. 1, 51; Tucker, *Chickamauga*, 202–3.

16. Sheridan, *Memoirs*, 1:279–80.

17. Newlin, *Seventy-third Illinois*, 230–31.

18. OR 30, pt. 2, 287; Sorrel, *Recollections of a Confederate Staff Officer*, 192.

19. Longstreet, *From Manassas to Appomattox*, 438; Sorrel, *Recollections of a Confederate Staff Officer*, 193.

20. OR 30, pt. 2, 32–33, 287–88; Polk, *Polk*, 2:241.

21. Polk, *Polk*, 2:241; see Connelly, *Autumn of Glory*, chapter nine, for an excellent discussion of the failures of the Confederate high command during the night of 19 September.

22. OR 30, pt. 2, 33, 52; Manigault, *Carolinian Goes to War*, 97; Polk, *Polk*, 2:242; Connelly, *Autumn of Glory*, 209.

23. Polk, *Polk*, 2:242; Bragg to Sykes, 8 February 1873, John F. H. Claiborne Papers, UNC; Polk to George Brent, 28 September 1863, George Brent Papers, DU; Bragg to his wife, 27 September 1863, Bragg Papers, MoHS.

24. Brent journal, 25 September 1863, Palmer Collection, WRHS.

25. Hood, *Advance and Retreat*, 62–63.

26. J. Stoddard Johnston, "General J. B. Hood and Chickamauga," CV 13, no. 12 (December 1905): 552; Thomas Claiborne to Henry Van Ness Boynton, 16 April 1891, Historical Files, CCNMP.

27. Sorrel, *Recollections of a Confederate Staff Officer*, 193; Longstreet, *From Manassas to Appomattox*, 438; OR 30, pt. 2, 287–88; Frank Burr, "Chickamauga,

The Bloody Field of Carnage and Death Revisited," Atlanta *Constitution*, 1 April 1883.

28. *OR* 30, pt. 2, 140; Hill, "Chickamauga," 652–53; Statement of Captain T. Coleman, D. H. Hill Papers, NCDAH.

29. *OR* 30, pt. 2, 58, 63; Polk to Brent, 28 September 1863, Brent Papers, DU; undated letter of W. J. Morris to William Polk, Polk Papers, US.

30. Hill, "Chickamauga," 653; Statements of Lieutenant J. A. Reid and Major A. C. Avery and Breckinridge to Hill, 16 October 1863, both in Hill Papers, NCDAH.

31. Hill, "Chickamauga," 653; *OR* 30, pt. 2, 140.

32. Connelly, *Autumn of Glory*, 213.

33. *OR* 30, pt. 2, 52.

34. Ibid., 198.

35. Ibid., 57–58.

36. Ibid., 60.

37. Statements of T. Coleman and Archer Anderson, 13 October 1863, Hill Papers, NCDAH; *OR* 30, pt. 2, 141; Hill, "Chickamauga," 653.

38. *OR* 30, pt. 2, 141; Davis, *Breckinridge*, 370–71.

Chapter Seventeen / We Will End It

1. Cooper memoirs, 34, CWC, TSLA; B. F. Sawyer, "Annals of the War: Chickamauga," Philadelphia *Weekly Times*, 13 March 1886; Freeman diary, 20 September 1863, CWC, TSLA; *Battery M, First Illinois Light Artillery*, 84; Wagner reminiscences, 78, *CWTI* Collection, USAMHI; Donahower, "Narrative, Volume 2" 124, Donahower Papers, MnHS.

2. Y. R. LeMonnier, "General Polk at Chickamauga," *CV* 9, no. 1 (January 1901): 17; Affidavit of Y. R. LeMonnier, 7 September 1913, Civil War Papers, Reminiscences: Army of Tennessee, TU.

3. Wheless to W. D. Gale, 8 October 1867, Polk Papers, US.

4. *OR* 30, pt. 2, 52.

5. Ibid., 61, 63, 79; Wheless to Gale, 8 October 1867, Polk Papers, US.

6. Bragg never accepted Polk's version of events. He repeated Lee's lie in a letter to his wife, written just after the battle, in which he railed against the Bishop, and he set it down as gospel truth in postwar correspondence as well. See Bragg to his wife, 27 September 1863, Bragg Papers, MoHS, and Bragg to Sykes, 8 February 1873, John F. H. Claiborne Papers, UNC; LeMonnier, "Polk at Chickamauga," 17; Polk, *Polk*, 2:250.

7. Wheless to Gale, 8 October 1867, Polk Papers, US; Hill, "Chickamauga," 653; *OR* 30, pt. 2, 141.

8. Wheless to Gale, 8 October 1867, Polk Papers, US.

9. *OR* 30, pt. 2, 53.

10. Wheless to Gale, 8 October 1867, Polk Papers, US; *OR* 30, pt. 2, 53, 60–62.

11. *OR* 30, pt. 2, 62; Wheless to Gale, 8 October 1867, Polk Papers, US; Beatty diary, 89, UNC.

12. *OR* 30, pt. 2, 141; Hill, "Chickamauga," 653.

13. LeMonnier, "Polk at Chickamauga," 17; *OR* 30, pt. 2, 63; Connelly, *Autumn of Glory*, 219.

14. *OR* 30, pt. 2, 33, 53; Connelly, *Autumn of Glory*, 220; Davis, *Breckinridge*, 372; Hill, "Chickamauga," 653.

15. Statement of Major A. C. Avery, 3 November 1863, Hill Papers, NCDAH; Connelly, *Autumn of Glory*, 220–21; Polk, *Polk*, 2:257–58.

16. Palmer, *Personal Recollections*, 181; Manigault, *Carolinian Goes to War*, 123; Connelly, *Autumn of Glory*, 220–21.

17. Sanderson, letter diary, 21 September 1863, OHS; Horace Porter to his sister, 3 October 1863, Porter Papers, DLC.

18. Quoted in Lamers, *Edge of Glory*, 336.

19. Kirk, *Fifteenth Pennsylvania Cavalry*, 234–35, 255; Lamers, *Edge of Glory*, 337; Sanderson, letter diary, 21 September 1863, OHS; *OR* 30, pt. 1, 402.

20. *OR* 30, pt. 2, 138, 277.

21. Ibid., pt. 1, 69, 70, 330, 342, 965; Rosecrans, "Chattanooga Campaign"; Cist, *Army of the Cumberland*, 202.

22. Lamers, *Edge of Glory*, 338; Hannaford, *Sixth Ohio*, 465.

23. Shanks, *Personal Recollections*, 66–67.

24. McKinney, *Education in Violence*, 240; Cist, *Army of the Cumberland*, 202.

25. Cist, *Army of the Cumberland*, 202.

26. James Henry Haynie, *The Nineteenth Illinois: A Memoir of a Regiment of Volunteer Infantry Famous in the Civil War of Fifty Years Ago for Its Drill, Bravery, and Distinguished Services* (Chicago: M. A. Donahue, 1912), 238–40; *OR* 30, pt. 1, 330, 355, 847, 1014; Cist, *Army of the Cumberland*, 202; Lamers, *Edge of Glory*, 338.

27. *OR* 30, pt. 1, 338, 343, 1021.

28. Rosecrans, "Chattanooga Campaign"; Dana, *Recollections*, 114–15; Cist, *Army of the Cumberland*, 202.

29. *OR* 30, pt. 1, 356, 1032. Wood makes no mention of this sorry affair in his report of the battle.

30. Rosecrans, "Chattanooga Campaign"; Cist, *Army of the Cumberland*, 202; *OR* 30, pt. 1, 58, 356.

31. *OR* 30, pt. 1, 330, 361, 693–94, 803.

32. Ibid., 803.

33. Ibid., 489, 952–53; Rosecrans, "Chattanooga Campaign."

34. Piston, *Lee's Tarnished General*, 71.

35. Ibid., 70; Longstreet, *From Manassas to Appomattox*, 440; *OR* 30, pt. 2, 288, 503.

36. *OR* 30, pt. 2, 363, 385; Longstreet, *From Manassas to Appomattox*, 440.

37. Connelly, *Autumn of Glory*, 222; Longstreet, *From Manassas to Appomattox*, 440; *OR* 30, pt. 2, 288, 503; "Few Survivors of Civil War Days Still Live on Chickamauga Battlefield," Chattanooga *News*, 22 September 1923.

38. Hood, *Advance and Retreat*, 63.

39. Aquila Wiley, "General Hill Answered," National *Tribune*, 19 May 1887; *OR* 30, pt. 1, 441, 540.

40. *OR* 30, pt. 1, 367–68.

41. Ibid., 277, 556, 561; Obreiter, *Seventy-seventh Pennsylvania*, 164. Left with no field officers, no flag, and fewer than one hundred men, the Seventy-seventh Pennsylvania of Dodge's brigade had ceased to exist as a regiment.

CHAPTER EIGHTEEN / THE LEFT MUST BE HELD

1. John Lavender, *The War Memoirs of Captain John W. Lavender, C. S. A. They Never Came Back; the Story of Co. F, Fourth Arks. Infantry, C. S. A., Originally Known as the Montgomery Hunters, as Told by Their Commanding Officer.* (Pine Bluff, Ark.: W. M. Hackett and D. R. Perdue, 1956), 79; Wagner reminiscences, 78, *CWTI* Collection, USAMIHI.

2. Lot D. Young, *Reminiscences of a Soldier of the Orphan Brigade* (Louisville: Courier-Journal Job Printing Company, 1918), 69; John Jackman journal, 20 September, DLC; Joyce, "Orphan Brigade at Chickamauga," 31; Charles W. Anderson, "Gracie — Chickamauga — Whitaker," *CV* 2, no. 8 (August 1895): 251–52.

3. R. Gerald McMurtry, "Confederate General Ben Hardin Helm: Kentucky Brother-in-Law of Abraham Lincoln," *The Filson Club Historical Quarterly* 32, no. 4 (October 1958): 311–13; Thompson, *Orphan Brigade*, 380–82.

4. John Jackman journal, 20 September 1863, DLC.

5. *OR* 30, pt. 2, 199, 215; W. W. Herr, "Kentuckians at Chickamauga," *CV* 2, no. 11 (October 1895): 294–95.

6. *OR* 30, pt. 1, 287, pt. 2, 199; Scribner, *How Soldiers were Made*, 155; Herr, "Kentuckians at Chickamauga," 295.

7. Herr, "Kentuckians at Chickamauga," 295; *OR* 30, pt. 2, 215–16.

8. Scribner, *How Soldiers Were Made*, 155, Perry, *Thirty-eighth Indiana*, 93; *OR* 30, pt. 2, 209.

9. Davis, *Breckinridge*, 374–75; McMurtry, "Confederate General Ben Hardin Helm," 320; *OR* 30, pt. 1, 277, pt. 2, 209.

10. Thompson, *Orphan Brigade*, 387–88.

11. *OR* 30, pt. 1, 368, 372, 375; Calkins, *One Hundred and Fourth Illinois*, 137; Douglas Hapeman diary, 20 September 1863, ISHL; *Indiana at Chickamauga*, 263.

12. *OR* 30, pt. 1, 368, 372, pt. 2, 203; Hapeman diary, 20 September 1863.

13. Calkins, *One Hundred and Fourth Illinois*, 152.

14. *OR* 30, pt. 1, 368, 375.

15. Young, *Reminiscences*, 64–65; Joyce, "Orphan Brigade at Chickamauga," 32.

16. Thompson, *Orphan Brigade*, 391; John Jackman journal, 20 September 1863, DLC; *OR* 30, pt. 2, 204.

17. Ibid., pt. 2, 204, 209, 214; Longstreet, *From Manassas to Appomattox*, 459.

18. Longstreet, *From Manassas to Appomattox*, 459; George Kirkpatrick, *The Experiences of a Private Soldier in the Civil War* (Chicago, n.p., 1924), 30, 60.

19. *OR* 30, pt. 2, 221, 224, 226; *Indiana at Chickamauga*, 263.

20. *OR* 30, pt. 1, 368; *Indiana at Chickamauga*, 263; Anderson, "Gracie — Chickamauga — Whitaker," 251; Grebner, *We were the Ninth*, 152.

21. Davis, *Breckinridge*, 374; *OR* 30, pt. 2, 199.

22. *OR* 30, pt. 1, 70; Rosecrans, "Chattanooga Campaign"; Lamers, *Edge of Glory*, 342.

23. Joseph Reynolds, "An Incident of the Second Day at Chickamauga," Historical Files, CCNMP; *OR* 30, pt. 1, 251, 402; McKinney, *Education in Violence*, 244; Piatt, *Thomas*, 408.

24. *OR* 30, pt. 1, 278; Palmer, *Personal Recollections*, 182.

25. *OR* 30, pt. 1, 251, 330, 338 356, 361, 375.

26. Ibid., 278–79, 369; Calkins, *One Hundred and Fourth Illinois*, 137.

27. Belknap, *Michigan at Chickamauga*, 114–15.

28. Haynie, *Nineteenth Illinois*, 229.

29. *OR* 30, pt. 2, 222, 224.

30. J. W. Allen, "A Bullet in a Testament," *CV* 6, no. 4 (April 1899): 154; *OR* 30, pt. 2, 225–26.

31. *OR* 30, pt. 2, 222; United States, Surgeon General's Office, *The Medical and Surgical History of the War of the Rebellion (1861–1865)*, 3 vols. in 6 (Washington: G.P.O., 1870–88): 2:669.

32. *OR* 30, pt. 2, 233, 235.

33. Ibid., pt. 1, 553, pt. 2, 237; Wilbur Goodspeed to Henry V. N. Boynton, n.d., Battery A, First Ohio File, CCNMP.

34. Wells, "Chickamauga," 219; Hannaford, *Sixth Ohio*, 466; *OR* 30, pt. 1, 781, 786, 801; Simmons, *Eighty-fourth Illinois*, 97; Suiter diary, 20 September 1863, ISHL.

35. Bishop, *Second Minnesota*, 105–6; Donahower, "Narrative, Volume 2," 125, Donahower Papers, MnHS.

36. Bishop, *Second Minnesota*, 106–7; Judson Bishop to his sister, 29 September 1863, Judson Bishop Papers, MnHs; Donahower, "Narrative, Volume 2," 127–28, Donahower Papers, MnHS; Wells, "Chickamauga," 225.

37. Bishop to his sister, 29 September 1863, Bishop Papers, MnHS; Donahower, "Narrative, Volume 2," 128, Donahower Papers, MnHS; *OR* 30, pt. 1, 1059.

38. *OR* 30, pt. 1, 570, pt. 2, 233; Francis A. Kiene, *A Civil War Diary. The Journal of Francis A. Kiene, 1861–1864. A Family History*, ed. Ralph E. Kiene, Jr. (Kansas City: Year Book House, Inc., 1974), 18.

39. Donahower, "Narrative, Volume 2," 130–31, and Frank Weinland to Donahower, 27 November 1900, both in Donahower Papers, MnHS; *OR* 30, pt. 1, 1059, pt. 2, 237–39; Stevens, "Chickamauga: A Wartime Letter"; Grebner, *We Were the Ninth*, 143.

40. *OR* 30, pt. 1, 570; Kiene, *Civil War Diary*, 18.

41. *OR* 30, pt. 2, 216, 222.

42. Haynie, *Nineteenth Illinois*, 233; *OR* 30, pt. 1, 369.

43. Tourgee, *Story of a Thousand*, 238; *OR* 30, pt. 1, 379; Haynie, *Nineteenth Illinois*, 221; Borden M. Hicks, "Personal Recollections of the War of the Rebellion," *Glimpses of the Nation's Struggle. Sixth Series. Papers Read before the Minnesota*

Commandery of the Military Order of the Loyal Legion of the United States, January, 1903–1908 (Minneapolis: Aug. Davis, 1909), 529.

44. U.S. Surgeon General's Office, *Medical and Surgical History of the Civil War,* 669.

45. OR 30, pt. 2, 200; Hay, "Campaign and Battle at Chickamauga," 229.

Chapter Nineteen / To Fire Seemed Foolish

1. Hazen, *Narrative of Military Service,* 129–30; Amasa Johnson, "Chickamauga. A Reply to General Wiley and a Defense of General Thomas," *National Tribune,* 16 June 1887; Wiley, "General Hill Answered." Wiley asserts, unconvincingly, that it was he who suggested to Hazen that the brigade build breastworks.

2. OR 30, pt. 1, 535, 568; Kern, *First Ohio,* 20; Hazen, *Narrative of Military Service,* 130.

3. OR 30, pt. 2, 155, 161, 177; Statements of J. T. Hearne, 23 September 1863 and of A. J. Vaughan, 13 October 1863, both in Hill Papers, NCDAH.

4. OR 30, pt. 2, 177, 180, 182, 185; W. E. Yeatman memoirs, 5, CWC, TSLA.

5. OR 30, pt. 2, 183.

6. Ibid., pt. 1, 732, 763; pt. 2, 177; William Volke, et al. to Absolom Baird, 9 September 1895, Twenty-fourth Illinois File, CCNMP; Johnston, "At Chickamauga. A Soldier's Story of the Battle," Lancaster *New Era,* 10 September 1892; Wiley, "General Hill Answered."

7. Henry Richards, *Letters of Captain Henry Richards of the Ninety-third Ohio Infantry* (Cincinnati: Press of Wrightson and Company, 1883), 22–23.

8. Kerns, *First Ohio,* 20.

9. Wagner reminiscences, 80, *CWTI* Collection, USAMHI; Wiley, "General Hill Answered."

10. OR 30, pt. 2, 161, 171; Edward E. Tinney to Charles Van Adder, 1 December 1978, courtesy of Charles Van Adder.

11. Mark Perrin Lowrey Autobiographical Essay, 30 September 1867, University of Southern Mississippi.

12. Charles Van Adder, "A Biographical Sketch of Captain John N. Sloan, C.S.A.," 1–3, unpublished article courtesy of author.

13. OR 30, pt. 2, 164, 166, 168; Preston, "Memoirs of the War," 20–21, Thirty-third Alabama Papers, ADAH.

14. OR 30, pt. 2, 155, 174, 156; Charles Van Adder to Peter Cozzens, 12 October 1990.

15. OR 30, pt. 2, 288, 364.

16. Ibid., 155, 161, 166, 264.

17. Ibid., 168–69.

18. Tourgee, *Story of a Thousand,* 222–23; OR 30, pt. 2, 164, 364.

19. OR, 30, pt. 1, 417, pt. 2, 166; Preston, "Memoirs of the War," 20–21, Thirty-third Alabama Papers, ADAH.

20. Floyd, *Seventy-fifth Indiana,* 158, 163; OR 30, pt. 2, 372, 380, 386; Cahal to Atkinson, 30 September 1863, CWC, TSLA.

21. OR 30, pt. 2, 372, 376, 379.

22. Cahal to Atkinson, 30 September 1863, CWC, TSLA; OR 30, pt. 2, 364, 410.

23. Gray reminiscences, 63, UNC; Cahal to Colonel Atkinson, 30 September 1863, CWC, TSLA.

24. OR 30, pt. 2, 397.

25. Ibid., 390.

26. Gray reminiscences, 63, UNC; OR 30, pt. 2, 393; Floyd, *Seventy-fifth Indiana*, 163.

27. OR 30, pt. 2, 164, 166, 374–83, 386; Longstreet, *From Manassas to Appomattox*, 459.

28. OR 30, pt. 1, 441.

29. Booth, "Chickamauga."

30. Floyd, *Seventy-fifth Indiana*, 165–66.

31. Collins, *Unwritten History of the War*, 158–59; OR 30, pt. 2, 156, 188.

32. OR 30, pt. 2, 156.

33. Ibid., 156, 188–90, 196.

34. Ibid., 142, 240.

35. Ibid., 142, 240–41, 245; Hill, "Chickamauga," 657; Polk, *Polk*, 2:258.

36. OR 30, pt. 2, 245; Warner, *Generals in Gray*, 106; A. M. Speer to Henry V. N. Boynton, 20 October 1894 and Elison Capers to Marcus Wright, 19 June 1891, both in Historical Files, CCNMP.

37. Liddell, *Liddell's Record*, 144–45; OR 30, pt. 2, 242, 245.

38. Polk, *Polk*, 2:258, OR 30, pt. 2, 242, 275, 278, 280; Hill, "Chickamauga," 657.

39. William Carnes, "Memoirs of William Watt Carnes, Captain of Artillery, C.S.A., Army of Tennessee," 144–45, Historical Files, CCNMP (photocopy, original in the possession of William W. Carnes II); W. W. Carnes, "Chickamauga. A Battle of which the Half Has Not Been Told," Atlanta *Constitution*, 8 April 1883.

40. R. J. Redding to Henry V. N. Boynton, 24 October 1894, Historical Files, CCNMP; OR 30, pt. 2, 242, 245.

41. Hannaford, *Sixth Ohio*, 466; Palmer, *Personal Recollections*, 182; *Indiana at Chickamauga*, 151.

42. OR 30, pt. 2, 246; Redding to Boynton, 24 October 1894, Historical Files, CCNMP.

43. Capers to Boynton, 19 June 1891, Historical Files, CCNMP.

44. OR 30, pt. 2, 246, 249; Redding to Boynton, 24 October 1894, Speer to Boyton, 26 October 1894, and James Boynton to Boynton, 29 October 1894, all in Historical Files, CCNMP.

45. OR 30, pt. 2, 253, 259.

46. Ibid., pt. 1, 250, and pt. 2, 259, 267; Kiene, *Civil War Diary*, 18.

47. Donahower, "Narrative, Volume 2," 132–34, Donahower Papers, MnHS; Stevens, "Chickamauga: A Wartime Letter"; Grebner, *We Were the Ninth*, 143.

48. OR 330, pt. 1, 369, 824; Beatty, *Citizen Soldier*, 338.

49. Beatty, *Citizen Soldier*, 344–45.

50. OR 30, pt. 1, 369.

51. Ibid., 369, 379, 824.

52. Ibid., 379, 824, 828, 829, 834; *Indiana at Chickamauga,* 189–90.,

53. OR 30, pt. 1, 544, 841; Wright, *Eighth Kentucky,* 192–93; Perry, *Thirty-eighth Indiana,* 93.

54. OR 30, pt. 1, 847, and pt. 2, 259, 267; Wright, *Eighth Kentucky,* 192–93.

55. OR 30, pt. 2, 259, 262, 265, 269.

CHAPTER TWENTY / THE FATAL ORDER

1. OR 30, pt. 1, 59, 610, 804, 949; Van Cleve to Edward Ruger, 24 May 1867, Thomas Papers, RG 94, National Archives; Lamers, *Edge of Glory,* 342–43; Tucker, *Chickamauga,* 255.

2. OR 30, pt. 1, 70; Lamers, *Edge of Glory,* 343.

3. OR 30, pt. 1, 448.

4. Pirtle, "Leaves from My Notebook," 68–69, Lytle Family Papers, CHS; Sheridan, *Memoirs,* 1:280; OR 30, pt. 1, 580.

5. Pirtle, "Leaves from My Notebook," 63–65, Lytle Family Papers, CHS; OR 30, pt. 1, 70, 139.

6. OR 30, pt. 1, 610, 622–23, 836, 983; O. H. Morgan to H. C. Grosvenor, 25 October 1911, Seventh Indiana Battery File, CCNMP; Skinner, *Pennsylvania at Chickamauga,* 368.

7. Reynolds, "Second Day at Chickamauga," 2, Historical Files, CCNMP.

8. Ibid.; OR 30, pt. 1, 102.

9. OR 30, pt. 1, 409.

10. Reynolds, "Second Day at Chickamauga," 4, Historical Files, CCNMP; Develling, *Seventeenth Regiment,* 102–3.

11. Lamers, *Edge of Glory,* 342. A popular misconception has long existed that Kellogg "discovered" a gap between Reynolds's right and Wood's left while riding from Thomas directly to Rosecrans to request Brannan's division. As the story goes, Kellogg, galloping in rear of the Union lines, saw Reynolds's line of battle but failed to notice that of Brannan on Reynolds's right. From this, Kellogg concluded that Brannan was out of line and that Reynolds's right was "in the air." This is the version presented in Tucker's *Chickamauga.*

This explanation is open to serious criticism on several levels. Most obvious, it ignores Reynolds's own version of events. That Kellogg did in fact speak with Reynolds is borne out in a letter from Rosecrans to the War Department of 13 January 1864, in which he says "General Reynolds sent me word by Captain Kellogg . . . that there were no troops on his immediate right, and that he wanted support there." See OR 30, pt. 1, 102. Moreover, Thomas had been granted the authority the night before to call on Brannan should the need arise; logically, with time of the essence, Kellogg would have ridden directly to Brannan. He probably decided to seek Rosecrans's formal approval (or rather notify him of a *fait accompli*) only after he found that Brannan was not in reserve as he and Thomas had assumed and that his departure would endanger Reynolds's right flank.

Finally, if Kellogg had ridden directly from Thomas to Rosecrans, the quickest and most logical route would have taken him away from the Glenn-Kelly road at a point nearly two hundred yards in rear of the Union lines and across the Dyer field. Even had he continued down the Glenn-Kelly road in rear of the lines as far as the Dyer road, the two hundred yards of heavy timber that intervened between the road and the Union breastworks would have rendered not only Brannan's division but all of King's brigade of Reynolds's division invisible as well.

12. Rosecrans, "Chattanooga Campaign."

13. Lamers, *Edge of Glory,* 343.

14. *OR* 30, pt. 1, 635.

15. Ibid., 983.

16. Ibid. Starling's testimony, given under oath at the Crittenden court of inquiry after the battle, refutes the assertions (which were never based on any evidence) of Garfield apologists that he had no knowledge of the order to Wood. That he actually read the order is unlikely; if he had, Garfield certainly would have clarified its language.

17. Ibid., 694.

18. Ibid., 660; Woodruff, *Fifteen Years Ago,* 285–86, 295–96.

19. *OR* 30, pt. 2, 474.

20. Ibid., pt. 1, 672; Woodruff, *Fifteen Years Ago,* 286.

21. *OR* 30, pt. 1, 635, 983–84.

22. Alexander D. Bache to Rosecrans, 12 January 1864, Rosecrans Papers, UCLA; Cist, *Army of the Cumberland,* 220–21; *OR* 30, pt. 1, 984; John McElroy, "Army of the Cumberland and the Great Central Campaign," *National Tribune,* 4 October 1906; J. T. Woods's manuscript account of Chickamauga, dated 17 October 1863, Laurence M. Strayer Collection.

23. *OR* 30, pt. 1, 500, 635; Lamers, *Edge of Glory,* 343; Cist, *Army of the Cumberland,* 221.

24. Quoted in Tucker, *Chickamauga,* 257.

25. Cist, *Army of the Cumberland,* 223.

26. Turchin, *Chickamauga,* 113–14.

27. McElroy, "Army of the Cumberland and the Great Central Campaign," *National Tribune,* 4 October 1906; *OR* 30, pt. 1, 635.

28. *OR* 30, pt. 1, 657; Woodruff, *Fifteen Years Ago,* 285–86.

Chapter Twenty-one / A Sickening Confusion

1. *OR* 30, pt. 2, 288; Longstreet, *From Manassas to Appomattox,* 447.

2. *OR* 30, pt. 2, 490; Tucker, *Chickamauga,* 265; Postwar schematic of the Brotherton Farm, Historical files, CCNMP.

3. *OR* 30, pt. 1, 500, 532, 534, and pt. 2, 474; Heg, *Civil War Letters,* 164; William C. Black Diary, 19 September 1863, Kansas State Historical Society.

4. *OR* 30, pt. 2, 490, 507.

5. Ibid., pt. 1, 657, 664, 673; *Indiana at Chickamauga,* 194.

6. Belknap, *Michigan at Chickamauga,* 128–29; *OR* 30, pt. 1, 667, 673, and pt. 2, 457.

7. Goodrich, "Gregg's Brigade," 265; OR 30, pt. 2, 495.

8. Oates, *War between the Union and the Confederacy*, 256; OR 30, pt. 1, 409; Develling, *Seventeenth Regiment*, 103.

9. Battlefield Marker 138, "Battery D, First Michigan Light Artillery, 20 September 1863," CCNMP; Belknap, *Michigan at Chickamauga*, 164.

10. OR 30, pt. 1, 411; Morton Hunter, "Chickamauga: Part Taken by Eighty-second Indiana," Bloomington *Telephone*, 14 October 1887.

11. OR 30, pt. 1, 809, 812, 816–17.

12. Van Cleve to Edward Ruger, 24 May 1867, Thomas Papers, RG 94, National Archives; OR 30, pt. 1, 611; Kirk, *Fifteenth Pennsylvania Cavalry*, 270.

13. OR 30, pt. 1, 402, 417, 423, 426.

14. Ibid., pt. 2, 517.

15. Polley, *Hood's Texas Brigade*, 210–11; Mills Lane, ed., *Dear Mother: Don't Grieve About Me . . . Letters from Georgia Soldiers in the Civil War* (Savannah: Beehive Press, 1977), 275.

16. Ibid.; OR 30, pt. 1, 423, 426–27.

17. OR 30, pt. 1, 421–23; *Indiana at Chickamauga*, 138–39.

18. Richard Boyle, "Chickamauga," *National Tribune*, 10 January 1907.

19. P. T. Martin, "Recollections of a Confederate, *CV* 15, no. 5 (May 1907): 564; Lane, *Dear Mother*, 275.

20. OR 30, pt. 2, 457–58.

21. Ibid; Battlefield Marker 177, "Sixth Ohio Battery, 20 September," CCNMP.

Chapter Twenty-two / A Broken-Backed Cat

1. James Fraser to his father, 26 September 1863, Fiftieth Alabama File, CCNMP; OR 30, pt. 2, 303; Warner, *Generals in Gray*, 70.

2. OR 30, pt. 1, 517, 525.

3. Ibid., 517, 522.

4. Ibid., 525.

5. Green, *Volunteer Service*, 36–37; Day, *One Hundred First Ohio*, 172–74.

6. Castle, "Comrade Castle's Address," 12–13.

7. Marcoot, *Five Years in the Sunny South*, 36; OR 30, pt. 1, 500, 590, 592–93, 600; Lamers, *Edge of Glory*, 348.

8. OR 30, pt. 1, 500; Fisher, *A Staff Officer's Story*, 66; Postwar photograph of the Tan Yard, Picture File, CCNMP.

9. Henry Castle, "Sheridan with the Army of the Cumberland," in *Minutes of Proceedings of the Twentieth Annual Reunion of the Survivors, Seventy-third Regiment Illinois Volunteer Infantry. Afternoon and Evening Tuesday, October 2, 1906* (n.p., n.d.), 11, 17.

10. Castle, "Comrade Castle's Address," 13–14; Marcoot, *Five Years in the Sunny South*, 36; OR 30, pt. 1, 592–93.

11. Dana, *Recollections*, 115.

12. Porter to his sister, 3 October 1863, Porter Papers, DLC; Sanderson, letter diary, 21 September 1863, OHS; Kirk, *Fifteenth Pennsylvania Cavalry*, 235; Lamers, *Edge of Glory*, 351; Thruston, "Chickamauga," 412.

13. OR 30, pt. 1, 938, 940-41; Cist, *Army of the Cumberland*, 212; Lamers, *Edge of Glory*, 350-51.

14. OR 30, pt. 2, 304; Manigault, *Carolinian Goes to War*, 98.

15. OR 30, pt. 1, 590, and pt. 2, 330, 336; George Kilmer, "Preacher Soldiers. Parson Jacques [sic] and his Illinoisans of the Seventy-Third," unidentified newspaper clipping (probably from *National Tribune*) in *War Department Pamphlet Number Twenty*, USAMHI.

16. Castle, "Comrade Castle's Address," 13, and "Sheridan and the Army of the Cumberland," 17-18.

17. OR 30, pt. 1, 591-93, 600, and pt. 2, 336, 339; Marcoot, *Five Years in the Sunny South*, 36; "Lieutenant Colonel John Weedon," *CV* 13, no. 10, (October 1905), 443.

18. Castle, "Sheridan and the Army of the Cumberland," 18; Sheridan, *Memoirs*, 1:282-83.

19. Pirtle, "Leaves from My Journal," 71-72, and Edwin Parsons to his parents, 1 October 1863, both in Lytle Family Papers, CHS; Lyman G. Bennett and William Haigh, *History of the Thirty-sixth Regiment Illinois Volunteers, during the War of the Rebellion* (Aurora: Knickerbocker and Hodder, 1876), 467-68.

20. Pirtle, "Leaves from My Journal," 72-73, Lytle Family Papers, CHS.

21. Bennett, *Thirty-sixth Illinois*, 469.

22. Oates, *War between the Union and the Confederacy*, 256.

23. Ibid., 256; OR 30, pt. 2, 334.

24. Bragg to Sykes, 8 February 1873, John F. H. Claiborne Papers, UNC; OR 30, pt. 2, 304; J. Patton Anderson, "Sketch of General Anderson's Life," James Patton Anderson Papers, UNC.

25. OR 30, pt. 2, 318; Manigault, *Carolinian Goes to War*, 98.

26. OR 30, pt. 1, 588, and pt. 2, 322; A. M. Chandler, "Reminiscences of Chickamauga, *CV* 2, no. 3 (March 1894): 79.

27. Edwin Parsons to Elizabeth Lytle Broadwell, 14 August 1888, Lytle Family Papers, CHS.

28. Pirtle, "Leaves from My Journal," 74-77, Lytle Family Papers, CHS; OR 30, pt. 1, 587; Robert S. Walker, "The Pyramids of Chickamauga (William H. Lytle)," Chattanooga *Sunday Times Magazine Section*, 9, 13 September 1936.

29. Howard Green to Nat Foster, 1 November 1863, Parsons to Broadwell, 14 August 1888, and Pirtle, "Leaves from My Journal," 77, all in Lytle Family Papers, CHS.

30. Pirtle, "Leaves from My Journal," 77, Lytle Family Papers, CHS.

31. Mrs. J. Patton Anderson, "Generals Anderson and Lytle — A Reminiscence," *CV* 12, no. 9 (September 1904): 442.

32. Ibid.; Walker, "Pyramids of Chickamauga (Lytle)," Chattanooga *Sunday Times Magazine Section*, 9, 13 September 1936; B. L. Archer, "Incidents of General Lytle's Burial, *CV* 12, no. 9 (September 1904): 442; Owen, *In Camp and Battle*, 286-87.

33. OR 30, pt. 1, 595.

34. Silas Miller to James Barr, 1 and 30 October 1863, Miller Papers, Grand Army of the Republic Memorial Hall and Military Museum, Aurora, Illinois.

35. Rosecrans, "Chattanooga Campaign"; *OR* 30, pt. 1, 58–59; Sanderson, letter diary, 21 September 1863, OHS; Porter to his sister, 3 October 1863, Porter Papers, DLC; Lamers, *Edge of Glory*, 351–53.

36. Dana, *Recollections*, 115; Porter to his sister, 3 October 1863, Porter Papers, DLC.

37. "Biography of General Horace Porter," 4–6, Porter Papers, DLC. The author of this essay is unknown; it may have been autobiographical.

38. *OR* 30, pt. 1, 516–17, 520; John A. Martin, "Some Notes on the Eighth Kansas Infantry and the Battle of Chickamauga. Letters of Colonel John A. Martin," *Kansas Historical Quarterly* 13 (1944): 141–42.

39. Marcoot, *Five Years in the Sunny South*, 37; Kirk, *Fifteenth Pennsylvania Cavalry*, 270.

40. Kirk, *Fifteenth Pennsylvania Cavalry*, 242.

41. Sanderson, letter diary, 29 September 1863, OHS.

42. Excerpts from diary and letters of John Levering, 20 September 1863, Historical Files, CCNMP; *OR* 30, pt. 1, 936, 950, 956; Kirk, *Fifteenth Pennsylvania Cavalry*, 264–65.

43. *OR* 30, pt. 1, 598; Smith, *Private Smith's Journal*, 98.

44. Manigault, *Carolinian Goes to War*, 98; *OR* 30, pt. 2, 346; Smith, *Private Smith's Journal*, 98–99; Cornelius I. Walker, *Rolls and Historical Sketch of the Tenth Regiment, So. Ca. Volunteers in the Army of the Late Confederate States* (Charleston: Walker, Evans and Cogswell, 1881), 50.

45. McGee, *Seventy-second Indiana*, 185; *Indiana at Chickamauga*, 206–7; *OR* 30, pt. 1, 448.

46. McGee, *Seventy-second Indiana*, 185; *OR* 30, pt. 1, 598–99, and pt. 2, 346; Gates Thruston to Henry V. N. Boynton, 14 October 1879, Seventy-second Indiana File, CCNMP.

47. Thruston, "The Crisis at Chickamauga," in *Battles and Leaders*, 3:664; Thruston to Boynton, 14 October 1879, Seventy-second Indiana File, CCNMP.

48. *OR* 30, pt. 1, 448, 462, 548; Thruston to Boynton, 14 October 1879, Seventy-second Indiana File, CCNMP; Orlando A. Somers, *A Protest against, and Appeal from the Action of the Indiana-Chickamauga Park Commissioners, and Others to the Commissioners of the National Military Park, Chickamauga, Georgia, together with Specifications of Errors, Citations of Proof, with Comment. By the Survivors' Association of the 8th Indiana Cavalry, 39th Regiment of Indiana Volunteers* (Kokomo, Ind.: Tribune Print, 1901), 7–11; J. N. Jones, "Chickamauga," *National Tribune*, 4 July 1901; Sketch map depicting charge of Wilder's brigade, Seventy-second Indiana File, CCNMP.

49. Atkins to Cist, 18 March 1898, Abraham Lincon Book Shop, Chicago; Manigault, *Carolinian Goes to War*, 99, 103.

50. Somers, *Protest against the Indiana-Chickamauga Park Commissioners*, 27–29; Manigault, *Carolinian Goes to War*, 99; Sunderland, *Wilder's Brigade*, 88–89.

51. McGee, *Seventy-second Indiana*, 185–86; Sunderland, *Wilder's Brigade*, 88–89.

52. Quoted in Sunderland, *Wilder's Brigade*, 89; *OR* 30, pt. 2, 318.

53. *Ninety-second Illinois,* 112; Atkins to Cist, 18 March 1898, Abraham Lincon Book Shop, Chicago; George Wilson, "Wilder's Brigade. The Mounted Infantry in the Chickamauga Campaign, III," *National Tribune,* 26 October 1893; McGee, *Seventy-second Indiana,* 186; Sunderland, *Wilder's Brigade,* 89–91; OR 30, pt. 1, 448–54, 462, 598.

CHAPTER TWENTY-THREE / THE SIGNS GREW WORSE

1. OR 30, pt. 1, 361, 622–23; O. H. Morgan to Henry Van Ness Boynton, 28 October 1893, Seventh Indiana Battery File, CCNMP.

2. OR 30, pt. 1, 412, 622–23; P. L. Hubbard, "The Capture of the Eighth Indiana Battery," *National Tribune,* 6 June 1907.

3. OR 30, pt. 1 664, 667, 673, 984; Stormont, *Fifty-eighth Indiana,* 191.

4. OR 30, pt. 1, 288–89, 453–56; Longstreet, *From Manassas to Appomattox,* 448–50.

5. OR 30, pt. 2, 459, 512, 519; Battlefield Marker 179: "Robertson's Brigade, September 20, 1863, 11:30 A.M." CCNMP; Theophilus F. Botsford and Joseph Q. Burton, *Historical Sketches of the Forty-seventh Alabama Infantry Regiment, C.S.A.* (Montgomery: Confederate Pub. Co., 1982), 9.

6. OR 30, pt. 1, 611, 984.

7. Ibid., 623, 673; Botsford and Burton, *Forty-seventh Alabama,* 9, 18.

8. Ibid.; OR 30, pt. 1, 623, 836; Skinner, *Pennsylvania at Chickamauga,* 368.

9. OR 30, pt. 1, 623, 667; Hubbard, "Capture of the Eighth Indiana Battery"; Gammage, *The Camp, the Bivouac, and the Battlefield,* 91; Lavender, *They Never Came Back,* 80; Walter Clark, ed., *Histories of the Several Regiments and Battalions from North Carolina in the Great War 1861–1865, Written by Members of Their Respective Commands,* 5 vols. (Goldsboro, N.C.: Nash Brothers, Printer, 1901), 2:713–15.

10. Ibid.; OR 30, pt. 2, 495, 498; J. G. McCown, "About Ector's and McNair's Brigades, *CV* 9, no. 3 (March 1901): 113.

11. OR 30, pt. 1, 611, 984–85.

12. Ibid., 60, 361, 849; Rosecrans, "Chattanooga Campaign."

13. OR 30, pt. 1, 59–60; Cist, *Army of the Cumberland,* 212, 224; Kirk, *Fifteenth Pennsylvania Cavalry,* 246.

14. So Garfield later told his friend and confidant, Major General Jacob Cox. See Cox, *Military Reminiscences,* 10; Lamers, *Edge of Glory,* 353.

15. William S. Rosecrans to Sylvester Rosecrans, 9 October 1893, Rosecrans Papers, UCLA.

16. Cist, *Army of the Cumberland,* 224–26; Rosecrans, "Chattanooga Campaign."

17. Rosecrans, "The Campaign for Chattanooga," *Century Magazine* (May 1887): 132. For a slightly different version of the Rosecrans-Garfield colloquy, see *Society of the Army of the Cumberland, Burial of General Rosecrans, Arlington National Cemetery, May 17, 1902* (Cincinnati: Robert Clarke, 1903), 87–89.

18. James R. Gilmore, "Garfield's Ride at Chickamauga," *McClure's Magazine* 5 (1895): 358; Cist, *Army of the Cumberland,* 225–26; "General Sherman's Letter,

What General Rosecrans Says of It," *National Tribune,* 8 October 1881; Calvin Goddard to Rosecrans, 8 December 1863 and Rosecrans to M. J. Patton, 18 February 1890, both in Rosecrans Papers, UCLA.

19. Cist, *Army of the Cumberland,* 225; Gilmore, "Garfield's Ride," 358; OR 30, pt. 1, 60.

CHAPTER TWENTY-FOUR / THEY CAN WHIP US NEVER

1. OR 30, pt. 1, 252.
2. Ibid., 635; Lamers, *Edge of Glory,* 345.
3. OR 30, pt. 1, 636.
4. "William A. Brown's Book," Stanford's Battery File, CCNMP; George T. Todd, *First Texas Regiment* (Waco, Tex.: Texiana Press, 1963), 18; W. M. Abernathy, "Our Mess: Southern Gallantry and Privations, 1861–1865," Abernathy Papers, MDAH.
5. OR 30, pt. 2, 636.
6. Snider, "Reminiscences of the War," 242; OR 30, pt. 2, 512, 514.
7. OR 30, pt. 1, 636–37, 708; Clark, *125th O.V.I.,* 106.
8. Giles, *Rags and Hope,* 207–8; Clark, *125th O.V.I.,* 106.
9. OR 30, pt. 2, 512, 515.
10. Clark, *125th O.V.I.,* 107; OR 30, pt. 1, 636, 640, and pt. 2, 517.
11. OR 30, pt. 1, 704, and pt. 2, 512–13; Giles, *Rags and Hope,* 201.
12. OR 30, pt. 1, 440; Clark, *125th O.V.I.,* 106, 126.
13. OR 30, pt. 1, 441, 470, 475; Tourgee, *Story of a Thousand,* 223–24; High, *Sixty-eighth Indiana,* 90–91; Charles Radcliffe, "Battle of Chickamauga," *National Tribune,* 1 September 1891.
14. Tourgee, *Story of a Thousand,* 225.
15. Sorrel, *Recollections of a Staff Officer,* 203–4; Longstreet, *From Manassas to Appomattox,* 448.
16. Hood, *Advance and Retreat,* 63–64; West, *Texan in Search of a Fight,* 109.
17. OR 30, pt. 2, 503; John Coxe, "Chickamauga," *CV* 30, no. 7 (July 1922): 291.
18. Hood, *Advance and Retreat,* 63–67; Dyer, *Gallant Hood,* 210; "Major Abner W. Wilkins," *CV* 16, no. 2 (February 1918): 78.
19. OR 30, pt. 2, 503–4; "Correspondence of the Charleston Courier, by Personne, 18 October 1863," in the Lancaster *Ledger,* 4 November 1863, James' South Carolina Battalion File, CCNMP.
20. Clark, *125th O.V.I.,* 107; OR 30, pt. 1, 637, 695.
21. OR 30, pt. 1, 252, 694; Clark, *125th O.V.I.,* 107–110.
22. OR 30, pt. 1, 706, 708; *The Military History of Ohio, Illustrated. Stark County Soldiers' Edition* (Toledo: A. H. Hardesty, 1886), 324.
23. Stormont, *Fifty-eighth Indiana,* 191–92; Coxe, "Chickamauga," 293.
24. OR 30, pt. 1, 704; "Correspondence of the Charleston Courier, by Personne," Lancaster *Ledger,* 4 November 1863, James' South Carolina Battalion File, CCNMP.
25. William D. Trantham, "Wonderful Story of Richard R. Kirkland," *CV* 16, no. 3 (March 1908): 105.

26. *OR* 30, pt. 1, 700.

27. Letter from an unidentified captain of the Third Kentucky to Henry V. N. Boynton, 9 October 1893, Third Kentucky File, CCNMP.

28. *OR* 30, pt. 1, 637, 708; Charles T. Clark to E. A. Carman, 12 February 1909; "Correspondence of the Charleston Courier, by Personne, 18 October 1863," Lancaster *Ledger*, 4 November 1863, in James' South Carolina Battalion File, CCNMP; Archibald Gracie, *The Truth about Chickamauga* (Boston: Houghton, Mifflin, 1911), 259–60.

CHAPTER TWENTY-FIVE / GIVE US A POSITION

1. "Few Survivors of Civil War Days Still Live in Vicinity of Chickamauga Battlefield," Chattanooga *News*, 22 September 1923.

2. Tucker, *Chickamauga*, 330.

3. Bishop, "Van Derveer's Brigade at Chickamauga," 65; John Rammage to Chickamauga-Chattanooga National Battlefield Park Commission, 17 March 1896, One Hundred Twenty-first Ohio File, CCNMP.

4. "Few Survivors of Civil War Days Still Live in Vicinity of Chickamauga Battlefield," Chattanooga *News*, 22 September 1863.

5. *OR* 30, pt. 1, 1040–41, 1047–48; Sturges Diary, 20 September 1863, *CWTI* Collection; Jerry Korn, *The Fight for Chattanooga: Chickamauga to Missionary Ridge* (Alexandria, Va.: Time-Life Books, 1985), 74–77; Canfield, *Twenty-first Ohio*, 142–43; Vance, "On Thomas' Right," 91.

6. See the testimony of various officers in the Negley Court of Inquiry for more details of Negley's actions on Horseshoe Ridge (*OR* 30, pt. 1, 385, 1040–47); Canfield, *Twenty-first Ohio*, 115; Ward, "The Storm Breaks," 114–15.

7. *OR* 30, pt. 1, 438, 1066; Skinner, *Pennsylvania at Chickamauga*, 224–25.

8. Walker, "History of the First Brigade," Thomas Papers, RG 94, National Archives; "Recollections of Colonel Walker," *Reunion Tribune*, 23 September 1886; Silas Canfield to Arnold McMahan, 7 June 1889, Sullivan Collection, BGSU; Vance, "On Thomas' Right," 90.

9. Canfield to McMahan, 7 June 1889, and Draft Report of the Twenty-first Ohio in the Battle of Chickamauga in McMahan's Libby Prison Notebook, both in Sullivan Collection, BGSU; Canfield, *Twenty-first Ohio*, 116, 136, 142–43; Isaac Cusac to Henry V. N. Boynton, 13 March 1909, Twenty-First Ohio File, CCNMP; Gracie, *Truth about Chickamauga*, 53–55.

10. Walker, "History of the First Brigade," Thomas Papers, RG 94, National Archives; Alfred Hunter, *History of the Eighty-second Indiana Volunteer Infantry, Its Organization, Campaigns and Battles* (Indianapolis: William B. Burford, Printer, 1893), 82–86.

11. *OR* 30, pt. 1, 424–25, 830–31; McElroy, *Chickamauga and Chattanooga*, 35.

12. *OR* 30, pt. 1, 370; Beatty, *Citizen Soldier*, 340; Calkins, *One Hundred and Fourth Illinois*, 139; Hunter, *Eighty-second Indiana*, 87.

13. *OR* 30, pt. 1, 701, 704–5, 708, 1008; A. Andrews to the Chickamauga-Chattanooga National Park Commission, 5 February 1909, Sixty-fourth Ohio File,

CCNMP; Clark to Carmen, 12 February 1909, and Whiteside Diary, 20 September 1863, both in One Hundred Twenty-fifth Ohio File, CCNMP; Letter from unidentified captain of the Third Kentucky to Henry V. N. Boynton, 9 October 1893, Third Kentucky File, CCNMP; Roland Critchfield to E. A. Carman, 16 February 1909, Sixty-fifth Ohio File, CCNMP; Gracie, *Truth about Chickamauga*, 54; George Dolton to Arnold McMahan, 6 June 1890, Sullivan Collection, BGSU.

14. *OR* 30, pt. 1, 638.

15. Letter from unidentified captain of the Third Kentucky to Boynton, 9 October 1893, Third Kentucky File, CCNMP; Shanks, *Personal Recollections*, 69; McKinney, *Education in Violence*, 247–48.

16. Hinman, *Sherman Brigade*, 429; Clark, *125th O.V.I.*, 117.

17. McKinney, *Education in Violence*, 207–8.

18. Ward, "The Storm Breaks," 107.

19. *Society of the Army of the Cumberland, Thirtieth Reunion, Louisville, Kentucky, October 8, 9 1901* (Cincinnati: Robert Clarke, 1902), 183.

20. Ward, "The Storm Breaks," 115; Sturges diary, 20 September 1863, *CWTI* Collection, USAMHI.

21. *OR* 30, pt. 1, 338.

22. Ibid., 331.

23. Ibid., 331, 339, 349, 409–10, 660, 1030–31, 1047–48; Sturges diary, 20 September 1863, *CWTI* Collection, USAMHI; Belknap, *Michigan at Chickamauga*, 128–29.

24. Ward, "The Storm Breaks," 115.

25. Coxe, "Chickamauga," 293; Vance, "On Thomas' Right," 91; Canfield, *Twenty-first Ohio*, 116; "Colonel Walker's Recollections," *Reunion Tribune*, 23 September 1886.

26. Coxe, "Chickamauga," 293; *OR* 30, pt. 1, 388–89; Canfield, *Twenty-first Ohio*, 136.

27. *OR* 30, pt. 2, 508.

28. Ibid., 504; "Correspondence of the Charleston Courier, by Personne, 18 October 1863," Lancaster *Ledger*, 4 November 1863, in James' South Carolina Battalion File, CCNMP; *Ceremonies at the Unveiling of the South Carolina Monument on the Chickamauga Battlefield, May 27th, 1901. Together with a Record of the Commission Who Suggested and Were Instrumental in Securing and Erecting the Monument, etc.* (n.p., n.d.), 17.

29. Benjamin Humphreys, "History of the Sunflower Guards," manuscript in John F. H. Claiborne Papers, UNC; Warner, *Generals in Gray*, 16, 144.

30. Humphreys, "History of the Sunflower Guards," John F. H. Claiborne Papers, UNC.

31. Oates, *War between the Union and the Confederacy*, 259.

32. Ibid., 260–61; "Correspondence of the Charleston Courier, by Personne, 18 October 1863," Lancaster *Ledger*, 4 November 1863, James' South Carolina Battalion File, CCNMP.

33. *OR* 30, pt. 2, 504; "Correspondence of the Charleston Courier, by Personne, 18 October 1863," Lancaster *Ledger*, 4 November 1863, James' South Carolina Battalion File, CCNMP.

34. Morton Hunter, "Address by General Hunter," Bloomington *Telephone*, 7 October 1887; Haynie, *Nineteenth Illinois*, 229; E. A. Carman to Albert Cone, 20 February 1909, Cone to Carmen, 1 March 1909, and James Whallon to James S. Fullerton, 26 May 1894, all in Nineteenth Illinois File, CCNMP; OR 30, pt. 1, 381.

35. OR 30, pt. 1, 370; Haynie, *Nineteenth Illinois*, 229.

36. Belknap, *Michigan at Chickamauga*, 117; Oates, *War between the Union and the Confederacy*, 261-62.

37. J. S. Gilbert to J. Fuller Lyon, undated letter entitled "Ensign Clark's Courage," in scrapbook of the same name, CCNMP; Archibald Gracie, Jr., to Robert R. Hemphill, 25 May 1907, Hemphill Family Papers, DU. Gracie believed the incident to have occurred between 3:30 and 4:00 P.M. However, Kershaw states in his report that the Seventh was no longer actively attacking Horseshoe Ridge at that hour.

38. Oates, *War between the Union and the Confederacy*, 262.

39. OR 30, pt. 2, 504; Clark to Carmen, 12 February 1909, One Hundred Twenty-fifth Ohio File, CCNMP.

40. OR 30, pt. 2, 504, 510.

41. Gracie, *Truth about Chickamauga*, 245; Humphreys, "History of the Sunflower Guards," John F. H. Claiborne Papers, UNC.

42. OR 30, pt. 2, 509; Humphreys, "History of the Sunflower Guards," John F. H. Claiborne Papers, UNC; Gracie, *Truth about Chickamauga*, 245-46.

43. Letter from unidentified captain of the Third Kentucky to Boynton, 9 October 1893, Third Kentucky File.

44. Canfield, *Twenty-first Ohio*, 116-18; Canfield to McMahan, 11 June 1889, and "A Memento of the 9th Reunion of the 21st Regiment O.V.I.," *Reunion Tribune*, 23 September 1886, both in Sullivan Collection, BGSU.

Chapter Twenty-Six / A Hell of a Fight

1. OR 30, pt. 2, 459.

2. Ibid., pt. 1, 459-60, 493-94.

3. Ibid., pt. 2, 460.

4. Connelly, *Autumn of Glory*, 224.

5. OR 30, pt. 2, 460; Gracie, *Truth about Chickamauga*, 56.

6. OR 30, pt. 2, 304, 460.

7. Ibid., pt. 1, 460-61, 476.

8. Elijah Wiseman, "Tennesseans at Chickamauga, Vivid Descriptions of the Sunday's Fighting," *CV* 2, no. 7 (July 1894): 205; OR 30, pt. 2, 482-83; Martin, "Recollections of a Confederate," 231; "Viditoe House," postwar photograph in Historical Files, CCNMP.

9. OR 30, pt. 2, 504; "Correspondence of the Charleston Courier, by Personne, 18 October 1863," Lancaster *Ledger*, 4 November 1863, James' South Carolina Battalion File, CCNMP.

10. OR 30, pt. 2, 318, 321, 327.

11. Vance, "On Thomas' Right," 91.

12. *OR* 30, pt. 2, 461; Martin, "Recollections of a Confederate," 231.

13. Canfield, *Twenty-first Ohio*, 120–21; *OR* 30, pt. 2, 318, 325; McMahan's Draft Report of Chickamauga, Sullivan Collection, BGSU.

14. *OR* 30, pt. 2, 318, 321–23, 327; Vance, "On Thomas' Right," 93; McMahan's Libby Notebook and an undated essay entitled "The Regiment," written by McMahan, both in Sullivan Collection, BGSU; Canfield, *Twenty-first Ohio*, 121.

15. Vance, "On Thomas' Right," 91.

16. Ibid., 91–92.

17. Ibid., 93; Canfield, *Twenty-first Ohio*, 144; H. H. Alban to McMahan, 12 June 1889, and McMahan's Draft Report, Sullivan Collection, BGSU; *OR* 30, pt. 2, 462, 496.

18. Partridge, *History of the Ninety-sixth Illinois*, 226–27.

19. *OR* 30, pt. 1, 69, 854, and pt. 3, 741; J. G. Taylor to John G. Mitchell, 8 March 1882, Strayer Collection; John M. Morgan, "Old Steady: The Role of General James Blair Steedman at the Battle of Chickamauga," *Northwest Ohio Quarterly* 22 (1950): 85.

20. *OR* 30, pt. 1, 69, 139–40.

21. Woods, "Chickamauga," 5–6, manuscript account dated 25 October 1883, Strayer Collection; "In Memoriam: Gordon Granger," *Society of the Army of the Cumberland. Fifteenth Reunion, Cincinnati, Ohio 1883* (Cincinnati: Robert Clarke, 1884), 214.

22. J. Gordon Taylor to John G. Mitchell, 8 March 1882, Strayer Collection.

23. J. S. Fullerton, "Reenforcing Thomas at Chickamauga," in *Battles and Leaders*, 3:666; *OR* 30, pt. 1, 854.

24. For a detailed treatment of the postwar claims and counterclaims of Granger and Steedman and their respective supporters in this matter, see Morgan, "Old Steady," 73–78.

A few contemporary opinions on the question are worth relating here. Captain William Avery, a member of Granger's staff, wrote Colonel John Mitchell that Henry Cist, who was voted the official historian of the Army of the Cumberland by its reunion society, had "gone over the controversy and he [found] the claim of Steedman is utterly groundless" (Avery to Mitchell, 18 March 1882, Strayer Collection). Mitchell agreed (Mitchell to Woods, 24 February 1882, Strayer Collection). Although he retained no special fondness for Granger, whom he called a "blatherskite" in a postwar letter, Rosecrans also sided with that general in the dispute. "Of my own knowledge I can tell you that Steedman was under Granger's command and would never have moved to the front under orders except through him" (Rosecrans to Silas Canfield, 14 January 1882, and to J. T. Woods, 15 February 1882, both in Strayer Collection). Finally, Colonel Henry Boynton, as historian of the Chickamauga-Chattanooga National Battlefield Park Commission, wrote: "Let the truth be stated plainly and with the utmost positiveness. General Steedman did not go to the battlefield either in defiance of or in disobedience to the orders of General Granger. The movement was ordered by Granger" (Boynton to Woods, 20 November 1883, Strayer Collection).

Finally, in his own report of the battle, Steedman himself says: "At 11:30,

General Granger becoming satisfied, from the heavy and receding sounds of artillery, that the enemy was pressing the left of our line severely, ordered me to move to the battlefield as rapidly as possible" (OR 30, pt. 1, 860).

25. Mitchell, quoted in an undated series of notes on Chickamauga by Arnold McMahan, Strayer Collection.

26. Taylor to Mitchell, 8 March 1882, Strayer Collection; OR 30, pt. 1, 854.

27. Fullerton, "Reinforcing Thomas at Chickamauga," 666; Taylor to Mitchell, 8 March 1882 and Mitchell to Woods, 9 March 1882, both in Strayer Collection; Morgan, "Old Steady," 87–88; Charles Partridge, "The Ninety-sixth Illinois at Chickamauga," Papers of the Illinois State Historical Society 15 (1912): 75.

28. Partridge, History of the Ninety-sixth Illinois, 177.

29. OR 30, pt. 2, 525; Anderson, "Gracie — Chickamauga — Whitaker," 251.

30. Woods, Steedman and His Men, 42–43; Partridge, "Ninety-sixth Illinois at Chickamauga," 75.

31. Battery M, First Illinois, 85–86; Partridge, History of the Ninety-sixth Illinois, 178–79; Dolton to McMahan, 3 February 1890, Sullivan Collection, BGSU.

32. Seth Moe to the editor, Cincinnati Commercial, 5 November 1883; OR 30, pt. 1, 854, 871; Fullerton, "Reinforcing Thomas at Chickamauga," 666–67.

33. Isaac Doan, Reminiscences of the Chattanooga Campaign, a Paper Read at the Reunion of Company B, Fortieth Ohio Infantry, at Xenia, O., August 22, 1894, by Sergeant Isaac C. Doan (Richmond, Ind.: N.p., 1894), 4; Holmes, 52nd O.V.I., 126; Isaac Royse, History of the 115th Regiment Illinois Volunteer Infantry (Terra Haute, Ind.: N.p., 1900), 124–25.

34. Edward Robbins, Civil War Experiences, 1862–1865 (Carthage, Ill.: n.p., 1919), 3.

35. John Patton Memoirs, 17, DLC; Shanks, Personal Recollections, 68–69; McKinney, Education in Violence, 249; Fullerton, "Reinforcing Thomas at Chickamauga," 667.

36. OR 30, pt. 1, 860; McKinney, Education in Violence, 250.

37. McKinney, Education in Violence, 250.

38. OR 30, pt. 1, 860; Fullerton, "Reinforcing Thomas at Chickamauga," 667.

39. George Green to E. D. Swain, 19 November 1898, Seventy-eighth Illinois File, CCNMP; OR 30, pt. 1, 1863.

40. Royse, 115th Illinois, 127–28.

41. Partridge, History of the Ninety-sixth Illinois, 184.

42. Ibid., 184–85; Royse, 115th Illinois, 127–28; James W. Dove, "Chickamauga, Another Account of General Steedman's Gallantry on that Bloody Field," National Tribune, 13 March 1884.

43. "Statement of William B. Hamilton," and a partial typescript of an address given at a reunion of Whitaker's brigade in Toledo, 18 September 1908, 4–5, both in Twenty-second Michigan File, CCNMP; John Robertson, Michigan in the War (Lansing: W. S. George and Company, State Printers, 1882), 424; McMahan Draft Report, Sullivan Collection, BGSU.

44. Partridge, History of the Ninety-sixth Illinois, 206; Whitaker's Brigade reunion address, 5–6, Twenty-second Michigan File, CCNMP; "Correspondence

of the Charleston Courier, by Personne, 18 October 1863," Lancaster *Ledger,* 4 November 1863, James' South Carolina Battalion File, CCNMP; OR 30, pt. 2, 504; N. H. Miller to McMahan, 12 June 1889, Sullivan Collection, BGSU.

45. Carlton to McMahan, 8 August 1889, and Dolton to McMahan, 25 June 1890, both in Sullivan Collection, BGSU; Gracie, *Truth about Chickamauga,* 405–6; McKinney, *Education in Violence,* 251; Joseph Foraker, *Notes of a Busy Life,* 2 vols. (Cincinnati: Stewart and Vidd, 1916), 1:25; Mabel Carlton Horner, "Caleb Henry Carlton," manuscript biography in Caleb Carlton Papers, DLC.

46. OR 30, pt. 1, 853; Partridge, *History of the Ninety-sixth Illinois,* 210; Thomas Eddy, *The Patriotism of Illinois, A Record of the Civil and Military History of the State in the War for the Union,* 2 vols. (Chicago: Clarke and Company, 1865), 1:75; "In Memoriam: Brigadier General Walter C. Whitaker," *Society of the Army of the Cumberland. Nineteenth Reunion, Chicago, Illinois, 1888* (Cincinnati: Robert Clarke, 1889), 190–93; George Dolton to McMahan, 6 June 1890, Sullivan Collection, BGSU.

47. Royse, *115th Illinois,* 139; OR 30, pt. 2, 496; G. S. Robinson, "Steedman's Charge at Chickamauga," *National Tribune,* 20 December 1906.

48. Royse, *115th Illinois,* 133.

49. Thomas J. Doughman Civil War Recollections, 7, Eighty-ninth Illinois File, CCNMP; Carlton to McMahan, 8 August 1889 Sullivan Collection, BGSU.

50. Partridge, *History of the Ninety-sixth Illinois,* 186, 206; J. Edward James to his sister, 24 September 1863, J. Edward James Letters, Memphis State University.

51. Carter Van Vleck to Sady Broaddus, 27 September 1863, William Broaddus Papers, DU; Extracts from letter of Colonel Darius Warner, One Hundred Thirteenth Ohio File, CCNMP; Francis McAdams, *Our Knapsack, Sketches for the Boys in Blue* (Columbus: Charles M. Cott, 1884), 42; Green to Swain, 19 November 1898, Ninety-Sixth Illinois File, CCNMP; OR 30, pt. 2, 462, 476, 482, 496; F. M. Kelso, "Tennesseans at Chickamauga, a Trio of Brave Staff Officers," CV 2, no. 7 (July 1894): 324.

52. McKinney, *Education in Violence,* 250; Fullerton, "Reinforcing Thomas at Chickamauga," 667.

53. Shanks, *Personal Recollections,* 275–76; Mitchell to Woods, 9 March 1882, Strayer Collection.

54. Extracts from letter of Colonel Warner, One Hundred Thirteenth Ohio File, CCNMP.

55. Partridge, *History of the Ninety-sixth Illinois,* 187, 206, 236–38; John Smith, *The Right of the Federal Army at Chickamauga* (Chicago: Knight, Leonard, and Company, 1894), 6, 11–13; George Dolton to McMahan, 22 January 1890, Sullivan Collection, BGSU; Gifford S. Robinson, "Chickamauga," manuscript recollections in Gifford S. Robinson Papers, ISHL.

56. Some accounts have erroneously placed the Ninety-eighth Ohio to the left of the One Hundred Thirteenth. For more on the correct positioning of the regiments of Mitchell's brigade, see J. L. Ervin to Senator Bledsoe, 11 February 1895, Ninety-eighth Ohio File and Extracts from Colonel Warner's Letter, One Hundred Thirteenth Ohio File, both in CCNMP; OR 30, pt. 1, 869; "Snodgrass

or Horseshoe Ridge," map by George Dolton, in Sullivan Collection, BGSU; Smith, *Right of the Federal Army,* 11–18; Doughman Recollections, 7, Eighty-ninth Ohio File, CCNMP; Sketch maps of Whitaker's position on Horseshoe Ridge drawn by Caleb Carlton and by McMahan, in Sullivan Collection, BGSU; W. G. McClellan, "Chickamauga," *National Tribune,* 14 February 1884. Veterans from the One Hundred Twenty-first Ohio also maintained that the Ninety-sixth Illinois never formed on their right. See Charles Webster to Boyton, 9 January 1896, and Jacob Rhodes, et al., to the Chickamauga-Chattanooga National Battlefield Park Commission, 10 February 1896, both in One Hundred Twenty-first Ohio File, CCNMP. The claim of the Ninety-sixth, however, has been substantiated by eyewitnesses from other units, including Battery M, First Illinois.

57. Taylor to Mitchell, 8 March 1882, Strayer Collection.

58. Donahower, "Narrative, Volume 2," 136, Donahower Papers, MnHS; Bishop, *Second Minnesota,* 108–9; Bishop to McMahan, 10 August 1889, Sullivan Collection, BGSU.

59. Walker, "History of the Second Brigade," Thomas Papers, RG 94, National Archives; *OR* 30, pt. 1, 424.

60. Alfred Hunter, *Eighty-second Indiana;* Morton Hunter, "At Chickamauga, The Part Taken by the Eighty-second Indiana," *National Tribune,* 24 November 1887.

61. Lieutenant Colonel Bishop and Captain Donahower of the Second Minnesota claimed that their regiment relieved the Twenty-first Ohio as soon as it came on the field. Major McMahan and the officers of the Twenty-first maintained that their regiment held the front line until after the next Confederate attack while the Minnesotans engaged the enemy from behind the Twenty-first. The weight of evidence seems to support the Ohioans' contention. *OR* 30, pt. 1 424; Donahower, "Narrative, Volume 2," 137, Donahower Papers, MnHS; Bishop to McMahan, 10 August 1889, Canfield to McMahan, 18 July 1889, Miscellaneous Notes in McMahan's Libby Prison Notebook, all in Sullivan Collection, BGSU (a number of other letters in the collection also deal with this question); Canfield, *Twenty-first Ohio,* 136; Isaac Cusac, "The Twenty-first Ohio at Chickamauga," *National Tribune,* 5 September 1907.

62. Thruston, "Chickamauga," 413; *OR* 30, pt. 1, 639; Bishop to McMahan, 10 August 1889, and miscellaneous notes in McMahan's Libby Notebook, both in Sullivan Collection, BGSU; Extracts from Colonel Warner's letter, One Hundred Thirteenth Ohio File, CCNMP.

63. McKinney, *Education in Violence,* 251.

Chapter Twenty-seven / A Few Are Holding Out

1. Tucker, *Chickamauga,* 337.

2. Longstreet, *From Manassas to Appomattox,* 450; *OR* 30, pt. 1, 289, 304–5, 492–93; Tucker, *Chickamauga,* 337; Claiborne to Boynton, 16 April 1891, Historical Files, CCNMP.

3. *OR* 30, pt. 2, 358; Longstreet, *From Manassas to Appomattox,* 450.

4. Owen, *In Camp and Battle*, 274–75, 281; Longstreet, *From Manassas to Appomattox*, 451.

5. Longstreet, *From Manassas to Appomattox*, 452; Hill, "Chickamauga," 659; Connelly, *Autumn of Glory*, 225; Frank Burr, "Chickamauga, The Bloody Field of Carnage and Death Revisited," Atlanta *Constitution*, 1 April 1883.

6. OR 30, pt. 1, 860, and pt. 2, 462, 304–5, 504.

7. Doughman recollections, 8–9, Eighty-ninth Ohio File, CCNMP.

8. William J. McKell, "The Journal of Sergt. Wm. J. McKell," *Civil War History*, 3 (September 1957): 317–18.

9. Woods, *Steedman and His Men*, 60.

10. Bishop to McMahan, 10 August 1889, Sullivan Collection, BGSU; OR 30, pt. 1, 424; Partridge, *History of the Ninety-sixth Illinois*, 211.

11. Patton Memoirs, Book 17, DLC.

12. Ibid.

13. Doan, *Reminiscences of the Chattanooga Campaign*, 6–7; *Battery M, First Illinois*, 88–89.

14. Woods, *Steedman and His Men*, 60–62; Doughman recollections, 9, Eighty-ninth Ohio File, CCNMP; J. C. Smith to the Editor, Toledo *Journal*, 12 December 1883.

15. Batchelor diary, 20 September 1863, ISHL.

16. OR 30, pt. 2, 463.

17. Manigault, *Carolinian Goes to War*, 100, 106.

18. OR 30, pt. 1, 867, and pt. 2, 337, 339, 470; Dolton to McMahan, 27 August 1890, Sullivan Collection, BGSU.

19. OR 30, pt. 2, 349–50, 353–54.

20. Ibid., 470.

21. J. C. Moore, "McNair's Arkansas Brigade, *CV* 14, no. 3 (March 1906): 124; OR 30, pt. 2, 463.

22. Oates, *War between the Union and the Confederacy*, 263.

23. Canfield, *Twenty-first Ohio*, 136; McMahan's Libby Notebook, Sullivan Collection, BGSU.

24. OR 30, pt. 2, 318–19, 325, 327; George Dolton to John C. Rietti, 22 April and 10 May 1890, John C. Rietti Papers, MDAH.

25. OR 30, pt. 2, 463–64.

Chapter Twenty-eight / I Never Saw Better Fighting

1. OR 30, pt. 1, 893.

2. Carter, *First Tennessee Cavalry*, 97; OR 30, pt. 1, 900.

3. Ibid.; E. H. Bowman to Rosecrans, 28 June 1882, Rosecrans Papers, UCLA.

4. OR 30, pt. 2, 520; John Chapin, "At Chickamauga," in *Tenth and Eleventh Reunions of the First Ohio Volunteer Cavalry, Covington, O., Oct. 8, 1889. Columbus, O., September 16, 1890* (Columbus, Ohio: Langdon Printing Company, 1891), 15.

5. Chapin, "At Chickamauga," 15–16; Eli Long Autobiography, Eli Long Papers, USAMHI.

6. Chapin, "At Chickamauga," 16–17.

7. Long autobiography, Long Papers, USAMHI; J. K. Womack, "Chickamauga as I Saw It," *CV* 25, no. 2 (February 1917): 74.

8. Womack, "Chickamauga as I Saw It," 74.

9. John Wyeth, *With Sabre and Scalpel, the Autobiography of a Soldier and Surgeon* (New York: Harper and Brothers, 1914), 247–48.

10. *OR* 30, pt. 521; Wyeth, *With Sabre and Scalpel,* 250–51.

11. *OR* 30, pt. 1, 507–8, 893, 896, 900, and pt. 2, 521; William McAfee, "Disobeyed Orders at Chickamauga," *National Tribune,* 28 March 1907.

12. *OR* 30, pt. 1, 339, 500–501, 504–5.

13. Thruston, "Chickamauga," 414; Thruston to Boynton, 14 October 1899, Historical Files, CCNMP; Gracie, *Truth about Chickamauga,* 72–73.

14. *OR* 30, pt. 1, 331, 339, 1022–23.

15. Ibid., 331, 1023, 1036; Hough, *Soldier in the West,* 150.

16. Thruston, "Chickamauga," 414; Thruston to Boynton, 14 October 1899, Historical Files, CCNMP.

17. *OR* 30, pt. 1, 501.

18. Smith, *Life and Letters of Garfield,* 1:342–43.

19. Kirk, *Fifteenth Pennsylvania Cavalry,* 257; McKinney, *Education in Violence,* 252; *OR* 30, pt. 1, 253; Tucker, *Chickamauga,* 358. For a highly fictionalized account of Garfield's ride, similar to those that circulated during his presidency, see Gilmore, "Garfield's Ride."

20. Kirk, *Fifteenth Pennsylvania Cavalry,* 257; *OR* 30, pt. 1, 141.

21. McKinney, *Education in Violence,* 252; Van Horne, *Army of the Cumberland,* 1:355.

22. Smith, *Life and Letters of Garfield,* 1:343.

23. *OR* 30, pt. 1, 141.

24. Cist, *Army of the Cumberland,* 225–26; Lamers, *Edge of Glory,* 356–57.

25. *OR* 30, pt. 1, 140.

26. Ibid., 978.

27. Ibid., pt. 2, 289, 358; Thomas Claiborne to Boynton, 16 April 1891, Historical Files, CCNMP.

28. *OR* 30, pt. 2, 420.

29. Quintard, *Doctor Quintard, Chaplain C.S.A.,* 89; *OR* 30, pt. 2, 419; Owen, *In Camp and Battle,* 274; Warner, *Generals in Gray,* 113–14.

30. *OR* 30, pt. 2, 415; "Few Families of Civil War Days Still Live in Vicinity of Chickamauga Battlefield," Chattanooga *News,* 22 September 1923.

31. *OR* 30, pt. 2, 416, 422, 505; Undated letter from Archibald Gracie to the Chickamauga-Chattanooga National Battlefield Park Commission, entitled "Suggested Inscription for the Bronze Tablet on the Summit of Gracie's Hill of Snodgrass Ridge," in "Ensign Clarke's Courage," CCNMP.

32. Shaver, *Sixtieth Alabama,* 20.

33. *OR* 30, pt. 2, 423, 426, 427.

34. John Davenport to his wife, 28 September 1863, John Davenport Letters, First Alabama Battalion File, CCNMP; *OR* 30, pt. 2, 424–25.

35. Haynie, *Nineteenth Illinois*, 225.

36. *OR* pt. 1, 381, and pt. 2, 422–26, 505; James Whallon to James Fullerton, 26 May, 1894, Nineteenth Illinois File, CCNMP; Belknap, *Michigan at Chickamauga*, 118–19; Hicks, "Personal Recollections of the War," 530; Shaver, *Sixtieth Alabama*, 16.

37. *OR* 30, pt. 1, 465, and pt. 2, 423, 429; Clark to Carmen, 12 February 1909, One Hundred Twenty-fifth Ohio File, CCNMP.

38. Dickert, *Kershaw's Brigade*, 280–81.

39. *OR* 30, pt. 1, 253; Smith, *Life and Letters of Garfield*, 1:345; Tucker, *Chickamauga*, 359; Walker, "History of the First Brigade," Thomas Papers, RG 94, National Archives.

40. *OR* 30, pt. 1, 253; Turchin, *Chickamauga*, 147; Gracie, *Truth about Chickamauga*, 95–97. Gracie's chapter entitled "Thomas' Unsupported Testimony" presents a well-documented, well-argued refutation of the claim that Thomas delayed his withdrawal until dark. Gracie errs only in asserting that Reynolds was forced to abandon his position behind the breastwork and in the time of Turchin's charge against Liddell.

Chapter Twenty-nine / Don't Waste Any Cartridges

1. *OR* 30, pt. 1, 155; Gracie, *Truth about Chickamauga*, 42.

2. *OR* 30, pt. 1, 948, 978.

3. Villard, *Memoirs*, 1:165–66.

4. *OR* 30, pt. 1, 142–43.

5. Villard, *Memoirs*, 1:165–66; Lamers, *Edge of Glory*, 358.

6. Palmer, *Personal Recollections*, 183; R. Johnson, "Chickamauga," *National Tribune*, 23 January 1896.

7. Kimberly, *Forty-first Ohio*, 51; *OR* 30, pt. 1, 764; Hazen, *Narrative of Military Service*, 132.

8. Hazen, *Narrative of Military Service*, 132; Wiley, "General Hill Answered"; *OR* 30, pt. 1, 764, 769; McConnell, "Ninth Indiana"; Clark to Carmen, 12 February 1909, One Hundred Twenty-fifth Ohio File, CCNMP.

9. *OR* 30, pt. 1, 708, 764, and pt. 2, 424, 429, 446, 508.

10. Calkins, *One Hundred and Fourth Illinois*, 149; *OR* 30, pt. 1, 381, and pt. 2, 425–27; Boatner, *Civil War Dictionary*, 820; Whallon to Fullerton, 26 May 1894, Nineteenth Illinois File, CCNMP.

11. *OR* 30, pt. 2, 416, 441; Liddell, *Liddell's Record*, 133; Warner, *Generals in Gray*, 416–17.

12. *OR* 30, pt. 1, 424, and pt. 2, 441, 445; John B. Palmer, "The Fifty-eighth North Carolina at the Battle of Chickamauga," *Our Living and Our Dead* 3, no. 4 (October 1875): 455; Canfield, *Twenty-first Ohio*, 144.

13. *OR* 30, pt. 2, 445.

14. Ibid., 447.

15. Thompson, *Orphan Brigade*, 226.

16. Canfield, *Twenty-first Ohio*, 121; McMahan, "Comments on General Brannan's Letter of May 3, 1864," McMahan Draft Report of Chickamauga, J. S. Ma-

honey to McMahan, 23 July 1889, and Canfield to McMahan, 18 July 1889, all in Sullivan Collection, BGSU.

17. Bishop, "Van Derveer's Brigade at Chickamauga," 68–69; Donahower, "Narrative, Volume 2," 141, Donahower Papers, MnHS.

18. OR 30, pt. 2, 441.

19. Ibid., 417, 431.

20. Wells, "Chickamauga," 229–30; Dolton to McMahan, 6 June 1890, Sullivan Collection, BGSU.

21. J. L. Erwin to Senator Bledsoe, 11 February 1895, Ninety-eighth Ohio File, CCNMP; James Dove, "Chickamauga, Another Account of General Steedman's Gallantry on that Bloody Field," National Tribune, 13 March 1884; Batchelor diary, 20 September 1863, ISHL.

22. Partridge, History of the Ninety-sixth Illinois, 217–18; Smith, Right of the Federal Army, 16, 20.

23. Dolton to McMahan, 3 February 1890, Sullivan Collection, BGSU.

24. OR 30, pt. 2, 347, 350, 464, 469.

25. G. S. Robinson, "Chickamauga," undated manuscript in Robinson Papers, ISHL; Dolton to McMahan, 6 June 1890, Sullivan Collection, BGSU; OR 30, pt. 2, 349–50.

26. Patton Memoirs, Book 17, DLC; Battery M, First Illinois, 88–89; Dolton to McMahan, 22 January and 6 June 1890, Sullivan Collection, BGSU.

27. OR 30, pt. 2, 464, 476; Battery M, First Illinois, 88–89; Wiseman, "Tennesseans at Chickamauga," 205.

28. Walker, "History of the First Brigade," Thomas Papers, RG 94, National Archives; OR 30, pt. 1, 856, 860.

29. Smith, Federal Right at Chickamauga, 14; Statement of William Hamilton, 10 November 1908, Twenty-second Michigan File, CCNMP; Morgan, "Old Steady," 91.

30. OR 30, pt. 2, 322, 441, 445; Robinson, "Chickamauga," Robinson Papers, ISHL; Palmer, "Fifty-eighth North Carolina at Chickamauga," 455; Dolton to McMahan, 16 June 1890, Sullivan Collection, BGSU.

31. Vance, "On Thomas's Right," 94; OR 30, pt. 1, 389; Canfield, Twenty-first Ohio, 120–21.

32. Bishop, "Van Derveer's Brigade at Chickamauga," 68–69; Dolton to McMahan, 6 June 1890, Sullivan Collection, BGSU; Canfield, Twenty-first Ohio, 136–37; George Dolton, "Chickamauga Battlefield — Snodgrass Ridge," CV 1, no. 12 (December 1893): 362–63.

33. Mahoney to McMahan, 23 July 1889, "Major McMahan's Response," undated clipping from the Toledo Daily Commercial, and McMahan, "Comments on General Brannan's Letter of May 3, 1864," all in Sullivan Collection, BGSU; Cusac to Carman, 13 March 1909, Twenty-first Ohio File, CCNMP; Canfield, Twenty-first Ohio, 136–37. In a postwar letter to McMahan, Van Derveer denied having given any orders to the major that afternoon. Neither Mahoney nor Cusac could make out the face of the colonel with whom they spoke in the dark, but both recalled that he wore colored glasses that looked like sun goggles. Both Van

Derveer and Boynton wore glasses. George Dolton said that those of Boynton were especially large and suggested to McMahan that it may have been Boynton who gave him the fateful command. See Van Derveer to McMahan, 15 July 1889, and Dolton to McMahan, 6 June 1890, both in Sullivan Collection, BGSU.

34. Cusac to Carman, 13 March 1909, Twenty-first Ohio File, CCNMP; Carlton to McMahan, 8 August 1889, and G. S. Robinson to McMahan, 13 July 1888, both in Sullivan Collection, BGSU; OR 30, pt. 1, 389, and pt. 2, 445–46; Canfield, *Twenty-first Ohio*, 123, 140.

35. Vance, "On Thomas's Right," 96–97.

Chapter Thirty / The Storm Broke Loose

1. OR 30, pt. 2, 34.
2. Ibid., 241; Hill, "Chickamauga," 661; Liddell, *Liddell's Record*, 144–45.
3. OR 30, pt. 2, 80, 96, 205.
4. Polk, *Polk*, 2:263; OR 30, pt. 2, 200.
5. Carnes, "Chickamauga, A Battle of Which the Half Has Not Been Told," Atlanta *Constitution*, 8 April 1883; Polk, *Polk*, 2:263.
6. OR 30, pt. 2, 85, 144; Polk, *Polk*, 2:263.
7. Carnes, "Chickamauga"; OR 30, pt. 2, 156.
8. OR 30, pt. 2, 253, 275; Holmes, *52nd O.V.I.*, 881; Oscar F. Harmon, *Life and Letters of Oscar Fitzhalan Harmon, Colonel of the One Hundred Twenty-fifth Regiment Illinois Volunteers* (Trenton: MacCrelish and Quigley, 1914), 155; Thaddeus Brown et al., *Behind the Guns, the History of Battery I, Second Regiment Illinois Light Artillery* (Carbondale: Southern Illinois University Press, 1965), 63; William Putney, "Chickamauga, The Bugler of the Second Illinois Light Artillery Has His Say," *National Tribune*, 24 September 1885.
9. OR 30, pt. 2, 253, 260, 275.
10. Manuscript History of the Thirty-sixth Ohio Volunteer Infantry, in John C. Booth Papers, OHS; OR 30, pt. 1, 1070.
11. High, *Sixty-eighth Indiana*, 94–96; *Indiana at Chickamauga*, 199–200.
12. Turchin, *Chickamauga*, 147; OR 30, pt. 1, 442; B. M. Clayton, "Turchin's Great Charge," *National Tribune*, 18 August 1921.
13. OR 30, pt. 1, 253; Turchin, *Chickamauga*, 148.
14. Tucker, *Chickamauga*, 363; OR 30, pt. 1, 253, 442.
15. Turchin, *Chickamauga*, 147–50; G. L. Camp, "Turchin's Brigade at Chickamauga," *National Tribune*, 22 October 1908; Clayton, "Turchin's Great Charge."
16. OR 30, pt. 2, 260.
17. Ibid., 267; Manuscript History of Thirty-sixth Ohio, Booth Papers, OHS; George B. Turner to his mother, 23 September 1863, Turner Papers, OHS; Turchin, "'A Monotony Full of Sadness,'" 65; Turchin, *Chickamauga*, 150–52.
18. OR 30, pt. 2, 265–66.
19. OR 30, pt. 1, 483, and pt. 2, 275; George Dolton, "A Desperate Field," *National Tribune*, 21 September 1893.
20. Turchin, *Chickamauga*, 151–52; OR 30, pt. 1, 482; Manuscript History of the Thirty-sixth Ohio, Booth Papers, OHS; Brown, *Behind the Guns*, 63–64.

21. *OR* 30, pt. 1, 442; Manuscript History of the Thirty-sixth Ohio, Booth Papers, OHS; Turchin, *Chickamauga,* 152.

22. Unidentified article by Booth (possibly from *National Tribune*), Booth Papers, OHS; Turchin, *Chickamauga,* 152.

23. Gracie, *Truth about Chickamauga,* 106–9; High, *Sixty-eighth Indiana,* 98; *OR* 30, pt. 1, 254.

24. Palmer, *Personal Recollections,* 184; *OR* 30, pt. 1, 715.

25. Sorrel, *Recollections of a Staff Officer,* 201; *OR* 30, pt. 2, 364.

26. Palmer, *Personal Recollections,* 184; *OR* 30, pt. 1, 715; Gracie, *Truth about Chickamauga,* 85; Sorrel, *Recollections of a Staff Officer,* 201–2.

27. Palmer, *Personal Recollections,* 184–85; *OR* 30, pt. 1, 754.

28. Palmer, *Personal Recollections,* 184–85; *OR* 30, pt. 2, 364, 386; Cooper memoirs, 35, CWC, TSLA.

29. *OR* 30, pt. 1, 536, 541, 556, 559; Gracie, *Truth about Chickamauga,* 85–90.

30. *OR* 30, pt. 2, 85.

31. Ibid., 183.

32. Carnes, "Chickamauga, a Battle the Half of Which Has Not Been Told," Atlanta *Constitution,* 8 April 1883; *OR* 30, pt. 2, 177.

33. John Johnston, "Chickamauga. A Soldier's Story of the Battle," Lancaster *New Era,* 10 September 1892; Gracie, *Truth about Chickamauga,* 91; *OR* 30, pt. 1, 279.

34. Watkins, *"Co. Aytch,"* 107; *OR* 30, pt. 1, 288, 291–93, 296, 299, and pt. 2, 178; Scribner, *How Soldiers Were Made,* 158–59; Augustus L. Waddle, *Three Years with the Armies of the Ohio and the Cumberland* (Chillicothe, Ohio: Scioto Gazette, 1889), 52; W. W. Carnes, "Chickamauga, A battle the Half of Which Has Not Been Told," Atlanta *Constitution,* 8 April 1883.

35. *OR* 30, pt. 2, 103, 120, 178–79, 220.

36. Scribner, *How Soldiers Were Made,* 158–59; *OR* 30, pt. 1, 279.

37. Cooper memoirs, 35–35, CWC, TSLA; Washburn, "Reminiscences of Confederate Service," 59; *OR* 30, pt. 2, 144–45, 156, 189, 200, 205, 217–18, 223; Polk, *Polk,* 2:266.

38. Walker, "History of the First Brigade," Thomas Papers, RG 94, National Archives; G. W. Steele to Boynton, 7 June 1895, One Hundred First Ohio File, CCNMP; High, *Sixty-eighth Indiana,* 98.

39. Sheridan, *Memoirs,* 2:286–87; Castle, "Sheridan with the Army of the Cumberland," 19; Gracie, *Truth about Chickamauga,* 110–12, 122–23; *OR* 30, pt. 1, 501, 581.

40. Boynton to Fullerton, 17 April 1896, Historical Files, CCNMP; McConnell, "Ninth Indiana."

41. *OR* 30, pt. 1, 417, 432, 441, 464, 476; Robert Watson's Journal, 20 September 1863, Seventh Florida File, CCNMP.

42. *OR* 30, pt. 2, 441–42, 432.

43. Ibid., 432.

44. Vance, "On Thomas' Right," 97.

45. McMahan to Dolton, 30 January 1890, and McMahan's Draft Report of Chickamauga, both in Sullivan Collection, BGSU; Vance, "On Thomas' Right," 97; Canfield, *Twenty-first Ohio*, 123, 140, 145; Watson journal, 20 September 1863, Seventh Florida File, CCNMP; *OR* 30, pt. 2, 432.

46. Carlton to McMahan, 8 August 1889, Sullivan Collection, BGSU; *OR* 30, pt. 2, 432.

47. William Hamilton to Edgar Spalding, 16 December 1908, and Spalding to Boynton, 21 November 1900, both in Twenty-second Michigan File, CCNMP; *OR* 30, pt. 2, 432.

48. Boynton to Fullerton, 17 April 1896, Historical Files, CCNMP; *OR* 30, pt. 1, 436; G. E. Dolton, "Chickamauga," *National Tribune*, 9 November 1893; Dolton to McMahan, 6 June 1890, Sullivan Collection, BGSU.

49. Boynton to Fullerton, 17 April 1896, Ninth Indiana File, CCNMP; Dolton to McMahan, 6 June 1890, Sullivan Collection, BGSU.

50. Gracie, *Truth about Chickamauga*, 176; Boynton to Fullerton, 17 April 1890, Ninth Indiana File, CCNMP. The adjutant of the Ninth, S. P. Hodson, thought it was Van Derveer with whom they had argued, but in the darkness, he was uncertain. Boynton, however, contended that it was he who exchanged words with Suman and his staff. The weight of evidence favors Boynton's claim.

51. Gracie, *Truth about Chickamauga*, 38, 180; Boynton to Fullerton, 17 April 1896, and McConnell to Boynton, 16 March 1894 and 17 July 1895, all in Ninth Indiana File, CCNMP; McConnell, "Ninth Indiana"; B. A. Dimm, "The Close of Chickamauga," *National Tribune*, 2 May 1907; R. M. Johnson, *In Matter of the Appeal to the Secretary of War, by the Indiana Chickamauga Park Commission* (N.p., n.d.), 14–15.

52. Gracie, *Truth about Chickamauga*, 328–29; McConnell to Boynton, 16 March 1894, and Thomas Madden to David Turpie, 5 May 1896, both in Ninth Indiana File, CCNMP; Dimm, "The Close of Chickamauga."

53. *OR* 30, pt. 1, 769, and pt. 2, 443; Gracie, *Truth about Chickamauga*, 321; Thomas Prickett to Dearest Matilda, 24 September 1863, Prickett Civil War File, InHS.

54. Boynton to Fullerton, 17 April 1896, and McConnell to Boynton, 17 July 1895, both in Ninth Indiana File, CCNMP; B. A. Dunn, "That Mysterious Volley," *National Tribune*, 17 September 1908; McConnell, "Ninth Indiana."

55. Vance, "On Thomas' Right," 97–98; T. B. Morton, "That Mysterious Volley," *National Tribune*, 25 July 1907; *OR* 30, pt. 1, 395, and pt. 2, 439; Turchin, *Chickamauga*, 234; Watson journal, Seventh Florida File, CCNMP; Canfield, *Twenty-first Ohio*, 123.

56. Carlton to McMahan, 8 August 1889, Sullivan Collection, BGSU; *OR* 30, pt. 2, 432, 439; Mabel Carlton Horner, "Caleb Henry Carlton," manuscript biography in Carlton Papers, DLC.

57. G. W. Steele to Boynton, 7 June 1895, and Boynton to Fullerton, 17 April 1896, both in Ninth Indiana File, CCNMP; Walker, "History of the First Brigade," Thomas Papers, RG 94, National Archives; John Beals to J. H. Gray, 19 February 1897, Beals Civil War File, InHS.

Chapter Thirty-one / God Help Me Bear It

1. Turner to his sister, 1 October 1863, Turner Papers, OHS; Patton Memoirs, Book 17, DLC.
2. Beatty, *Citizen Soldier*, 343–44.
3. Sheridan, *Memoirs*, 1:287; Hough, *Soldier in the West*, 150.
4. Scribner, *How Soldiers Were Made*, 162–63.
5. Partridge, *History of the Ninety-sixth Illinois*, 189–90.
6. Beatty, *Citizen Soldier*, 345.
7. William Gale to William Polk, 28 March 1882, and O. B. Spence to William Polk, 3 September 1874, both in Polk Papers, US; *OR* 30, pt. 2, 34; Polk, *Polk*, 2:266.
8. *OR* 30, pt. 2, 465, 505; Connelly, *Autumn of Glory*, 227–28; Hill, "Chickamauga," 659.
9. Gale to his wife, 28 September 1863, Gale to William Polk, 28 March 1882, Spence to William Polk, 3 September 1874, and Leonidas Polk to his wife, 21 September 1863, all in Polk Papers, US; Polk, *Polk*, 2:267. After the war, Gale told Polk's son that the alleged meeting with Bragg had taken place between 11:00 P.M. and midnight, rather than after 1:00 A.M.
10. Green, *Johnny Green of the Orphan Brigade*, 99; Lavender, *They Never Came Back*, 84, 85; Dickert, *Kershaw's Brigade*, 277.
11. Watkins, "Co. Aytch," 108–9.
12. Shaver, *Sixtieth Alabama*, 18–19.
13. Lindsley, *Military Annals of Tennessee. Confederate*, 344.
14. Coleman diary, 20 September 1863, 117–18, UNC.
15. Coxe, "Chickamauga," 294; Wyeth, *With Sabre and Scalpel*, 252; Giles, *Rags and Hope*, 108.
16. Doughman recollections, 10, Eighty-ninth Ohio File, CCNMP.
17. Morton, *Artillery of Forrest*, 125–26; August Bratnober diary, 20 September 1863, Tenth Wisconsin File, CCNMP; Heartsill, *Fourteen Hundred and Ninety-one Days*, 159; *OR* 30, pt. 2, 418.
18. Wyeth, *With Sabre and Scalpel*, 254–55; *OR* 30, pt. 2, 418; Cooper Memoirs, 35–36, CWC, TSLA; John Snow to his sister, 23 September 1863, John Snow Papers, DU.
19. Liddell, *Liddell's Record*, 146–47; *OR* 30, pt. 2, 34–35.
20. *OR* 30, pt. 2, 35; Connelly, *Autumn of Glory*, 229.
21. Longstreet gave several, rather contradictory accounts of his conversation with Bragg. Each varied somewhat with regard to what precisely the army should do once it crossed the Tennessee. The account related here is that from Longstreet's Memoirs. However, in a letter to Secretary of War Seddon written after the battle, he said he counseled Bragg to move first against East Tennessee and then against Rosecrans's line of communications. Twenty years later, he told Hill that his intention had been either to interpose the army between Rosecrans and Nashville or to move directly against Chattanooga. Yet another version, supplied by one of Hill's staff officers who talked with Longstreet during the day, said he had intended for the army to invade Middle Tennessee and perhaps move as far north as

Nashville or Louisville. See Connelly, *Autumn of Glory*, 229–30; *OR* 30, pt. 4, 711; James A. Goggin, "Chickamauga — A Reply to Major Sykes," *SHSP* 12 (1884), 221.

22. Connelly, *Autumn of Glory*, 230–31; *OR* 30, pt. 2, 37; Oates, *War between the Union and the Confederacy*, 265; Goodson to his niece, 28 September 1863, Forty-fourth Alabama File, CCNMP.

23. Forrest to Polk, 21 September 1863, Leonidas Polk Papers, DLC; Morton, *Artillery of Forrest*, 126–27; B. L. Ridley, "Daring Deeds of Staff and Escort," *CV* 4, no. 10 (October 1896): 358–59; Wyeth, "Appearance and Characteristics of Forrest," 43.

24. Wyeth, "Appearance and Characteristics of Forrest," 43; Ridley, "Daring Deeds of Staff and Escort," 359; Morton, *Artillery of Forrest*, 127.

25. Hough, *Soldier in the West*, 150; Royse, *115th Illinois*, 167.

26. Hough, *Soldier in the West*, 150–52.

27. Lamers, *Edge of Glory*, 361.

28. Hay, *Letters and Extracts*, 2:92.

29. *OR* 30, pt. 1, 254–55; Lamers, *Edge of Glory*, 366–67; Royse, *115th Illinois*, 167.

30. *OR* 30, pt. 1, 255.

CHAPTER THIRTY-TWO / DENUNCIATIONS

1. Sanderson, letter diary, 21 September 1863, OHS.

2. Lamers, *Edge of Glory*, 367.

3. *OR* 30, pt. 1, 150; Lamers, *Edge of Glory*, 366; Beatty, *Citizen Soldier*, 350.

4. Lamers, *Edge of Glory*, 367; *OR* 30, pt. 1, 146, 155, and pt. 3, 755.

5. Hay, *Letters and Extracts*, 2:92–93, 102; Dana to Rosecrans, 21 March 1882, Rosecrans Papers, UCLA.

6. *Rosecrans's Burial Service*, 96–98; Gideon Welles, *The Diary of Gideon Welles, Lincoln's Secretary of the Navy*, 3 vols. (Boston: 1911), 2: 447; "Garfield-Rosecrans," *National Tribune*, 18 March 1882; Cox, *Military Reminiscences*, 2:10–19; Dana to Rosecrans, 18 March 1882, Rosecrans Papers, UCLA.

7. Hay, *Letters and Extracts*, 2:102; Welles, *Diary*, 2:447.

8. *OR* 30, pt. 1, 168.

9. Lamers, *Edge of Glory*, 379–80; *OR* 30, pt. 4, 57.

10. McKinney, *Education in Violence*, 269.

11. Wilson, manuscript of *Life of Dana*, appendix 38–39, Wilson Papers, DLC; Villard, *Memoirs*, 2:186–89; Welles, *Diary*, 2:446–47; Morgan, "Old Steady," 92.

12. Villard, *Memoirs*, 2: 191–92; *OR* 30, pt. 1, 1005–53; Hough, *Soldier in the West*, 155, 161; Warner, *Generals in Blue*, 342.

13. Wilson, manuscript of *Life of Dana*, appendix, 65.

14. Welles, *Diary*, 2:442.

15. Lamers, *Edge of Glory*, 380.

16. McKinney, *Education in Violence*, 270; *OR* 30, pt. 1, 404.

17. Rosecrans to McCook, 8 November 1879, and Dana to Rosecrans, 18 March,

1882, both in Rosecrans Papers, UCLA; McKinney, *Education in Violence*, 270; Lamers, *Edge of Glory*, 391–92.

18. Sanderson, letter diary, 20 October 1863, OHS; Lamers, *Edge of Glory*, 394–95; Rosecrans to Garfield, 29 October 1863, Rosecrans Papers, UCLA.

19. Connelly, *Autumn of Glory*, 235.

20. Mary Chesnut, *A Diary from Dixie* (New York: D. Appleton, 1914), 307.

21. Connelly, *Autumn of Glory*, 235.

22. Brent journal, 22 September 1863, Palmer Collection, WRHS; Lafayette McLaws, "After Chickamauga," in *Addresses Delivered before the Confederate Veteran Association of Savannah, Georgia, to Which is Appended the President's Annual Report* (Savannah: Braid and Hutton, Printers, 1898), 52.

23. OR 30, pt. 2, 54.

24. Connelly, *Autumn of Glory*, 236.

25. Polk to Bragg, 28 September 1863, Polk Papers, US; McLaws to Hill, 25 January 1864, Hill Papers, NCDAH; "Charge Specifications Preferred against Major General T. C. Hindman," and "Charges Preferred against Lieut. Gen. L. Polk," both in John F. H. Claiborne Papers, UNC; Brent journal, 28 and 29 September 1863, Palmer Collection, WRHS.

26. Davis, *Jefferson Davis, Constitutionalist*, 6:53; Connelly, *Autumn of Glory*, 236; Bragg to Davis, 1 October 1863, J. T. Claiborne Papers, UNC.

27. OR 30, pt. 2, 55–56; Connelly, *Autumn of Glory*, 236.

28. Davis, *Jefferson Davis, Constitutionalist*, 6:55.

29. Polk to his daughter, 10 October 1863, Polk Papers, US; Hill to his wife, 25 September 1863, D. H. Hill Papers, USAMHI; Richmond *Enquirer*, 13 October 1863; Connelly, *Autumn of Glory*, 236–37; William Preston to William Preston Johnston, 3 October 1863, Mrs. Mason Barret Collection of Albert Sidney and William Preston Johnston Papers, TU.

30. OR 30, pt. 2, 705–6; Thomas R. Hay to D. H. Hill, Jr., 17 June, 1923, D. H. Hill, Jr., Papers, NCDAH.

31. Polk to Lee, 27 September 1863, Polk Papers, US.

32. Hay to Hill, Jr., 17 June 1923, D. H. Hill, Jr., Papers, NCDAH; McLaws to Hill, 25 January 1864, Hill Papers, NCDAH; Connelly, *Autumn of Glory*, 238–39.

33. Brent journal, 4 and 5 October 1863, Palmer Collection, WRHS.

34. Connelly, *Autumn of Glory*, 241.

35. Polk to his daughter, 10 October 1863, Polk Papers, US; Connelly, *Autumn of Glory*, 242.

36. Horn, *Army of Tennessee*, 286–87.

37. Ibid.; Brent journal, 9–11 October 1863, Palmer Collection, WRHS; Sorrel, *Recollections of a Confederate Staff Officer*, 200; Connelly, *Autumn of Glory*, 245–46; Longstreet, *From Mannassas to Appomattox*, 465–66.

38. OR 30, pt. 2, 148.

39. McLaws to Hill, 25 January 1864, Hill Papers, NCDAH; Bragg to Sykes, John F. H. Claiborne Papers, UNC.

40. Warner, *Generals in Gray*, 137.

41. Preston to Will Preston Johnston, 3 October 1863, Barret Collection, TU.

42. Davis, *Jefferson Davis, Constitutionalist,* 6:65–66; Lucius Polk to Mrs. Leonidas Polk, 5 November 1863, Polk Papers, US.

43. Turchin, *Chickamauga,* 238–39; Tucker, *Chickamauga,* 389; Thomas Livermore, *Numbers and Losses in the Civil War—1861–1865* (Boston: Riverside Press, 1901), 69.

44. Tucker, *Chickamauga,* 389.

45. OR 30, pt. 1, 542, and pt. 2, 305; Tucker, *Chickamauga,* 388.

46. OR 30, pt. 1, 148; Hazen, *Narrative of Military Service,* 120; Rosecrans, "Chattanooga Campaign."

47. Polk to Davis, 6 October 1863, Polk Papers, DLC.

48. Hill, "Chickamauga," 662.

BIBLIOGRAPHY

MANUSCRIPTS

Abraham Lincoln Book Shop, Chicago
>Smith Atkins Letter

Alabama Department of Archives and History, Montgomery
>Twenty-Eighth Alabama Infantry Papers
>Thirty-Third Alabama Infantry Papers
>Thirty-Ninth Alabama Infantry Papers

W. Stanley Hoole Special Collections Library, University of Alabama, Tuscaloosa
>Henry D. Clayton Papers

Bowling Green State University, Bowling Green, Ohio
>William J. Sullivan Collection of Twenty-first Ohio Volunteer Infantry Papers

University of California at Los Angeles
>William Starke Rosecrans Papers

Special Collections Department, Chicago Public Library
>Army of the Cumberland Photograph Album

Chickamauga-Chattanooga National Military Park Library
>August Bratnober Diary
>Thomas J. Doughman Civil War Recollections
>John Ely Diary
>Alexis H. Reed Diary
>Edwin Reynolds Diary
>William R. Talley Autobiography
>Robert Watson Journal
>E. G. Whiteside Diary
>Miscellaneous Correspondence, Historical and Regimental Files

Cincinnati Historical Society
>Cist Family Papers
>Lytle Family Papers

DePauw University, Greencastle, Indiana
>William D. Ward Recollections

Duke University Library, Durham, N.C.
    George Brent Papers
    William L. Broaddus Letters and Papers
    John Magee Diary
    Eugene Marshall Papers
    James Nourse Diary
    Pope-Carter Family Papers
    John Snow Papers
    Samuel Stout Papers
    James A. Wiswell Papers
Emory University Library, Atlanta
    James Longstreet Papers
Grand Army of the Republic Memorial Hall and Military Museum, Aurora, Illinois
    Silas Miller Letters
Illinois State Historical Library, Springfield
    John Batchelor Diary
    Douglas Hapeman Diary
    Gifford S. Robinson Papers
    James P. Suiter Diary
University of Illinois Library, Urbana-Champaign
    John Hoch Papers
    Montraville Reeves Papers
Smith Memorial Library, Indiana Historical Society, Indianapolis
    Civil War Files of:
    John Beals
    James C. Essington
    William B. Graham
    Peter B. Kellenberger
    Robert C. Price
    Thomas Prickett
    James S. Thomas
    William D. Ward
    John C. Wysong
Kansas State Historical Society
    William C. Black Diary
Knox College Archives, Galesburg, Illinois
    Philip Sidney Post Papers
Library of Congress, Washington, D.C.
    Caleb Henry Carlton Papers
    Josiah Dexter Cotton Papers
    James A. Garfield Papers
    Charles C. Hood Collection
    John Jackman Journal
    McCook Family Papers

John Wesley Marshall Journal
John Patton Memoirs
Leonidas Polk Papers
Horace Porter Papers
Louis T. Wigfall Family Papers
James H. Wilson Papers
Samuel S. Yoder Family Papers
Massachusetts Historical Society, Boston
Henry Hall Papers
Memphis State University, Memphis
J. Edward James Letters
Michigan Historical Collections, Bentley Historical Library, University of Michigan, Ann Arbor
Richard B. Robbins Papers
Minnesota Historical Society, St. Paul
Judson Bishop Papers
Jeremiah Chester Donahower Papers
Mississippi Department of Archives and History, Jackson
W. M. Abernathy Papers
T. Otis Baker Papers
John C. Rietti Papers
Missouri Historical Society, St. Louis
Braxton Bragg Papers
James E. Love Papers
National Archives, Washington, D.C.
Record Group 94, George Thomas Papers
North Carolina Department of Archives and History, Raleigh
Daniel Harvey Hill Papers
Daniel Harvey Hill, Jr., Papers
Southern Historical Collection, University of North Carolina, Chapel Hill
James Patton Anderson Papers
Taylor Beatty Diary
Benjamin Franklin Cheatham Papers
J. T. Claiborne Papers
John F. H. Claiborne Papers
Daniel Coleman Diary
Joseph B. Cumming Recollections
Gale-Polk Family Papers
Daniel Chevilette Govan Papers
R. M. Gray Reminiscences
Leroy Moncure Nutt Papers
Henry C. Semple Papers
Thomas B. Wilson Reminiscences
Marcus Wright Papers
Ohio Historical Society, Columbus

John C. Booth Papers
John P. Sanderson Letter Diary
George B. Turner Papers
Private Collection
    J. T. Woods Scrapbook, Collection of Laurence M. Strayer
South Caroliniana Library, University of South Carolina, Columbia
    John H. Stenmeyer Recollections
McLain Library and Archives, University of Southern Mississippi, Hattiesburg
    Mark Perrin Lowrey Autobiographical Essay
University of the South, Sewanee, Tennessee
    Leonidas Polk Papers
Tennessee State Library and Archives, Nashville
    Benjamin Franklin Cheatham Papers
    Civil War Collection:
        William Gibbs Allen Memoirs
        David S. M. Bodenheim Memoirs
        Terry H. Cahal Letter
        Newton Cannon Memoirs
        Carroll Henderson Clark Memoirs
        Samuel Alonzo Cooke Memoirs
        James L. Cooper Memoirs
        George Washington Dillon Papers
        John Freeman Diary
        D. G. Goodwin Letters
        John Harris Letter
        Milton Preston Jarnagin Memoirs
        Philip N. Matlock Memoirs
        Nat G. Pierce Letter
        W. M. Pollard Diary
        William E. Sloan Diary
        J. F. Wheless Reminiscences
        W. E. Yeatman Memoirs
University of Tennessee, Knoxville
    Henry Cushing Letters
Tulane University, New Orleans
    Mrs. Mason Barret Collection of Albert Sidney and William Preston Johnston
        Papers
    Jefferson Davis Papers, Louisiana Historical Association Collection
    Civil War Papers, Reminiscences: Army of Tennessee
United States Army Military History Institute, Carlisle Barracks, Pennsylvania
    Luther P. Bradley Papers
    Civil War Miscellaneous Collection:
        Thomas Green Papers
        Jacob Miller Papers
    Civil War Times Illustrated Collection:

Eben P. Sturges Diary
Levi Wagner Reminiscences
James E. Edmonds Papers
Harrisonburg Civil War Round Table Collection:
Alan Griest Journal
D. H. Hill Papers
Eli Long Papers
Richard F. Mann Collection: William E. Stahl Diary
Robert Minty Papers
War Department Pamphlet Number Twenty
Virginia State Library, Richmond
D. H. Hill Papers
Wabash College, Crawfordsville, Indiana
Henry Campbell Papers
Western Reserve Historical Society, Cleveland
William P. Palmer Collection of Braxton Bragg Papers
State Historical Society of Wisconsin, Madison
John Henry Otto Memoirs
Wyoming Historical Society, Cheyenne
Henry B. Freeman Papers
Yale University Library
Civil War Miscellaneous and Manuscripts Collection: Arthur Carpenter Papers

NEWSPAPERS

Aberdeen (Alabama) *Examiner*
Atlanta *Constitution*
Bloomington (Indiana) *Telephone*
Cincinnati *Commercial Gazette*
Chattanooga *News*
Chattanooga *Times*
Indianapolis *Journal*
Lancaster (Pennsylvania) *Ledger*
Lancaster (Pennsylvania) *New Era*
Muskegon (Michigan) *Chronicle*
National Tribune
Noblesville (Indiana) *Republican Ledger*
Philadelphia *Weekly Times*
San Francisco *Examiner*
Toledo *Blade*
Toledo *Daily Commercial*
Toledo *Journal*

NATIONAL TRIBUNE

The *National Tribune*, published by John McElroy, a former member of the Sixteenth Illinois Cavalry, was the precursor of *Stars and Stripes*. Each issue featured front-page stories of the war by veterans, many of whom were prominent, as well as numerous shorter pieces and letters. Although occasionally embellished, the accounts nonetheless constitute an important and generally neglected source of primary materials for the Union side. Both a comprehensive index and a selected reprinting of the paper's better articles would be valuable additions to Civil War literature. To give the reader an idea of the wealth of information contained in the *National Tribune*, I have compiled this list of the articles I consulted in my research on Chickamauga.

J. N. Abbott. "Opening of Chickamauga Fight." 9 April 1914.

Booth, John. "Chickamauga, A Campaign Unrivaled in the Annals of War." 2 October 1890.

Boyle, Edward. "Chickamauga." 10 January 1907.

Brasher, C. A. "Chickamauga." 9 May 1889.

Burke, James. "Chickamauga: The Troops that Successfully Resisted the Charge of Longstreet's Veterans." 19 May 1887.

Camp, G. L. "Turchin's Brigade at Chickamauga" 22 October 1908.

Carlin, William P. "Military Memoirs." 16 April 1885.

Clayton, B. M. "Turchin's Great Charge." 18 August 1921.

Cusac, Isaac. "The Twenty-first Ohio at Chickamauga." 5 September 1907.

Dickennan, Albert. "The Ninth Ohio at Chickamauga." 13 October 1906.

Dimm, B. A. "The Close of Chickamauga." 2 May 1907.

Dolton, George. "Chickamauga." 9 November 1893.

————. "A Desperate Field." 21 September 1893.

Dove, James W. "Chickamauga, Another Account of General Steedman's Gallantry on that Bloody Field." 13 March 1884.

Dunn, B. A. "That Mysterious Volley." 17 September 1908.

"Garfield — Rosecrans." 18 March 1882.

"General Sherman's Letter, What General Rosecrans Says of It." 8 October 1881.

Hill, H. H. "The Second Minnesota: Reminiscences of Four Years' Service at the Front." 13 July 1899.

Hubbard, P. L. "The Capture of the Eighth Indiana Battery." 6 June 1907.

Hunter, Morton. "At Chickamauga, the Part Taken by the Eighty-second Minnesota." 24 November 1887.

————. "Chickamauga." 21 May 1888.

Johnson, Amasa. "Chickamauga. A Reply to General Wiley and a Defense of General Thomas." 16 June 1887.

Johnson, Richard. "Chickamauga, Sketch of the Campaign and Famous Battle." 23 January 1896.

————. "Men and Events. Recollections of Distinguished Generals of the Civil War." 15 August 1895.

Jones, J. N. "Chickamauga." 4 July 1901.

Keeran, Samuel. "Chickamauga." 10 September 1891.

Kemper, A. C. "General W. H. Lytle." 5 July 1883;

McAfee, William. "Disobeyed Orders at Chickamauga." 28 March 1907.

McClellan, W. G. "Chickamauga." 14 February 1884.

McConnell, D. B. "The Ninth Indiana." 11 November 1886.

McElroy, John. "Army of the Cumberland and the Great Central Campaign." 4 October 1906.

McNeil, S. A. "At Chickamauga." 14 April 1887.

———. "The Thirty-first Ohio at Chickamauga." 9 February 1888.

Miller, G. W. "The Thirty-first Ohio at Chickamauga." 21 February 1907.

Morton, T. B. "That Mysterious Volley." 25 July 1907.

Pease, G. M. "Chickamauga. The Part Taken by the Sixty-ninth Ohio and McCook's Brigade." 3 July 1890.

Perry, F. W. "Chickamauga. Toilsome March of the Fourteenth Corps Over the Mountains." 28 June 1883.

Putney, William. "Chickamauga, The Bugler of the Second Illinois Light Artillery Has His Say." 24 September 1885.

Radcliffe, Charles. "Battle of Chickamauga." 1 September 1891.

Rea, William. "Roasted Bacon at Bridge." 15 October 1914.

Reed, A. H. "Chickamauga. The Fourteenth Corps' Magnificent Stand Against Overwhelming Forces." 21 September 1916.

Robinson, G. S. "Steedman's Charge at Chickamauga." 20 December 1906.

Rosecrans to the Editors. 31 March 1870.

Rosecrans, William S. "The Chattanooga Campaign." 6 March 1882.

Stevens, John. "Chickamauga: A Wartime Letter from an Indiana Boy." 28 May 1908.

Walker, I. B. "Chickamauga. Going into Action with Hands Full of Bacon and Coffee." 2 July 1891.

Wiley, Aquila. "General Hill Answered." 19 May 1887.

Wilson, George. "Wilder's Brigade. The Mounted Infantry in the Tullahoma-Chickamauga Campaigns." 12, 19, and 26 October 1883.

Young, I. K. "Chickamauga. The Battle as I Saw It." 22 April 1886.

Zehring, S. P. "Chickamauga: The Conspicuous Gallantry of Van Derveer's Brigade." 13 October 1887.

OFFICIAL DOCUMENTS

United States. Surgeon General's Office. *The Medical and Surgical History of the War of the Rebellion (1861–1865).* 3 vols. in 6. Washington: U.S. Government Printing Office, 1870–88.

The War of the Rebellion: A Compilation of the Official Records of the Union and Confederate Armies. Washington, D.C.: U.S. Government Printing Office, 1880–1901.

ADDRESSES, ARTICLES, AND ESSAYS

Allen, J. W. "Bullet in a Testament." *Confederate Veteran* 6, no. 4 (April 1898): 154.

Anderson, Archer. *The Campaign and Battle of Chickamauga, an Address Delivered before the Virginia Division of the Army of Northern Virginia Asso-*

ciation, at Their Annual Meeting, in the Capitol at Richmond, Virginia, October 25, 1881. Richmond: William Ellis Jones Printers, 1881.

Anderson, Charles W. "Gracie — Chickamauga — Whitaker." *Confederate Veteran* 3, no. 8 (August 1895): 251–52.

Anderson, Mrs. J. Patton. "Generals Anderson and Lytle — A Reminiscence." *Confederate Veteran* 12, no. 9 (September 1904): 442.

Archer, B. L. "Incidents of General Lytle's Burial." *Confederate Veteran* 12, no. 9 (September 1904): 442.

Atkins, Smith. *Chickamauga. Useless, Disastrous Battle. Talk by Smith D. Atkins, Opera House, Mendota, Illinois, February 22, 1907, at Invitation of Woman's Relief Corps, G.A.R.* N.p., 1907.

"Autobiography of General Patton Anderson." *Southern Historical Society Papers* 24 (1896): 57–72.

Avery, Alphonso Calhoun. "Memorial Address on Life and Character of Lieutenant General D. H. Hill, May 10, 1893." *Southern Historical Society Papers* 21 (1893): 110–50.

Baird, John A., Jr. " 'For Gallant and Meritorious Service,' Major General Absalom Baird." *Civil War Times Illustrated* 15, no. 3 (June 1976): 4–9.

Bell, G. W. R. "Reminiscences of Chickamauga." *Confederate Veteran* 12, no. 2 (February 1904): 71.

Berney, Saffold. "Major Henry Churchill Semple." *Alabama Historical Quarterly* 18 (1956): 552–58.

Berry, J. M. "The Quiet Humor of General Pat Cleburne." *Confederate Veteran* 12, no. 4 (April 1904): 176.

Blegen, Theodore. "Colonel Hans Christian Heg." *Wisconsin Magazine of History* 4, no. 2 (December 1920):

Bramblitt, W. H. "General Lytle's Body on the Battlefield." *Confederate Veteran* 10, no. 1 (January 1902): 22.

Brown, W. C. "How Confederates Treated a Federal." *Confederate Veteran* 13, no. 5 (May 1905): 228.

"Captain W. W. Carnes — In Memoriam." *Confederate Veteran* 15, no. 7 (July 1907): 245.

Carnahan, James. "Indiana at Chickamauga." In *War Papers, Read before the Indiana Commandery, Military Order of the Loyal Legion of the United States*, vol. 1, 86–116. Indianapolis: By the Commandery, 1898.

———. "Personal Recollections of Chickamauga." In *Sketches of War History, Papers Read Before the Ohio Commandery, Military Order of the Loyal Legion of the United States*, vol. 1, 401–22. Cincinnati: By the Commandery, 1888.

Carnes, W. W. "Chickamauga." *Southern Historical Society Papers* 14 (1886): 398–402.

Castle, Chauncey H. "Comrade Castle's Address." In *Minutes of Proceedings of the Fourteenth Annual Reunion, Survivors Seventy-third Regiment Illinois Infantry Volunteers, Held Afternoon and Evening, Wednesday, September 27, 1900.* N.p., n.d.

Castle, Henry. "Sheridan with the Army of the Cumberland." In *Minutes of*

Proceedings of the Twentieth Annual Reunion of the Survivors Seventy-third Regiment Illinois Infantry Volunteers. Afternoon and Evening Tuesday, October 2, 1906. N.p., n.d.

Chandler, A. M. "Reminiscences of Chickamauga." *Confederate Veteran* 2, no. 3 (March 1894): 79.

Chalaron, J. A. "Vivid Experiences at Chickamauga." *Confederate Veteran* 3, no. 9 (September 1895): 278–79.

Chapin, James. "With the Army of the Cumberland in the Chickamauga Campaign, the Diary of James Chapin." *Georgia Historical Quarterly* 59 (1975): 223–42.

Chapin, John. "At Chickamauga." In *Tenth and Eleventh Reunions of the First Ohio Volunteer Cavalry, Covington, O., Oct. 8, 1889. Columbus, O., September 16, 1890.* Columbus, Ohio: Landon Printing Company, 1891.

Clay, H. B. "Concerning the Battle of Chickamauga." *Confederate Veteran* 13, no. 2 (February 1905): 72.

"Colonel Robert C. Trigg, of Virginia." *Confederate Veteran* 17, no. 2 (February 1909): 65.

Coxe, John. "Chickamauga." *Confederate Veteran* 30, no. 7 (July 1922): 291–94.

Crippen, Edward W. "The Diary of Edward W. Crippen, Private, Twenty-seventh Illinois Volunteers, War of the Rebellion, August 7, 1861 to September 19, 1863." *Publications of the Illinois State Historical Society* 14 (1909): 220–82.

Dent, J. H. "General Lytle's Sword." *Confederate Veteran* 9, no. 6 (June 1901): 248.

Doan, Isaac. *Reminiscences of the Chattanooga Campaign, a Paper Read at the Reunion of Company B, Fortieth Ohio Infantry, at Xenia, O., August 22, 1894, by Sergeant Isaac C. Doan.* Richmond, Ind.: N.p., 1894.

Dolton, George E. "Chickamauga Battlefield — Snodgrass Ridge." *Confederate Veteran* 1, no. 12 (December 1893): 362–63.

Findley, R. P. "The Story of a March." In *Grand Army of the Republic War Papers, Papers Read before Fred C. Jones Post, No. 401, Department of Ohio, G.A.R.,* 351–66. Cincinnati: Fred C. Jones Post, No. 401, 1891.

"Gallant Mississippians at Chickamauga." *Confederate Veteran* 7, no. 12 (December 1899).

"General Walthall." *Illinois Central Magazine* 4, no. 8 (February 1916): 9–12.

"General William B. Bate." *Confederate Veteran* 2, no. 11 (November 1894): 336–37.

Gilmore, James R. "Garfield's Ride at Chickamauga." *McClure's Magazine* 5 (1895): 357–60.

Goggin, James M. "Chickamauga — A Reply to Major Sykes." *Southern Historical Society Papers* 13 (1884): 219–24.

Goodrich, John T. "Gregg's Brigade in the Battle of Chickamauga." *Confederate Veteran* 22, no. 6 (June 1914): 263–64.

Green, B. W. "Two Armies—A Comparison." *Confederate Veteran* 16, no. 3 (March 1918): 101.

Green, Curtis. "Sixth Georgia Cavalry at Chickamauga." *Confederate Veteran* 8, no. 7 (July 1900): 324.

Hay, Thomas Robson. "The Campaign and Battle of Chickamauga." *Georgia Historical Quarterly* 7 (1923): 213–50.

Heg, E. B. "Stephen O. Himoe, Civil War Physician." *Norwegian American Studies and Records* 11 (1940): 30–56.

Herr, W. W. "Kentuckians at Chickamauga." *Confederate Veteran* 3, no. 10 (October 1895): 194–95.

Hicks, Borden M. "Personal Recollections of the War of the Rebellion." In *Glimpses of the Nation's Struggle. Sixth Series. Papers Read before the Minnesota Commandery, Military Order of the Loyal Legion of the United States, January, 1903–1908*, 519–44. Minneapolis: Aug. Davis, 1909.

"Hindman's Successful Strategy." *Confederate Veteran* 16, no. 6 (June 1918): 248–49.

Hosea, Lewis. "The Regular Brigade of the Army of the Cumberland." In *Sketches of War History, 1861–1865. Papers Prepared for the Ohio Commandery of the Loyal Legion of the United States*, vol. 5, 328–60. Cincinnati: Robert Clarke Company, 1903.

Hunter, Morton. "Battle of Chickamauga. The Part Taken by the Eighty-second Indiana — Address Delivered by General Morton C. Hunter at Columbus, Indiana, October 7, 1887." Bloomington *Telephone*, 14 October 1887.

Inzer, John W. "Colonel Robert C. Tyler." *Confederate Veteran* 15, no. 5 (May 1907): 237.

Johnston, J. Stoddard. "General J. B. Hood and Chickamauga." *Confederate Veteran* 13, no. 12 (December 1905): 550–52.

Jones, J. William. "Chickamauga — a Reply to Major Sykes." *Southern Historical Society Papers* 12 (1884): 221.

Joyce, Frederick. "The Orphan Brigade at Chickamauga." *Southern Bivouac* 3 (1884/85): 29–32.

Kane, John A. "From Chickamauga to Chattanooga, the Battlefield Account of Sergeant John M. Kane." Edited by Joseph E. Suppiger. *East Tennessee Historical Society Publications* 45 (1973): 99–108.

"Kansas at Chickamauga and Chattanooga." *Transactions of the Kansas State Historical Society* 8 (1904): 271–75.

Kegley, Tracy M. "Bushrod Rust Johnson, Soldier and Teacher." *Tennessee Historical Quarterly* 7 (1948): 249–58.

Kelso, F. M. "Tennesseans at Chickamauga, a Trio of Brave Staff Officers." *Confederate Veteran* 2, no. 7 (July 1894): 324.

LeMonnier, Y. R. "General Leonidas Polk at Chickamauga." *Confederate Veteran* 24, no. 1 (January 1916): 17–19.

"Lieutenant Colonel John Weedon." *Confederate Veteran* 13, no. 10 (October 1905): 443.

"Lieutenant Colonel W. W. Carnes, Memphis, Tennessee." *Confederate Veteran* 6, no. 8 (August 1898): 384.

McKell, William J. "The Journal of Sergt. Wm. J. McKell." *Civil War History* 3 (September 1957): 315–39.

McCown, J. G. "About Ector's and McNair's Brigades." *Confederate Veteran* 9, no. 3 (March 1901): 113.

McLaws, Lafayette. "After Chickamauga." In *Addresses Delivered before the Confederate Veteran Association of Savannah, Georgia, to Which Is Appended the President's Annual Report.* Savannah: Braid and Hutton, Printers, 1898.

McMurray, W. J. "The Gap of Death at Chickamauga." *Confederate Veteran* 2, no. 11 (November 1894): 329–30.

McMurtry, Robert G. "Confederate General Ben Hardin Helm, Kentucky Brother-in-Law of Abraham Lincoln." *Filson Club Historical Quarterly* 32 (1958): 311–28.

"Major Abner Williams." *Confederate Veteran* 26, no. 2 (February 1918): 78.

Martin, J. H. "Longstreet's Forces at Chickamauga." *Confederate Veteran* 20, no. 12 (December 1912): 563–65.

Martin, John A. "Some Notes on the Eighth Kansas Infantry and the Battle of Chickamauga. Letters of Colonel John A. Martin." *Kansas Historical Quarterly* 13 (1944): 141–45.

Martin, P. T. "Recollections of a Confederate." *Confederate Veteran* 15, no. 5 (May 1907): 231–32.

Martin, Will T. "A Defense of General Bragg's Conduct at Chickamauga." *Southern Historical Society Papers* 11 (1883): 200–205.

Massenberg, T. L. "Captain W. W. Carnes' Battery at Chickamauga." *Confederate Veteran* 12, no. 11 (November 1904): 517–18.

Minnich, Jay. "Liddell's Division at Chickamauga." *Confederate Veteran* 13, no. 1 (January 1905): 22–24.

———. "Unique Experiences in the Chickamauga Campaign." *Confederate Veteran* 35, no. 6 (June 1927): 222–25.

Minty, Robert. *Remarks of Brevet Major General R. H. G. Minty, made September 18, 1895, at the Dedication of the Monument Erected to the Fourth Michigan Cavalry, at Reed's Bridge, Chickamauga National Park.* Ogden, Utah: Brantley Paper Company, 1896.

"Mississippians in the Battle of Chickamauga." *Confederate Veteran* 14, no. 8 (August 1906): 342.

Morgan, John M. "Old Steady: The Role of General James Blair Steedman at the Battle of Chickamauga." *Northwest Ohio Quarterly* 22 (1950): 73–94.

Morton, D. B. "Last Surviving Confederate Lieutenant General." *Confederate Veteran* 17, no. 2 (February 1909): 83.

Moore, J. C. "McNair's Arkansas Brigade." *Confederate Veteran* 14, no. 3 (March 1906): 123–24.

Mosley, F. A. "Strained Relations between Generals Forrest and Wheeler." *Confederate Veteran* 14, no. 8 (August 1906): 360.

Otey, W. N. Mercer. "Operations of the Signal Corps." *Confederate Veteran* 8, no. 3 (March 1900): 129–30.

———. "Story of Our Great War." *Confederate Veteran* 11, no. 8 (August 1906): 342–43.

Palmer, John B. "The Fifty-Eighth North Carolina at the Battle of Chickamauga." *Our Living and Our Dead* 3 (1875): 454–55.

Parson, Edwin. "Chickamauga." In *War Papers Read before the Commandery of the State of Wisconsin, Military Order of the Loyal Legion of the United States,* vol. 2, 438–43. Milwaukee: Burdick, Armitage, and Allen, 1896.

Partridge, Charles A. "The Ninety-sixth Illinois at Chickamauga." *Papers of the Illinois State Historical Society* 15 (1912): 72–80.

Polley, J. B. "A Battle 'Above the Clouds.'" *Confederate Veteran* 5, no. 3 (March 1897): 104–5.

———. "Reminiscences of Chickamauga." *Confederate Veteran* 5, no. 1 (January 1897): 11–12.

Ridley, Bromfield L., Jr. "Daring Deeds of Staff and Escort." *Confederate Veteran* 4, no. 10 (October 1896): 358–59.

———. "Southern Side at Chickamauga, Article I," *Confederate Veteran* 6, no. 9 (September 1898): 407–9.

———. "Southern Side at Chickamauga, Article II." *Confederate Veteran* 6, no. 11 (November 1898): 513–16.

Rone, John T. "First Arkansas Brigade at Chickamauga." *Confederate Veteran* 8, no. 4 (April 1905): 166–67.

Rosecrans, William S. "The Campaign for Chattanooga." *Century Magazine* (May 1887): 130–35.

Shackelton, Robert. "The Battlefield of Chickamauga." *Blue and Gray* 1 (1893): 488–89.

Shook, Robert. "Timely Information to General Bragg." *Confederate Veteran* 18, no. 7 (July 1910): 39.

Sloan, John M. "A Most Worthy Plea for Help." *Confederate Veteran* 2, no. 2 (February 1894): 37.

Smith, J. D. "Walthall's Brigade at Chickamauga." *Confederate Veteran* 7, no. 10 (October 1904): 483–84.

Smith, W. H. "Melanchthon Smith's Battery." *Confederate Veteran* 12, no. 11 (November 1904): 532.

Snider, S. P. "Reminiscences of the War." In *Glimpses of the Nation's Struggle, Military Order of the Loyal Legion of the United States, Minnesota Commandery, Second Series.* St. Paul, Minn.: By the Commandery, 1890.

Stewart, Charles. "A Bachelor General." *Wisconsin Magazine of History* 17 (1933): 131–34.

Sykes, Edward T. "Walthall's Brigade, a Cursory Sketch with Personal Experiences of Walthall's Brigade, Army of Tennessee, C.S.A., 1862–1865." *Publications of the Mississippi Historical Society, Centenary Series* 1 (1916): 477–623.

Thruston, Gates P. "Chickamauga." *Southern Bivouac,* no. 2 (1886/1887): 406–15.

Tourgee, Albion. "A Civil War Diary of Albion W. Tourgee." Edited by Dean H. Keller. *Ohio History* 74, no. 2 (Spring 1965): 99–131.

Trantham, William D. "Wonderful Story of Richard R. Kirkland." *Confederate Veteran* 16, no. 3 (March 1908): 105.

Turchin, Nadine. "'A Monotony Full of Sadness': The Diary of Nadine Turchin, May 1863–April 1864." Edited by Mary Ellen McElligott. *Journal of the Illinois State Historical Society* 70, no. 1 (February 1977): 27–89.

Van Adder, Charles. "A Biographical Sketch of Captain John N. Sloan, C.S.A." Unpublished article, courtesy of author.

Vance, Wilson J. "On Thomas' Right at Chickamauga." *Blue and Gray* 1, no. 2 (February 1893): 87–99.

Vaulx, Joseph. "Commander of Memphis Encampment." *Confederate Veteran* 14, no. 4 (April 1906): 151.

Washburn, Wiley A. "Reminiscences of Confederate Service." *Arkansas Historical Quarterly* 35 (Spring 1976): 47–90.

Wells, E. T. "The Campaign and Battle of Chickamauga." *United Service* 16 (September 1896): 205–33.

Wilder, John T. "The Battle of Hoover's Gap." In *Sketches of War History 1861–1865. Papers Prepared for the Commandery of the State of Ohio, Military Order of the Loyal Legion of the United States, 1903–1908*, vol. 6, 168–73. Cincinnati: Monfort and Company, 1908.

Wilder's Brigade Reunion. Effingham, Ill., September 17, 1909. Remarks by Smith D. Atkins, Late Colonel of the Ninety-second Illinois Volunteer Infantry (Mounted). N.p., 1909.

Williams, Samuel C. "General John T. Wilder." *Indiana Magazine of History* 31, no. 3 (September 1935): 169–203.

Wiseman, Elijah. "Tennesseans at Chickamauga, Vivid Descriptions of the Sunday's Fighting." *Confederate Veteran* 2, no. 7 (July 1894): 205.

Womack, J. K. "Chickamauga as I Saw It." *Confederate Veteran* 25, no. 2 (February 1917): 74.

Wyeth, John. "Appearance and Characteristics of Forrest." *Confederate Veteran* 4, no. 2 (February 1896): 42–43.

AUTOBIOGRAPHIES, COLLECTED WORKS, DIARIES, LETTERS, MEMOIRS, AND PERSONAL NARRATIVES – BOOKS AND PAMPHLETS

Beatty, John. *The Citizen Soldier; or, Memoirs of a Volunteer*. Cincinnati: Wilstach, Baldwin, 1879.

Berry, Thomas. *Four Years with Morgan and Forrest*. Oklahoma City: Harlow-Ratliff Company, 1914.

Bevens, W. E. *Reminiscences of a Private, Company "G," First Arkansas Regiment Infantry*. N.p., 1913.

Bierce, Ambrose. *The Collected Writings of Ambrose Bierce*. New York: Citadel Press, 1946.

Bircher, William. *A Drummer Boy's Diary*. St. Paul: St. Paul Book and Stationery Company, 1889.

Buckner, Allen. *Memoirs of Allen Buckner*. Lansing: Michigan Alcohol and Drug Information Foundation, 1982.

Buell, Clarence, and Robert Johnson, eds. *Battles and Leaders of the Civil War*. 4 vols. New York: Thomas Yoseloff, 1956.

Butler, Marvin. *My Story of the Civil War and the Underground Railroad*. Huntington, Ind.: United Brethren Publishing Establishment, 1914.

Chesnut, Mary. *A Diary from Dixie*. New York: D. Appleton, 1914.

Collins, R. M. *Chapters from the Unwritten History of the War between the States; or, Incidents in the Life of a Confederate Soldier, in Camp, on the March, in the Great Battles, and in Prison.* St. Louis: Nixon-Jones Printing Company, 1893.

Connolly, James Austin. *Three Years in the Army of the Cumberland, the Letters and Diary of Major James A. Connolly.* Bloomington: Indiana University Press, 1959.

Cort, Charles E. *"Dear Friends," the Civil War Letters and Diary of Charles Edwin Cort.* Edited by Helyn W. Tomlinson. Minneapolis: N.p., 1962.

Cox, Jacob. *Military Reminiscences of the Civil War.* 2 vols. New York: Charles Scribner's Sons, 1900.

Cumming, Kate. *Gleanings from the Southland.* Birmingham, Ala.: Roberts and Son, 1896.

Dana, Charles. *Recollections of the Civil War.* New York: Boughmans, 1898.

Davis, Jefferson. *Jefferson Davis, Constitutionalist: His Letters, Papers and Speeches.* Edited by Dunbar Rowland. 10 vols. Jackson, Miss.: Mississippi Department of Archives and History, 1923.

Dornblaser, Thomas. *Sabre Strokes of the Pennsylvania Dragoons in the War of 1861–1865.* Philadelphia: Lutheran Publication Society, 1884.

Eby, Henry H. *Observations of an Illinois Boy in Battle, Camp and Prisons, 1861–1865.* Mendota, Ill.: By the author, 1910.

Fisher, Horace Cecil. *The Personal Experiences of Colonel Horace Newton Fisher, A Staff Officer's Story.* Boston: N.p., 1960.

Fitch, Michael. *Echoes of the Civil War as I Hear Them.* New York: R. F. Fenno, 1905.

Fletcher, William Andrew. *Rebel Private, Front and Rear.* Austin: University of Texas Press, 1954.

Foraker, Joseph. *Notes on a Busy Life.* 2 vols. Cincinnati: Stewart and Vidd, 1917.

Giles, Valerius C. *Rags and Hope, the Recollections of Val C. Giles, Four Years with Hood's Brigade, Fourth Texas Infantry, 1861–1865.* Edited by Mary Laswell. New York: Coward-McCann, 1961.

Green, Charles R. *Volunteer Service in the Army of the Cumberland.* Olathe, Kans.: N.p., 1913–14.

Green, Johnny Williams. *Johnny Green of the Orphan Brigade: The Journal of a Confederate Soldier.* Lexington: University of Kentucky Press, 1956.

Harmon, Oscar F. *Life and Letters of Oscar Fitzalan Harmon, Colonel of the One Hundred Twenty-fifth Regiment Illinois Volunteers.* Trenton: MacCrelish and Quiqley Company, 1914.

Hay, John. *Letters of John Hay and Extracts from Diary.* 3 vols. Washington, D.C.: N.p. 1908.

Hazen, William. *A Narrative of Military Service.* Boston: Ticknor, 1885.

Heartsill, William W. *Fourteen Hundred and Ninety-one Days in the Confederate Army, a Journal Kept by W. W. Heartsill, for Four Years, One Month, and One Day; or, Camp Life, Day-by-day, of the W. P. Lane Rangers, from April 19, 1861, to May 20th, 1865.* Jackson, Tenn.: McCowat-Mercer Press, 1954.

Heg, Hans Christian. *The Civil War Letters of Colonel Hans Christian Heg.* Edited by Theodore C. Blegen. Northfield, Minn.: Norwegian-American Historical Association, 1936.

Hood, John Bell. *Advance and Retreat. Personal Experiences in the United States and Confederate States Armies.* Philadelphia: Press of Burke and M'Fetridge, 1880.

Hough, Alfred L. *Soldier in the West: The Civil War Letters of Alfred Lacey Hough.* Philadelphia: University of Pennsylvania Press, 1957.

Houghton, William R. and M. B. *Two Boys in the Civil War and After.* Montgomery, Ala.: Paragon Press, 1912.

Imboden, C. M. *With the Army of the Cumberland, A Review of the Last Eight Months of My Service in the War of 1861–1865* Blandinsville, Ill.: N.p., 1969.

Johnson, Richard W. *A Soldier's Reminiscences in Peace and War.* Philadelphia: J. R. Lippincott, 1886.

Kell, William H. *Military Record of Lieutenant Colonel William H. Kell.* N.p., n.d.

Kelly, Gene, compiler. *Collection of Civil War Letters Written by Mercer County Soldiers.* N.p., n.d.

Kiene, Francis A. *A Civil War Diary. The Journal of Francis A. Kiene, 1861–1864. A Family History.* Edited by Ralph E. Kiene, Jr. Kansas City: Year Book House, 1974.

Kirkpatrick, George. *The Experiences of a Private Soldier in the Civil War.* Chicago: N.p., 1924.

Lane, Mills, ed. *Dear Mother: Don't Grieve About Me . . . Letters from Georgia Soldiers in the Civil War.* Savannah: Beehive Press, 1977.

Liddell, St. John Richardson. *Liddell's Record.* Edited by Nathaniel C. Hughes. Dayton, Ohio: Morningside, 1985.

Lincoln, Abraham. *The Collected Works of Abraham Lincoln.* Edited by Roy Basler. 8 vols. New Brunswick, N.J.: Rutgers University Press, 1953.

Longstreet, James. *From Manassas to Appomattox, Memoirs of the Civil War in America.* Philadelphia: J. B. Lippincott, 1896.

Lyle, William W. *Lights and Shadows of Army Life; or, Pen Pictures from the Battlefield, the Camp, and the Hospital.* Cincinnati: R. W. Carroll, 1865.

McAdams, Francis. *Our Knapsack, Sketches for the Boys in Blue.* Columbus, Ohio: Charles M. Cott, 1884.

Manigault, Arthur Middleton. *A Carolinian Goes to War: The Civil War Narrative of Arthur Middleton Manigault.* Columbia: University of South Carolina Press, 1983.

Marcoot, Maurice. *Five Years in the Sunny South, Reminiscences of Maurice Marcoot.* N.p., n.d.

Oates, William C. *The War between the Union and the Confederacy and Its Lost Opportunities, with a History of the Fifteenth Alabama and the Forty-eight Battles in Which It Was Engaged.* New York: Neale, 1905.

Palmer, John M. *Personal Recollections of John M. Palmer: The Story of an Earnest Life.* Cincinnati: Robert Clarke, 1901.

Partridge, Charles A. *The Battle of Chickamauga.* Waukegan, Ill.: Gazette Printing Establishment, 1881.

Petzoldt, Theodore. *My War Story, As Told Fifty Years After the War to Tracy B. Caswell at Denver, Colorado, 1911–1913.* Portland, Ore.: N.p., 1913.

Phillips, Alfred R. *Fighting with Turchin.* N.p., n.d.

Polley, Joseph Benjamin. *A Soldier's Letters to Charming Nellie.* New York: Neale, 1908.

Quintard, Charles Todd. *Doctor Quintard, Chaplain C.S.A. and Second Bishop of Tennessee, Being His Story of the War.* Sewanee, Tenn.: University Press, 1905.

Richards, Henry. *Letters of Captain Henry Richards of the Ninety-third Ohio Infantry.* Cincinnati: Press of Wrightson and Company, 1883.

Robbins, Edward. *Civil War Experiences, 1862–1865.* Carthage, Ill.: N.p., 1919.

Scribner, Benjamin. *How Soldiers Were Made; or, the War as I Saw It under Buell, Rosecrans, Thomas, Grant and Sherman.* Chicago: Donohue and Henneberry, 1887.

Shanks, William. *Personal Recollections of Distinguished Generals.* New York: Harper, 1866.

Sheridan, Philip Henry. *Personal Memoirs of P. H. Sheridan.* 2 vols. New York: Charles L. Webster, 1888.

Smith, Benjamin T. *Private Smith's Journal, Recollections of the Late War.* Edited by Clyde Walton. Chicago: R. R. Donnelly, 1963.

Sorrel, G. Moxley. *Recollections of a Confederate Staff Officer.* New York: Neale, 1905.

Stanley, David Sloane. *Personal Memoirs of Major General D. S. Stanley, U.S.A.* Cambridge, Mass.: Harvard University Press, 1917.

Stebbins, Jerome K. *Diary of Jerome K. Stebbins from Date of Enlistment September 12, 1861 to October 27, 1863. Also Captain Joseph W. Miller's Account of the Battle of Chickamauga the 18th and 20th of September 1863.* Marietta, Ohio: N.d.

Stevens, John W. *Reminiscences of the Civil War, by J. W. Stevens, a Soldier in Hood's Texas Brigade, Army of Northern Virginia.* Hillsboro, Tex.: Hillsboro Mirror Print, 1902.

Strong, Benjamin T. *Three Years During the War, Sergeant Benjamin T. Strong's Biography.* Olathe, Kans.: C. R. Green, 1913.

Taylor, Richard. *Destruction and Reconstruction: Personal Experiences of the Late War.* New York: D. Appleton, 1879.

Toney, Marcus. *The Privations of a Private.* Nashville: For the Author, 1905.

Villard, Henry. *Memoirs of Henry Villard, Journalist and Financier, 1855–1900.* 2 vols. Boston: Houghton-Mifflin, 1904.

Waddle, Augustus L. *Three Years with the Armies of the Ohio and the Cumberland.* Chillicothe, Ohio: Scioto Gazette, 1889.

Welles, Gideon. *Diary of Gideon Welles, Lincoln's Secretary of the Navy.* 3 vols. Boston: Houghton, Mifflin, 1911.

West, John C. *A Texan in Search of a Fight.* Waco, Tex.: Texiana Press, 1961.

Womack, John J. *The Civil War Diary of Captain J. J. Womack, Company E. Sixteenth Regiment, Tennessee Volunteers*. McMinnville, Tenn.: Womack Printing Company, 1961.

Wyeth, John Allen. *With Sabre and Scalpel, the Autobiography of a Soldier and Surgeon*. New York: Harper and Brothers, 1914.

Young, Lot D. *Reminiscences of a Soldier of the Orphan Brigade*. Louisville: Courier-Journal Job Printing Company, 1918.

Unit Histories

Aten, Henry. *History of the Eighty-fifth Regiment Illinois Volunteer Infantry*. Hiawatha, Kans.: N.p., 1901.

Beach, John N. *History of the Fortieth Ohio Volunteer Infantry*. London, Ohio: Shepherd and Craig, 1884.

Bennett, Lyman G. *History of the Thirty-sixth Regiment Illinois Volunteers During the War of the Great Rebellion*. Aurora, Ill.: Knickerbocker and Hodder, 1876.

Bishop, Judson. *The Story of a Regiment, Being a Narrative of the Services of the Second Regiment, Minnesota Veteran Volunteer Infantry in the Civil War of 1861–1865*. St. Paul: N.p., 1890.

———. *Van Derveer's Brigade at Chickamauga*. St. Paul: N.p., 1903.

Botsford, Theophilus F., and Joseph Q. Burton. *Historical Sketches of the Forty-seventh Alabama Infantry Regiment, C.S.A.* Montgomery: Confederate Publishing Company, 1982.

Brown, Thaddeus, et al. *Behind the Guns, the History of Battery I, Second Regiment Illinois Light Artillery*. Carbondale: Southern Illinois University Press, 1965.

Buck, Irving. *Cleburne and His Command*. Dayton: Morningside, 1982.

Burke, William. *The Military History of Kansas Regiments During the War for the Suppression of the Great Rebellion*. Leavenworth, Kans.: W. S. Burke, 1868.

Calkins, William Wirt. *The History of the One Hundred and Fourth Regiment of Illinois Volunteer Infantry, War of the Great Rebellion, 1862–1865*. Chicago: Donohue and Henneberry, 1895.

Canfield, Silas S. *History of the Twenty-first Regiment Ohio Volunteer Infantry*. Toledo: Vrooman, Anderson and Bateman, 1893.

Carter, William R. *History of the First Regiment of Tennessee Volunteer Cavalry in the Great War of the Rebellion, with the Armies of the Ohio and Cumberland, under Generals Morgan, Rosecrans, Thomas, Stanley and Wilson, 1862–1865*. Knoxville: Gaut-Ogden Company, 1902.

Chase, John. *History of the Fourteenth History Regiment, O.V.V.I., from the Beginning of the War in 1861 to Its Close in 1865*. Toledo: St. John Printing House, 1881.

Cist, Henry. *The Army of the Cumberland*. New York: Charles Scribner's Sons, 1882.

Clark, Charles. *Opdycke Tigers, 125th O.V.I., a History of the Regiment and the Campaigns and Battles of the Army of the Cumberland*. Columbus, Ohio: Spahr and Glenn, 1895.

Clark, Walter, ed. *Histories of the Several Regiments and Battalions from North Carolina in the Great War, 1861–1865, Written by Members of Their Respective Commands.* 5 vols. Goldsboro, N.C.: Nash Brothers, Printer, 1901.

Cope, Alexis. *The Fifteenth Ohio Volunteers and Its Campaigns, War of 1861–1865.* Columbus, Ohio: Press of Edward T. Miller, 1916.

Curry, William. *Four Years in the Saddle, History of the First Regiment Ohio Volunteer Cavalry, War of the Rebellion, 1861-1865.* Columbus, Ohio: Champlin Printing Company, 1898.

Davidson, Henry. *History of Battery A, First Regiment Ohio Volunteer Light Artillery.* Milwaukee: Daily Wisconsin Printing House, 1865.

Day, Lewis. *Story of the One Hundred and First Ohio Infantry, a Memorial Volume.* Cleveland: William Bayne, 1894.

Demoret, Alfred. *A Brief History of the Ninety-third Regiment Ohio Volunteer Infantry, Recollections of a Private.* Ross, Ohio: Graphic Printing, 1898.

Develling, Charles T. *History of the Seventeenth Regiment, First Brigade, Third Division, Fourteenth Corps, Army of the Cumberland.* Zanesville, Ohio: E. R. Sullivan, 1889.

Dickert, D. Augustus. *History of Kershaw's Brigade, with Complete Roll of Companies, Biographical Sketches, Incidents, Anecdotes, Etc.* Newberry, N.C.: Elbert H. Aull Company, 1899.

Dodge, William Sumner. *History of the Old Second Division, Army of the Cumberland.* Chicago: Church and Goodman, 1864.

Douglas, Lucia Rutherford. *Douglas's Texas Battery, C.S.A.* Tyler, Tex.: Smith County Historical Society, 1966.

Floyd, David Bittle. *History of the Seventy-fifth Regiment of Indiana Volunteers, Its Organizations, Campaigns, and Battles (1862–1865).* Philadelphia: Lutheran Publishing Society, 1893.

Gammage, Washington L. *The Camp, the Bivouac, and the Battlefield, Being a History of the Fourth Arkansas Regiment.* Little Rock, Ark.: Southern Press, 1958.

Gibson, Joseph. *History of the Seventy-eighth Pennsylvania Volunteer Infantry.* Pittsburgh: Pittsburgh Printing Company, 1905.

Grebner, Constantin. *We Were the Ninth: A History of the Ninth Regiment, Ohio Volunteer Infantry, April 17, 1861 to June 7, 1864.* Edited and translated by Frederic Trautmann. Kent, Ohio: Kent State University Press, 1987.

Grose, William. *The Story of the Marches, Battles and Incidents of the Thirty-sixth Regiment Indiana Volunteer Infantry.* New Castle, Ind.: Courier Printing Company, 1891.

Hamilton, D. H. *History of Company M, First Texas Volunteer Infantry, Hood's Brigade, Longstreet's Corps, Army of the Confederate States of America.* Kansas City, Mo.: E. L. Mendenhall, 1925.

Hannaford, Ebenezer. *The Story of a Regiment, a History of the Campaigns, and Associations in the Field, of the Sixth Regiment, Ohio Volunteer Infantry.* Cincinnati: By the Author, 1868.

Harden, Henry. *History of the Ninetieth Ohio Volunteer Infantry in the War of the Great Rebellion in the United States, 1861–1865*. Stoutsville, Ohio: Press of Fairfield-Pickaway News, 1902.

Haynie, James Henry. *The Nineteenth Illinois: A Memoir of a Regiment of Volunteer Infantry Famous in the Civil War of Fifty Years Ago for Its Drill, Bravery, and Distinguished Services*. Chicago: M. A. Donahue, 1912.

High, Edwin W. *History of the Sixty-eighth Regiment Indiana Volunteer Infantry, 1862–1865, with a Sketch of E. A. King's Brigade, Reynolds's Division, Thomas's Corps in the Battle of Chickamauga*. Metamora, Ind.: Sixty-eighth Indiana Infantry Reunion Association, 1902.

Hinman, Wilbur F. *The Story of the Sherman Brigade. The Camp, the March, the Bivouac, the Battle; and How the Boys Lived and Died during Four Years of Active Field Service*. Alliance, Ohio: Press of Daily Review, 1897.

History of the Organization, Marches, Campaigns, General Services and Final Muster Out of Battery M, First Regiment of Illinois Light Artillery. Princeton, Ill.: Mercer and Dean, 1892.

History of the Seventy-ninth Regiment Indiana Volunteer Infantry in the Civil War of 1861 in the United States. Indianapolis: Hollenbeck Press, 1899.

Holmes, James T. *52d O.V.I., Then and Now*. Columbus, Ohio: Berlin Print Company, 1898.

Horrall, Spillard. *History of the Forty-second Indiana Volunteer Infantry*. Chicago: Donahue and Company, 1892.

Horton, Joshua. *A History of the Eleventh Regiment (Ohio Volunteer Infantry) Containing the Military Record . . . of Each Officer and Enlisted Man of the Command*. Dayton: W. J. Shuey Printer, 1866.

Hunter, Alfred. *History of the Eighty-second Indiana Volunteer Infantry, Its Organization, Campaigns, and Battles*. Indianapolis: William B. Burford, Printer, 1893.

Keil, Frederick W. *Thirty-fifth Ohio, a Narrative of Service from August 1861 to 1864*. Fort Wayne, Ind.: Archer, Housh and Company, 1894.

Kern, Albert. *History of the First Regiment Ohio Volunteer Infantry in the Civil War, 1861–1865*. Dayton: N.p., 1912.

Kimberly, Robert L. *The Forty-first Ohio Volunteer Infantry in the War of the Rebellion, 1861–1865*. Cleveland: W. R. Smellie, 1897.

Kinnear, John. *History of the Eighty-sixth Regiment Illinois Volunteer Infantry, During Its Term of Service*. Chicago: Tribune Book and Job Printing Office, 1866.

Kirk, Charles. *History of the Fifteenth Pennsylvania Volunteer Cavalry, which was Recruited and Known as the Anderson Cavalry in the Rebellion of 1862–1865*. Philadelphia: N.p., 1906.

Lathrop, David. *The History of the Fifty-ninth Regiment Illinois Volunteers; or a Three Years' Campaign through Missouri, Arkansas, Mississippi, Tennessee and Kentucky, with a Description of the Country, Towns, Skirmishes and Battles . . .* Indianapolis: Hall and Hutchinson, 1865.

Lavender, John. *The War Memoirs of Captain John W. Lavender, C.S.A. They Never Came Back; the Story of Co. F, Fourth Arks. Infantry, C.S.A., Originally*

Known as the Montgomery Hunters, as Told by Their Commanding Officer. Pine Bluff, Ark.: W. M. Hackett and D. R. Perdue, 1956.

Lewis, George. *The Campaigns of the One Hundred Twenty-fourth Ohio Volunteer Infantry.* Akron: Werner, 1894.

Lindsley, John. *The Military Annals of Tennessee. Confederate. First Series: Embracing a Review of Military Operations, with Regimental Histories and Memorial Rolls.* Nashville: J. M. Lindsley, 1886.

McAdams, Francis. *Every-Day Soldier Life; or, a History of the 113th Ohio Volunteer Infantry.* Columbus, Ohio: Charles M. Cott and Company, 1884.

McGee, Benjamin. *History of the Seventy-second Indiana Volunteer Infantry.* Lafayette, Ind.: S. Vatter and Company, 1882.

Mauzy, James. *Historical Sketch of the Sixty-eighth Regiment Indiana Volunteers, with Personal Recollections by Members of Company D, and Short Biographies of Brigade, Division and Corps Commanders.* Rushville, Ind.: Republican Company, Printers, 1887.

Morris, George W. *History of the Eighty-first Regiment of Indiana Volunteer Infantry.* Louisville: Franklin Printing Company, 1901.

Morton, John. *The Artillery of Nathan Bedford Forrest, "Wizard of the Saddle."* Nashville: Publishing House of M. E. Church, South, 1909.

Newlin, William H. *History of the Seventy-third Regiment of Illinois Infantry Volunteers, Its Services and Experiences in Camp, on the March, on the Picket and Skirmish Lines, and in Many Battles of the War, 1861–1865.* Springfield, Ill.: The Regimental Reunion Association, 1890.

Ninety-second Illinois Volunteers. Freeport, Ill.: Journal Publishing House and Bookbindery, 1875.

Obreiter, John. *The Seventy-seventh Pennsylvania at Shiloh. History of the Regiment.* Harrisburg, Pa.: Harrisburg Publishing Company, 1908.

Otto, John. *History of the Eleventh Indiana Battery, Connected with an Outline History of the Army of the Cumberland.* Fort Wayne, Ind.: W. D. Page, 1891.

Owen, William M. *In Camp and Battle with the Washington Artillery of New Orleans, a Narrative of Events During the Late Civil War.* Boston: Ticknor and Company, 1885.

Partridge, Charles. *History of the Ninety-sixth Regiment Illinois Volunteer Infantry.* Chicago: Brown, Pettibone, and Company, 1887.

Perry, Henry. *History of the Thirty-eighth Regiment Indiana Volunteer Infantry.* Palo Alto, Ind.: F. A. Stuart, 1906.

Polley, Joseph Benjamin. *Hood's Texas Brigade, Its Marches, Its Battles, Its Achievements.* New York and Washington: Neale, 1910.

Puntenney, George. *History of the Thirty-seventh Regiment of Indiana Volunteer Infantry, Its Organization, Campaigns, and Battles, Sept. '61 to Oct. '64.* Rushville, Ind.: Jackson Book and Job Department, 1896.

Robertson, Jerome B. *Touched with Valor, Civil War Papers and Casualty Reports of Hood's Texas Brigade, Written and Collected by General Jerome B. Robertson, Command of Hood's Texas Brigade, 1862–1864.* Edited by Harold B. Simpson. Hillsboro, Tex.: Hill Junior College, 1964.

Rogers, Robert M. *The One Hundred Twenty-fifth Regiment Illinois Volunteer Infantry. Attention Battalion!* Champaign, Ill.: Gazette Printing, 1882.

Rowell, John. *Yankee Artilleryman, Through the Civil War with Eli Lilly's Indiana Battery.* Knoxville: University of Tennessee Press, 1975.

Royse, Isaac. *History of the 115th Regiment Illinois Volunteer Infantry.* Terra Haute, Ind.: N.p., 1900.

Shaver, Lewellyn A. *A History of the Sixtieth Alabama Regiment, Gracie's Alabama Brigade.* Montgomery: Barrett and Brown, 1867.

Simmons, Louis A. *The History of the Eighty-fourth Regiment Illinois Volunteers.* Macomb, Ill.: Hampton Brothers, 1866.

Simpson, Harold. *Hood's Texas Brigade, Lee's Grenadier Guard.* Waco, Tex.: Texiana Press, 1970.

Smith, John. *A History of the Thirty-first Regiment of Indiana Volunteer Infantry in the War of the Rebellion.* Cincinnati: Western Methodist Book Concern, 1900.

Stewart, Nixon. *Dan McCook's Regiment, Fifty-second O.V.I., a History of the Regiment.* Alliance, Ohio: Review Print., 1900.

Stormont, Gilbert R. *History of the Fifty-eighth Regiment of Indiana Volunteer Infantry, Its Organizations, Campaigns, and Battles, from 1861–1865.* Princeton, Ind.: Press of Clarion, 1895.

Sunderland, Glenn. *Wilder's Lightning Brigade—And Its Spencer Repeaters.* Washington, Ill.: The Book Works, 1984.

Todd, George T. *First Texas Regiment.* Waco, Tex.: Texian Press, 1963.

Tourgee, Albion. *The Story of a Thousand, Being a History of the Service of the One Hundred Fifth Ohio Volunteer Infantry, in the War for the Union.* Buffalo, N.Y.: McGerald and Son, 1896.

Vale, Joseph. *Minty and the Cavalry, a History of Cavalry Campaigns in the Western Armies.* Harrisburg, Pa.: Edwin K. Meyers, 1886.

Van Horne, Thomas. *History of the Army of the Cumberland, Its Organizations, Campaigns, and Battles.* 2 vols. Cincinnati: Robert Clarke, 1875.

Walker, Cornelius I. *Rolls and Historical Sketch of the Tenth Regiment, So. Ca. Volunteers in the Army of the Late Confederate States.* Charleston, S.C.: Walker, Evans, and Cogswell, 1881.

Watkins, Samuel. *"Co. Aytch," Maury Grays, First Tennessee Regiment; or, a Side Show of the Big Show.* Chattanooga: Times Printing Company, 1952.

Winkler, Angelina V. *The Confederate Capital and Hood's Texas Brigade.* Austin: E. Von Boeckman, 1894.

Woodruff, George H. *Fifteen Years Ago; or the Patriotism of Will County.* Joliet, Ill.: Joliet Republican Book and Job Steam Printing House, 1876.

Worsham, William. *The Old Nineteenth Tennessee Regiment.* Knoxville: Press of Paragon Printing Company, 1902.

Wright, Thomas J. *History of the Eighth Regiment Kentucky Volunteer Infantry, During Its Three Campaigns, Embracing Organizations, Skirmishes, and Battles of the Command, with Much of the History of the Old Reliable Third Brigade, Commanded by Hon. Stanley Matthews, and Containing Many*

Interesting and Amusing Incidents of Army Life. St. Joseph, Mo.: St. Joseph Steam and Printing Company, 1880.

SECONDARY SOURCES — BOOKS

Andrews, J. Cutler. *The North Reports the Civil War*. Pittsburgh: University of Pittsburgh Press, 1955.

Belknap, Charles. *History of the Michigan Organizations at Chickamauga, Chattanooga and Missionary Ridge, 1863*. Lansing: Robert Smith Printing Company, 1897.

Bickham, William D. *Rosecrans' Campaign with the Fourteenth Army Corps, or the Army of the Cumberland: a Narrative of Personal Observations . . .* Cincinnati: Moore, Wilstach, Keys, 1863.

Black, Robert Clifford. *The Railroads of the Confederacy*. Chapel Hill: University of North Carolina Press, 1952.

Boatner, Mark M., III. *The Civil War Dictionary*. New York: David McKay, 1959.

Boynton, Henry Van Ness. *Dedication of the Chickamauga and Chattanooga National Military Park September 18–20, 1895. Report of the Joint Committee to Represent the Congress at the Dedication of the Chickamauga and Chattanooga National Military Park*. Washington: G.P.O., 1896.

Bridges, Hal. *Lee's Maverick General, Daniel Harvey Hill*. New York: McGraw-Hill, 1961.

A Brief Historical Sketch of the "Fighting McCooks," Reprinted from the Proceedings of the Scotch-Irish Society of America. New York: James Kempster Printing Company, n.d.

Burr, Francis A. *The Great Battle of Chickamauga*. Memphis: Tracy Printing Company, 1883.

Ceremonies at the Unveiling of the South Carolina Monument on the Chickamauga Battlefield, May 27, 1901. Together with a Record of the Commission Who Suggested and Were Instrumental in Securing and Erecting the Monument, etc. N.p., n.d.

Cleaves, Freeman. *Rock of Chickamauga: The Life of General George H. Thomas*. Norman: University of Oklahoma Press, 1948.

Connelly, Thomas Lawrence. *Autumn of Glory: The Army of Tennessee, 1862–1865*. Baton Rouge: Louisiana State University Press, 1971.

Connelly, Thomas Lawrence, and Archer Jones. *The Politics of Command, Factions and Ideas in Confederate Strategy*. Baton Rouge: Louisiana State University Press, 1982.

Cozzens, Peter. *No Better Place to Die: The Battle of Stones River*. Urbana: University of Illinois Press, 1990.

Cummings, Charles M. *Yankee Quaker, Confederate General: The Curious Career of Bushrod Rust Johnson*. Rutherford, N.J.: Fairleigh Dickinson University Press, 1971.

Daniels, Larry J. *Cannoneers in Gray. The Field Artillery of the Army of Tennessee, 1861–1865*. University, Ala.: University of Alabama Press, 1984.

Davis, William C. *Breckinridge: Statesman, Soldier, Symbol.* Baton Rouge: Louisiana State University Press, 1973.

Dyer, John. *The Gallant Hood.* Indianapolis: Bobbs-Merrill, 1950.

Eddy, Thomas. *The Patriotism of Illinois, A Record of the Civil and Military History of the State in the War for the Union.* 2 vols. Chicago: Clarke and Company, 1865.

Federal Writers' Project, WPA. *Georgia. A Guide to Its Towns and Countryside.* Athens: University of George Press, 1940.

Fitch, John. *Annals of the Army of the Cumberland, Comprising Biographies, Descriptions of Departments, Accounts of Expeditions, Skirmishes, and Battles.* Philadelphia: J. B. Lippincott, 1863

Fitch, Michael. *The Chattanooga Campaign, with Special Reference to Wisconsin's Participation Therein.* Madison: Wisconsin History Commission, 1911.

Govan, Gilbert E., and James W. Livingood. *The Chattanooga Country, 1540–1976: From Tomahawks to TVA.* Knoxville: University of Tennessee Press, 1977.

Gracie, Archibald. *The Truth about Chickamauga.* Boston: Houghton, Mifflin, 1911.

Green, Francis Arthur. *The Witness of a House.* Chickamauga, Ga.: Gordon-Lee House, 1984.

Hattaway, Herman, and Archer Jones. *How the North Won: A Military History of the Civil War.* Urbana: University of Illinois Press, 1983.

Horn, Stanley. *The Army of Tennessee.* Norman: University of Oklahoma Press, 1952.

Indiana at Chickamauga, 1863–1900. A Report of the Indiana Commissioners, Chickamauga National Military Park. Indianapolis: Sentinel Printing Company, 1900.

Johnson, R. M. *In Matter of the Appeal to the Secretary of War, by the Indiana Chickamauga Park Commission.* N.p., n.d.

Johnson, Sidney. *Texans Who Wore the Gray.* Tyler, Tex.: N.p., 1907.

Keifer, Joseph Warren. *Slavery and Four Years of War. A Political History of Slavery in the United States, Together with a Narrative of the Campaigns and Battles of the Civil War in Which the Author Took Part: 1861–1865.* 2 vols. New York: G. P. Putnam's Sons, 1900.

Korn, Jerry. *The Fight for Chattanooga: Chickamauga to Missionary Ridge.* Alexandria, Va.: Time-Life Books, 1985.

Lamers, William. *The Edge of Glory: A Biography of General William S. Rosecrans, U.S.A.* New York: Harcourt, Brace and World, 1961.

Livermore, Thomas. *Numbers and Losses in the Civil War—1861–1865.* Boston: Riverside Press, 1901.

Losson, Christopher. *Tennessee's Forgotten Warriors: Frank Cheatham and His Confederate Division.* Knoxville: University of Tennessee Press, 1989.

McElroy, Joseph. *Chickamauga. Record of the Ohio Chickamauga and Chattanooga National Military Park Committee.* Cincinnati: Earhart and Richardson, 1896.

McKinney, Francis. *Education in Violence: The Life of George H. Thomas and the History of the Army of the Cumberland.* Detroit: Wayne State University Press, 1961.

McWhiney, Grady. *Braxton Bragg and the Confederate Defeat. Volume 1. Field Command.* New York: Columbia University Press, 1969.

The Military History of Ohio, Illustrated. Stark County Soldiers' Edition. Toledo: A. H. Hardesty, 1886.

Nash, Charles E. *Autobiographical Sketches of Gen. Pat Cleburne and Gen. T. C. Hindman, Together with Humorous Anecdotes and Reminiscences of the Late Civil War.* Little Rock, Ark.: N.p., 1898.

Neff, Robert O. *Tennessee's Battered Brigadier: The Life of General Joseph B. Palmer.* Murfreesboro, Tenn.: Historic Travellers' Rest, 1988.

O'Connor, Richard. *Ambrose Bierce: A Biography.* Boston: Little, Brown, 1967.

Owen, Ira S. *Greene County in the War.* Xenia, Ohio: Torchlight Job Rooms, 1872.

Piatt, Donn. *General George H. Thomas, a Critical Biography. With Concluding Chapters by Henry V. Boynton.* Cincinnati: Robert Clarke, 1893.

Piston, William. *Lee's Tarnished General: James Longstreet and His Place in Southern History.* Athens: University of Georgia Press, 1987.

Polk, William. *Leonidas Polk, Bishop and General.* 2 vols. New York: Longmans, Green, 1893.

Reid, Samuel C. *Great Battle of Chickamauga, A Concise History of Events from the Evacuation of Chattanooga to the Defeat of the Enemy.* Mobile, Ala.: F. Titcomb, 1863.

Reid, Whitelaw. *Ohio in the War: Her Statesmen, Her Generals, and Soldiers.* 2 vols. Cincinnati: Moore, Wilstach, and Baldwin, 1868.

Robertson John. *Michigan in the War.* Lansing: W. S. George and Company, State Printers, 1882.

Sartrain, James Alfred. *History of Walker County, Georgia, Volume 1.* Dalton, Ga.: A. J. Showalter, 1932.

Scott, William F. *Philander P. Lane, Colonel of Volunteers in the Civil War, Eleventh Ohio Infantry.* New York: Privately Printed, 1920.

Seitz, Donn C. *Braxton Bragg, General of the Confederacy.* Columbia, S.C.: The State Company, 1924.

Skinner, George W. *Pennsylvania at Chickamauga and Chattanooga. Ceremonies at the Dedication of the Monuments Erected by the Commonwealth of Pennsylvania to Mark the Positions of the Pennsylvania Commands Engaged in the Battles.* Harrisburg, Pa.: Wm. Stanley Ray, State Printer, 1900.

Smith, John. *The Right of the Federal Army at Chickamauga.* Chicago: Knight, Leonard, and Company, 1894.

Smith, Theodore C. *The Life and Letters of James Abram Garfield.* 2 vols. New Haven: Yale University Press, 1925.

Society of the Army of the Cumberland. *Burial of General Rosecrans, Arlington National Cemetery, May 17, 1902.* Cincinnati: Robert Clarke, 1903.

————. *Reunion Proceedings.*

Somers, Orlando A. *A Protest against, and Appeal from the Action of the Indiana-Chickamauga Park Commissioners, and Others to the Commissioners of the National Military Park, Chickamauga, Georgia, Together with Specifications of Errors, Citations of Proof with Comment. By the Survivors' Association of the 8th Indiana Cavalry, 39th Regiment of Indiana Volunteers.* Kokomo, Ind.: Tribune Print, 1901.

Stickles, Arndt. *Simon Bolivar Buckner, Borderland Knight.* Chapel Hill: University of North Carolina Press, 1940.

Tucker, Glenn. *Chickamauga: Bloody Battle in the West.* Indianapolis: Bobbs-Merrill, 1961.

Turchin, John B. *Chickamauga.* Chicago: Fergus Printing Company, 1888.

Waggoner, Clark. *Honors at Chickamauga, The Claim of "Hero" at that Battle. Delayed Justice to the Memory of a Brave and Gallant Soldier.* Toledo: N.p., 1883.

Warner, Ezra. *Generals in Blue: Lives of the Union Commanders.* Baton Rouge: Louisiana State University Press, 1964.

————. *Generals in Gray: Lives of the Confederate Commanders.* Baton Rouge: Louisiana State University Press, 1959.

Williams, Samuel. *General John T. Wilder, Commander of the Lightning Brigade.* Bloomington: Indiana University Press, 1936.

Wingfield, Marshall. *General A. P. Stewart, His Life and Letters.* Memphis: Privately printed, 1954.

Woodward, Steven E. *Jefferson Davis and His Generals: The Failure of Confederate Command in the West.* Lawrence: University of Kansas Press, 1990.

Woods, J. T. *Steedman and His Men at Chickamauga.* Toledo: Blade Printing and Paper Company, 1876.

MAP

Atlas of the Battlefield of Chickamauga, Chattanooga and Vicinity. Published . . . by the Chickamauga and Chattanooga National Park Commissions. Washington: G.P.O., 1901.

INDEX

Individual regiments are indexed alphabetically and identified parenthetically as to army by the abbreviations AC for Army of the Cumberland and AT for Army of Tennessee. Italicized page numbers at the end of entries in this index refer to the Appendix, which lists officers and units participating in the Battle of Chickamauga. For additional information about particular actions, see names of specific battle units as well as the names of individuals and places.

A Note on the Author

Peter Cozzens, a summa cum laude graduate of Knox College with a degree in international relations, is a foreign service officer with the U.S. Department of State. Prior to joining the Foreign Service, he served as a military intelligence officer in the United States Army. Cozzens has contributed articles to the *Illinois Historical Journal* and has written historical introductions to modern editions of Thomas Van Horne's *History of the Army of the Cumberland* and Henry Cist's *Army of the Cumberland*. He is the author of *No Better Place to Die: The Battle of Stones River* and is writing a history of the Chattanooga campaign.